The WTO and India

The WTO and India

Issues and Negotiating Strategies

Edited by

ALOKESH BARUA
and
ROBERT M. STERN

Orient BlackSwan

THE WTO AND INDIA

ORIENT BLACKSWAN PRIVATE LIMITED

Registered Office
3-6-752 Himayatnagar, Hyderabad 500 029 (A.P.), India
e-mail: centraloffice@orientblackswan.com

Other Offices
Bangalore, Bhopal, Bhubaneshwar, Chennai,
Ernakulam, Guwahati, Hyderabad, Jaipur, Kolkata,
Lucknow, Mumbai, New Delhi, Patna

© Orient Blackswan Private Limited 2010

First Published 2010

ISBN 978 81 250 4042 2

Typeset by
Le Studio Graphique, Gurgaon 122 001
in Adobe Caslon Pro 10/12

Printed at
Aegean Offset Printers
Greater Noida

Published by
Orient Blackswan Private Limited
1/24 Asaf Ali Road
New Delhi 110 002
e-mail: delhi@orientblackswan.com

Contents

List of Tables, Figures, Maps and Boxes	*ix*
Acknowledgements	*xiii*
List of Abbreviations	*xv*
Short Explanations of Important Terms	*xxi*

Introduction *Alokesh Barua and Robert M. Stern*	1

SECTION I: A DEVELOPING COUNTRIES PERSPECTIVE

1. The WTO and Trade Negotiations: A Developing Country Viewpoint *Manoj Pant*	31
2. The WTO and our Role in the World Economy of the Future *Ashok Guha*	44

SECTION II: NEGOTIATING OPTIONS AND STRATEGIES

3. India and Coalitions in Multilateral Trade Negotiations *Manmohan Agarwal*	53
4. Searching for the Missing Link: India's 'Negotiation Strategy' at WTO? *Debashis Chakraborty*	65
5. Designing a Proactive Stance for India in the Doha Development Agenda Negotiations *Alan V. Deardorff and Robert M. Stern*	88

6. India at Doha: Retrospect and Prospect 106
   Arvind Panagariya

SECTION III: MARKET ACCESS: AGRICULTURE, MANUFACTURES AND TEXTILES

7. WTO Agriculture Negotiations and India 123
   Ramesh Chand

8. Trade and Industrial Performance since the WTO Reforms: What Indian Evidences Suggest? 142
   Alokesh Barua, Debashis Chakraborty and Pavel Chakraborty

9. How Big is the Bang for India? Market Access in Textiles 170
   Samar Verma

SECTION IV: TRADE FACILITATION AND GOVERNMENT PROCUREMENT: SINGAPORE ISSUES OF FUTURE CONCERN

10. Regional Integration through Trade Facilitation: Integrating East India with Bangladesh and North India with Central Asia 199
    Pritam Banerjee, Dipankar Sengupta and Phunchok Stobdan

11. Transparency in Government Procurement: A Case Study of India 221
    Sandwip Kumar Das

SECTION V: TRIPS AND GATS

12. The TRIPS Agreement: Public Health Concerns for India 241
    Amit Shovon Ray

13. GATS and India: Negotiations in Mode 3 255
    Rashmi Banga

14. GATS Negotiations in Environmental Services: A Developing Countries Perspective with Special Reference to India 279
    Aparna Sawhney

Section VI: Growth, Poverty and Inequality

15. Trade and Poverty in the Poor Countries 297
    Jagdish Bhagwati and T. N. Srinivasan

16. Globalisation, Growth and the Poor 302
    T. N. Srinivasan and Jessica Seddon Wallack

17. Income Distribution, Structural Change and 321
    International Trade: A Developing Countries
    Perspective with Special Reference to India
    Ananya Ghosh Dastidar

18. Trade Liberalisation and Income Inequality: 347
    An Analysis of Inter-Regional Income Inequality in India
    Alokesh Barua and Pavel Chakraborty

Bibliography 373
List of Contributors 397
Index 399

Tables, Figures, Maps and Boxes

TABLES

4.1	An analysis of India's submissions at WTO	71
4.2	An analysis of trade scenario between India and proposed partners	76
4.3	An analysis of current cooperation between India and potential partners at WTO negotiations	78
4.4	Comparison of anti-dumping cases—the EU, India and the US	80
5.1	Bound tariff rates and effective rates of duty for India (average unweighted tariffs, per cent)	95
5.2	Indicators of Indian agricultural trade	96
	(a) Difference in Uruguay Round final bound rates and MFN tariff rates: Number of lines by different range groups	96
	(b) Aggregate measure of support to Indian agriculture (selected crops)	96
5.3	Anti-dumping initiations by economy taking action	99
5.4	Anti-dumping initiations by selected exporting economies	100
7.1	India's agriculture trade before and after WTO, in million USD	126
7.2	Input subsidies in Indian agriculture in relation to value of output	132
7.3	Standard rates of duty on import of selected agricultural commodities in India during 1991–92 to 2002–3	133
7.4	Matrix showing bands and cuts in overall trade distracting support and in AMS	136
7.5	Bands and cuts in tariffs proposed for developed and developing countries	137
8.1	Tariff reforms of select countries during the nineties	143
8.2	The openness measures for Indian economy (Rs in crore)	147
8.3	A comparative analysis: Country review	149
8.4	Cases at DSB involving India (updated upto 21 March 2007)	149
8.5	Exports and imports of India by destination	152
8.6	Export ratios of India by HS sections	153
8.7	Import Ratios of India by HS sections	154
8.8	The indices of IIT	157
8.9	IIT trends (1987–88 to 2002–3)	158
8.10	Horizontal and vertical specialisation trend	160
8.11	The trends in scale efficiency of the industrial sector	161

9.1	Integration programmes at a glance (Integration as a percentage of the volume of 1990 imports)	173
9.2	Average US and EU tariff rates (in percentage) on ATC products by liberalisation tranche and categories: 1995–2004 (US)	176
9.3	Comparative tariffs by selected products, pre- and post-Uruguay Round (all figures in percentage)	177
9.4	Impact of Greater China's WTO accession on textile exports—per cent change	186
9.5	Impact of Greater China's WTO accession on clothing exports—percentage change	187
9.6	The direction of exports of readymade garments from India to quota countries	188
9.7	Estimated annual manufacturing costs in garment making 1999 (USD '000)	189
10.1	Potential growth sectors for Bangladeshi exports to West Bengal and Assam	202
10.2	Potential growth sectors for West Bengal and Assam exports to Bangladesh	203
10.3	Transaction costs vis-à-vis shipment value in India-Bangladesh trade	205
10.4	Bottlenecks at the India-Bangladesh border	205
10.5	Comparative time and cost of North-East India routes to rest of the subcontinent	206
10.6	Xinjiang's transportation links	214
11.1	Value of government expenditure	225
13.1	Average annual growth rates in services	264
13.2	Percentage distribution of workers in India: 1991–2001	266
13.3	Trends in employment elasticity	268
13.4	India's share in world services exports	269
13.5	Categorisation of services: extent of trade liberalisation and growth	272
13.6	Major external and domestic constraints to trade	273
13.7	Major external and domestic constraints in health and educational services	274
13.8	Constraints in construction, engineering services and transport	275
13.9	Constraints in legal services	275
14.1	The global environmental market by region, 2004	282
16.1	Development outcomes in the 1980s and 1990s, by growth class (unweighted means)	308
17.1	Results of fixed effect panel regression	333
17.2	Results of random-effects and pooled least squares regression	336
17.3	Results of least squares regression using the Sachs-Warner measure of openness	338
17.4	Results of least squares regression using trade shares as a measure of openness	339

18.1	Inequality index at constant prices for 20 regions (1993–94=100)	351
18.2	Inequality trends (1993–94=100)	352
18.3	Non-linearity of inequality index, 1980–81 to 2005–6 (1993–94=100)	353
18.4	Causality of inequality for 20 regions, 1980–81 to 2005–6 (1993–94=100)	356
18.5	Structural change equation: Random effect model, (1990–91 to 2005–6)	360
18.6	Elasticity openness with openness dummy (1991–2006)	365
18.7	Non-linear estimates of inequality measure on trade/NSDP ratio (1991–2006)	366

FIGURES

1.1	Model 1	32
1.2	Model 2	33
5.1	Cross-country comparison of average tariff rates	95
7.1	Indices of global trade in agriculture, base 1985=100	127
7.2	India's share in global agriculture trade (in percentage)	128
7.3	Export of agricultural products: 1991–92 to 2003–4	129
7.4	Import of selected agricultural products: 1991–92 to 2003–4	129
7.5	Real prices of selected agricultural products adversely affected by WTO	130
7.6	Production of oilseeds and raw cotton in India, before and after WTO	131
9.1	Average hourly wages in the apparel industry, selected countries ($, 2000)	184
9.2	Per cent impact of ATC phase-out and China's accession on total exports	188
11.1	Transparency in government procurement	223
13.1	Average sectoral growth rates (1994–2004)	263
13.2	Average sectoral contribution to GDP	264
13.3	Share of services in GDP	264
13.4	Sectoral growth of employment in organised sector	267
13.5	Average share in total services exports	269
13.6	Average net export earnings (USD billion)	270
13.7	Share of services in inward FDI (1991 to 2002)	271
18.1	Unregistered manufacturing	355
18.2	Infrastructure	355
18.3	Manufacturing share and per capita income (structural change results, 1991–2006)	361
18.4	Service share and per capita income (structural change results, 1991–2006)	362
18.5	Manufacturing share and population (structural change results, 1991–2006)	363
18.6	Services share and population (structural change results, 1991–2006)	363
18.7	Services inequality and trade/NSDP	367

MAP

10.1 Trade route between North-East India and the rest of
the India through Bangladesh ... 203

BOX

11.1 Transparent procurement rules ... 222

Acknowledgements

This book is partly but not entirely based on a two day outreach conference that was held on 11–12 August 2004 in Guwahati, Assam. It was organised by the Center for International Trade and Development, School of International Studies, Jawaharlal Nehru University in collaboration with the Department of Economics, Cotton College, Guwahati and the Cotton College Alumni Association. We gratefully acknowledge the financial supports that we had received from the Jawaharlal Nehru University and from the Indian Council of Social Sciences Research, New Delhi. We had also received generous logistical supports from many institutions and organisation from Delhi as well as from Assam. The institutions like the UNCTAD, Oxfam and the Center de Sciences Humaine inspired us by their active participation in the conference. It is a heartening fact to put on record that in both days of the conference we had witnessed a very large participation of people from all walks of life. We had never seen such a massive gathering of people in any academic seminar anywhere in India. The participants representing the entire North-east India included college teachers, students, researchers, bureaucrats, business people, NGO activists and various other stake holders. It was an eye opening for us to notice the enthusiasm of the people to know and to understand the implications of various WTO agreements for the country. Interestingly, many people had raised their eyebrows when someone from the audience wanted to find if the calamities like the Tsunami was also caused by the WTO liberalisation! It is certainly not a travesty of fact that such wild anticipation often blurs political debates on WTO reforms. We realised how little people know about the role of WTO in their lives. It seems therefore that it is a mere wastages of resources to hold such seminars and conferences in big cities where a few and the same sort of people keep turning up each time. Rather, one should consider organising more such outreach awareness programs in remote areas for proper dissemination of knowledge about the WTO agreements. After all, the ultimate success of the WTO induced liberalisation processes shall depend on how the stake holders can extract the benefits from the economic liberalisation process and safe guard themselves through democratisation and participatory process of governance against any possible ill effects of liberalisation. We take this opportunity to gratefully thank all the participants whose presence made the conference a great success. In particular we wish to acknowledge the contribution made by the faculty of economics, Cotton College, and the Cotton College Alumni Association.

In all fairness to the contributors of the present volume, it must be said that the book in its present form was an afterthought. The conference had left with many gaps which needed to be filled to make a complete work on the WTO and India encompassing not only the broad issues relating to the WTO liberalisation process but also analyses of the nitty-gritty of the negotiating processes, evaluation of the actual impact of WTO-induced liberalisation on the different sectors of the economy and also on social well-being of the people. Therefore, we had to be selective in choosing the papers presented in the conference for this volume since we did not have enough papers to cover all the above areas. So we had invited papers from different scholars to fill the vacuum. We are very much thankful to Arvind Panagariya, Jagdish Bhagwati and T. N. Srinivasan and Jessica Seddon Wallack for positively responding to our request and for permitting us to include in the book their already published papers on specific topics with some updating in some cases. We are happy to acknowledge that Aparna Swahney, Ananya Ghosh Dastidar, Debashis Chakraborty and Rashmi Banga have contributed papers on selective issues on our request. We owe a great deal of indebtedness to all of them.

We are thankful to the Jawaharlal Nehru University and particularly to Professor Rajendra Prasad, Rector, JNU, for extending a generous financial support for the publication of the book without which the publication attempt would have been a far cry. Of course, we must not fail to appreciate the support and enthusiasm that we had received from others whom we are not able to acknowledge individually due to space constraint but for which this endeavour would not have been successful. We also like to thank our publisher, Orient Blackswan, for showing interest in the publication of this book. Lastly, a very special thank is due to our student Mr Hariprasad C. G. for editing and painstakingly preparing the manuscript for the press.

ALOKESH BARUA   ROBERT M. STERN

Abbreviations

AB	appellate body
ABI	Argentina, Brazil and India
ACP	African, Caribbean and Pacific
ACS	Association of Caribbean States
AD	anti-dumping
ADB	Asian Development Bank
AG	Andean Group
AIP	Apparel Industry Initiative
AMS	Aggregate Measure of Support
AOA	Agreement on Agriculture
APEC	Asia Pacific Economic Cooperation
APEDA	Agricultural and Processed Food Products Export Development Authority
ASEAN	Associations of Southeast Asian Nations
ATC	Agreement on Textiles and Clothing
ATMI	American Textile Manufacturing Industry
AVE	Ad Valorum Equivalent
BCT	Berne convention treaty
BIMSTEC	Bay of Bengal Initiative for Multi-Sectoral Technical and Economic Cooperarion
BITs	bilateral investment treaties
BOP	balance of payments
BOT	build-operate-transfer
BPO	business process outsourcing
BRO	Border Road Organisation
BSNL	Bharat Sanchar Nigam Limited
CAG	Comptroller and Auditor General of India
CAP	common agricultural policy
CARICOM	Caribbean Community and Common Market
CBD	Convention on Biodiversity
CBI	Cross-Border Initiative
CDF	conventional dosage forms
CDRI	Central Drug Research Institute
CEFTA	Central European Free Trade Area
CGE	computational general equilibrium

CII	Confederation of Indian Industries
CMIE	Centre for Monitoring the Indian Economy
CMP	Common Minimum Programme
CNPC	China's National Petroleum Corporation
CSS	contractual service suppliers
CTD	committee on trade and development
CTE	committee on trade and environment
CTG	Council for Trade in Goods
CTH	change in tariff heading
CVC	Central Vigilance Commission
DDA	Doha Development Agenda
DGCIS	Directorate General of Commercial Intelligence and Service
DGFT	Director General of Foreign Trade
DGS&D	Directorate General of Supplies and Disposal
DOT	Department of Telecommunications
DPCO	Drug Price Control Orders
DSB	Dispute Settlement Body
DSM	dispute settlement mechanism
EACS	East Asian Economic Caucus
EC	European Community
ECOWAS	Economic Community of West African States
EDI	Economic Data Interchange
EEA	European Economic Area
EEC	European Economic Community
EEP	export enhancement programme
EFTA	European Free Trade Association
EGS	Environmental Goods and Services
EIB	Eastern India-Bangladesh
ENT	Economic Needs Test
EP	European Pharmacopoeia
EPM	export performance measure
ESCAP	Economic and Social Commission for India and the pacific
EU	European Union
FCI	Food Corporation of India
FDB	Friends of the Development Box
FDI	foreign direct investment
FEMA	Foreign Exchange Management Act
FERA	Foreign Exchange Regulation Act
FGI	Friends of Geographical Indications
FGLSM	Feasible Generalized Least Square Method
FIPS	Five Interested Parties
FTAs	free trade agreements
GATS	General Agreement on Trade in Services
GATT	General Agreement on Tariffs and Trade
GDP	gross domestic product
GFRs	General Financial Rules

GMP	Good Manufacturing Practices
GMS	Greater Mekong Sub region
GNS	Group of Negotiations on Services
GPA	Agreement on Government Procurement
GSP	Generalised System of Preference
GTAP	Global Trade Analysis Project
HOS	Heckscher-Ohlin-Samuelson
IBSAC	India, Brazil, South Africa and China
ICH	International Conference on Harmonisation
ICMR	Indian Cotton Mills' Federation
ICT	information and communication technology
IDA	International Development Assistance
IIT	intra-industry trade
ILO	International Labour Organisation
IOC	Indian Oil Corporation
IP	intellectual property
IPRs	intellectual property rights
ISI	import substitution industrialisation
ITA	information technology agreement
ITC	International Trade Centre
ITCB	International Textile and Clothing Bureau
IWT	Inland Water Transport
J&K	Jammu and Kashmir
LDCs	less developed countries
LMG	Like Minded Group
MEAs	multilateral environmental agreements
MFA	Multi-Fibre Arrangement
MFN	most-favoured-nation
MNCs	multi-national corporations
MOA	mechanism of action
MoU	memorandum of understanding
MR	medical representative
MRTP	Monopolies and Restrictive Trade Practices
MTNs	multilateral trade negotiations
NAFTA	North American Free Trade Agreement
NAMA	Non-Agricultural Market Access
NAS	National Accounts Statistics
NATO	North Atlantic Treaty Organization
NBER	National Bureau of Economic Research
NCB	National Competitive Bidding
NDDR	new drug discovery research
NDDS	novel drug delivery systems
NE	North-Eastern
NSDP	Net State Domestic Product
NTBs	non-tariff barriers
NTMs	non-tariff measures

OECD	Organization for Economic Co-operation and Development
OPEC	Organisation of the Petroleum Exporting Countries
OPT	Outward Processing Traffic
OVB	omitted variables bias
PNTR	permanent normal trade relations
PoK	Pakistan occupied Kashmir
PRC	People's Republic of China
PSEs	public sector enterprises
PTA	Preferential Trading Agreement
PWD	Public Works Department
QR	quantitative restrictions
R&D	research and development
RBI	Reserve Bank of India
RCA	elative comparative advantage
RCA	revealed comparative advantage
RCA	Revealed Comparative Advantage
RIS	Research and Information System for Developing Countries
RoO	Rules of Origin
RTA	Regional Trading Arrangement
S&DT	Special and Differential Treatment
SAARC	South Asian Association for Regional Cooperation
SACU	Southern African Customs Union
SAFTA	South Asia Free Trade Agreement
SCO	Shanghai Cooperation Organization
SEZs	special economic zones
SITC	Standard International Trade Classification
SP	special product
SPS	sanitary and phyto-sanitary
SPS	Sanitary and Phytosanitary Agreement
SRE	Silk Route Extension
SSC	Special Safeguard Clause
SSG	special safeguards
SSM	special safeguard mechanism
STEs	state trading enterprises
TBT	technical barriers to trade
TEDs	turtle exclusion devices
TF	trade facilitation
TFP	total factor productivity
TIC	Trade Indifference Curve
TMB	Textiles Monitoring Body
TNCs	Transnational National Corporations
TPA	Trade Promotion Authority
TPEDB	Tarim Petroleum Exploration and Development Bureau
TRIMs	Trade Related Investment Measures
TRIPS	Trade related Intellectual Property Rights
TRQ	tariff rate quota

TTF	Trade and Transport Facilitation
UK	United Kingdom
UN	United Nations
UNCITRAL	United Nations Centre for International Trade Law
UNCTAD	United Nations Conference on Trade and Development
UPA	United Progressive Alliance
UPOV	International Union for the Protection of New Varieties of Plants
US	United States
USAID	United Stated Agency for International Development
USFDA	US Food and Drug Administration
USP	US Pharmacopoeia
USTR	United States Trade Representative
WBIDC	West Bengal Industrial Development Corporation
WCO	World Customs Organization
WIPO	World Intellectual Property Organization
WRAP	Worldwide Responsible Apparel Production
WRAP	Worldwide Responsible Apparel Production
WTO	World Trade Organization
XUAR	Xinjiang Uighur Autonomous Region
VRA	voluntary restraint arrangement
VER	voluntary export restraint
OMA	orderly marketing arrangement

Short Explanations of Important Terms

ABI: Argentina, Brazil and India, formed to negotiate on NAMA.

Aggregate Measurement of Support (AMS): AMS mean the annual level of support that have direct effects on production and trade, expressed in monetary terms, provided for an agricultural product or non-product specific support given in favour of agricultural producers other than support provided under programmes that qualify as exempt from reduction under Annex 2 to the AOA. Total Aggregate Measurement of Support means (Total AMS)—all product-specific support and non-product-specific support in one single figure. Members with a Total AMS have to reduce base period (1995) support by 20 per cent over 6 years (developed country members) or 13 per cent over 10 years (developing country members). Least-developed countries do not need to make any cuts.

Agreement on Agriculture (AOA): The original GATT did apply to agricultural trade, but it contained loopholes. For example, it allowed countries to use some non-tariff measures such as import quotas, and to subsidise. In particular, developed countries like the EU and the US had developed a complicated system of subsidising agriculture either through production or through exports subsidies. It was in the Uruguay Round that the AOA was introduced specifically to quotas and exports subsidies. The AOA was to be implemented by 2001 by developed countries and 2005 by developing countries.

The discussion on modalities began with technical work on the three elements of AOA viz. domestic support, market access and export subsidies/competition. Special treatment for developing countries was treated as an integral part of all the three pillars of AOA and non-trade concerns were also included. But positions taken by different members remained wide apart and no consensus could be reached on the draft on modalities, and the deadline passed. The differences prevailed over almost all the areas like various boxes of domestic support, tariff, tariff quotas, export credits, food aid and various provisions for developing countries.

The AOA was intended to operate on three levels: first, to ensure market access, second, to reduce domestic support in the form of subsidies and third to reduce export subsidies.

Agreement on Textiles and Clothing (ATC): By this agreement the WTO members have committed themselves to remove the quotas by 1 January 2005. This obviously means the end of the MFA. The textile sector will be fully integrated into normal GATT rules.

Amber Box: Agricultural support of trade-distorting kinds is referred to as 'Amber Box' measures. For example, government buying-in at a guaranteed price ('market price support') falls into the category of support.

Andean Group: Bolivia, Colombia, Ecuador, Peru and Venezuela.

Anti-Dumping Duties: Article VI of the GATT 1994 permits the imposition of anti-dumping duties against dumping. Dumping means whenever any article is exported from any country or territory to another at less than its normal value then it is called dumping. The country where the goods are dumped can impose an anti-dumping duty not exceeding the margin of dumping, if dumping causes injury to producers of competing products in the importing country.

Asia Pacific Economic Cooperation (APEC): Australia, Brunei Darussalam, Canada, Chile, China, Hong Kong (China), Indonesia, Japan, Republic of Korea, Malaysia, Mexico, New Zealand, Papua New Guinea, Peru, Philippines, the Russian Federation, Singapore, Taiwan (China), Thailand, US and Vietnam.

Association of Caribbean States (ACS): Antigua and Barbuda, the Bahamas, Barbados, Belize, Colombia, Costa Rica, Cuba, Dominica, the Dominican Republic, El Salvador, Grenada, Guatemala, Guyana, Haiti, Honduras, Jamaica, Mexico, Nicaragua, Panama, St. Kitts and Nevis, St Lucia, St Vincent and the Grenadines, Suriname, Trinidad and Tobago and Venezuela.

Association of South-East Asian Nations (ASEAN): Brunei Darussalam, Cambodia (from October 2004), Indonesia, Laos, Malaysia, Myanmar, Philippines, Singapore, Thailand and Vietnam.

Bangkok Agreement: Bangladesh, India, Republic of Korea, Lao People's Democratic Republic, Philippines, Sri Lanka and Thailand.

BIMSTEC: In the name of the founder members the group was originally known as Bangladesh India Myanmar Sri Lanka Thailand Economic Cooperation. However, with the entry of Bhutan and Nepal, its name was changed to Bay of Bengal Initiative for Multi-Sectoral Technical and Economic Cooperation.

Blue Box: Direct payments under production limiting programmes referred to as 'Blue Box' measures, which are exempt from commitments if such payments are made on fixed areas and yield or a fixed number of livestock.

Cairns Group: The Cairn Group is a coalition of 19 agricultural exporting nations accounting for one-third of world's exports of agricultural exports. It is a diverse coalition bringing together developed and developing countries from Latin America, Africa and the Asia-Pacific region and has been an influential voice in the agricultural reform debate since its formation in 1986 and has continued to play a key role in pressing the WTO membership to meet in full the far-reaching mandate set in Doha. The current members of this group are: Australia, Argentina, Brazil, Canada, Chile, Colombia, Fiji, Indonesia, Malaysia, New Zealand, Pakistan, Paraguay, Peru, the Philippines, South Africa, Thailand and Uruguay.

Caribbean Community and Common Market (CARICOM): Antigua and Barbuda, the Bahamas (part of the Caribbean Community but not of the common market), Barbados, Belize, Dominica, Grenada, Guyana, Jamaica, Montserrat, St Kitts and Nevis, St Lucia, St Vincent and the Grenadines, Suriname and Trinidad and Tobago.

Central European Free Trade Area (CEFTA): Bulgaria, the Czech Republic, Hungary, Poland, Romania, the Slovak Republic and Slovenia.

Circumvention: Avoiding quotas and other restrictions by altering the country of origin of a product

Common Agricultural Policy (CAP): The EU's comprehensive system of production targets and marketing mechanisms designed to manage agricultural trade within the EU and with the rest of the world.

Countervailing Measures: Action taken by the importing country, usually in the form of increased duties to offset subsidies given to producers or exporters in the exporting country

Cross-Border Initiative (CBI): Comoros, Kenya, Madagascar, Malawi, Mauritius, Namibia, Rwanda, Seychelles, Swaziland, Tanzania, Uganda, Zambia and Zimbabwe.

De minimis: Under the *de minimis* provisions of the AOA there is no requirement to reduce trade-distorting domestic support in any year in which the aggregate value of the product-specific support does not exceed 5 per cent of the total value of production of the agricultural product in question. In addition, non-product specific support which is less than 5 per cent of the value of total agricultural production is also exempt from reduction. The 5 per cent threshold applies to developed countries whereas in the case of developing countries the *de minimis* ceiling is 10 per cent.

Dispute Settlement Understanding: Crucial feature of the Uruguay Round agreement was to put in place a sophisticated DSM. Under this a Dispute Settlement Body (DSB) is set up to manage trade disputes between WTO signatories. Once the dispute settlement board gives the ruling then the aggrieved party has the right to retaliate against the offending party.

Dumping: Occurs when goods are exported at a price less than their normal value, generally meaning they are exported for less than they are sold in the domestic market or third-country markets, or at less than production cost.

East Asian Economic Caucus (EACS): Brunei Darussalam, China, Hong Kong (China), Indonesia, Japan, Republic of Korea, Malaysia, Philippines, Singapore, Taiwan (China) and Thailand.

Economic Community of West African States (ECOWAS): Benin, Burkina Faso, Cape Verde, Cote d'Ivoire, the Gambia, Ghana, Guinea, Guinea-Bissau, Liberia, Mali, Mauritania, Niger, Nigeria, Senegal, Sierra Leone and Togo.

European Free Trade Association (EFTA): The group was formed in 1960 by Austria, Denmark, Norway, Portugal, Sweden, Switzerland, and Britain as an alternative to the European Economic Community (EEC). Some members joined the EEC subsequently. Currently the members are Iceland, Liechtenstein, Norway, and Switzerland. During 1990s Iceland, Liechtenstein, and Norway had joined the European Economic Area (EEA), which also include all members of the EU.

European Union (EU): Austria, Belgium, Denmark, Finland, France, Germany, Greece, Ireland, Italy, Luxembourg, the Netherlands, Portugal, Spain, Sweden and the United Kingdom were the original EU (15). However, in April 2004 ten East European Republics have joined the Union as well to make it EU (25)—Cyprus, Czech Republic, Estonia, Hungary, Latvia, Lithuania, Malta, Poland, Slovakia and Slovenia.

Exceptions: Some exceptions in trade are allowed under the WTO regime. For example, countries can set up a free trade agreement that applies only to goods traded within the group—discriminating against goods from outside. Or they can give developing countries special access to their markets. Or a country can raise barriers against products that are considered to be traded unfairly from specific countries. And in services, countries are allowed, in limited circumstances, to discriminate. But the agreements only permit these exceptions under strict conditions.

Export enhancement programme (EEP): A programme of US export subsidies given generally to compete with subsidised agricultural exports from the EU on certain export markets.

Export subsidies: Under the AOA, taking averages for 1986–90 as the base level, developed countries agreed to cut the value of export subsidies by 36 per cent over the six years starting in 1995 (24 per cent over 10 years for developing countries). Developed countries also agreed to reduce the quantities of subsidised exports by 21 per cent over the six years (14 per cent over 10 years for developing countries). Least developed countries do not need to make any cuts. It must be clearly recognised that least developed countries have no obligation to reduce subsidies; other developing countries like India that give almost no subsidies and with their per capita income below 1000 dollars, are not obliged to reduce any agriculture subsidies.

Five Interested Parties (FIPS): Australia, Brazil, the EU, India and the US.

Food security: Concept which discourages opening the domestic market to foreign agricultural products on the principle that a country must be as self-sufficient as possible for its basic dietary needs

Friends of Geographical Indications (FGI): Dominican Republic, Egypt, Honduras, India, Jamaica, Kenya, Pakistan, Sri Lanka and Thailand. Similar views were expressed also by some of the transition economies like Bulgaria, Czech Republic, Romania, Slovakia and Slovenia.

Friends of the Development Box (FDB): Cuba, Dominican Republic, El Salvador, Haiti, Honduras, Kenya, Nicaragua, Nigeria, Pakistan, Peru, Senegal, Sri Lanka, Uganda and Zimbabwe.

G-10: Bulgaria, Iceland, Israel, Japan, Korea, Republic of Liechtenstein, Mauritius, Norway, Switzerland, Chinese Taipei (also referred as 'European-East Asian grouping').

G-10: Argentina, Brazil, Cuba, Egypt, India, Nicaragua, Nigeria, Peru, Tanzania and Yugoslavia (formed during the Uruguay Round).

G-110: The developing country coalition formed at Hong Kong Ministerial (2005) by G-20 and G-90 coming together.

G-15: A 15 member group formed in 1989. There are now 19 members. The current members are Algeria, Argentina, Brazil, Chile, Colombia, Egypt, India, Indonesia, Iran, Jamaica, Kenya, Malaysia, Mexico, Nigeria, Peru, Senegal, Sri Lanka, Venezuela and Zimbabwe.

G-20: Argentina, Bolivia, Brazil, Chile, China, Cuba, Egypt, India, Indonesia, Mexico, Nigeria, Pakistan, Paraguay, the Philippines, South Africa, Thailand, Venezuela, and Zimbabwe (formed in 2003).

G-24: Argentina, Bolivia, Brazil, Colombia, Cuba, Dominican Republic, Ecuador, Salvador, Honduras, India, Indonesia, Malaysia, Mexico, Nicaragua, Pakistan, Panama, Paraguay, Peru, the Philippines, Sri Lanka, Thailand, Uruguay and Venezuela.

G-33: The G-33 is also known as the SP/SSM, an alliance to champion the concepts and provisions of special products and special safeguard mechanisms. The group comprises 42 developing countries of the WTO. They are: Antigua and Barbuda, Barbados, Belize, Benin, Botswana, China, Cote d'Ivoire, Congo, Cuba, Dominican Republic, Grenada, Guyana, Haiti, Honduras, India, Indonesia, Jamaica, Kenya, Korea, Mauritius, Mongolia, Montserrat, Mozambique, Nicaragua, Nigeria, Pakistan, Panama, The Philippines, Peru, Saint Kitts, Saint Lucia, Saint Vincent and the Grenadines, Senegal, Sri Lanka, Suriname, Tanzania, Trinidad and Tobago, Turkey, Uganda, Venezuela, Zambia, and Zimbabwe.

G-6: Australia, Brazil, the EU, India, Japan and the US

G-7: Group of seven leading industrial countries: Canada, France, Germany, Italy, Japan, United Kingdom, US.

G-77: Developing country grouping in UNCTAD with Brazil and India as members.

G-8: G 7 + Russia

G-9: Australia, Austria, Canada, Finland, Iceland, New Zealand, Norway, Sweden, and Switzerland (formed during Uruguay Round).

G-90: African Union/, ACP and least developed countries (also known as 'G-90', but with 64 WTO members): Angola, Antigua and Barbuda, Bangladesh, Barbados, Belize, Benin, Botswana, Burkina Faso, Burundi, Cambodia. Cameroon, Central African Republic, Chad, Congo, Cote d'Ivoire, Cuba, Democratic Republic of the Congo, Djibouti, Dominica, Dominican Republic, Egypt, Fiji, Gabon, The Gambia, Ghana, Grenada, Guinea (Conakry), Guinea Bissau, Guyana, Haiti, Jamaica, Kenya, Lesotho, Madagascar, Malawi, Maldives, Mali, Mauritania, Mauritius, Morocco, Mozambique, Myamnar, Namibia, Nepal, Niger, Nigeria, Papua New Guinea, Rwanda, Saint Kitts and Nevis, Saint Lucia, Saint Vincent and the Grenadines, Senegal, Sierra Leone, Solomon Islands, South Africa, Suriname, Swaziland, Tanzania, Togo, Trinidad and Tobago, Tunisia, Uganda, Zambia, Zimbabwe.

Generalised Scheme of Preferences (GSP): This was a treatment introduced specifically in the Tokyo round (also known as the developing country round). Under this clause, specific concessions were extended to the developing countries by the developed countries in terms of tariff concessions, which allowed developing countries to export to developed countries at import duties lower than the MFN import duty applicable to other developed countries. However, as and when developing countries graduated to developed country status these GSP preferences were withdrawn. For example in 1984, Hong Kong and Singapore lost their GSP status in exports of textiles to developed countries. In general, the GSP preference is based on the countries' per capita income in US Dollars. Countries lose their GSP status when their per capita income exceeds $1000.

Geographical indications: Certain products are known by the place where they are produced. Well-known examples include Champagne or Scotch. TRIPS agreement contains special provisions for these products.

Green Box: Agricultural support with no, or minimal, distortive effect on trade is referred to as 'Green Box' measures. For example, support provided for agricultural research or training is considered under this type.

Harmonised system: An international nomenclature developed by the World Customs Organization, which is arranged in six digit codes allowing all participating countries to classify traded goods on a common basis. Beyond the six digit level, countries are free to introduce national distinctions for tariffs and many other purposes.

Information technology agreement (ITA): Formally the ministerial-declaration on trade in information technology products under which participants will remove tariffs on IT products by the year 2000

Internal support: Encompasses any measure which acts to maintain producer prices at levels above those prevailing in international trade; direct payments to producers, including deficiency payments, and input and marketing cost reduction measures available only for agricultural production.

Market access: The AOA commits all WTO members to long-term reforms which would make agricultural trade fairer and more market-oriented. The main elements of AOA relate to the following three areas of policy:

- Market access, i.e., opening markets by removing various restrictions on imports.
- Domestic Support, i.e., reducing import subsidies and output price support operations so that the relative profitability is least disturbed.
- Export Subsidies, i.e., reducing the subsidies on export operations.

Developing countries do not have to cut the subsidies or lower their obligations. Least-developed countries don't have to do this and special provisions deal with the interests of countries that rely on imports for their food supplies. There is a 'peace provision' under which disputes on agriculture subsidies cannot be responded to by anti-dumping actions till the end of 2003.

Agricultural trade in the international markets before the WTO era was extremely restrictive and protected. The earlier era allowed far greater protection against agricultural imports like quantitative restrictions (QRs) through canalisation, licensing, quotas, etc. extending even to complete import bans on some commodities.

Most favoured nation (MFN) Clause: Under this clause, all tariff and other reforms agreed to by any country in the round of trade negotiations are extended to all signatories to a trade agreement. In other words, no bilateral agreements are normally permitted.

Multi-Fibre Agreement (MFA): Before the WTO Agreement took effect in 1995, a large portion of textiles and clothing exports from developing countries to the industrial countries was subject to quotas under a special regime outside normal GATT rules. Much of the trade in this sector prior to 1995 was subject to bilateral quotas negotiated under the MFA. The MFA governed the trade in textiles since 1974 until its end in 1995. The MFA essentially means an arrangement by which countries are allocated Quotas by the quota imposing countries. It can be a bilateral agreement or unilateral action.

National treatment (NT): The principle of giving others the same treatment as one's own nationals. GATT Article III requires that imports be treated no less favourably than the same or similar domestically-produced goods once they have passed customs. GATS Article XVII and TRIPS Article 3 also deal with national treatment for services and intellectual property protection. This is an extension of MFN principle to the domestic market. This principle entails that imported and domestic commodities must be treated equally. The principle is also applicable to foreign and domestic services and foreign and domestic legal trademarks, patents, etc. For example, one cannot have stipulation that imported goods will be charged a different sales tax from a domestic good or to take another example, one cannot in general say that foreign company resident in India will be subjected to different laws than a wholly owned Indian Company.

As in the case of MFN a country can specify exceptions to National Treatment. These exceptions are not normally of indefinite duration.

Non-reciprocity clause: This was also inserted in the Tokyo Round. It implies that developing countries do not have to reciprocate tariff concessions offered by developed countries. While this non-reciprocity implied that developing countries could keep the markets protected from exports from developed countries, it also implied that developing countries had no incentives to negotiate on trade issues

Non-tariff measures (NTMs): Quotas, import licensing systems, sanitary regulations, prohibitions, etc.

Nullification and impairment: Means damage to a country's benefits and expectations from its WTO membership through another country's change in its trade regime or failure to carry out its WTO obligations.

Price undertaking: Undertaking by an exporter to raise the export price of the product to avoid the possibility of an anti-dumping duty is called price undertaking.

PSI: Pre-shipment inspection—the practice of employing specialised private companies to check shipment details of goods ordered overseas—i.e. price, quantity, quality, etc.

Quantitative restrictions (QRs): Specific limits on the quantity or value of goods that can be imported (or exported) during a specific time period.

Regional trade agreements of India:

Agreement	*Date Signed*	*Partners*
Indo-Sri Lanka Free Trade Agreement	28 December 1998	India, Sri Lanka
Framework agreement with Chile	20 January 2005	India-Chile
Free Trade Agreement on Trade and Commerce	28 February 1995	India-Bhutan
Framework Agreement for Free Trade Area	10 September 2003 (amended on 30 August 2004)	India-Thailand
Agreement on Trade and Economic Cooperation	16 September 1996	India-Mongolia

(Contd)

(Table Contd)

Agreement	Date Signed	Partners
India-Bangladesh Trade Agreement	4 October 1980 (renewed from time to time and now valid up to 30 October 2001)	India-Bangladesh
India-Maldives Trade Agreement	31 March 1981	India- Maldives
Indo-Nepal Treaty of Trade	6 December 1991	India-Nepal
Framework Agreement on India-Egypt Preferential Trade Area	30 April 2001	India-Egypt
India-Singapore Comprehensive Economic Cooperation Agreement	29 June 2005	India-Singapore
Framework Agreement for Comprehensive Economic Cooperation between India and ASEAN Nations	8 October 2003	India- Brunei Darussalam, Cambodia, Indonesia, Lao PDR, Malyasia, Myanmar, Philipines, Singapore, Thailand, Vietnam.
India-MERCOSUR Preferential Trade Agreement	25 January 2004	India-Argentina, Brazil, Paraguay, Uruguay
India- GCC Framework Agreement on Economic Cooperation	25 August 2004	India-UAE, Baharain, Saudi Arabia, Oman, Qatar, Kuwait
Framework Agreement on BIMST Economic Cooperation FTA	8 February 2004	Bhutan, India, Myanmar, Nepal, Sri Lanka, Thailand
Agreement on South Asian Free Trade Area	January 2004	India, Pakistan, Srilanka, Bangladesh, Bhutan, Maldives, Nepal
India-SACU (Southern African Customs Union) Framework Agreement	September 2004	India- South Africa, Lesotho, Swaziland, Botswana and Namibia
Bangkok Agreement	31 July 1975 (latest negotiation in October 2001)	Now operational between five countries: Bangladesh, China, India, Republic of Korea and Srilanka
India-ASEAN Free Trade Agreement in goods	To be signed in April 2009	Brunei, Cambodia, Indonesia, Laos, Malaysia, Myanmar, the Philippines, Singapore, Thailand and Vietnam

Rules of origin: Laws, regulations and administrative procedures are used to determine a product's country of origin. A decision by a customs authority on origin can determine whether a shipment falls within a quota limitation or qualifies for a tariff preference or is affected by an anti-dumping duty. These rules can vary from country to country.

Safeguard measures: Action taken to protect a specific industry from an unexpected build-up of imports—governed by Article XIX of the GATT 1994 is known as safeguard measures.

Sanitary and phyto-sanitary (SPS) measures agreement: To prevent entry of products, which are sub standard. The SPS agreement allows countries to set their own standards. But it also says regulations must be based on science. They should be applied only to the extent necessary to protect human, animal or plant life or health. Member countries are encouraged to use international standards if there is scientific justification.

'Single-Undertaking' Clause: This clause has been inserted in all trade-agreements under the Uruguay Round in 1995. Specifically, it implies that countries undertake to implement the full text of an agreement and not part of it.

Tariff binding: Commitment not to increase a rate of duty beyond an agreed level. Once a rate of duty is bound, it may not be raised without compensating the affected parties.

Tariff escalation: Higher import duties on semi-processed products than on raw materials, and higher still on finished products. This practice protects domestic processing industries and discourages the development of processing activity in the countries where raw materials originate.

Tariff peaks: Relatively high tariffs, usually on 'sensitive' products, compared to generally low tariff levels. For industrialised countries, tariffs of 15 per cent and above are generally recognised as 'tariff peaks'.

Tariffication: Procedures relating to the agricultural market-access provision in which all non-tariff measures are converted into tariffs.

Tariffs: Customs duties on merchandise imports levied either on an ad valorem basis (percentage of value) or on a specific basis (e.g. $7 per 100 Kgs.). Tariffs give price advantage to similar locally-produced goods and raise revenues for the government.

Technical barriers to trade agreements (TBT): The objective of the agreement is to attempt some harmonisation of domestic regulations, standards, testing and certification procedures etc., to ensure that these standards cannot be used as artificial trade restrictions. The agreement says the procedures used to decide whether a product conforms with national standards have to be fair and equitable. It discourages any methods that would give domestically produced goods an unfair advantage. The agreement also encourages countries to recognise each others testing procedures.

Textiles Monitoring Body (TMB): If taken, the level of restraints should be fixed at a level not lower than the actual level of exports or imports from the country concern

Trade Facilitation: Removing obstacles to the movement of goods across borders (e.g. simplification of customs procedures).

Trade Negotiations: The time period involved in the initial agreement and the final implementation of the agreement is called a Round of Trade Negotiations. There have been eight rounds of trade negotiations since 1947 the details of which are given below by year, name of the place where the round was held, main issues of negotiations and number of contracting parties, that is, formal members of the GATT:

1947	1st Conference on multilateral trade negotiations (Geneva)	23
1949	2nd Conference on multilateral trade negotiations (Annecy)	23
1951	3rd Conference on multilateral trade negotiations (Torquay)	32
1956	4th Conference on multilateral trade negotiations (Geneva)	34
1960–61	Dillon Round	37
1964–67	Kennedy Round	76
1973–79	Tokyo Round	85
1982 (November)	Ministerial meeting, establishment the Preparatory Committee for a New Round	
1986 (September)	Launch of the Uruguay Round (Punta del Este)	
1994 (April)	Signaturs (Marrakesh)	95
1995 (January)	Establishment of the World Trade Organization	
1996 (December)	Ministerial Meeting (Singapore)	
1998 (May)	Ministerial Meeting (Geneva)	
1999 (November–December)	Ministerial Meeting (Seattle)	
2001 (November)	Ministerial Meeting (Doha)	
2003 (September)	Ministerial Meeting (Cancun)	
2005 (December)	Ministerial Meeting (Hong Kong)	

Trade Policy Review Body: It is also agreed that trade policies of the government are to be periodically reviewed. The Trade Policy Review Body is meant to serve this purpose. The objectives are: (i) to increase the transparency and understand of countries' trade policies and practices, though regular monitoring; (ii) to improve the quality of public and intergovernmental debate on the issues; (iii) to enable a multilateral assessment of the effects of policies on the world trading system.

Trade Related Intellectual Properties (TRIPS): Knowledge is an important part of trade in certain commodities and high technology products, because these products are based upon invention, innovation, research design and testing. Films, music recording, books, computer software and on line services are bought and sold because of the information and creativity they contain. Creators of such inventions and designs are given a right known as intellectual property rights. For instance, books, paintings and films have copyright, inventions are patented, brand names and product logos are registered as trademarks.

Transitional safeguard mechanism: Allows members to impose restrictions against individual exporting countries if the importing country can show that both overall imports of a product and imports from the individual countries are entering the country in such increased quantities as to cause—or threaten—serious damage to the relevant domestic industry.

Uruguay Round: Multilateral trade negotiations launched at Punta del Este, Uruguay in September 1986 and concluded in Geneva in December 1993, adoption of the final Act. Signed by ministers in Marrakesh, Morocco, in April 1994.

VRA, VER and OMA: Voluntary restraint arrangement, voluntary export restraint and orderly marketing arrangement, mean bilateral arrangements whereby an exporting country (government or industry) agrees to reduce or restrict exports without the importing country having to make use of quotas, tariffs or other import controls.

World Customs Organization (WCO): A multilateral body located in Brussels through which participating countries seek to simplify and rationalise customs procedures.

The World Trade Organization (WTO):

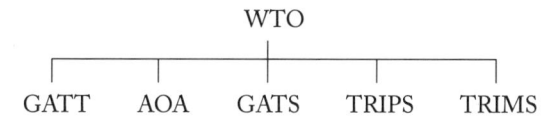

```
                        WTO
         ┌──────┬────────┼────────┬──────┐
        GATT   AOA      GATS    TRIPS  TRIMS
```

GATT: General Agreement on Tariffs and Trade: this is carried over from the earlier agreement and deals with trade in commodities.

AOA: Agreement on Agriculture covers trade agreement relating to exports and imports of agricultural goods.

GATS: General Agreement on Trade in Services: this agreement applies to trade in services like software exports, insurance etc.

TRIPS: Trade Related Intellectual Properties: this relates to trade in commodities where some patent protection is necessary.

TRIMS: Trade Related Investment Measures: this is related to those investment measures that complied with GATT provisions.

Introduction

ALOKESH BARUA AND ROBERT M. STERN

"I don't think they play at all fairly," Alice began in a rather complaining tone, "and they all quarrel so dreadfully one can hardly hear oneself speak—and they don't seem to have any rules in particular; at least, if there are, no one attends to them...."

Lewis Carroll, *Alice's Adventures in Wonderland*, p. 112

THE WTO IN THE MAKING

The Global Trading System: Yesterday and Today

To a reader in the nineteenth century the above quote might well have seemed a fair description of global trading relations at the time rather than of a game of croquet in the Queen of Hearts' court. It was only in the course of the nineteenth century that the beginnings of some order, as we know it today, began to emerge. Industrialisation had been taking hold in several countries, and it generated an intensified search for foreign markets and sources of supply. Governments in Europe were faced with calls for lower tariff barriers on imported inputs and to negotiate reductions in tariffs protecting foreign markets. But in a nationalistic world of vying states—as it still is today—governments were not about to ease access to their markets in the absence of some quid pro quo.

The way forward had been found in the adoption of two instruments of policy—reciprocity and non-discrimination—which had set off a wave of trade liberalisation. These two ideas had enabled countries to surmount their innate distrust of each other and to engage in mutually beneficial and generalised reductions in tariff barriers. Reciprocity—meaning, contingent and equivalent concessions—had assuaged the fear of governments that they might not be receiving, at least as much, from others as they were giving themselves, and non-discrimination had reassured them that they were enjoying the same treatment as had been won by other competing states. Neither of these ideas was a sudden intellectual invention; they had long been known to guide human affairs. But, their application to trade relations had been comparatively new and has done much to advance global trade liberalisation.

Historians have usually identified the signing of the Anglo-French Treaty of 1860 as the landmark that signalled the new era of trade relations. Besides, the need for a political gesture of friendship, the immediate cause for the signing of the treaty, had been a decision by the French government to follow Britain's policy of trade liberalisation that had been introduced following the repealing of the British Corn Laws in the 1840s. This had marked the end of British mercantilism that had been criticised many decades earlier, in the writings of Adam Smith and David Ricardo. The French leaders had been persuaded at the time by the popular, but mistakenly simplistic and mono-causal, belief that Britain's superior industrial performance owed much to its free trade policy. However, in undertaking to reduce tariffs on British manufactures, the French government had sought some concession from Britain in order to win the support of its export interests in getting the lower tariffs passed through the Parliament. Although, Britain had already nailed the flag of free trade to its mast—and had firmly, but exceptionally, believed that others in their own interest should also reduce their tariffs unilaterally—it had accommodated the French political need. Further, when other European countries had anxiously sought comparable access to the French market, France had offered them the same tariff rates that it had set for Britain. Thereafter, the inclusion of such a most-favoured-nation (MFN) clause in commercial treaties had become common practice among the European states. It also had the advantage of preventing treaties from being in a constant state of flux, with tariff schedules having to be repeatedly renegotiated bilaterally.

What had emerged, in industrialising Europe from the struggle of countries to gain market access for their exports of manufactured goods, was a network of bilateral, commercial treaties linked together through the MFN clause. While this had been a step towards more predictable trade relations, the system however, was not notable for its stability. Apart from Britain—which had adhered with almost religious fervour to free trade—most European countries had found their treaty obligation hard to live with. After a drift towards freer trade in the 1850s and 1860s, most countries had later, assumed more protectionist stances. Commercial treaties had been frequently denounced or renegotiated, and some lengthy and bitter trade wars had broken out. Still, while every country had valued the freedom to make unilateral decisions about its national trade barriers, all had been driven reluctantly to accept certain constraints on their behaviour, in order to gain access to others' markets.

The outbreak of World War I in 1914 and the subsequent political upheaval engendered in its aftermath, had disrupted trade relations for some years. Nevertheless, in the peace conferences following the war, the avowed goal of governments had been to restore the pre-1914 order in international monetary, financial and trade relations. But economic conditions had militated against a restoration of the minimal levels of mutual trust necessary for agreements. In the unstable monetary conditions of the early 1920s, countries had engaged in currency depreciations that had been seen by others as competitive and, in line with economic thinking of the time, and thus made the negotiation of tariff reductions pointless. For a while, in the later 1920s, restoration of the gold standard made the outlook, for trade relations, appear more hopeful. But the differences in tariff levels between the high and low tariff countries had been sizable, and governments could not agree on a common formula for tariff cutting. The onset of the Depression in the 1930s and early responses to it, with tariff increases and currency devaluations, had put an end to any hope for normal trade relations. Some countries, led by Germany, had resorted to bilateral barter or clearing arrangements that had necessarily been discriminatory. Others, like Britain, had sought to revive trade through the creation of preferential trading areas. In these circumstances of worldwide inadequacies in domestic demand, trade relations had largely ceased to be conducted within a multilateral framework based on non-discrimination.

Introduction 3

It is notable that the United States (US) had virtually played no part in the evolution of trade relations before World War I and remained largely aloof from international trade affairs in the inter-war years. American manufacturing and marketing skills had become internationally evident as early as the 1890s, but the US had principally remained, for many years, an exporter of primary commodities. It had been fortunate that agricultural exports had generally met with low trade barriers before World War I, so there were few restraints on the US' pursuit of a high tariff policy on imported manufactures. Indeed, the US Congress could then interpret reciprocity as the negotiation of reductions in foreign tariffs, with the threat of increases in American tariffs. MFN treatment had also been offered only conditionally, so that to qualify for a new MFN tariff rate, all trading partners had to offer equivalent tariff reductions.

However, by the 1920s the interest of US manufacturing industries in foreign markets had grown substantially, with the share of manufactured goods having risen to nearly two-thirds of total exports. A latecomer to the world of trade relations, it was only then that the US gradually begun to accommodate the accepted international norms while trading with other countries. With the adoption of the Fordney-McCumber Tariff Act in 1922, the principle of unconditional MFN treatment had been adopted. And, in 1934, the passage of the Reciprocal Trade Agreements Act had made reciprocity—understood as equivalence in concessions—the accepted means of gaining improved access to foreign markets.

The New Era of the General Agreement on Tariffs and Trade

Following World War II, which ended in 1945, the US had launched its grand design to establish an orderly multilateral framework for international monetary, financial, and trade relations. The ideas of non-discrimination and reciprocity had again become central to global arrangements for trade. But now, they had been formally embodied in a multilateral agreement—the General Agreement on Tariffs and Trade (GATT). Two factors had reinforced the great importance given by US policy makers, at the time, to the principle of non-discrimination. One had been the conviction, of the Roosevelt administration's Secretary of State, Cordell Hull, that the trade discrimination practiced internationally in the 1930s, had exacerbated the bitter political rivalries in a period that had finally terminated in war. The other had been the more commercial reason that US manufacturers had particularly resented the British imperial preferences, erected in the early 1930s.

The ideas of non-discrimination and reciprocity have substantially contributed to the progressive reduction of trade barriers on manufactured goods, among the core industrialised countries, including North America, Western Europe and Japan, since the end of World War II. The core countries, until very recently, had dominated trade relations within the GATT framework, and their central focus had been on the reduction of industrial tariffs. These tariffs have been significantly reduced, as a result of the periodic GATT negotiations that were carried out between 1947 and 1994, with the conclusion of the Uruguay Round negotiations. In the early years of the post-World War II GATT negotiations, these tariff reductions had been negotiated bilaterally, on a reciprocal basis. Later, in the Kennedy Round in the 1960s, reciprocity had been expressed in the adoption of a common tariff formula that had replaced or supplemented bilateral negotiations. In principle, the core countries likewise had largely adhered to non-discrimination in their trade with each other. But, subsequently, in practice, they had deviated substantially in the 1970s and 1980s, by resorting to measures outside the framework of the GATT. These measures had mainly taken the form of voluntary export restraints or orderly marketing agreements. While their incidence fell more on Japan and some of the newly industrialising countries in East Asia and elsewhere, this evasion of GATT rules became so prevalent that it seriously undermined the respect for the system on which its existence depended. It was partly for this reason that governments during the Uruguay Round negotiations (1986–94) had agreed to eschew these practices and thereby, reaffirm adherence to non-discrimination.

Thus, up to and even including the Uruguay Round, it could be fairly said that the ideas of reciprocity and non-discrimination largely shaped international trade relations. But the increasing resort especially to preferential trading arrangements before and after the Uruguay Round changed these governing ideas. Reciprocity, as a guiding principle, had lost some of its relevance and clarity; and, in the face of the proliferation of free trade agreements (FTAs), non-discrimination in trade relations among states, appeared to fade into the background.

Reciprocity and the Changing Character of Trade Negotiations

Two changes that had taken place during and since the Uruguay Round, muddied the nature of reciprocity as an idea guiding multilateral trade relations. The first had been that at the behest of the industrial countries, the content of trade negotiations had been substantially broadened; and the second had been that the developing countries, largely due to their emergence as significant exporters of manufactures, had become influential participants in these negotiations.

Among the major industrial countries, the negotiation of improved market access for service industries and for capital, had continued to be based on a clear recognition of reciprocity. Countries had agreed to a mutual widening of markets, yielding potential advantage to producers and investors on all sides. In this regard, even the new Uruguay Round Agreement, on the protection of intellectual property rights (IPRs), had only reaffirmed a mutually advantageous form of cooperation that had long been in place.

For the developing countries, however, the question of reciprocity had been more complex and uncertain. Developing countries had earlier sought a special status within the GATT, claiming that the industrial countries should reduce their trade barriers for them, keeping in line with the principle of non-discrimination. But, the developing countries in turn, would not adhere to the condition of reciprocity. The exceptional status of the developing countries had been taken further in the 1970s, when the industrial countries introduced the Generalised System of Preferences. This had also been given formal recognition during the Tokyo Round in the late 1970s when clauses relating to Special and Differential Treatment were incorporated into the GATT. Further, particular groups of developing countries had been given additional preferential access to industrial countries' markets. The other side of the coin had been that the industrial countries felt free to disregard the spirit of the GATT whenever it proved politically expedient to do so. They had not hesitated to practice extensive discrimination against specific exports from developing countries, most egregiously, when they had imposed restrictions on textiles and apparel in the 1960s that burgeoned into the Multi-Fibre Arrangement (MFA).

Before the launching of the Uruguay Round in 1986, however, these unequal relations had begun to change. Many developing countries had made progress in modernising their economies through industrialisation; and they were all influenced, to varying degrees, by the worldwide shift in beliefs about economic policy that, among other things, favoured more outward-oriented growth. Indeed, several developing countries had unilaterally lowered their trade barriers and most had become members of, or sought membership in, the GATT.

During and after the Uruguay Round, some 'rebalancing' in trade relations began to take place, though it remains highly controversial whether the negotiations had satisfied the condition of reciprocity. While developing countries generally did not fully reciprocate in tariff reductions, they had agreed, in principle, to the opening up of market access to service industries and to limitations on the conditions that could be imposed on foreign direct investment (FDI). These were both concessions that had appeared to largely benefit producers and investors in the industrial countries. When the new international rules on IPRs had been added to the list, the grounds for questioning the reciprocal character of the negotiations appeared substantial to many observers.

But there has been another, and less obvious, reason why the idea of reciprocity has lost much of its clarity. This was because the Uruguay Round also gave weight to rules—like those relating to subsidies and FDI—which, while relating to issues of market access, had also directly impinged on domestic policies and practices. Together with revisions of domestic laws and regulations, required by the liberalisation of the service industries, these had initiated, what some commentators have dubbed as the 'deeper integration' of markets. They have marked the beginning of a new development in trade relations, in which actual or proposed trade rules could penetrate more deeply into the management of national economic and social affairs. Some of the issues later raised by the industrial countries for inclusion in the Doha Round negotiations have borne the same stamp.

While some developing countries may have tacitly accepted these changing rules, others have voiced serious misgivings. As in all countries, the desire to protect entrenched domestic interests for internal political reasons has no doubt been an active consideration. But there have also been other, more valid reasons. Of central concern, were the limitations that these changes had imposed on the development policies, which these countries had been pursuing. Since the early years after World War II, most developing countries have used their powers to establish national firms in non-traditional sectors. They have created investment opportunities for the domestic business community (or political elite) through the use of a range of measures including tariffs, subsidies in one form or another, quantitative restrictions and limitations on foreign investment. Accordingly, there has been considerable concern that the freedom to pursue such development policies has been jeopardised by some of the rules that had been adopted in the Uruguay Round.

Some of these new rules were apparently extending the principle of national treatment beyond its traditional, and limited, meaning through added restrictions on the freedom of governments to discriminate in favour of national firms by means of domestic measures. In effect, the leading industrialised-country governments were collectively seeking to create an international framework of rules and procedures within which their own markets could be more closely integrated with each other. It was, in more popular terms, to establish a 'level playing field' in which the firms of each country would ideally compete everywhere on the same terms. The incipient framework drew on the ideas that guided the industrialised countries, and in particular, the US, in the management of their own domestic markets.

This represents a new paradigm in trade relations. It has been advocated by those who lean towards a cosmopolitan view of the global economy; a view that sees the emergence of an increasingly integrated world market governed by common rules that regulate transactions in this single market. It has a view that coincides with exporting interests, especially those of multinational corporations. But, almost all countries also have national aims that they were not willing to surrender in order to accommodate their trading partners. Some of these aims were rightly dismissed by cosmopolitan proponents as essentially being obstructive rent-seeking activities, agricultural protectionism and anti-dumping measures. But, it needs to be understood that there was a global diversity in such aims and policies. Many of these aims and policies have deep roots in national societies, and it can be argued that they should therefore be afforded legitimacy. This has been a reality that was reflected in the historically more familiar view of the world as composed of separate nation states, each with its own national market. In this view, it was for each country to decide—in the light of its own social norms and economic aims—how far it wanted to adjust its own domestic laws and practices in order to accommodate its trading partners and to gain a comparable adjustment from them. It has been a view that has long been the basis for achieving the reciprocal liberalisation of trade.

Establishing the World Trade Organization

The World Trade Organization (WTO), created in 1995, was thus the successor to, and incorporates within it, the GATT which was a treaty among Western market economies at the end of World War II. In the GATT, member countries agreed to abide by the rules relating to when they could increase trade barriers, especially tariffs, in order to prevent them from using trade policies that would harm other countries. The GATT was also a forum for the negotiation of the reduction of trade barriers. Presumably, the WTO was to ensure this as well, although it has not yet done so to any great extent. The GATT oversaw eight rounds of multilateral trade negotiations, culminating in the Uruguay Round that created the WTO. The WTO also took on issues that GATT had not covered, including trade in services, tariffication in agriculture and intellectual property protection. The most important change in the WTO, compared to the GATT, may have been its dispute settlement mechanism (DSM). The GATT permitted countries to complain against other countries for violating its rules. Each complaint was handled by a 'panel' of experts who issued a report that, if adopted unanimously by GATT members, would require the offending party to either change its behaviour or be subject to sanctions. However, securing unanimity meant that the offending party could block a report, in effect giving every country veto power over findings against itself. The surprise was that this had ever worked at all, which it had.

The WTO reversed this bias, requiring instead a unanimous decision to block a report, and it therefore, made the DSM much more effective. It also made other improvements, including the right to appeal. The intent was to provide viable enforcement for WTO rules, and it appears to have worked. The DSM has been used much more often than under the GATT, both by and against a wide range of countries, as is shown in the 'Overview of the State-of-play of WTO Disputes'. Just as importantly, large countries (the US) have stopped going outside the GATT with their most important complaints.

Inevitably, however, the DSM has not worked to everyone's satisfaction. The WTO restricts policies that harm other countries, not only deliberately, but also inadvertently, such as when policy restricts the options of another country's citizens. A contentious example was the 'shrimp-turtle' case. A US law protected sea turtles from death in the nets of shrimp fishermen by prohibiting imports of shrimp caught without 'turtle exclusion devices' (TEDs). Since it is impossible to tell from looking at a shrimp how it was caught, the law restricted imports from certain countries altogether. These countries took the case to the WTO, which decided against the US. In effect, this decision struck down US law, an intrusion into sovereignty that offended environmentalists and others. There have been other, similar examples since.

The potential of the WTO to intrude in national affairs was also increased by its expanded coverage. The GATT was limited to trade in goods, excluding certain sectors such as agriculture and textiles/apparel. The latter was covered instead by the GATT-sanctioned MFA, which restricted developing-country exports to developed countries. The WTO changed all this, or at least it promised to. The Uruguay Round scheduled the elimination of the MFA, though the most difficult liberalisation was postponed ('back-loaded') for ten years to 2005, when the MFA was finally rescinded. First steps were also taken in agriculture, which converted existing non-tariff barriers (NTBs) to tariffs (tariffication) so that later they could be negotiated downward; and trade in services was covered in a parallel agreement to the GATT, and the General Agreement on Trade in Services (GATS).

The WTO also expanded to new areas. Most prominent has been its Trade Related Intellectual Property (TRIPS) Agreement that covered intellectual property—primarily patents, copyrights and trademarks. In addition, the WTO included (as the GATT had before) some small ways in which countries could use trade policies for environmental purposes. However, the one area much discussed, where the WTO has *not* been extended is labour standards and rights. Even though there were many interest groups in the developed countries who favoured using trade policies for this purpose, resistance from the developing world, as well as from corporations who employed labour there, had prevented it from even being discussed.

Whom Does It Help and Hurt?

With its expanded role, the WTO affects many groups. But, fundamentally it has been, like the GATT, a force for increased trade and thus, a force for increased globalisation. The WTO has not yet, done much on international capital movement, although its agreement on financial services lowers transaction costs for movements of financial capital. But, it has done a great deal to facilitate international trade. Those who gain and lose from the WTO, then, are also those who gain and lose from globalisation. That is, there has been gains and losses to abundant and scarce factors, to industry-specific factors, and to factors unable to move or retrain. Because the WTO extends to previously excluded sectors—textiles, apparel, agriculture and services—these principles have applied especially strongly to them. For example, developed-country textile workers, who have been protected for decades, have had particular reason to be concerned, since the MFA ceased to exist. Developing-country textile workers have had a corresponding reason to be hopeful.

More generally, however, the WTO has had an important institutional role beyond merely fostering trade between countries—by constraining countries from using trade policies that would hurt others and themselves. Without such constraints, two things would guide countries' uses of trade policies. First, large countries would be able to use policies to gain at the expense of small countries. Second, weak and misguided governments would be able to use policies to benefit themselves and their 'cronies'. The WTO, with its rules and its DSM for enforcement, has deterred both. It has protected weak countries from strong countries, and also weak countries from themselves. This has been true especially for poor countries. Thus, even though the WTO was mostly designed by rich countries and even corporations, its greatest beneficiaries may well have been in the developing world.

Who loses from the WTO? Again, some of the losers have simply been those who lose most from trade, and here we must point again to relatively unskilled labour in developed countries. It makes perfect sense that organised labour in developed countries should be sceptical of the benefits from the WTO, for theory predicts that greater trade would indeed hurt their members, at least relatively.

Aside from these effects of globalisation itself, the rules of the WTO would also hurt those who would wish to break them. If large countries sought to use their economic size at the expense of other countries, then they would be frustrated by the WTO. Fortunately, there is little evidence that the most powerful countries have sought to do this, in recent decades. More likely losers, therefore, have been those who tried to use trade policy for other legitimate purposes but ran afoul of the WTO, as in the shrimp-turtle case. Those who sought to halt environmental degradation naturally wished to use trade policies to pursue their aims, since few other policies worked across borders. Yet to do so, risked violating the strictures of the WTO. Environmentalists have therefore, sometimes been hamstrung by WTO rules, and they believe that they—or the environment—are hurt by the WTO.

It is true that the WTO has made the objectives of environmentalists harder to attain. Policies imposed costs, and some of these costs have been borne by other countries when one country unilaterally used trade policies for environmental purposes. The WTO has given these costs more weight than if countries could act alone. This has meant that a lower level of environmental protection would result when these costs would be factored in. This is as it should be, since global policy decisions should be based on global costs and benefits, including all aspects of all people's lives, not just the environment of one country. Environmentalists, whose role is narrower, would indeed make less progress when their interests were balanced against those of others.

Environmentalists might say: Fine, but the WTO does not just balance other interests against the environment; it rules the environment out of court. All we want is for environmental concerns to be heard in the WTO. In fact, the WTO has not included several environmental clauses, so even here the question is one of balance. How much of a role should environmental concerns play in justifying trade policies? Arguably, the current system has not done badly. The problem with using trade policies for environmental and other purposes has been that they pushed the cost onto others too easily. The WTO has forced their advocates to find fairer ways to achieve those purposes. For example, the shrimp-turtle brouhaha led, more quietly, to shrimp fishermen being equipped with turtle-exclusion devices (TEDs) at the expense of the developed country. One could say that this was the right solution all along.

There have been other issues, besides the environment, whose advocates wished to use trade policies, including human rights and labour standards. For both of these, the United States especially, has used trade policies in the past, against a number of developing countries and in the implementation of preferential trading arrangements. Some have seen the WTO as an enemy of human rights and labour standards. That conclusion is much too strong, but as with the environment, the WTO interferes with policies that would have otherwise been available to pursue these ends, and the ends themselves will not be attained as fully.

In the case of human rights, the WTO has permitted some use of trade policies, such as the economic sanctions that were used against Rhodesia in 1965 and against South Africa in 1985. Formally, these were permitted under GATT Article XXI, based on actions under the United Nations (UN) Charter for purposes of peace and security. The WTO has not permitted unilateral sanctions for human rights, however.

In the case of labour standards and labour rights, the issue has been more complex, partly because it has been so difficult to separate the moral from the economic, and partly because of the different views of what labour standards mean economically. Some labour standards questions, such as the prohibition of slave labour and exploitative child labour, are clearly moral issues. Others, such as minimum wages, are economic. And still others, such as working conditions and child labour with the approval of caring parents, are somewhere in between. It has been hard to say where to draw the line, and who should draw it.

Economically, most labour standards affect the cost of labour, even when not explicitly about wages. But their effects depend on how one believes that wages are determined. From the perspective of competitive markets, which has guided most economists on this issue, labour standards are mostly about the remuneration of labour in poor versus rich countries, and higher labour standards in the former primarily benefits the latter, putting developing country workers out of work. Another view, however, has been that all labour remuneration is at the expense of capital, so higher labour standards merely reduce profits. In economics, this second view has made most sense if employers have market power, something that globalisation is, in fact, likely to undermine. But not everyone believes in market economics, especially non-economists, and there are plenty of subscribers to this second view among opponents of the WTO. In their view, by having excluded labour standards as a basis for trade policy, the WTO has helped capitalists and hurt workers, everywhere. But modern economics suggests that only developed-country workers may have been hurt, while the true beneficiaries of the WTO have been the developing-country workers for whom labour standards were ostensibly meant to help.

The latter view has been voiced prominently by economists and by most leaders of the developing countries. They have perceived labour standards, when enforced by trade sanctions, as thinly disguised protection for developed-country labour. The WTO has excluded labour standards as part of its broader role of protecting the weak from the strong, and it has been noteworthy that, at the 1996 WTO Ministerial Meeting in Singapore, it was decided that issues of labour standards would be handled in the International Labour Organization (ILO), which was designed to deal with the broad range of labour issues.

Other Objections to the WTO

Even among those who think that the WTO has had it right on environment and labour standards, there is an agreement that it, nonetheless, does have flaws. One has been its lack of transparency. The proceedings of the DSM panels have generally been secret, and the panellists have got information mostly from governments. Some have regarded this mechanism as non-democratic, and have feared its capture by corporations with financial stakes in the outcome. They would like interested NGOs to be able to provide greater input to the process, and perhaps to have the panellists themselves selected by a process that NGOs could influence.

The complaint about non-democratic procedures is ironic, since the WTO has been working by consensus among mostly democratic governments, whereas NGOs are by definition, self-appointed special interests. More important, however, has been a concern of the developing countries that opening the DSM to public scrutiny and influence would cause its capture by precisely these special interests, at the expense of the developing countries. Nonetheless, even defenders of the WTO are coming to see the DSM's secrecy as possibly counterproductive. It has also been inconsistent with other WTO procedures, which have always been open if anyone cared to look at them. Therefore, many have said that the DSM should expand the role of NGOs and others in being permitted to file 'friend of the court briefs'. Some have also argued that a more permanent body should replace the panels themselves, instead of being assembled case-by-case. If so, then greater public input to selection of that body might be natural.

Another concern has long been that a few rich countries have dominated the WTO, while developing countries have had little role. This has been true in spite of—or even because of—its formal reliance on consensus. With 150 member countries, consensus is not practical, and therefore a smaller group has typically sought agreement among themselves and then come to the larger group for approval. This smaller group, often referred to as the 'green room group', after the room in which they have sometimes met at WTO headquarters in Geneva, has been assembled on an ad hoc basis by the Director General and has included both developed and developing countries, based on their interest in the issues being addressed. However, many developing countries—especially smaller ones—have been excluded and thus not formally represented. This has not by design because there was no design, but by default. Exactly how to change this has not been clear, but something surely needs to be done.

As already noted, a common objection to the WTO has been that it overruled domestic laws. This is true, for that is its purpose. The GATT was a treaty among countries to prevent them from using certain laws and policies that would adversely affect other countries. The WTO has continued that purpose. However, while the original GATT dealt only with tariffs, over time the GATT/WTO has expanded to many other policies, such as environmental laws, whose main purposes have not been international. Critics object that the WTO has undermined domestic policies, not just tariffs. Countries might well want to reconsider their membership if these new restrictions are too onerous. Had the WTO existed for 50 years without the opportunity to withdraw, this might have been a big concern. However, since all members joined only in 1995, it would be surprising if many were now to pull out.

A troubling feature of the WTO for many has been that countries may not restrict imports based upon the processes by which they were produced. The WTO has permitted countries to exclude goods deemed harmful to health or the environment, for example, but only based on observable characteristics of the products themselves. In practice, countries have often wanted to exclude imports that were produced by a process that has harmed the environment, has violated labour standards or human rights, has adverse health consequences for consumers, or may be otherwise undesirable. These are often legitimate concerns, and if the process could be inferred from a product characteristic at the border, the WTO might permit their exclusion. But without that, exclusion must be based on the country where they were produced and some judgment about practices there. This has run the risk of excluding products that did not use the offending process, and also of undermining a producing country's legitimate comparative advantage.

A final concern of many WTO critics has been that it is dominated by large corporations. This is true and probably inevitable, since it is large corporations that do most trade. Corporations have both the incentive and the resources to influence policies, and they do, both within countries and internationally. This means that the WTO has elements that would not be there without corporate lobbying, and some of these elements are undesirable. For example, anti-dumping statutes have been economically nonsensical and pernicious, and yet the GATT has always permitted them, for the obvious reason that many corporations wanted them. More recently, in response to corporate lobbying, the Uruguay Round added intellectual property rights to the WTO, in spite of strong resistance from developing countries that was ultimately overcome by the promise of market opening in textiles and apparel.

The WTO, then, has not been a perfect organisation. It could be improved, but many of its flaws would inevitably remain, because they were there in response to political realities. Overall, it seems clear that the WTO has served an extremely useful purpose, and that it has served it surprisingly well. One indication that the WTO has not been too far off the mark comes from its opponents. Although they share unhappiness with the WTO, some have said that it does too much, others that it does too little. Environmentalists have usually complained that it does too much, by ruling against national efforts to improve the environment, and they want it to be weakened or destroyed so that national policies could proceed unhindered. Labour activists, on the other hand, have complained that it does too little, by not enforcing labour standards around the world. They want the WTO to take on more issues, and interfere more with national policies.

The WTO Ministerial Meetings: Seattle and Beyond

With this as background, it is of interest to consider the issues that have been taken up in the periodic WTO ministerial meetings. Ministerial meetings are held regularly, every two years in a different location for the purpose of moving ahead with the agenda for further multilateral negotiations. The first ministerial meeting was held in Singapore in 1996, and this had set out the objectives for a post-Uruguay Round negotiating agenda. The next ministerial meeting took place in Seattle in December 1999, with the ostensible purpose to agree on the parameters of a new round of negotiations. But this had not happened. The meeting attracted protestors, who demonstrated in the streets of Seattle and even prevented the opening session. The negotiators nonetheless did have extensive discussions, but they failed to reach agreement and left Seattle empty-handed.

One issue is, why? The protestors naturally took credit for derailing the new round and for having stopped the WTO in its tracks. However, most of those who were involved in the negotiations have said that the protests had little to do with the failure. The first problem was that the countries of the WTO had failed to agree beforehand on an agenda for the meeting. They had met at WTO headquarters in Geneva for months, trying to reach an agreement, but they had failed even then, long before the Seattle protests. The ministerial meeting nonetheless went ahead, but it has been crippled by this failure in the preparations, which in turn was due both, to bad luck and to the depth of the disagreements that divided the participants.

The bad luck was that the United States had been distracted by its talks with China on terms of entry to the WTO. These negotiations had been expected to finish long before, but were instead delayed by the accidental bombing of the Chinese embassy in Belgrade. The negotiations with China had been stalled, then continued, and finally concluded just shortly before the WTO Ministerial. This prevented the US from making all of the efforts that were needed to reach agreement on an agenda.

But an agreement might have been elusive in any case. Large differences had divided the participants, including even whether to discuss certain issues. In agriculture, the US and the less developed countries (LDCs) had sided with other agricultural exporters wanting to push ahead with the negotiations. The European Union (UN) and Japan had nothing to do with that. The EU was however, on the side of the US on another issue: labour standards. Both had wanted at least to talk about them in a new round, while LDCs, as noted here, were firmly opposed to it. LDCs, the EU and Japan had sided together, against the US, on anti-dumping. They wanted to reopen negotiations on this, in the hopes of restricting the increasing use of these policies, but the US had refused. Finally, LDCs had been unhappy with the back-loading of the textile agreement and had wanted to renegotiate the timetable, feeling that they acquired very little market access in return for their acceptance of the TRIPS agreement. Here too, the US and EU had refused. On all of these issues, one of the parties did not even wanted them to be discussed.

There were also other problems encountered in Seattle. The US, as the host of the meeting, had been pushing for a new round that would include many issues and proceed rapidly, perhaps causing some countries to feel they were being railroaded. Key players in the negotiations were new to their jobs, including Mike Moore, who had been appointed as the director general of the WTO only a short time before. Finally, the desire for further multilateral liberalisation may have been diminished by many countries' participation in various regional agreements, such as the North American Free Trade Agreement (NAFTA), Mercosur and the various free trade agreements of the EU.

Meanwhile, the protestors had gathered in unprecedented abundance. They had included representatives of US labour unions, labour rights activists, environmental groups, human rights advocates and anti-corporate interests. Their disruption of the meeting had been confined to conventional forms of protest, such as picketing, chanting and blocking streets. However, the event and publicity had also attracted a group of self-described anarchists. They had no particular interest in trade or the WTO, but were bent only on destruction, and they had made news and enemies by throwing rocks and breaking windows. This had drawn more attention than peaceful protest ever would have, but it was clear what effects it really had.

Towards the end of the week of meetings, with the negotiations having made little progress, President Clinton arrived in Seattle and made a speech that seems to have derailed them completely. Previously, the US and EU had both hoped to insert labour rights into the negotiations, but only in a small way. They had tried to persuade the developing countries that the issue would only be discussed, not negotiated, and that there certainly would not be any use of trade sanctions in pursuit of labour rights. Whether this could have succeeded has been unclear, but in any case, Clinton's speech had explicitly mentioned using trade sanctions to enforce labour rights. From then on the opposition, developing countries hardened, even to discussions, and it became clear that no agreement on an agenda for a new round would be reached.

As mentioned, the protestors have taken credit for this failure, while the negotiators have said that the protestors made little difference. It has been difficult to know who was right. It seemed that Clinton's speech was the final straw that prevented agreement, and that he may have been influenced by the protests. On the other hand, even if he had been responding to the protests, he may have decided that the meetings were going to fail in any case, and thus opted to collect political points for presidential candidate, Al Gore, from the opportunity. Or his first priority may have been permanent normal trade relations (PNTR) with China, and he had not wanted to antagonise the labour force further until after the election. There has been no way of knowing.

It should be noted, however, that a failure of trade negotiations is hardly unprecedented. In the early 1980s, the United States had also failed to initiate a new round, at another ministerial meeting. Later, with the Uruguay Round underway, negotiations had collapsed several times, with no apparent hope of being restarted. Nonetheless they had, and the round had eventually concluded successfully.

Following the Seattle Ministerial Meeting, the next ministerial had been convened in Doha, Qatar, in November 2001. There were high hopes that real progress would be made, both by and for developing countries, with the launch of the so-called Doha Round. Although many issues were on the table, the central issues that were so contentious in Seattle, again proved to be difficult to address, namely, developed country protection and subsidies in industries of interest to developing countries, especially agriculture; and developing country tariffs on non-agricultural products and other restrictions on market access, including in services. In the event, these issues had proven to be so contentious that the Doha Round negotiations have been characterised more by the lack of progress. At the Cancun Ministerial in 2003, the meeting ended without even the beginnings of a negotiating text being agreed upon. Such a text had been achieved during the following year, but the next ministerial, in Hong Kong in 2005, had ended in success only because the criteria for success had been almost reduced to the level of meaninglessness. In July 2006, WTO Director GeneralPascal Lamy had finally acknowledged that the negotiations had been going nowhere and would fail to meet the deadline imposed by the expiration of US Trade Promotion Authority in mid-2007. He had, therefore, suspended the negotiations. Today, although various efforts have been made to revive them, the negotiations remain in a state of suspended animation.

While the Doha Round had been officially named as the Doha Development Agenda (DDA), this had not been done because its purpose was to achieve the policies that would stimulate development. Rather, it had intended to pursue the usual objective of trade liberalisation with the unusual proviso that developing countries would not be sidelined or put at a disadvantage. Trade liberalisation may well be necessary for economic development, but it has hardly been sufficient. The best that could have been hoped for from the Doha Round was therefore, to remove barriers to development.

Those barriers have existed—and may continue to exist, due to the Doha Round's failure—because developing countries had failed to participate in previous negotiating rounds, where they might have pushed for the opening up of markets to their exports. Instead, first because they had been late to sign the GATT, and then later because they had sought and were granted 'special and differential treatment' that exempted them from the negotiations, they sat on the sidelines while developed countries had negotiated down those trade barriers that had been in their mutual interest to eliminate. Developing countries had benefited from these negotiations, to some extent, as their MFN status had allowed them the same market access that was granted to others. But, this was usually not in the sectors where developing countries themselves were able to export the most. As a result, the world today has been characterised by the highest tariffs in developed countries on goods exported by developing countries, both labour-intensive manufactures such as textiles and apparel, and various agricultural products. The latter are also subject to significant subsidies provided by developed country governments to their agricultural interests. In addition, and also because they had not participated actively in the previous rounds, many developing countries also have high tariffs on numerous imports. If the Doha Round is not successfully revived, this unsatisfactory state of affairs would continue, and the developing countries of the world would continue to be hobbled in their efforts to escape poverty.

By remaining exempt from the negotiations, developing countries have not only failed to secure the benefits of foreign liberalisation on their exports but they have also failed to secure the benefits from the liberalisation they might themselves have undertaken, although some countries have eventually, seen the benefits of liberalisation and have adopted it unilaterally. But, by having avoided the negotiated commitment to liberalise, they have also avoided the international discipline that might have assisted them in achieving reforms of internal policies as well.

The Future of the WTO

It should have been evident from the preceding discussion that the WTO has been a remarkable institution but, that it has been stalled in its efforts to promote the continuing liberalisation of international trade. The main features and accomplishments of the WTO include:

- The WTO had been formed by governments for the purpose of promoting globalisation and preventing countries from doing harm with their trade policies.
- Those who have gained most from the WTO are those who have gained from globalisation, especially small, poor countries, who would be most affected by nationalistic trade policies.
- The WTO has restricted those who would use trade policies for other goals, including the environment, labour standards and human rights, forcing them to pursue their objectives at less cost to other countries.
- The WTO has provided a that has been quite effective, although its operation has been less transparent than it could be.
- The WTO has operated by consensus, but its large membership makes that process unwieldy and exclusionary in practice, leaving many developing countries especially without a voice.

The current impasse in the Doha Round negotiations has put the WTO under stress. It would take considerable political will on the part of both, the developed and developing countries, to move ahead and to recognise the mutual benefits, which they may realise, by addressing the reduction and removal of the existing barriers that inhibit their trade in agricultural products, manufactures and services.

A BRIEF OVERVIEW ABOUT THE PRESENT VOLUME

The present volume has been designed to examine the experiences of the Indian economy of trade liberalisation, since the formation of the WTO in 1995. We have cast India as one amongst the many developing countries in the world so as to compare India's performance in relation to other countries. The book has been organised as the following: Section I has addressed the long-run interests of the developing countries and argued that these countries should try, rather aggressively, to achieve a liberalised world trade regime to maximize their gains from trade; Section II has considered the various negotiating options available for India and how best India can formulate its strategies to achieve the desired results. In particular, it has addressed the question why India, and the other developing countries, should actively and constructively participate in the Doha negotiations to further their own interests; with regard to the specific interests of the Indian economy in relation to the WTO reforms, we have considered the issues relating to market access in agriculture, textiles, and industry in general in Section III; Section IV has dealt with the new emerging issues of concern for India, in particular trade facilitation and government procurement; the implications of the TRIPS and GATS have been considered in Section V; and finally, in Section VI we have considered issues relating to growth, poverty, and inequality, with particular reference to the Indian economy.

Section I: A Developing Countries Perspective

The developing countries have certain common features and interests. First of all, many of these countries have attained their independence from colonial rule towards the middle of the twentieth century and have since, engaged themselves in the process of catching up with the West by means of more rapid rates of economic growth. Second, these countries have tended to be relatively labour abundant and characterised by low income, low savings, unemployment and poverty. These factors have been primarily responsible for their industrial backwardness and specialisation in primary production. Third, as a consequence of their specialisation on primary products, they have mainly exported primary commodities and imported manufactures. Fourth, with rising income and the operation of Engels' law and technical progress in the developed countries, there has at times been a decline in their terms of trade, vis-à-vis manufactures. Fifth, the foregoing factors have served to create the demand for an import-substitution strategy of development and direct import-control measures. As a result, prior to the Uruguay Round, most of these countries had shown very little interest in the GATT rounds, in which reciprocal trade liberalisation among the developed countries, in manufactures, had received prime importance. However, many developing countries had been original members of the GATT, and their interests in those rounds were mainly in securing special and more favourable treatment for their exports and imports. Since world trade mainly catered to the interests of the developed world, the developed countries have, therefore, not paid sufficient attention to the interests of the developing countries' trade and industrial policies.

However, certain changes have taken place in both the developed as well as the developing countries in recent decades. In the developing countries, it had increasingly become recognised that the import-substitution strategy had resulted in serious micro- and macro-economic problems for these countries. A series of empirical studies found that producing goods under tariff protection had contributed to the expansion of high cost and inefficient industrial structures in many countries. As a consequence, many developing countries had experienced continuous balance-of-payments and foreign exchange crises, inflationary pressures and fiscal deficits. In these circumstances, it was difficult for them to sustain their economic growth. However, a few developing countries, especially in East Asia, had taken bold initiatives to discontinue their import-substitution strategy and instead, had adopted an export-led, outward-looking growth strategy that resulted in unusually high rates of economic growth. This East Asian 'miracle' has turned several countries in the region into major trading countries in the global system. Increasingly, policy makers in the developing world have realised that their complementary demographic relations, with respect to the West, have given them an edge over the developed countries particularly in low technology and labour-intensive manufactures. Therefore, they could expect to do better by adopting an export-led rather than import-substitution strategy of growth. As a consequence, the interests of many developing countries have shifted towards seeking greater market access for their labour-intensive products, such as textiles and clothing, in the markets of developed countries.

In recent decades, several developed countries have experienced lower rates of economic growth and a slowing down in the volume of their mutual trade. Labour has become increasingly scarce in these countries due to their demographic transition and lower rates of population growth. Consequently, multinational firms have increasingly sought out low-wage-cost locations in the developing countries, for greater profit opportunities. Since some developing countries had been experiencing very high GDP growth, multinational firms from the developed countries also looked for market access for their technology-intensive products in the markets of developing countries. Thus, there has been a convergence of interests in both developing as well as developed countries for a more liberal international trading regime.

It is noteworthy that, unlike the previous GATT negotiations, in the Uruguay Round negotiations (1986–94), the developing countries had actively participated to enhance their interests. Despite their diversities and differences in interests, they tried to act in a coordinated manner on many issues, vis-à-vis the developed nations in the negotiation process.

Taking a general developing countries perspective, Manoj Pant, in Chapter 1, has drawn attention to the fact that, since the Uruguay Round, the subsequent trade negotiations have been marred by acrimony. He has argued that this is partly due to the fact that the 'single undertaking' clause in the WTO, has deprived developing countries the use of the non-reciprocity clause that they could previously resort to in the GATT. In addition, as it has become more common for countries to negotiate on the basis of trading blocs, negotiations have necessarily taken on considerable political dimensions. Tracing developments in international negotiations from the Uruguay Round to the 2003 WTO Ministerial Meeting in Cancun, Pant has argued that, while many developing countries may lack the intellectual capital to understand the nuances of the negotiation processes and agreements, developed countries have consistently sought to evade liberalisation, especially of their agricultural policies, with respect to their developing country trading partners. Consequently, trade negotiations have now been beset with the problem of lack of 'trust' between developed and developing countries. Agricultural trade liberalisation has, thus, become the litmus test of a successful pursuit of post-Uruguay Round multilateral trade negotiations.

In Chapter 2, Ashok Guha has argued that the old nation-state system has become an obsolete framework to deal with the complex web of international transactions and the conduct of multilateral trade negotiations. The WTO has been the architectural foundation for the world economy of the future, and India's attitude to it must, accordingly, be informed by a long-run perspective on the WTO system and what India's role should be in this system. Trends in population growth, savings and economic growth has suggested that Asia, and in particular China and India, would dominate the world economy of the twenty first century. It has been important, therefore, that the multilateral trading system be strengthened and kept viable. Further, in terms of the ethnicity of the Western world and the ownership of its capital, the importance of the people of Asian origin has been growing rapidly. Soon, boundaries between geographical units would decline in importance, and the precise distribution of the benefits of trade between countries would become less significant than the maximisation of its volume. Thus, it would be, in India's interest, to do everything possible to sustain the momentum of the expansion of international trade, to resist the attempts of the West to restrict trade on a variety of pretexts, and also to control India's own protectionist pressures.

Section II: Negotiating Options and Strategies

The GATT had provided a forum for countries to negotiate and exchange their trade commitments. It had been a forum in which countries could express their different opinions and conflicting interests, and engage in a negotiating process with a scope for the resolution of the conflicting interests through bargaining and compromises to make rules regulating international trade and trade relations. Once the negotiating process had stopped, it collapsed and required a new negotiating process to begin. For instance, the WTO Seattle Ministerial Conference (1999) had considered the possibility of including social clauses under the ambit of the WTO, but this had to be dropped in view of the opposition of India and many other developing countries. During the Doha Ministerial (2001), the launching of a new round had been questioned by the developing countries, on the ground that the market-access issues originating from the Uruguay Round commitments needed to be materialised first (Chapter 4). Then, in Cancun (2003), the developed-developing country gap had widened greatly over the question of loss of market access for developing countries due to the EU and US agricultural import tariffs and domestic subsidies. And, even the July 2004 WTO meeting had left many unresolved areas open. In short, the debates and disputes over market-access issues have been far from being over and have threatened the conduct of the ongoing DDA negotiations.

India has continuously been showing active interest in the negotiating process towards formalising an efficient and rule-based world trade regime. There have indeed been differences within the domestic economy, marked by acrimonious debates on the issue of India joining the WTO. But, the Indian parliamentary democracy has succeeded in arriving at a broad consensus in favour of signing the WTO agreement and thereby, becoming its member. In addition, in spite of the global trend to form regional trade agreements, India has remained loyal, until recently, to the multilateral system for the most part of the last decade (WTO 2003). From an initial position of hesitation as was seen in the first WTO Ministerial Conference held in Singapore in 1996, India has succeeded in achieving a position of leadership of the developing country bloc in the Cancun Ministerial

Meeting in 2003. Thus, while India has remained inactive by not protesting against the inclusion of four new issues, namely, trade and investment, competition policy, transparency in government procurement, and trade facilitation at the Singapore meeting in 1996, it has played a somewhat active role in the Geneva (1998) Ministerial Conference and has thus, become a part of the Global E-commerce Agreement. Similarly, in response to the non-realisation of the promised market access under the Uruguay Round and also to a number of cases it faced at the WTO, India was forced to adopt a proactive approach in Seattle (1999) by raising its voice against incorporation of social aspects under the WTO ambit. In the same way, in Doha (2001), when developed countries had been willing to begin discussion for launching a new round, India with a handful of developing country partners opposed it, demanding realisation of market access as promised under the Uruguay Round. The concern over TRIPS and public health had also played a major role (Chapter 6). Finally, in Cancun (2003), the G-20 group, led by Brazil, China and India, had made an alternative proposal against the EU-US proposal for reducing their domestic agricultural subsidies. Also, during the last week of July 2004, ministers from Australia, Brazil, the EU, India and the US, had reached an agreement to keep the DDA negotiations going, a much-needed step to initiate fresh talks. In the G-20 ministers meeting in New Delhi (18–19 March 2005), the ministerial declaration had decided to keep the pressure on developed countries for increased market access.

Manmohan Agarwal, in Chapter 3, has maintained that the developing countries faced a new situation in the run up to the Uruguay Round and during the negotiations. This had forced developing countries to be more active in the negotiations than they had been in earlier rounds. One of the issues facing these countries had been, how were they to participate in the negotiations. Developing countries have been individually small and have needed to form coalitions to bargain effectively. Before the Uruguay Round, all developing countries had formed a bargaining group, just as they had in the UN. But, this approach had appeared to be inadequate. Some developing countries broke away from this pattern and formed mixed coalitions, in which developed and developing countries were partners. Such coalitions had seemed to be the way of the future. But, later experience has shown weaknesses in such mixed coalitions, and the search for an effective way for developing countries to negotiate has continued. In the run up to the Doha Round, and in the preliminary stage of negotiations, the older method of developing countries to participate as a group had made a comeback. But, it has been an open question whether their unity would survive in the long run. It seems that single-issue groups have coherence, whether the group consists only of developing countries or is a mixed group. The problem arises when compromises have to be made with other single issue, perhaps partly overlapping groups.

The Indian approach to the negotiations had been to develop a joint developing country stance. While it had failed in this endeavour during the Uruguay Round, it has played a more important role during the Doha Round. It has been part of the coalition of developing countries that successfully prevented the inclusion of most of the Singapore issues in the Doha Round negotiations. India has also been a member of the Group of 5 important countries, that has discussed the overall state of the negotiations. Its membership in this group may create dilemmas for its negotiating position—should it push for the goals of the developing countries even when these may conflict with its own interests? In particular, India has developed many industries which are not internationally competitive at this stage and may need protection. Countries that have already been competitive in these industries or those who have not yet invested in these industries, would have different interests from those of India. It would be a challenge to Indian negotiators to develop positions that harmonise the different interests as well as protect India's national interest.

Debashis Chakraborty, in Chapter 4, has pointed out that, although India was one of the founding members of the GATT, it has never been enthusiastic towards multilateral negotiations during the GATT period and the early days of the WTO. The scenario has changed from the Doha Round onwards, and since the Cancun Ministerial, India has been actively engaged in negotiations with developed countries as a part of several developing-country coalitions. This change has outwardly testified to an evolution of India's negotiating strategy at the WTO. However, looking at the negotiating stances that India has adopted over the last decade and the various compulsions it faced, the author has argued that many of these negotiating stances have been generated from a contemporary political perspective, rather than from well-conceived cost-benefit analysis, although, they may have nonetheless contributed to India's national interest. The reversal of India's negotiating stance on a couple of issues has been proof of that. The paper has attempted to present a critical analysis of India's changing perspective over three issues, namely, trade and investment, regional trade blocs and anti-dumping investigations. Not surprisingly then, India's claimed 'achievements' have been subject to questions in this light. The paper concludes that adoption of a need-based negotiating approach, unilaterally or in association with other developing countries, as demanded by the situation, is what is needed for India.

The Doha Round

The WTO Doha Round of multilateral trade negotiations has been called the 'Doha Development Agenda' (DDA), since it has promised to 'place [developing countries'] needs and interests at the heart of the Work Programme adopted in this Declaration'. Robert M. Stern and Alan V. Deardorff, in Chapter 5, have summarised the framework that has been agreed upon as the basis for the WTO Doha Development Agenda (DDA) negotiations; then they have discussed the design and mission of the WTO and the economic effects of multilateral trade liberalisation. Keeping in view India's interests, they have examined the conditions for India's realisation of the maximum benefits from the DDA negotiations and the implications for broader Indian domestic policy reforms. They have suggested a set of recommendations for India's proactive involvement and negotiating strategies in the DDA negotiations for multilateral trade liberalisation in agricultural products, manufactures and services, and for improvements in WTO rules governing trade and related issues. The chapter concludes with a brief discussion of the policy agenda that has been adopted by India's newly elected coalition parties, the implications of the emphasis on social reform and equity for India's negotiating strategies in the DDA negotiations, and a vision of the role that India might play in the global trading system and in world politics.

Arvind Panagariya, in Chapter 6 provides an overview of what was achieved at Doha and examines critically India's negotiating stance. He has argued that while India's opposition to the inclusion of the Singapore issues in the negotiating agenda had been defensible, certain aspects of India's stance had also been disturbing. For example, India's stance that the developed countries should eliminate their tariff peaks without asking India to liberalise its own tariffs further, had been against the spirit of multilateralism. Such a demand, he has suggested, is unrealistic. Similarly, having pushed for the 'implementation issues' and by taking a position that India may not have any interest for negotiations beyond the Uruguay Round built-in agenda, was a tactical mistake. This had been because it had given the impression that India was not in favour of another trade round, even though, behind the scenes, this may not have been the case. Panagariya has argued that, despite power asymmetries, the WTO has been the 'best hope for protection of our trading rights', and faster economic growth in the developing countries could only be guaranteed by a liberalised trading regime. Therefore, India should keep this fact in mind while negotiating about the future of the world trading regime; and it could achieve its desired goal if it has a well-calculated negotiating agenda which gives a positive impression and is also credible.

Section III: Market Access: Agriculture, Manufactures and Textiles

Increased market access via reduction of trade barriers—mainly tariffs—in industrial products had been the central point of negotiations on trade liberalisation in all previous GATT rounds, prior to the Uruguay Round. As a result, at the time of the Uruguay Round negotiations, tariffs in the industrial countries on manufactured goods had already been reduced to quite a low level. Thus, from the viewpoint of the developing countries, market access and lower tariffs on industrial products had not been the key issues of importance in the negotiations. Rather, what had been important for many developing countries was the removal of the quantitative restrictions on textiles and clothing exports; and the freeing of trade in agriculture from domestic supports and other non-tariff distortions. Interestingly, as has been noted by the WTO (2001), despite low average tariffs in the industrial countries, the level of realised market access has been significantly lower than the predicted one, and, that there are areas where barriers have been quite significant. Because of the discrepancy between the potential and the actual market-access conditions, considerable discontentment seems to have prevailed among the developing countries. Their major unhappiness had arisen from the very slow pace of implementation of the Agreement on Textiles and Clothing (ATC) that had been promised in the Uruguay Round. The developing countries have been particularly concerned about the relatively high tariff and non-tariff barriers retained by the two major trading entities, EU and US (Chapter 8). The abuse of anti-dumping measures as instrument of protection in the developed countries has also been a major issue of concern.

Agriculture

The WTO Agreement on Agriculture (AOA) covers: (1) domestic support, (2) market access (that is, tariffs and restrictions on imports and exports) and (3) export subsidies. The agreement had sought reductions in such trade-distorting domestic policies as price interventions and subsidies; reductions in export subsidies; replacing quantitative restrictions on trade with tariffs, and reductions in tariffs to encourage more and freer trade. Thus, the Uruguay Round had successfully brought under its purview issues relating to trade liberalisation in agricultural products, something that had been kept out of all previous multilateral trade negotiations. Previously, under the auspices of the GATT, agriculture had been highly protected in the developed countries, particularly in the EU and Japan, by means of a variety of policy measures such as agricultural subsidies and other non-tariff barriers to trade. Therefore, developing countries perceived a clear advantage in the removal of those trade-distorting agricultural restrictions.

At the time of the Uruguay Round negotiations, India's main concern regarding market access had been greater access for its agricultural and textiles and clothing products in the developed countries' markets. Presumably, as Ramesh Chand points out in Chapter 7, the expectations regarding agriculture had been based on the fact that at the time of the Uruguay Round negotiations, international prices of most of the farm commodities were significantly above the domestic prices in India. And, of course, the desire for greater access in textiles exports had been moulded by India's presumed comparative advantage in labour-intensive products. Undoubtedly, the prospects of increased exports of agricultural goods had been affected by the prevailing subsidies and various NTBs in the markets of developed countries, apart from the existence of a plethora of domestic restrictions on agricultural exports. However, as India had initiated domestic reforms in 1991 and the ban on exports of agricultural goods had been withdrawn, the country experienced an upward swing in agricultural exports because of the differential price impact. However, as Chand argues, this price advantage had not lasted long and farm exports, which more than doubled in dollar terms during the first four years between 1992–93 to 1996–97, started declining during the post-WTO period.

In view of the Doha Round negotiations, Chand expresses his anxiety over the implications of the evolving international trade regime and focuses on how India should try effectively to adjust to the new global trade situation and accordingly work out effective domestic and external trade policy measures to meet the challenges of trade liberalisation.

Manufactures

The Uruguay Round induced reciprocal tariff reduction policies have led to increased market access in manufactures for Indian goods in foreign markets and also increased market access for imports in Indian markets. The increased competition therefore has been expected to result in price declines and, therefore, increased consumer welfare, increased trade volume, increased efficiency and realisation of scale economies, and restructuring of industries according to India's presumed comparative advantage in labour-intensive manufactures. It should, therefore, lead to a decline in those industries, in which India may no longer have a comparative advantage; and at the same time, expansion of those lines of industries in which the country enjoys a comparative advantage. How India has actually performed in response to the reforms, is studied by Alokesh Barua, Debashis Chakraborty and Pavel Chakraborty, in Chapter 8. Interestingly, they have observed that the proportions of labour-intensive manufacturing products have been rising in India's export basket, which has been consistent with expectations. Yet, they further noted that, despite India's overall trade pattern appearing to be of the Heckscher-Ohlin type, the proportion of intra-industry trade (IIT) also seems to have increased, leaving scope for forces of market imperfections perhaps to play an important role in Indian industries. Some indication of intra-industry specialisation in production was also indicated. The presence of market imperfection in domestic industries, which have still been segmented from the world market, has been further supported by high concentration ratios in the early 1990s, followed by continuous decline of industry concentration over the decade. The authors argue that this process has been facilitated by both, increased competition from imports as well as entry of foreign firms, since the initiation of WTO-induced reform.

Textiles and Clothing

Before the WTO agreement took effect in 1995, a large proportion of textiles and clothing exports, from developing countries to the industrial countries, had been subject to quotas under a special regime outside normal GATT rules. Much of the trade in this sector prior to 1995, had been subject to bilateral quotas negotiated under the MFA. The MFA had governed trade in textiles from 1974 until its end in 1995. With the ATC, WTO members had committed themselves to remove the quotas by 1 January 2005. That is, the system of import quotas that had dominated trade in textiles and clothing, since the early 1960s, had to be phased out over a ten-year period following conclusion of the Uruguay Round after 1995. Thus, the textile and clothing sectors had to be fully integrated according to normal GATT rules. In particular, importing countries would no longer be able to discriminate between exporters. As a consequence of the agreement, trade in textiles and clothing had been poised to undergo fundamental changes in the 10 years after 1995. The likely effects of the dismantling of the MFA on India's textile and clothing production and exports have been considered by Samar Verma in Chapter 9.

Verma has noted that the quota phase-out, as proposed under the ATC, was heavily back-loaded; as a result of which about 94 per cent of the value of products, that had been restricted by quotas, would be 'integrated' into the WTO rules only on 1 January 2005. This phenomenon, described by Verma, would be akin to the 'Big Bang' in trade, production and consumption patterns in textile and clothing globally, since the US and the EU together import over 60 per cent of world textiles and almost 75 per cent of world clothing imports directly, and much more indirectly. Since India relies heavily on these two markets for its textile and clothing exports, the 'Big Bang' according to Verma, would be very critical for Indian exports. However, notwithstanding such expected gains from the MFA phase out, there have remained several concerns on the 'real' increase in market access to the US and the EU. According to Verma, the last decade's experience of the implementation of the ATC, and emerging new, 'non-traditional' forms of protectionism by the world's largest markets, have cast serious doubts over the promise of increased real market access of textile and clothing exports into these markets. He has argued that such developments would be tantamount to the continuation of an era of protectionism. Verma has further looked at how India should prepare itself to compete with the newly emerging Chinese economy and other countries in the international arena.

Section IV: Trade Facilitation and Government Procurement: Singapore Issues of Future Concern

The Singapore Ministerial Meeting of the WTO that had been held in 1996, immediately after the formation of the WTO, took up new issues like the link between trade and investment and competition for future consideration for negotiations. Investment and competition policy have been, of course, a part of the built-in-agenda of the WTO. The Singapore issues included a set of four issues, namely, investment, competition, transparency in government procurement and trade facilitation.

The draft WTO General Council Decision of 31 July 2004, had stated that investment, competition and government procurement would not form part of the Work Programme and hence no negotiations on any of these issues would take place within the WTO during the Doha Round. Trade facilitation, the General Council had decided by explicit consensus, however, would remain and therefore, negotiations on this issue may continue. The decision taken on the modalities of trade facilitation had emphasised the need for special and differential treatment for developing and least developed countries. According to the decision, developing countries needed to only adopt commitments according to their capacity to implement them. This had given rise to an interesting hypothesis—whether other Singapore issues could also be resolved on similar lines if brought up for negotiations in the future. Thus, trade facilitation has been the only surviving element of the Singapore issues and has been examined in this section, although, issues relating to transparency in government procurement have also been considered.

Trade Facilitation

Pritam Banerjee, Dipankar Sengupta and Phunchok Stobdan, in Chapter 10, have analysed the role of trade facilitation in promoting regional integration, especially in restoring India's economic ties with Bangladesh and of Ladakh with Central Asia. They have argued that these regions had originally been a part of the same socio-economic unit and were linked by a common trade route that was interrupted by political events. With India and its neighbours increasingly integrating their economies with the rest of the world, the authors have argued that it might be economically logical, from the national and regional points of view, that these old ties be restored. They have highlighted the trade facilitation measures necessary for this integration to take place, pointing out that the measures would include strengthening the provisions in the WTO that deal with transit issues; as well as, the infrastructural and domestic regulatory structures, which would have to be dealt with if regional integration is to become a reality.

Government Procurement

In Chapter 11, Sandwip Kumar Das has considered government procurement policy in the context of the Indian economy. He has maintained that India has had no policy regulating government procurement; and that there have been only numerous rules and procedures made by central, sub-central and regional authorities at multiple layers of the federal economy. There has been no Act of the parliament in this regard. These rules have been non-uniform, outmoded and complex, leaving scope for favouritism, political pressure and corruption. The system could not guarantee neutrality and fairness in public purchasing decisions. However, regulatory bodies, audits and vigilance have posed credible threats for those who might engage in corrupt practices. Whether or not all this should restrict corruption is difficult to say, but the procurement system is such that agents may have to cheat to get a fair deal. There have also been indications that excessive vigilance has restricted innovation in public procurement. A survey conducted at both, the central and state level, has revealed a chaotic purchasing environment. So far as a multilateral agreement on government procurement is concerned, India should have no problem with transparency as well as MFN. The basic problem that would arise is in giving national treatment, as India's concern with certain protected sectors is justified.

Section V: TRIPS and GATS

The Uruguay Round had considered some new issues that were traditionally excluded from the purview of the GATT. Two major agreements came into being as a consequence:

namely, GATS and TRIPS. These two important agreements and their implications for the Indian economy have been considered in this section.

TRIPS

The TRIPS agreement under the WTO has been one of the most contentious and highly debated agreements, right from its introduction during the Uruguay Trade Round in the 1980s. Under this agreement, all WTO member nations were required to provide a uniform standard of protection for a wide range of IPRs including patents, copyrights, trademarks, industrial designs, geographical indications, IC designs and undisclosed information. Amit Shovan Ray, in Chapter 12, has drawn attention to the patents provision of the TRIPS agreement.

Ray has maintained that intellectual property (IP) requires protection in terms of granting property rights to the innovator, as it has important implications for economic development. He has focused on the public health concerns arising out of a TRIPS compatible patent regime in India, against the backdrop of the evolution of the Indian pharmaceutical industry post-1970, as well as, WTO-driven challenges and adjustments that have been taking place in this industry since 1990.

Ray has argued that the WTO-led new international economic order would have a profound impact on the structure and functioning of the Indian pharmaceutical industry, with serious implications for India's health care. He has shown how quality, and research and development (R&D) have become the twin pillars of success and survival for the Indian pharmaceutical industry in the post-reform period. He has concluded that, while the emerging international economic order has been likely to promote the discovery and introduction of new drugs worldwide, in India it is unlikely to have any perceptible favourable impact on India's health, given the market-driven therapeutic focus of new drug-discovery research. More alarming has been the tendency of market forces in the new era, to perpetuate a vicious circle of antibiotics through the discovery of newer generations of antibiotics. In addition, he has indicated that under the new world order, price and quality of drugs would move in a direction that favours the rich and discerning patients, while the poor may be deprived of affordable medicines of acceptable quality.

GATS

For many reasons, the issues relating to trade in services had been kept out of the GATT and had only been raised in the early 1980s, with primarily US support. But in the course of the Uruguay Round negotiations, by December 1993, 95 participants had submitted their schedule of offers under the new GATS Agreement. Therefore, negotiations on the liberalisation of trade in services began only after the Round had concluded in 1994. Rashmi Banga, in Chapter 13, has argued that India, unlike other developing countries, had been playing a proactive role in the multilateral negotiations on trade in services under the GATS. She has noted that, given the comparative advantage in Mode 1 (that is, cross-border trade) and Mode 4 (which is temporary movement of persons), India would obviously need to negotiate actively in these Modes to remove the non-tariff barriers faced while dealing with its major trading partners. However, with respect to Mode 3 (that is, allowing commercial presence), India has had a defensive interest. Under the new plurilateral approach to services negotiations, India has received most of the requests under Mode 3. In view of this, Banga has focused on trade liberalisation in Mode 3 to provide a policy framework to identify the sectors where such commitments can be undertaken and sectors that may require significant domestic reforms before subjecting them to liberalisation.

Aparna Sawhney, in Chapter 14, has examined the current environmental services negotiations under the Doha agenda from the perspective of a developing country like India. It has begun with the classification of environmental services under the GATS, the nature of the global environmental services industry, and liberalisation interests of developed and developing countries in the negotiaitons. It has then considered the case of the emerging Indian environmental services sector, and the country's negotiation stance at the WTO. India has adopted a fairly liberal foreign investment regime, along with increasing private participation in infrastructure services like water, sanitation, and sewage. Upgrading domestic capability in environmental technology has been the main import need of developing countries like India, while export interest lay mostly in labour-intensive professional services like environmental consulting and management under Mode 4 (de-linked from Mode 3). Considering the similar challenges and concerns of developing countries in the liberalisation of environmental services, a coalition along the lines of the G-20 would be a powerful means of overcoming the current negotiation impasse and ensuring a developing country-friendly outcome.

Section VI: Growth, Poverty and Inequality

The normative issues of greatest concern for developing countries have been related to the links between trade and growth, and trade and income distribution. While concerns with the rise or decline in the poverty ratio as globalisation proceeds have relatively been given more importance, in the developed world, relative income distribution has received prime importance as well. Relative income distribution has been viewed from two different angles, namely, inter-personal distribution or distribution according to the broad factors of production, capital and labour, and inter-regional income distribution. The four papers in this section have dealt with these issues both at theoretical and empirical levels.

Growth and Poverty: Theoretical Views

Jagdish Bhagwati and T. N. Srinivasan, in Chapter 15, have analysed the static and dynamic effects of globalisation on poverty. They have assumed that the effects on poverty can be examined by looking at the effects of globalisation on the real wages of unskilled workers. Then, following the standard Stolper-Samuelson argument, they have concluded that free trade should help in the reduction of poverty in the developing countries. They have further pointed out that if a country follows an open-economy policy with proper macroeconomic stability, then free trade is definitely bound to reduce poverty. On the other hand, the dynamic effects have been related to the trade-growth relationship. They have argued that the theoretical relationship depends on the characteristics of the growth model that one considers, that is, whether one considers a Harrod-Domar type or a Solow type growth model. Similarly, the effects of growth on poverty have depended on the type of growth model one considers. Because of such theoretical ambiguities, the pertinent issues have been empirical, and they have provided a survey of empirical findings on these issues. Drawing from the experiences of the two giant Asian developing countries—China and India—Bhagwati and Srinivasan have argued that greater integration into the world economy may lead a country to a higher growth path and also a reduction poverty.

Poverty and Inequality: Empirical Findings

T. N. Srinivasan and Jessica Seddon Wallack, in Chapter 16, have considered the possible causal relationships and empirical association between globalisation and growth, growth and poverty, and globalisation and poverty reduction. They have argued that globalisation can reduce poverty directly and also, by accelerating growth. They have further suggested that redistributive policies may be much less effective in poverty reduction in comparison to greater access to markets, more competitive insurance and financial markets, and improved institutions. They have viewed the effectiveness of international integration in helping to reduce poverty, although it may be limited by domestic policy failures and continuation of protectionism.

Ananya Ghosh Dastidar has argued in Chapter 17, that certain structural characteristics of developing countries may have had an important influence on the overall distribution of income, and that these have been likely to influence the way in which income distribution is affected by greater openness to international trade. Her empirical study has used a panel data set based on 34 developing countries (including India), spanning the course of 1970 and 1990, to examine whether trade has had any systematic impact on income distribution. Her regression results have ruled out any such impact of trade openness on income distribution. Moreover, she has found that the composition of exports, especially with respect to primary goods, rather than the extent of openness per se, is what matters while evaluating the distributional consequences of international trade.

With respect to the Indian economy, she has observed that income distribution within the country is determined largely, by the forces governing the evolution of inter-regional disparities between rural and urban areas and among different states. In particular, she has argued that as long as globalisation is accompanied by economic growth and foreign capital inflows that are urban centric and that targets the better endowed (with respect to infrastructure) states, income inequality in the country is likely to increase with openness. She has pointed out in this context that education may well become an extremely important tool for individuals to acquire skills that are in greater demand, and therefore, to improve their chances of moving up the income ladder.

Openness and Regional Inequality

In Chapter 18, Alokesh Barua and Pavel Chakraborty have analysed the issue of the impact of trade liberalisation on regional inequality in India. There is a large literature pertaining to increasing regional inequality in India. Recently, it has been observed that trade liberalisation has led to a further increase in regional inequality. While the inequality trend has merely been a statistical construct, it does not explain by itself the causes of rising inequality in India. Theoretical analyses offer conflicting views on this. Similarly, most empirical research for various countries on the link between trade liberalisation and inequality also, provides opposite trends. The present study has examined inequality in a Chenery-Syrquin type of structural framework, in which income inequality results from manufacturing inequality insofar as the rise in per capita income is determined by the increase in the share of manufactures in the gross domestic product (GDP). The study confirms this hypothesis using a pooled sample of data on state GDP and its various components over a 20-year period. It has been shown that trade liberalisation has significantly contributed to a rise in the share of manufacturing in GDP for all the states of India, and it confirms that per capita income is positively, and significantly, related to the share of manufacturing. The non-linear trends in the Theil measure of income inequality and manufacturing inequality have indicated that both indices have shown a downturn after the initiation of WTO reforms. Thus, the authors conclude that trade liberalisation has not increased regional inequality and perhaps, helps in decreasing regional inequality. This result has been consistent with the standard neoclassical prediction on the effects of trade liberalisation on production and confirms the view shared by many contemporary economists that trade liberalisation reduces income inequality.

References

WTO. 2001. *Doha Round Declaration*, Geneva: WTO.
———. 2003. *Annual Report*, Geneva: WTO.

SECTION I

A Developing Countries Perspective

1

The WTO and Trade Negotiations: A Developing Countries Viewpoint

Manoj Pant

Never in the past have successive rounds of trade talks led to the kind of violent acrimony that was witnessed in Seattle and Genoa. Even though the Doha Round was concluded peacefully, the Canadians had offered to hold the next round of trade talks at an almost inaccessible mountain resort! Surprisingly, the activist-opponents of the WTO today draw from the civil society in both, developed and developing countries. Even prior to the Doha Round of negotiations, there was a debate on whether this would be a new round or a continuation of the Uruguay Round. Not all the dissension can be explained by political motivation alone. There is some perceived threat from the full application of the Uruguay Round agenda. Removal of these perceived threats is crucial to the success of the Doha (See Chapters 5 and 6 for details on the Doha Round). This article looks at the reasons for some of the dissatisfaction expressed by both developing and developed countries in successive rounds of trade negotiations. In particular, it will argue how the negotiating positions are so radically different today than they were about ten years ago. The issues facing developing countries today are now coming into sharp focus. But first it is necessary to clarify why there is a need for the WTO.

THE THEORY OF MULTILATERAL NEGOTIATIONS

It may be noted that even the perfectly competitive neo-classical model of trade does not say that free trade is the optimal (best) policy. This proposition is valid only for a small country. For a large country (which can influence world prices by buying or selling more or less) the optimal policy is one of optimal tariff. Yet, this is true only if there are no tariff wars. In the presence of such competitive tariff wars, all countries can be shown to be worse off than before.

In Figure 1.1, while OH is the home country's offer curve, OF refers to that of the foreign country (assuming a two-country, two-commodity framework). We measure the home country's exports, OE, on the horizontal axis and its imports (foreign country's exports), OM on the vertical. The offer curves thus indicate each country's exchange offers.

Figure 1.1 Model 1

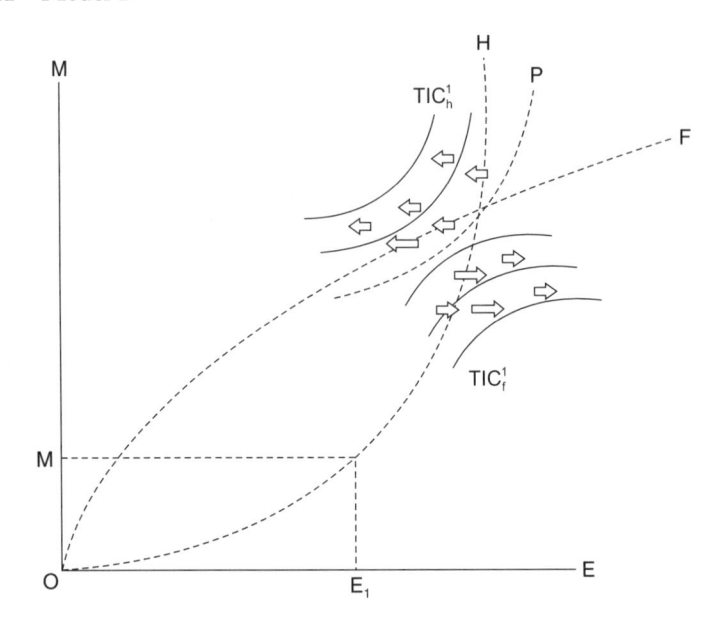

In other words, OH represents the quantum of its exports, the home country is willing to forgo (OEI) for the corresponding amount of its imports (OMI). The shape of OH as drawn is based on the assumption that as a country gives up successive units of its exports, the corresponding quantum of imports it will require becomes larger and larger. This is somewhat like a case of 'diminishing returns' to exporting. However, unlike microeconomic theory, the possibility of the export offer actually declining (beyond point X on the OH curve) is a distinct possibility. This reflects the fact that as a country becomes richer (the 'terms of trade effect') its consumption of its own products would tend to increase. In a similar fashion, OF represents the foreign country's offer curve. While I do not intend to get into the finer aspects of derivation of the offer curves here, it is important to note that OF, for example, represents the foreign country's demand for the products of the home country ('reciprocal demand curve'). Thus, it represents the demand curve facing the home country.

To define the home country's equilibrium, we must define its 'indifference' map. This is given by the so-called Trade Indifference Curves (TICs). TIC_h^1 is one such curve for the home country. The curves are upward sloping, indicating that if a country gives up one more unit of exports (E), it must get an additional amount of imports to be on the same TIC. By symmetry, the foreign country's offer curve would be of the same shape but with reference to the vertical axis.

Finally, as in microeconomic theory, the equilibrium is defined as the point of tangency of its demand curve and the indifference curve.

We can now define two kinds of equilibrium. Trading equilibrium requires that the home country's offer of exports be exactly matched by the demand of the foreign country. This, in Figure 1.2, allows for only one equilibrium, $Q\underline{h}$, where OF and OH intersect.

FIGURE 1.2 Model 2

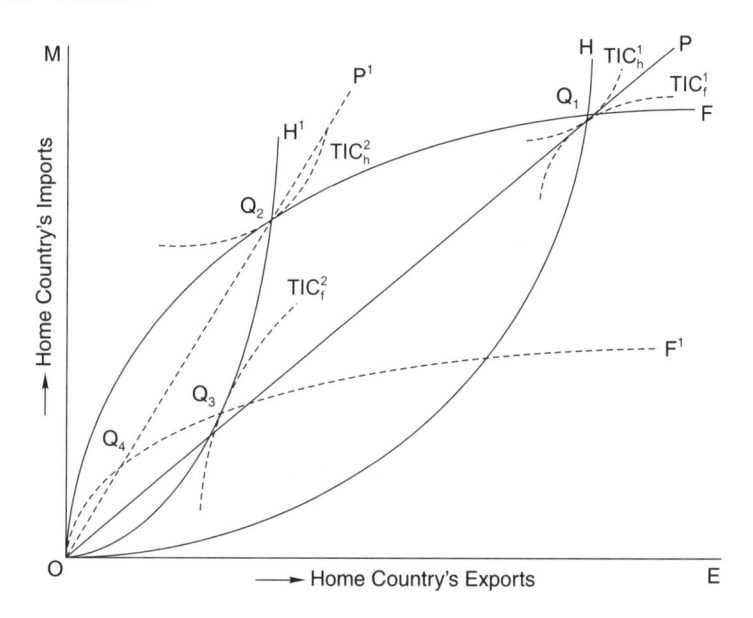

The slope of line OP then describes the equilibrium terms of trade (the value in terms of M of one unit of the home country's exports). Second, as discussed earlier, the optimum of the country is defined by the point at which its TIC is tangential to its demand curve. In case of the home country, this equilibrium is defined as the tangency of some TIC_h to OF. Figure 1.2 shows that while Q_1 is an equilibrium, it is not a stable equilibrium. At Q_1, TIC_h^1 cuts OF. An inspection reveals that the optimum welfare level for H is the point Q_2, where TIC_h^2 is tangential to OF. H can move to this point from Q_1 by imposing an optimum tariff which shifts its offer curve to OH^1. Country H finds its terms of trade improve to OP', as also its welfare.

However, from the perspective of country F, the welfare level falls below the free trade level of TIC_f^1. Since it now faces the offer curve OH^1, it can improve its own welfare by imposing an optimum tariff which takes it to welfare level TIC_f^2 the point of tangency with OH at Q_3. This would invite retaliation from H, leading to a new point Q_4, and so on. Game theorists would interpret this as a non-cooperative Cournot game.

The end result is that total world trade would fall below the free trade level at Q_1, and in fact, both countries might be worse off than at Q_1. Two main points emerge. First, the free trade equilibrium at Q_1 is not a stable equilibrium. Second, in unilateral tariff wars, both countries lose, but it is never in the interest of any one country to unilaterally cut its tariff even as the world (and its own) welfare levels are falling. However, if countries were to negotiate a multilateral tariff reduction from a point like Q_3, then both countries could improve their tariff levels to the free trade level of Q_1. The point is that the free trade equilibrium is maintainable only in a setting of multilateral tariff negotiations.

To put it briefly, this was the logic behind GATT earlier and remains so behind the WTO now. There may be some justification for arguing that the distribution of gains from trade in multilateral tariff negotiations have not been fair, but to conclude from this that a country should withdraw from the WTO, is a remedy worse than the disease. What seems more important is whether developing countries can make common cause in the negotiations. The following sections will look at the changes in international economic relations which shaped negotiating positions prior to the Uruguay Round; will look at the main features of the crucial Uruguay Round; will look at negotiations in the Doha Round and the post-Doha developments; finally conclude with some suggestions as to how the developing countries need to look at future negotiations.

BACKGROUND TO THE URUGUAY ROUND

It is important to understand that in the six rounds after GATT (upto the Kennedy Round), there was almost no disagreement on tariff negotiations. To begin with, most countries were too busy reconstructing their economies after World War II to resist the US, which was the driving force behind the trade negotiations. Second, the devastation caused by tariff wars during the Great Depression was not yet forgotten. Finally, the US gave major tariff concessions without asking for much in return, as its objectives were to break into the Imperial Preferences—under which Canada and United Kingdom (UK) had preferential trade with the colonies—and to bring Japan into the mainstream of trading nations.

The first signs of disagreement emerged with the Tokyo Round of 1973. This was the first time that developing countries emerged as bargaining partners. However, based on the perceived threat of the 'oil weapon', and the fiscal stagnation in the developed economies, developing countries were able to extract one major concession: while they benefited from the MFN status of tariff reductions in developed countries, they did not have to reciprocate (non-reciprocity clause). It would be naive to argue that the developing countries did not benefit from the tremendous growth of world trade from 1955 to 1975. This was particularly true of the trade-oriented economies of East and Southeast Asia. During this period, manufactured exports from less developing countries (LDCs) grew much faster than world trade.

The benefits of multilateral tariff reductions shown in the previous section are available only at a cost. The gains from trade of the standard neoclassical model, discussed above, are predicated on the presumption that countries undergo a structural change. In the context of the developing economies, trade benefited the one factor that was then in surplus—labour. The manufactured exports from the LDCs were largely mass-produced, labour intensive items like toys, garments, electronics and so on. It is now well recorded that wages increased in most of the East Asian 'tigers' in this period, relative to developed countries like the US (Ethier 1983). However, the corresponding structural change required in the developed countries was not easy to sell to the labour constituency in these countries. The main concession obtained by the developed countries to ease the pain of labour restructuring was the MFA of 1974. In the case of exports of agricultural commodities from developing countries, the developed countries reacted to developing country exports with NTBs. Various studies, particularly by the UNCTAD, have documented the growth of these NTBs since 1979 (UNCTAD 1993). The other response of the developed countries was to subsidise their agriculture exports. Finally, the structure of GDP had changed radically in most developed countries and in the newly rich, newly industrialised economies (NIEs) by the end of the 1980s: the dominant sector in these countries was the services sector.

The conflict inherent in North-South trade ultimately found its expression in the Uruguay Round and the formation of the WTO in 1995. While the inclusion of services in trade negotiations was imminent, US-EU trade frictions saw agriculture being brought into trade negotiations for the first time. It is instructive that while the negotiations on a new Uruguay Round began in 1986, it was only in 1995 that the Dunkel Draft became the Final Act of the Uruguay Round and the WTO was formed.

The purpose of providing a detailed background above, is to indicate that while the benefits of multilateral tariff reductions are as high as ever before, the attitude of the developed countries is very different. A number of historical developments made the initial conditions very different in the 1990s as compared to the 1970s and the 1980s. First, the bogey of the oil weapon had been exposed by 1985. The oil producing countries did not realise that control of distribution channels was as important as control of the production of oil wells. In addition, massive technological progress in fuel efficiency has led to a relative decline in the demand for oil. Today, at its highest levels, oil prices have not reached the same nominal levels as in 1979. Second, the 'single undertaking' clause of the Uruguay Round does not allow LDCs the exclusionary benefits of earlier rounds. Third, economics is dominant in this round as the political compulsions of the Cold War era are absent. Fourth, technological progress since 1955, particularly in the developed countries, does not make cheap labour as important to mass consumer goods production as it was in the 1950s (Whalley 1999b). Finally, the tremendous growth of Regional Trading Arrangements (RTAs), under Article XXIV of the GATT, implies that the negotiators are trading blocs and not countries.

The negotiating groups in the WTO are thus, very different from those in previous rounds. The main groups are the EU, the North American Free Trade Area (NAFTA) (read: US), the Cairns Group and Japan. Association of Southeast Asian Nations (ASEAN) has never been a true RTA (bilateral trade deals are common), while SAARC has not taken any shape as yet. In addition, the tremendous growth of the Transnational National Corporations (TNCs), who control a major part of world trade, has added one more bargaining force influencing country positions at the WTO (Pant 1995). Finally, we have the growth of an international civil society (represented by NGOs), which has made its presence felt at Seattle and at Genoa. Economists have argued that developed country labour has as much to lose from the WTO as that of developing countries (Roderick 1995). This has important implications for the articulation of a developing country position in future talks.

THE URUGUAY ROUND

This section will discuss the two main agreements of the Uruguay Round that were supposed to benefit developing countries: the AOA and the MFA; and the not so favourable TRIPS and Trade Related Investment Measures (TRIMS).

Agreement on Agriculture

Seen from the perspective of the economic arguments put forward by developed and developing countries, the final act, giving shape to the WTO and the Uruguay Round of trade negotiations, was easy to understand. The most contentious issue in the Uruguay Round was the AOA. The AOA was the consequence of the US making common cause with the agriculture-based Cairns group to force the EU to cut its common agricultural policy (CAP). It would be a mistake to regard the AOA as the result of any pressure exerted by developing countries. The EU was in any case looking for a way out as its agricultural subsidy programme was becoming far too expensive.[1] The core issues of the AOA (the 'built-in' agenda) were market access, export competition, and domestic support. In the AOA, it was decided that countries would grant market access upto 3 per cent of the domestic market to other countries. Presumably to end the 'subsidy war', it was decided to cut export subsidies (on 1986–88 base) by 36 per cent while reducing the volume of exports subject to subsidies by 20 per cent in the six-year period till 2001. Finally, countries had to calculate their domestic agriculture support expenses in 1986–88. This Aggregate Measure of Support (AMS) was to be reduced by 20 per cent over a six-year period.

The actual benefits for developing countries were minimal. First, in the case of export subsidies, by defining the cuts in the aggregate rather than the product-specific (which was only 15 per cent) way, the measure was biased in favour of cutting the low rather than high tariffs (Tangermann 1994). Consequently, tariffs on products of interest to developing countries, like sugar, tobacco, cotton, cereals, and prepared fruits and vegetables had the highest tariff peaks (Josling 1999; UNCTAD/WTO 1997). Second, the actual reduction of export subsidies was avoided by using the 'carry over' provision through which unused subsidies of one year could be carried over to another year. It is not often realised that developed country subsidies are concentrated on a few items like cheese, butter, beef and wheat, and tend to be high when world prices are low (Panagariya 1999). Third, the stipulations regarding the reduction in AMS were systematically bypassed by the creation of the various boxes such as the blue box, green box and amber box. This in effect implied that the EU compensation programme under the 1992 CAP and the US deficiency payment programme were not included while calculating the AMS. Such exclusions were typical in the fruition of free trade agreements, which lead to reduced protection for domestic producers (Grossman and Helpman 1995). Finally, if all other measures failed, direct import restrictions were permitted only to developed countries under the Special Safeguard Clause (SSC) in the case of sudden disruptions due to out of quota imports (for India see Chapter 7).

Multi Fibre Agreement

One of the major factors that led developing countries to acquiesce to such controversial agreements as TRIPS and TRIMs was the commitment given by the developed countries to phase out quota-based MFA by 2004. This phasing out was to be done by periodically releasing items subject to MFA restrictions and subjecting them to WTO regulations. The trouble was that once again these phasing-out programmes were specified at the aggregate rather than the product-specific level. Consequently, most of the products of interest to developing countries will be phased out only by 2004 or so (Whalley 1999a). Interestingly, the agreement does not say whether some new agreement will replace the MFA. What is more likely, is the use of anti-dumping measures and high duties by developed countries to prevent imports from developing countries. It is difficult to understand why the developing countries attached so much importance to the phasing out of the MFA especially in view of the fact that there are very few studies (See Chapter 9 for India) which suggest that the gain from the phasing out process would be substantial (Francois et al. 1996; Harrison et al. 1996). It is possible that the phasing out of the MFA will divide the least developing countries further (Whalley 1999b).

TRIPS and TRIM

The single undertaking' clause enabled the developed countries to bring in their own agenda on industrial goods and services, TRIPS and TRIM along with the GATS. As is well known, the extension of the 20-year product patent regime was primarily pushed by the pharmaceutical and biochemical companies. This is the agenda of one of the latest participants in trade talks, the TNCs. It is also now acknowledged, that particularly in the context of pharmaceutical products, TRIPS would reduce global welfare (Juma 1999; Maskus and Konan 1994; Pant 1996; Subramaniam 1994). It is a measure of the ill preparedness of the developing countries that they agreed to the 10-year implementation of the new patent regimes on the basis of unknown and unguaranteed benefits from the phasing out of MFA and the new AOA. I have already argued that none of the benefits have so far materialised for reasons stated above. It is also worth restating that, 28 years after the installation of the MFA regime, the developed countries are still not ready for a structural adjustment to free trade in textiles and apparel. In a recent statement, the American Textile Manufacturing Industry (ATMI) says it will vehemently oppose any attempts to advance the timetable for phasing out the MFA (*Economic Times* 2001). Yet, developing countries are expected to undertake structural adjustments to the new patent regime in just 10 years!

THE DOHA ROUND: WHY DEVELOPING COUNTRIES WERE DIVIDED

Initially, many developing countries seemed to think that the issue of non-implementation of the Uruguay Round commitments would be the principal agenda at Doha. However, just prior to the Doha meeting, the US agreed with the EU on the need for a new round and the US trade representatives were busy moving round the world to convince developing countries of the same. At Doha itself, the differences among developing countries were evident. While India stood steadfast till the end in opposing a new round and inclusion of new issues, it was soon isolated. The developing countries of Asia, Latin America and Africa did not support India, as their own bilateral interests were taken care of by the EU and the US. Why were the developing countries so divided?

The most important factor appears to be the RTAs that have proliferated, particularly in the last 20 years or so. The basis of an RTA is free trade among member countries, which maintain a common tariff vis-à-vis the rest of the world. The two largest RTAs today are the EU and the NAFTA. Both have provided preferential (quota) access to developing countries as this qualifies for tariff reduction under GATT. For example, the out of (preferential) quota tariff rate in the EU for bananas is around 160 per cent. The EU has similar preferential arrangements for some of its erstwhile colonies in Africa. Similarly, the NAFTA offers similar preferential treatment to some Latin American countries, while Mexico is already a member. In the context of the MFA, countries of East Asia and Southeast Asia no longer benefit, as in the 1970s and 1980s, from reduced tariffs. For some of the least developed countries (for example, Bangladesh), there is already preferential access in the EU and removal of the MFA might in fact harm rather than help them. In short, through trade-distorting preferential tariffs, the developing countries are now divided into the developing and least developing countries. The latter are particularly averse to losing the benefits that accrue from preferential access to RTAs. Therein, lies the problem. While most developed countries are in one of the two major RTAs, most neighbouring developing countries (in

Latin America and in Central Europe) are bargaining for entry into one or the other. On the other hand, ASEAN in Asia is divided into the least developing, developing, and developed countries, and does not negotiate as a group. In any case, it is largely driven by Singapore, whose interests lie more with the US than with any other country. It is hoped that the South Asian Association for Regional Cooperation (SAARC) may now realise the need to sink their differences and present a united stand in future negotiations.

Probably because of India's protest, the final Doha Declaration did ensure that some of the core developing country interests were taken care of (See Chapter 5 and 6 for details about India). First, the separately adopted declaration on health for poorer developing countries clearly marked a turning point in the decade-old fight on the impact of the TRIPS on the pricing of health care. Clauses 5b and c of the declaration effectively implied that compulsory licensing could be imposed in the case of 'national emergency' and countries had the 'freedom to determine the grounds' for compulsory licensing. In addition, Clause 5c widened the cases of 'national epidemics' to a whole host of diseases beyond HIV/AIDS. The issue of 'parallel imports' was recognised in Clause 6 and the Council of TRIPS is expected to find a solution.

A second contentious issue in the context of TRIPS has been the issue of patenting plant life forms. Clause 19 of the Doha Declaration required the Council on TRIPS to examine the relationship between the Convention on Biodiversity (CBD) and the TRIPS, and stated that the council would 'take fully into account the development dimension'. The CBD requires that firms take the permission of the state governments before exploiting the natural biodiversity of any country.

Third, the concerns of many developing countries like India were addressed in Clause 18, which recognised the need to extend the protection of geographical indications to products other than wine and spirits.

Fourth, despite a strong ED bid, the issue of the social clause and core labour standards was left out of the work programme though it found its place in the preamble. It is now clear that the ED plans to use trade incentives to address its prime social clause agenda (Pant 2002a).

Finally, the initial fear with regard to the issue of government procurement proved ill founded. The declaration recognised the right of governments to give preference to domestic suppliers, but called for the transparency of procedures. Given the corruption in public procurement operations in many developing countries, this 'transparency clause' is to be welcomed.

These successes for developing countries, by no means inconsequential, were achieved at the expense of allowing environment issues and the Multilateral Agreement on Investment (MAI) on the WTO agenda. However, while the environment issues were on the agenda of the next (fifth) ministerial, the discussion on the MAI were to begin only after a consensus on the modalities of negotiations was reached at the Fifth Ministerial.

POST-DOHA DEVELOPMENTS.

Subsequent developments showed that the achievements at Doha were primarily a consequence of the US preoccupation with the 'war on terror', after the incidents of 11 September, 2001 and their need to win friends around the globe. This became clear in the next ministerial meeting at Cancun, Mexico, in September, 2003.

Expectedly, the main issues for the developing countries at Cancun was the non-implementation (in spirit if not the letter) of the Uruguay Round agreement on agriculture and textiles by the developed countries. The major difference, from the earlier meetings, from the point of view of negotiating strategies, was the formation of the new negotiating group of developing countries variously called G-20 or G-21. The viability of this new group stemmed from the presence of four main developing country stalwarts, namely, China, India, South Africa and Brazil. The crucial issue at Cancun were the factors that led to the cementing of this group over the next few months aided by an attempt by the developed countries to stall progress in implementation of the Uruguay Round agreements on agriculture and textiles.

The Cancun Ministerial was slated for an unruly end when the developed countries attempted to begin negotiating on proposals related to what had then come to be called 'The Singapore Issues'. The two most contentious ones were related to multilateral agreements on investment and competition. The other two issues were related to government procurement and trade facilitation. What cemented the G-21 alliance was the attempt by the US and EU to bring both investment and competition on the negotiating table. The provocation was the fact that at Doha it was agreed that even the modalities of discussion of an agreement on the Singapore issues (apart from the agreement itself) was to begin in Cancun only after an 'explicit consensus' was reached on such discussion. It was clear at Cancun that the developing countries were unwilling to be a party to this consensus. In any case, a number of studies have indicated that there is no theoretical or historical basis for a multilateral agreement on either competition or investment (see, for example, Pant and Nunnenkamp 2003).[2] In the light of this the attempt to bring multilateral agreements on investment and competition onto the WTO agenda smacked of backdoor attempts to stall implementation of the Uruguay Round agreements on agriculture and textiles.

This was particularly true given the implications of the 'single undertaking' clause introduced from the Uruguay agreement. In any case, the method of discussion at Cancun reaffirmed the fears of developing countries in general, and Africa in particular, of lack of transparency in WTO negotiations (Trotman 2004; also see Ostry 2004). It is interesting to note that at Cancun, it was the walkout of the African representatives, which led to a premature end to the meeting. This walkout was prompted by the unwillingness of the US to end the subsidy regime for their cotton farmers that severely impacted the cotton exporters of Africa.

For the first time, then, a major ministerial failed to come to any kind of agreement. However, in terms of negotiating strategies the most important development at Cancun was the emergence of the G-21 as a new group. It is interesting to note that today, more than one year after Cancun, this group has maintained its cohesion despite attempts by the US in particular to break it up. Since Cancun only a few inconsequential members of the G-21 (largely small Latin American countries) have left the group. More importantly, the G-21 completed the process of formation of negotiating groups at the WTO. It was the incompleteness of this group formation which had led to the division at Doha discussed in the previous section. The stability of the G-21 has implied that developed countries are not going to find it easy to progress further in trade negotiations without final implementation of the AOA and the ATC.

The strength of the G-21 was apparent at the end of Cancun when it was agreed that of the Singapore issues only the issue of trade facilitation would be included in trade negotiations. To quote the framework agreement on the Doha work programme finalised in Geneva on 31 July, 2004:

> [...] the Council agrees that these issues (*Trade and Investment, Trade and Competition Policy and Transparency in Government Procurement*) mentioned in the Doha Ministerial Declaration in paragraphs 20–22, 23–25 and 26 respectively, will not form part of the Work Program set out in that Declaration and therefore no work towards negotiations on any of these issues will take place within the WTO during the Doha Round. (emphasis added).

In addition, as agreed at Cancun, even the progress of developing countries on trade facilitation measures would depend on funding from multilateral agencies like the World Bank. In fact, a perusal of the 31 July framework agreement makes it clear that the dominant theme is the modalities of defining and reducing protection in agriculture. As expected the infamous MFA quota system in textile trade came to an end on 1 January, 2005. However, it was clear that the developing countries had to generate much domestic intellectual capital (especially within the G-21) to ensure that the letter of the agreement to be reached in Hong Kong in December 2005 incorporated their interests. Such intellectual capital had so far been seriously deficient (Pant 2002b).

The Hong Kong Ministerial of December 2005 was preceded by a number of mini-ministerials and bilateral meetings in Geneva and China. As the proceeding of the Hong Kong Ministerial clearly showed, the developing countries had made non-implementation of the AOA, by developed countries, the litmus test of the seriousness of developed countries in implementing a free trade agenda, which encompassed all sectors of the economy. The G-20, which emerged in Cancun, was the primary force behind the Hong Kong declaration which concentrated on defining the formula by which agricultural tariff reductions could be defined. It is to the credit of the G-20 that, at Hong Kong, they were able to commit developed countries to agree to eliminate all cotton subsidies by end 2006. This was of particular interest to African LDCs.

Hence, the G-20 has emerged as the group which also has the responsibility of taking on board the developing countries of Africa which felt that reduction of agricultural subsidies in developed countries could raise the price of agricultural commodities which would harm them as net food importers. The role of developing countries like India was further enhanced in that they would make specific efforts to accommodate the least developed countries. In this regard the Hong Kong declaration specified that 'developed-country Members, and developing-country Members declaring themselves in a position to do so, agree to implement duty-free and quota-free market access for products originating from LDCs' (WTO). While some discussion also took place on negotiations on Non-Agricultural Market Access (NAMA) and the modalities of implemented the GATS, it is now clear that implementing the AOA in both spirit and letter is crucial to a successful completing of the Doha Round. What the Hong Kong Ministerial also indicated is the firming up of the new G-20 negotiating group which meant that developing countries also now have a strong representation in all green room negotiations.

CONCLUSION

The purpose of this article has been to see how negotiating strategies have changed subsequent to the Uruguay Round agreement in 1995. The principle point made is that the logic of multilateral negotiations remains as strong as in 1948 when the GATT was negotiated. However, since then major changes have taken place which makes negotiation a much more difficult task.

The most important change after 1995 has been the introduction of the 'single undertaking' clause in all subsequent trade agreements which nullifies all the benefits of the 'non-reciprocity' clause for developing countries first introduced in the Tokyo Round agreement. The fall out of this clause has been that developing countries have so far not had any incentive to engage the developed countries in trade negotiations. As a consequence, developed countries have unilaterally built up an extensive system of tariff and non-tariff barriers to exports from developing countries particularly in the case of agriculture and textile exports.

Second, the 'single undertaking clause' has gone along with an expansion of the areas where trade agreements are binding to include virtually all sectors of the economy including services and investment. Given the impact that expanded trade would have on their own domestic political economy, developing countries have now had to concentrate negotiations to first end the bias against their exports in developed countries, and then to try to ease the pain of structural adjustment via the Special and Differential Treatment (S&DT) provisions of subsequent agreements. However, given the nature of negotiations such S&DT provisions are no longer available in perpetuity.

Third, the nature of negotiations in the WTO today implies that it is the trading blocs rather than individual countries that determine the outcome. Till Cancun, the emergence of a strong developing country bloc was in doubt. This was so, particularly because the developed countries (the US and EU in particular) used the system of preferential tariff arrangements to divide the developing countries. This system of preferential trading arrangements, particularly in the context of the explosive growth of regional trading areas in the 1990s, nullified the other major benefit that developing countries had obtained in the Tokyo Round: the system of Generalised System of Preferences (GSPs). The formation of the G20 has ended this serious lacuna in trade negotiations.

To sum up, negotiations today do not allow the escapism that the Tokyo round agreement had permitted to developing countries. With the single undertaking clause allowing cross sectoral bargaining the art of negotiations is something that developing countries have to learn. The first task in this process is the development of strong negotiating groups. The Cancun negotiations probably constituted the start of this process of learning. The Hong Kong Ministerial reflected the first assertion by developing countries in finalising negotiating agendas.

Endnotes

[1] Statements by Tony Blair and Agricultural Commissioner, Franz Fischler, on http://www.Ellbusiness.com.

[2] For papers on multilateral competition policies see Alan Winters and P. Mehta (2003).

References

Economic Times, 11 August 2001.
Ethier, S. 1983. *Modern International Economic*, New York: W.W. Norton and Co.

Francois, J. R., B. MacDonald and H. Nordstorm. 1996. 'The Uruguay Round: A Numerical based Qualitative Assessment', in *The Uruguay Round and Developing Economies*, edited by W. Martin and L. A. Winters, Cambridge: Cambridge University Press.

Grossman, G. M. and E. Helpman. 1995. 'The Politics of Free Trade Agreement', *American Economic Review*, vol. 85, no. 4, pp. 667–90.

Harrison, G. W., T. E. Rutherford and D. G. Tarr. 1996. 'Quantifying the Uruguay Round', in *The Uruguay Round and Developing Economies*, edited by W. Martin and L. A. Winters; Cambridge: Cambridge University Press.

Josling, T. 1999. 'Developing Countries and the New Round of Multilateral Trade Negotiations: Background Notes on Agriculture', paper presented at the conference on Developing Countries in the Next WTO Trade Round, Harvard University, November.

Juma, C. 1999. 'Intellectual Property Rights and Globalization: Implications for Developing Countries', paper presented at the conference on Developing Countries in the Next WTO Trade Round, Harvard University, November.

Maskus, K. E. and D. E. Konan. 1994. 'Trade Related Intellectual Property Rights: Issues and Exploratory Results, in *Analytical and Negotiating Issues in the Global Trading System*, edited by A. Deardorff and R. Stem, Michigan: Ann Arbor.

Ostry, Sylvia. 2004. 'External Transparency: The Policy Process at the National Level of the Two-Level Game', in *Doha and Beyond: The Future of the Multilateral Trading System*, edited by Mike Moore, Cambridge: Cambridge University Press.

Panagariya, A. 1999. 'The Millenium Round and Developing Countries: Negotiating Strategies and Areas of Benefit', paper presented at the conference on Developing Countries in the Next WTO Trade Round, Harvard University, November.

Pant, Manoj. 1995. *FDI in India: The Issues Involved*, New Delhi: Lancer Books.

_____. 1996. 'TRIPS and TRIMs: India's Threat Perceptions', in *Egypt and India in the Post Cold War World*, edited by M. E. Selim, Centre for Asian Studies, Cairo: Cairo University.

_____. 2002a. 'First the Stick and Now the Carrot: Labour Standards in WTO', *Economic Times*, vol. 3, August.

_____. 2002b. 'Millenium Round of Trade Negotiations: A Developing Country Perspective', *International Studies*, vol. 39, no. 3, pp. 1–32.

Pant, Manoj and P. Nunnenkamp. 2003. 'Why the Case for a Multilateral Agreement is Weak', Working Paper no. 400, Kiel Institute for World Economics, March.

Roderick, D. 1999. 'Globalization and Labour', in *Market Integration, Regionalism and the Global Economy*, edited by R. E. Baldwin, D. Cohen, A. Sapir and A. Venables, Cambridge: Cambridge University Press.

Subramaniam, A. 1994. 'Putting Some Numbers on the TRIPS Pharmaceutical Debate', *International Journal of Technology Management*, vol. 10, no. 10, pp. 252–68.

Tangermann. 1994. *An Assessment of the Uruguay Round on Agriculture*, report prepared for the Agricultural Directorate, OECD, Paris.

Trotman, LeRoy. 2004. 'The WTO: The Institutional Contradictions', in *Doha and Beyond: The Future of the Multilateral Trading System*, edited by M. Moore, Cambridge: Cambridge University Press.

UNCTAD. 1993. *Trade and Development Report*, Geneva: UNCTAD.

UNCTAD/WTO. 1997. *Market Access Development since the Uruguay Round: Implications, Opportunities and Challenge*, Geneva: UNCTAD.

Whalley, J. 1999a. 'Note on Textiles and Apparel in the Next Trade Round', paper presented at the conference on Developing Countries in the Next WTO Trade Round, Harvard University, November.

———. 1999b. 'Developing Countries and Systems Strengthening in the Uruguay Round', in *Uruguay Round and the Developing Economies*, edited by W. Martin and L. A. Winters, Washington DC: The World Bank.

Winters, Alan and P. Mehta (eds). 2003. *Bridging the Differences*, Jaipur: Centre for International Trade, Economics and Environment.

WTO. *Hong Kong Ministerial Declaration: Annex F*, available at www.wto.org.

2

The WTO and our Role in the World Economy of the Future

Ashok Guha

THE WTO AND THE LONG RUN FUTURE OF THE WORLD ECONOMY

The WTO is the first supranational institution with coercive powers in the domain of international economic relations. It is based on a surrender of sovereignty by its member states and embodies as such, a totally new principle of governance in the world economy. This principle however has now become an imperative. In a world increasingly unified by the revolutions in information and communication technology following upon the earlier revolution in transport, most of our everyday transactions have repercussions that reach across borders and indeed often circle the globe. The old nation-state system has become an obsolete framework for the governance of this vast and complex web of international transactions. The WTO lays the basis of an alternative order. It is the foundation of the economic architecture of the world of the twenty-first century.

The structure of the WTO and the provisions of the treaty on which it is based, thus have very long run implications. Their consequences will extend beyond the immediate present, not only to future decades and generations but to distant posterity as well. In evaluating these consequences, we need to look beyond the world economy as presently constituted, to discern, howsoever dimly, the unfolding pattern of the future world. And to understand the likely impact on India, we require a clearer vision of India's likely place in this emerging global mosaic.

INTERNATIONAL DEMOGRAPHIC DISPARITIES AND THE WORLD OF THE FUTURE

Prophecy on such a scale is a hazardous venture, smacking astrology at its most occult. Yet over the last few decades, so unmistakable have been the trends, that it is perhaps possible to make a few projections about the contours of the world economy of the future with some degree of assurance. We focus here on the trends in three main areas, demography, savings and growth. Of these, demographic trends are perhaps the most exogenous, and are least likely to be affected by the processes of globalisation of which the WTO is a by-product. Yet even here, it is the triumphal march of the market that is perhaps the trigger. An episode in the market's all-consuming growth has been its penetration in the modern household.

As demand for labour has risen, wages and employment opportunities for women outside the home have grown, while labour-saving gadgets have taken over household chores. In the advanced world where this process has progressed furthest, it has led to the increasing economic independence of women, the breakdown of the traditional division of labour between the sexes and the disintegration of the nuclear family. As marriage has become an anachronism, the basic support structure for child-bearing and rearing has crumbled away. The incentives for child-bearing have collapsed; birth rates in rich countries have plunged quite as dramatically as they did following the dissolution of the extended family in the less developed world. In very few advanced societies today the total fertility rate (the number of children born to the average woman during her entire reproductive life span) is above the replacement level (of about 2) (Bezruchka 2005). In Japan, where prohibitive housing costs are an added factor, it is as low as 1.38. In the US, total fertility has fallen from 3 in 1980 to 1.9 in 2000—though the latter figure is buoyed up by a Latino fertility rate of 3 and a black fertility rate of 2.4. The flow of babies into the advanced world is drying up.

Coupled with increasing longevity, the collapse of the birth rate has totally changed the age structure of Western society. In the US, there are now three times as many elders over 60 as there are children below 4. The West, as we knew it, is aging and will soon be dead.

The aspect of this problem that has been most widely discussed is the growing burden of old age support. A rapidly shrinking working population must provide for a swelling horde of retirees. The elderly exercise their claims on current output through social security and pensions, as well as through their ownership of most of the nation's wealth. A class division between rentiers and workers is thus superimposed on the generation gap—hardly a prescription for social harmony.

DISPARITIES IN SAVINGS RATES

Even more significant is the impact on the savings rate. As Nobel laureate Franco Modigliani argued, a declining and aged population is one in which retirees who are consuming their wealth, outnumber workers who are adding to it. If the older generation plans to bequeath a legacy to its heirs rather than to exhaust its wealth over its lifetime, its savings, though declining, may still be positive. But as fertility declines, the bequest motive weakens. Dynasties disappear; even children become scarce; who after all do you leave your money to?

In the US, the fading of the bequest ethic is well-attested by the evidence (Bureau of Economic Analysis, various years). In 1960, retirees were consuming their resources at the rate of 6–7 per cent a year; in 1990, they were doing so at the rate of 12–14 per cent. This was reflected in the collapse of the aggregate rate of personal savings—from 11 per cent of disposable income in 1970 to −1 per cent in 2000.

The US is not unique in this respect either. All the Organisation for Economic Co-operation and Development (OECD) countries have low and falling savings ratios to match their low and falling birth rates and aging populations. Contrary to received wisdom, the lavish consumption ratios of the rich countries stand in starkly paradoxical contrast to the parsimonious poors of Asia—where the Chinese save 35–40 per cent of their incomes and even India's personal savings rates approach 25 per cent.

There are of course non-demographic factors behind this paradox as well. The well-developed credit institutions of rich countries—hire purchase, credit cards, housing mortgages and so on, minimise the need for precautionary savings or for savings to fund lumpy expenditures. Social security and medicare reduce the need for private savings to finance retirement or health care. Yet, it is difficult to argue that such factors can account for a difference in savings rates as vast as that between the US and the Chinese figures or explain the dramatic fall in US savings rates between 1970 and 2000, a period when public policy was largely directed at dismantling the welfare state.

With savings so low, even the barest minimum of investment can be sustained only through large trade deficits. The US current account deficit, for instance, averaged 1.4 per cent of GDP throughout the 1990's. These in turn imply substantial inflows either of loan or of equity capital. The OECD countries face a future in which they will either be owned by foreigners or be deeply indebted to them.

What is more, as their populations age, their ethnic composition is changing. Immigrants account for an ever-growing proportion of the OECD work force. In the US, the Chinese are everywhere: no longer confined to the East and West coasts, they have invaded Kansas, Missouri and Iowa, those once-inviolate bastions of heartland America. The 'Yellow Peril', the specter that so haunted the lily-white Australia of the thirties, has silently engulfed large districts of Melbourne and Sydney. The Hispanics are flooding into the US, not just into inner-city ghettos, but into hitherto-white suburbia as well. South Asians are becoming politically significant minorities in England and the US, Turks and Arabs in Europe and Greeks and Italians in Australia.

However, the racial balance of the Western world will be unsustainable even without immigration. Even if the US is sealed off to immigrants, non-Hispanic whites, at present levels of total fertility, will lose 10 per cent of their number in every generation, while Hispanics add 50 per cent. The white Anglo-Saxon Protestants, the community most deeply penetrated by the market, will account for an ever-narrowing segment of the population, while more prolific groups increase their share. Natural selection will work to temper the impact of the market on fertility.

DIFFERENCES IN GROWTH RATES

Quite as spectacular as the differences in demographics and savings, have been the world-wide disparities in growth rates. Over the last four decades, East Asia has developed at an astronomical rate, several times faster than that of the advanced West. Over the last twenty years, South Asia too has far outstripped the West. India's growth performance since its recovery from the foreign exchange crisis of 1991–93 and the simultaneous collapse of its rupee trade has been most remarkable. Skeptics like Paul Krugman, who believed that the Asian miracle was merely transient, that it would run out of steam as the technological gap between Asia and the West narrowed, and that the Asian crisis of 1997 represented the exhaustion of the sources of Asian growth have been surprised and silenced by the renewed vigour of Asia's recovery over the last five years.

In stark contrast, Western economies have stagnated for well over a generation. Real wages in the US have not risen since the 1960',s while Western Europe has been in the throes of chronic unemployment and recession. Surprisingly, all this has occurred in the age of the most dazzling scientific and technological accomplishments in human history, the era when the West has explored interstellar space and unlocked the secrets of the atom, cracked the genetic code and conjured up life in the laboratory, unleashed the Information

Revolution and magically transformed communications, agriculture and medicine. Yet in this age, low-tech Asia has comprehensively outperformed the high-tech West in the realm of economics. No paradox can be more striking than this geographical mismatch between the scientific miracles of the twentieth century and its economic miracles.

TECHNOLOGY, TRADE AND GROWTH IN ASIA AND THE WEST

What lessons do these trends teach and what kind of a future world do they portend? It is evident from the contrast between the Asian experience and the Western that high technology is not the secret of growth today. Indeed, the calculations of Alwyn Young and Lawrence Lau have conclusively established that the contribution of technical progress to East Asia's economic success have been minor, if not negligible. Asia's economic development has in fact been powered by an explosion in labour-intensive manufactured exports. It is part of an unfolding pattern of international specialisation that is integrating the labour surpluses of Asia into the mainstream of world trade. Over the last forty years, a new international division of labour has been emerging with first labour-intensive industries and then standardised manufacturing migrating to low-wage economies. The advanced countries are concentrating increasingly on services, R&D and research-intensive industries. The momentum of this process is unlikely to be exhausted as long as international wage differentials persist—provided the growth of international trade is sustained. The continuation and extension of the Asian economic miracles are therefore crucially dependent on the continued expansion of free multilateral trade. Our economic future, more than that of any other part of the world is bound up with, not, as is often believed, the frustration of the basic stated objectives of the WTO, but with their fulfillment.

If world trade continues to expand and intensify, we can look forward to a future in which Asia, and in particular China and India, will be economic superpowers. However, our crystal-ball-gazing into the future of the world's population and its savings tells much more than this. It indicates that the ethnic character of the advanced world will change, that the youth and workers of the West will increasingly be immigrants and that the wealth of the West will increasingly be owned by foreign investors. Such changes in the composition of Western populations and in the ownership of their property would strip the boundaries between nations of their significance. The distribution of the world's income between nations would matter less and less relative to the maximisation of its aggregate. The case for an extension and intensification of world trade would be strongly reinforced.

IMPLICATIONS FOR THE WTO

It is in this perspective that the negotiations on the future shape of the WTO need to be approached. Whether they will be is another question—since the negotiating parties are nation-states with their vested interest in the preservation and perpetuation of the old politico-economic order based on nation-states and since the pressures to which they are exposed emanate essentially from established interest groups that have benefited from the old order and are therefore eager to resist change. However, for Asia at least, our stake in the expansion of multilateral trade is too overwhelming to be ignored.

What are the implications of this, with regard to the objectives we should adopt on the major issues confronting the WTO? First, all measures that seek to restrict free trade on a variety of pretexts need to be adamantly opposed. These include anti-dumping duties, agricultural subsidies and 'social clauses' that seek to restrict labour-intensive exports from poor countries on the pretext of unfair wages or working conditions. Measures that seek to restrict trade on the pretext of protecting the environment should be rejected in favour of an international environmental regime that constrains domestic environmental policy to the extent that it has cross border repercussions.

Secondly, a multilateral investment agreement that limits the terms under which different countries could attract foreign investment should be rejected. Such an agreement amounts essentially to an effort to restrain free competition between agents in a market: different countries now can offer alternative menus to foreign investors; free choice by the latter should ensure an optimally diversified investment regime, much better at any rate than one designed by negotiation between bureaucracies and imposed uniformly on all members of the WTO.

A third and more complex issue revolves around intellectual property. How strong a protection of new technology is desirable from the point of view of countries like India? Received wisdom asserts that we, as consumers rather than producers of technology, stand to gain more from a weak patent regime that facilitates the diffusion of innovations than from a strong regime that stimulates the incentive to innovate. A weak regime, so it is believed, would not only cheapen the products of new technology; it would also facilitate our acquisition of the technology and, in the long run, strengthen our own R&D capacity. In the light of our analysis of the trends in the world economy, this is a view that needs qualification. Asia's past economic success and her future prospects are linked to the rapid expansion of world trade, not to the ownership of new technologies. The major obstacle to our continued development is likely to be international recession—the persistent stagnation of the high-tech West fuelling the growth of protectionist sentiment. It may be therefore in our own interest to offer the West concessions that strengthen its comparative advantage in R&D and encourage it to become more dependent on the labour-intensive goods that we are well-equipped to supply efficiently. Our future depends not on zero-sum games designed to carve out a larger slice of a stagnant world output but on maximising the size of the pie itself while maintaining our relative share.

As our time-horizon lengthens, these considerations will be strongly reinforced. With Asians producing ever more of the output of the West and claiming ever more of its wealth, the geographic distribution of the gains from the growth of the world economy will matter less and less.

Unfortunately, the constraints of geography and the compulsions of the immediate present are likely to play a much larger role than we have envisaged in determining the attitudes of different governments to the evolving negotiations on the future of the WTO. Nation-states are bound to be primarily concerned about the volume of output they will control within their own jurisdictions, and governments, the chief actors in the negotiating process, have time-horizons bounded essentially by the next election. The hard realities of political economy may lead therefore to an outcome very different from what would appear to be optimal in the long run to a mere economist.

References

Bezruchka, Stephen A. 2005. 'Fertility Table', OECD Social Indicators edition, http://mailman1.u.washington.edu/pipermail/pophealth/2005-March/001071.html and http://www.oecd.org/dataoecd/34/28/34542290.xls.

Bureau of Economic Analysis. various years. *Savings Data*, US Department of Commerce, http://www.bea.gov/national/nipaweb/Nipa-Frb.asp.

Section II

Negotiating Options and Strategies

3

India and Coalitions in Multilateral Trade Negotiations

Manmohan Agarwal

INTRODUCTION

The coalition of developing countries failed to make any headway with their proposals for a New International Economic Order in the seventies. They failed to prevent the inclusion of services, TRIPS and TRIMs in the agenda for multilateral trade negotiations (MTNs) at Punta del Este in 1986. This is in contrast with the seeming success of the Cairns group in negotiations for reducing distortions in agricultural trade and of the 'café au Lait' group in dealing with the issues involved in services trade. Both developed and developing countries were members of the Cairns and Café au Lait groups. This contrasting experience resulted in considerable analysis of appropriate coalitions for developing countries, given that, individually most of them are too small to be able to play any significant role in the negotiations.

The changing nature of MTNs over the years has necessitated shifts in negotiating strategies and tactics. This chapter will analyse briefly, the approach of developing countries to multilateral negotiations over the years as the nature of these negotiations has changed. It will then look at the differing stages of negotiations and how the nature of coalitions changes with the stage of negotiations. The chapter will finally discuss India's approach to coalition formation.

The Uruguay Round intensified changes in the nature of MTNs to which developing countries could not adequately respond. Three phases can be distinguished in the development of MTNs. In the initial phase, negotiations were undertaken by offers and bids by major suppliers. The major suppliers of a good would ask for lower tariffs on these goods by their partners and would offer tariff cuts on their imports. By the very nature of this approach, negotiations were confined to the major trading countries, and countries participating in these negotiations could clearly see the benefits of engaging in such negotiations, as it was relatively easy to see the benefits to their exports. The negotiations were restricted to manufactured goods as agriculture was kept out of the negotiations at the insistence of the US. Developing countries were on the sidelines, not that they had any objections to this. Agriculture, as already noted, was kept out of the negotiations and exports of developing countries consisted mainly of primary products.[1] Furthermore, developing countries were all embarking on a policy of industrialisation under high protective barriers and their objective in MTNs was to be allowed to do so.

In the next phase mainly by the fourth round, it was realised that this method of negotiating tariff cuts was very limited (Evans 1971). Consequently, a formula approach was adopted. Tariffs would be cut according to a formula; the negotiations were about what formula to be used, the extent to which a limited number of commodities could be exempted from the formula approach and what commodities should be exempted. For instance, during the Kennedy Round, according to the Congressional Act that gave the administration the authority to negotiate tariff cuts, the administration could not negotiate on cuts in tariffs on textile imports. Countries proposed formulae that would, in turn, help them. Countries with very high tariffs on some imports, often did not want to reduce these tariffs on industries, which were protected for important economic or political reasons and would rather propose a proportional tariff cut, so that tariffs on all imports would be cut by the same percentage. In a relative sense the country could go on protecting the industry. The exporters of this commodity would propose a formula whereby high tariffs would be cut proportionately more leading to a degree of harmonisation in tariff levels. Tariffs cuts in manufactures, and since the Uruguay Round on agriculture, are cut by some formula approach. This approach required countries to formulate or at least to analyse the effects of various formulae on their economy in order to establish their negotiating position. However, developing countries do not seem to have usually undertaken such exercises as they did not really participate in the negotiations on tariff cuts.

But since the Tokyo Round, and much more since the Uruguay Round, the nature of MTNs has changed significantly.[2] More sectors are covered by the negotiations. This by itself may not lead to a substantial increase in the complexity of the negotiations. A formula approach could be adopted for each new sector and a similar analysis be undertaken to find the advantages and disadvantages of adopting different formulae. But once more sectors are covered, there will be much greater scope for trade-offs between sectors. It could be that losses in one sector could be more than offset by gains in another sector. Such trade-offs obviously occurred within the manufacturing sector earlier. But trade-offs between different sectors such as agriculture and manufactures may be more difficult to handle, as factor mobility between the two sectors may be limited and policies to compensate losers in a sector may be more difficult to implement.

But the inclusion of TRIPS and services in the negotiations for the Uruguay Round further complicated the nature of the negotiations. While there is general consensus that some protection is needed to encourage innovative activity, it is not clear what the optimum level of protection is.[3] An increase in the level of protection may encourage more innovation as it increases the gains from innovation. But the larger gains may encourage innovators to sit back and relax, an argument similar to the one used to partly explain low rates of improvement of productivity, under import substitution industrialisation strategies. The lack of clarity of the effects of a stricter TRIPS regime made the negotiations very difficult. This vagueness has come back to haunt the negotiations. The handicaps that the TRIPS regime poses for tackling serious public health dangers, such as HIV/AIDS, has forced recognition of the need to modify some of the provisions of the TRIPS agreement. Also countries such as India faced losses in some sectors, for example, pharmaceuticals, and gains in others, such as entertainment and software, making it difficult to balance the different effects. Furthermore, within the pharmaceutical sector, large firms were expected to be gainers while small firms were the losers.

The implications of negotiations on services were even more difficult to gauge. Liberalisation of service trade seemed to be almost inextricably tied to factors like movements either of capital and labour and would in many cases require substantial modification of domestic legislations and regulations (Bhagwati 1984; Sampson and Snape 1985). Here there seemed, a priori, scope for successful exchange of obligations with the developed countries winning agreement for movement of capital and developing countries for movement of labour. But it did not work out in that fashion. Developing countries themselves needed foreign investment and, though they had maintained their right to impose conditions on capital inflows, such conditions had been liberalised over time. The developed countries were much more reluctant to permit freer movement of persons. The implications of trade in services were much more serious for the domestic policy regimes and many countries, both developed and developing, were initially hesitant to engage in negotiations on services. But, eventually a group of developed and developing countries came together to discuss the issues and implications of negotiations on services. The work of this group was instrumental in the inclusion of services in the Uruguay Round agenda. Its success caused many trade policy analysts to conclude that such mixed issue based coalitions were the way for the future.

The increased complexity of the negotiations had particularly severe adverse effects on developing countries who had limited capabilities to undertake the preliminary analysis in order to design a negotiating position and negotiating strategy. They often had insufficient people to participate meaningfully in all the negotiating groups.

BRIEF OVERVIEW OF DEVELOPING COUNTRIES IN ECONOMIC NEGOTIATIONS

Initially developing countries only had a limited interest in MTNs. They were not major exporters of any manufactured good, so under the rules of negotiations in force in the initial rounds, they were sidelined. They were also not interested in reducing import duties, and so were not in a position to engage in reciprocal bargaining, even though they would have liked to improve market access for their exports. Agriculture was excluded from negotiations. A three member expert committee of the GATT had made recommendations for improving market access for their primary exports (Haberler 1958). But, these could not be implemented because the structure of GATT does not allow for unilateral concessions. The developing countries concentrated their attention to get special and differential treatment in the sense of not having to make any tariff reductions and to derive unilateral benefits from tariff cuts by the developed countries.

Most developing countries faced balance of payments (BOP) problems in their attempts to accelerate growth in the 1950s and 1960s. Investment programmes needed for growth were stepped up and resulted in increased physical capital imports. These imports together with those of industrial intermediate goods quickly outpaced the growth of exports, which were anyway discriminated against by the import substitution industrialisation (ISI) strategy adopted by the developing countries. The ISI strategy also implied that developing countries were not interested in opening up their markets in reciprocal liberalisation bargain. Financing of these deficits through suppliers' credits (much of so-called aid from Europe and Japan, during the early period, had terms close to suppliers' credits) and borrowing from the World Bank at market related interest rates soon resulted in unsustainable debt levels and BOP crises.

In these circumstances, developing countries sought unilateral concessions for access to the markets of the developed countries and soft aid. On both fronts, there was some success. International Development Assistance (IDA), the soft arm of the World Bank was set up and also gradually terms on which the developed countries offered bilateral aid were improved. Moreover, the (GSP), which gave preferential access to exports from developing countries into the developed country markets, was established. This departure from the GATT's MFN principle was given legal sanction by the enactment of the enabling clause in the Tokyo Round agreement.

Though the increase in aid was significant, the benefits from GSP were very limited (Murray 1977). Furthermore, additional progress on both fronts, hit a roadblock in the 1970s, with serious repercussions on developing countries. The slow growth of aid, particularly for higher income developing countries, forced them to borrow more in commercial markets, which contributed to the debt crisis in the 1980s and had very deleterious effects on the economic performance of most of such countries.

Many analysts have claimed that developing countries did not benefit from GATT negotiations because they were not willing to engage in serious negotiations, particularly in reciprocal negotiations, which was the style at the GATT (Sally 2004). They also argued that the bloc style of negotiation adopted by developing countries was not appropriate as this made it difficult to make concessions on any item on the agenda, as every item represented the interest of some bloc members. This became an increasingly important constraint as, over time, developing countries became more heterogeneous, and their interests diverged.

Others refute the above claims.[4] Negotiations for GSP and Part IV were hard negotiations in accord with the interest of developing countries because of their ISI strategy. Part IV allowed trade preferences to be granted to developing countries even though these would be against the GATT's MFN principle. But it is still a moot point whether developing countries could have got greater market access, had they engaged in reciprocal bargaining.

Agriculture, which accounts for most of GDP and exports in most developing countries, was kept out of the GATT at the insistence of the US, with the EU following suit in adopting very distortionary policies in the sector. So, it is not clear what inducement, if any, developing countries could have offered to the US and EU to engage in bargaining that included agriculture.[5] Within the manufacturing sector, the developed countries took the textile and clothing sector, the major sector of interest to developing countries, outside the GATT and constructed on elaborate quantitative restrictions (QR) regime, which was in violation of GATT rules.[6] It is doubtful whether any reciprocal negotiations by developing countries could have prevented this behaviour.[7] Developing countries found that while their demands for liberalisation achieved no success, they did achieve some success in the case of their demand for special and different treatment (Tussie and Lengyel 2001).

In the face of this failure, developing countries concentrated their efforts at the United Nations Conference on Trade and Development (UNCTAD). They adopted a negotiating strategy that tried to use the advantage of numbers. So the developing countries tried to negotiate as a group. But to keep the group together they had to include demands that any of the members made. This made their demands read like a laundry list without any prioritisation within the list. It also meant that there was no flexibility to their negotiating position. Their negotiating position was rigid, as is often the negotiating position of the EU. A change required that all the participants agree. The combined negotiating position had another weakness, one that became more apparent during the discussions on the agenda for the Uruguay Round. The group of developing countries initially was an informal group with no fixed membership, rules or procedures. The leaders of the informal group were Argentina, Brazil, Egypt, India erstwhile and Yugoslavia, and the group also induced Chile, Jamaica, Pakistan, Peru and Uruguay as other prominent members. In the pre-negotiations for the Uruguay Round, it became somewhat more formal and came to be known as the G-10.

Since different countries had different interests, individual countries could be broken from the coalition by being offered deals that met their particular needs. For instance, 10 developing countries till the ministerial at Punta del Este had resisted the demands of the developed countries for TRIPS, TRIMs and services to be included in the negotiations. But, Argentina's interest was mainly liberalisation of agricultural trade and inclusion of this item in the negotiations resulted in Argentina dropping out from the G-10. Gradually other countries also dropped out and the agenda demands of the developed countries were met.

Furthermore, developing countries did participate in reciprocal bargaining during the Uruguay Round and studies suggest that the costs and benefits from the Uruguay Round agreements have been most unevenly distributed. This seems to be inconvertible though one may debate about the line of action one should adopt to rectify the problem.

This sorry record has forced developing countries to look carefully at how to form coalitions. Since the Uruguay Round, developing countries have become convinced of the need to become more engaged in MTNs as the negotiations are not only about tariff cuts and market access, but also about rules governing various international transactions. Developing countries could stay out of tariff negotiations and the developed countries also did not mind this because the markets of the developing countries are small. Rules are needed and staying out of negotiations would mean that adopted rules would not take into account interests of developing countries.

The much greater scope of trade negotiations has also meant that bargains can be made across sectors. Also developing countries are more heterogeneous today and often it is easier to make alliances between a group of developing countries and a group of developed countries that have a similar interest such as the Cairns group. Both developed countries such as the EU and Japan and developing countries that import food such as Jamaica have a common interest in not removing agricultural subsidies as that would raise the cost of food imports in Jamaica. But, on certain issues, the developing countries have taken a common stand, for example, the Singapore issues. The presence of major developing countries, such as, Brazil, China, India and South Africa that seem to have a common interest, has helped to develop a common negotiating stance among developing countries.

NEGOTIATING STAGE AND COALITION FORMATION

Negotiations can be divided into four stages—the work programme of the WTO, the agenda, the modalities and the final agreement. The experience with the Uruguay Round suggested that it would be difficult to keep out of the work programme issues of interest to a sufficiently large number of countries. It was also implied that stopping the progression from inclusion of an issue in the work programme to its inclusion in the agenda for negotiations would be difficult. It followed from these beliefs that developing countries should not act as blocking coalitions, but should develop their own proactive agenda. The contrast between the apparent success of the Cairns and Café au Lait groups in contrast to the failure of the blocking G-10 developing countries at Punte del Este seemed to bolster this belief. The Café au Lait Group was successful as it provided a forum for a detailed analysis of the nature of service trade and the issues involved in services trade, since there was an area where knowledge was limited.

But the experience since then has shown that the belief that items could not be prevented from being included in the agenda was unfounded. Developing countries were successful in preventing the inclusion of trade and labour standards as well as three of the four Singapore issues—competition policy, government procurement and investment.

The coalition of developing countries has survived the stage of establishing the work programme, the agenda and in the process that resulted in the framework agreement. At an earlier stage, environmental standards were included in the work programme but work on labour standards was postponed, but raised particularly vociferously by President Clinton at the Seattle Ministerial. Then, many in developing countries feared that at every meeting fresh concessions would be wrested from developing countries till ultimately the entire agenda of the developed countries was adopted. Similarly, when at Doha it was decided to postpone the decision on inclusion of the Singapore issues till a later ministerial, many trade policy analysts in developing countries feared that this postponement was merely a fig leaf and the later ministerial would include these issues in the negotiating agenda (Agarwal 2004). The time interval would be used by the developed countries to break the unity of the developing countries. But, this has not happened, and the developing countries have maintained their unity.

Developing countries have been successful in their defensive strategy for a number of reasons:

First, many countries during the run up to the Uruguay Round believed that the international economy was becoming more integrated to the advantage of all countries. There was a particularly strong belief bolstered by substantial research that more open economies performed better, and so developing countries that were more cautious or openly skeptical about liberalisation found themselves swimming against the current and were unsuccessful. But experience over the past two decades has shown that trade liberalisation by itself may not be sufficient to result in improved economic performance.[8] Per capita incomes in Latin America and Sub-Saharan Africa have declined or remained stagnant over the past two decades despite the substantial reforms that have occurred. This, together with much lower rates of protection currently prevalent in developing countries, seem to have removed the urgency for engaging in MTNs to reduce protection.

Second, the movement for liberalisation in the developed countries, particularly the US, has slackened, and the interests of specific sectors are sought to be met either by sectoral agreements as in telecommunications or financial services or by preferential (bilateral) trading agreements. The actions of the developed countries, such as the highly publicised laws against business process outsourcing (BPO) in US legislatures weaken the hands of liberationists in domestic debates in developing countries.

Third, trade liberalisation in particular was considered to be a win-win situation. The outcome of the Uruguay Round negotiations has belied this optimistic picture. Developing countries were expected to gain from liberalisation of the agricultural and textile sectors. But the structuring of the agreements resulted in limited gains to developing countries (Dubey 2005). Of course, there may be no point in caviling at this, and the matter can be rectified only in future negotiations. But, an important lesson is that even within an overall win-win situation, a country may have to act very mercantilistically to get benefits. The developed countries had done so, while the developing countries, many of whose residents live at the margin of subsistence, did not do so. Developing countries, therefore, have become more cautious in MTNs.

Fourth, the experience with coalitions between developed and developing countries has not been very encouraging. The final agriculture agreement The Blair House agreement during the Uruguay Round was a deal between the US and EU in which the Cairns group seems to have played a minimal role. This deal essentially postponed liberalisation of agricultural trade. Tariffication of all trade barriers laid the foundation for future negotiations. But the tariffication at inflated levels, and the very limited cuts negotiated and the language of the agreed cuts all conspired to result in very limited liberalisation. The sidelining of the Cairns group exposed differences among the group, those between exporters of temperate products and exporters of tropical products, as also between the developed and developing countries.[9] Similarly, the Café au Lait group does not seem to have been very successful when it came to the nitty gritty of final negotiations. Negotiations were often at the sub-sectoral level and few countries had similar interests at the sub-sectoral level. Furthermore, the smaller developed countries particularly in Europe saw their future in closer European integration, and so were no longer able to form coalitions with developing countries.

So, fifth, European integration has reduced the scope for coalitions among developed and developing countries.

Sixth, it has been realised that log rolling of interests of different countries is not necessarily bad. That is how a common European negotiating position is achieved. Even on a grander scale, the US and EU agreement on including the Singapore issues on the agenda of the MTNs was a log-rolling exercise since initially the US was against a large round. What are needed are mechanisms for resolving differences. This may not be easy, as the European experience with France illustrates.

The G-20 developing countries has been able to protect the interest of developing countries in the ongoing agricultural negotiations. It seems to be the continuation of a process whereby single interest groups are able to function effectively. The problem, however, arises when cross sectoral trade-offs are required.

The formulation of more homogeneous groups of developing countries, such as the group of small vulnerable economies, the African group, and the ACP group, should make it easier to alter the negotiating position of developing countries taking into account the interests of the different groups. Also the presence of some common countries in different groups might make it easier to carry out the adjustments in negotiating positions of the developing countries which will be necessary during the process of reaching the final agreement. Such groupings seem to have provided greater coherence to the negotiating position of developing countries, particularly during the negotiation on the modalities for negotiation. Whether these groups can lead to more meaningful participation in the actual negotiations is something to be seen.

INDIA'S NEGOTIATING POSITION

India, in common with other developing countries, did not play a very significant role in negotiations before the Uruguay Round though, it was an important member (See Chapter 6). During the Uruguay Round it realised the need to be more active. But it was not prepared for the negotiations. The bureaucracy was not prepared for the negotiations—the negotiating unit at Geneva was severely understaffed. Nor were many group outside the government extensively consulted in the charting of India's negotiating position. There seem to have been no extensive studies of the costs and benefits of different proposals discussed during the negotiations. The general opinion among trade policy analysts is that India had no fall back position, so that when it had to make concessions on TRIPS it ended up by ceding to everything the US wanted. This time the Indian government is more organised. Studies have analysed the import of various proposals on India, particularly in the area of tariffs cuts in manufactures. Also, the government has had extensive discussions with business groups as to what India's negotiating position should be. But, other civil society groups are still outside the consultation procedure. Furthermore, there still seems to be inadequate analysis as to whether a particular position would increase income in India or decrease it; by how much and what might be the distributional consequences of various negotiating positions. In this context, it is not clear from available information, as to what extent the states have been consulted and how much their interests have been taken into account.

India has an exceptional and difficult negotiating problem. It is a large country with the potential for development of most industries. During its import substitution regime, considerable resources were devoted to developing modern high technology industries. These industries are not yet internationally competitive but have the potential to become so and keep the growth momentum going and would lead to much higher incomes in the future. Indian policy makers wish to protect these industries while improving the market access for labour intensive industries which are already competitive. Its negotiating strategy has to be different from that of the typical developing country, which is small and therefore, can establish only a few industries and needs to import products of other industries. By its very position, such a small country would gain considerably from an open system under which it can specialise and export a few products to the rest of the world, while importing commodities which it cannot produce. So whether it is already competitive in a sector and seeks market access or does not produce good and wishes to import it cheaply, its interest is in liberalisation.[10]

At the time of the Uruguay Round, India and Brazil were two countries in a similar situation of having established many high-tech industries that were not yet internationally competitive. This commonality of interest was often exhibited during the Uruguay Round negotiations, though Brazil has a more open economy than India and had experienced very rapid growth of exports during the late 1960s and 1970s. Brazil, however, faced a severe disadvantage during the Uruguay Round negotiations. It was in the throes of a debt crisis whose resolution required the cooperation of the developed countries, particularly the US, as US banks were the major creditors. It is unclear whether there was any linkage between the Uruguay Round negotiations and resolution of the debt crisis. But, towards the end of the Uruguay Round negotiations, India seemed to have been isolated, and could not be seen as the only hold out. It ultimately, for instance, agreed to the TRIPS agreement.

In the current Round, India and Brazil are joined by South Africa and China who perhaps face, a similar situation. The economic performance and situation of these countries make them less vulnerable to pressure from the developed countries. The example of China is particularly telling. It shows the benefits of liberalisation when the liberalisation is carried out in conjunction with other reforms and when it is controlled by the government. While it is difficult to prove, economically well to do countries are in a better position to play a leading role. At the time of the Uruguay Round, India was perceived as performing badly and could not be considered as a role model. The pride of place was held by the East Asian, and partly the Southeast Asian, countries. Indian performance today is rated highly as the economy has grown at about 6 per cent a year for almost a quarter of a century, whereas the East and Southeast Asian economies have been facing difficulties partly because of very rapid liberalisation of the capital account. There thus, seems to be a possibility of these four larger developing countries, which face many similar problems, forming a negotiating group. Together, they account for 6 to 7 per cent of trade, larger than that of Canada which is a member of the QUAD.[11] China has a large public sector which needs reorganisation. The Chinese government seems much more inclined to let inefficient industries decline, and may thus, have a different interest than the other three.

Brazil and India also seem to have learnt from the experience of the Uruguay Round. There are greater consultations with a broader group of countries such as the G-20. There has been changes at the WTO as well. Groups of developing countries seem to almost have an official position, whereas earlier this was not so. Recognition by the WTO would give these groups greater coherence and provide an incentive to stay together. Furthermore, under pressure from the African countries, procedures seem to have become more transparent and participatory.

India's difficulties are compounded in the current Round because of its membership of the P-5, the five major countries that have a leadership role. Here it has to act as a representative of the developing countries. Championing the cause of developing countries may clash with its own self-interest. A similar situation had risen in the 1970s in the negotiations about the new international economic order. India supported the Organization of the Petroleum Exporting Countries (OPEC) in these negotiations, even though the actions of OPEC of raising oil prices was against Indian interests and OPEC deposited the surpluses with Western banks and agencies, and did relatively little to assist developing countries facing BOP difficulties. A specific example of such a dilemma is that many developing countries may wish India to lower its tariff, which is much higher than most other developing countries. Particularly, many other important developing countries such as Brazil and China may seek access in high technology industries in which companies in these countries are not yet internationally competitive. Policy makers in Brazil and China may see exporting to India as enabling these companies to benefit from economies of scale and thereby, become more competitive, internationally. Indian policy makers may wish to protect these industries for some more time. Preferential agreements with Brazil or China may be one way out of the dilemma. The Indian decision to negotiate free trade agreements more vigorously may be a move in this direction, because analysis suggests that India gains little from these agreements due to the diversified destination of its exports.

The coalition of developing countries seemed to be more effective during the Doha Round. Their effectiveness at the Cancun Ministerial came from their willingness to let the negotiations be deadlocked rather than compromise on an agreement which was unfavourable to them. But, this apparently changed during the concluding stages of the Hong Kong Ministerial. At that stage, countries such as Brazil and India changed tack to prevent a collapse of the talks. The final outcome as represented in the concluding declaration suggests compromises by developing countries for little substantive gain. For instance, the EU only agreed to eliminate export subsidies by 2013, to which they were already committed by internal budgetary policies. They did not budge on domestic support or on placing limitations on the blue and green boxes. Similarly, the acceptance of plurilateral approaches to service negotiations, a proposal developing countries had resisted earlier, opens particular developing countries to the combined demands and pressures from a group of developed countries, which may be difficult to resist. The press also reported that India was accused by Pakistan and Malaysia of looking after its own interests and betraying the interests of developing countries, though it was in the P-5 as a representative of developing countries. India obviously concluded that it had more to gain from some forward movement of the overall negotiations than from a stalemate.

Despite the trade liberalisation that has occurred and the increasing importance of exports of goods and commercial services, it is unclear what role trade plays in the current development strategy of the Indian government. But still, exports can play an important role in India's growth, particularly in employment. Increase in exports of labour intensive manufactures and commercial services have been important as employment in the organised sector declined in the 1990s. Employment in export industries can be a major way to raise incomes and reduce poverty. So, India has a large interest in improving access for these industries. For instance, the sudden dismantling of the MFA in 2005 may lead to a surge in textile exports to the developed countries and result in imposition of contingent protection measures, as is happening to China. India thus has a joint interest with China to prevent restriction of access for labour intensive manufactures. As already mentioned, India has a common interest with Brazil in protecting their higher technology sectors. South Africa can be an important contribution to the coalition, as it may have a commonality of interest with Brazil, China and India in protecting some industries established during the apartheid era. However, South Africa is also an important and influential member of the African group and this group, with almost 50 members, can add strength to the cause as there is a need to have a democratic decision making system.

Endnotes

[1] The way to deal with trade in primary commodities has always been a contentious issue both within the GATT and later, in the 1970s during negotiations on the New International Economic order (Bhagwati and Ruggie 1984).

[2] See Winham (1986) for negotiations during the Tokyo Round and for discussions on the Uruguay Round see Martin and Winter (1996).

[3] Even theoretical analysis has resulted in ambiguous answers. Some have argued stricter TRIPS standards would help developing countries, whereas others have reached the opposite conclusion (Helpman 1993).

[4] Comment by Professor M. Dubey on paper by R. Sally in a seminar on the WTO at the Centre for International Trade and Development, School of International Studies, JNU held in 2004.

[5] The waiver to impose import quotas was granted to the US so that Congress could continue its price support programme. In 1955, the US was granted a very broad waiver to

impose import quotas. The exclusion of agriculture was almost complete with the formation of the European Common Agricultural Policy.

[6] At the time of accession of Japan in 1955, some members were allowed to impose controls on Japanese goods including textiles. This was followed by the Short Term Arrangement in 1961 and the Long Term Arrangement in 1962, directed against the textile and clothing exports of developing countries. It culminated in the Multi Fibre Arrangement of 1974.

[7] For instance, only 160 bindings of some 20,000 tariff concessions were on goods of interest to developing countries (Williams 1994).

[8] Careful trade analysts had always placed trade policy within the broader policy framework, whereas enthusiasts often stressed trade policy only. For instance, share of exports in GDP in Sub-Saharan African countries has not increased despite the reforms, and this requires further analysis.

[9] For instance, developed members such as Canada and Australia, did not wish to use agriculture for cross sectional bargains because of their interest in other bargaining groups as well (Tussie and Glover 1993; Narlikar 2003). Also Canada as net agricultural importer had an equivocal position and differed from Australia (Narlikar 2003).

[10] India's position is akin to the problem that bedeviled all preferential trading arrangements among developing countries. Members sought to allocate industries in order to have a more equal distribution of benefits, but could not agree to any allocation as no country seemed to be willing to give up the option of setting up an industry (Agarwal 1991).

[11] The members of the QUAD are the US, the EU, Canada and Japan. The four together manage the MTNs.

References

Agarwal, Manmohan. 1991. 'South-South Trade: Building Block on Bargaining Chip', in *Rules, Power and Credibility*, edited J. Whalley, Toronto: Macmillan, pp. 196–99.

———. 2004. 'Regional Trading Arrangements in the Era of Globalisation: An Indian Perspective', *International Studies*, vol. 41, no. 4, pp. 411–23.

Bhagwati, J. 1991. 'Splintering and Disembodiment of Services and Developing Nations', *World Economy*, vol. 7, no. 2, pp. 133–43.

Bhagwati, J. and Ruggie. 1984. *Powers, Passions and Purpose: Prospects for North South Negotiations*, Mass.: MIT Press.

Dubey, M. 2005. 'India and WTO Negotiations in the Doha Round', paper presented at the seminar on The Indian Experience of Liberalisation, Institute for Advanced Studies, Shimla.

Evans, John W. 1971. *The Kennedy Round in American Trade Policy: The Twilight of the GATT*, Cambridge and Mass.: Harvard University Press.

Gary, Sampson and Richard Snape. 1985. 'Identifying the Issues in Trade in Services', *The World Economy*, vol. 8, no. 2, pp. 171–82.

Haberler, G. 1958. *Trends in International Trade*, Geneva: GATT.

Helpman, E. 1993. 'Innovation, Imitation and Intellectual Property Rights', *Econometrica*, vol. 61, no. 6, pp. 1247–80.

Hoekman, B., A. Mattoo and P. English (eds). 2002. *Development Trade and the WTO: A Handbook*, Washington DC: The World Bank.

Martin, Will and L. Alan Winters (eds). 1996. *The Uruguay Round and the Developing Countries*, Cambridge: Cambridge University Press.

Murray, T. 1977. *Trade Preferences for Developing Countries*, New York: John Wiley and Sons.

Narlikar, A. 2003. *International Trade and Developing Countries: Bargaining Coalitions in the GATT and the WTO*, London: Routledge.

Sally, R. and P. Draper. 2004. 'China, ASEAN, India: Trade Policies and Coalition Building in Asia', paper presented at the seminar on WTO: India's Post Cancun Concerns, jointly organised by the Planning Commission and Centre for International Trade and Development, School of International Studies, JNU, New Delhi, 18–19 October.

Tussie, D. and M. Lengyel. 2001. *Developing Countries and the WTO Participation versus Influence*, Buenos Aires, Argentina: Latin American Trade Network, and Facult and Latin America Canada Cencios Social.

Tussie, D. and D. Glover (eds). 1993. *The Developing Countries in World Trade: Policies and Bargaining Strategies*, Boulder: Lynne Riennes Publishers.

Williams, M. 1994. *International Economic Organisations and the Third World*, New York: Harvester Wheatsheaf.

Winham, Gilbert R. 1986. *International Trade and the Tokyo Round Negotiation*, Princeton: Princeton University Press.

4

Searching for the Missing Link: India's 'Negotiation Strategy' at WTO?[1]

DEBASHIS CHAKRABORTY

INTRODUCTION

It is needless to add that the absence of mutual consensus on modalities of future reform at WTO (which, in plain words implies persistence of some of the trade barriers) affects the developing countries much more severely, than their developed counterparts (Stiglitz 2001, 23; RIS 2003, 1). With the completion of the ten-year long transitory phase of WTO on 31 December 2004, the fluid state of multilateral negotiations on various modalities,[2] even after the Hong Kong Ministerial in December 2005, necessitates formulation of a suitable negotiating strategy by the part of developing countries. The statement applies to India, a developing country member of WTO, as well. It has been observed at times that India usually responds to the economic need with a time lag—the economic liberalisation programme initiated in 1991 could serve an example in this regard—where the government opted for the reform exercise only when the situation reached an extreme (Joshi and Little 1996). The current paper looks into the negotiating strategies followed by India over the years at the multilateral forum, and attempts to analyse whether the same has undergone any qualitative change, or if the case be so, the determinants behind it. It further attempts to analyse the difference in India's response pattern with respect to three different areas under WTO.

INDIA AT THE MULTILATERAL FORUM DURING THE GATT DAYS

It is indeed worth noting that despite being a founder member, India never considered the option of negotiating actively at the GATT forums. Since the country was following an import-substituting development strategy, opening up the domestic market to foreign competition was thought to be harmful, while export promotion was never a priority. However, the country at times discussed trade and development issues at United Nations Conference on Trade and Development (UNCTAD) forums in collaboration with other developing countries like Brazil (primarily through the G-77 network) (Draper and Sally 2004). It should be mentioned that even today India feels comfortable to discuss trade-related issues at UNCTAD forums in association with other developing countries.[3]

India's uneasiness towards opening up of trade barriers came to forefront during the Uruguay Round. During the initial years, India was quite unsure of the future implications of including provisions on agriculture, TRIPS and services in the Dunkel Draft, and hence could not adopt a suitable negotiating strategy (Sharma 1995). Although it occasionally attempted to collaborate with other developing countries (G-10), most of the time the intended agenda was not fulfilled, partly because of the absence of boldness in the approach on the part of the members (Blinova et al. 2006). In particular, it needs to be mentioned that in association with Brazil and Egypt, India attempted to obstruct the US initiative for liberalisation of trade in services by including it in the GATT framework (Chisti 1991). This looks ironic today, as India is currently one of the biggest beneficiaries of liberalisation of 'mode four' of services trade and is negotiating for further liberalisation of the same in relevant forums. At the end of the discussion on the Dunkel Draft, the country became a contracting party to the WTO, when it signed the final text in 1994 at Marrakesh.

FROM MARRAKESH TO DOHA

During the initial years of WTO, pre-reform notions were to some extent still guiding the official mindset in India and hence active negotiations at multilateral levels were not readily forthcoming. As a part of the Like Minded Group (LMG), India mostly kept focusing on the high cost of the Uruguay Round commitments and the unrealised promises. The outlook continued duirng the Singapore (1996) and Geneva (1998) ministerial meetings respectively. However, at the Seattle Ministerial (1999), India became visible at the negotiating scene for the first time by opposing the inclusion of labour and environmental concerns under the wings of WTO. The country expressed satisfaction over the developing country solidarity generated over this issue and hoped that in future new topics would be put in the discussion agenda of the ministerial meetings only after realisation of the market access level promised during the Uruguay Round negotiations.[4] It also collaborated with a number of developing country groupings during this period (for example G-15, Friends of Geographical Indications, G-24), focusing on common concerns on S&DT, GI and so on. (Narlikar 2003).

However, India's negotiating strategy, or the absence of it, faced serious challenge at the Doha Ministerial (2001). Before Doha, India raised concern over three broad points, namely: (i) non-realisation of anticipated benefits (e.g. ATC and AOA), (ii) inequities and imbalances in several agreements (e.g. TRIPS, Subsidies and Countervailing Measures, Anti-dumping Agreement, and so on) and (iii) non-operational and non-binding nature of S&DT provisions.[5] With this perspective, at Doha, India opposed initiation of discussion on a new round, as well as on the four new areas (Singapore issues), much to the annoyance of a number of developed and developing country members. This blanket opposition was not appreciated and other members on most of the points rejected India's stance (Singh 2001). However, India remained contented with her performance at the negotiating table since the ministerial declaration (DDA) finally included a number of its key agendas (e.g.—giving importance to implementation issues; discussion on market access issues in agricultural and non-agricultural products, with focus on S&DT for developing countries; inclusion of a separate declaration on TRIPS and Public Health; acknowledgement of the importance of ensuring free movement of natural persons in service trade).[6]

Not surprisingly, the academia has hardly shared the official euphoria in the post-Doha period. Anant (2001) heavily criticised the inflexibility in Indian position on implementation issues, blaming that for India's failure at Doha by saying, 'The consequence of the government's approach to the WTO and to trade negotiations is to create a self-fulfilling prophecy. Our flawed rejectionist approach to negotiations, with the absurd threats to leave, imply that we are unable to address our own immediate trading concerns.' Mattoo and Subramanian (2003) also described India's position at Doha to be, 'characteristically but perhaps not unjustifiably defensive'.

The causes of the inflexibility in India's negotiating stance could be explained by focusing on the determinants of the transition from a submissive to a pro-active mode of participation (Chakraborty 2005). First, the country initially preferred to adopt the route of demanding increased market access from the partners depending heavily on S&DT provision,[7] rather than negotiating on a give-and-take basis. However, the growth rate of Indian exports slumped during late nineties, especially after the East Asian economic crisis, thereby necessitating the need for increasing market access. Second, despite reduction in tariff barriers in the post-WTO period, various procedural as well as newer forms of NTBs substantially affected the 'effective' market access, both in case of trade in goods and services.[8] On the other hand the remaining barriers on imports in India were being increasingly questioned (Mehta 1999, *USTR* various issues). A total of thirteen cases were lodged against the WTO-incompatibilities of several Indian provisions before Seattle (e.g. compliance with TRIPS—DS 50 and DS 79; removal of quantitative restrictions on imports of agricultural, textile and industrial products—DS 90–94 and DS 96; measures affecting the automotive sector—DS 146 and DS 175), most of which had to be withdrawn after conceding defeat (or, at best after notifying 'amicable settlement') at the dispute settlement body (Chaisse and Chakraborty 2004). As against this backdrop, liberalisation in export markets was perceived as the due compensation by India. Simultaneously, opposition of the idea of including environmental and labour-standard related issues under the WTO at Seattle was quite natural, as these barriers affected a significant proportion of India's exports. Third, India was not a member of any major trade bloc up to the Doha Round and relied mostly on multilateral liberalisation for export growth. The adverse impact of differential rules of origin requirements in a number of partner countries, forced it to lay more stress on ensuring multilateral liberalisation through faster realisation of implementation issues.

Apart from the direct market access related concerns, the patenting of a variety of *Basmati rice* ('Texmati', by Ricetec Inc.) in the US during late nineties was a major incident, which India attempted to counter on the ground of violation of geographical indications. However, it was felt that the required level of protection (e.g. in line with *wine* and *spirits* in the west) for Indian products, be it Darjiling Tea or Basmati, was not available and India identified the indication of upcoming patent applications in traditional medicinal plants like *neem* (*Azadirachta indica*) and *haldi* (*Curcuma longa*) and so on to be a major threat in the coming future. This understandably led to the adoption of a pro-active approach in case of geographical indications.[9] In addition, given the steady outflow of professional service providers to the developed countries from India, the major negotiating agenda became ensuring free mobility of natural persons (that is, Mode 4 of service trade) right from the beginning.

In short, while India, under threats from a plethora of external events, rightly identified enhancement of market access as the solution, it was still not ready to negotiate on the barriers remaining in its economy. The reliance for this enhancement was mostly on realisation of implementation issues and S&DT. It is observed from the WTO *Annual*

Report (2003) that the average tariff in India was almost three-fold of even a number of developing countries, and that way its opponents in Doha had a point. However, the inflexibility on India's part paid it an appreciable dividend as the DDA promised to initiate discussion on a number of key concern areas raised by it.

DOHA TO HONG KONG

The Doha experience was a morale booster for India, and the country began to participate actively in the subsequent WTO negotiations advocating for reform of several areas during the next two years. Before the Cancun Ministerial (2003), India's negotiating strategy focused explicitly on lowering of agricultural subsidy in the developed countries; improvement of non-agricultural market access; liberalisation of service trade (mainly movement of natural persons) and acknowledgement of public health concerns in developing countries; calling for discussion on these issues at the upcoming ministerial.[10]

It became increasingly clear from 2002 onwards that liberalisation of the agricultural subsidy regime in the developed countries would be the central question at the Cancun, and a couple of failed attempts of the EU to undertake this task made a number of members (developed as well as developing countries) quite unhappy (Chakraborty 2004). The EU-US joint proposal on liberalisation of agricultural trade released a few days before Cancun Ministerial was completely unacceptable to the developing countries, and they submitted an alternate proposal on the modalities for future reform (the G-20 proposal by countries including Brazil, China, India and South Africa) calling for immediate action to end export dumping and production subsidies in agriculture apart from improvement of market access.[11] The EU and the US submitted a revised declaration at the ministerial only to be rejected by the developing countries, and the ministerial draft issued on 13 September 2003 (known as the 'Derbez Draft'; Document no. JOB (03)/156/Rev. 2) disappointed developing and developed countries alike. While developing countries termed the draft as another version of the EU-US submission and insisted on considering the G-20 draft as the basis of negotiation instead, the EU and the US were uncomfortable with the draft's proposals on domestic support reform. It was perceived that there exists tremendous scope for improving various aspects of the draft.[12]

India refused to consider the Derbez Draft as a basis for future negotiations owing to three basic reasons. First, it believed that the draft did not properly acknowledge the developing country perspective on domestic support to agriculture. Second, while DDA assured that the future negotiations on Singapore issues would be initiated only after arriving at an explicit consensus, the Derbez Draft moved ahead on that front on its own without consulting the developing country members. Finally, the developing countries had been vocal on ensuring special treatment for their 'strategic' products for sometime and the consequences of subsidisation of cotton cultivation in developed countries was at the forefront in that matter. However, instead of asking the developed countries to ensure WTO-compliance with respect to their cotton-subsidisation schemes, the Derbez Draft adopted the long-route of promising advisory supports to the affected economies for crop diversification. Clearly this stand was unacceptable to the developing countries. All these issues prompted India to maintain a hard stance against adoption of the Derbez Draft.[13] Although the multilateral negotiation was stalled for almost a year due to these differences among member countries, India as a part of the G-20 initiative remained active in the process of reaching an agreement through informal negotiations during this period.[14] Another developing country group named G-33 evolved in the following period, whose main agenda was ensuring 'special products' (SP) and 'special safeguard mechanism' (SSM) as an integral part of S&DT in the agriculture framework, in which India functioned as a prominent member.

When the deadlock in the negotiating process was broken in July 2004 at Geneva, India played a key role during the discussion along with Australia, Brazil, the EU and the US India expressed disappointment initially as the preliminary drafts of the meeting did not reflect her concerns on the need for setting disciplines on blue and amber boxes for the developed countries and inclusion of 'SSM' and 'SP' provisions for developing countries properly.[15] However, it believed the finally agreed upon draft (known as July 2004 Draft), which formed the framework of future negotiations, was much more sensitive to developing country interests as compared to the Derbez Draft in terms of all three pillars of agricultural trade. In addition, the draft proposals on acknowledging developing country sectoral concerns (e.g. cotton) and enhancement of non-agricultural market access were also welcomed.[16] Furthermore, India was quite happy with the omission of three Singapore issues (barring trade facilitation) from the negotiating agenda for the time being. This is again quite ironic in a sense, as India was the only country opposing inclusion of trade facilitation in the negotiating agenda at Doha (2001).

Just before the Hong Kong Ministerial, on 6 December 2005 the General Council of WTO approved to change TRIPS provisions relating to patents and public health (WTO, 6 December 2005). The provision will formally be a part of TRIPS agreement, when two-third of the Members ratify it by 1 December 2007. Once implemented, this would mark the first amendment of a core WTO agreement and therefore marks a landmark for the developing countries.

The Hong Kong Ministerial in December 2005 witnessed a north-south divide once more, with G-20 and G-90 coming together to form G-110. In addition, the Ministerial also witnessed the emergence of the developing country grouping NAMA-11, focusing on non-agricultural market access issues. The stage for such a grouping was set earlier that year, when Argentina, Brazil and India formed the ABI group on NAMA. The ministerial resulted formation of a task force with a recommendation deadline of July 2006 and decision on elimination of agro export subsidies by 2013. However, all the available facts emerging from the ministerial, taken together, do not necessarily signify a major gain for the developing countries. At best, it could be argued that some deal is probably better than a Cancun-type no-deal, thereby portraying the result of the ministerial as only a second-best outcome (Debroy and Chakraborty 2006). The negotiation to wind up the modalities on agriculture and non-agricultural products by end of April 2006 is yet to deliver a solution, both agreeable to developed and developing countries. The visit of the WTO Secretary General Pascal Lamy to India a couple of times during 2006 and 2007 failed to generate anything positive in this regard. The comment of the trade reprehensive Rob Portman threatening in early 2006 that the US might abandon WTO if other countries do not show more willingness to open their markets (Hindustan Times 2006a) was not particularly helpful. Subsequently it refused to bring down its subsidies (especially in agriculture) further, claiming that their offer made during October 2005 is yet to get matching response from other developed countries (Hindustan Times 2006b).

The trade ministers of G-6 met in Geneva during July 2006 where Brazil and India were to push the G-20 agenda and ask the US to undertake real reform commitments

(Hindustan Times 2006c). Unfortunately, the discussion failed to generate any agreement, following which the trade talks had to be suspended (Hindustan Times 2006d). To make things worse, the U.S. recently threatened to withdraw the preferential trade benefits to 13 developing countries (actually covering major G-20 players) under GSP by ordering a review whether to 'limit, suspend or withdraw' it (Hindustan Times 2006e).[17] Needless to add, this further necessitates the need for adoption of a joint negotiating approach by developing countries in order to extract tangible market access benefits from their developed counterparts.

Clearly Indian negotiating strategy registered a qualitative change in the post-Doha period, and the determinants of the same would be interesting to look at. Firstly, IPR concerns played a key role in that process. On the face of HIV/AIDS epidemic in 2001, South Africa started importing a cheaper generic version of the patented medicines from an Indian firm Cipla, through The Medicines and Related Substances Control Amendment Act. However, rising protests from various quarters through legal and diplomatic channels caused South Africa to terminate this process (Dasgupta 2003). This event led India to submit a proposal on 'TRIPS and Public Health' in association with several developing countries, asking the WTO to ensure that the TRIPS Agreement does not infringe upon the sovereign right of the members to formulate their own public health policies and adopt measures for providing affordable access to medicines.[18] The potential threat to a major component of the export basket caused India to act fast and henceforth it started to raise the public health related concerns in the appropriate forums.

Secondly, India emerged as a major victim of anti-dumping investigations in the post-WTO period, and the leading export-earning sectors like textile suffered in particular.[19] The country had to move to the Dispute Settlement Body (DSB) in a number of textile-related cases as complainant, and termination of the alleged measures, after winning several of them (for example DS 33 involving the US; DS 34 involving Turkey; DS 141 involving the EU) encouraged it further to adopt pro-active strategies. On the other hand, the defeat in a case on application of rules of origin on textile products (DS 243 involving the US) caused India to focus on market access concerns.[20] Thirdly, increasing participation at the DSB made India aware of the loopholes in the system, and negotiations on that front also began from 2002 onwards. Fourthly, slow progress of MFA phase-out was another major concern area, which called for active negotiation by the developing countries (Commonwealth Business Council 2001). It was observed that in the EU and the US market, quotas on most of the key products of India's export basket were liberalised only after 31 December 2004. Last but not the least, from mid-2003 onwards the negotiation pattern of the developing countries (including India) focused extensively on agriculture, which has been a direct consequence of the EU-US joint submission before Cancun. In brief, the active participation of India in the WTO in the post-Doha period was influenced both by the pertinent concerns as well as contemporary incidents.

A SECTORAL PERSPECTIVE OF INDIA'S NEGOTIATING STRATEGY

The priority areas of Indian negotiation are analysed with the help of Table 4.1, where its submissions to WTO are summarised. The increase in the number of submissions over the years testifies the increased participation of the country in the negotiating process. Apart from the increase in the number of submissions and the number of focal areas, it could be argued that their effectiveness has also improved appreciably, as the number of joint submissions (numbers shown in parenthesis) has escalated in the post-Doha period. It could be claimed that the possibility of success is now much higher through joint negotiations through the developing country groupings (G-20, G-33 and so on.), as compared to the lone walk of India during the pre-Doha days.

TABLE 4.1 An analysis of India's submissions at WTO[21]

(Number of submissions)

Category	1997	1998	1999	2000	2001	2002	2003	2004	2005	2006	Total
Agriculture	7 (–)	7 (–)	0	4 (2)	6 (1)	1 (–)	6 (4)	2 (2)	0	0	33 (9)
Competition policy	1 (–)	3 (–)	0	1 (–)	0	2 (–)	0	0	0	0	7 (–)
Dispute settlement	0	0	0	0	0	4 (3)	1 (1)	1 (1)	2 (2)	0	8 (7)
Environment	2 (–)	2 (–)	0	3 (–)	0	0	1 (–)	0	3 (–)	1 (–)	12 (–)
General Council	0	4 (–)	29 (9)	1 (–)	7 (5)	1 (1)	8 (7)	1 (1)	0	0	51 (23)
Investment	1 (–)	1 (–)	4 (–)	1 (–)	1 (–)	4 (1)	0	0	0	0	12 (1)
NAMA	0	0	0	0	0	1 (0)	4 (1)	0	3 (3)	3 (3)	11 (7)
WTO rules	0	0	0	0	0	2 (–)	3 (–)	0	2 (–)	3 (2)	10 (2)
Services	3 (–)	1 (–)	0	2 (1)	1 (1)	1 (–)	5 (3)	5 (4)	7 (6)	0	25 (15)
TRIPS	0	0	2 (–)	7 (2)	4 (4)	4 (3)	1 (1)	1 (1)	3 (3)	1 (1)	23 (15)
Trade facilitation	0	0	0	0	0	0	0	0	3 (2)	8 (1)	11 (3)
Trade and development	0	0	0	0	0	3 (2)	0	0	1 (1)	0	4 (3)

Source: (Chakraborty 2007)

While in agriculture the Indian submissions during initial years consisted of notifications; in the later period the focus shifted towards export and domestic subsidy, market access and non-trade concerns like food security, and further to S&DT and identification of special products for developing countries in recent years. Although explicit focus on NAMA was missing earlier and the focus concentrated mostly on anti-dumping issues, in 2003, before the Cancun ministerial, India submitted a number of proposals in order to free the trade in manufacturing products. During the last two years, a total of six joint proposals on NAMA has been made.

In case of services, while eight submissions were made over 1997–2002, seventeen submissions during 2003–05 alone highlight the growing importance of the sector in Indian economy. The stress has primarily been laid on mode 1 (cross-border supply) and mode 4 (movement of natural persons), both of which are subject to certain barriers.[22] It can be argued that the Mode 4 process became partly victim of India's success in BPO (Mode 1), which is also being threatened in certain US states and some European countries on the ground of domestic job losses.[23] This caused India to focus more on liberalisation of Mode 1 of services in the recent period.[24] In addition, India has also concentrated on de-linking of the practice of independent professionals from the requirements under commercial presence.[25] Currently the country is submitting 'requests' to a number of countries for a wide range of service categories, while simultaneously receiving the same. Some partners have questioned India's hesitancy in posting 'offers' for freeing services trade, the probable reason being the MFN clause, that is, the requirement of granting the same level of market access to all members. This gives rise to free rider problem, that is., a country can restrain from posting 'requests' but nonetheless could enjoy increased market access once its export market opens itself to any negotiating third country. Also in case of environmental services the country is now favouring 'project approach', which does much more justice towards developing countries. (Chakraborty 2007).

In case of TRIPS, the Indian communications revolved around public health implications, protection of biological diversity and traditional knowledge. Although the country resisted introduction of product patent regime during the transitory phase fearing adverse price implications of the new regime; the new ordinance, coming into effect from 1 January 2005 (and later with passing of the product patent bill in parliament), paves the way for examination of product patent applications submitted. However, certain provisions of the new ordinance have already generated criticisms from various quarters (Dhar and Rao 2004). India is currently negotiating at the WTO on the conditions for granting of compulsory licenses for foreign suppliers to provide medicines in the domestic market.[26] The recent focus of negotiation on TRIPS front further includes various traditional knowledge related concerns including evidence requirement for determination of patent right over TK in another country, responsibility for burden of proof and the legal implications for providing wrongful evidences, and so on.[27]

Although competition policy, environment or investment issues were not among the priority areas, India contributed to the ongoing discussion from time to time, especially in its communications during 2003. A number of joint submissions on dispute settlement in association with other developing countries testify India's concern towards improving the procedural framework as well. The negotiations on dispute settlement focus on modification of the agreement so as to ensure S&DT for developing countries and prevention of the misuse of the provisions. The evolution of the practical mindset and readiness to respond to the challenges is particularly evident from India's experience at the trade facilitation (TF) front. While the country resisted inclusion of TF in the negotiating agenda since Doha Ministerial, once it was included in the forum, it has submitted eleven proposals in this area during 2005–6.

A 'TREMBLING HAND' APPROACH TOWARDS NEGOTIATIONS?

While the qualitative change in India's negotiating strategy could be ascertained from the earlier analysis, at times the viewpoint pursued by the country has been questioned. A very classic example could be the fact that India opposed liberalisation of services during the Uruguay Round, or discussion on TF during the Doha Ministerial, while the importance of both for Indian economy is enormous. However, India fortunately moved forward abandoning those inflexible positions in the subsequent period. While the subsequent change testifies adaptability on India's part, it nonetheless also indicates selection of a wrong strategy earlier in the first place. In other words, the initial positions were arrived at, perhaps without undertaking proper assessment of economic needs. In the following sections, we will briefly discuss the changing perspective of India's external strategy in three cases—trade and investment, regional trade agreements and anti-dumping. While in case of the first, it could be argued that India ultimately moved towards the 'steady state', the future of the second path is slightly uncertain, while the third has certainly led to an 'explosive' situation. It could be argued that the sooner the negotiating position of the country in all issues reaches the steady state, the better.

Trade and Investment

It has been argued at times that developing countries should link capital mobility with labour mobility (Hoekman and Saggi 2000). However, this view has been challenged on the ground that, as long as developing countries like India need the technical know-how and FDI from developed countries, there is no point in linking labour mobility with capital mobility (Das 2003). After the Singapore Ministerial (1999), given the relatively lower FDI inflow as compared to several Asian neighbours, India for a brief period considered the possibility of linking capital and labour mobility as seen from its submission to the Working Group on Trade and Investment:

> Even if the Working Group considers ways for the mobility of capital, there is little or no guarantee that appropriate labour inputs would become available for utilization of that capital. Hence, the Working Group can help align grassroots realities and suggest easy mobility of selected categories of labour apart from the higher categories of personnel for which most Member countries of the WTO have already undertaken commitments under the GATS. For complementing immediate production purposes, the Working Group can suggest ways for selected labour to move from surplus regions to deficit regions (Government of India 1998).

India further stressed its position in a later submission by claiming (Document no. WT/WGTI/W/72, dated 13 April 1999), '... mobility of labour should be inextricably linked with the discussions on trade-investment linkage if the WTO is to go beyond looking at delivery systems to look at production systems.' Even after the failure of the Seattle ministerial (1999), it did not abandon the idea, as during the Seattle-Doha period it focused on (Document no. WT/WGTI/W/86, dated 22 June 2000) a number of questions involving optimality of barrier-free FDI inflow in developing countries, foreign investors' obligations, issues pertaining to investment incentives, the costs of adjustment and impact on social gains in developing countries and the comparative flexibility with bilateral investment agreements, and so on. It claimed that there is a need to check:

> Whether mobility of labour should also not be meaningfully addressed when movements relating to the other three factors of production namely, goods, services and capital are being taken up in one form or the other.

However, in the following period, India started slowly moving away from this position, probably in the light of the capital flight experienced during the East Asian crisis. Perhaps the realisation of the potential impacts of free capital mobility occurred a bit later. Before the Doha Round, India expressed dissatisfaction over the progress of technology transfer in developing countries, and cited it as an obvious reason for regulating FDI inflow (Document no. WT/WGTI/W/105, dated 26 June 2001):

> One major reason why FDI is sought by countries, especially developing countries, is that FDI generally brings with it the much needed state-of-the-art technology that developing countries lack. However, available facts and figures do not vindicate this expectation of developing countries ... more striking, particularly for the developing countries, is the fact that while their share of FDI inflows has gone up, their share in global technology transfers has come down.... [T]he inevitable conclusion that developing countries should preserve their right and ability to influence foreign direct investment flows into their territories with a view to ensuring that it is accompanied by appropriate technology.

At the Doha Ministerial (2001), India decided against discussion on any of the Singapore issues, until and unless the level of market access promised to the developing countries at the Uruguay Round are realised.[28] It is interesting to note that apart from developed countries, a number of developing countries like Chile, Costa Rica, South Korea, Morocco, Czech Republic and Hungary were quite keen to the idea of discussing trade and investment in the ministerial meeting (Singh 2001). India's demand was incorporated in the ministerial declaration, known as DDA, which agreed that the negotiations on trade and investment would take place after the Fifth Session of the Ministerial Conference (paragraph 20–22) and further promised to take note of the development policies and objectives of host governments as well as their right to regulate FDI in the public interest. Subsequently India relied on the argument of worsening of BOP in case of a potential crisis (Document no. WT/WGTI/W/148, dated 7 October 2002) to keep control on capital movement:

> Any movement of capital that would cause serious damage to the domestic industry, particularly small and medium-sized enterprises and have adverse effects on employment would need to be carefully regulated. Developing countries need to retain the ability to screen and channel foreign investment in accordance with their domestic interests and priorities. Another point to which attention needs to be drawn is the possible damaging effect of capital outflows on balance-of-payments.... [T]here is also a strong case for performance requirements such as export obligations and foreign exchange neutrality to moderate the adverse effects of capital outflows.

It has already been noted that India's attempt to retain control over merchandise trade on BOP grounds has been defeated at the dispute settlement body earlier. Subsequent submissions of the country to the WTO stressed on the advantages of bilateral investment treaties (BITs) over the proposed options as mentioned in the following (Document no. WT/WGTI/W/150, dated 7 October 2002). The stance is hardly surprising since between 1995 and 2001, India entered into BITs with 41 countries (Das 2003).

> Developing countries need to retain the ability to screen and channel FDI in tune with their domestic interests and priorities. Bilateral investment treaties have been favoured the world over for precisely the flexibility they provide to the host country while at the same time extending necessary protection to foreign investors.

Before the Cancun Ministerial, India focused on a wide range of issues spanning over the extent of constitutional powers available to the authorities to make rules and regulations related to foreign investment, disclosure and accounting procedures, effects of technology transfer, restrictive business practices and several other areas (Document no. WT/WGTI/W/152, dated 19 November 2002). It further pointed out that the developed countries favouring multilateral agreement on investment should keep the special characteristic of capital and past experiences of other forums, for example, the OECD in mind:

> the question of non-discrimination in capital flows becomes more complex. There is no clear buyer-seller linkage, as is the case of goods and services, and no certainty regarding the source of funds. There is also no certainty regarding the manner in which funds will be retained in the host country and at what point in time, in what manner, and to what extent funds will flow out.... A certain degree of discrimination between different kinds of investment is unavoidable... A case in point is the OECD Code for the Liberalization of Capital Movements in which right of establishment was introduced

in 1984. Another instance is that of the APEC non-binding investment principle. A multilateral Agreement on Investment under the auspices of the economically well-off countries of the OECD, which envisaged in the draft agreement binding national treatment obligations, did not find favour with many of these countries, and had to be abandoned. How then can an agreement of this nature, envisaging national treatment and MFN provision of a binding nature, be considered in a much more heterogeneous group like WTO? (Government of India 2002)

While the July 2004 declaration of WTO decided that no negotiation on trade and investment would take place within the WTO during the Doha Round, the issue was not raised at the Hong Kong Ministerial (2005) as well, thereby giving India some time to decide whether it wants to go for BITs or a multilateral approach on this question. Interestingly, the statement of the Prime Minister of India during March 2006 on consideration of full capital account convertibility of the rupee might mark yet another change in India's approach towards trade and investment at the multilateral forums in coming future.

Regional Trade Blocs

During the pre-Doha period, India relied mostly on multilateral liberalisation for export growth and was not part of any active trade bloc. However, given the increase in RTAS and Preferential Trade Agreements (PTAs) from 1995 onwards, India started voicing its concerns over circumvention of procedural liberalisation undertaken due to RTAs, especially in textile products, at several occasions.[29] Since the experience of Doha and later Cancun, India started to get involved in various RTAs on both counts—(i) to ensure an assured export market, (ii) to enhance bilateral relation with other developing countries. The proposed partners of India are spread over Asia (ASEAN, Bay of Bengal Initiative for Multi-Sectoral Technical and Economic Cooperation (BIMSTEC)), Africa (South African Customs Union (SACU)) and Latin America (Mercosur) (Nag and Chakraborty 2006, Chakraborty and Sengupta 2006). This recent regionalism move has been criticised by scholars, who argued that India should continue on the track of multilateral liberalisation (Agarwal 2004). It is indeed worth checking whether the RTA policy of the country is on the right track.

Table 4.2 shows the trade scenario of India with the proposed partners for the years 1996–97 and 2005–6, both in terms of trade ranks and market shares. The analysis showed that barring a handful of exceptions like Brunei, Paraguay, and so on, the importance of proposed partners in India's trade basket is generally showing an increasing trend (measured in terms of either export or import ranking of the proposed partners or both). Second, a number of major negotiating partners are climbing up in the rankings both in terms of exports and imports (China, Sri Lanka, Singapore, Thailand, Brazil, and so on). Furthermore, as of 2005–6, the total shares of the intended partners account for nearly 42 and 33 per cent of India's total export and import respectively. It is therefore logical to expect that the preferential agreements would provide further boost to bilateral trade and investment among them. It is further expected that the internal objection to the adverse impacts of RTA liberalisation in the initial years would be minimum, since negotiations in most of these proposed blocs would be completed over a long period, usually a decade.[30] The increased 'bloc-wardness' is not likely to affect the incentive for multilateral negotiation since at least for trade in services, India would still be looking towards liberalisation of the EU and US market, given its current export pattern.

TABLE 4.2 An analysis of trade scenario between India and proposed partners

Countries	Export 1996–97 Share	Rank	Export 2005–6 Share	Rank	Import 1996–97 Share	Rank	Import 2005–6 Share	Rank
West Asia								
Afghanistan	0.0679	78	0.1384	66	0.0078	100	0.0392	74
Bahrain	0.1875	55	0.1865	60	0.3393	37	0.1271	55
Kuwait	0.4623	37	0.4983	37	2.4253	12	0.3096	38
Oman	0.3495	43	0.3962	43	0.0309	79	0.1780	47
Qatar	0.0953	68	0.2516	51	0.3140	39	0.6044	28
Saudi Arabia	1.7245	16	1.7555	15	4.6500	6	1.0943	21
United Arab Emirates	4.4100	6	8.3342	2	3.3929	8	2.9190	10
Total	7.2970		11.5607		11.1602		5.2716	
South Asia								
Bangladesh	2.5962	10	1.6145	16	0.1590	50	0.0852	60
Bhutan	0.0657	81	0.0962	77	0.0863	60	0.0595	67
Maldives	0.0310	97	0.0656	92	0.0004	130	0.0013	150
Nepal	0.4951	33	0.8342	28	0.1637	49	0.2546	42
Pakistan	0.4697	36	0.6686	32	0.0924	58	0.1204	56
Sri Lanka	1.4264	20	1.9640	13	0.1095	57	0.3873	34
Total	5.0841		5.2431		0.6113		0.9083	
East And South-East Asia								
Australia	1.1513	24	0.7966	29	3.3660	9	3.3171	7
Brunei Darussalam	0.0180	108	0.0417	101	0.0001	142	0.0006	162
Cambodia	0.0047	141	0.0235	121	–	–	0.0005	165
China, PR	1.8369	14	6.5565	3	1.9342	17	7.2859	3
Indonesia	1.7683	15	1.3388	19	1.5257	19	2.0166	15
Japan	5.9933	3	2.4069	10	5.5899	4	2.7225	12
Lao People's Democratic Republic	0.0011	184	0.0053	163	–	–	0.0001	190
Malaysia	1.5869	17	1.1270	22	2.8194	11	1.6194	17
Mongolia	0.0021	168	0.0011	181	0.0001	136	0.0011	155
Myanmar	0.1350	61	0.1074	74	0.4528	34	0.3526	36
Philippines	0.5487	31	0.4798	38	0.0420	72	0.1579	50
Republic of Korea	1.5491	18	1.7724	14	2.2580	14	3.0596	9
Singapore	2.9204	8	5.2626	4	2.1494	16	2.2484	14
Thailand	1.3358	21	1.0431	24	0.5039	32	0.8122	23
Vietnam	0.3528	42	0.6700	31	0.0043	105	0.0881	59
Total	19.2044		21.6327		20.6458		23.6826	
Africa								
Botswana	0.0020	170	0.0105	148	–	–	0.0001	186
Mauritius	0.4820	34	0.1935	59	0.0102	92	0.0049	121
Namibia	0.0028	161	0.0142	138	0.0001	140	0.0139	101
South Africa	0.9447	26	1.4811	18	0.8204	25	1.6571	16
Swaziland	0.0086	130	0.0051	165	0.0182	84	0.0158	96
Total	1.4401		1.7044		0.8489		1.6918	

(Contd)

(Table 4.2 Contd)

Countries	Export				Import			
	1996–97		2005–6		1996–97		2005–6	
	Share	Rank	Share	Rank	Share	Rank	Share	Rank
Latin America								
Argentina	0.1753	57	0.1935	58	0.5144	30	0.5055	31
Brazil	0.3959	41	1.0579	23	0.3900	35	0.5987	29
Chile	0.1974	53	0.1476	64	0.2495	43	0.2913	41
Paraguay	0.0186	107	0.0159	133	0.0004	129	0.0028	130
Uruguay	0.0480	93	0.0271	116	0.0038	106	0.0027	131
Total	0.8352		1.4420		1.1581		1.4010	
Overall	**33.8608**		**41.5829**		**34.4243**		**32.9553**	

Source: Constructed from India's trade data.

It needs to be further analysed whether the bond between India and the proposed members are really strong. Table 4.3 looks at the existing level of cooperation among India and its partners considering the number of joint submissions by India and a particular country as a suitable proxy. The level of cooperation is quite appreciable with a number of African, Southeast Asian and Latin American partners as well as two regional neighbours— Pakistan and Sri Lanka. The West Asian countries however are yet to enter into any such negotiating collaboration.[31] The areas characterised by maximum cooperation are agriculture, issues under General Council (mainly trade in textile and garments, increasing use of contingency measures, and so on) and services. Interestingly, regional neighbours like Pakistan and Sri Lanka have rallied heavily behind India on the TRIPS front, clearly owing to similarity in export pattern. Given the dominance of labour-intensive products in the export basket of the proposed partners, the cooperation is likely to be strengthened further in future.

The bond between India and the partners is likely to remain strong owing to a number of reasons. First, there exist a striking similarity between the NTBs imposed on exports of India and the partner countries in the EU and the US market, which calls for adoption of a joint negotiating approach (ESCAP 2000; Mehta and George 2005). Second, there is a growing concern among the developing countries that even after the removal of the MFA quota regime, the expected level of market access will not be forthcoming, and the major exporters of textiles and garments, located mostly in South and Southeast Asia, need to collaborate on this issue.[32] Third, apart from material areas of cooperation, the importance of institutional areas of cooperation like dispute settlement are also worth mentioning.[33] Last but not the least, apart from demanding market access for exports, the developing countries (G–33) have also been vocal on ensuring sufficient protection to their domestic entities, as evident from the joint submissions to WTO regarding SP, SPM and S&DT. Clearly, this is another area where India and most of the partners stand to gain extensively by pursuing a joint negotiating agenda (Chakraborty and Hazra 2005). The other concern areas include TRIPS. In 2005 India made two joint submissions with Brazil, which has a rich history of fighting with the developed countries on this front (Raizada 2001), and India is likely to benefit extensively from this association.

TABLE 4.3 An analysis of current cooperation between India and potential partners at WTO negotiations[34]

Countries	\multicolumn{8}{c}{WTO Disciplines}
	A	B	C	D	E	F	G	H
West Asia								
Afghanistan	–	–	–	–	–	–	–	
Bahrain	–	–	–	–	–	–	–	
Kuwait	–	–	–	–	–	–	–	
Oman	–	–	–	–	–	–	–	
Qatar	–	–	–	–	–	–	–	
Saudi Arabia	–	–	–	–	–	–	–	
United Arab Emirates	–	–	–	–	–	–	–	
South Asia								
Bangladesh	–	–	8	–	–	–	1	
Bhutan	–	–	–	–	–	–	–	
Maldives	–	–	2	–	–	–	–	
Nepal	–	–	–	–	–	–	–	
Pakistan	5	2	15	1	2	17	7	1
Sri Lanka	4	2	11	–	–	1	7	1
East And South-East Asia								
Brunei Darussalam	–	–	–	–	–	–	–	
Cambodia	–	–	–	–	–	–	–	
China, PR	3	–	5	1	1	5	1	1
Indonesia	4	1	21	–	6	8	1	
Japan	1	–	–	–	–	2	–	
Lao PDR	–	–	–	–	–	–	–	
Malaysia	2	3	15	–	1	4	1	
Mongolia								
Myanmar	–	–	–	–	–	–	–	
Philippines	4	–	5	–	5	11	1	
Republic of Korea	3	–	–	–	–	4	–	
Singapore	–	–	–	–	–	4	–	
Thailand	2	–	5	–	–	14	7	
Vietnam	–	–	2	–	–	–	–	
Africa								
Botswana	2	–	5	–	–	–	1	
Mauritius	2	–	4	–	1	–	4	
Namibia	1	–	1	–	4	–	1	
South Africa	2	–	1	–	5	–	1	
Swaziland	1	–	1	–	–	–	1	
Latin America								
Argentina	3	3	–	–	7	6	1	
Brazil	3	3	2	–	7	6	10	
Chile	3	–	–	–	–	16	–	
Paraguay	3	–	1	–	–	1	–	
Uruguay	1	–	–	–	–	2	–	

Source: Compiled from India's proposals to WTO, 1995–2006.

While it can be argued that the recent RTA drive will be beneficial for the Indian economy as a whole, the procedure for identifying the potential partners has been questioned at times (Nag and Chakraborty 2006). It has become quite evident that the proposed blocs, once in force, would lead to overlapping RTAs. For instance, India is in the process of entering into an FTA with ASEAN, in which case the need for separate FTAs with Thailand or Singapore does not make much sense. Similarly, going for BIMSTEC undermines the working of South Asia Free Trade Agreement (SAFTA), proposed Indo-ASEAN FTA and Indo-Sri Lanka FTA. One of the major discontents of India against RTAs during late nineties was the potential trade diversion through complexities of the overlapping blocs (World Bank 2000). In future, India might as well attract criticism on similar ground from various quarters. India has already witnessed frictions over the determination of rules of origin with ASEAN and Thailand. India usually applies twin criteria for determining rule of origin in FTAs—(i) value addition method and (ii) change in tariff heading (CTH), arguing that the value addition method alone is not adequate for the purpose as high wage rates or high rent can increase the product value even without substantial physical value addition. However, ASEAN in mid-2005 strongly noted that only value addition norm should be included. As a result of this debate, a new set of rules of origin had to be formulated (Nag and Chakraborty 2006). Moreover, the negotiation on the 'negative list' under Indo-ASEAN FTA had also been a frustrating experience for India.

Anti-Dumping

The 'perverse' learning from the multilateral forum is perhaps most evident in case of anti-dumping (Chakraborti and Sengupta 2005). The textile and garment exports of India in earlier period have been the major victim of anti-dumping investigations abroad, and the country had dealt with a number of such initiations through WTO DSB. Although India has won a number of cases (DS 141—EC), and opted for mutual settlement on some occasions (DS 140—EC; DS 168—South Africa), it had to concede defeat in one case involving textile and garment products (DS 206—US). At the multilateral forums, India has raised concern over the increasing use of anti-dumping measures on several occasions.[35] The submissions highlighted problems in determination of dumping, imposition of duty and other procedural problems. However, since post-Doha period, India itself emerged as a major user (or, 'misuser', as some trade partners often point out) of this provision. The trend becomes clearly visible from Table 4.4, where the cases faced and imposed by three countries, EU, India and U.S. are compared. The WTO Annual Report (2004) noted that 'Of the 1323 (anti-dumping) measures in force reported, 21% were maintained by the United States, 16% by India, 15% by the European Communities, 7% each by South Africa and Canada, and 6% by Argentina. Other Members reporting measures in force each accounted for 5% or less of the total' (WTO 2004). The EU, China and the have already voiced their discontent to India over this issue on several occasions, and the WTO *Trade Policy Review* (2002) had also been vocal on this issue. The chemical imports of the country have been the worst sufferer from this measure. Recently, EU (DS 304), Bangladesh (DS 306) and Taiwan (DS 318) have moved to DSB against the anti-dumping procedure followed in India, and currently, consultations are in progress. The results of these three cases would have profound implications for all future cases lodged against India in this area. The fact that till date India has failed to win a single case as respondent puts it in a sticky wicket.

It is observed that the use of this provision by India over the last two years is showing a declining trend, which is a welcome move.

TABLE 4.4 Comparison of anti-dumping cases—the EU, India and the US.

Period	India		E.U.36		U.S.A.	
	A	B	A	B	A	B
1 January 1995–31 December 1995	5	3	33	21	13	6
1 January 1996–31 December 1996	20	10	23	35	21	21
1 January 1997–31 December 1997	13	7	41	59	16	15
1January 1998–31 December 1998	33	12	21	42	22	15
1 January 1999–30 June 1999	40	6	32	20	28	7
1 July 1999–30 June 2000	27	11	49	32	29	10
1 July 2000–30 June 2001	37	–	29	–	77	–
1 July 2001–30 June 2002	76	12	23	39	58	11
1 July 2002–30 June 2003	67	12	15	32	29	12
1 July 2003–30 June 2004	37	14	18	19	42	23
1 July 2004–30 June 2005	30	12	32	19	9	13

Note: A—Initiations of anti-dumping actions by a country
B—Initiations of anti-dumping investigations against a country
Source: WTO Annual Reports (various issues)

The Future Concerns

While the adoption of pro-active approach at the WTO, as well as the grouping with other developing countries could be considered as a major qualitative change, the achievements so far, in practical terms, are still limited. For instance, while the formation of G-20 at Cancun was a much-hyped event, de facto, the failure of WTO members to arrive at a conclusion provided the EU and US the perfect excuse to delay the liberalisation of domestic support and export subsidy provided to their agricultural sector for ten valuable months. Moreover, in spite of providing certain leverages to the developing countries, the July 2004 draft contains a number of gray areas, which could give rise to disputes in future (Chakraborti 2004). The outcome of the Hong Kong Ministerial is also limited in that sense. Therefore, without belittling the achievements, it could be said that the actual gains in future would extensively depend on the negotiating skill of the newly formed coalitions/groupings in coming multilateral negotiations (G-20, G-33 and so on).

It seems the developing countries are already on the right track as the G-20 meet at New Delhi (18–19 March, 2005) reaffirmed the negotiating position of the group for the Hong Kong Ministerial to ensure, 'the need to observe necessary sequencing of issues identified in the "July Framework" so as to ensure progress in each of the three pillars'.[37] The document also expressed concern over the pace of lowering of subsidies on cotton and elimination of tariff escalation in developed countries, and stressed the need to ensure S&DT for developing countries for preserving food security, rural development and livelihood concerns within their territories. The challenge for the G-20 would be to formally extend the understanding in case of agriculture to the case of services and other areas, which is not easily forthcoming. Nonetheless, a cross-sympathisation of interest is observed to some extent. For instance, Brazil is returning India's support in case of agriculture at negotiations on Mode 4 in services. (Draper and Sally 2004) In addition, several G-20 partners, namely, Pakistan, China, Indonesia, Thailand and the Philippines are fast emerging as strong negotiating partners in case of trade in services with an explicit focus on liberalisation of mode 4, where India's prime interest lies.[38]

However, questions are already being raised on the future of the group on various grounds (Ranjan 2005). Given the wide variation in export orientation of G-20 members, the chances of arriving at a consensus on any issue are limited. Part recognition of the statement comes from the fact that although the G-20 Ministers at New Delhi in March 2005 discussed issues relating to services export and non-agricultural market access, these areas were not included in the final declaration.[39] Alternatively, G-20 consensus in case of agriculture is 'negative' in character, that is, it generally opposes the EU-US joint proposal (both during Cancun and the Hong Kong Ministerial), the consensus on which is easier to form. Replicating the same in case of services through 'positive' measures, that is., through offers by consensus among the members of the group would not be so easy.

The state of affairs strongly suggests that India needs to adopt a true pro-active approach towards negotiations. Despite the outward changes in attitude towards negotiations, the attachment towards S&DT and the hesitation in making offers at negotiation table is likely to affect its potential gains in future. In addition, India's current uneasiness towards opening the agricultural and certain services sectors at negotiations is unrealistic.[40] Furthermore, while India has been vocal on the prevalence of NTBs in the markets of the developed country for quite some time, the presence of the same at its domestic market might trigger dissatisfaction, and ultimately lead to disputes in future (Das 2003; USTR 2004). Three complaints against India on anti-dumping procedure within a very short span strengthen this point. Therefore, the need of the hour is to adopt a focused 'request-and-offer' approach, in association with other developing countries and sometimes even unilaterally, as the situation demands, at future negotiations.

Endnotes

[1] An earlier version of the paper has been published in the July 2005 issue of the *Taiwanese Journal of WTO Studies*. The views expressed in the paper are personal.

[2] '... in general the negotiations did not move forward as far or fast as anticipated, with important spring deadlines in agricultural and non-agricultural market access and on dispute settlement being missed.' WTO *Annual Report*, 2004, p. 2. The lack of agreement on reform modalities even during early 2007 is a worrying concern.

[3] See 'Developing Countries at UNCTAD call for the WTO Doha Programme to Realize (not just reflect) Development' 19 October 2004, http://twnside.org.sg/title2/twninfo171.htm.

[4] *India and the WTO*, November–December 1999, pp. 4–5 (the Commerce and Industry Minister Murasoli Maran's reply to the short-duration discussion on the Seattle meet in the Rajya Sabha on 9 December 1999).

[5] *India and the WTO*, June–July 2001, pp. 3–5 (Letter of the Minister of Commerce of India to G-77 Trade Ministers dated 14 June 2001).

[6] The Minister of Commerce Mr Maran commented in New Delhi that, 'In sum, the Doha mandate will not in any way harm us; on the contrary, we have substantial gains'. *India and the WTO*, October–November 2001, pp. 1–2 (Statement by Mr Murasoli Maran, Minister for Commerce and Industry, in the Rajya Sabha on 21 November 2001 and in Lok Sabha on 21 November 2001, Regarding the Fourth Ministerial Conference of the WTO).

[7] *India and the WTO*, April 1999, 'Differential and more Favourable Treatment for Developing and Least Developed Countries in various WTO Agreements—Concerns regarding Implementation', pp. 1–7.

[8] Bhattacharyya (1999), Ministry of Commerce (1999), Mehta (1999). The NTBs are still operational on Indian exports, as seen from R. Mehta (2005).

[9] Khan and Debroy (2004); India's communication, dated 29 March 2001 (Document no. IP/C/W/247).

[10] *India and the WTO*, 'Issues in the run up to Cancun (Replies given in Parliament during May, 2003), vol. 5, no. 5, May 2003, pp. 3–8.

[11] For the detailed proposal, see *India and the WTO*, vol. 5, no. 8, August 2003, pp. 5–7.

[12] International Food & Agricultural Trade Policy Council (2004) showed that there are twenty-five ways to improve the draft.

[13] *India and the WTO*, vol. 5, no. 10–11, October–November 2003, pp. 1–6 (Text of keynote address by the Commerce Minister Mr Arun Jaitley at FICCI-UNCTAD Seminar on 'Reflections on post-Cancun Agenda: The Way Ahead', 22 October 2003, New Delhi).

[14] 'On the occasion of the Ministerial Meeting of the G-20 held in Brasilia, on December 11 and 12 2003, the group had the opportunity to meet with Commissioner Lamy to discuss the present status of the Doha Round and how to move forward in the negotiations on agriculture.' *India and the WTO*, vol. 5, no. 12, December 2003.

[15] 'India Rejects WTO Draft', *Hindustan Times*, July 31, 2004.

[16] *India and the WTO*, vol. 6, no. 8, August 2004, 'Statement by Kamal Nath, Minister for Commerce and Industry, in the Parliament on the WTO Framework Agreement' (New Delhi, 16 August 2004).

[17] The 13 countries are Argentina, Brazil, Croatia, India, Indonesia, Kazakhstan, Philippines, Romania, Russia, South Africa, Thailand, Turkey and Venezuela.

[18] India's communication to WTO with African and other developing countries dated 29 June 2001 (Document no. IP/C/W/296).

[19] India's communication to WTO dated 14 July 2003 (Document no. WT/GC/W/503).

[20] India claimed that the rules of origin requirement in US on imports of textiles and apparel products were inconsistent with paragraphs (b), (c), (d) and (e) of Article 2 of the Agreement on Rules of Origin. However, the Panel ruled that India failed to establish its claims.

[21] Submissions under service trade include informal submissions to WTO as well. The numbers in the parenthesis indicate the number of joint submissions.

[22] India's communication dated 24 November 2000 (Document no. S/CSS/W/12), communication dated 3 July 2003 (Document no. TN/S/W/14), communication dated 31 March 2004 (Document no. TN/S/W/19), communication dated 29 September 2004 (Document No TN/S/W/23).

[23] 'California Senate passes Anti-BPO Bill', *Hindustan Times*, 25 August 2004.

[24] India's communication dated 28 June 2004 (Document no. JOB(04)/87).

[25] India's Communication dated 31 March 2004 (Document no. TN/S/W/19).

[26] India's communication dated 30 October 2002 (Document no. IP/C/W/385); communication dated 24 June 2002 (Document No IP/C/W/355).

[27] India's communication dated 2 March 2004 (Document no. IP/C/W/420).

[28] '... negotiations (on Singapore Issues) can be launched in these areas only if there is explicit consensus. As far as the proposal to negotiate rules on foreign direct investment is concerned, I would at the outset like to request everybody not to mix up two different issues namely, willingness of a country of receive foreign direct investment and willingness of a country to accept binding multilateral rules on foreign direct investment in the WTO. I would also like

to point out that India has a fairly open and liberal foreign investment regime but does not believe that there is need for negotiating rules on this subject in the WTO. In our assessment, the only purpose of such an exercise would be to protect the interests of foreign investors and to take away the policy flexibility available to the developing countries.' Statement by Mr Prabir Sengupta, Commerce Secretary, Government of India, at the informal General Council Meeting of the WTO held in Geneva on 25 June 2001. *India and the WTO*, June–July 2001, p. 6.

[29] *India and the WTO*, vol. 1, no. 8, August 1999, p. 3.

[30] The tariff elimination on goods trade between India and ASEAN countries would be complete by 2016, starting from January 2006, although in case of some countries, it will be achieved by 2011. In case of BIMSTEC, the tariff elimination for developing country imports under normal track will be achieved by June 2012, starting from July 2007. In case of Indo-Thailand FTA, the zero-duty imports will be achieved by 2010. However, the creation of a FTA cell in the Ministry of Commerce and Industry to deal with the adverse impact, if any, of FTAs on specific sectors and also, to obtain suggestions for amendments to the agreements for inclusion or exclusion of items of concern to domestic industry in 2005 is part recognition of the producers' anxiety.

[31] It seems India's decision to enter into RTAs with the GCC countries is more influenced by the economic need of mineral fuel importation from most of these countries.

[32] See the proposal submitted by India and other developing countries on 14 July 2003 (Document No. WT/GC/W/503). India already holds trade ties with Maldives and Pakistan and is in the process of entering in preferential arrangement with Indonesia, People's Republic of China, Thailand and Vietnam. Also the Commerce Minster recently has talked about the need to resist new forms of protectionism in post-MFA era at the India economic Summit Plenary Session on 'International Trade: A New Voice of Emerging Markets', organised by Confederation of Indian Industries and the World Economic Forum, New Delhi on 6 December 2004. *India and The WTO*, vol. 6, no. 11–12, November–December 2004.

[33] Hoekman and Mavroidis (2001), p. 23. Also see Chaisse and Chakraborty (2004). So far among the proposed partners, Malaysia, Pakistan, Sri Lanka and Indonesia have jointly submitted proposals with India to WTO in this regard.

[34] A—Agriculture; B—Dispute Resolution; C—General Council (Special and Differential Treatment, Singapore Issues, Anti-Dumping, Trade in Textiles, Modalities, Preparation for Ministerial Conferences and so on); D—Investment; E—Non-Agricultural Market Access; F—Services; G—TRIPS, H—Trade Facilitation.

[35] India's communication dated 8 May 2003 (Document no. TN/RL/W/106); communication dated 17 October 2002 (Document no. TN/RL/W/26); communication dated 25 April 2002 (Document no. TN/RL/W/4).

[36] The data includes the anti-dumping measures imposed on individual EU member states as well.

[37] 'G-20 Ministerial Declaration', http://www.commerce.nic.in/wto_sub/g20/min_decln.htm.

[38] See the developing country joint proposals entitled, 'Review of Progress in Negotiations, Including Pursuant to Paragraph 15 of the Guidelines for Negotiations', 29 September 2004 (Document no. TN/S/W/23); Informal Paper on 'Mode 4-Transparency Issues', 29 September 2004 (Document no. JOB(04)/142); 'Review of Progress as Established in Paragraph 15 of the Guidelines and Procedures for the Negotiations on Trade in Services', 31 March 2004 (Document no. TN/S/W/19); 'Implementation of Paragraph 15 of the Guidelines and Procedures for the Negotiations on Trade in Services', 25 July 2003 (Document no. TN/S/W/16) and 'Proposed Liberalization of Mode 4 Under GATS Negotiations', 3 July 2003 (Document no. TN/S/W/14).

[39] 'G-20 adopts New Delhi Declaration', *The Hindu*, Sunday, 20 Mar 2005, http://www.thehindubusinessline.com/2005/03/20/stories/2005032001810300.htm.

[40] In late nineties, after India conceded defeat in DS 90 against the US, it had to remove the import restriction on agricultural items, and it was widely believed that the agricultural sector might be ruined. See Binu S. Thomas, 'Flood of food imports could destroy Indian agriculture', http://www.twnside.org.sg/title/flood-cn.htm. However, contrary to popular belief, the opening up of imports did not create any major problem for the agriculture sector.

References

Agarwal, Manmohan. 2004. 'Regional Trading Arrangements in the Era of Globalizations: An Indian Perspective' *International Studies* vol. 41, no.4, pp. 411–23.

Anant, T. C. A. 2001. 'India and the WTO: Flawed Rejectionist Approach', *Economic and Political Weekly*, vol. 36, nos 46 and 47, pp. 4243–45.

Baru, Sanjaya. 2003. 'India Launches FTA Spree Before Cancun', *The Financial Express*, Friday, 20 June, http://fecolumnists.expressindia.com/print.php?content_id=36543.

Barua, Alokesh and Debashis Chakraborty. 2004. 'Liberalization, Trade and Industrial Performance in India: An Empirical Study', paper presented in the seminar on 'WTO Negotiations: India's Post-Cancun Concerns', jointly organised by the Planning Commission and International Trade and Development Division, JNU, 18–19 October.

Bhattacharyya, B. 1999. 'Non-Tariff Measures on Indian Exports: An Assessment', Occasional Paper no. 16, Indian Institute of Foreign Trade, New Delhi.

Blinova, Natalia, Nicolas Dorgeret and Razvan-Florian Maximiuc. 2006. 'The EU in the Complex WTO', paper presented at the WTO seminar, Geneva, 11–13 May, http://hei.unige.ch/sections/sp/agenda/wto/wto2006/Paper%20-%20EU%20%20in%20the%20complexWTOr.pdf.

Chaisse, Julien and Debashis Chakraborty. 2004. 'Disputes Resolution in the WTO: In the Light of Chinese and Indian Involvements', in *Future Negotiation Issues at WTO: An India-China Perspective*, edited by Bibek Debroy and Mohammad Saqib, New Delhi: Globus Books, pp. 377–432.

Chakraborty, Debashis. 2003. 'The Changing Face of Indian Negotiation Strategy in WTO', paper presented in the seminar on NDA Government's Foreign Policy, organised by SPANDAN in association with Ministry of External Affairs, Government of India, JNU, New Delhi, 30 July.

_____. 2004. 'Recent Negotiation Trends on Agriculture under WTO', RGICS Working Paper 47.

_____. 2005. 'India's Participation in WTO Negotiations: The Changes in Attitude and Emphasis', *Taiwanese Journal of WTO Studies*, vol. 3, pp. 119–63.

_____. 2007. 'India's Negotiations on Trade and Environment Issues at WTO: A Decade Long Experience', *GALT Update*, vol. 1, no. 2, pp. 12–17.

_____. 2007b. 'Misuse of Anti-Dumping Provisions: What do the WTO Disputes Reveal?', in *Anti-Dumping: Global Abuse of a Trade Policy Instrument*, edited by B. Debroy and D. Chakraborty, New Delhi: Academic Foundation, pp. 155–83.

Chakraborty, Debashis and Julien Chaisse. 2005. 'Trade Policy Review Mechanism and Dispute Settlement System: A Cross-Country Analysis of Enforcing WTO Rules between Negotiations and Sanctions', in *WTO at Ten: Looking Back to Look Beyond*, edited by Bibek Debroy and Mohammad Saqib, New Delhi: Konark Publishers, pp. 210–78.

Chakraborty, Debashis and Pavel Chakraborty. 2005. 'Indian Exports in the Post-Transitory Phase of WTO: Some Exploratory Results and Future Concerns', *Foreign Trade Review*, vol. 40, no. 1, pp. 3–26.

Chakraborty, Debashis and Arnab Kumar Hazra. 2005. 'Preferential Trade Agreements and India: A Review of Issues', Rajiv Gandhi Institute for Contemporary Studies (RGICS) Working Paper no. 48, New Delhi.

Chakraborty, Debashis and Dipankar Sengupta. 2006. 'IBSAC (India-Brazil-South Africa-China): A Potential Developing Country Coalition in WTO Negotiations', Centre de Sciences Humaines (CSH) Occasional Paper no. 18, New Delhi.

———. 2005. 'Learning Through Trading? India's Decade-Long Negotiation Strategy at WTO', *South Asian Survey*, vol. 12, no. 2, pp. 223–46.

Chand, Ramesh. 2005. 'India's Agricultural Trade during Post-WTO Decade: Lessons for WTO Negotiations', paper presented at the conference on Off the Starting Block to Hong Kong: Concerns and Negotiating Options on Agriculture and NAMA for India, organised by Centre for Trade and Development (CENTAD), New Delhi, 22 July.

Chisti, Sumitra. 1991. *Restructuring of International Economic Relations: Uruguay Round and the Developing Countries*, New Delhi: Concept Publishing Company.

Commonwealth Business Council. 2001. *Developing Countries and the WTO Trade Debate: Compelling Case for Full Participation in the New Round*, London, Commonwealth Business Council.

Das, Deb Kusum. 2003. 'Quantifying Trade Barriers: Has Protection Declined Substantially in Indian Manufacturing?', Indian Council for Research on International Economic Relations (ICRIER) Working Paper no. 105, New Delhi.

Das, S. P. 2003. 'An Indian Perspective on WTO Rules on Foreign Direct Investment', in *India and the WTO*, edited by A. Mattoo and R. M. Stern, Washington DC: The World Bank and Oxford University Press, pp. 141–68.

Dasgupta, Subhendu. 2003. 'Their Rules, Our Rights: Intellectual Property Rules and Right to Health', in *WTO and TRIPS: Indian Perspective*, edited by Byasdeb Dasgupta et al., Kalyani: University of Kalyani, pp. 33–34.

Deardorff, Alan V. and Robert M. Stern. 2004. 'Designing a Pro-active Stance for India in the Doha Development Agenda Negotiations', paper presented in the seminar on WTO Negotiations: India's Post-Cancun Concerns jointly organised by the Planning Commission and International Trade and Development Division, JNU, 18–19 October.

Debroy, Bibek and Debashis Chakraborty (eds). 2007. *The Trade Game: Negotiation Trends at the Multilateral Level and Concerns for Developing Countries*, New Delhi: Academic Foundation.

Dhar, Biswajit and C. Niranjan Rao. 2004. 'Third Amendment to 1970 Patent Act: An Analysis', EPW Commentary, *Economic and Political Weekly*, vol. 39, no. 52, 25 December, http://www.epw.org.in/showArticles.php?root=2004&leaf=12&filename=8076&filetype=html.

Draper, Peter and Razeen Sally. 2004. 'Developing-Country Coalitions in Multilateral Trade Negotiations', paper presented in the seminar on WTO Negotiations: India's Post-Cancun Concerns, jointly organised by the Planning Commission and International Trade and Development Division, JNU, 18–19 October.

Economic and Social Commission for Asia and the Pacific (ESCAP). 2000. 'Non-tariff Measures with Potentially Restrictive Market Access Implications Emerging in a Post-Uruguay Round Context', Studies in Trade and Investment no. 40, ESCAP, New York.

Government of India. 1998. 'Global Relationship between the Mobility of Capital and the Mobility of Labour: Selected Issues for Consideration', submission by India to the WTO

Working Group on the Relationship between Trade and Investment, Document No. WT/WGTI/W/39, 4 June.

Government of India. 2002. 'Investors' and Home Governments' Obligations', submission by China, Cuba, India, Kenya, Pakistan and Zimbabwe to the WTO Working Group on the Relationship between Trade and Investment, Document No. WT/WGTI/W/152, 19 November.

Government of India, Ministry of Commerce, 'G-20 Ministerial Declaration', http://www.commerce.nic.in/wto_sub/g20/min_decln.htm.

_____. Ministry of Commerce, Various submissions made to WTO, http://www.commerce.nic.in/indian_wtopaper.htm.

_____. various issues. *India and the WTO*, Newsletter of Ministry of Commerce.

_____. 1999. 'Non-Tariff Barriers faced by India', Preliminary Report, Ministry of Commerce, New Delhi, November.

_____. 2005. 'Kamal Nath constitutes FTA Cell to Deal with Industry Grievances', press release, 7 January, http://www.commerce.nic.in/Jan05_release.htm#h7.

Hindustan Times. 2006a. 'US May Walk out of WTO', 16 February.

_____. 2006b. 'US Refusal to Bring Down Subsidies May Extend Deadlock on Trade Talks', 31 May.

_____. 2006c. 'Trade Talks Gain Momentum with Ministers' Conclave', 22 July.

_____. 2006d. 'India Plans Alternative Strategy with EU, Japan', 26 July.

_____. 2006e. 'US May Make India Pay for WTO Intransigence', 9 August.

Hoekman, Bernard M. and Petros C. Mavroidis. 2001. 'WTO Dispute Settlement, Transparency and Surveillance', in *Developing Countries and the WTO: A Pro-Active Agenda*, edited by B. Hoekman and W. Martin, Oxford: Blackwell Publishers, p. 23.

Hoekman, B. and K. Saggi. 2000. 'Assessing the Case for Extending WTO Disciplines on Investment-Related Policies', *Journal of Economic Integration*, vol. 15, no. 4, pp. 629–53.

International Food & Agricultural Trade Policy Council. 2004. 'Twenty-Five Ways to Improve the Derbez Draft on Agriculture', 10 February, http://www.agritrade.org/Doha/Derbez/Assessment%20Paper.pdf.

Joshi, Vijay and I. M. D. Little. 1996. *India's Economic Reforms: 1991–2001*, New Delhi: Oxford University Press.

Khan, Amir Ullah and Bibek Debroy. 2004. *Intellectual Property Rights Beyond 2005: An Indian Perspective on the Debate on IPR Protection and the WTO*, Kottayam: DC School of Management and Technology.

Mattoo, Aaditya and Arvind Subramanian. 2003. 'India and the Multilateral Trading System Post-Doha: Defensive or Pro-active?', in *India and the WTO*, edited by A. Mattoo and R. M. Stern, Washington DC: the World Bank and Oxford University Press.

Mehta, Dewang. 1999. 'Non-Tariff Trade Barriers in I.T. Trade', paper presented in the seminar on WTO Information Technology Symposium, Geneva, 16 July, www.wto.org/english/tratop_e/inftec_e/mehta.ppt.

Mehta, Rajesh and J. George (eds). 2005. *Food Safety Regulation, Concerns and Trade: The Developing Country Experience*, New Delhi: Macmillan.

Mehta, Rajesh. 1999. *Tariff and Non-Tariff Barriers of Indian Economy: A Profile*, New Delhi: Research and Information System for Developing Countries (RIS).

_____. 2005. 'Non-Tariff Barriers Affecting India's Exports', RIS Working Paper no. 97, New Delhi.

Nag, Biswajit and Debashis Chakraborty. 2006. 'India's Approach to Asian Economic Integration', paper presented in the conference on Globalization, Blocization, and East

Asian Economic Integration, at the Center for WTO Studies, National Chengchi University, Taipei, 31 March.
Narlikar, Amrita. 2003. *International Trade and Developing Countries: Bargaining Coalitions in the GATT and WTO*, London: Routledge.
Nordas, Hildegunn Kyvik. 2004. *The Global Textile and Clothing Industry Post the Agreement on Textile and Clothing*, Geneva: WTO.
Ranjan, Prabhash. 2005. 'How Long Can the G-20 Hold Itself Together? A Power Analysis', Working Paper no. 1, Centre for Trade and Development, an Oxfam GB Initiative, New Delhi.
Raizada, B. K. and Javed Sayed. 2002. 'IPR and Drugs and the Pharmaceutical Industry: Concerns for Developing Countries', in *Salvaging the WTO's Future: Doha and Beyond*, edited by Amit Dasgupta and Bibek Debroy, New Delhi: Konark Publishers pp. 274–89.
Research and Information System for the Non-Aligned and Other Developing Countries. 2003. *World Trade and Development Report 2003: Cancun and Beyond*, New Delhi: Academic Foundation.
Sally, Razeen. 2000. 'Developing Country Trade Policy Reform and the WTO', *Cato Journal*, vol. 19, no. 3, pp. 403–23.
Sharma, Devinder. 1995. *GATT-WTO: Seeds of Despair*, New Delhi: Konark Publishers.
Singh, Yashika. 2001. 'India at the Fourth Ministerial Meeting in Doha: Déjàvu Again?', RGICS Working Paper no. 32, New Delhi.
Stiglitz, Joseph E. 2001. 'Two Principles for the Next Round or, How to Bring Developing Countries in from the Cold', in *Developing Countries and the WTO: A Pro-Active Agenda*, edited by B. Hoekman and W. Martin, Oxford: Blackwell Publishers.
Tangermann, Stefan. 2001. 'Agriculture: New Wine in New Bottles?', in *The World Trade Organization Millenium Round: Freer Trade in the Twenty-First Century*, edited by K. G. Deutsch and Bernhard Speyer, London: Routledge, pp. 199–212.
The Hindu. 2005. 'G-20 Adopts New Delhi Declaration', Sunday, 20 March, http://www.thehindubusinessline.com/2005/03/20/stories/2005032001810300.htm.
Verma, Samar. 2004. 'How Big is the Bang for India: Market Access in Textiles Post 2004', paper presented in the seminar on The WTO and India: Issues and Negotiating Strategies, jointly organised by JNU, ICSSR and Cotton College, Guwahati, 11–12 August.
United States Trade Reprehensive. various issues. 'National Trade Estimate: Foreign Trade Barriers', in *Report on India*, www.ustr.gov, accessed 15 September 2006.
World Bank. 2000. 'Trade Blocs Policy Research Report', http://www.worldbank.org/research/trade/pdf/trade_blocs2.pdf, accessed 7 February 2003.
WTO. various issues. *WTO Annual Report*, Geneva: WTO.
———. 1998. *Trade Policy Review, India*, Geneva: WTO.
———. 2002. *Trade Policy Review, India*, Geneva: WTO.
———. 'Members OK Amendment to Make Health Flexibility Permanent', press release, http://www.wto.org/English/news_e/pres05_e/pr426_e.htm, accessed 19 December 2005.

5

Designing a Proactive Stance for India in the Doha Development Agenda Negotiations

ALAN V. DEARDORFF AND ROBERT M. STERN

INTRODUCTION

In this paper, we focus on the potentially significant gains for India from a strategy of proactive pursuit of its national interests in the WTO DDA negotiations. Being proactive means that these gains can be realised by negotiations for greater market access for India's exports of goods and services to its major trading partners in conjunction with reciprocal offers to these trading partners of greater access to the Indian markets.

In the following sections we summarise the framework that has been agreed upon as the basis for the DDA negotiations; the design and mission of the WTO and the economic effects of multilateral trade liberalisation; the conditions for India's realisation of the maximum benefits from the DDA negotiations and the implications for broader Indian domestic policy reforms; set out our recommendations for India's negotiating strategies in the DDA negotiations for multilateral trade liberalisation in agricultural products, manufactures, and services, and for improvements in WTO rules governing trade and related issues. The last section will summarise the findings of the paper.

THE FRAMEWORK OF THE DDA NEGOTIATIONS

Almost ten years have now passed since the conclusion of the WTO Ministerial Meeting held in Qatar in November 2001 that was designed to launch the DDA negotiations. It had been hoped that the negotiations would be energised by the WTO meeting in Cancún in September 2003, but agreement could not be reached there on the negotiating framework. After a series of subsequent meetings, it was announced on 31 July 2004 that agreement had been reached on a framework for the final phase of the DDA. As indicated by the United States Trade Representative (USTR) (2004; 1–4), the main features of this framework include the reform of agricultural trade, new market access for manufactures, opening of services markets and trade facilitation for the movement of goods across borders.

Agricultural Trade Reform

- All countries, except the least developed, will reduce agricultural tariffs, with deeper cuts in higher tariffs, a 'banded' formula to achieve greater tariff harmonisation across countries, consideration of a tariff cap, and selective expansion of tariff quotas for

'sensitive' products. Developing countries will be subject to lesser tariff reduction commitments.
- Elimination of agricultural export subsidies.
- Disciplines for export credits and export guarantee programs.
- Disciplines for the trade-distorting practices of State Trading Enterprises.
- Reductions, caps and harmonisation of levels of domestic support overall and for specific commodities, with 20 per cent reductions by all WTO members in the first year of implementation.
- Maintenance of the viability of food aid programmes.
- Changes in national policies for cotton to address issues of market access, domestic support and export competition.

Manufactured Products

- Negotiation of a tariff-cutting formula for industrial products under which higher tariffs will be cut more than low tariffs.
- Sectoral initiatives to fully eliminate or harmonise tariffs in particular industry areas.
- Developing countries will be allowed longer implementation periods and flexibility on percentages of their tariff lines. Least developed countries will be encouraged to bind more of their industrial tariffs.
- NTBs will be identified and subjected to reductions in later negotiations.

Services

- Intensify negotiations to open global services markets and to achieve progressively higher levels of liberalisation.

Trade Facilitation

- Update and modernise current WTO rules on border procedures.
- Cut red tape and unnecessary formalities at the border.
- Advance reforms to promote anti-corruption efforts.

In keeping with the professed objectives of the DDA, it is stated in USTR (2004, 5) that:

- 'The framework encourages expanded trade between developed and developing countries, as well as expanded "South-South" trade. Open markets and domestic reform go hand in hand, offering the best means for further integrating developing countries into the global economy'.
- 'This reflects the recent commitment of G-8 Leaders to ensure that the poorest are not left behind but that they too develop the capacity to participate in the global trading system. The framework recognizes that different countries will need to move at different speeds toward open trade.'

Now that the framework for the DDA negotiations has been established, it is essential for the WTO member countries to design their strategies in order to pursue their national interests in the negotiations. We turn next accordingly, for background purposes, to outline briefly the design and mission of the WTO, discuss conceptually what the economic effects of trade liberalisation may be, and then consider the conditions needed for India in particular to maximise the benefits from its involvement in the DDA negotiations.

THE DESIGN AND MISSION OF THE WTO AND THE ECONOMIC EFFECTS OF TRADE LIBERALISATION

Design and Mission of the WTO

Srinivasan (2004, 18) has noted that '[...] the WTO is a misunderstood and maligned institution in much of the debate on it in India.' It may be useful, therefore, to review briefly the main features and mission of the WTO, as set out on the WTO website:

> The World Trade Organization (WTO) is the only international organisation dealing with the global rules of trade between nations. Its main function is to ensure that trade flows as smoothly, predictably and freely as possible.
>
> The result is assurance. Consumers and producers know that they can enjoy secure supplies and greater choice of the finished products, components, raw materials and services that they use. Producers and exporters know that foreign markets will remain open to them.
>
> The result is also a more prosperous, peaceful and accountable economic world. Virtually all decisions in the WTO are taken by consensus among all member countries and they are ratified by members' parliaments. Trade friction is channeled into the WTO's dispute settlement process where the focus is on interpreting agreements and commitments, and how to ensure that countries' trade policies conform with them. That way, the risk of disputes spilling over into political or military conflict is reduced.
>
> By lowering trade barriers, the WTO's system also breaks down other barriers between peoples and nations.
>
> At the heart of the system—known as the multilateral trading system—are the WTO's agreements, negotiated and signed by a large majority of the world's trading nations, and ratified in their parliaments. These agreements are the legal ground-rules for international commerce. Essentially, they are contracts, guaranteeing member countries important trade rights. They also bind governments to keep their trade policies within agreed limits to everybody's benefit.
>
> The agreements were negotiated and signed by governments. But their purpose is to help producers of goods and services, exporters, and importers conduct their business.
>
> The goal is to improve the welfare of the peoples of the member countries. (WTO 2004)

As the foregoing statement indicates, the WTO is an inter-governmental organisation that establishes the rules governing international trade and seeks to enhance the welfare of its members by pursuing the reductions of trade barriers and hence the liberalisation and expansion of trade. It is in this context that WTO member countries, India included, can be engaged in and benefit from the process of trade liberalisation. Next, in this connection, it may be helpful to consider briefly some of the ways in which multilateral trade liberalisation can be expected to work and the impacts involved.

Economic Effects of Trade Liberalisation

When tariffs or other trade barriers are reduced, domestic buyers (both final and intermediate) substitute towards imports, and the domestic competing industry contracts production while foreign exporters expand. Thus, in the case of multilateral liberalisation that reduces tariffs and other trade barriers simultaneously in most sectors and countries, each country's industries share in both of these effects, expanding or contracting depending primarily on their export or import orientation and on whether their protection is reduced more or less than in other sectors and countries.

Worldwide, these changes cause increased international demand for all sectors. World prices increase most for those sectors where trade barriers fall the most. This, in turn, causes changes in the relative prices of countries' exports compared to their imports—their 'terms of trade'—that can be positive or negative. Those countries that are net exporters of goods with the greatest degree of liberalisation will benefit from increases in their terms of trade, as the world prices of their exports rise relative to their imports. The reverse occurs for net exporters in industries where liberalisation is slight—either because liberalisation in these sectors is resisted or perhaps because it has already taken place in previous trade rounds.

The effects on the welfare of countries arise from a mixture of these terms-of-trade effects, together with the standard efficiency gains from trade and also from additional benefits due to the realisation of economies of scale. Thus, we expect on average that the world will gain from multilateral liberalisation, as resources are reallocated to those sectors in each country where there is comparative advantage. In the absence of terms-of-trade effects, these efficiency gains should raise national welfare for every country,[1] although some factor owners within a country could lose. However, it is possible for a particular country whose net imports are concentrated in sectors with the greatest liberalisation to lose overall, if the worsening of its terms of trade swamps these efficiency gains.

On the other hand, if markets are imperfectly competitive, multilateral trade liberalisation permits all countries to expand their export sectors at the same time, as all sectors compete more closely with a larger number of competing varieties from abroad. As a result, countries as a whole may gain from lower costs due to increasing returns to scale, lower monopoly distortions due to greater competition, and reduced costs and/or increased utility due to greater product variety. All of these effects make it more likely that countries will gain from liberalisation in ways that are shared across the entire population.

The various effects just described in the context of multilateral trade liberalisation will also take place when there is unilateral trade liberalisation. However, these effects will then depend on the magnitudes of the liberalisation in relation to the patterns of trade and the price and output responses involved between the liberalising country and its trading partners. Similarly, many of the effects described will take place also with the formation of bilateral or regional FTAs. But in these cases, there will be both trade creation and trade diversion, with consequent positive and negative effects respectively on the economic welfare of FTA-member countries. At the same time, trade diversion has negative effects on the economic welfare of non-member countries. The net effects on economic welfare for individual countries, and also globally, will thus, depend on the economic circumstances and policy changes implemented.

In reality, of course, all of the various effects just described will occur over time, some of them more quickly than others. It is important accordingly to specify the time horizon over which the trade liberalisation takes place, taking into account how the economy and its various sectors do and do not adjust to changing market conditions, as well as the short- or long-run nature of these adjustments. In the context of the WTO negotiations, it is typically the case that the reductions in trade barriers are phased in over an extended period of time. Thus, in the Uruguay Round, which was completed in 1994, the liberalisation was to be phased in over a period of 10 years. As indicated above, there will similarly be an extended period of phase-in especially for developing countries in the implementation of the DDA negotiations. It is also important to bear in mind that there may be longer-run adjustments that could occur through capital accumulation, population growth, and technological change, and that the longer-run growth paths of individual economies may themselves be influenced by trade liberalisation.

CONDITIONS FOR INDIA'S REALISATION OF MAXIMUM BENEFITS FROM THE DDA NEGOTIATIONS AND DOMESTIC POLICY REFORMS

The foregoing discussion has sketched the framework for the DDA negotiations and the ways in which significant benefits can be realised by countries participating in the process of multilateral trade liberalisation. It should be emphasised in this context that there are two basic pillars of the multilateral trading system and of trade negotiations that are important to bear in mind: reciprocity and non-discrimination (most-favored-nation (MFN) treatment). Reciprocity, in multilateral trade negotiations, means that there is a bargaining process in the negotiations, in which WTO member countries exchange concessions for the expansion of mutual market access by means of reductions in their trade barriers. Non-discrimination (MFN treatment) means that all reductions in trade barriers made by WTO member countries are extended to all WTO members irrespective of whether they themselves have made concessions. In this connection and with reference especially to India's involvement in the DDA negotiations, we have the benefit of the writings by such influential, US academic economists as T. N. Srinivasan (2003; 2004) and Jagdish Bhagwati and Arvind Panagariya (2003) and by World Bank/IMF staff members such as Aaditya Mattoo and Arvind Subramanian (2003), who remain in close contact with policy issues and developments in the Indian economy. We draw to a large extent on their various writings in our following discussion, as well as on Deardorff and Stern (2004).

In particular, Srinivasan notes, from India's standpoint:

> We should offer proposals of our own that further our interests rather than merely reacting to others. Offering little in exchange while asking a lot of others is a sure way of becoming a marginal player with negligible influence on the outcome of negotiations. Since unilaterally opening our markets to international competition is in our own interest regardless of whether our access to markets of others is enhanced, getting such enhanced access in return in negotiations is a bonus.
>
> [...] The Doha negotiations offer us an opportunity to reach for our legitimate position in global trade and finance and to compete effectively in world markets. But to avail ourselves of this opportunity, we have to articulate a consistent position that would promote our interests on various items of the negotiating agenda. (Srinivasan 2003, 1–2)

The question, then, is how the policy makers view the country's interests in the negotiations (See Chapter 5 for more details on this issue). In order to realise the maximum potential gains from the negotiations, it is essential that the leading policy makers have the willpower to look across and beyond the interests of the different groups in society, to build domestic coalitions to support continued and greater openness of the economy, and to devise programs to assist sectors and workers and their families to adjust to the changes that may be engendered in the liberalisation process. In this connection, Bhagwati and Panagariya (2003, 1) stress that:

> Our liberalization is in our own interests. How well we are able to exploit the markets of our partners depends not just on how open those markets are but also on how open our markets are. This is amply illustrated by our own success in the last decade under progressive opening of our markets. With the economic reforms taking root, our ability to benefit from increased openness at home and abroad is likely to be that much greater in the future.

In building support for a more proactive role in the DDA negotiations, the policy makers need accordingly to document and publicise the domestic and external benefits that the Indian economy has already realised, both from its unilateral policy reforms undertaken since 1991 and from the implementation of the Uruguay Round multilateral agreements in the past decade. This will necessitate the identification and measurement of the orders of magnitude of the sectors, geographic regions, and individuals and groups who have benefited from the domestic policy reforms and the multilateral trade liberalisation. At the same time, it is essential that the policy makers be up front about identifying the sections of society that have done less well or perhaps have even been harmed by liberalisation. In the course of gathering and disseminating this information, efforts can be made to establish coalitions representing the interests of the major beneficiaries of the liberalisation in support of the DDA negotiations. It will also be essential to devise programs and policies to address problems of adjustment to the possibly adverse changes that may be experienced. Finally, estimates can be made of the economic effects of the DDA negotiations on India and its major trading partners. Presumably, it will be possible to show that the benefits stemming from proactive participation in the DDA negotiations will be sufficiently large so that the gainers can potentially compensate the losers and the economy as a whole will be better off than would otherwise be the case.

So far we have sought to develop in broad outline, the rationale for India's proactive participation in the DDA negotiations. In this connection, Mattoo and Subramanian (2003) stress the central importance of instituting and sustaining 'good' domestic economic policies that will inject greater competition into the domestic economy, together with judicious regulation to remedy market failures and achieve efficient realisation of desired social objectives.[2] The issue then is whether and how multilateral engagement can be designed to contribute meaningfully to overall domestic policy reform. In this connection, Mattoo and Subramanian provide a number of arguments to bolster their position.

First, they argue that multilateral engagement can facilitate domestic reform if governments are able to demonstrate the payoffs resulting from increased access to foreign markets and thereby encourage the formation of countervailing interests to counteract groups that resist economic reform. By demonstrating the external payoffs from greater openness domestically, India can become a more credible bargainer in the multilateral negotiations and thereby be in a better position to induce its major trading partners to provide access to their own markets. Second, multilateral engagement can provide the basis for a commitment to good domestic policies. The point here is that external commitments may provide guarantees against the reversal of current policies and provide a credible promise of future reform. This may help to provide time for competitive conditions to become established, for firms to adjust to market changes, and to neutralise vested interests in maintaining the status quo.

Third, by creating and securing greater foreign market access, multilateral engagement in the WTO framework can help to overcome the asymmetric power differences between stronger countries and less powerful countries. This can be achieved by means of resort to the rules-based WTO dispute settlement system that can be used to help protect the weaker party in cases of trade disputes. Finally, multilateral engagement is a means of fending off or reducing the distorting effects of preferential trading arrangements. That is, as mentioned above, one of the two basic pillars of multilateralism is non-discrimination, which can serve to reinforce the conditions of competition for all countries and thereby provide the foundation for the realisation of greater economic efficiency and global welfare.[3]

RECOMMENDATIONS FOR INDIA'S NEGOTIATING STRATEGIES IN THE DDA

Having established the case to be made for India's proactive participation in the DDA, we turn now to consider the particular strategies to be recommended for India to pursue its interests in the multilateral liberalisation of agricultural products, manufactures, and services and for improvements in the WTO rules governing trade and related issues and selected WTO Secretariat estimates.

Table 5.1 indicates India's effective (applied) rates of duty and bound tariff rates for the whole economy and broken down by sector—agriculture, mining, manufacturing—and by stage of processing. It is evident that India's tariff rates are relatively high and, as noted in Figure 5.1, which they rank among the highest in the world compared to other emerging-market/developing economies (see Chapter 8). There is considerable scope therefore for significant reductions in India's tariffs in the DDA negotiations.

Agricultural Liberalisation

As noted in Table 5.1, India's average applied tariffs in agriculture are 33 per cent while its average bound tariffs in the WTO are 94 per cent. Thus, there is a significant wedge overall between the applied and bound rates, and, as shown in Table 5.2(a), the wedge exceeds 50 percentage points in 556 out of the total 673 agricultural tariff lines. With respect to domestic support, shown in Table 5.2(b), India's total AMS is negative and thus indicative of taxation of Indian agriculture. Mattoo and Subramanian (2003, 340) note that Indian exporters do receive some direct and indirect export subsidies. They also note that, despite high bound tariff rates, India's production of such major crops as rice, wheat, pulses, and sugar were for the most part fully integrated with world markets, and that India has significant actual and potential comparative advantage in rice, sugar, dairy products, cotton, processed foods, and cereals. India therefore is in a position both to consider reductions in its tariff rates on agricultural imports and to seek greater foreign market access for its agricultural exports (See Chapter 7).

TABLE 5.1 Bound tariff rates and effective rates of duty for India (average unweighted tariffs, per cent)

	Effective rate of duty[a] 1993/94	Effective rate of duty[b] 1997/98	Effective rate of duty 2001/2	Bound rate of duty[c] by year 2005
Whole economy	71	35 (15)	32	54 (42)
By sector				
Agriculture	43	26 (16)	33	94 (33)
Mining	70	25 (13)	22	36 (9)
Manufacturing	73	36 (10)	33	52 (41)
By stage of processing				
Unprocessed	50	25 (16)	29	74 (40)
Semiprocessed	75	35 (9)	32	44 (23)
Processed	73	37 (17)	33	56 (51)

Notes: Standard deviations appear in parentheses. Tariff averages consider only those tariff lines with ad valorem rates (year beginning April 1).

a. Following the reform package contained in the 1993/94 budget. The auxiliary duty was merged with the basic customs duty in the 1993/94 budget.

b. Effective MFN rate (that is, actual rates applied where basic rates have been reduced by exempt rates). However, many exempt rates cannot be incorporated, such as where the exempt rate applies to only a part of the Harmonised Commodity Description and Coding System six-digit tariff line. The effective rate also excludes specific exemptions.

c. Includes only items bound during the Uruguay Round. The bound rates do not include the commitments under the Information Technology Agreement.

Source: Mattoo and Subramanian (2003: 337), based on UNCTAD, World Bank, Government of India

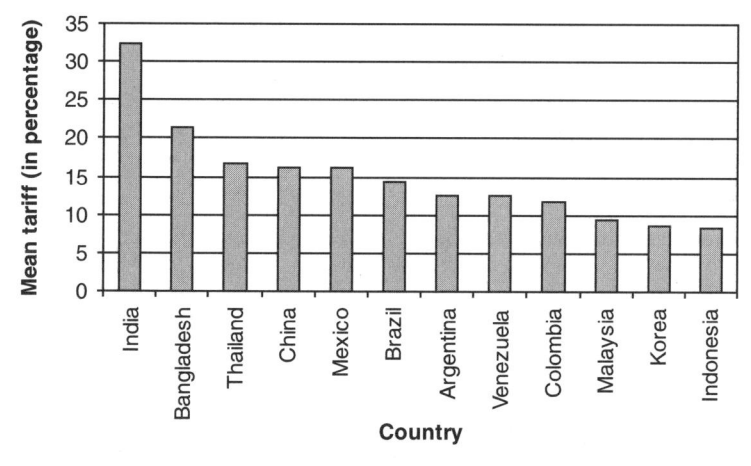

FIGURE 5.1 Cross-country comparison of average tariff rates

Note: Tariff data are for 2000, except for Malaysia (1997), India (1999), and the Republic of Korea (1999).

Source: Mattoo and Subramanian (2003, 336) based on *World Development Indicators*, 2002.

TABLE 5.2 Indicators of Indian agricultural trade

(a) Difference in Uruguay Round final bound rates and MFN tariff rates: Number of lines by different range groups

Range (UR-TR)	Number of Lines[a]
UR-TR > = 75	401
50 = < UR-TR < 75	155
25 = < UR-TR < 50	29
10 = < UR-TR < 25	39
0 = < UR-TR < 10	41
UR-TR < 0	8
Total	673

Note: Tariff Lines at six-digit Harmonised Commodity Description and Coding System (HS) or subgroups of six-digit HS including only agricultural products.
Source: Mattoo and Subramanian (2003, 341), based on Gulati (1999).
TR = MFN tariff rate as announced in the Government of India Budget, 1999/2000.
UR = Uruguay Round final bound rates.

(b) Aggregate measure of support to Indian agriculture (selected crops)

Year	Product-specific support (as % of value of agricultural output)	Non-product-specific support (as % of value of agricultural output)	Total AMS (as % of value of agricultural output)
1986	−34.29	2.25	−32.04
1987	−32.08	3.2	−28.88
1988	−35.54	3.32	−32.22
1989	−36.97	3.39	−33.58
1990	−31.78	3.36	−28.42
1991	−62.23	3.6	−58.63
1992	−69.31	3.46	−65.85
1993	−54.75	3.14	−51.61
1994	−43.27	3.4	−39.87
1995	−44.09	3.9	−40.19
1996	−45.84	3.62	−42.22
1997	−32.16	4.12	−28.04
1998	−41.89	3.49	−38.4

Source: Mattoo and Subramanian (2003: 341), based on Gulati (1999).

In devising its strategy for agricultural negotiations, it is important to acknowledge that Indian agriculture accounts for nearly one-fourth of the GDP, and that more than one-half of India's total population is in the agricultural sector. In this light, former commerce minister, Arun Jaitley has reflected the political concerns involved:

> Some countries have been strongly pushing for greater market access for their products as far as agriculture is concerned. But under the present circumstances, with high levels of subsidies, with very high levels of our population in India involved in agriculture, if we open up our farmer to competition with highly-subsidised economies, perhaps we could even be pushing him to a situation, which could create acute social distress, let alone the economic consequences of the same.

And, therefore, when these negotiations are completed, we do hope—and this is one of the points that we've been trying to explain to our colleagues in the developed world—that an adequate understanding of India's position would be accommodated in terms of market access, which really results from the extent to which tariffs are to be reduced and in identifying certain sensitive products as special products where an adequate amount of protection would have to be assured. Apart of course from creating a special safeguard mechanism whereby a surge of imports to our market could be checked. In terms of sheer volume, a surge in any one of the sensitive items can actually cause distress to ... millions of farmers. These are the sensitivities that we have to keep in mind. We do not wish to stall the negotiations on agriculture, but we do hope adequate windows of exception for economies like India that are highly dependent on agriculture, are created. (Jaitley 2003)

In addressing these concerns, Srinivasan has noted that:

The sustenance of our rural economy ... should not be equated with keeping the current large share ... of our labour force and rural households continuing to earn their living directly or indirectly from agriculture. That so large a proportion of our labour force is still employed in agriculture ... is a telling indicator of the failure of our development strategy in enabling workers to move from agriculture to more productive employment elsewhere in the economy. ... We should focus on increasing agricultural productivity, and, at the same time, generate productive employment opportunities in rural areas outside of agriculture. We should recognise that greater integration of our markets for agricultural inputs and outputs with world markets would provide greater incentives for productivity raising investment and innovation in agriculture. In sum, issues of food security, creation of a safety net for the poor, addressing risks and returns in farming of small and marginal farmers, and rural development are objectives that fall largely in the domain of domestic policy. Using trade policy would be far more costly and less effective in achieving them. Our negotiating partners can easily see through the tenuous connection between the objectives and trade policy.

... the adjustment problem in exposing our farmers to world prices is real and could be serious if the opening is sudden. By announcing the opening in advance and phasing it in over a reasonable time, it can be largely contained. Given the opportunity our diverse agriculture can be very competitive internationally and there is no need to fear competition. (Srinivasan 2003)

As noted above, the framework for agricultural trade reform in the DDA negotiations calls for reductions in import tariffs, elimination of export subsidies, and reductions in domestic supports. In our judgment, India has much to gain by proactive engagement in the agricultural negotiations by means of bargaining with the major industrialised countries. It should emphasise especially the reduction of both import barriers and domestic agricultural supports in the industrialised countries, so as to expand the market access for India's agricultural exports. To achieve this, India should be prepared to offer reciprocal concessions to bind its applied agricultural import tariffs and to reduce these applied tariffs over an extended period of time. To achieve effective results from the agricultural negotiations, India could also consider allying with members of the Cairns group and of the group of 21 that have much to gain from agricultural liberalisation.

Manufactured Products Liberalisation

As already indicated, India's tariffs are among the highest of the world's major trading countries. Mattoo and Subramanian (2003, 336–38) argue in this connection that it is clearly in India's interest actively to seek reductions in tariffs on manufactured products. First, while India's manufactures tariffs are high and may be difficult politically to reduce, India's concessions in the DDA negotiations could provide useful bargaining leverage. Second, given the large wedge between India's applied and bound tariffs noted in Table 5.1, the current situation could lead to uncertainty and unpredictability about India's trade policy on the part of investors. Reducing bound levels of tariffs could thus improve India's investment climate. Third, reductions in tariffs in the major industrialised country markets, especially in labor-intensive manufactures such as textiles and clothing, leather products and footwear, and so on, will directly benefit Indian export industries (See Chapter 8). Finally, there is evidence that India has been affected adversely by the trade diversion resulting from the NAFTA and other preferential trading arrangements. The most effective way to ameliorate and possibly completely to eliminate the trade diversion effects of the preferential arrangements is to negotiate MFN tariff reductions in the DDA negotiations.

Services Liberalisation

Mattoo and Subramanian (2003) note that India's services commitments in the Uruguay Round negotiations, completed in 1993–94, were rather limited. As they state:

> The government will need to decide whether to offset to bind the current regime and, more important, whether to liberalise further either unilaterally or as part of the Doha negotiations. The challenge is to ensure that these decisions reflect good economic policy rather than the dictates of political economy or negotiating pressures. It is useful, therefore, to recall what we have learned about services liberalisation:
>
> - There are substantial gains both from successful domestic liberalisation, especially in key infrastructure services like telecommunications, transport, and financial services, and from improved access to foreign markets.
> - Successful domestic liberalisation requires:
>   - Emphasis on competition more than a change of ownership
>   - Credibility of policy and liberalisation programs
>   - Domestic regulations to remedy market failure and pursue legitimate social goals efficiently
> - Effective market access requires:
>   - Elimination of explicit restrictions
>   - Disciplines on implicit regulatory barriers. (Mattoo and Subramaniam 2003: 346)

In recent years, Mattoo and Subramanian cite some significant changes in services policy, including telecommunications, maritime transport services, and to some extent in banking and insurance services. As the result of these changes, they stress that India may now be in a good position in the services negotiations to address foreign services barriers. This is especially the case with regard to the temporary movement of natural persons, given that India is so well endowed with labor with many different skill levels. There are also concerns about the protectionist backlash against outsourcing, especially in the US, that may need to be addressed from India's standpoint in the DDA negotiations (See Chapters 13 & 14).

WTO Rules Governing Trade and Related Issues

Anti-Dumping

As indicated in Table 5.3, India has the distinction of having initiated 206 anti-dumping actions in 1999–2002. This compares to 192 actions initiated by the US and 134 by the EU. It is well known that the only economic justification for anti-dumping measures is in cases of 'predatory' dumping, in which an exporter intends to drive competitors permanently out of the market so as to secure monopoly advantage and the ability subsequently to raise price. As Srinivasan (2003) and Mattoo and Subramanian (2003, 345) note, the occurrence of predatory pricing is unlikely because of the difficulty of keeping other rivals from entering the market. It is also the case that India has been singled out as the object of anti-dumping actions.

TABLE 5.3 Anti-dumping initiations by economy taking action

Economy	Number of anti-dumping initiations 1991–94	1995–98	1999–2002	Index of anti-dumping initiations (1995–98) per dollar of imports, USA = 100*
Industrial Economies				
Australia	213	77	65	1,096
Canada	84	39	68	199
EU	135	122	134	210
US	226	94	192	100
All industrial economies	678	353	489	74
Developing Economies				
Argentina	59	72	105	2,627
Brazil	59	54	46	871
India	15	78	206	1,875
Republic of Korea	14	34	13	204
Mexico	127	31	30	275
South Africa	16	113	44	2,324
All developing economies	394	509	612	313

Notes: *Based on numbers of anti-dumping initiations from 1995 to 1998 and values of merchandise imports for 1996.
Source: Mattoo and Subramanian (2003: 344), based on WTO Secretariat, Rules Division, Anti-Dumping Measures Database.

As noted in Table 5.4, per dollar of exports India was impacted more than any other country by the anti-dumping actions of others. Given that anti-dumping actions are taken almost always for protectionist purposes, the issue is what alternatives there may be to these actions. Most economists would recommend using competition laws on predation, but it is unlikely that this option is feasible because competition laws are currently not part of the WTO rules and have been set aside as far as the DDA negotiations are concerned. Under the circumstances, the best that might be done is for India to join with like-minded countries in the DDA negotiations and urge that anti-dumping be removed as an instrument of trade policy. In its place, safeguard measures could be used to deal with problems posed by surges in imports. Safeguard measures are permitted under Article XIX of the GATT, and, as Srinivasan (2003) notes, they would be much less damaging than anti-dumping measures.

TABLE 5.4 Anti-dumping initiations by selected exporting economies

Economy	Number of anti-dumping initiations			Index of anti-dumping initiations (1995–98) per dollar of imports, US = 100
	1991–94	1995–98	1999–2002	
Industrial economies				
France	26	8	13	34
Germany	35	30	28	70
Italy	16	16	14	77
Japan	32	23	46	67
United Kingdom	20	16	18	74
United States	70	48	42	100
Developing economies				
Brazil	50	23	38	585
China	115	94	154	751
India	24	21	43	779
Korea, Rep. of	50	40	81	385
Taiwan, China	31	30		323
Thailand	26	21	50	451

Source: Mattoo and Subranian (2003, 345), based on WTO Secretariat, Rules Division, Anti-Dumping Measures Database.

Preferential Trading Arrangements

It is well known that there has been a plethora of PTAs negotiated especially in the past decade. The WTO has reported that, by its definition, there were 250 preferential agreements that had been notified, and that the number could rise to 300 by the end of 2005. The number may thus, have roughly trebled since the WTO was first established in 1995. Until recently, India had confined its PTA activities mainly to South Asia, but it has now signed and is actively pursuing bilateral FTAs with a number of countries in Southeast Asia. As noted above, there is some evidence that Indian exports have been unfavorably impacted by the NAFTA and by the arrangements negotiated by the EU. There could be some benefits for India from forming FTAs with countries in South-East Asia, but these benefits are likely to be relatively small.

Till date, India has not become involved in FTAs with any of the major industrialised countries. It is noteworthy though that Lawrence and Chadha (2004) have set forth a detailed case for India and the United States to establish a bilateral FTA. They argue in particular that this would provide an impetus for domestic policy reform in India, and, based on some computable general equilibrium (CGE) modelling, a US-India FTA might yield welfare gains for India that are comparable to what might be expected to result from the DDA multilateral negotiations. In our view, there are important drawbacks to a US-India FTA. In particular, it is unlikely that agricultural reforms can be dealt with effectively on a bilateral basis. The DDA multilateral negotiations on agricultural liberalisation can be expected to offer greater potential benefits for India. Also, a US bilateral FTA would be very intrusive in requiring that India adapt its domestic policies on matters like government procurement, intellectual property rights, investment, competition policy, and possibly social measures covering labor standards and the environment, so as to conform to US institutions and regulatory principles and practices.

Accordingly, as Srinivasan (2003) and Bhagwati and Panagariya (2003) argue, it would be in India's interest to push for making the existing PTAs open-ended, by allowing expanded membership on an MFN basis and by 'killing preferences at source' by vigorous pursuit of the multilateral reduction and removal of existing barriers to trade in agricultural products, manufactures, and services.

TRIPS

In the run-up to the WTO ministerial meeting in Cancún in September 2003, there was a prolonged controversy related to the public health provisions of the TRIPS Agreement in order to provide medicines to poor countries to deal with HIV/AIDS, tuberculosis, malaria and other epidemics. It was finally agreed that pharmaceutical firms in countries like India that are able to produce good-quality and low-cost generic drugs could export these drugs to certifiably poor countries unable to produce the drugs themselves. While this was a laudable relaxation of the TRIPS Agreement, Srinivasan (2003) argues there are some larger and fundamental issues that need to be addressed. He notes that:

> ... unlike commodity or service trade in which both exporter and importer benefit, TRIPS in effect would result in transfer to patent holders in a handful of rich countries from ... purchasers from a large number of poor countries. The potential benefit, if any, accruing to innovators in poor countries from stronger IP protection is largely uncertain in the distant future.
>
> The most unsatisfactory aspect of TRIPS was that it was thrust, largely by the US, on the developing countries in the Uruguay Round in return for the phasing out of the Multifibre Arrangement and agricultural trade liberalisation. Apart from the fact that the latter was illusory and the former was back loaded with most of the benefits to developing countries coming after 2005, no convincing case was made for mandating a uniform patent life regardless of whether it was for a process or product innovation, and whether the product was a lifesaving drug or a new nail clipper! Most egregiously, the overwhelming empirical evidence that the link between the monopoly rights granted through patents and incentive to innovate was weak at best and varied between industries, was completely ignored. Even where there was an apparent link, such as in pharmaceuticals, grant of patents has not been shown to be the most cost-effective policy of promoting innovation. In short, the developing countries got a very raw deal when they accepted TRIPS. Taking TRIPS out of the WTO is politically impossible. However, India can once again claim moral high ground by pointing out the lack of a strong economic argument for patent protection and its enforcement through TRIPS. (Srinivasan 2003)

In addition to the foregoing, Mattoo and Subramanian (2003, 342) suggest that India might consider changing its IP legislation so as to permit retaliation by withdrawing IP protection in cases in which partner countries do not comply with commitments affecting the market access of Indian exports. They also recommend that India should design its domestic competition law so as to use compulsory licensing to address anti-competitive practices involving IP protection. Finally, they recommended that India should actively pursue its national interests with regard to proprietary protection of its genetic resources, indigenous knowledge, and geographic indications (See Chapter 12).

Trade Facilitation

It is widely agreed that many countries, including India, have customs and related arrangements that can be very costly and thus inhibit trade. As noted above, trade facilitation has been included as part of the framework for the DDA negotiations. It is certainly in India's interest to institute reforms that will cut red tape and eliminate unnecessary formalities at the border and to promote anti-corruption efforts (See Chapter 10).

Other Issues

Prior to the September 2003 Cancún Meeting, the EU especially was actively promoting inclusion of the so-called Singapore issues as part of the DDA multilateral negotiations. These issues involved competition policy, investment, government procurement, and trade facilitation. But because of widespread opposition at Cancún, generally from developing countries, including India, it was decided subsequently to drop the first three of the Singapore issues. Thus, only trade facilitation was incorporated into the framework for the DDA negotiations.

In our judgment, we concur with the decision to put the other Singapore issues on hold, since there is so much else that needs to be done to bring about trade liberalisation. This is not to say, however, that issues of competition policy, investment, and government procurement are unimportant for India. Rather, as pointed out by Bhattacharjea (2003), Das (2003), and Srivastava (2003), India may have much to gain by instituting measures to deal with these issues as part of its domestic policy reforms and in the context of the WTO rules and agreements.

We should also note that issues of labour and environmental standards have been excluded from the DDA negotiating framework. Here again, these are issues that can be addressed as parts of India's domestic reform agenda. But, in our view, India should hold fast in keeping these issues outside the boundaries of the WTO rules and procedures.

CONCLUSION AND A VISION FOR INDIA

In this paper, we began by summarising the framework that has been agreed upon as the basis for the DDA negotiations. We then discussed briefly the design and mission of the WTO and the economic effects of multilateral trade liberalisation. Thereafter, we discussed the conditions for India's realisation of the maximum benefits from the DDA negotiations and the implications for broader Indian domestic policy reforms. Finally, we set out our recommendations for India's proactive involvement and negotiating strategies in the DDA negotiations for multilateral trade liberalisation in agricultural products, manufactures, and services, and for improvements in WTO rules governing trade and related issues.

Now that the DDA negotiations are underway, the question is how the Congress Party leadership and membership of the governing coalition of political parties will decide to pursue India's interests in the negotiations. In this connection, Srinivasan (2004) has reviewed the Common Minimum Programme (CMP) agreed to by the constituents of the United Progressive Alliance (UPA) that formed the government. He notes that the CMP has 'a strong secular and populist flavor' that is reflected in the following governing principles of the UPA government:

- To preserve, protect and promote social harmony and to enforce the law without fear or favour to deal with all obscurantist and fundamentalist elements who seek to disturb social amity and peace.

- To ensure that the economy grows at least 7–8 per cent per year in a sustained manner over a decade or more and in a manner that generates employment so that each family is assured of a safe and viable livelihood.
- To enhance the welfare and well being of farmers, farm labour and workers, particularly those in the unorganised sector, and assure a secure future for their families in every respect.
- To fully empower women politically, educationally, economically and legally.
- To provide for full equality of opportunity, particularly in education and employment for Scheduled Castes, Scheduled Tribes, OBCs and religious minorities.
- To unleash the creative energies of our entrepreneurs, businessmen, scientists, engineers and all other professionals and productive forces of society. (Srinivasan 2004' 3–4)

There is a 'solemn pledge of the UPA government to provide a government that is free of corruption, transparent, accountable and responsive at all times.' There is a commitment to the continuance of economic reforms that '[...] will be oriented to spreading and deepening rural prosperity and to bringing about a visible and tangible difference in the quality of life of ordinary citizens' (Srinivasan 2004).

Given the orientation of the UPA governing principles, Srinivasan notes:

> Other than pointing out the need for tripling the current level of FDI, and promising to protect national interest, particularly of farmers in all WTO negotiations and to use the flexibility in existing WTO agreements to protect Indian agriculture and industry fully, and to a play a proactive role in strengthening the solidarity of developing countries in the shape of G-20 in the CMP does not have much to say on external trade and investment issues. (Srinivasan 2004, 6–7)

Srinivasan concludes:

> The protectionist language of the CMP unfortunately is suggestive, *not* of India playing a proactive and aggressive role in resuming the Doha Round for reducing trade barriers everywhere, but of a return to its traditional defensive stance. This stance was futile in the past and would be in the future. (Srinivasan 2004, 19–20)

We can only hope that Srinivasan's conclusion is overly pessimistic, and that as the DDA negotiations unfold, the coalition government will recognise what India has to gain from the negotiations and can then implement the appropriate steps to pursue its interests in a forceful and proactive manner. Indeed, it seems fitting for us to conclude by citing the vision that Srinivasan has expressed of 'India's Legitimate Position in the Global Economic System':

> Undoubtedly, our greatest achievement since independence is that India continues to be a thriving democracy. We are the second most populous country and the largest democracy in the world. India was ranked by the World Bank as 162nd in terms of per capita gross national income (GNI) in 2001, and 12th in terms of absolute GNI; the corresponding ranks for China were 123rd and 6th, respectively. In world merchandise trade, we were the world's 30th largest exporter in 2002 with a share of 0.8%, having only slightly improved our position of 32nd largest trade in 1994 with a share of 0.6%. On the other hand, China significantly improved its position from being the 11th largest trader with a share of 2.9% in 1994 to the 5th with a share of 5.1%. Although it is not possible to set a specific number as our legitimate share of

world trade, there is no doubt our share is not commensurate with our being the 12th largest economy in the world. More importantly, we should aspire to be seen by the rest of the world as an economy from which they can buy a range of quality products at attractive prices, and to which they can sell their products in a stable market and policy environment with virtually no barriers. We should also be seen as an attractive destination for investment as well as a source for investment finance. The rupee should become a stable 'hard' currency which the rest of the world would gladly hold as part of their foreign exchange reserves. We should be playing a major role in the decision making organs of the WTO, World Bank and the IMF. In short, we have the potential to be, and should have the aspiration to become, one of the major global economic powers. On the other hand, a slow progress towards realizing our potential and, worse still, failure to realize it, would put paid our dreams of becoming a major world power and a permanent member of the United Nations Security Council. The world will then say of us...that 'India is an economy with great potential and is likely to remain so! (Srinivasan 2003, 3–4)

In the final analysis, as Panagariya (2002, 22) has noted, it is essential that India should think hard about the end game in the negotiations and then define its negotiating position accordingly.

POSTSCRIPT ON CONCLUDING THE DOHA ROUND

Since this chapter was originally written in 2004–5, the Doha negotiations have remained stalled (as of May 2010). The issue is what will be impact of the current economic crisis on the negotiations in the near future. While there was a flurry of small protectionist measures by the major trading countries during the crisis, these were much smaller than many feared and seems now to have abated. Governments apparently realise that it is in their interest to at least maintain the status quo. The situation demands that a conclusion to the Doha negotiations with developed country abandoning their demand for market access in developing and emerging economies. Emerging economies should be encouraged to take measures to reduce and bind their tariffs at lower levels and to narrow the range of exceptions of reductions to be allowed. In addition, there is a need for mutually beneficial liberalisation of trade in services, which may offer the largest potential benefits, given the importance of services in most countries, the role of services as inputs in the production process, and the fact that protection of services is significantly higher as compared to industrial products; putting services negations on a different negotiating track in order to concentrate on the Doha negotiations on agricultural and industrial products. Once these latter negotiations have been underway and may be nearing conclusion, services issues could then be addressed in a wider forum (see Hoekman, Martin and Mattoo, 2010).

Endnotes

[1] Welfare is measured by the 'equivalent variation,' which is defined as the amount of income that would have to be given or taken away from an economy instead of a change in policy in order to leave the economy as well off as it would be after the policy change has taken place. If the equivalent variation is positive, it is indicative of an improvement in economic welfare resulting from the policy change, in the sense that those who gain from the change could afford to compensate those who lose and still remain better off.

[2] As noted in Lawrence and Chadha (2004, 23–24):

The list of areas for Indian reform is long. It includes the need for additional trade and services liberalisation, customs reform, measures to attract foreign investment, privatisation and reform of public sector enterprises, adoption of competition and regulatory policies, liberalisation of small-scale sector reservation policies, labor market reforms, reforms of policies for sick industries, reform of relations between the central and state governments, changes in the investment environment for power, telecommunication, and transportation, tax reform and agricultural sector reform. Aside from specific actions in each area, there is a need to improve government performance by reducing corruption, increasing transparency, and providing opportunities for judicial review.

[3] Lawrence and Chadha (2004) provide an extensive discussion in support of a bilateral free trade agreement between the US and India that they argue could contribute to high-quality institutional reform of the Indian economy.

References

Bhagwati, Jagdish and Arvind Panagariya. 2003. 'Defensive Play Simply Won't Work', *Economic Times*, 29 August.
Bhattarcharjea, Aditya. 2003. 'Trade, Investment, and Competition Policy', in *India and the WTO*, edited by A. Mattoo and R. M. Stern, Washington DC: The World Bank and Oxford University Press.
Das, Satya P. 2003. 'An Indian Perspective on WTO Rules on Foreign Direct Investment', in *India and the WTO*, edited by A. Mattoo and R. M. Stern, Washington DC: The World Bank and Oxford University Press.
Deardorff, Alan V. and Robert M. Stern. 2004. 'Enhancing the Benefits for India and Other Developing Countries in the Doha Development Agenda Negotiations', paper presented at the conference on The WTO and India: Issues and Negotiating Strategies, Cotton College, Guwahati, Assam, 11–12 August.
Gulati, Ashok. 1999. *Agriculture and the New Trade Agenda in the WTO 2000 Negotiations: Interests and Options for India*, New Delhi: Institute for Economic Growth.
Hoekman, Bernard, Will Martin and Aaditya Mattoo. 2010. 'Conclude Doha: It Matters!', CEPR Discussion Paper DP7788.
Jaitley, Arun. 2003. 'Will We Step Out and Drive at Cancun?', *Economic Times*, 29 August.
Mattoo, Aaditya and Arvind Subramanian. 2003. 'India and the Multilateral Trading System post-Doha: Defensive or Proactive?', in *India and the WTO*, edited by A. Mattoo and R. M. Stern, Washington DC: The World Bank and Oxford University Press.
Office of the United States Trade Representative. 2004. 'Charting a Course to Prosperity: WTO Agrees on Detailed Plan to Open Markets, Expand Trade', *Trade Facts*, www.ustr.gov.
Panagariya, Arvind. 2002. 'India at Doha: Retrospect and Prospect', *Economic and Political Weekly*, vol. 37, no. 4, pp. 279–84.
Srinivasan, T. N. 2003. 'India in the Doha Round', *Financial Express*, 4 September 2003.
_____. 2004. 'Indian Economy, Economic Reforms and Change in Government', paper presented at the Annual Conference on the Indian Economy, Center for Research on Economic Development and Policy Reform (CREDPR), Stanford, 1 June.
Srivastava, Vivek. 2003. 'India's Accession to the Government Procurement Agreement: Identifying Costs and Benefits', in *India and the WTO*, edited by A. Mattoo and R. M. Stern, Washington DC: The World Bank and Oxford University Press.
WTO. 2004. 'The World Trade Organisation in Brief', www.wto.org, accessed on 1 July 2009.

6

India at Doha: Retrospect and Prospect[1]

Arvind Panagariya

Doha is behind us. But it is also ahead of us. With the Doha dust settled, however, it is a good time to reflect on what has been achieved, how it was achieved, what was India's role, how this role was perceived and why? It is also a good time to draw lessons from the experience since we must get down to the business of developing positions on the negotiations to which we have committed ourselves along with other WTO members in Doha.

The following sections will provide an overview of what was achieved in Doha; will outline India's negotiating stance and subject it to critical examination; will dissect carefully the origins of the scathing criticisms India received in the Western press and will conclude with lessons for the future.

WHAT WAS ACHIEVED IN DOHA?

The Doha Ministerial produced three key documents: (i) Decision on Implementation-Related Issues and Concerns, which addresses a number of complaints of developing countries with respect to the implementation of the Uruguay Round Agreement; (ii) Declaration on the TRIPS Agreement and Public Health, which weakens some of the provisions of the TRIPS Agreement; and (iii) Doha Ministerial Declaration, which outlines the work program for the new round.[2]

In assessing the Decision on Implementation-Related Issues and Concerns and the Declaration on the TRIPS Agreement and public health, it must be kept in mind that WTO decisions and declarations do not have the same legal status as the WTO agreements. It is not entirely clear what weight the WTO dispute settlement panels and the Appellate Body will give to these documents relative to the WTO Agreements. More concretely, in a WTO dispute, if the provisions in the Declaration on the TRIPS Agreement and public health suggest an outcome different from that in the TRIPS Agreement itself, we do not know which of the two documents will prevail. Against this background, let me offer a brief description of each of the three documents.

Decision on Implementation-Related Issues and Concerns

The decision on Implementation-Related Issues and Concerns had been pushed heavily by India with the backing of many developing countries, especially in Asia and Africa.

Spanning over eight single-space pages, it substantively offers several relatively minor, often inconsequential concessions to developing countries with respect to the implementation of the Uruguay Round agreements. I will discuss some of the provisions of the declaration in greater detail later in my critique of India's negotiating stance.

Declaration on the TRIPS Agreement and Public Health

The initiative for the Declaration on the TRIPS Agreement and Public Health was led by Brazil, India and South Africa, and it enjoyed wide support among developing countries.[3] Setting aside the caveat noted above on its legal standing relative to the TRIPS Agreement, the Declaration was a significant victory for developing countries. The Declaration acknowledges the primacy of the member countries' right to protect public health and promote access to medicines for all. More concretely, it recognises each member's 'right to grant compulsory licenses and the freedom to determine the grounds upon which such licenses are granted.' It also gives each member the 'right to determine what constitutes a national emergency or other circumstances of extreme urgency' for the purpose implementing the TRIPS Agreement (WTO 2001a).

The Doha Ministerial Declaration

The Doha Ministerial declaration is a long and complex document and I will not discuss the parts that are marginal to the future negotiations. The main negotiating agenda in the declaration can be divided into four parts: (i) trade liberalisation, (ii) trade and environment, (iii) WTO rules and (iv) the so-called 'Singapore issues' comprising investment, competition policy, trade facilitation and transparency in government procurement. Negotiations on the first three items constitute a single undertaking and are to be concluded by 1 January 2005. As regards the Singapore issues, negotiations on them may not start until after the fifth ministerial in 2003 and even then it is not a forgone conclusion. This is explained later in greater detail.

Trade Liberalisation

The trade liberalisation agenda is wide ranging and includes industrial goods, agricultural goods and services. The last two of these items have been under negotiation since 1 January 2000 as a part of the Uruguay Round built-in agenda. In the area of industrial goods, developing countries have complained since the Uruguay Round agreement that peak tariffs in developed countries were concentrated in labour-intensive goods, textiles and clothing, leather and leather products and footwear. The ministerial declaration gave this complaint due consideration by agreeing to negotiate reductions or elimination of tariffs including tariff peaks, high tariffs and tariff escalation, particularly in products of export interest to developing countries.

In the area of agriculture, the members committed themselves to comprehensive negotiations aimed at substantial improvements in market access, reductions, with a view to phasing out, in all forms of export subsidies and substantial reductions in trade-distorting domestic support measures. The EU vehemently opposed the insertion of the phrase 'with a view to phasing out' and agreed to it only after other members agreed to the qualification that the declaration would not prejudge the outcome of negotiations.

In services, the declaration recognised the ongoing negotiations since 1 January 2000 and referred to the large number of proposals submitted by members on a wide range of sectors and several horizontal issues including the movement of natural persons. It asked participants to submit initial requests for specific commitments by 30 June 2002 and initial offers by 31 March 2003.

Trade and Environment

The subject of environment has been under study at the WTO under the auspices of the Committee on Trade and Environment for sometime. But the Doha Declaration brought it into the negotiating agenda for the first time. India and most other developing countries had been opposed to bringing environment into the negotiating agenda in any form but the EU had insisted on it. Fortunately, the negotiating mandate was quite limited and unlikely to damage the interests of developing countries. It called for negotiations on (a) the relationship between existing WTO rules and specific trade obligations set out in multilateral environmental agreements (MEAs); (b) procedures for regular information exchange between MEA secretariats and the relevant WTO committees, and the criteria for the granting of observer status; and (c) the reduction of tariff and non-tariff barriers to environmental goods and services. With respect to the first subject, the Declaration explicitly noted that the negotiations shall not prejudice the WTO rights of any Member that is not a party to the MEA in question. This meant that trade sanctions by MEA signatories on non-signatories were ruled out.

WTO Rules

The Declaration opens WTO rules in three areas to negotiation: (1) anti-dumping, (2) subsidies and countervailing measures and (3) regional trade agreements. The first of these was a major concession by the US to Japan and the developing countries. Under the second item, members agreed to open up the issue of fisheries subsides, which was an important concession to developing countries. The third item was under discussion at WTO under the auspices of the Committee on Regional Trade Agreements; India was one of the countries to have urged its inclusion into the negotiating agenda.

Singapore Issues

EU had insisted on the inclusion of negotiations for multilateral agreements on investment, competition policy, trade facilitation and transparency in government procurement. A large number of developing countries, especially from Asia and Africa, had opposed the EU demand. India was the most vocal opponent and persisted in its demand to keep the four issues out of the negotiating agenda until the end. According to the deliberately vague compromise language in the declaration, members 'agree that negotiations will take place after the fifth Session of the Ministerial Conference on the basis of a decision to be taken, by explicit consensus, at that Session on modalities of negotiations (WTO 2001b).' Developed countries interpret this phrasing to mean that the fifth ministerial in 2003 is to decide only on the modalities while the agreement to kick off the negotiations is already in place. Many developing countries take the view that the decision on modalities by explicit consensus gives them a veto against the launch of the negotiations themselves. The following clarification, issued by Yussef Hussain Kamal, the Chair of the Conference, at the urging of India, favoured the latter interpretation. Its legal standing however was tenuous:

Let me say that with respect to the reference to an "explicit consensus" being needed ... for a decision to be taken at the Fifth Session of the Ministerial Conference, my understanding is that, at that Session, a decision would indeed need to be taken, by explicit consensus, before negotiations on Trade and Investment and Trade and Competition Policy, Transparency in Government Procurement, and Trade Facilitation could proceed. In my view, this would give each Member the right to take a position on modalities that would prevent negotiations from proceeding after the Fifth Session of the Ministerial Conference until that Member is prepared to join in an explicit consensus.(Kamal 2001)

INDIA'S NEGOTIATING STANCE

Negotiating positions are difficult to state precisely since they evolve continuously until an agreement is reached. Prior to the Doha meeting, India had publicly stated that it did not support the launch of a round that went beyond the built-in agenda of the Uruguay Round agreement. Yet, in the end, Commerce Minister Murasoli Maran not only supported a round that included some new issues but also wisely claimed its launch a victory for India.

Nevertheless, it can be safely asserted that India joined the talks leading up to the Doha Ministerial with a rather extreme position, taking a very hard line. India's position was most clearly outlined in the press brief entitled 'Why India is Opposing Negotiations on New Issues,' posted on the Ministry of Commerce website and issued by Press Information Bureau, Government of India on 7 November 2001 (See Chapter 3).

The title of this brief made clear India's unequivocal opposition to the expansion of the negotiating agenda beyond the built-in Uruguay Round agenda, which included market access negotiations in agriculture and services and reviews of and negotiations on some narrowly specified aspects of a small number of Uruguay Round agreements. But the contents of the press brief listed more explicitly the areas India opposed going into the Doha meeting: investment, competition policy, transparency in government procurement, trade facilitation, environment, labour and industrial tariffs. In the case of investment and competition policy, the brief expressed India's opposition to even 'plurilateral' agreements within the WTO.

This position was more or less reiterated in the statement delivered by Maran at Doha on behalf of India. In a key paragraph of the statement, he noted, 'Rather than charting a divisive course in unknown waters, let this Conference provide a strong impetus to the on-going negotiations on agriculture and services, and the various mandated reviews that by themselves form a substantial work programme and have explicit consensus.' Later, he expressed explicit opposition to the inclusion of the so-called Singapore issues into the agenda: 'In the areas of Investment, Competition, Trade Facilitation or Transparency in Government Procurement, basic questions remain even on the need for a multilateral agreement.'

The statement by Maran is not explicit on either support for or opposition to the negotiations on market access in industrial goods. The only paragraph dealing with this subject states,

> In relation to market access, even after all the Uruguay Round concessions have been implemented by industrialized countries, significant trade barriers in the form of tariff peaks and tariff escalation continue to affect many developing country exports.

These will clearly need to be squarely addressed. Meanwhile, sensitive industries in developing countries including small scale industries sustaining a large labour force cannot be allowed to be destroyed.(Maran 2001)

Since tariff peaks and tariff escalation could not be addressed outside of new negotiations, this statement would seem to suggest support for the inclusion of industrial tariffs into the negotiating agenda. Yet, in the absence of an explicit statement to that effect and the clear opposition expressed in the 7 November 2001 brief—'We are not convinced about the need for tariff negotiations when even Uruguay Round phase-out has not been yet completed for certain products', an unambiguous conclusion to this effect cannot be drawn.

The fact that the draft ministerial declaration presented at Doha at the opening of the conference did not place the negotiations on industrial tariffs into square brackets, and used to signal disagreement on the part of some members, it may also suggest that all countries including India were on board in this area. But again, this was not a litmus test: Maran himself lamented at the beginning of his statement that the draft Ministerial declaration is 'negation of all that was said by a significant number of developing countries and least-developing countries.'

Finally, India pushed hard for both implementation issues and the weakening of the TRIPS Agreement in the area of public health and medicines. With regard to the former, starting prior to the Seattle Ministerial, India had begun to lobby heavily for an agreement. This push culminated in the Decision on Implementation-Related Issues and Concerns at Doha. With respect to the TRIPS Agreement, along with Brazil and South Africa, India took the position that the TRIPS Agreement should be interpreted and implemented in a manner supportive of WTO Members' right to protect public health and ensure access to medicines for all. This effort led to the Doha Declaration on the TRIPS Agreement and Public Health.

Two lesser demands related to intellectual property that Maran also put on the table in his Doha statement were the extension of geographical indications to products other than wines and spirits and restrictions on the misappropriation of the biological and genetic resources and traditional knowledge of the developing countries. It is not clear whether these were serious demands or were intended merely to satisfy certain domestic lobbies.

QUESTIONING INDIA'S STANCE

Let me begin by noting that Maran's opposition to the inclusion of the Singapore issues into the negotiating agenda is quite defensible. I have written on this subject in greater detail elsewhere and I will not repeat it here (Panagariya 2000). But let me note two key points. First, if multilateral agreements on investment, competition policy, trade facilitation and transparency in government procurement are forged, it is the developing countries that will have to undertake substantial new obligations. It is not immediately clear why these countries should subject themselves to such obligations without systematic reciprocal commitments by developed countries. More importantly, many developing countries may not be able to fulfill these obligations and will be exposed to the risk of trade sanctions and hence loss of market access in goods and services. Second, in so far as the investment agreement is concerned, the slow pace of liberalisation in the area of services, which inevitably require opening the market to foreign investment and labour movements, indicates that countries find it much harder to open factor markets than goods markets.

The opposition to WTO agreements on investment, competition policy, trade facilitation and transparency in government procurement is not to imply opposition to liberalising policy changes in these areas. For instance, foreign investment liberalisation and trade facilitation are not only eminently sensible policies for developing countries but also a part of their ongoing policy reforms. Likewise, while competition policy at the national level exists in many developing countries, transparency is desirable in all aspects of the government business including procurement. Nevertheless, acceptance of such obligations under a WTO agreement before these countries are able to implement them in the form required by WTO agreements places their access to markets in goods and services at risk. For instance, time bound clearance of goods at the border sought under trade facilitation may be beneficial (though even here the country must decide whether its scarce resources should be deployed to speed up the internal movement of goods or at the movement the border) but countries have to be sure that they can implement them before signing on to a WTO agreement to this effect. We have already seen that the TRIPS obligations have been sufficiently onerous that the least developed countries had to be given an extra ten years of reprieve under the Doha Declaration on the TRIPS Agreement and Public Health. But for this extension, many of them would have faced the prospects of trade sanctions.

While India's opposition to the Singapore issues is, thus, defensible, at least three aspects of its stance at Doha remain disturbing: (i) failure to lend unequivocal support to liberalisation in industrial products and, indeed, outright opposition to such liberalisation where India was concerned; (ii) unduly large dispensation of the negotiating capital on the virtually empty box of implementation issues; and (iii) posturing that seemed to convey the impression that India was opposed to the launch of the round altogether. Let me elaborate on each of these points.

Tariffs on Industrial Products

Further liberalisation in industrial products is in India's own interest. Compared to virtually every major, economically resilient country, India's industrial tariffs remain astronomically high. As witnessed by our own experience during 1990s, there is much to be gained in terms of productive efficiency and benefits of consumers through further liberalisation. Politically, Finance Minister Yashwant Sinha had publicly stated his commitment to bringing the top tariff rate from the current level of 35 per cent to 20 per cent by the year 2004. By making such tariff reductions a part of a future WTO round, we only stand to double our benefits by gaining greater access to the US and EU markets as a part of an overall bargain.

Instead, India implicitly took the position that while developed countries must eliminate tariff peaks, India should not be asked to liberalise any further. This meant asking developed countries to eliminate tariff peaks unilaterally. While there is much to be said for unilateral liberalisation, in practice, large countries have only rarely lowered their tariffs unilaterally. As such the demand by India was unrealistic. Indeed, tariff peaks in textiles and clothing exist today not because developed countries are inherently inclined towards discrimination against imports from developing countries. Instead, they exist because until recently, developing countries chose not to participate in multilateral negotiations in any meaningful way. As a result, liberalising bargains were limited to developed countries and hence the products exported principally by the developing countries remained subject to the previous high levels of protection (Bhagwati and Panagariya 2002).

Indeed, when developing countries did finally join the negotiations actively in the Uruguay Round, they got the commitment from developed countries to phase out the Multi-fiber Arrangement (MFA) and thus return this sector to the full discipline of the General Agreement on tariffs and Trade (GATT). There remain complaints that developed countries have back loaded the liberalisation, pushing much of the substantive liberalisation to the last two installments due on January 1, 2003 and January 1, 2005. But fearing that less efficient suppliers—India among them—might lose rather than gain market share with the end of the quotas, this is precisely what developing countries had bargained.

Implementation Issues

India pushed heavily a number of demands under the rubric of "implementation issues". In my personal judgment, this was a tactical mistake. To be sure, there are more than 50 paragraphs in the declaration listing large number of items. But these are lot of nothings that do not add up to something. Substantive concessions in the document are few and far between and surely not enough to justify more than two years worth of negotiating capital which was spent to achieve them. Indeed, somewhat perversely, the decision allows developed countries to convey the impression that having conceded to the demands of developing countries without insisting on something in return they have been generous.

The first point to remember while evaluating the achievements in this area is that, as noted earlier, WTO decisions do not enjoy quite the same legal status as WTO agreements. While ruling on a dispute, dispute settlement panels and the Appellate Body are likely to rely principally on the WTO agreements rather than decisions. But even leaving that consideration aside, the decision on Implementation-Related Issues and Concerns is long on the expression of good intentions but short on actual commitments.

As an example, consider what may be the most substantive part of the Decision: the provisions relating to the implementation of the Uruguay Round ATC. There are three items in this part of the Decision: (i) developed country members should effectively utilise the provisions in the ATC for early elimination of quota restrictions; (ii) they should exercise particular consideration before initiating antidumping investigations of textile and clothing exports from developing countries previously subject to quantitative restrictions under ATC for a period of two years; and (iii) they shall notify any changes in their rules of origin concerning products falling under the coverage of the Agreement to the Committee on Rules of Origin which may decide to examine them.

These provisions add little to what exists in ATC currently. Provision (i) gives developing countries no extra leeway in challenging developed countries on the speed of elimination of quota restrictions over and above that granted by ATC. Precisely how, except as already provided in ATC, is one to determine that a country has failed to use the provisions relating to the elimination of quotas 'effectively'? Likewise, how is it to be determined that a country did not exercise 'particular consideration' before initiating antidumping investigation? The provision on the rules of origin is even less of a concession than the preceding two.

The only substantive concession in the area of textiles and clothing sought by developing countries as a part of implementation issues was a 'growth-on-growth' provision amounting to the compounding of the annual growth of quotas. Currently, textiles and clothing quotas are allowed to grow annually at a pre-specified rate with the growth rate applied to the initial base in the bilateral quota agreement. Developing countries had sought that growth be built on not just that base but also on growth in the previous years. However, this concession was not granted in the decision. Instead, it was referred to the Council for Trade in Goods for examination and recommendation by 31 July 2002.

The view that the decision carries few substantive benefits for developing countries is perhaps not particularly contentious. Even prior to its finalisation in Doha, Abdul Razak Dawood, Pakistan's minister for dommerce, Industries and production, who was India's ally in pushing for the decision, noted in the official statement of his government: 'The package of implementation measures proposed for adoption at Doha is almost a bare cupboard. Some major countries want to take away what little it contains—such as the provision for 'growth on growth' in textiles(Dawood 2001).'

Posturing Against the Round

With less than 1 per cent share in the world trade, India would have had almost insignificant power to influence the negotiations under normal circumstances. But two factors, both unique to Doha, made India a player of some significance. First, in the wake of the 11 September events, Bush administration had assigned the launch of a new round the highest priority. In retrospect, it is fair to speculate that Robert Zoellick, the USTR, arrived in Doha with the intention not to return home empty handed. This fact gave each country, including India, some leverage. This was confirmed by the fact that the United States gave special concessions to virtually all members that they possibly could.

Second, repeated assertions by both the US and EU that the next round must be a development round left them boxed in their own rhetoric: they would not look good launching a development round without the endorsement of a poor country with one billion people. A development round that left out one fifth of the humanity would be a joke. Bringing India on board was essential.

Given these facts and India's stance prior to the arrival at Doha, there was some measure of discomfort on the part of some developed countries in Doha that India might become the ultimate stumbling block to the launch of the new round. Therefore, India already ran the risk that as a pressure tactic, developed countries would try to discredit it as obstructionist. By failing to take a clear public stance in favour of a round that will squarely focus on trade liberalisation in all sectors and conveying it forcefully to the press and returning repeatedly to the theme of restricting the negotiations to the Uruguay Round built-in agenda and implementation issues, India made itself highly vulnerable to the charge of obstructionism.

Lest this diagnosis should appear an afterthought, let me remind that many, including the author, had advocated the strategy of supporting aggressively a trade liberalisation round well before the Doha meeting. I cannot resist reproducing some key passages from my monthly column in the Economic Times:

> Two years ago, prior to the WTO ministerial in Seattle, I had argued that developing countries should support a minimalist negotiating agenda that includes the UR built-in agenda plus trade liberalisation in industrial goods. The built-in agenda requires negotiations in agriculture and services and reviews of certain aspects of the Dispute Settlement Understanding and Agreement on TRIPS. This agenda still makes sense for India.
>
> As a part of its economic reforms, India is likely to continue liberalising its trade in industrial goods, agriculture and services. The benefit from this liberalisation can be greatly leveraged by pursuing it in the context of a multilateral negotiation. This way,

we will benefit not only from our own liberalisation but from the liberalisation of our trading partners as well. The dividend on the latter is double nowadays since it helps dilute trade preferences which have proliferated lately and discriminate against our exports in North America, Europe and other parts of the world. (Panagariya 2001)

I went on to conclude thus:

It is also important to recognize that most developing countries do not want a round that includes labour standards in any form whatsoever. Prospects for a round consistent with this goal have never been better. As a part of the mandate for the next round, developing countries may be able to assign this subject to the International Labour Organization once and for all.

This leaves principally the subjects of investment, competition policy and environment and trade on which the European Union is insistent. Even here, compromise may be possible. One option is to place these latter subjects on a second track and make participation in negotiations on issues on the second track optional. Alternatively, sufficiently tight wording could be chosen to limit the scope of negotiations in these areas.

The key element of our strategy must be to identify attainable objectives that best serve our interests. The negotiating strategy should be then targeted to achieve these objectives. (Panagariya 2001)

QUESTIONING THE COVERAGE IN THE WESTERN PRESS

During and immediately after the Doha meeting, India was subject to scathing criticism by the Western news media. The *Financial Times* (15 November 2001) called the country the 'worst villain' and 'the only real loser,' the *Economist* (17 November 2001) chastised it for having 'almost scuttled' the launch of the round and the *Wall Street Journal* (16 November 2001) described Maran as 'the man who rattled the WTO in Doha'. How do we explain this hostile treatment?

To be sure, India was partly responsible. By giving the distinct impression publicly that it was against negotiations beyond the Uruguay Round built-in agenda, even if this may not have been its actual negotiating position behind the scenes, India made itself vulnerable to these criticisms. But this is only half the story. Let me explain why.

While Maran was surely the most vocal opponent of the Singapore issues, he was scarcely alone. The US itself did not want the expansionist agenda but acquiesced to EU demand as a price of launching the round. More importantly, Egypt, Pakistan, Indonesia, Malaysia, Thailand, Nigeria, Kenya, and a host of other countries from Africa and Asia had expressed unequivocal opposition to the inclusion of these issues in the negotiating agenda. The main difference between these countries and India was that having been promised their respective favourite concessions, they were willing to go along with the compromise worked out by the US and EU on the Singapore issues, while India chose to stick to its original position.

In view of the fact that five years earlier India had accepted Singapore issues as study topics in the Singapore Declaration on the condition that negotiations on them will be launched by 'explicit consensus', Maran cannot be faulted for demanding the continuation of this provision in the Doha Declaration. After all, EU had also insisted on the language on the phase out of export subsidies until end and, indeed, delayed the Doha ministerial by almost a full day. Likewise, a day earlier, African, Caribbbean and Pacific (ACP) countries, which had been demanding an Article I waiver for their preferential Cotonou trade arrangement with EU, had threatened to walk out of the negotiations if the waiver was not granted to them. In this last case, technically the issue was not even formally linked to the ministerial package. Maran's misfortune was that the issue that concerned him most lingered till the end. That made him the last signatory to the Doha Declaration, leaving the distinct impression that he, and not Pascal Lamy of EU, was to be blamed for the delay.

There is one further disadvantage India faced in Doha in so far as its public image was concerned. At least technically speaking, the WTO secretariat is supposed to act as a neutral facilitator, a clearinghouse of sorts, for the negotiations. Nevertheless, the success of its Director General is ultimately measured by his ability to advance the negotiations. Therefore, Mike Moore, who was attending his last ministerial meeting as director feneral, had a heavy stake in the launch of the round. This fact made the WTO Secretariat potentially unsympathetic to a member viewed as a threat to the launch of the round.

Additionally, bureaucracies are inherently expansionist. Like the TRIPS agreement, the Singapore issues offer a large scope for the expansion of the policy space over which WTO can have its sway. This makes the WTO bureaucracy naturally inclined towards the inclusion of the Singapore issues into the negotiating agenda. This natural inclination is complemented by the location of WTO in Geneva. The staff can scarcely escape what they observe in their backyards: EU's fervor for the expansionist agenda.

These factors made India potentially a target of criticism by WTO staff in their informal contacts with the press. Lest this might appear entirely speculative, let me offer a concrete example. Following the attacks on India in the *Financial Times*, Per Gahrton, member of the European Parliament (Greens, Sweden) wrote in a letter to the newspaper:

> Sir, in your editorial on the World Trade Organization meeting in Doha (November 15), you named India as the "villain" of the meeting.
>
> Having followed the deliberations as a member of the European parliament delegation I would rather consider Mr Maran, head of the Indian delegation, as a defeated hero of a common Third World cause. I would propose another candidate for the pejorative label: Pascal Lamy, trade commissioner of the European Union.
>
> On the morning of the last official day of negotiations, Mr Lamy admitted to MEPs that the EU "is the problem", being at loggerheads with others on several crucial points, including its defense for the protectionist interests of certain member countries, such as agriculture, fisheries and textiles. (Gahrton 2001)

Astonishingly, four days later, Mike Moore came to the defense of Pascal Lamy. In a letter published in the *Financial Times* and reproduced below in its entirety, Moore wrote:

> Sir, It has not been my practice to involve myself in domestic political differences but the sheer magnitude of the injustice in the letter of November 24 from Per Gahrton, an MEP at the Doha ministerial, attacking Pascal Lamy, the European Union trade commissioner, has moved me to comment.
>
> It was Mr Lamy who led the battle for market access for least developed countries (Everything But Arms). Commissioner Lamy's role in brokering the waiver for African, Caribbean and Pacific (ACP) countries on preferential access to the EU market was widely acclaimed and the first ministers speaking in favor of the deal were from Africa. It was Mr Lamy who fought for and won advances on trade and the environment,

public access to medicines and the trade-related intellectual property rights agreement. He fought but was less successful on labour issues. He has led on matters of internal governance and transparency and the involvement of the World Trade Organization and civil society.

Europe had other agenda items that it promoted one way or another. Mr. Gahrton must have been at a different ministerial from the rest of us. (Moore 2001)

In defending Lamy, Mike Moore seemed to also defend his agenda extending to environment and labour, something that has been inimical to the position of virtually all developing countries. Additionally, by neither coming to Maran's defense following the original attacks on him in the *Financial Times* nor stating a single kind word for him while aggressively defending Lamy, he also conveyed a clear preference for the latter's position over Maran's. This is a far cry from what WTO is supposed to do: be an honest broker and clearinghouse for its member countries.

CONCLUDING REMARKS: THE WAY FORWARD

Continued asymmetries between the influence of the rich and poor countries notwithstanding, WTO is by far our best hope for protecting our trading rights. It is not a 'necessary evil' as our leaders sometimes describe it; instead, it is a godsend. A key condition for faster economic growth in countries such as India is guaranteed access to open world markets. And the only institution that can deliver this access is WTO. In spite of the pressures we face from the rich countries through WTO as reflected, for example, in the demand for trade-labour link, WTO remains the best guarantor of our trading rights. Anyone who thinks otherwise only need to contemplate a world without WTO. In that world, rich countries would not need to *demand* the trade-labour link; they will simply *impose* it. It is the power of the WTO rules that protects smaller nations from unilateral trade sanctions by rich and powerful nations.

In developing our future negotiating positions, we need to think far more systematically than we seem to have done to-date. At least three strategic conclusions can be drawn from the Uruguay Round and Doha experiences. First, we need to consider direct benefits for us of any demands that we put forward in the negotiations. Any time we demand something, we are using up our negotiating capital and we must be sure that there is a commensurate benefit in store for us. For example, consider our demand for growth-on-growth of MFA quotas. Did we analyse if this would generate benefits for us? From the information I have been able to collect, during the last two years, most of our MFA quotas have remained underutilised, presumably because of our high costs of production. Therefore, *prima facie* it is questionable whether we would have been able to export more, had developed countries conceded the growth-on-growth demand. On the contrary, increased exports by other countries under faster quota expansion would have even lowered the prices, making us relatively less competitive. Did we even consider such calculations?

In the same vein, we have made demands for the extension of protection to geographical indications for products other than wines and spirits and for rules against misappropriation of the traditional knowledge and genetic resources? How do these demands square with our complaints against the very inclusion of intellectual property rights into the WTO? Have we done the cost-benefit analysis of expanding intellectual property protection in these areas?

Second, diplomacy requires that we define our negotiating position positively rather than negatively. Our approach should be to state clearly the agenda on which we are willing to support a round. Only after we have stated our affirmative position clearly, should we proceed to the negative, with clear reasons for our objections. Without precluding an inflexible position on certain issues such as trade-labour link, it also does not make sense for us to lock ourselves publicly into a very inflexible overall position prior to the round. Countries such as Malaysia, Thailand, Pakistan, Nigeria and Egypt had taken positions quite similar to ours in their official statements but avoided giving the impressions of inflexibility in their public statements.

Finally and most importantly, prior to defining the negotiating position, we must think hard about the end game. For example, before we took the hard-line position in Doha, we should have asked ourselves: are we willing to walk out of the negotiations even if we are the only country to do so and if yes at what point? Is trade-labour link the make or break issue? Or is it the environment? Or Singapore issues? Or trade liberalisation in industrial goods? We should have defined our negotiating position based on the answers to these questions. By repeatedly staking a position that is far from what we eventually accept, as has been the case in the Uruguay Round agreement and the Doha Declaration, we lose credibility in the future negotiations and risk being isolated.

This risk has now increased manifold with the entry of China into WTO. As the largest developing country in terms of population, India enjoyed some advantage in the past negotiations. Now it will have to share this advantage with China. For instance, if China decides to take an essentially pro-negotiations stance towards the Singapore issues, it is unlikely that India will be able to stop negotiations on them from proceeding despite the 'explicit consensus' provision in the Doha Declaration. Are we willing to walk out of negotiations then even if we are the only country to do so? Our negotiators must think through that question before they arrive in Mexico in 2003 for the fifth WTO ministerial.

A POSTSCRIPT (25 FEBRUARY 2007)

Much has changed during the five years since I had originally written this article. Commerce Minister Murasoli Maran who had valiantly fought against the inclusion of the Singapore issues in the Doha Declaration passed away on 23 November 2003. But he scored a victory even as he fought prolonged illness first at the Methodist Hospital in Houston, Texas from November 2002 to September 2003 and later at the Apollo Hospital in Chennai. The vague wording upon which he had insisted in the Doha Declaration allowed the developing countries to kill three of the four Singapore issues at the WTO ministerial meeting in Cancun. Only the relatively benign issue of trade facilitation among the Singapore issues survived on the negotiating agenda. As one of a tiny minority of Maran's defenders on this score immediately following his return from Doha, I too am vindicated by his victory.

In the last five years, India has emerged as a major player in the Doha negotiations. With the emergence of the developing country grouping G-20, the developing countries came of age at Cancun. The traditional Quad countries—the US, EU, Japan and Canada—that called the shots in the past negotiating rounds have been essentially replaced by what I call the New Quad—the USA, EU, India and Brazil.

In turn, India has risen to the occasion playing its role responsibly. While firm in his stance, the current commerce minister, Kamal Nath, has been a constructive player at the various negotiating meetings. He has consistently stated that India will give its share of concessions in industrial products and services but cannot be expected to open up its agriculture. My personal view is that an agreement that brings the EU and US agricultural subsidies and tariffs considerably down will go a long way towards making the Indian farmers competitive on the world markets in a variety of agricultural products. Therefore, some opening up in agriculture by India as a part of a future Doha agreement will be to its advantage.

Nevertheless, Nath's position is entirely defensible on political grounds. When the Doha Round was launched, the developing countries were consistently told that agricultural protectionism was a problem of the developed countries and that they were the ones in need of offering concessions in this sector. Therefore, the expectation in the developing countries was that their concessions would be largely limited to industrial products and services. The politicians have done no groundwork to prepare the public for liberalisation in agriculture. This makes genuine agricultural liberalisation a political hot potato. Besides, even developed countries are currently far from placing major concessions in agriculture on the table. The US position has been particularly odd: it demands an ambitious agreement which implies large concessions by other countries without matching concessions by the US!

The original deadline for the conclusion of the Doha Round has passed. But this in itself is neither surprising nor significant. No round in the recent years has concluded in less than five years. As such the original deadline itself was unrealistic. But there is a catch—the Trade Promotion Authority (TPA) of the USTR would expire at the end of June 2007. Completion of the round is now a virtual physical impossibility without some the renewal of the TPA in some form.

There are signs that the US Congress may renew the TPA but with the requirement that the future agreements have tougher provisions for labour standards. The position of India in this respect is clear, however: it rejects any agreement that links trade and labour standards. Therefore, the US will still have to limit its demands for higher labour standards to bilateral dree trade area agreements if it wants the Doha round to come to a successful conclusion.

At the time of writing, the expectations of progress towards an agreement had risen considerably. The US is keen to make progress and has been in active negotiations with the EU to sort out its differences with the EU, especially on agriculture. If this is accomplished the burden is likely to shift to India regarding what concessions, if any, it is willing to grant in agriculture. We shall see.

Endnotes

[1] An earlier version of this paper was published in the *Economic and Political Weekly*, vol.37, no.4, 26 January–1 February 2002. I would like to thank Jagdish Bhagwati for numerous helpful discussions and comments on an earlier draft of the original paper.

[2] Doha also produced two waivers, a GATT Article XIII waiver for the EC banana regime and a GATT Article I waiver for the ACP-EC Partnership (Cotonou) Agreement. These waivers have no direct link to the ministerial declaration and could have been handled within the normal WTO procedures. But they had to be moved forward to Doha to get support of

the ACP countries for the round. A final document on which agreement had been reached in Doha but was not issued until 20 November 2001 deals with procedures for extension of Article 27.4 of the Subsidies and Countervailing Measures Agreement for certain developing member countries. This document is also without direct bearing on the ministerial declaration.

[3] Contrary to the impression conveyed in some news reports in the Western media, India did play a significant role in pushing the declaration. It was one of the eight WTO members—four developing and four developed—which drafted the final compromise language of the document. The eight countries in the group were Brazil, India, Kenya, Zimbabwe, Canada, the EU, New Zealand, and the US. South Africa was missing from the list presumably because it has the developed country status in WTO though it was with developing countries on this issue.

References

Bhagwati, Jagdish and Arvind Panagariya. 2002. 'Wanted: Jubilee 2010, Dismantling Protection', *OECD Observer*, no. 231/232, 27–29 May.

Dawood, Abdul Razak. 2001. Statement delivered by H. E. Mr Abdul Razak Dawood, Minister for Commerce, Industries and Production at the WTO Ministerial Conference, Doha, 10 November, WTO Document no. WT/MIN(01)/ST/6.

Kamal, Yussef Hussain. 2001. Speech delivered by Yussef Hussain Kamal, Finance Minister of Qatar and the Chair of the WTO Ministerial Conference at the closing plenary session, Doha, 14 November.

Gahrton, Per. 2001. 'Letter to the Editor', *Financial Times*, 24 November.

Maran, Murasoli. 2001. Statement delivered by Murasoli Maran, Honourable Minister of Commerce and Industry at the WTO Ministerial Conference, Doha, 10 November, WTO Document no. WT/MIN(01)/ST/10.

Moore, Mike. 2001. 'Letter to the Editor', *Financial Times*, 28 November.

Panagariya, Arvind. 2000. *The Millennium Round and Developing Countries: Negotiating Strategies and Areas of Benefits*, G-24 Discussion Paper Series, Cambridge and Mass.: UNCTAD and Center for International Development, University of Harvard.

WTO. 2001a. 'Declaration on the Trips Agreement and Public Health', adopted by the Ministerial Conference of the WTO, WTO Document no. WT/MIN(01)/DEC/2.

——— 2001b. 'Doha Ministerial Declaration', WTO Document no. WT/MIN(01)/DEC/W/1.

Section III

Market Access: Agriculture, Manufactures and Textiles

7
WTO Agriculture Negotiations and India

Ramesh Chand

BACKGROUND

Agriculture was included in the multilateral trade agreement (GATT) for the first time in the Uruguay Round and now it is firmly rooted in the WTO framework. Article XX of the Uruguay Round agreement on agriculture required WTO members to review the agreement after about five years, that is, by the end of 1999 or beginning of 2000, for continuing the reforms started with the UR. This gave opportunity to review the effect of implementation of Uruguay Round AOA, and in the light of that experience move further towards establishing a free, fair, and market oriented agricultural trading system. Negotiations for the next round of AOA were started in March 2000 and have entered tenth year now. During this period, these negotiations passed through several phases but could not reach a final agreement. The first phase began in early 2000 and ended with the stock taking meeting on 26–27 March 2001. About 90 per cent of the member governments, individually and/or in groups, submitted 45 proposals and three technical documents containing their starting position for the negotiations. India took active interest in putting forth its views on various issues and proposals for the new AOA and submitted a couple of proposals on its own and also with a group of some other developing countries. Likewise, other countries also submitted their proposals and views on various aspects related to negotiating agenda. These proposals and views were discussed in series of informal meetings and special sessions. This enabled WTO members to understand the position of each other and the complexities involved in reaching consensus on rules and commitments in agriculture. Specific proposals were developed and submitted by members to the WTO Secretariat during 2001–2, based on which the fourth WTO ministerial conference was held in Doha, on 9–14 November 2001, to finalise the modalities for fresh negotiations. The Doha Declaration had laid down the new mandate (Doha Mandate) and set following deadlines for further negotiations and conclusion of the round:

- Formulas and other modalities for commitments by the participating countries: 31 March 2003
- Comprehensive draft commitments of the countries: before fifth ministerial conference, 10–14 September 2003, in Cancun
- Stock taking: fifth ministerial conference, 10–14 September 2003 in Cancun
- Deadline: by 1January 2005.

The modalities programme began with technical work on three elements of AOA, namely, domestic support, market access, and export subsidies/competition. Special treatment for developing countries was treated as an integral part of all the three pillars of AOA and certain non-trade concerns were also included. Again, several meetings and sessions were held and efforts were made to come out with a consensus draft on modalities for further discussion by the deadline of 31 March 2003. But, positions taken by different members remained wide apart and no consensus could be reached on the draft on modalities, and the deadline passed. The differences prevailed over almost all areas like various boxes of domestic support, tariff, tariff quotas, export subsidies and credits, food aid, various provisions for developing countries. In addition, countries that recently joined WTO asked for certain provisions.

Subsequently, agriculture and Doha agenda issues were brought together for the 11–15 September Cancun Ministerial Conference. Intense discussions were held again and there was some narrowing down of position but not enough to reach consensus. The impasse continued for six months till March 2004. In the meantime several realignments took place among members and various positions were, by and large, represented by following: (i) G-20 group of developing countries that include Brazil, India, South Africa and Pakistan (ii) G-33 group led by Indonesia including Pakistan and Sri Lanka and pressing for special and differential treatment for developing countries (iii) the African group (iv) the African-Carribean-Pacific group (v) G-10 mainly developed countries including Switzerland, Norway, Japan (vi) G-90 comprising small, poor countries, less developed countries (LDC), African, Carribean and Pacific (ACP), and African groups (vii) USA and (viii) EU. Fresh round of negotiations on agriculture was taken up during 22–26 March 2004. There have also been interactions and discussions within countries, between countries, and between capitals and the Geneva process.

While serious differences persisted among members, WTO headquarters continued efforts to strike a common ground. After intense discussion for one week, WTO General Council came up with some broad agreement on a framework for further negotiations in the meeting of General Council that took place in the last week of July 2004. This framework, known as the 'July Package' was again examined by members and different position papers were prepared again by group of countries and by individual countries. In the aftermath of the July Package, a group of developing countries known as G-20, became quite strong and started articulating interests of developing countries quite forcefully. G-20 succeeded in pushing some of its important agenda and a new element has been introduced in the discussion on domestic support, which deals with domestic support by putting it in three to four different bands irrespective of size of country or volume of production. Different elements of the July Package took up the proposal of G-20, views of the US, EU and other groupings in the Ministerial meeting held in Hong Kong, 13–18 December 2005. However, once again, no consensus could be reached on the modalities, even though there was some convergence in positions taken by major groups.

Obviously, the reason for the delay in concluding the new round was the sharp differences among members on various aspects of AOA. Implementation of the Uruguay Round commitments has been a tough task for several member countries and it has exposed vulnerability of various segments of agriculture to global market forces. In most of the cases, expectations placed in the Uruguay Round AOA or promises related to this did not materialise. There is a widespread view that the Uruguay Round was a disappointment

(Grimwade 2004). The promise was that trade liberalisation and implementation of the AOA would bring large benefits to developing countries through improved access to the markets of the developed countries, increased trade and better pricing environment for tropical and other products of interest to developing countries. However, there was a distinction between reality and the promise. The biggest challenge to the agriculture of developing countries, in the post-WTO period, was posed by unprecedented and unforeseen decline in international agricultural prices. Because of this, exports of developing countries were badly hit and several countries were taken aback by import influx of those commodities in which they thought they had strong competitive edge. This caused adverse impact on farmers' income and employment. Developed countries could safeguard their agriculture against low global prices by providing huge support to their farmers but developing countries neither had mechanism nor resources to protect their agriculture and farmers against such adverse trading and pricing environment. The entire blame for this outcome is put on the Uruguay Round AOA. There is a feeling that developing countries did not bargain properly in the Uruguay Round and developed countries secured the balance of the AOA in their favour. Besides being discriminatory, the agreement is said to be ably manipulated by developed countries to benefit their agriculture at the cost of developing countries. Such threats and fears are further reinforced by the World Bank study (2002), which predicts that the greatest beneficiaries of Doha Round of WTO negotiations would be the rich economies of Western Europe. This time the member countries have turned highly conscious and are very careful about the minute details of various provisions of any future AOA and they are trying hard to protect their interests adequately (Finger 2001 and Finger and Nogues 2002). This has led to hardening of positions particularly relating to high level of domestic support and export subsidies in OECD countries, access to market of developed countries, and S&DT.

This paper analyses the implications of various proposals in the Hong Kong Ministerial for Indian agriculture and suggests broad agenda that India should follow in the future negotiations. The paper begins by looking at the changes in agricultural trade associated with the implementation of WTO AOA, which came into effect on 1 January 1995. It discusses the challenges thrown by WTO and how India adjusted to the global liberalisation in agriculture. This is followed by Indian perspective on main elements of AOA. The next section discusses the ministerial declaration adopted in Hong Kong round in December 2005 and discusses its implications. Last section proposes the agenda that India should follow and push in the future and final negotiations on AOA.

AGRICULTURE TRADE: BEFORE AND AFTER WTO

Implementation of the Uruguay Round AOA started from 1 January 1995. India, by then, had already initiated liberalisation of its economy and trade with economic reforms in June 1991. As a part of these reforms India adjusted its exchange rate to market rate and relaxed restrictions on agricultural exports. This created a favourable environment for agricultural exports. From 1993–94, agricultural exports started increasing in leaps and bounds. Export earnings doubled in three years between 1992–93 and 1995–96. Imports also increased at almost the same pace and net surplus generated by agriculture trade increased from USD 2 billion during 1992–93 to USD 4.33 billion during 1995–96 (Table 7.1).

Post-WTO Trade Performance

High growth in agricultural exports that resulted from domestic liberalisation during 1992–93 to 1994–95, witnessed further increase in the initial years of WTO and reached historical peak of USD 6.8 billion in 1996–97. However, after 1996–97 earnings from agricultural exports started moving downward (Table 7.1). This happened despite further liberalisation in agricultural exports as a part of Export-Import policy 1997–2002 announced in 1997. This raises several questions. Why have agricultural exports declined after 1996–97? Does this decline have something to do with the Uruguay Round AOA? Is the impact same on export of different commodities?

Table 7.1 India's agriculture trade before and after WTO, in million USD

Year	Import	Export	Net surplus
1990–91	672	3352	2680
1991–92	604	3203	2599
1992–93	938	2950	2012
1993–94	742	4013	3271
1994–95	1891	4211	2320
1995–96	1761	6098	4337
1996–97	1863	6806	4943
1997–98	2364	6685	4321
1998–99	3462	6064	2602
1999–2000	3708	5842	2134
2000–1	2646	6273	3627
2001–2	3408	6183	2775
2002–3	3542	6826	3302
2003–4	4781	8110	3329
2004–5	4909	8872	3963

Source: Department of Agriculture and Cooperation, *Agricultural Statistics at a Glance 2005*, New Delhi: Ministry of Agriculture, 2005

In order to find answers to these questions we begin by looking at the global agricultural trade since 1974,[1] representing the period before and after WTO. The scene is presented by indices of value (in nominal USD), volume (quantity) and unit value (price) (Figure 7.1). All the three indices moved on a rising trend till 1995, though there were phases of stagnation or small decline. After 1996, unit value in nominal USD term, which represents average global agricultural prices, followed a sharp downward turn, which was unprecedented. Successive decline in the unit value index was 5 per cent in 1997, 11 per cent in 1998, and 12 per cent in 1999. During 1999 to 2002, prices remained 21 to 23 per cent lower than the level reached in 1996.[2] Surprisingly, the large decline in prices in the post-WTO period did not dampen the growth in volume (quantity) of global export. However, the price decline was so strong that it brought down value of global agricultural trade despite increase in the trade volume. The detailed study of trade trends before and after WTO leads to the following inferences. First, implementation of the Uruguay Round caused unprecedented decline in global prices of agricultural products. Second, the WTO led to intense competition in global trade among various countries. Hopes of gains from the WTO led all countries, induced by global liberalisation, to push exports. This is the

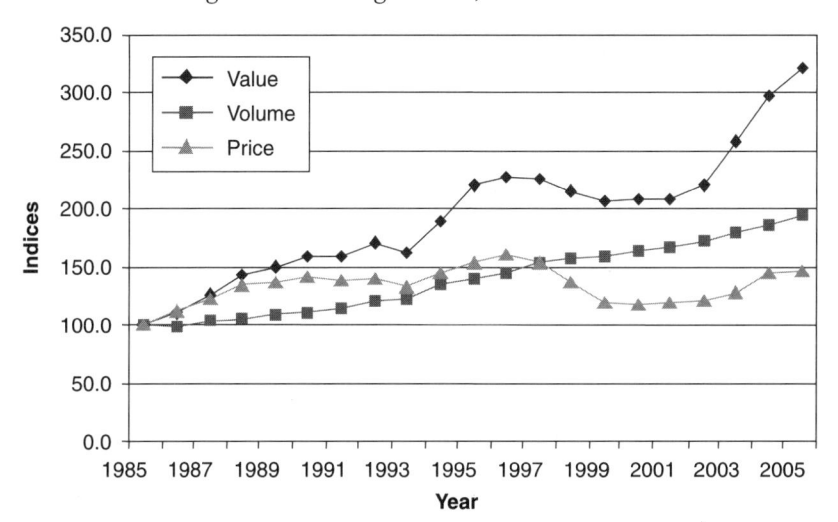

FIGURE 7.1 Indices of global trade in agriculture, base 1985=100

Source: WTO, *International Trade Statistics 2006*, Geneva: WTO, 2006.

reason that despite more than 25 per cent decline in average prices of agricultural group, continuing for a fairly long time, export volume maintained robust growth. Third, earnings from agricultural exports have been hit badly and increased sale brought less revenue.

As can be seen from Figure 7.1 and Table 7.1, India's agricultural exports followed world trend during 1990s. In fact, decline in the global agricultural price, in the aftermath of the WTO, affected India's exports more severally than world export. This is evident from the share of India in global agricultural exports (Figure 7.2). The reason for this was that while other countries maintained growth in volume of export despite adverse global price situation, quantity of Indian exports became stagnant with wide swings.

Several OECD countries continued and even raised export subsidies to protect their producers against increased competition in the post-WTO period. As far as the first two factors are concerned, much cannot be done to mitigate their impact on international prices. However, domestic support and export subsidies are open to be disciplined in the future negotiations.

There were considerable variations in export performance of various commodities. Non-basmati rice and wheat could not face global competition and their export was promoted by providing large subsidies (Chand 2002). Export of oilmeal, which was the second biggest item of export after marine products, suffered a serious setback due to decline in international prices and quantity of exports. Export earnings from traditional group consisting of tea, coffee, spices and tobacco suffered, mainly due to sharp fall in international prices as quantity of export in most cases did not decline. Export (value in USD) of marine products, and groups of livestock and horticultural products maintained the tempo of growth, continuing from pre-WTO period. This shows that post-WTO situation was favourable to export of high-value food products. Moreover, this growth was mainly market driven as there is little direct government intervention in these products.

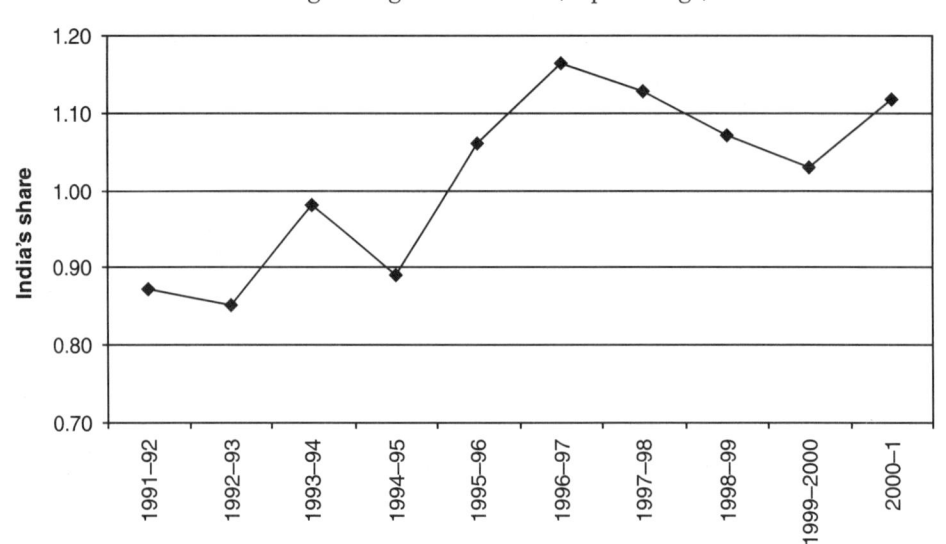

FIGURE 7.2 India's share in global agriculture trade (in percentage)

Source: Computed from Ministry of Finance, *Economic Survey*, New Delhi: Government of India, various issues.

Export of cotton almost dried up in the post-WTO period due to increased demand from domestic textile industry and decline in domestic production. Sugar exports remained occasional as the surplus arose temporarily. This scenario of India's agricultural exports indicate that future negotiations should focus on taking advantage in export of high value food products.

In the case of imports, liberalisation of trade did not cause much difficulty in the initial years of the WTO because international prices of bulk products were quite high in the first three post-WTO years. Imports hovered around USD 1.8 billion during 1994–95 to 1996–97. Subsequently, as international prices started falling, India's imports started rising. Level of imports doubled in three years between 1996–97 and 1999–2000 and reached a peak of USD 3.7 billion. This caused a lot of disappointment to the country which expected big gains in export earnings in the post-WTO period through increased market access into the markets of the developed countries. Domestic production of staples came under threat of disruption. International prices of cereals towards the year 2000 and 2001 turned out to be almost half of what they were in the beginning of the WTO. This happened when India had a very large stock of rice and wheat. Tariffs were not found adequate to keep a check on import of cereals and India had to resort to desperate measures like reimposing QRs on imports of foodgrains to keep a check on cheap imports. An important lesson from this experience is that India was not able to safeguard itself against imports with usual tariff when international prices went low. In order to deal with this kind of situations, India needs either high bound tariff so that applied tariffs can be raised appropriately or special safeguards.

WTO Agriculture Negotiations and India 129

FIGURE 7.3 Export of agricultural products: 1991–92 to 2003–4

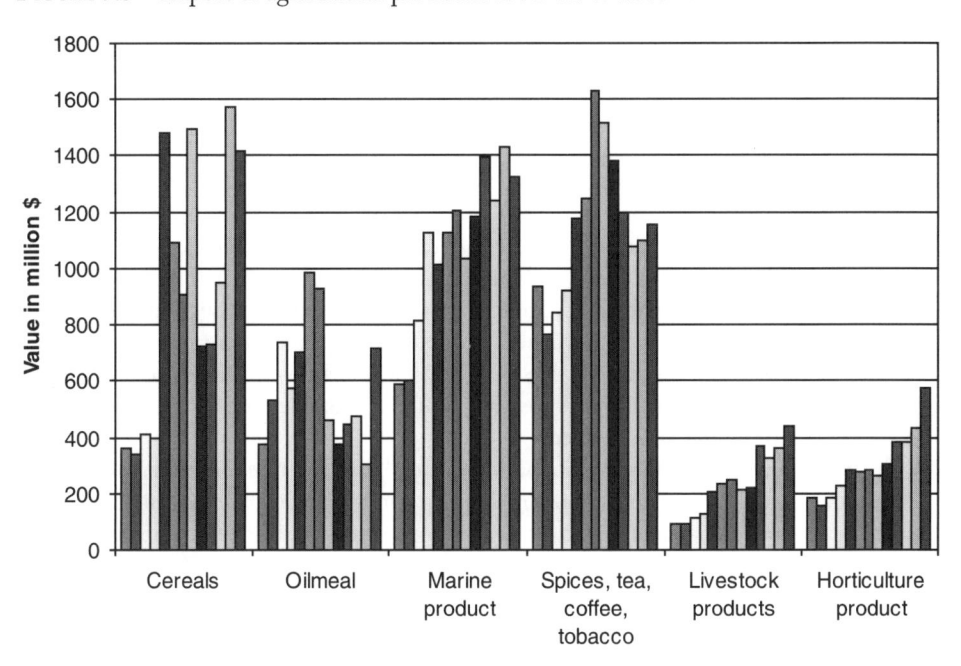

FIGURE 7.4 Import of selected agricultural products: 1991–92 to 2003–4

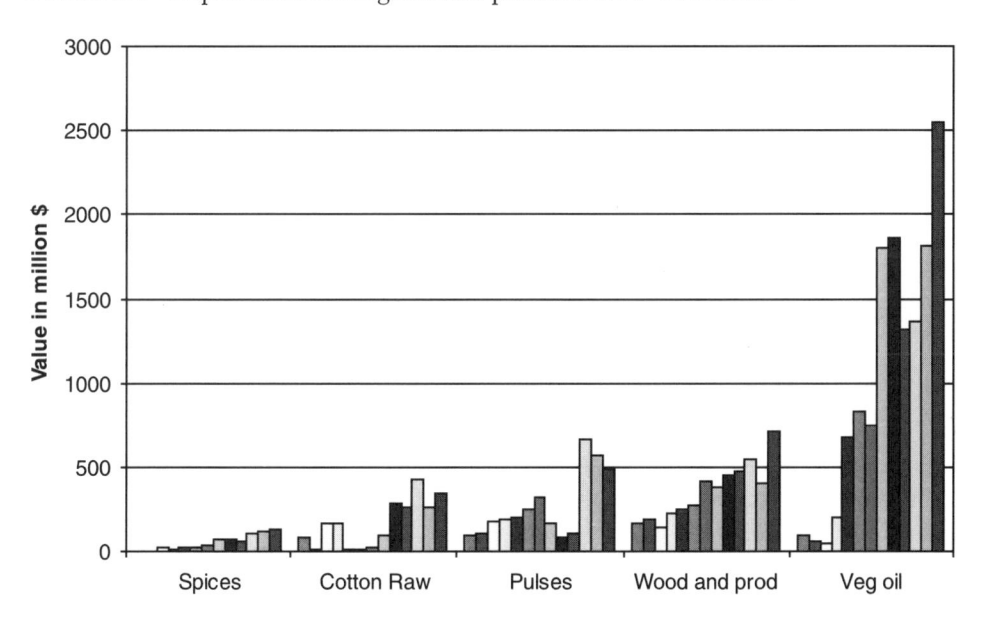

The composition of imports shows that most of the increase in agricultural imports took place due to increase in import of edible oil. Vegetable oils accounted for more than three fourth of the total increment in agriculture imports in the post-WTO period. The other items whose imports increased significantly are pulses, spices, cotton, and wood and wood products. There is also noticeable increase in imports of fruits and nuts. In this group, increase in cashew nut import is mainly for re-exporting of processed cashew nuts.

Imports of items like vegetable oils and wood/wood products have depressed domestic prices and caused adverse impact on domestic production (Figures 7.5 and 7.6). The import of wood/wood products have almost resulted in a collapse of the domestic prices of agro–forestry species like poplar.[3] In the case of pulses, imports did not help in lowering domestic prices. Imports of edible oil were much more than the reduction in production of edible oil. This is evident from the per capita availability of edible oil in the country which remained between 5 to 5.8 kg for a decade till 1992–93 and then steadily increased to more than 9 kg by 2002–3. Thus, edible oil imports have been quite favourable for consumers who could increase consumption due to low prices.

Experience with agricultural imports indicates that because of high volatility in international prices in some years even high-bound tariff is not adequate to regulate imports. In such a situation, India needs special safeguard or protection. Similarly, due to volatility in international prices, domestic prices of exportables also got depressed (for instance, see tea prices in Figure 7.5). As price volatility is the most important factor in affecting India's export and import and in turn domestic prices and production, the country should suggest measures in the AOA negotiations to reduce volatility and to guard against it.

FIGURE 7.5 Real prices of selected agricultural products adversely affected by WTO

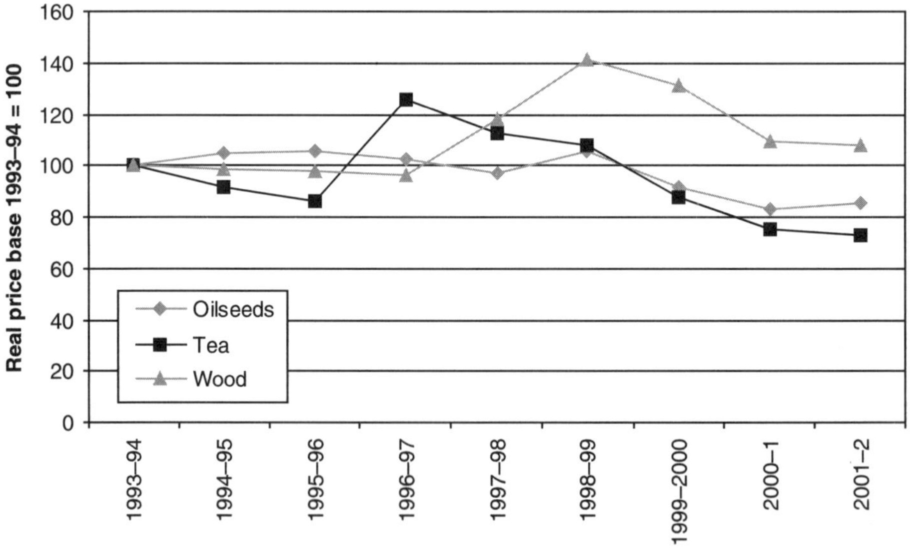

Source: Ministry of Finance, *Economic Survey*, New Delhi: Government of India, various issues.

FIGURE 7.6 Production of oilseeds and raw cotton in India, before and after WTO

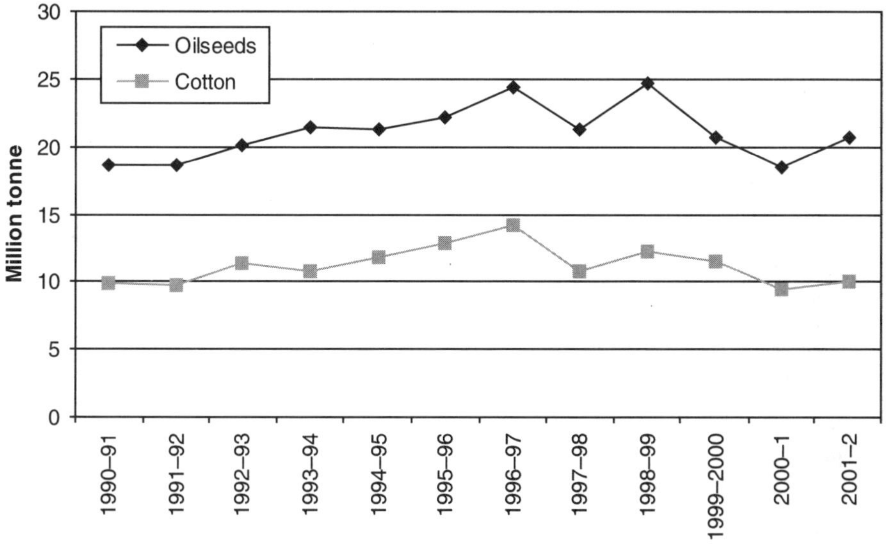

Source: Same as in Table 7.1.

INDIAN PERSPECTIVE

Prominent issues in the negotiations on agriculture are (i) reduction in domestic support, (ii) improved market access through substantial reduction in tariff and (iii) export subsidies and competition. Besides these there are some non-trade concerns like food security, structural adjustment, poverty alleviation, safety net for vulnerable population.

Domestic Support

Domestic policies in India have been such that domestic prices of major agricultural produce were kept lower than global prices. This resulted in negative product specific support or net taxation on agriculture. India provides some non-product specific support by subsidising inputs like fertiliser, irrigation, power and credit supplied to agriculture. The magnitude of non-product specific support remained quite small compared to the negative product specific support which rendered AMS negative.

So far AMS in India remained within permissible, *de minimus*, level of support as per the Uruguay Round AOA. However, the situation may change with the change in fixed reference price particularly because of volatility in international prices. Sometimes international prices turn out to be awfully low and they can deviate from normal level by as much as 50 per cent. If that level is used to compute AMS, it can turn out to be highly positive and much more than *de minimus* level of 10 per cent for developing countries which is exempted now. Thus, countries like India need to have some cushion in this. There is also no justification for treating product specific negative support as zero in AMS computation. It should be counted as such so that any negative product specific support is adjusted against non-product specific support.

Non-product specific support in India has increased from Rs 16706 crore during 1995–96 to Rs 43562 crores during 2003–4 (Table 7.2). This includes subsidies on fertiliser, irrigation, electricity, and credit supplied to agriculture. These subsidies, as per cent of value of agricultural output, are well below the level of 10 per cent, which is *de minimus* limit set for developing countries by the Uruguay Round AOA. India has scope to raise input subsidies by about 45 per cent of the current level without violating WTO limits.

TABLE 7.2 Input subsidies in Indian agriculture in relation to value of output

Year	Input subsidies Rs crore	Value of output Rs Crore	Subsidies as a percentage of output value
1993–94	13340	271839	4.91
1994–95	14739	312650	4.71
1995–96	16706	342535	4.88
1996–97	18935	399902	4.73
1997–98	22424	424094	5.29
1998–99	26079	488731	5.34
1999–2000	27305	514718	5.30
2000–1	30870	518693	5.95
2001–2	36331	562024	6.46
2002–3	42699	557035	7.67
2003–4	43562	635104	6.86

Note: Agriculture output includes crop and livestock.
Source: Central Statistical Organisation, *National Accounts Statistics*, New Delhi: Governemnt of India, various issues.

Agriculture in most parts of India is in a transitional stage. A large segment is still underdeveloped and requires a lot of governmental assistance in the initial stages for harnessing its potential and for development. Huge investments are required in infrastructure and institutional development as farmers generally have poor resources and do not have enough capital for investing in agriculture. As markets are not well developed, in several cases government intervention is needed to ensure remunerative price environment that leads to adoption of improved technology. Therefore, India needs provisions for product specific as well as non-product specific support to its agriculture. Similarly, there are special needs of agriculture which require assistance in the form of infrastructure development, research, extension, insurance and market development. India requires the Green Box for providing such assistance.

In a liberalised trade regime, competitiveness is affected by both, domestic policies and policies followed by others. Therefore, there is a need to see what a country's commitments are and what kind of rules and regulations would govern other countries. In this context, it is important to see how various provisions of domestic support have been used by other countries.

OECD countries particularly, EU members, the US, Canada and Japan provide huge subsidy to their farmers in various forms that put their production in an advantageous position vis-à-vis farmers in developing countries (Chand and Linu 2001). Moreover, Green and Blue boxes have been used to compensate for any reduction in the Amber Box. This support enables farmers from developed countries to reduce the cost of production and to offer their produce at a lower price. The net result for developing countries is the disadvantage in export and in competing with imports.

There is no justification for developed countries to provide such support to their farmers and to the agriculture sector because their agriculture is highly commercialised and is at an advanced stage of development. Infrastructure and markets are well developed and farmers are resourceful and capable to operate without government assistance. Therefore, in the new AOA, developed countries should not be allowed to give any kind of support in Green Box and Blue Box. Some well-defined measures can be considered under Green Box but their level should be capped to avoid their misuse as in the past.

Market Access

India has implemented its commitments in the area of market access (i) replacing non-tariff border measures with tariffs, (ii) removing QRs and (iii) liberalising trade by lowering applied tariffs, even though these were below bound rates as can be seen from Table 7.3. QRs were maintained on agricultural imports because of adverse balance of payment (BOP) situation till 2000 and then replaced QRs with tariffs.

India has mainly three slabs of bound tariffs; 100–4 per cent for raw products like cereals, most of the vegetables and fruits, oilseeds, pulses, 150 per cent for semi processed like tea, chicken, wheat flour, and 300 per cent for processed products like vegetable oils and fats. There is a deviation from these broad norms for some individual products. Actual and bound rate of duty for specific products is shown in Table 7.3. Actual rate of duty has been kept much below the bound rate except in a few cases.

TABLE 7.3 Standard rates of duty on import of selected agricultural commodities in India during 1991–92 to 2002–3

Commodity	1991–92	1995–96	1999–2000	2000–1	2001–2	2004–5	Bound tariff
Rice (non-basmati)	0	0	0	92	77	70–80	70–80
Wheat	0	0	0/50	108	100	50	100
Maize	0	0	0	60	50	50	70
Pulses	10	10	5	5	5	10	104
Oilseeds	55	50	35	35	35		100
R/M oil	45	30	18	35	35	75	75
Soybean oil	45	30	18	45	38	45	45
Groundnut oil	45	30	18	35	35	75	300
RBD Palm oil				75	75	65	300
Refined Palm oil				100	85	75–85	300
Onion	100	10	10	10	0	5	104
Potato	100	10	10	10	15	30	104
Cotton	35	50	40	25	5–35	30	
Sugar	35	0	40	100	60	60	150

Source: Same as in Table 7.1.

In the initial years of WTO, international prices were above long-term trend and liberalisation of trade did not cause any adverse impact on exports or through imports. Subsequently, international prices dropped to a very low level. This made export very difficult and domestic prices became attractive for large scale imports. Domestic production of staples also came under threat of disruption and India had to resort to desperate measures to keep a check on cheap imports. Important lessons from this experience is that, due to high volatility in international prices, tariffs are not enough to safeguard domestic production against imports when international prices go low. In order to deal with this kind of situations, India needs either very high bound tariff so that applied tariffs can be raised appropriately or special safeguards to regulate imports of sensitive products.

Setback to export occurs because of poor or reduced access in markets of other countries. Developed countries have very high bound tariff for selected products and they also have special safeguard to stop imports of some products (WTO 2002). Some countries have variable tariff which rises in response to the fall in price. All these measures reduce access to the markets in developed countries. When all such measures fail then sometimes sanitary and phyto-sanitary (SPS) measures are invoked without justification to check imports.

Based on this experience, Indian strategy should be to get adequate protection for its own market and seek more market access in the market of the developed countries.

Export Competition and Subsidies

The EU and US, which are among the big trading groups, along with 23 other countries, can subsidise exports. EU export subsidies have particularly caused concern to developing countries. India provides income tax exemptions for profit from agricultural export, domestic and international freight subsidy for some export commodities. These are not direct export subsidies which are provided by industrialised countries (Gulati 2004).

Export subsidies are highly trade distorting. India should strongly plead for immediate and complete elimination of export subsidies. Due to underdeveloped infrastructure, markets, and trade institutions in developing countries, government intervention at times, in terms of providing freight subsidy, incurring some marketing cost, and providing incentive for export in the initial stages, becomes essential to develop export potential. India should seek exemption in these as a part of for them.

State Trading Enterprises

State trading enterprises (STEs) have played an important role in creating a remunerative price environment for producers resulting in growth of output, commercialisation, promotion of trade in agriculture, and in improving food security. Main operations of STE included price administration, procurement and sale of significant part of domestic production, maintenance of commodity stock, and monopoly in import and export. Some operations of STEs are considered trade distorting while most of those were of regulatory and promotional categories. Food Corporation of India (FCI) plays a predominant role in price administration of wheat and paddy/rice in the country through bulk purchase of marketed surplus at predetermined prices, maintenance of large stocks and release of stock for public distribution, open market sales, and of late for exports. FCI has import monopoly through canalisation to import cereals, which was partly lifted in 1999 and resumed back after a short time as cheap imports hit coastal areas, despite government having enough stocks in its warehouses. India has almost eliminated the role of several other STEs in the import and export of vegetable oil, cotton, sugar and so on.

It is in the long-run interest of India to reduce the role of STEs and promote private enterprise in agriculture marketing and trade. However, due to volatility in prices, the stronghold of commodity cartels over global trade. While the capacity of India's producers and consumers to absorb big supply and demand shocks is limited, the global market is not very reliable either for addressing food security concerns of the country. Therefore, India requires some STE to address food security concerns particularly of weaker sections of society. These STE should play a minimalist role and they should operate along with private trade, without having monopoly in domestic or international trade.

Food Security

India has striven hard to attain food security by acquiring food self sufficiency. Significant proportion of the population is not only dependent on grain production for their livelihood but also for survival. Therefore, domestic capacities in grain production need to be strengthened and further developed. However, these should be done in an efficient manner so that the domestic produce is capable to compete with normal international prices.

India advocates flexibility in domestic support, renegotiation and maintenance of appropriate tariff binding, special safeguards (SSG) including QRs, and several other ideas on the grounds of food security. Maintaining a fair degree of grain self-sufficiency would need domestic interventions and institutional support. To ensure these, developing countries should not compromise on institutional interventions in grain sector. Trade has an important role in food security by way of stabilisation of domestic prices and in meeting food deficiency. In fact, meeting small fraction of demand through trade can have desirable impact on improving efficiency of domestic production and should not be seen as a threat to domestic producers. However, dependence on trade should not stifle domestic capacity for food production. India needs to strike a balance between grain self-sufficiency and trade by carefully weighing crop production choices.

HONGKONG MINISTERIAL DECLARATION

The General Council of WTO, in its meeting in the last week of July 2004, reached a broad agreement on a framework to move ahead on trade in agriculture. This framework, along with other proposals, was taken up for discussion in the Hong Kong Ministerial Conference, 13–18 December 2005. However, no consensus could be reached once again and the meeting ended up with a resolve to complete Doha Work Programmes and to conclude negotiations successfully in year 2006. To pursue this objective the ministerial meeting came up with a declaration (hereafter referred to as Hong Kong declaration). The document is available at the WTO site (WTO 2005). Broad elements of agriculture negotiations in the Hong Kong Round are discussed below. Under each element, a separate treatment is proposed for developing countries, which can be considered as S&DT for these members.

Domestic Support

The Hong Kong declaration includes two aspects of domestic support. One is, the overall support as given by the sum of Final Bound Total AMS, *de minimus* support, and Blue Box support capped at 5 per cent of the value of a member's average total value of agricultural production, during a historical period, as proposed in July 2004 by WTO General Council. Two, AMS.

The Hong Kong declaration proposes to first divide overall support in developed countries in three bands consisting of threshold support in the range of (i) USD 0–10 billion (ii) USD 10–60 billion and (iii) more than USD 60 billion, while cuts in these bands are proposed to be between 31 to 70 per cent, 53 to 75 per cent, and 70 to 80 per cent, respectively. According to these bands, European Community (EC) comes in the highest band (iii), the US and Japan come in the middle band (ii) and all other developed countries in band (i).

The second aspect of reduction in domestic support applies to AMS. As is the case with overall cut, the Hong Kong declaration mentions three bands for AMS with progressive cuts as shown in Table 7.4.

TABLE 7.4 Matrix showing bands and cuts in overall trade distracting support and in AMS

Particular	Band	Threshold US $	Cuts (in percentage)
a. Overall Trade Distracting Support	1	0–10	31–70
	2	10–60	53–75
	3	more than 60	70–80
b. AMS	1	0–12/15	37–60
	2	12/15–25	60–70
	3	more than 25	70–83

Note: For AMS reduction there could be possibility of putting EC in band three and the US in the second tier. Basis for putting in Japan is yet to be resolved.
Source: WTO Ministerial Conference, Sixth Session, Hong Kong, 13–18 December 2005. Document No. WT/MIN(05)/DEC, WTO.

As is obvious, the bands proposed in Table 7.4 are not related to the size of agriculture in a member country. Thus, there is the possibility of a smaller size country, even with higher support, to fall in the lower band as compared to a country with larger size of agriculture and relatively less support. In such cases, the Hong Kong declaration seeks complimenting band related reduction with additional criteria. No discernable convergence is yet seen in respect of review and clarification commitment on green box.

Further, developed countries are to apply 50 per cent and 80 per cent cut in product specific *de minimis* and non-products specific *de minimis* support.

There is still lot of divergence for discipline in domestic support given in developing country. One view is that, there should be no cut in *de minimis* at all for developing countries. The second view on this is that there should be no cut for developing countries with no AMS, and two-third of the cut accepted for developed countries in the case of developing countries having AMS.

Regarding the Blue Box, there are a couple of suggestions like further constraining Blue Box payments from the current 5 per cent ceiling to 2.5 per cent of a member's average total value of agricultural production during a historical period, and, additional criteria to discipline a new Blue Box.

The Green Box criteria will be reviewed and clarified with a view to ensuring that Green Box measures have no, or at most minimal, trade-distorting effects or effects on production.

Export Competition

Members are in agreement to ensure parallel elimination of all forms of export subsidies and disciple on all export measures having a sort of indirect effect like subsidies to be completed by the end of 2013. There are suggestions for front loading, that is, most of the reduction in the initial years, particularly in the case of cotton.

In order to ensure STEs do not adopt trade distorting practices, the proposal seeks to eliminate monopoly power of STE's in the future.

While for developed countries, progressive and parallel elimination of export subsidy is proposed, members of developing country will continue to benefit from the provision of article 9.4 of the AOA for five years, after end date for elimination of all forms of export subsidies.

Market Access

There are four aspects of market access, namely, tariff cut, sensitive product, special product and special safeguard mechanism. At present, tariff on some of the lines is imposed on per unit basis rather than on value of product. This poses serious difficulty in putting tariff lines in tariff bands. The proposal establishes method for calculating Ad Valorum Equivalent (AVE's) where tariffs are not computed on value, except in the case of sugar lines. This creates basis for putting tariff lines into bands for tariff cuts. There is considerable convergence on adopting linear cuts within the band but disagreement on level of cut is still high as can be seen from the matrix below.

TABLE 7.5   Bands and cuts in tariffs proposed for developed and developing countries

Band	Developed countries Threshold in percentage	Range of cut	Developing countries Threshold in percentage	Range of cut
1	0–20/30	20–65	0–20/30	15–25
2	20/30–40/60	30–75	20/50–40/100	20–30
3	40/60–60/90	35–85	40/100–60/150	25–35
4	> 60/90	42–90	> 60–150	30–40

The matrix illustrates the prevalent differences among members in the threshold, as well as the level of cuts. For instance, various proposals suggest first band to have upper limit of 20–30 per cent and the proposed cut again range form 20–65 per cent in the case of developed countries. There is also disagreement on concept and level of tariff caps.

As for developed countries, there is a working hypothesis of four bands for developing countries which proposes lower cut and higher threshold for these members. The proposal emphasises that each member (including members from developed countries) can declare certain percentage of the tariff line as a sensitive product, which would have flexibility from tariff reduction commitments. The proposals vary from 1 to 15 per cent of tariff lines.

The Hong Kong declaration provides for a sort of S&DT for developing country members in two ways. One, developing country members have flexibility to designate an appropriate number of lines as special product which are related to food security, livelihood security and rural development. Two, these countries will have the right to have recourse to a special safeguard mechanism based on quantity and price. This provision was earlier available only to 38 member countries.

Cotton

In order to address the plight of cotton farmers in developing countries, cotton was taken up separately in the AOA. The Hong Kong declaration called for elimination of all forms of export subsidies on cotton, by developed countries, in 2006.

Developing countries, particularly G-20, emerged as a strong group in articulating the agenda for WTO negotiations in Hong Kong round. Because of this, the July Package of 2004 got significantly changed and developing countries were able to push several of their proposals in the negotiations. It is now clear that because of very heavy domestic support in various forms and export subsidies in developed countries, agriculture in developing countries is not facing a leveled field. Because of this, developed countries have to accommodate the interests of developing countries and agree to different rules and obligations for this group. Despite full recognition of this aspect, consensus could not be reached on most of the issues and the Hong Kong declaration clearly shows that member countries have to show lot of flexibility to reach final agreement. There are also cases of different groups putting conditions to agree to some clauses, for instance the US agrees to do something if the EU does a particular thing, and vice versa.

The HD's main achievement is in the area of export competition and in having different set of obligations and provisions for developed and developing countries. There would be some complications in respect of domestic support as the reduction is proposed based on an absolute amount rather than considering domestic support relative to value of agriculture output. Similarly, separation of trade distorting domestic support and AMS for reduction commitment complicates the implementation. Further, inclusion of blue box in overall support for estimating the cut is not clear when there is a separate box for blue box support. The agreement institutionalises the Blue Box to provide assistance upto 5 per cent of the value of produce. The Green Box would also be there though the package seeks only non-trade distorting or minimal trade distorting measures in it. It needs to be noted that even in the Uruguay Round agreement, the Green Box was defined only to include non- or minimal trade distorting support but subsequently the box was used to shift amber box support to exempt green box. Therefore, the Green Box measure must be defined very clearly to avoid any ambiguity. In the area of market access, tariff reduction formula is yet to be decided. The framework permits developing countries to designate a list of SPs which would not be subject to market access commitments. In the same breathe the package retains a sort of special safeguard mechanism for 'sensitive products', which would allow developed countries to deny market access to the products defined as sensitive in their countries.

INDIA'S AGENDA FOR FINAL NEGOTIATIONS

Implementation of Uruguay Round AOA has been a mixed blessing for India. It created a favourable environment for trade reforms and for initiating trade liberalisation in agriculture, which was considered highly desirable for these countries. However, what was projected as a benefit from the AOA for developing countries like India and expectations based on that did not come true. There are several reasons for this; the major ones are:

1. Volatility in international prices, which further increased in post-WTO period;
2. Unexpectedly low prices of agricultural commodities beginning in the late 1990s;

3. Intense competition among developing countries to promote export;
4. Heavy subsidies in OECD countries; and
5. Lack of promised market access in markets of developed countries.

However, implementation of the Uruguay Round AOA has provided lot of experience to operate in liberalised global trade. This experience should be used in the ongoing negotiations on AOA so that India's concerns are adequately and appropriately addressed.

India needs to pay equal attention to what it agrees to do in its own market and economy and what other countries should be doing in their market. In liberalised trade, both import and export are equally important. Nature of popular opinion in the country is such that any deal that secures protection or freedom from commitment is considered as a great achievement. However, this is only one side of the story. The other side is what protection and freedom from commitment other countries get. Sometimes it is beneficial to go for a trade-off between, say making commitment to reduce subsidies and reducing protection in own market if it results in enough gain in market access in other countries. Second, India need not be extremely defensive and inward looking. Indian agriculture has some strength, which needs to be appropriately used to compete in the global trade. In this background, India should pursue the following agenda for negotiations in the AOA:

1. In the case of domestic support, the Blue Box should not be included in the calculation of overall support. India should seek elimination of the Blue Box which indirectly distorts trade. Green box should include purely non-trade distorting measures like training, inspection, extension services, infrastructure services, public stockholding for food security purpose. It should not include payment to producers in any form; all such payments should be included in the Amber Box. There should be a cap on Green Box assistance in developed countries. A developing country should have the freedom to provide assistance under the Green Box measures, as agriculture sector in these countries is in transition and it needs public support for harnessing its potential. In order to keep a check on concentrating support on one or a few products, AMS commitment should also apply at product level.
2. All export subsidies should be eliminated at the earliest. Measures like export credit guarantee and insurance should be allowed only to developing countries.

    Tariff reduction should be based on bound tariff and not applied tariff. India need not ask for unreasonably high tariffs particularly those above 100 per cent. Market access to developed countries markets through tariff rate quota (TRQ) causes several problems. In place of this India should ask for duty free import of tropical products from developing countries to developed countries; such products should be included in the duty free lines.
3. India requires some STE to address food security concerns particularly of weaker sections of society. However, India should agree to abolish monopoly of STEs in domestic or international trade.
4. S&DT to developing countries is a must in order to provide flexibility and to address livelihood concerns of a vast majority of the population, which is dependent on agriculture in these countries. This should include (i) An enlarged Green Box for developing countries (ii) exemption to selected SPs, related to food

security and livelihood, from market access commitments (iii) special safeguard mechanism to protect against flood of imports and injury to domestic product.
5. India should not seek too much protection for developing countries as it may go against its exports. OECD countries account for less than 40 per cent of India's agricultural exports. Developing countries are the major markets for India's agricultural exports. Increased competition to India's agricultural exports in the post-WTO period has also come from developing countries. Therefore, any concession that India seeks for developing countries goes to the countries of its export destination and its competitors. Composition of India's export to various destinations show that developed countries import mainly high value food products like marine products, cashew, tea, spices, coffee and basmati rice while the imports of developing countries mainly consists of products like rice, sugar, wheat, and oilmeal. Developing countries are likely to designate bulk products like cereals, sugar, oilseeds as "special products" to seek an exemption from market access commitments. Therefore, the more protection India seeks for developing countries, the more problems it is going to face in export to developing countries. India's strategy should be to seek reduction in domestic support and subsidies and improved market access in developed countries. The list of "special products" should be kept at a minimum and this offer should be used to eliminate or reduce special safeguards for sensitive products proposed in the July Package.

Endnotes

[1] The reason for choosing 1974 as the starting point is that agricultural prices and value of trade witnessed break in the past trend with sizable upward shift in early 1970s. After showing violent fluctuations for four years (1970–73) the trends stabilised in 1974.

[2] This decline refers to the average price of agricultural products. Among some individual commodities the decline was much higher and prices in the late 1990s turned out to be less than half of what they were during 1996–97.

[3] This timber species became very popular in North-west India during the last two and half decades for raising on field bunds and also in block plantation. The price of poplar logs in North West India has crashed to below Rs1500/tonne after 2002 as compared to more than Rs. 7000/tonne earlier.

References

Chand, Ramesh. 1999. 'Effect of Trade Liberalisation on Indian Agriculture: Institutional and Structural Aspects', Working Paper 39, CGPRT Centre, ESCAP, Bogor, Indonesia.
_____. 2002. *WTO, Trade Liberalization and Indian Agriculture*. New Delhi: Mittal Publications.
Chand, Ramesh and Mathew Philip Linu. 2001. 'Subsidies and Support in Agriculture: Is WTO Providing Level Playing Field?', *Economic and Political Weekly*, vol. 36, no. 32, pp. 3014–16.
Finger, J. M., 2001. 'Implementing the Uruguay Round Agreement: Problems for Developing Countries', *The World Economy*, vol. 24, no. 9, pp. 1097–108.
Finger, J. M. and J. J. Nogues. 2002. 'The Unbalanced Round Outcome: The New Areas in Future WTO Negotiations', *The World Economy*, vol. 25, no. 3, pp. 321–40.
Grimwade, Nigel. 2004. 'The GATT, the Doha Round and Developing Countries', in *The WTO and Developing Countries*, edited by H. Katrak and Roger Strange, New York: Palgrave Macmillan.

Gulati, Ashok. 2003. 'India', in *Agriculture, Trade and WTO in South Asia*, edited by D. I. Merlinda, Washington DC: The World Bank.

World Bank. 2002. *Global Economic Prospects and the Developing Countries 2002: Making Trade Work for the World's Poor*, Washington DC: The World Bank.

WTO. 2002. 'Special Agricultural Safeguard', background paper by the Secretariat, G/AG/NG/S/9/Rev.1, Revision, February.

WTO. 2005. Ministerial Conference Sixth Session, Hongkong, 13–18 December 2005, Document No. WT/MIN(05)/DEC, 22 December.

8

Trade and Industrial Performance since the WTO Reforms: What Indian Evidences Suggest?

Alokesh Barua, Debashis Chakraborty and Pavel Chakraborty

INTRODUCTION

The Uruguay Round of MTNs had led to a substantial improvement in market access for manufacturing in global trade mainly due to the reductions in tariffs barriers. The world trade regime as a consequence has become much freer than ever before. By ensuring the MFN treatment, the WTO has created a non-discriminatory trading regime. As a consequence of such increase in market access, Indian manufacturing sector may presumably have succeeded in exploiting the advantages of greater degree of openness for increasing its manufacturing exports. This chapter therefore will attempt to evaluate the kinds of quantitative and qualitative changes that may have taken place in the direction and the patterns of trade and resource allocation in Indian manufacturing. The chapter will provide a brief overview of the post-Uruguay Round market access situations in both the developed and the developing economies; will discuss India's role in the WTO policy negotiations for manufacturing market access and also how India had responded to its commitments in the implementation of the reform measures; will we try to provide some quantitative estimates of the effects of increased market access for Indian manufacturing under the assumptions of competitive market framework and constant returns to scale; will try to incorporate monopolistic market conditions and increasing returns to scale to find out if the conclusions based on competition differ greatly in presence of market imperfections and increasing returns to scale. We will end the chapter with a summary our main findings.

MARKET ACCESS IN MANUFACTURING: AN OVERVIEW

The issue of the reduction of tariffs on industrial products assumed the centrality of negotiations on trade liberalisation since the GATT days, understandably due to the fact that manufacturing products account for about 8 per cent of the global merchandise trade. A comparison of the share of exports of manufactures in total world exports in 1990 and 2000 reveals that the manufacturing share far exceeded the overall share in exports for the Western Europe and Asia and just exceeded in case of the North America. What this implies is that the other regions such as the Latin America, Central/Eastern Europe,

Middle East and Africa have shares in manufactures much lower than their shares in total exports to the world (Alburo 2003, 57). Interestingly, the shares of manufacturing in world exports have also been increasing for the developing countries and this must be due to increased market access in manufacturing. The developed countries have reduced their tariffs on imports of industrial products by an average of 40 per cent, i.e. from 6.3 per cent to 3.8 per cent following the Uruguay Round negotiations. But the developing countries on the other hand reduced their tariffs on imports of industrial products by an average of 20 per cent, that is, from 15.3 per cent to 12.3 per cent (UNCTAD 1996). Thus, while percentage reduction in tariff is smaller in developing countries than their industrial counterparts, the absolute reduction in their tariff rate is of course much greater. As a result, the post-Uruguay Round average tariff levels in the developing countries are much above the developed countries' tariffs levels. Table 8.1 gives some idea about the changing tariff structure of several developed and developing countries including India. It is seen that the average tariff rate has come down significantly for most of the countries.[1] However, WTO (2001) has clearly noted that *the level of realised market access is significantly lower than the predicted one* and there are areas where barriers quite significantly affect trade. For instance, although the average tariff rate has come down, 'numerous *tariff peaks*, mainly in the textiles and clothing and in the leather sectors' (WTO 2001, 2), affected the trade volume considerably. In addition, *tariff escalation* is turning out to be a major hindrance to trade in recent years. The WTO study (2001) notes:

> For certain products, such as textiles, clothing, leather, leather products and metals, most developed countries' tariffs increase with the level of processing. Many developing countries in Asia and Africa also exhibit escalating tariffs for these products. Developing countries argue that tariff escalation biases their production structure towards less refined products and thus represents a major impediment to their industrialisation (WTO 2001, 3).

TABLE 8.1 Tariff reforms of select countries during the nineties[2]

Year	All products					Primary products			Manufactured products		
	A	B	C	D	E	A	B	C	A	B	C
Australia											
1991	13.1	14.3	9.1	30.3	1.4	3.2	–	1.6	14.3	–	10.3
1993	9.8	11.9	7.7	–	–	2.5	–	1.3	11.7	–	9.7
1998	5.3	7.4	3.7	–	–	1.2	–	0.7	6.4	–	4.4
2004	5.1	–	3.8	5.9	2.9	1.4	–	0.7	5.6	–	4.4
Canada											
1989	8.6	7.4	6.0	14.6	3.4	5.1	5.9	2.5	9.9	7.1	6.7
1995	10.1	24.2	7.2	–	–	14.2	49.3	5.5	8.9	6.6	7.7
1998	7.5	26.5	3.8	–	–	16.1	54.9	6.7	5.1	6.1	3.2
2003	3.9	–	0.9	6.5	3.6	1.9	–	0.4	4.2	–	1.0
China											
1992	41.0	30.6	32.2	77.6	0.0	35.4	–	13.9	42.3	–	36.5
1994	36.3	27.9	35.5	–	–	32.2	24.3	19.6	37.6	28.8	40.6
1996	23.6	17.4	22.6	–	–	25.4	22.1	20.0	23.1	15.8	23.2
2004	9.8	–	6.0	16.0	0.0	10.0	–	5.6	9.7	–	6.0

(Contd)

Market Access: Agriculture, Manufactures and Textiles

(Table 8.1 Contd)

Year	All products					Primary products			Manufactured products		
	A	B	C	D	E	A	B	C	A	B	C
EU											
1989	4.1	5.9	3.8	3.9	18.2	8.7	–	2.7	2.7	–	4.4
1994	7.7	6.3	6.6	–	–	10.3	–	4.9	6.9	–	7.0
1998	6.0	5.6	3.5	.	.	9.4	.	3.4	4.8	.	3.5
2003	1.4	.	1.3	1.9	10.6	2.2	.	0.9	1.2	.	1.4
India											
1990	79.0	43.6	49.6	97.0	0.9	69.1	.	25.4	80.2	.	69.9
1997	30.0	14.0	27.7	.	.	25.7	22.6	22.6	31.3	9.8	29.5
2004	28.3	.	28.0	92.4	0.0	30.0	.	36.9	27.9	.	25.3
Japan											
1989	5.6	7.9	3.0	9.1	3.3	8.3	.	3.3	4.7	.	2.7
1998	5.7	7.7	2.0	.	.	8.9	.	4.5	4.5	.	1.5
2004	2.9	.	2.4	8.1	2.8	5.3	.	3.9	2.4	–	1.6
US											
1989	5.6	6.8	3.8	8.0	12.7	3.7	–	2.0	6.0	–	4.1
1995	5.9	7.0	4.1	–	–	5.5	–	2.7	6.0	–	4.4
1998	5.2	11.8	2.8	–	–	6.4	–	3.2	4.9	–	2.7
2004	3.2	–	1.8	4.0	6.8	2.7	–	1.1	3.3	–	1.9
Brazil											
1989	42.2	17.2	31.9	92.2	0.5	37.9	–	18.8	42.5	–	37.9
1997	11.9	7.7	14.6	–	–	8.6	5.7	7.1	12.6	7.8	16.4
2004	13.2	–	8.0	38.0	0.0	9.1	–	2.0	13.6	–	10.2
South Korea											
1989	14.8	5.3	10.5	11.8	12.5	14.6	–	5.5	14.9	–	13.5
1996	11.1	26.1	9.5	–	–	21.0	47.2	17.0	8.2	13.5	7.8
2002	9.5	–	10.0	5.3	0.5	20.9	–	19.0	7.8	–	5.0
Indonesia											
1989	21.9	19.7	13.0	50.3	0.3	19.9	–	5.8	22.3	–	15.6
1996	13.0	16.7	13.8	–	–	12.3	19.6	9.3	13.2	15.7	14.9
2003	6.4	–	5.2	3.5	0.2	8.0	–	3.1	6.1	–	5.8
Malaysia											
1988	17.0	15.1	9.4	46.1	7.2	15.2	–	4.6	17.4	–	10.5
1993	14.3	14.1	11.1	–	–	10.9	12.7	6.0	15.3	14.3	12.6
2003	7.3	–	4.2	21.1	1.0	4.5	–	2.1	7.8	–	4.6
Philippines											
1989	28.0	14.2	22.4	77.2	0.1	29.6	–	18.5	27.7	–	23.6
1995	20.0	11.0	18.4	–	–	21.6	12.8	16.8	19.5	10.4	18.9
2003	4.5	–	2.6	1.6	0.0	5.7	–	5.0	4.2	–	2.0

Source: World Bank, *World Development Indicators* Washington DC: The World Bank, various Issues.

Because of such discrepancies between the potential and the actual market access conditions in the developed countries' markets for the industrial products of the developing countries, the developing countries often expressed their strong discontentment with the developed world. The major source of unhappiness had of course been with the very slow pace of implementation of important agreement such as the ATC (see Chapter 9 for details). Since the ATC came to an end by 31 December 2004, the current concern was with the remaining tariffs and NTBs maintained by two major trading entities, the EU and the US, which are quite high.[3] The abuse of the anti-dumping measures as instrument of protection in the developed countries had also been a major point of concern (Aggrawal 2002; Chakraborty 2007).

Although no major tussle was experienced during Singapore (1996) and Geneva (1998) ministerial meetings of the WTO, discontents became perceptible from the Seattle Ministerial Conference (1999) onwards, where the possibility of including social clauses under WTO ambit was discussed (See Chapter 4). The proposal had to be dropped on the face of huge protest from various quarters. During the Doha Ministerial (2001), the launching of a new round was not accepted by the developing countries on the ground that the market access issues originating from the Uruguay Round commitments need to be ensured first (see Chapter 5 and 6 for details).[4] In Cancun Ministerial (2003), the developed-developing gap became too wide over the question of loss of market access due to agricultural subsidisation in the EU and the US, and even the July 2004 meeting left so many unresolved areas. Moreover, the timelines set for the conclusion of the negotiations at the Hong Kong Ministerial (2005) has been missed, as the WTO members failed to agree on the reform modalities. In short, the debates and disputes over market access issues are far from being over.

THE WTO AND INDIA

India at the WTO

India had all along been actively participating in the multilateral negotiations for formalising an efficient and rule-based world trade regime. There were indeed differences within the domestic economy marked by acrimonious debates on the issue of whether India should join the WTO or not. At the end of course the Indian parliament has ratified the proposal of India signing the WTO agreement. India did not succumb to the global trend towards formations of RTAs and instead remained loyal to multilateralism for the most part of the last decade. So India did not consider obtaining membership of regional blocs as an export expansionary strategy.[5] However, this outlook changed from 2003 onwards and currently India is part of a number of overlapping trade blocs, mostly in Asia (Nag and Chakraborty, 2006). From an initial position of hesitation as seen in the first WTO Ministerial Conference held in Singapore (1996), India has succeeded in achieving a position of leadership among the developing countries bloc in the Cancun Ministerial (2003). Thus, while India remained inactive by not majorly protesting against the inclusion of four new issues, namely, trade and investment, competition policy, transparency in government procurement, and trade facilitation, in the Singapore Ministerial (1996), it did play a somewhat active role in the Geneva Ministerial (1998) and became a part of the Global E-commerce Agreement. Subsequently, in response to the non-realisation of the promised market access under the Uruguay Round and also owing to a number of challenges it had faced at the WTO Dispute Settlement Body, India was forced to adopt a proactive approach in Seattle (1999) by raising its voice against the incorporation of social aspects under the WTO ambit. In the same way, in Doha (2001), when developed countries were willing to begin discussion for launching a new round, India with a handful of developing country opposed the move and demanded realisation of market access as promised under the Uruguay Round. The concern over TRIPS and Public Health also played a major role in this regard.[6] Finally, in Cancun (2003), the G-20 group led by Brazil, China, India and South Africa laid an alternate proposal against the EU-US proposal for removing agricultural subsidies in their domestic market. Also during July 2004, the commerce ministers from Australia, Brazil, the EU, India and the US discussed in a meeting, and reached an agreement; a much-needed step to initiate fresh talks. In the G-20 ministers meet in New Delhi (18–19 March 2005), the ministerial declaration further decided to keep the pressure on developed countries for increased market access, the line which was eventually followed at the Hong Kong Ministerial (2005):

> ... the tariff reduction formula must contain: (i) progressivity—deeper cuts to higher bound tariffs; (ii) proportionality—developing countries making lesser reduction commitments than developed countries and neutrality in respect of tariff structures; and (iii) flexibility—to take account of the sensitive nature of some products without undermining the overall objective of the reduction formula and ensuring substantial improvement in market access for all products.[7]

WTO-induced Reform in India

India had initiated a series of reforms including tariff reforms even before 1995. Historically it had adopted highly protective tariff policies for encouraging the domestic industries as a strategy of industrialisation. This however led to a gradual shrinkage of India's share in the world market since 1950s.[8] Apart from the protective tariff policies, India also had adopted various restrictive entry policies such as the reservation policies to protect the small-scale sector and the industrial licensing policies to restrict free entry of firms. These two sets of entry restriction policies had drastically reduced competition in the internal domestic market. In other words, the entry and exit decisions of the firms were influenced not by the market forces but by the whims of the bureaucratic decisions.[9] Consequently, a number of large business houses emerged in capital-intensive sectors. Although the Monopolies and Restrictive Trade Practices (MRTP) Commission was operational in this period, the domestic competition was heavily influenced by government policies in particular markets. Similarly, the strict regulations on foreign currency resulted in poor FDI inflow as compared to other Asian economies. Coupled with the lack of competition due to import restrictions, the inefficiency in manufacturing sector and the consequent low productivity had been a major problem for India. Concerned with the twin problems of slow growth and BOP constraint, India was compelled perhaps by the forces of circumstances to initiate certain reform measures both at the internal and external fronts. On the internal front the new industrial policy of 1991, removing the earlier licensing system and reservation of industries, had paved the way for adopting a liberalised economic system and as a result presently the government retains exclusive monopoly only for railways. The banking sector is gradually being opened up for private investors. In addition, replacement of Foreign Exchange Regulation Act (FERA by new Foreign Exchange management Act (FEMA), disinvestment in several public sector enterprises, reforms in direct and indirect taxes, building up infrastructure through liberalised policy framework, etc. has increased the reliability of the reform policies.[10] De-reservation of small-scale sectors over the last couple of years is considered to be a major step for promoting efficiency.[11] Finally, the government opened up a number of key sectors to attract FDI, and this result in an increase in the number of foreign players in the market.[12]

On the external front, more stress was laid on formulating an export-led growth strategy. Indian rupee was devalued in 1991, and the control over it was gradually loosened. The current account was made fully convertible in August 1994. Although discussions were going on for capital account convertibility, the South East Asian crisis in 1997 and the resulting capital flight caused India to adopt a cautious approach.[13] However, external reform was effectively locked in because of India's participation in WTO, as it was a signatory member of GATT since 1947 and became part of the WTO commitments from 1995. The statement of the Prime Minister of India in March 2006 on consideration of full capital account convertibility of the rupee might perhaps be followed by certain concrete policies in this front.

Thus, at the beginning of the WTO, India had already liberalised the economy to a large extent which was further accentuated by the tariff commitments made under the multilateral body from 1995 onwards. For instance, India lowered its (un-weighted) applied tariff rate for the overall economy from 125 per cent in 1990–91 to 71 per cent in 1993–94, and further to 22.2 per cent in 2004–5. Similarly, the maximum tariff rate has declined from 355 per cent in 1990–91 to 45 per cent in 1997–98 and further to 30 per cent in 2004–5 (Chadha et al. 2003, 15–16; World Bank reports, various years). In the same way, imports of previously restricted items were liberalised[14] and the coverage of tariff lines was gradually expanded, and India bounded around 73 per cent of its tariff lines compared to only 6 per cent bound tariff lines in the pre-Uruguay Round period. The ceilings for industrial goods are generally at 40 per cent *ad valorem* for finished goods and 25 per cent on intermediates. The phased reduction to these bound levels would be achieved during the 10-year period beginning from 1995 onwards.

The relative openness of the Indian economy in the post-1995 period in comparison to the previous epoch becomes obvious from Table 8.2, which shows export plus import as a share of GDP has increased three-fold over a major part of the last two decades. The tariff reform in the post-WTO accession period has resulted in a massive decline in average as well as peak tariff rates.[15] Buoyed with this advantage, the volume of import has increased at a higher rate as compared to export growth rate. Although the volume of trade balance is worsening over time, the increasing dependence on trade is a good sign.

TABLE 8.2 The openness measures for Indian economy (Rs in crore)

Year	Export (X)	Export growth (percentage)	Import (M)	Import growth (percentage)	Trade balance (TB)	TB Growth (percentage)	GDP at factor cost	TB as a percentage of GDP	X+M as a percentage of GDP
1983–84	9771	11.00	15831	10.76	–6060	10.38	471191	–1.29	5.43
1984–85	11744	20.19	17134	8.23	–5390	–11.06	490027	–1.10	5.89
1985–86	10895	–7.23	19658	14.73	–8763	62.58	514059	–1.70	5.94
1986–87	12452	14.29	20096	2.23	–7644	–12.77	536337	–1.43	6.07
1987–88	15674	25.88	22244	10.69	–6570	–14.05	556874	–1.18	6.81
1988–89	20232	29.08	28235	26.93	–8003	21.81	615206	–1.30	7.88
1989–90	27658	36.70	35328	25.12	–7670	–4.16	656469	–1.17	9.59
1990–91	32553	17.70	43198	22.28	–10645	38.79	693051	–1.54	10.93

(Contd)

(Table 8.2 Contd)

Year	Export (X)	Export growth (percentage)	Import (M)	Import growth (percentage)	Trade Balance (TB)	TB Growth (percentage)	GDP at factor cost	TB as a percentage of GDP	X+M as a percentage of GDP
1991–92	44041	35.29	47851	10.77	−3810	−64.21	702067	−0.54	13.09
1992–93	53688	21.90	63375	32.44	−9687	154.25	738003	−1.31	15.86
1993–94	69751	29.92	73101	15.35	−3350	−65.42	781345	−0.43	18.28
1994–95	82674	18.53	89971	23.08	−7297	117.82	888031	−0.82	19.44
1995–96	106353	28.64	122678	36.35	−16325	123.72	899563	−1.81	25.46
1996–97	118817	11.72	138920	13.24	−20103	23.14	970083	−2.07	26.57
1997–98	130101	9.50	154176	10.98	−24075	19.76	1016266	−2.37	27.97
1998–99	139753	7.42	178332	15.67	−38579	60.25	1083047	−3.56	29.37
1999–2000	159561	14.17	215236	20.69	−55675	44.31	1148367	−4.85	32.64
2000–1	203571	27.58	230873	7.27	−27302	−50.96	1198664	−2.28	36.24
2001–2	209018	2.68	245200	6.21	−36182	32.53	1268175	−2.85	35.82
2002–3	255137	22.06	297206	21.21	−42069	16.27	1316270	−3.20	41.96
2003–4	293367	14.98	359108	20.83	−65741	56.27	1428667	−4.60	45.67
2004–5	375340	27.94	501065	39.53	−125725	91.24	1536058	−8.18	57.06
2005–6	456418	21.60	660409	31.80	−203991	62.25	1674177	−12.18	66.71

Note: GDP figures from 1999–2000 onwards have been calculated in 1993–94 prices
Source: Calculated from Ministry of Finance, *Economic Survey*, New Delhi: Government of India, Various issues. P—Provisional Estimates, Q—Quick Estimates

Disputes and Concern Areas

Increasing trade is associated with disputes on newer areas, where trade is created. India has been very much concerned with certain global streams of events since 1995. In particular, various trade-distorting policies of partner countries have led to huge market access loss for India.[16] On the other hand, India's domestic policies have come under fire on various occasions, and questions have been raised on the WTO-compatibility of its various measures. In Table 8.3, a comparative analysis of the two Trade Policy Reviews on India undertaken in 1998 and 2002 is presented, which shows that despite the decline in the extent of WTO-inconsistency in Indian policies, concern areas still remain (e.g., contingency measures, entry restrictions, etc.). The concern is quite legitimate since Table 8.4 shows that as respondent India has lost most of the cases at the WTO forum, thereby implying the validity of the claims of the complainant countries.

As seen in Table 8.4, India has so far been involved in a total of 36 cases at the WTO Dispute Settlement Body. An analysis of the time trend of cases against India reveals that its trade policy is increasingly becoming WTO-compatible, during June 1999–January 2003 not a single case was registered. However, recently India's anti-dumping policy is increasingly coming under fire.[17] Second, while cases filed by India involves imposition of anti-dumping and other type of duties and WTO-incompatibility of import measures on textile products among other members, the cases filed against India centres on three broad issues, namely, import restrictions, patent regime and anti-dumping.[18] Third, while India has won 7 cases out of 17 as a complainant, it has not won a single case as respondent and lost 5 cases out of 19.[19] Finally, as third party, India had participated in disputes over TRIPS, textile products, primary products and allegations of dumping; i.e., the issues pertaining to its immediate interest. From the analysis in Tables 8.3 and 8.4, it appears that India may face a number of fresh disputes in coming years, as various countries have expressed their open dissatisfaction over the pace of India's external reform and the level of market access realised so far.[20] On the other hand, as mentioned earlier, various non-tariff barriers imposed on Indian exports caused the realised market access for the country to shrink by a considerable amount, which potentially opens areas of future dispute.

TABLE 8.3 A comparative analysis: Country review

Trade Policy Review (1998)	
Policies Praised	Policies where Further Reform Advocated
• Rapid reform in tariff rates over 1993–94 to 1997–98. • Overall economic reform measures. • Amendment in Copyright law in line with TRIPS.	• Complex structure of tariff regime and tariff escalation. • Import restriction on consumer goods. • Restrictive import licenses and other procedural hassles on imports. • Presence of indirect subsidies, export subsidies and other incentives. • Unfinished compliance with TRIPS. • Reform in case of agricultural products. • Transparency in decision-making. • Reform in services.
Trade Policy Review (2002)	
Policies Praised	Policies where Further Reform Advocated
• Simplification of tariff structure. • Complete elimination of quantitative restrictions. • Reduction in export restrictions. • Review of FDI policy. • Move towards full conformity with TRIPS. • Significant reform in certain key service sectors e.g. telecommunication, financial services and to some extent in infrastructural services.	• Increase in use of contingency measures on imports. • Wide range of price and distribution controls in agriculture. • Existence of certain commodity specific entry restrictions.

Source: Chaisse and Chakraborty (2004)

TABLE 8.4 Cases at DSB involving India (updated upto 21 March 2007)

	Cases involving India as Respondent			
Complaint by:	Win	Loss	Amicably settled	Continuing/ Recent Request	Total
Developed countries	0	5	9	4	18
Developing countries	–	–	–	1	1
	Cases involving India as Complainant			
Respondents:	Win	Loss	Amicably settled	Continuing/ Recent Request	Total
Developed countries	6	1	5	1	13
Developing countries	1	0	3	–	4

Source: Compiled from WTO documents.

EFFECTS OF INCREASED MARKET ACCESS IN MANUFACTURING
A Review of CGE Results

For analysing the possible effects of increased market access conditions on trade and industrial structure we first of all consider the standard Heckscher-Ohlin-Samuelson (HOS) framework of trade. This model predicts that trade liberalisation would shift resources away from the industries intensive in the use of relatively scarce factor to those industries which use the relatively abundant factor of the economy intensively. *The change in resource allocation results from the changes in relative commodity prices due to reduction in trade barriers* and it would improve the allocative efficiency of the economy in the use of resources. The improvement in efficiency is seen in terms of industrial adjustments through specialisation in industries in which the country has comparative advantage. Under the assumptions of perfect competition and constant returns to scale, such changes in relative commodity prices would lead to changes in the relative factor rewards according to the Stolper-Samuelson theorem. Thus, India being a relatively labour-abundant economy, trade liberalisation is expected to shift resources away from the capital-intensive industries towards the labour-intensive industries and consequently the rewards (both nominal and real) to labour would rise and to capital will decline following the Stolper-Samuelson hypothesis. The theory also suggests that such liberalisation will generally increase the welfare level of the economy. Thus, as we have noted above, the *price effects of the reduction of tariffs* may not be very significant for the developed countries as they have already lowered their tariff rates substantially before the Uruguay Round (Rodrik 1999) and moreover until the other obstacles to trade—MFA and anti-dumping measures—are removed, the market will be insulated from such price effects. Thus, Rodrik argues that increased openness in these countries affects the elasticity of (labour demand in his case) demand due to increased competition from the cheap labour-intensive products of the developing countries. On the other hand, as Wood and Ridao-Cano (1999) argues, the price changes may be substantial for developing countries as these countries begin the process of lowering their tariffs from very high initial tariff rates.

The quantitative analysis of the possible effects of unilateral and multilateral tariffs reductions as proposed under the Uruguay Round could be estimated through a computational general equilibrium (CGE modelling) framework. The broad findings of the CGE model by Chadha and others (2003) have been in line with the HOS predictions (shifting of resources towards labour-intensive products, increase in real returns to both labour and capital, growth in output and exports for exporting industries, increase in welfare, etc.). However, the projected decline in output and employment in several industrial sectors have not materialised. The discrepancy with the real world scenario may originate from the essentially static framework of CGE models and their dependence upon the assumed elasticity parameters, apart from the particular model specification underlying the exercise. Moreover, the implicit assumption of perfect competition leading to exit (not just decline) of import competing industries and the rise of export industries is not without its limitations.

It is important to note that the market even after liberalisation is segmented from the world market by tariff and other barriers like transport cost and to that extent the domestic firms can discriminate between the world and domestic markets (Agarwal and Barua 1993;

1994 and 2004). This implies that the domestic firms can charge higher price than the tariff inclusive foreign price, which gives certain freedom to firms to survive despite foreign import competition. While the distinction between the firm and the industry becomes blurred under the assumption of perfect competition, it now plays an important role under market imperfections. When both export and import competing firms are subject to increasing returns to scale, they face decreasing average cost curves. In the post-liberalisation period as the exporting firms expand they move along the downward slope of the decreasing average cost curve while the import competing firms move up the contour. Thus, while one set of firms is enjoying economies of scale, the other set of firms suffers from diseconomies of scale. The real benefits from increasing returns are therefore not unambiguous as scale advantage from increased production in export goods must be balanced against the diseconomies from the decline in the production of import competing goods (Rodrik 1988). Chakraborty (2002) provides some evidence of increasing returns in export industries and decreasing returns in import competing goods in India. The net welfare effects are therefore not known. However, this may not happen if industries are such that the import competing firms without any cost can easily adjust itself to produce the exporting variety. So if liberalisation does not lead to exit of the import competing firm then increased openness under the assumption of market imperfections and scale economies is expected to lead to increase in scale efficiency through intra-industry specialisation and improvement in welfare via the effects of increased varieties on consumer demand. A substantial increase in the levels of intra-industry trade has been observed in India since 1991 (Chakraborty 2002). The cost of adjustments may be minimal if the industrial structures in import and export goods are similar and this would limit the adverse implications on income distribution due to increased openness.

As argued by Agarwal and Barua (2003), openness also plays an important disciplining role in the market. It breaks domestic monopoly and forces market to behave competitively. If this happens then one would observe reduction in the monopoly power in industries reflected in the decline in market concentration due to globalisation.

We however cannot decide a priori which particular framework will be the appropriate one to examine the possible implications of globalisation on Indian industries and firms. The existence of market imperfection does not necessarily preclude the relevance of the HOS framework to analyse the effects of globalisation. The relative price effect may play a far more dominating role than the standard conclusions based on market imperfection. The issue is therefore open to empirical verification.

The Realised Impact of Trade Liberalisation

We first consider here the changing pattern and direction of India's trade. Then we will attempt to analyse whether India's net trade can be explained in terms of factor intensities. For the analyses, we use the trade figures provided under the HS system from various issues of Directorate General of Commercial Intelligence and Service (DGCIS) Monthly Statistics of Foreign Trade.[21] First, we consider the changing pattern in India's trade direction. As seen in Table 8.5, the export shares to Africa, Latin America and Asia are increasing in the post-WTO accession period, while the same to former USSR, North America and the EU has gone down. A similar trend is observed in case of imports as well, where shares of Africa and Asia are increasing in India's trade basket at the cost of North America and the EU.

TABLE 8.5 Exports and imports of India by destination

Region	Export 1960–61	Export 1990–91	Export 2005–6	Import 1960–61	Import 1990–91	Import 2005–6
EU	36.2	27.5	16.0	37.1	29.4	22.3
North America	18.7	15.6	6.1	31.0	13.4	17.7
Eastern Europe, Russia and Baltic States	7.0	17.9	2.2	3.4	7.8	1.3
Africa	6.3	2.1	2.7	5.6	2.2	5.4
Asia including OPEC	11.0	19.9	35.2	10.3	30.3	48.5
Latin America	1.6	0.4	1.7	0.4	2.3	2.9

Source: Ministry of Finance, *Economic Survey*, New Delhi: Government of India, various years.

The increase in trade shares of Asia, particularly Southeast and East Asia has been the direct result of the 'Look East' policy followed by India since 1991. The collapse of Soviet Union, a major trade partner, coupled with the increasing trend in regionalism in the world caused India to focus its attention to the hitherto unexplored quarters. In the pre-1991 days, India deliberately maintained a distance with the countries located in this region. However, since the initiation of economic reform process in 1991, India is trying to attract FDI inflow in the country and was keen to repeat a 'flying geese' phenomenon through East Asian capital (Saint-Mezard 2003, 26). Singh (2004) shows that from 1992 onwards, Indian prime ministers have regularly visited the region, so as to facilitate increasing bilateral associations.[22]

Next, we focus on the pre- and post-reform trends in India's trade pattern. In Tables 8.6 and 8.7, the trends in export and import shares of HS sections have been provided. It is clearly seen from Table 8.6 that the percentage share of HS-sections I–V, i.e. primary commodities comprising animal products and processed foodstuffs in India's export, have declined. Among the intermediate and light manufacturing products, while sections VI, VII and X have shown proportionate increase, sections VIII and IX have declined. Export of section XI (textile and textile articles) has declined, while the same for section V (mineral fuels) has increased considerably. Section XIV (gems and jewellery) is found to be more or less constant over the period. On the whole, the major export items consist of labour-intensive light manufacturing products.[23]

It is observed from Table 8.7 that imports of section I–IV, i.e., the primary commodities, are declining. A similar trend is noticed in the other sections barring the exceptions of V (mineral products), VIII (hides and skins, leather products, fur skins and articles thereof), XI (textile & textile articles). Import of section VI (products of the chemical and the allied industries) and XII (footwear, headgear, umbrellas; prepared feathers and articles thereof) in proportional terms did not show any appreciable change over time. Import of section XIV (gems and jewellery) has undergone a changing trend.

The export and import dynamics at HS 2-digit level provides some interesting results. The prominent export items are mineral fuels (HS-27), chemical products (HS-29), articles of leather (HS-42), articles of apparel and clothing (HS-61 and 62), gems and jewellery (HS-71), and machinery and equipment (HS-84 and 85). It is observed that import share of manufacturing items are increasing in general. The most significant import items are mineral fuels (HS-27), gems and jewellery (HS-71), and machinery and equipment products (HS-84 and 85).

TABLE 8.6 Export ratios of India by HS sections[24]

Year	1987–88	1989–90	1990–91	1991–92	1992–93	1993–94	1994–95	1995–96	1996–97	1997–98	1999–2000	2000–1	2001–2	2002–3	2003–4	2005–0
I	4.237	3.125	3.605	4.018	4.020	4.324	4.930	3.929	4.188	4.280	3.891	4.016	3.613	3.405	2.719	2.265
II	14.582	10.848	9.734	9.856	6.514	8.131	7.796	11.177	9.713	9.722	8.889	7.021	6.892	7.077	6.232	4.750
III	0.136	0.285	0.270	0.406	0.313	0.472	0.603	0.848	0.585	0.506	0.714	0.522	0.395	0.292	0.335	0.272
IV	2.708	3.430	3.227	3.715	4.867	4.797	3.122	3.757	5.244	4.388	2.309	2.357	3.057	2.306	2.631	2.203
V	9.118	7.629	7.543	6.991	6.336	5.628	5.028	4.543	4.227	3.439	2.194	6.382	7.247	8.111	8.875	16.711
VI	4.646	8.399	7.864	8.621	6.968	7.080	7.853	7.746	8.793	9.448	9.510	9.538	9.711	10.239	10.370	10.436
VII	0.784	1.127	1.207	1.137	1.839	2.000	2.599	2.467	2.210	2.084	1.983	2.394	2.643	2.903	3.135	3.100
VIII	5.584	5.068	5.392	4.712	5.000	4.011	4.293	3.837	3.256	3.385	2.925	3.029	3.062	2.516	2.442	1.801
IX	0.117	0.087	0.080	0.092	0.074	0.227	0.168	0.118	0.128	0.099	0.080	0.080	0.077	0.092	0.099	0.101
X	0.208	0.193	0.186	0.203	0.259	0.836	0.384	0.476	0.433	0.334	0.449	0.542	0.572	0.605	0.0572	0.539
XI	26.506	23.989	27.433	27.236	28.120	25.738	27.298	25.625	27.391	26.897	26.001	26.038	23.624	22.491	21.114	17.316
XII	2.877	2.457	2.864	2.684	2.369	2.270	2.181	1.918	1.760	1.589	1.756	1.551	1.613	1.292	1.328	1.126
XIII	0.308	0.384	0.434	0.571	0.719	0.795	0.996	1.024	0.974	0.944	1.066	1.180	1.150	1.176	1.162	0.975
XIV	16.772	19.175	16.205	15.387	16.942	18.035	17.179	16.643	14.183	15.327	20.951	16.710	16.748	17.247	16.856	15.383
XV	2.409	3.987	4.088	4.541	6.065	6.243	5.528	5.583	5.827	6.203	6.249	6.677	6.525	8.016	8.819	9.316
XVI	4.707	5.293	5.230	4.849	4.311	4.349	4.656	5.047	5.555	5.826	5.401	6.121	6.464	6.020	6.901	6.747
XVII	1.622	1.957	2.218	2.769	2.927	2.659	2.933	2.815	2.889	2.664	2.226	2.378	2.327	2.538	3.064	4.193
XVIII	0.627	0.684	0.464	0.416	0.319	0.359	0.374	0.377	0.435	0.449	0.675	0.737	0.819	0.808	0.862	0.741
XIX	0.002	0.003	0.001	0.001	0.005	0.003	0.002	0.001	0.003	0.011	0.002	0.005	0.014	0.004	0.005	0.002

TABLE 8.7 Import Ratios of India by HS sections

Year	1987–88	1989–90	1990–91	1991–92	1992–93	1993–94	1994–95	1995–96	1996–97	1997–98	1999–2000	2000–1	2001–2	2002–3	2003–4	2005–6
I	0.667	0.175	0.022	0.075	0.093	0.048	0.064	0.092	0.033	0.066	0.097	0.063	0.055	0.066	0.067	0.031
II	2.121	2.127	1.062	1.616	2.870	2.247	2.023	1.629	1.991	2.561	1.725	1.240	2.193	1.979	1.597	1.183
III	4.569	0.710	0.865	0.715	0.453	0.472	0.979	2.014	2.209	1.816	3.930	2.793	2.887	3.046	3.305	1.537
IV	1.284	0.661	0.410	0.466	0.487	0.493	3.103	0.520	0.359	0.642	0.758	0.285	0.342	0.314	0.274	0.410
V	21.349	22.078	30.406	32.266	31.616	28.888	25.918	24.577	30.607	25.649	30.357	36.047	32.276	33.471	30.211	35.274
VI	8.329	11.986	9.774	13.396	12.784	11.388	13.161	16.388	11.283	12.219	10.740	8.442	9.461	8.517	8.683	8.003
VII	3.382	3.719	3.509	3.666	2.658	2.694	3.012	3.355	2.823	2.479	2.132	1.856	2.128	2.036	2.209	2.211
VIII	0.113	0.300	0.437	0.401	0.390	0.496	0.443	0.370	0.366	0.365	0.316	0.394	0.441	0.347	0.313	0.225
IX	1.081	1.126	1.091	0.875	0.907	0.620	0.792	0.666	0.696	1.025	0.929	0.973	1.076	0.675	0.929	0.643
X	2.664	2.156	2.475	1.851	1.789	1.915	1.811	2.217	2.084	2.237	1.684	1.814	1.867	1.612	1.726	1.317
XI	2.032	2.189	2.126	1.726	2.211	2.320	2.957	2.558	2.005	2.022	2.266	2.309	2.980	2.673	2.580	1.793
XII	0.063	0.065	0.083	0.086	0.084	0.111	0.108	0.103	0.079	0.076	0.070	0.069	0.058	0.051	0.055	0.071
XIII	0.456	0.482	0.480	0.457	0.413	0.304	0.470	0.399	0.330	0.364	0.348	0.367	0.459	0.399	0.441	0.453
XIV	9.159	12.137	8.924	10.168	12.239	12.441	8.306	7.979	10.139	15.895	20.592	19.149	18.189	17.057	18.113	13.871
XV	11.556	13.315	11.494	8.668	8.600	7.741	9.193	8.592	8.793	7.847	4.972	4.223	4.969	4.333	4.996	6.608
XVI	17.489	14.736	13.825	11.518	11.793	13.015	14.997	16.664	14.968	15.566	12.425	14.063	14.454	16.606	17.272	17.306
XVII	3.417	4.220	3.966	1.916	2.114	5.444	3.908	2.925	3.798	2.538	2.294	1.883	2.240	3.092	4.133	5.932
XVIII	2.266	2.565	2.573	2.030	2.290	1.997	1.893	1.995	1.543	2.020	1.968	1.958	2.361	2.259	2.048	1.836
XIX	0.003	0.002	0.001	0.001	0.002	0.000	0.000	0.001	0.001	0.002	0.003	0.001	0.002	0.004	0.004	0.001

An Analysis Based on Net Trade Flows

It is observed from the earlier analysis that India's trade in manufacturing products has increased gradually in the post-WTO period, but the trade balance was never in India's favour. On the other hand, although trade with developed countries still accounts for a major proportion of total trade, the share of developing countries is on the rise. Broadly, the trade pattern is in line with the traditional HOS theorem, which predicts that, a labour-abundant country like India will export labour-intensive products, while importing capital-intensive products.[25]

In order to check the relevance of the theorem for India, we undertake the following estimation exercise. India being a developing country, the net export of a particular product group should bear a positive relationship with the unskilled-skilled wage ratio of the group, and a negative relationship with its capital-labour ratio. Based on this assumption, we calculate net trade figures of India at HS 4-digit level for all industries. The industry-related data is collected from the *Annual Survey of Indian Industries* (NIC-87 classification), and matched with the trade data through a minor modification over the concordance table prepared by Debroy and Santhanam (1993). Since the industry classification system has undergone a change from 1998–99 onwards, to obtain a comparable dataset on trade and industry, we select the 11-year period (1987–88 to 1997–98) as the sample. From the set of 175 industries at 3-digit level of industrial classification, a balanced panel is prepared with 135 industries.[26] We estimate the following model:

$$NT_{it} = \mu_i + \beta_1 \cdot (SK/USK)_{1it} + \beta_2 \cdot E(K/L)_{2it} + \beta_3 \cdot S_{it} + V_{it} + \varepsilon_{it} \quad \ldots (1)$$

Where, i = 1 (1) 135, and t = 1 (1) 11.

Where NT_{it} is net trade deflated by total trade for the i-th industry in period t, μ_i is constant over time and specific to the individual cross-section unit, known as individual effect,[27] $(SK/USK)_{it}$ is the skilled to unskilled labour wage ratio, $E(K/L)_{it}$ is the estimated capital-labour ratio, and S_{it} represents the percentage share of a sector's gross value added in the aggregate gross value added of the industry sector.[28] We include a WTO reform dummy V_{it} in the analysis, which takes the value of 1 after 1995 and 0 beforehand. We estimate the equation in Generalized Least Square framework, and usual corrections for autocorrelation and heteroskedasticity are made. The result is reported in the following:[29]

$$NT_{it} = 0.524 - (0.005) \cdot (SK/USK)_{1it} - (0.060) \cdot E(K/L)_{2it} + (0.052) \cdot S_{it} + 0.196 (V_{it})$$
$$(***) \quad (***) \quad (***) \quad (***) \quad (***) \quad \ldots (2)$$

Number of observations = 1479   Wald Chi^2 (4) = 341.27   Prob. > Chi^2 = 0.0000

The empirical findings indicate that net export items are labour-intensive products usually produced by unskilled labours. Moreover, there is a significant impact of the size of the industries in determination of its trade-intensity, as industries with larger size tend to export more. In addition, the WTO dummy is highly significant, implying that WTO accession has favoured export of products intensive in abundant factors.

The Stolper-Samudson theorem in international trade predicts that there will be a distributional impact on the factor prices in the aftermath of free trade. The price of the relatively abundant input would rise while the same for the relatively scarce input will fall, responding to which industries might modify their input requirements. Capital-labour ratio in Indian industries has gradually increased over time (Chakraborty 2002),[30] although both the cost of capital (rate of interest) and real wage has gradually declined over the years.[31] Hazra and Chakraborty (2005) showed that from 1982 onwards (also in the post-liberalisation period) new industrial units tend to be more capital-intensive owing to the inflexibility in labour market.[32] In other words, domestic policy inflexibility has deprived the relatively abundant factor the full effect of economic liberalisation.

INCREASING RETURNS AND IMPERFECT COMPETITION

Implicit in the above analysis are the assumptions of perfect competition and constant returns to scale, which implies that IIT has to be completely ruled out. If however IIT exists then the netting of trade flows in the above analysis will eliminate a large quantity of trade from our analysis. Secondly, intra-industry trade means countries are having simultaneous comparative advantage as well as disadvantage in the same industry, which is not permissible under HOS framework. Grubel and Lloyd (1975), Dixit and Stiglitz (1977), Krugman (1979 and 1980) and Lancaster (1980) theorised this phenomenon by assuming imperfect competition, product differentiation and economies of scale. As argued by Grubel and Lloyd (1975), IIT can be intensified by trade liberalisation and its presence minimises the problems of adjustment, which we have discussed above. Expansion of trade in such a situation does not involve inter-sectoral changes in resource allocation as in the HOS model but only reduction of product varieties within the industry.

Since mid-seventies, research on IIT focused on its determinants and impact. Generally trade reform enhances IIT in manufactures, both in case of developed and developing countries (Balassam 1966; Willmore 1970; Grubel and Lloyd 1975; Globerman 1990; Musonda 1997; Faustino et al. 1998 and Andresen 2001).

Focusing on the Indian data over 1960–80, Pant and Barua (1986) observed that increased trade resulted in no appreciable change in IIT level barring a few commodity groups owing to (a) specialisation in narrow product lines, (b) trade bias towards developed countries and (c) worsening of export potentials of the manufacturing sector. Bhattacharyya (1994) showed that the IIT index is rather skewed in favour of a few selected industry groups, and is considerably higher with developed countries and NICs vis-à-vis the same with developing countries and LDCs (Veeramani 2001).[33] The finding was supported by Kantawala (1997), which reported an insignificant intra-SAARC IIT level for India.

Analysing IIT trends in the capital goods industries, Veeramani (1999) noted a marginal increase over the years and found the trade to be predominantly vertical in nature; both in case of multilateral and bilateral trade.[34] It has been observed that for manufacturing products, the relatively higher IIT indices is associated with a rising share in the export basket in general (Veeramani 2001; Chakraborty 2002).

In Table 8.8, the aggregate IIT trends for Indian economy over the last decade are provided where we report Grubel-Lloyd (uncorrected), Grubel-Lloyd (corrected) and Aquino indices. It is observed that overall index is showing an increasing trend by all three measures. In Table 8.9, we report the IIT indices at HS sectional level.[35] It is seen that the IIT indices across individual HS sections are also rising over time and quite high for manufacturing items.

TABLE 8.8 The indices of IIT

Year	Grubel-Lloyd (U)	Grubel-Lloyd (C)	Aquino
1987–88	24.43	29.63	24.25
1988–89	26.41	30.23	25.46
1989–90	29.37	33.47	28.59
1990–91	25.47	29.29	25.12
1991–92	25.44	26.58	25.14
1992–93	27.13	29.90	26.60
1993–94	26.74	27.41	26.55
1994–95	22.92	23.90	22.90
1995–96	22.98	25.19	22.98
1996–97	25.02	27.15	24.84
1997–98	26.82	29.35	26.52
1998–99	26.19	29.72	25.54
1999–2000	28.53	33.77	27.26
2000–1	30.29	32.41	29.48
2001–2	30.32	32.94	29.60
2002–3	32.40	35.08	31.48
2003–4	34.20	40.29	32.75

The IIT indices could qualitatively be further segregated in two categories, namely—horizontal and vertical. Horizontal IIT is generally associated with trade in commodities differentiated by attributes. On the other hand, vertical IIT is prevalent when trade in commodities differentiated by quality takes place. Horizontal IIT are supposed to be more relevant when countries at similar stage of economic development are engaged in trade with each other. Vertical IIT becomes particularly important when trade among countries unequal in terms of development takes place. The recent empirical literature has, however, shown that even in trade among developed countries, vertical IIT could explain a substantial proportion.[36] The recent literature on IIT assumes that the differences in unit values (UV) of the commodities represent the quality difference among them. If UV^X and UV^M represent the unit values of export and import items of an industry at the same level of industrial classification respectively, then the trade is regarded as horizontal, if the ratio of the unit values differs by less than α percentage, and vertical, if otherwise.[37] In other words, for the trade to be horizontal, the following condition must hold:

$$1 - \alpha \leq (UV^X / UV^M) \leq 1 + \alpha \qquad \ldots (3)$$

If the above condition is violated, then the trade is vertically differentiated. The arbitrary parameter α could take different values. However, throughout the literature on horizontal and vertical IIT, two values, 15 per cent and 25 per cent, have been used most widely. The 15 per cent threshold is used when the price differences are supposed to reflect only quality differences, based on the assumption of perfect competition, i.e., consumers will not purchase a similar or lower quality good at a higher price. However, in case of imperfect information, where price difference could result from brand names as well, the 15 per cent difference is too narrow. Instead of using 15 per cent as the threshold limit, 25 per cent should be the accurate level for this purpose. Both of these values could be used in order to check the robustness of the result.

TABLE 8.9 IIT trends (1987–88 to 2002–3)

Year	1987–88	1988–89	1989–90	1990–91	1991–92	1992–93	1993–94	1994–95	1995–96	1996–97	1997–98	1998–99	1999–2000	2000–1	2001–2	2002–3
I	1.99	2.00	2.29	1.70	1.96	1.81	3.42	5.34	2.62	5.32	6.33	3.44	6.05	9.03	19.53	16.64
II	23.74	25.36	32.78	34.97	27.30	33.67	32.49	30.06	20.03	26.62	21.59	21.89	34.45	34.32	22.38	27.49
III	3.70	6.30	5.79	8.78	9.54	23.92	18.53	15.54	12.72	3.25	5.55	2.50	3.60	6.63	18.76	10.04
IV	10.43	9.18	6.95	8.18	7.30	6.49	8.92	6.79	17.12	9.70	12.68	9.79	10.69	22.59	22.46	25.15
V	22.27	29.89	31.95	37.52	34.27	35.42	34.87	37.16	36.25	36.81	32.93	17.09	12.80	8.67	9.56	11.59
VI	25.27	14.49	23.35	28.87	23.64	24.04	27.04	31.24	31.13	31.47	33.60	33.61	33.63	40.61	39.50	42.81
VII	18.03	16.77	17.62	16.79	19.23	21.76	19.79	32.12	31.89	28.33	33.69	36.57	41.91	50.88	49.01	50.95
VIII	50.08	32.30	38.83	25.78	20.81	18.65	22.53	26.70	21.86	20.79	16.61	14.24	16.15	21.52	25.79	27.87
IX	3.81	11.46	4.70	3.54	11.98	2.29	3.45	5.78	7.79	12.38	10.36	62.01	7.96	10.59	10.14	15.74
X	22.75	27.98	20.58	25.12	24.85	23.60	22.94	29.74	28.02	26.04	30.65	31.82	35.77	34.22	32.18	29.78
XI	8.84	9.40	11.84	9.97	12.73	12.17	12.90	11.16	11.72	14.65	19.94	19.78	14.48	15.77	18.09	22.10
XII	63.83	68.43	67.29	63.77	61.54	51.06	44.54	39.00	42.02	38.70	49.15	50.01	41.44	49.44	53.22	42.58
XIII	24.21	19.64	23.65	22.75	21.24	17.34	21.84	21.49	21.60	23.75	21.40	25.44	29.09	31.63	34.86	39.73
XIV	96.71	95.59	94.48	93.23	87.92	89.76	91.04	69.59	70.41	74.45	50.98	42.31	53.57	50.71	49.92	58.54
XV	21.79	20.86	30.23	22.73	26.54	23.83	30.40	31.22	35.52	36.10	39.87	40.48	39.29	43.53	43.28	48.83
XVI	52.70	50.56	53.57	57.12	53.51	58.36	58.41	57.66	59.93	58.10	60.44	60.94	59.68	60.14	67.28	61.21
XVII	38.65	46.19	29.22	37.13	37.20	29.00	18.78	23.70	27.63	28.92	39.18	39.20	44.54	43.86	38.30	29.98
XVIII	37.00	35.47	49.50	51.85	47.87	53.28	52.42	53.46	56.12	58.19	59.68	55.98	57.71	57.10	66.71	62.63
XIX	26.01	33.51	27.53	36.01	2.63	35.52	54.05	40.85	34.41	44.44	87.75	50.43	44.90	36.97	80.25	57.59

In Table 8.10, the overall vertical IIT trends in twelve manufacturing industries with high trade share and IIT indices are reported using UV method at three cross-sections of time—1988–89, 1999–2000 and 2003–4. While the first period gives an impression about the pre-reform scenario, the other two depict the same in the post-WTO framework. The increase in market access through tariff liberalisation in the post-1995 period has caused Indian export of manufacturing products to increase, not only in developing countries, but also in developed countries as well. The fact is part represented by the steady increase in the number of both-way traded items over the sample period. In addition, over 1999–2000 to 2003–4, the proportion of both-way trade as a percentage of all traded lines has declined for certain commodities, signifying trade in newer varieties. The analysis reveals that a major proportion of India's trade in the sample groups is vertical in nature. It is further interesting to note that while the proportion of vertical trade increased over 1988–89 to 1999–2000 for most of the industries, it marginally declined over 1999–2000 to 2003–4 for a number of industries both at 15 per cent and 25 per cent level of difference. The decline is particularly marked for HS 42. In other words, for a significant number of commodity groups, the unit price levels of exports and imports at 6-digit level of aggregation moved closer.

INDUSTRY LEVEL ANALYSIS

Rodrik (1988) had made an important point on the effects of trade liberalisation under monopolistic competition and economies of scale by arguing that trade liberalisation may not lead to the exit of the relatively inefficient firms; which do not export but remain import competitive within the domestic market. The segmentation of markets due to tariffs and other barriers make it possible for the non-exporting firms to exist along with the exporting firms. In such a situation, trade liberalisation while enables the exporting firms to move down along the downward sloping average cost curve and enjoy scale economies, the import competing firms will be forced to move up along the average cost curve and suffer from the diseconomies of scale. Thus, the producer's surplus will increase for the exporting firms and will decrease for the import competing firms. The net welfare impact of trade will therefore not be unambiguous. We make an effort to explore whether such scale effects can be seen in the Indian industrial sector in the aftermath of reform. For this we estimate a production function for each industry at NIC 2-digit level and examine if any appreciable changes in scale efficiency can be noticed. The estimation is performed in a two-input framework, with the assumption of a Cobb-Douglas Production function of the following form:

$$Y = A \cdot K^{\alpha} \cdot L^{\beta}$$

Y, K and L being output, capital and labour respectively, then, sum of the powers of the inputs, i.e., $(\alpha + \beta)$ represents the economies of scale. The production function is subject to increasing, constant or decreasing returns to scale depending on the fact whether $\alpha + \beta$ is greater than, equal to or less than one. In the proposed model, gross-value added data is taken as an indicator to represent output Y. The price changes have been corrected by deflating it by the yearly price index of the manufactured products. Of the two inputs considered for analysis, while the calculation of labour is done directly, i.e., the number of employees is taken as a representative of labour input, measurement of capital is done following the Perpetual Inventory Method.

TABLE 8.10 Horizontal and vertical specialisation trend[38]

HS-Digit	Both way Trade (Number of HS 6-digit lines)			Proportion of Both way Trade (percentage of all 6-digit lines)			Proportional of 6-digit lines with Vertical trade (15 per cent)			Proportional of 6-digit lines with Vertical trade (25 per cent)		
	1988–89	1999–2000	2003–04	1988–89	1999–2000	2003–04	1988–89	1999–2000	2003–04	1988–89	1999–2000	2003–04
28	44	61	153	70.97	95.31	85.00	88.64	86.89	90.20	77.27	80.33	85.62
29	76	129	287	77.55	98.47	91.69	85.53	91.47	86.41	77.63	70.07	76.31
30	–	16	26	–	100.00	89.66	–	81.25	100.00	–	75.00	100.00
39	39	47	119	92.86	100.00	94.44	79.49	93.62	91.60	69.23	80.85	79.83
40	20	24	70	86.96	100.00	95.89	100.00	91.67	85.71	100.00	87.5	78.57
42	–	12	10	–	92.31	100.00	–	91.67	70.00	–	91.67	50.00
71	6	14	39	46.15	77.78	79.59	83.33	85.71	92.31	83.33	64.29	82.05
72	61	63	155	63.54	94.03	91.18	88.52	90.48	77.42	78.69	80.95	67.10
73	33	50	111	67.35	96.15	92.50	96.97	94.00	96.40	87.88	88.00	91.89
84	167	198	471	90.76	98.02	92.90	97.6	97.47	95.75	96.40	95.96	93.84
85	78	99	275	93.98	99.00	94.18	96.15	92.93	89.82	93.59	87.88	83.27
87	19	27	65	65.52	96.43	89.04	94.74	96.30	93.85	89.47	81.48	86.15

For estimating the production function at 2-digit level, data at 3-digit level is considered for the industries (NIC-1987) taken from the factory sector.[39] From the 183 industries, 15 industries have been dropped, as they are not economically productive uniformly throughout the period. We define 1987–88 to 1991–92 to be the pre-reform period, while 1992–93 to 1997–98 is considered as the post-reform period.[40] The production function is written in logarithmic form in the following way:

$$Y_{it} = \mu_i + \beta_l \cdot K_{it} + \beta_K \cdot L_{it} + \varepsilon_{it} \qquad \ldots (4)$$

Where, i = 1 (1) n, and t = 1 (1) T

Where Y is the logarithm of output and K and L are the logarithms of inputs, μ_i is constant over time and specific to the individual cross-section unit, known as individual effect. 'n' is the number of industries in a particular group.

As noted by Rodrik (1995), the scale efficiency should rise in the post-liberalisation period, in particular for a country like India, where policy restrictions played a major role in the pre-reform days. The results of economies of scale estimation are briefly summarised in Table 8.11. First, it is checked whether a sector is subject to scale economies, i.e., whether $(\alpha + \beta - 1)$ is significantly different form zero. On the basis of that test, we drop HS 22 (beverages and tobacco), HS 33–34 (basic metal and metal products) and HS 38 (other manufacturing industries) from the analysis, and proceed with the remaining seven sectors.

TABLE 8.11 The trends in scale efficiency of the industrial sector

		Industries with $(\alpha + \beta - 1)$ significantly different from zero		
Industry code	Description	Trends in Net Trade	$(\alpha + \beta)$ in pre-reform period	$(\alpha + \beta)$ in post-reform period
20–21	Manufacture of food products	Negative in mid-eighties, but becomes positive from early nineties.	1.0971	1.1423
23–26	Cotton Textile and other fabrics	The trade balance was always positive, the increasing in recent years.	1.0543	1.1435
27–28	Wood and Paper industries	The trade balance was always negative, and increasing in the recent period.	1.0704	1.1287
30–31	Chemicals, rubber and plastic	Positive in mid-eighties, but becomes negative since early nineties. The balance is worsening in recent period.	1.2372	0.8481
32	Non-metallic mineral products	Negative in mid-eighties, but becomes positive afterwards. The trade balance is fluctuating.	0.9852	1.4640
35–36	Machinery and equipment	The trade balance was always negative, and worsening in recent period.	1.1947	1.0492
37	Transport Equipments	The trade balance was always negative, and worsening in recent period.	1.1537	1.0661

	Industries with $(\alpha + \beta - 1)$ not significantly different from zero
Industry code	Description
22	Manufacture of beverages, tobacco and related products
33–34	Basic metals and manufactures of metal products
38	Other manufacturing industries

It could be seen from Table 8.11 that the scale efficiency of the factory sector does not show a uniform trend. Certain sectors show an increase in scale efficiency while the others have shown decrease in efficiency. For a number of sectors, the liberalisation dummy has been found to be statistically non-significant. We compare the result of scale efficiencies of the manufacturing industries at 2-digit NIC level with the trade balances of the corresponding HS-industries at 2-digit level in the same table. The observation reveals that, in general, the NIC-industries with decrease in scale efficiency are associated with a declining trend in net trade of the corresponding HS-industries over the sample period. The only exception is the wood and paper industry, for which the economies of scale has increased in the post-liberalisation period, despite a negative trade balance. In other words the import-competing sectors in the post-liberalisation period have suffered to certain extent, while the net exporter industries reaped the advantages of increased scale efficiency. The result broadly in line with the findings of Krishna and Mitra (1998), which found that although the rate of growth of productivity has increased weakly in the post-liberalisation period, the returns to scale expressed as a sum of factor shares has actually declined.[41]

CONCLUSION

From the above analysis the following conclusions can be drawn. First, the Indian economy is much more liberalised today in comparison to the pre-1991 situation. This has happened partly because of the internal compulsions created by the serious BOP crisis in 1991 and the slowing down of productivity growth over decades and partly by the external forces due to the obligatory commitments under the WTO. Second, by focusing on the manufacturing sector only, it is observed that trade liberalisation has led to increase in the net exports of the labour-intensive products across the spectrum of industries. Third, by introducing possibilities of increasing returns and market imperfection, it is seen that trade liberalisation does not lead to extinction of import competing industries from the economy as would be predicted by the traditional theory. Rather, it forces the import competing industries to move upwards along their downward sloping average cost curves. This had led to a decrease in the scale of production of the import competing goods and consequently loss of efficiency. On the other hand, the exporting industries realised economies of scale from their expansion of production and as a result experienced efficiency gains. The net effect of trade liberalisation, both unilateral as well as WTO-induced, on welfare therefore is ambiguous.

Endnotes

[1] India being a developing country is entitled to use a higher WTO Bound rate.

[2] A—Simple Mean Tariff, B—Standard Deviation of Tariff Lines, C—Weighted Mean Tariff, D—Share of Tariff Lines with International Peaks, E—Share of Tariff Lines with Specific Tariffs.

[3] The detailed account of EU and US barriers could be obtained from the *National Trade Estimate* report published by the USTR and the *Report on United States Barriers to Trade and Investment* published by the European Commission, apart from the respective trade policy reviews brought out by WTO from time to time. WTO trade policy review of EU (2000) deserves special mention in this regard.

[4] In particular, the developing countries were against inclusion of the Singapore issues, i.e., trade and investment, competition policy, transparency in government procurement, and trade facilitation and trade and environment related discussions at the proposed new round.

[5] 'As some members (notably Australia, Hong Kong, China, India and Singapore) have shown, unilateral liberalisation can also be in their national interest' WTO 2003, 11).

[6] Indian pharmaceutical sector has suffered heavily on this count. The Cipla-South Africa incidence as quoted in Dasgupta (2003) is the best example of it.

[7] 'G-20 Ministerial Declaration', available at http://www.commerce.nic.in/wto_sub/g20/min_decln.htm.

[8] The export and import share of India stood at 2.2 and 3.1 respectively in 1948. However, it stood at 0.5 and 0.6 per cent in 1992. After ten years of reform experience, the shares have increased marginally to 0.8 and 0.9 per cent in 2002.

[9] For instance, Chapter V(b) of Industrial Dispute Act might be cited, which directed that for factories with more than 100 workers, prior permission from government is a must before retrenching them in order to make the firm viable. Hazra (2001) shows that even if a firm foresees higher demand for its products in a given period, it would be reluctant to employ more workers because retrenching them during lean periods could be impossible, which leads to increasing capital/labour ratio in the factory sector over time.

[10] Now, private investment in power is unrestricted with 100 per cent foreign equity allowed. Moreover, foreign investment in mining is allowed up to 50 per cent equity.

[11] During 2000–1, the government de-reserved the readymade garments sector from SSI list. Next year, de-reservation was done in the field of 14 items related to leather goods, shoes and toys. Finally during 2002–3, 51 more items were removed from the list. The acceptance of the Competition Act (2002) by the lower house of the parliament also had a significant impact on the market structure.

[12] FDI policy in initial years allowed automatic approval of foreign investment in various sectors up to 51 per cent, and the limit is being raised in recent years to 100 per cent in select sectors and special economic zones (SEZs), apart from introduction of one-window facilities instead of time-consuming lengthy bureaucratic channels. In addition, during 2002–3, FDI has been allowed in print media up to 26 per cent, which was not implemented earlier due to national security concerns.

[13] The Tarapore Committee report (1997) recommended that a number of precautionary measures should be gradually implemented before making capital account fully convertible.

[14] WTO-induced reforms played a crucial role in this regard. Restriction on several import items on BOP grounds were withdrawn after losing the case against US (DS 90). Similarly, the impetus for reforms in the domestic IPR regime came in the aftermath of losing two cases on patent protection for pharmaceutical products to US (DS 50) and EC (DS 79).

[15] Virmani et al (2004) has shown that Indian industry would gain from further reduction of tariffs in the coming years in terms of efficiency.

[16] For a detailed analysis, see Bhattacharya (1999). Bhattacharya estimated the total NTM affected exports from India to EU, US and Japan to be Rs 155,910.7 million, Rs 81,623.78 million and Rs 33,350.06 million respectively during 1996–97.

[17] Taiwan (DS 318—1 November 2004), Bangladesh (DS 306—2 February 2004) and EU (DS 304—11 December 2003) has lodged three cases against India complaining its initiation of Anti-Dumping measures to be WTO-incompatible. Bangladesh is the first developing country to lodge a case against India at the dispute settlement body.

[18] The quantitative restrictions on import of primary and other commodities had to be removed in 2000, as India lost the case on 'Quantitative restrictions on imports of agricultural, textile and industrial products' (DS 90) against US in 1999. The list of the 714 items at HS 8-digit level, which were free from QR with effect from 31 March 2000, are provided in the March 2000 issue of *India and the WTO*, the monthly newsletter of Ministry of Commerce, Government of India.

[19] It needs to be mentioned that in two cases, (DS58, import prohibition of shrimp and shrimp products against US, and DS206, anti-dumping and countervailing measures on steel plate against US), although certain US procedures in force were ruled WTO-inconsistent, some of India's claims were rejected by the panel in the latter while certain panel rulings were reversed by the Appellate Body in the former.

[20] China is not happy with India's anti-dumping policy for a long time. US has raised voice on a couple of occasions that the level of market access proposed in India through some liberalised measure is often nullified because of restrictive policies in other fields.

[21] The *International Trade Statistics Yearbook*, United Nations, provide Standard International Trade Classification (SITC) data, it does not publish export and import figures of the traded items, whose values are less than 0.3 per cent of total trade. Hence, a number of commodities will remain excluded, if the UN data is to be used.

[22] The initiative of the policy makers was adequately supported by the business community, as Confederation of Indian Industries (CII), which accompanied the prime ministers in all these trips, played a crucial role in this period.

[23] The 'Revealed Comparative Advantage' (RCA) indices of Kumar et al. (2000) showed improvement mainly in labour-intensive products, with a specialisation trend in narrow product lines. However, it was observed that India does not possess competitiveness in a vast number of commodities.

[24] HS I—Live animals, animal products; HS II—Vegetable products; HS III—Animal or vegetable fats, and oils and their cleavage products; HS IV—Prepared foodstuffs, beverages and tobacco; HS V—Mineral products; HS VI—Products of the chemical and the allied industries; HS VII—Plastics and rubber; HS VIII—Hides and skins, leather products, furskins and articles thereof; HS IX—Wood, cork & articles thereof, manufacture of plaiting materials; HS X—Paper, paper-board and articles thereof, HS XI—Textile and textile articles; HS XII—Foorwear, headgear, umbrellas, prepared feathers and articles thereof, HS XIII—Stone, cement and similar materials, ceramic products, glass and glassware; HS XIV—Pearls, precious and semi-precious stones/metals amd articles thereof; HS XV—Base metals & articles of base metals, HS XVI—Machinery & their parts, electrical & electronic equipment, parts thereof; XVII—Transport equipment; XVIII—Instrument and apparatus, clocks and watches, parts and accessories thereof; XIX—Arms and ammunition, parts and accessories thereof.

[25] However, Bharadwaj (1962) by analysing Indo-US bilateral trade arrived at a conclusion that the trade pattern refutes HOS theorem, since India export capital-intensive products and imports labour-intensive products.

[26] A number of industries have been merged and some others are dropped, as they were not operational for a major portion of the sample period.

[27] In the fixed-effect approach, μ_i is considered to be a group-specific constant, whereas in random effect model μ_i is considered to be a group-specific disturbance term.

[28] The capital-labour ratio is estimated by using Perpetual Inventory Method following Hashim and Dadi.

[29] '***' implies significance at 1 per cent level.

[30] The increasing trend was observed not to be restricted to machinery, chemical or metal products, but equally strong in relatively labour-intensive sectors like plastic products and food industries as well.

[31] The report on the Second National Commission on Labour (2002, 1348) notes, 'As a result of increase in prices, there is an erosion in the wage levels in real terms, and in order to prevent such an erosion, dearness allowance is paid and it is linked to the consumer price index.'

[32] According to Chapter V-B of the Industrial Dispute Act (1947), a firm employing more than 300 workers needed prior permission of the government to retrench the excess labours, which was further amended to 100 in 1982. According to Hazra (2001), even if a firm foresees higher demand for its products in a given period, it will be reluctant to employ more workers because retrenching them in lean period could be impossible, as the government never permits retrenchments owing to political compulsions.

[33] The empirical finding also suggested that the link between industrial organisation and international trade, which was so effectively established for developed countries, does not hold good in the Indian scenario.

[34] The study came out with the policy prescription that future export promotion strategies should exploit the comparative advantage at the finer industry level rather than focusing any sector as a whole.

[35] However, at the sectional level it is seen that under a few circumstances, the value of export or import items at the 4-digit level are uniformly higher than the corresponding import or export items. Under these circumstances, using G-L index may not be the appropriate method. Hence, for calculating the IIT values at the sectional level the Acquino method (1978), which allows for correction of overall imbalance at the elementary level, is used as the more appropriate measure.

[36] The vertical or horizontal specialisation in recent literature is defined in the following way by calculating unit value index, which is discussed in detail in chapter 2. This method has been adopted by Abed-el-Rahman (1991), Greenaway, Hine and Milner (1995), Aturupane et al (1997), Andresen (2001) and others.

[37] The rationale for using UVs is that assuming perfect information, a variety sold at a higher price is in general associated with a higher quality, or, stated otherwise, relative prices reflect relative qualities. This notion is in line with the findings of Stiglitz (1987), which states that even with imperfect information, prices tend to reflect quality.

[38] HS 28—Inorganic chemicals, HS 29—Organic chemicals; HS 30—Pharmaceutical products; HS 39—Plastics and articles thereof; HS 40—Rubber & articles thereof; HS 42—Articles of leather, saddilry harness and animal gut; HS 71—Pearls, precious and semi-precious stones/metals & articles thereof; HS 72—Iron and steel; HS 73—Articles of Iron and steel; HS 84—Nuclear reactors, boilers, mechanery and mechanical appliances, parts thereof; HS 85—Electrical machinery and equipment and parts thereof, sound and TV recorders, and reproducers and parts thereof; HS 87—Road vehicles and parts.

[39] The repair and servicing sector, included in 39–43, 74, 91 and 95–97, is dropped, and we concentrate on industries ranging from 20–21 to 38.

[40] 1991–92 has been defined as the liberalisation year, since several reform measures in industrial policies were initiated from that point.

[41] However, the authors believed that the reduction does not necessarily mean lower scale efficiency but may indicate an increased exploitation of returns to scale by firms, which may have been operating at too small a scale before initiation of reforms. It could also reflect the relatively inflexible capacity constraints in the industries.

References

Abed-el-Rahman, K. 1991. 'Firms Competitive and National Comparative Advantages as Joint Determinants of Trade Composition', *Weltwirtschaftliches Archiv*, vol. 127, pp. 83–97.

Agarwal, Manmohan and Alokesh Barua. 1993. 'Trade Policy and Welfare in Segmented Markets', *Keio Economic Studies*, vol. 30, no. 2, pp. 95–108.

_____. 1994. 'Effects of Entry in a Model of Oligopoly with International Trade', *Journal of International Trade & Economic Development*, vol. 3, no. 1, pp. 1–13.

_____. 2002. 'Firm and Industry Response to Liberalization in India: Theory and Evidence', paper presented in an international seminar organised by the CSH on Globalization of Firms: India, China and Russia, New Delhi, 19–20 December.

_____. 2004. 'Entry Liberalization and Export Performance: A Theoretical Analysis in a Multimarket Oligopoly Model', *Journal of International Trade and Economic Development*, vol. 13, no. 3, pp. 287–303.

Aggarwal, Aradhna. 2002. 'Anti-Dumping Law and Practice: An Indian Perspective', ICRIER Working Paper no. 85, April.

Alburo, Florian A (2003)

Andresen, Martin A. 2001. 'Canada, the United States and NAFTA: The Effects on Trade Patterns', Working Paper, Department of Economics, Simon Fraser University.

Aquino, Antonio. 1978. 'Intra-industry Trade and Inter-industry Specialisation as Concurrent Sources of International Trade in Manufactures', *Weltwirtschaftliches Archiv*, vol. 114, pp. 275–96.

Aturupane, Chonira, Simion Djankov and Bernard Hoekman. 1997. 'Determinants of Intra-industry Trade between East and West Europe', draft paper, The World Bank.

Balassa, Bela. 1966. 'Tariff Reductions and Trade in Manufactures among the Industrial Countries', *American Economic Review*, vol. 56, pp. 466–73.

Bharadwaj, R. 1962. 'Factor Proportions and the Structure of Indo-US Trade', *Indian Economic Journal*, vol. 10, October.

Bhattacharya, B. 1999. 'Non-Tariff Measures on Indian Exports: An Assessment', Occasional Paper no. 16, Indian Institute of Foreign Trade, New Delhi.

Bhattacharyya, R. 1994. 'India's Intra-Industry Trade: An Empirical Analysis (1970–1987)', *Indian Economic Journal*, vol. 42, no. 2, pp. 54–74.

Chadha, R. et al. 2003. 'Computational Analysis of the Impact on India and the Uruguay and the Uruguay Round and the Doha Development Agenda Negotiations', in *India and the WTO*, edited by Aaditya Mattoo and Robert M. Stern, New Delhi: Oxford University Press, pp. 13–46.

Chaisse, Julien and Debashis Chakraborty. 2004. 'Disputes Resolution in the WTO: In the Light of Chinese and Indian Involvements', in *Future Negotiation Issues at WTO: An India-China Perspective*, edited by Bibek Debroy and Mohammad Saqib, New Delhi: Globus Books, pp. 377–432.

Chakraborty, Debashis. 2002. 'India's Intra-industry Trade: An Analysis of the Pre-reform and Post-reform Trends', unpublished M.Phil dissertation, International Trade and Development Division, School of International Studies.

_____. 2007. 'Misuse of Anti-Dumping Provisions: What do the WTO Disputes Reveal?', in *Anti-Dumping: Global Abuse of a Trade Policy Instrument*, edited by B. Debroy and D. Chakraborty, New Delhi: Academic Foundation, pp. 155–83.

Das, D. K. 2003. 'Manufacturing Productivities under Varying Trade Regimes: India in the 1980s and 1990s', ICRIER Working Paper no. 107, July.

Das, S. K. and Alokesh Barua. 1996. 'Regional Inequalities, Economic Growth and Liberalization: A Study of the Indian Economy', *Journal of Development Studies*, vol. 32, no. 3.

Dasgupta, Subhendu. 2003. 'Their Rules, Our Rights: Intellectual Property Rules and Right to Health', in *WTO and TRIPS: Indian Perspective*, edited by Byasdeb Dasgupta et al., Kalyani: University of Kalyani, pp. 27–41.

Debroy, Bibek and A. T. Santhanam. 1992. 'Matching the Codes of the ITC (Revision 2) with the ITC (Harmonized System)', *Foreign Trade Bulletin*, Indian Institute of Foreign Trade, January.

———. 1992. 'Concordance between National Industrial Classification and India Trade Classification (Revision 2)', *Foreign Trade Bulletin*, Indian Institute of Foreign Trade, July.

———. 1993. 'Matching Trade Codes with Industrial Codes', *Foreign Trade Bulletin*, Indian Institute of Foreign Trade, July.

Dixit, Avinash and Joseph Stiglitz. 1977. 'Monopolistic Competition and Optimum Product Diversity', *American Economic Review*, pp. 297–308.

Faustino, H. C., J. R. Silva and R. V. Carvalho. 1999. 'Testing Intra-Industry Trade between Portugal and Spain: 1990–1996', Working Paper, Instituto Politenico De Portalegre.

Globerman, Steven and J. W. Dean. 1990. 'Recent Trends in Intra-industry Trade and their Implications for Future Trade Liberalization', *Weltwirtschaftliches Archiv*, pp. 25–49.

Goldar. 2004. 'Productivity Trends in Indian Manufacturing in the Pre and Post Reform Periods', ICRIER Working Paper no. 137, June.

Ministry of Finance. various years. *Economic Survey*, New Delhi: Government of India

Ministry of Labour. 2002. *Second Labour Commission Report*, New Delhi: Government of India, http://labour.nic.in/lcomm2/nlc_report.html.

Greenaway, David, Robert Hine and Chris Milner. 1995. 'Vertical and Horizontal Intra-industry Trade: A Cross Industry Analysis for the United Kingdom', *Economic Journal*, vol. 105, pp. 1505–18.

Grubel, Herbert G. and P. J. Lloyd. 1975. *Intra-industry Trade: The Theory and Measurement of International Trade in Differentiated Products*, New Delhi: Macmillan.

Hazra, Arnab Kumar. 2001. 'Industrial Disputes Act: A Critical Appraisal', RGICS Working Paper no. 29.

Joshi, Vijay and I. M. D. Little 1998. *India Economic Reforms 1991–2001*, New Delhi: Oxford University Press.

Kantawala, Bhavana S. 1997. 'Inter and Intra-industry International Trade among SAARC Countries: 1981–1992', *Foreign Trade Review*, vol. 32, nos. 1 & 2, pp. 29–72.

Krishna, Pravin and Devashish Mitra. 1998. 'Trade Liberalisation, Market Discipline and Productivity Growth: New Evidence from India', *Journal of Development Economics*, vol. 56, pp. 447–62.

Krugman, Paul R. 1979. 'Increasing Returns, Monopolistic Competition and International Trade', *Journal of International Economics*, vol. 9, no. 4, pp. 469–79.

———. 1980. 'Scale Economies, Product Differentiation, and the Pattern of Trade', *American Economic Review*, no. 5, pp. 950–59.

Kumar, A. G., K. Sen and R. Vaidya, 2000. 'India's Export Competitiveness and Finance', in *India Development Report*, Mumbai, pp. 177–90.

Lancaster, K. 1966. 'A New Approach to Consumer Theory', *Journal of Political Economy*, vol. 74, pp. 132–57.

———. 1980. 'Intra-industry Trade under Perfect Monopolistic Condition', *Journal of International Economics*, vol. 10, 1980 pp. 151–75.

Nag, Biswajit and Debashis Chakraborty. 2006. 'India's Approach to Asian Economic Integration', paper presented in the conference on Globalization, Blocization, and East Asian Economic Integration, Center for WTO Studies, National Chengchi University, Taipei, 31 March.

Naik, Gopal and Yashika Singh. 2003. 'Doha Round Negotiations: Agriculture', Working Paper no. 217, Indian Institute of Management, Bangalore, November.

Pant, Manoj and Alokesh Barua. 1986. 'India's Intra-Industry Trade: 1960–80', Discussion Paper no. 8, International Trade and Development Division, School of International Studies, JNU.

Raizada, B. and Javed Sayed. 2002. 'IPR and Drugs and the Pharmaceutical Industry: Concerns for Developing Countries', in *Salvaging the WTO's Future: Doha and Beyond*, edited by Amit Dasgupta and Bibek Debroy, New Delhi: Konark Publishers, pp. 274–89.

Rao, Padma Arti. 2001. 'A Study of the Determinants of Firm Profitability in Selected Industries in Post-Reform India', unpublished M.Phil. dissertation, Delhi School of Economics, University of Delhi.

Ridao-Cano (1999)

Rodrik, D. 'Imperfect Competition, Scale Economies, and Trade Policy in Developing Countries', in *Trade Policy Issues and Empirical Analysis*, edited by R. E. Baldwin, Chicago and London: University of Chicago Press, 1988.

Rodrik, D. 1995. 'Trade and Industrial Policy Reform', in *Handbook of Development Economics*, vol. III, edited by J. Behrman and T. N. Srinivasan, pp. 2925–82.

Rodrik, D. 1999. 'Making Openness Work: The New Global Economy and the Developing Countries', Overseas Development Council, Washington DC, 1999.

Saint-Mezard, Isabelle. 2003. 'The Look East Policy: An Economic Perspective', in *Beyond the Rhetoric: The Economics of India's Look East Policy*, vol. III, edited by Frederic Grare and Amitabh Mattoo, New Delhi: Centre de Sciences Humaines and Manohar, pp. 21–43.

Singh, Swaran. 2004. 'Factoring Taiwan in India's Look East Policy', in *India and ASEAN: Foreign Policy Dimensions for the 21st Century*, edited by K. Raja Reddy, New Delhi: New Century Publications, 2004.

Singh, Yashika. 2000. 'EU Trade: Tariff and Non-tariff Hurdles', RGICS Working Paper no. 13.

Srivastava, Vivek, Pooja Gupta and Arindam Datta. 2001. *The Impact of India's Economic Reforms on Industrial Productivity, Efficiency and Competitiveness: A Panel Study of Indian Companies, 1980–97*, New Delhi: National Council of Applied Economic Research.

Stiglitz, Joseph. 1987. 'The Causes and Consequences of the Dependence of Quality on Price', *Journal of Economic Literature*, vol. 25, pp. 1–48.

Tata Services Limited. 2003. *Reforms and Productivity Trends in Indian Manufacturing Sector*, Mumbai: Department of Economics and Statistics.

Topalova, Petia. 2003. 'Trade Liberalization and Firm Productivity: the Case of India', Yale University, www.econ.yale.edu/seminars/NEUDC03/topalova1.pdf.

UNCTAD (1996).

Unel, Bulent. 2003. 'Productivity Trends in India's Manufacturing Sectors in the last Two Decades', IMF Working Paper no. WP/03/22.

Veeramani, C. 1999. 'Intra-Industry Trade under Economic Liberalisation: The Case of Indian Capital Goods Industries', *Journal of Indian School of Political Economy*, vol. 11, no. 3, pp. 455–73.

———. 2001. 'India's Intra-Industry Trade Under Economic Liberalisation: Trends and Country Specific Factors', Working Paper no. 313, Centre for Development Studies.

Virmani, A., B. Goldar, C. Veeramani and V. Bhatt. 2004. 'Impact of Tariff Reforms on Indian Industry: Assessment Based on a Multi-sector Econometric Model', ICRIER Working Paper no. 135, July.

Willmore, L. N. 1972. 'Free Trade in Manufactures among Developing Countries: The Central American Experience', *Journal of Economic Development and Cultural Change*, vol. 20.

Wood, Adrian and Ridao-Cano Cristobal. 1999. 'Skill, Trade and International Inequality', Oxford Economic Paper no. 51, pp. 89–119.

World Bank. various years. *World Development Indicators*, Washington DC: The World Bank.

WTO. various issues. *WTO Annual Report*, Geneva: WTO.

——. 1999. *WTO: Trading into the Future*, Geneva: WTO.

——. 2000. *Trade Policy Review, European Union*, Geneva: WTO.

——. 2001. 'Market Access: Unfinished Business—Post-Uruguay Round Inventory and Issues', Special Studies no.6.

9

How Big is the Bang for India? Market Access in Textiles

SAMAR VERMA

INTRODUCTION

Since 1974, the MFA—as an egregious exception to GATT principles—largely influenced the international production and trade flows in textile and clothing products. This arrangement provided a framework, under which the developed countries imposed quotas on exports of textiles and apparel, from the 'low cost developing countries'. The US imposed quotas on 46 countries including 6 non-WTO members, whereas, the EU maintained quotas on textile and clothing imports from 21 countries including 5 non-WTO members (Elbehri 2004). Following the Uruguay Round negotiations, for increasing market access in textiles and clothing in the developed country markets, a new agreement named ATC, was devised to terminate the MFA. The ATC was formulated chiefly for (i) gradual phase-out of the quotas over a period of ten years ending on 31 December 2004 and (ii) acceleration of growth rates in quotas for restricted products during the transition period (1995–2004). Due to several provisions in the ATC, the quota phase-out was heavily 'back loaded', as a result of which, about 94 per cent of the quota items were 'integrated' into the WTO rules only on 1 January 2005! And that phenomenon was akin to the 'Big Bang' in the trade, production and consumption patterns in textile and clothing globally, since the US and the EU together import over 60 per cent of world textile and almost 75 per cent of world clothing imports directly, and much more indirectly.[1] India relies heavily on these two markets for its textile and clothing exports, which makes the 'Big Bang' very critical for Indian exporters.

In addition, since the EU and the US, amongst other developed countries, had decided to reduce tariffs on all industrial products by 38 per cent, it is also expected to favourably affect exports of the textile and clothing industry. India's interests is obvious, because the country being a labour-abundant economy, expects its exports of textiles and clothing products to go up as a result of increased market access in textiles. The textile and clothing sector[2] contributes about four per cent of GDP and 14 per cent of industrial output. By providing direct employment of 35 million people it enjoys the status of the second largest employing sector in India only next to the agriculture. With a very low import-intensity of about 1.5 per cent, it is the largest *net* foreign exchange earner in India (almost 35 per cent of foreign exchange). This is the only industry that is self-reliant and complete in value chain—producing everything from fibres to the highest value added finished product of garments. Its growth and vitality therefore has critical bearings on the Indian economy at large. The question then is how 'Big' would this 'Bang' actually be for Indian textiles and clothing exporters?

Although, it is indeed too early to empirically assess, in any meaningful fashion, the impact of the 'big bang', this paper makes an attempt to evaluate the possible impact on India's textile production and export after the abolition of the existing quota restrictions. The paper is thus organised as follows: In Section I we shall examine, first of all, the evolution of textiles and clothing policies and the forces that had led to its eventual incorporation within the GATT system. We will then look at the possible ramifications of this on other policy changes that might affect trade and production of the textiles and clothing industry globally in general and the Indian textile industry in particular. Section II is devoted to quantitative evaluation of the impact of the new textile policies on Indian textile and clothing industry.

SECTION I

In this section, we will broadly deal with the forces that led to the collapse of the MFA, through a gradual process via the ATC, the implementation experience of the ATC, impact of the reductions in tariffs for textile and clothing products and the impositions of various new barriers to entry on textile products in the markets of the developed countries.

The Process of the Final Eclipse of the MFA

The MFA agreement and its subsequent renewals emerged out of the volatile economic climate of the early 1970s and the ongoing influence of the textile coalition on the trade-policy making of the US The US was clearly the driving force behind MFA I, motivated by the apparently perpetual need to contain Congressional fervour for even greater levels of control over imports and the desire to seek multilateral legitimacy for an overtly protectionist project. (Underhill 1998 160–62).[3]

Thus, neither the rhetoric nor the reality of the GATT system prevailed in textile and clothing over a period of some thirty years, as trade policy-making remained embedded in the distributional politics of industrial adjustment in the sector across a series of key advanced economies. It is argued that the protectionist policies at best bought time and at worst aggravated the crisis for western textile sectors. To quote Underhill:

> The so called new protectionism of the MFA became the principal policy tool for the avoidance of economic adjustment, a process which would have effaced many firms and traditional industry practices in a whirlwind of bankruptcies, mergers/takeovers and capital-intensive investment programmes. Powerful domestic interests representing economic liabilities were able to command sufficient political resources so as to constitute a political blockage to the process of economic change, preserving domestic industrial structures beyond their sell-by dates.[4] (Underhill 1998, 10)

Specifically, four factors appear to be responsible for the final demise of the MFA and its takeover by the ATC. First, since the MFA was never extended to the OECD countries, and also since significant proportion of trade took place among the developed countries,[5] the MFA did not shield the developed countries' textile and clothing sectors from competitive pressures altogether. Competition from the high-wage countries on account of ongoing trade liberalisation, even during the MFA period, as well as from the low-wage developing country producers in limited segments of this industry, was very much there. This resulted in increasing capital and technology intensive nature of yarn and fabric production, and dislocation of clothing production through foreign sourcing strategies (Underhill 1998: 212, 244 and fn 4).[6] The latter implied that the clothing firms themselves became big importers of low-cost textiles from low-wage producers like developing countries, Eastern European countries, or Mediterranean producers.[7]

Second, firms, employers' organisations and state governments increasingly perceived the MFA as having had a limited success as an instrument of protectionism. The developing countries were one step ahead in improvising and innovating to circumvent the quota barriers imposed under the MFA. In fact, the quota system fostered new producer countries of textile and clothing products (Underhill 1998, 201).[8] And this was reflected in the increase of total imports of textile and clothing products to the advanced economies. The MFA, as a state-based instrument of trade policy, was less and less suitable for a global economy, characterised by transnational integration of production and trade.

Third, the dynamics of the Uruguay Round negotiations themselves were responsible for the ATC. Developed countries in return for allowing a phased quota liberalisation in textile and clothing sectors, bargained for inclusion of 'new' issues such as the GATS and the TRIPS. Besides, the high-wage producers focused on tightening the WTO-compatible trade remedies, like anti-dumping and safeguard measures as a better alternative to the MFA for protecting their industry interests.

And finally, and perhaps most significantly, access to the markets of the developing countries became important for growth of firms in developed countries. And this too could be obtained within the ambit of the Uruguay Round negotiations. Indeed, the EU had officially made it its plan, to meaningfully liberalise its quota even within the ATC period, on the condition of guaranteed and meaningful market access of the EU producers to markets of developing countries.

The ATC Implementation Experience[9]

The ATC was initially applauded as a major achievement of developing country exporters of textiles and clothing products. It did not, however, take long before scepticism crept in. And the fears in respect of developed countries' intentions, are turning out to be true one after another. The importers of the developed countries followed the ATC (and other WTO agreements having a bearing on textiles and clothing trade)[10] prescriptions in letter and not in spirit. Given the past performance in connection with the ever-widening spectrum of protection applied in the course of MFA, the ATC increasingly began to be viewed as a way of faking liberalisation and finagling protectionism (Spinanger 1999). The implementation experience could be categorised under following categories (ITCB 2001).[11]

Dismantling of Quota Restrictions

The fundamental objective of the ATC was to secure progressive dismantling of the GATT—inconsistent quota restrictions on the global trade of the textile and clothing sectors. Towards achieving that objective, the ATC laid out a clearly defined roadmap for integrating the textile and clothing sector into the GATT fold. The experience so far, however, has been considerably disappointing for the exporters of the developing countries.

The minimum threshold requirements have no doubt been met, but the primary objective of ensuring greater market access in commercial sense has been belied.[12]

Moreover, the product coverage under the ATC included restrained (by quotas) as well as non-restrained items. Products that were never covered under quota restrictions comprised over 40 per cent of each restraining country's base year volume imports of 1990. The restraining countries took advantage of this and 'frontloaded' their integration programmes with such non-restrained items during the first three stages. They had to include only 11 per cent of restrained imports (in volume terms), during the first three stages together, to establish fulfilment of the threshold requirements. Thus, the US and the EU integrated only 19.52 per cent and 20.98 per cent of their restrained imports respectively during the first three stages; and these items consist mainly of textiles (not clothing). In other words, about 80 per cent of restrained imports were integrated only on the last day of ten-year phase-out schedule, that is, on 31 December 2004.

The same fact becomes evident if one looks at the number of quotas that have been eliminated in the first three stages (See Table 9.1).

TABLE 9.1 Integration programmes at a glance
(Integration as a percentage of the volume of 1990 imports)

Restraining Member	Yarns	Fabrics	Made-ups	Clothing	Total
U.S.A.	19.72	8.06	17.12	6.45	51.35
EU	18.82	14.77	9.76	9.27	52.62
Canada	13.28	9.8	24.3	6.4	53.78
Norway	12.83	20.53	19.75	11.88	64.99

Note: Data for the EU are of 1995, the year from which its membership has increased to EU-15.
Source: ITCB/CR/BRA/4, 7 May 2001, Annex Table 1.

Out of the total number of quotas as on 1 January 1995, the US and the EU eliminated none (zero) during the first stage. During the first three stages together, they have removed only 56 and 52 out of 757 and 219 quotas respectively (that is, 7.4 per cent and 24 per cent respectively). This cannot be conceived of as progressive dismantling of quotas by any stretch of imagination. As Spinanger holds, '...the USA is faking liberalisation and finagling protectionism just as much if not more so than the EU' (Spinanger 1997).

Finally, since the entire programme was couched in volume terms, and developed countries had chosen to backload the phase-out schedule, most of high value items of clothing and made-ups were be integrated only at the end of the transition period. The first ones to be integrated were yarn and fabrics, which are relatively low value items.

State of Quota Access

Developed countries have often quoted the 'growth-on-growth' provision in the ATC as large increase in quota access even during the phase-out period. There is little doubt that compared to the low and fixed quota growth rates allowed under the MFA, the ATC was more liberal in ensuring enhancement of quota growth rates by clearly defined percentages during phase-out schedule—by 16 per cent from 1995, by 25 per cent from 1998 and by

27 per cent from 2002. Least developed countries and small suppliers had been granted a faster access in the ATC by advancing the increase in quota growth rates by one stage.

However, it deserves mentioning that the least developed countries like Bangladesh had not been granted the extra access at par with small suppliers by either the US or Canada. Moreover, a large number of quotas continued to be utilised in full. Hence, quotas did bite despite the enhanced market access. India too utilised its garment quotas in full since the late 1980s. And finally, it is important to note that the Base growth rate in quota allowed to different exporting nations, was critical to determining the extent of additional quota access due to 'quota enhancement' in the ATC. It is not surprising that the economies, which had received high rates of quota growth, tended to be less dynamic exporters.

New Restrictions/Safeguard Actions

The Article 6 of the ATC permitted introduction of new QRs by all WTO members (who decided to retain such a right)[13] on products that were not integrated under the ATC. This article also marked a significant qualitative improvement[14] in the use of transitional safeguard actions over its MFA predecessor. This was exemplified in the continuous deceleration in number of transitional safeguard actions invoked since 1995, as well as clarifications by the WTO rulings on stringent requirements of the Article 6.

Between 1995 and 2000, the EU, Canada and Norway did not use safeguard measure at all, whereas the US invoked it 24 times within months after the ATC came into effect, against 14 WTO members, of which ten actions were against five Asian exporting nations. It is also noticeable that only a handful of safeguard actions invoked by the US stood the test of scrutiny. Moreover, there was a substantial decline in number of safeguard actions invoked since 1995.

Furthermore, during investigations, the WTO panels have made significant rulings, which diminish the possibility of misuse of safeguard actions in the hands of countries such as the US For instance, one WTO panel ruled that the ATC being an integral part of the WTO, its interpretation would be within the GATT and the WTO agreements, and not 'within the four corners of the ATC' (as argued by the US). On the other hand, the MFA could not be a part of the 'context' of the ATC since it was neither an integral part of the WTO, nor was it made 'in connection with the conclusions' of the WTO agreements.

Circumvention

Exporting countries do not condone any circumvention of quotas. In fact, they allow their factory on-site inspection and audit for meeting detailed requirements under different WTO obligations. However, the 'alleged' circumvention had been used as a 'defensive tactic' by developed countries, to justify their back-loaded quota phase-out programmes, as well as to delay any meaningful market access to exporters. A variety of procedures and requirements had been established with the ostensible purpose of preventing circumvention/transhipment, causing adverse consequences to exporters as well as importers.

Reciprocal Market Access

Failure of developing countries to allow improved market access into their own domestic markets is cited as a proof, that developing countries have not fulfilled their requirements under Article 7 of the ATC. However, aside from this general assertion, developed countries could not mention even one specific instance to buttress their claim. The EU went to the extent of proclaiming that its strategic criterion for inclusion of products in phase-out schedule was based on using existing quotas as a bargaining chip to obtain improved market accesses. In fact, the EU-Pakistan memorandum of understanding (MoU) signed in 2001 corroborates the EU stand.

However, the linking of quota liberalisation by the EU to reciprocal market access by developing exporting countries is, according to the UN Economic and social Commission for Asia and the Pacific (ESCAP) (1996), 'in effect, making an incongruous proposition'.

It is true that tariffs in the ESCAP region remain higher on average than other regions but given the strong competitiveness of those economies in clothing, many of the high tariff rates could be redundant. However, it appears unjustified to demand additional market access in exchange for the already accepted obligation of meaningful liberalisation.

During the Uruguay Round of negotiations, the Asian countries were subject to intensive negotiations for market access, and they made substantial tariff concessions in the sector. While India reduced its trade-weighted tariff average by 52 per cent, Indonesia bound 100 per cent of its tariffs to an average rate of 39.9 per cent and Malaysia bound 100 per cent of its tariffs to 19.4 per cent, to mention a few.

Rules of Origin

The Rules of Origin (RoO) determine which country/area quotas should be charged for particular imports, when manufacturing of the products occurs in more than one country. The uncertainty surrounding the working of such process is a major problem, and it was estimated that the total costs of rules of origin for firms would be at least 2 per cent of the value of the imported goods. While prior to 1 July 1996, US determined RoO on the basis of location of substantial transformation of the product, in subsequent period it was changed to the location of complete production/assembly. However, following strong EU protest, the US and the EU entered into a bilateral deal, restoring pre-1996 rules for products of interest to the EU. It is striking that wool fabrics, cotton and wool made-ups and apparel products are subject to more stringent/vaguely defined RoO, apparently because these have been of particular interest to exports o the developing country.

The complexity of the current rules of origin adds strength to the argument that rich countries are exploiting them as protectionist tools, rather than using them in good faith. Rules of origin are not based on logical principles, but on political expediency. Thus, the US has different rules of origin for different trade agreements. Moreover, it also has different rules for different products even within individual trade agreements. Likewise the EU has different rules for different trading partners, often quite different from those of the US. In addition, the provisions within any trade agreement may be extremely intricate, for example., the RoO provisions in the recent US-Singapore FTA, run to more than 240 pages of detail. With such complexity, it is hard for developing countries to be involved in the determination of these rules, and in practice they rarely are.

Tariffs

Tariff reductions were not a part of the ATC and average tariff on textile and clothing products continue to be considerably higher than that for industrial products. The gap has only widened due to the Uruguay Round tariff reduction commitments in textile and clothing sector being only half of that for industrial products.

However, averages conceal the true incidence in individual markets, due to a high degree of skewedness in tariff rates across products, especially in clothing.

Table 9.2 shows the average of the US and the EU tariff rates on the ATC products, according to the ATC mandated liberalisation stages. Tariffs on clothing are higher than on textiles everywhere, in each stage. Second, the average tariff rate on all products (and the four categories of yarns, fabrics, made-ups and clothing) to be integrated last, have on an average, higher tariffs compared to those that are integrated in earlier stages. Among the four product categories, tariff on clothing is highest. This is true for both the EU and the US, though more significant in case of the US

TABLE 9.2 Average US and EU tariff rates (in percentage)[a] on ATC products by liberalisation tranche and categories: 1995–2004 (US)

Liberalisation Trench	Categories	1996	1997	1998	1999	2000	2001	2002	2003	2004
I	Tops/yarns	5.7	5.4	5.2	5.0	4.7	4.5	4.2	4.0	3.7
	Fabrics	6.5	5.3	4.9	4.6	4.2	3.9	3.6	3.2	2.9
	Made-ups	6.8	6.4	6.0	5.6	5.2	4.9	4.5	4.2	3.9
	Clothing	5.0	4.7	4.5	4.2	4.0	3.8	3.6	3.4	3.1
	Total	6.2	5.5	5.2	4.8	4.5	4.2	3.9	3.6	3.3
II	Tops/yarns	4.9	4.7	4.5	4.3	4	3.8	3.6	3.4	3.2
	Fabrics	9.4	9.1	8.7	8.3	8	7.7	7.3	7	6.7
	Made-ups	8	7.6	7.3	6.9	6.5	6.2	5.8	5.4	5.1
	Clothing	11.7	11.3	10.8	10.3	9.9	9.4	9	8.6	8.1
	Total	9.6	9.2	8.8	8.5	8.1	7.7	7.3	6.9	6.5
III	Tops/yarns	10	9.8	9.5	9.3	9	8.8	8.6	8.3	8.1
	Made-ups	9.9	9.7	9.4	10.7	8.9	8.6	8.3	8.1	7.8
	Clothing	8.9	8.5	8	7.6	7.3	6.9	6.6	6.2	5.8
	Total	9.5	9.2	8.9	9	8.2	7.9	7.6	7.3	7.1
IV	Tops/yarns	9.3	9.1	8.9	9.9	8.4	8.2	7.9	7.7	7.5
	Fabrics	16	15.4	14.8	14.3	13.7	13.2	12.6	12	11.5
	Made-ups	10.2	9.9	9.7	9.5	9.2	9	8.8	8.6	8.3
	Clothing	15.2	14.6	14.2	13.9	13.5	13.2	12.9	12.5	12.2
	Total	14.8	14.2	13.8	13.5	12.9	12.5	12.1	11.7	11.3

Note: [a] unweighted average.
Source: Spinanger 1999.

Table 9.3 shows tariff peaks for clothing imports for individual products by the four major markets. The tariff peaks are glaring in clothing imports in both these markets. This table also highlights the comparative difference in tariffs across the four major markets. Existence of substantially higher tariff in one market would discourage other restraining members to advance the quota dismantling, due to fear of trade diversion. Country with lower tariff would, for the same reasons, resist any further lowering of tariff.

Tariff preferences are granted rather generously, on an average, by developed countries to developing countries, through preferential schemes such as Generlised System of Preferences (GSP). However, this is not the case for tariff peak items, as 'sensitive' products are excluded from these schemes or some type of quantitative limitation is imposed, either as tariff rate quota or in terms of eligibility requirements. Preferential schemes offer little protection against tariff peaks in Quad countries,[15] with the exception of the EU, which is generous even in respect of peak tariff items (Hoekman et al. 2001). The existing tariff structure fuels the doubt, that it would continue to influence the course of international trade in textile and clothing much beyond 2004. Thus, international trade in textile and clothing products from 2005 would not be free, but only quota-free.

TABLE 9.3 Comparative tariffs by selected products, pre- and post-Uruguay Round (all figures in percentage)

Product Description	US Pre	US Post	EU Pre	EU Post	Japan Pre	Japan Post	Canada Pre	Canada Post
Knit apparel:								
Trousers WG								
Wool	17.0	14.9	14	12	14	10.9	25	18
Cotton	16.7	14.9	14	12	14	10.9	25	18
Synthetic	30.0	28.2	14	12	14	10.9	25	18
Shirts MB								
Wool	17.0	14.9	13	12	14	10.9	25	18
Cotton	21.0	19.7	13	12	14	10.9	25	18
MMF	34.6	32.0	13	12	14	10.9	25	18
Blouses/shirts WG								
Wool	17.0	13.6	14	12	14	10.9	25	18
Cotton	21.0	19.7	14	12	14	10.9	25	18
MMF	34.6	32.0	14	12	14	10.9	25	18
T-shirts								
Wool	6.0	5.6	13	12	14	10.9	25	18
Cotton	21.0	16.5	13	12	14	10.9	25	18
MMF	34.0	32.0	13	12	14	10.9	25	18
Pullovers								
Wool	17.0	16.0	14	12	14	10.9	25	18
Cotton	20.7	16.5	14	12	14	10.9	25	18
MMF	34.2	32.0	14	12	14	10.9	25	18
Non-knit apparel:								
Overcoats MB								
Wool	52.9c/kg+21	41c/kg+16.3	14	12	14	9.1	25	18
Cotton	10.0	9.4	14	12	14	9.1	22.5	17
MMF	29.5	27.7	14	12	14	9.1	25	18
Overcoats WG								
Wool	46.3c/kg+21	41c/kg+16.3	14	12	14	9.1	25	18
Cotton	9.5	8.9	14	12	14	9.1	22.5	17
MMF	29.5	27.7	14	12	14	9.1	25	18
Anoraks MB								
Wool	52.9c/kg+21	49.7c/kg+19.7	14	12	14	9.1	25	18
Cotton	10.0	9.4	14	12	14	9.1	22.5	17
MMF water resist.	7.6	7.1	14	12	14	9.1	22.5	17
MMF other	29.5	27.7			14	9.1	22.5	18

(Contd)

(Table 9.3 Contd)

Product Description	US Pre	US Post	EU Pre	EU Post	Japan Pre	Japan Post	Canada Pre	Canada Post
Anoraks WG								
Wool	46.3c/kg+21	36c/kg +16.3	14	12	14	9.1	25	18
Cotton	9.5	8.9	14	12	14	9.1	22.5	17
MMF water resist.	7.6	7.1	14	12	14	9.1	25	18
MMF other	29.7	27.7			14	9.1	25	25
Trousers MB								
Wool	52.9c/kg+21	41.9c/kg+16.3	14	12	14	9.1	25	18
Cotton	17.7	16.6	14	12	14	9.1	22.5	17
Synthetic fibres	29.7	27.9	14	12	14	9.1	25	18
Artificial fibres	29.7	27.9	14	12	14	9.1	25	18
Trousers WG								
Wool	17.0	13.6	14	12	14	9.1	25	18
Cotton	17.7	16.6	14	12	14	9.1	22.5	17
Synthetic fibres	30.4	28.6	14	12	14	9.1	25	18
Artificial fibres	30.4	28.6	14	12	14	9.1	22.5	17
Jackets WG								
Wool	46.3c/kg+21	17.5	14	12	14	9.1	25	18
Cotton	10.0	9.4	14	12	14	9.1	22.5	17
Synthetic fibres	29.0	27.3	14	12	14	9.1	25	18
Artificial fibres	29.0	27.3	14	12	14	9.1	22.5	17
Dresses								
Wool	17.0	13.6	14	12	14	9.1	25	18
Cotton	12.6	8.4	14	12	14	9.1	22.5	17
Synthetic fibres	17.0	16.0	14	12	14	9.1	25	18
Artificial fibres	17.0	16.0	14	12	14	9.1	25	18
Skirts WG								
Wool	17.0	14.0	14	12	14	9.1	25	18
Cotton	8.7	8.2	14	12	14	9.1	22.5	17
Synthetic fibres	17.0	16.0	14	12	14	9.1	25	18
Artificial fibres	17.0	16.0	14	12	14	9.1	22.5	17
Shirts MB								
Wool	52.9c/kg+21	17.5	13	12	11.2	7.4	25	18
Cotton	21.0	19.7	13	12	11.2	7.4	22.5	17
MMF	30.9c/kg+27.5	29.1c/kg+25.9	13	12	11.2	7.4	25	18
Blouses WG								
Wool	82.7c/kg+21	17.0	14	12	14	9.1	25	18
Cotton	16.4	15.4	14	12	14	9.1	22.5	17
MMF	28.6	26.9	14	12	14	9.1	25	18
Brassieres	18.0	16.9	6.5	6.5	12.8	8.4	22.5	17

(Contd)

(Table 9.3 Contd)

Product Description	US		EU		Japan		Canada	
	Pre	Post	Pre	Post	Pre	Post	Pre	Post
Made-ups:								
Bed linen								
Cotton embroid.	23.8	20.9	13	12	11.2	4.5	22.5	17
Cotton not embr.	7.6	6.7	13	12	11.2	4.5	22.5	17
MMF embroid.	17.0	14.9	13	12	8	5.3	25	18
MMF not embr.	13.0	11.4	13	12	8	5.3	25	18
Toilet and kitchen linen cttn terry tow.	10.3	9.1	13	12	11.2	7.4	22.5	17
Woven fabrics of:								
Carded wool	36.1	25	13	8	8	5.3	25	14
Combed wool	36.1	25	13	8	8	5.3	25	14
Cotton (HS 5208)	9.0	9	10	8	5.6	3.7	15	12
Blue demin	8.9	8.4	10	8	5.6	3.7	17.5	12
Synth. filam. yarn	17.0	14.9	11	8	8	5.7	25	14
Synthetic fibres	17.0	14	11	8	12.5	8.8	25	14
Artif. staple fibres	17.0	10	11	8	10	6.6	25	14
Yarns of:								
Wool	9.0	6	3.8	3.8	4	2.7	12.5	8
Cotton	7.3	7.3	6	4	2.8	1.9	12.5	8
Synth. filament	10.0	8	9	4	10	6.6	10	8
Synth. staple fib.	12.0	10	9	4	10	6.6	10	8
Synthetic staple fibres	4.9	4.3	7.5	4	6–10	4–6.6	8.5	5

Notes:
1. The products selected are the most representative in terms of trade.
2. Abbreviations: MB: Men and boys; WG: Women and girls; MMF: Man-made fibres.

Source: WTO, Uruguay Round of Multilateral Trade Negotiations, Legal Instruments Embodying the Results of the Uruguay Round.

2.4 Trade Defence Mechanism

Anti-Dumping and Countervailing Measures

There has been an apprehension among exporting countries, that with the imminent loss of quota protection by 2005, GATT-consistent trade defence mechanism of anti-dumping (AD) could provide a convenient recourse to alternative methods of protection (Oxfam 2004). Most 'analysts of the US industry expect that these (anti-dumping and countervailing) actions will be increasingly used as products are integrated into the GATT' ... (Baughman 1997). Experience with the ATC implementation[16] so far does lend credence to these suspicions. The imposition of anti-dumping duty by EU on bed linen exports from India (1997) is a classic case exemplifying the protectionist tendencies in the EU policies. Although the DSB ruled in India's favour in 2001, by that time exports of bed linen had fallen from USD 127 million in 1998 to USD 91 million in 2001. The revenue of 'Anglo-French Textiles', one of the affected Indian companies, fell by more than 60 per cent in the three years, when the duties were imposed. It was forced to shed more than 1,000 jobs, with a severe economic impact on the southern Indian town of Pondichery where the company is located, as it was both the biggest industry and employer. Furthermore, despite defeat at WTO, the EU merely altered the terms of the complaint slightly and reapplied the duties. It is ironic to note, the EU is now challenging the US in WTO forum for using a particular method to judge whether dumping is happening ('zero dumping' assessment), the very method which the EU originally used against Indian bed linen back in 1997.

The US further banned the import of Indian Skirts claiming that the fabrics out of which these skirts were made, did not fulfil their inflammably standards. It has lately alleged that Indian exports benefited from subsidies and has recently lodged an anti-subsidy complaint against Indian exports, and safeguard measures will be more significant than anti-dumping measures.

Safeguard Measures

Under Article XIX, countries can legitimately take emergency actions on imports of particular products to prevent or remedy serious injury caused or threatened by increased imports to domestic producers. This could take the form of tariffs, or QRs on the imports of particular products concerned, subject to fulfilment of a number of obligations.[17] Unlike the ATC and its predecessor arrangements, these actions under the GATT Art. XIX however can be implemented on MFN basis. Since the inception of the WTO, over 62 safeguard actions have been invoked under the Agreement on Safeguards.

Non-Traditional Measures

While looking beyond the ATC on conditions likely to affect the global trade in textile and clothing sectors, apart from the issues discussed above, the emerging trend towards a variety of formal and informal requirements under the guise of environmental, social or other conditional ties needs to be mentioned. These new 'requirements' may include documentation formalities, licenses, certificates, marks of origin and so on, as per the provisions of Article VIII and XIX of GATT.[18]

Documentation obligations, which add to the cost of doing business, include maintenance of complete records of production, such as the place of production, number and identification of the type of machinery used in production, the number of workers employed in production, certification from both manufacturer and exporters regarding working conditions and quality for work life of employees and workmen and so on, They can be—and often have been-used to cause delays in customs clearances, and uncertainty for importers, exporters and other businesses involved. Thus, for true and effective liberalisation, it is necessary that along with quotas and tariffs, these non-traditional barriers also be minimised.

Among the emerging requirements general and care labelling, applied generally non-discriminatorily, could be mentioned, which apart from protecting consumer rights, are increasingly seen by companies as marketing tools. Various documentation requirements like source of raw materials, proofs regarding processing of inputs, transfer documents and so on, is among the major procedural hassles. In addition, introduction of a number of a number of eco-labelling schemes for promoting products based on technologies that reduce water pollution in key production processes is a major issue.[19] For instance, in February 1999, the EC has adopted comprehensive criteria for award of eco-label across the entire value chain of textile and clothing sectors.

Linking labour standard with textile trade is another concern, since both the EU and the US have long sought to use their GSP and other preferential schemes ostensibly to promote observance of core labour standards.[20] For instance, US-Cambodia Textile Agreement provides that the latter shall support the implementation of a programme to improve working conditions in the textile and clothing sectors. On compliance with core labour standards, Cambodia is entitled to 14 per cent enhancement in its quota. Africa Growth and Opportunity Act of the US could also be mentioned in this regard. Apart from direct government participation, private social codes are also quite frequent, for example, 'Worldwide Responsible Apparel Production (WRAP)', the certification of which is factory-based, and represent core standards for production facilities to ensure that 'sewn products are produced under lawful, humane, and ethical conditions'. In fact, a number of bills[21] were introduced in the US Congress as early as in 1995–96, that would take action against use of child labour in imported products (Baughman 1997). However, the efficacy of these measures are often questioned and it is argued that the best help that developed countries could provide would be allowing greater and more meaningful market access to labour intensive products from developing countries (Panagariya 1999).

Preferential Trading Arrangements (PTAs)

While there have been spurts in formation of RTAs in the past decade, the collapse of multilateral negotiations at Cancun exacerbated the process. According to the annual report (2000) of the WTO committee on RTAs, 220 RTAs have been notified to the GATT/WTO.[22] Of these, 191 agreements were notified under GATT Article XXIV, of which 109 are still in force today, 18 agreements were notified under the Enabling Clause;[23] and 11 were under GATS Article V. It is estimated that the share of preferential trade in the world increased from 40 per cent during 1988–92 to 42 per cent during 1993–97 (Grether et al. 1998). There have been several studies on the possible effect of some of the PTAs on non-members' exports. These studies report that trade diversion of exports is heavily concentrated in textiles and clothing sectors. Upto 31 December 2004, the quotas on exports of textile and clothing products on non-members in case of NAFTA often constituted a barrier higher than its tariff counterpart.

SECTION II

Impact of Quota Abolition on Indian Textile Industry

Indian Textile Industry

The structure of the Indian textile industry is extremely complex in character (Verma 2002). For instance, while the yarn-manufacturing sector is almost entirely in the organised sector, the cloth-manufacturing sector in India is almost wholly in the unorganised sector. The share of organised composite mills in total cloth manufacturing is just 4.4 per cent (Office of Textile Commissioner 2000).[24] The share of decentralised powerlooms was 59 per cent in 1999–2000, up from 39 per cent in 1980–81. Hosiery, handloom and khadi, wool, and silk accounted for the rest. Garments too are extremely fragmented sector, with over 60 per cent of all garment units engaged only as fabricators, while independent units engaged in sewing operations. The lop-sided government policy has been held to be the chief reason for this skewed industrial structure of both textile and garment industries.

India has a wide range of domestically produced fibres. As the world's third largest cotton producer, India's fibre basis is mainly cotton oriented, but includes to a lesser extent also wool, silk, jute and ramie. India's strong cotton orientation constitutes both strength (availability of low-cost raw materials) and an obstacle for export development due to a lack of product diversification in terms of fibre composition. Hence, India is not well prepared to take advantage of the increasing global demand for blended and synthetic textile and clothing products. For several decades, domestic policies deliberately favoured cotton over man-made fibres, through discriminatory policies, a trend that has recently been discontinued. Also, quality problems in India's cotton translate into quality deficiencies with yarns and fabrics that are either directly exported or indirectly used as input into Indian clothing products.

India has the second largest yarn spinning capacity in the world (after China) and accounts for 25 per cent of world's spindle capacity. It has a strong infrastructure base in textile spinning with 38.58 million spindles of which 94 per cent are export oriented units accounting for 2.20 million spindles. India is emerged as the largest exporter of cotton yarn, accounting a share of 25 per cent in world. Despite the prevalence of low productivity, low rates of modernisation and low profit margins due to suffering from discriminatory government policies, it is expected that (cotton) yarn exports will be among India's main winners of ATC quota removal.

With about 64 per cent of the world's installed looms, India accounts for the largest number of looms to weave fabrics world-wide. The small-scale power looms and handloom producers using old equipment account for 98 per cent of installed looms, and produce mainly low-value unfinished fabrics for the domestic market. Composite mills in the organised sector account for only 2 per cent of installed looms, but for 85 per cent of India's fabric exports. The total number of shuttle less looms in the organised and decentralised sector is around 20,000. Although, this gives massive capacity to cater to India's own as well as export requirements, many mills will simply not be able to benefit from quota removal in 2005 (Institut Francais de la Mode 2004) and will have to go out of business unless they quickly restructure and modernise. The sector's poor performance (composite mills and others) also poses a risk to the future export performance of India's woven clothing manufacturers. Furthermore, lack of access to flawless, uniform, long-length and high-quality fabrics made in India, puts firms in a tough scenario, vis-à-vis their counterparts in China or Pakistan.

The processing of fibers, yarns, fabrics and garment/made-ups is one of the primary design aspects which contribute to the significant value addition in terms of colours, motifs, geometrical design and so on, India had 12,600 process houses in the country comprising 133 in the composite mill sector, 2066 independent process units and about 10,400 hand processors. Even though the processing stage is the most significant process in the value added chain of various textile products, the technological input is very low making it the weakest link in the textile production chain. This means a loss of potential gains in value added products as well as valuable foreign exchange earnings through high valued exports. The current proportion of average value added in the processing units in India is a mere 100 per cent, where as in a high tech processing unit, target average value addition of 300 per cent is easily feasible. A consequence of this is that the share of processed cotton fabrics in our fabric export is only 46 per cent (Sathyam Committee Report 2001). This segment of the textile and clothing sector needs to follow best practices taking special care in environmental and health issues. A facilitating role of the Government is awaited in the processing segment, to place correct incentives for fresh investment.

Clothing Industry: Woven and Knitted Apparel

Apparel sector employs directly or indirectly four million people and the total turnover is around USD 16 million. With an increasing production volume (3000 million pieces/ year), this sub-sector experiences the best growth rate within the textile and clothing chain (+ 20 per cent/year). Woven apparel is the sector, best prepared for quota removal. The quality consciousness is growing from a low level, with apparel producers being more conscious about the fabric quality and the necessity to adopt fashion trends. The industry also benefits from the experience of a skilled and relatively low cost labour force. However, it is highly unorganised and deeply fragmented due to the government restriction on large companies' development in woven apparel (Small Scale Industry norm). Consequently, the volumes produced remain small and the sector has not grown at its potential. In general, the level of automation in apparel remains low and the average investment by machine is inferior to China or Thailand, with a lower productivity.[25] It is hoped that the recent lifting of SSI reservation offers opportunities to local producers and foreign investors to shift into a larger production base, thereby benefiting from economies of scale.[26] Indian apparel exporters work mainly as subcontractors for foreign apparel companies or retailers, which has increased their experience, flexibility and knowledge of European and US markets.

The knitwear sector is still partially covered by the system of small-scale industry (SSI) reservation, which limits the size of knitting units. The main centres of Indian knitting industry are Tirupur (cotton) and Ludhiana in Punjab (wool), where hundreds and thousands of small knitting units have set up co-operative arrangements for production and finishing, up-gradation of quality, marketing, and exporting. The knitting sector is still small but quickly gaining in importance. Products such as leisurewear have become very competitive on the international markets. In addition, there is a trend moving towards higher quality and value added products (for example, Pashmina), and a UNDP project for upgrading the technology has been recently implemented. However, backward technology and low rate of modernisation hinder the development of the sector, particularly as long as SSI reservation will prevent companies to set up larger and modern knitting units. On the other side, price sensitiveness becomes a source of concern (in particular with the impact of tariff preferences granted by the EU to certain other suppliers).

Labour Productivity

Although the absolute cost of hiring labour in India is low, the labour cost per unit of production is higher due to the low productivity of labour. A comparison of different countries on the basis of labour productivity shows that India has an advantage over other countries like Thailand, Turkey, and Hong Kong. However, countries like Indonesia, Pakistan and Sri Lanka have even lower wage costs and labour productivity is unfavourable vis a vis China, Korea and Indonesia and so on.

FIGURE 9.1 Average hourly wages in the apparel industry, selected countries ($, 2000)

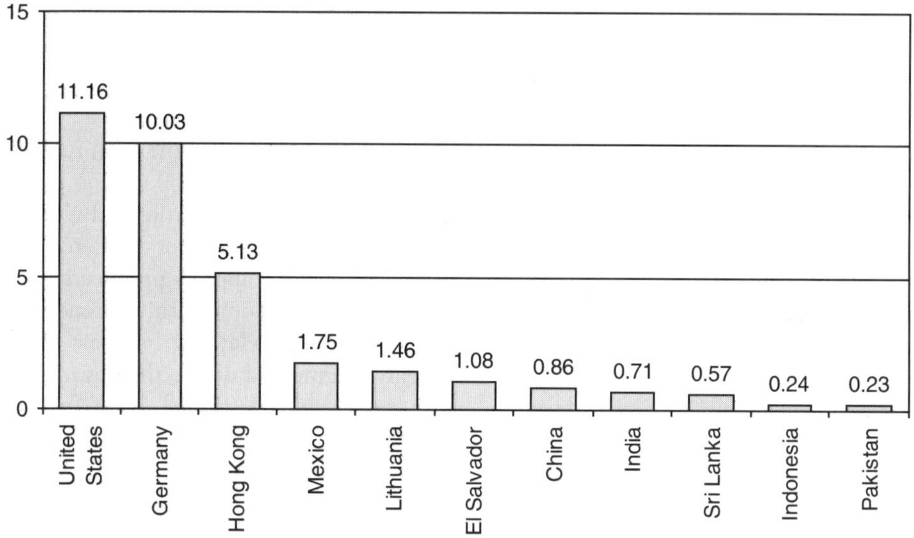

United States	11.16
Germany	10.03
Hong Kong	5.13
Mexico	1.75
Lithuania	1.46
El Salvador	1.08
China	0.86
India	0.71
Sri Lanka	0.57
Indonesia	0.24
Pakistan	0.23

Source: OXFAM 2004.

Productivity in Indian apparel sector is lower compared to other countries. For instance, compared to 20.6 ladies blouses produced by Hong Kong manufactures per machine per day, India manufactures only 10.2. Similar figures in case of trousers for Hong Kong and India are 19.3 and 6.8, or in gents shirts are 20.9 and 9.1 in that order. A Mckinsey study (2001), using number of shirts produced per day as a measure, noted that productivity in India is 16 per cent of that in US, which is alarmingly low. Another major factor affecting the industry, which can be the reason for the low levels of productivity, could be the government policy to overprotect labour in the organised sector, thus discouraging the generation of productive employment. Consequently, there has also been less foreign investment inflow to the sector even after it's de-reservation from the SSI list in 2001–2.

IMPACT OF QUOTA ELIMINATION[27]

Several studies have cited the fact of MFA-quotas being a constraint to Indian exports; the competitive performance of Indian textile and clothing sectors is likely to improve when the quotas are dismantled beginning 2005. Although, India ranks first in terms of world's installed capacity in weaving and shuttle-less looms and jute production, the export performance of the industry falls short of expectation. Indian share of export in global trade is very poor. In the year 1999, while India exported only 3 per cent of world textile exports in value terms, its share in clothing was 2.6 per cent only. It is also noteworthy that India's export of textiles was showing a continuously declining trend in the 1990s.[28]

Although MFA created an egregious exception to the *most favoured nation* principle of GATT, the WTO ATC marked a significant turnaround as scholars put:

> The dismantling of the quota regime represents both an opportunity as well as a threat. An opportunity because markets will no longer be restricted; a threat because markets

How Big is the Bang for India?   185

will no longer be guaranteed by quotas, and even the domestic market will be open to competition. (Kathuria and Bharadwaj 1998)

The reality, that from 1st January 2005 onwards all textile and clothing products are being traded without quota-restrictions, brings the issue of competitiveness to the fore for all firms in the textile and clothing sectors, including those in India.

Numerous studies have been conducted on impact of quota abolition on international trade in this sector. However, the few common conclusions of almost all studies are that the quota phase-out would bring about a massive restructuring in production and exports, a price fall in clothing and textile products, and significant gains to at least two countries from the Asian region, that is, China and India.

Since the existence of multilateral restraints on textiles and clothing exports in 1973 (that is,. the Multi-fibre Arrangement) trade in clothing products has overtaken trade in textile products. Furthermore, whereas textile products have lost shares in world trade since the second half of the 80s, the share of clothing products has remained roughly the same in this time period. The degree to which the trade restrictions themselves were responsible for these shifts has not been determined. However, it can be contented that currently the trend is toward just-in-time production, so the textile production is moving all the more closer to where clothing products are manufactured, which is likely to continue.

A recent study by Spinanger and Verma (2003) computes, using Computable General Equilibrium Model, the gainers and losers from the quota phase-out. The Global Trade Analysis Project (GTAP) 5 model use, belongs to a family of economic models characterised by an input-output structure (based on regional and national input-output tables), that explicitly links industries in a value added chain from primary goods, over continuously higher stages of intermediate processing, to the final assembling of goods and services for consumption. Linkages between sectors are both direct (like the input of textiles in the production of automobiles) and indirect (like the use of mining inputs into steel, which feeds into machines, which weaves the textiles). The model captures these linkages by use by modelling firms of factors and intermediate inputs while producing goods and services. The results of the model calculations on export growth in textiles and clothing can be summarised as follows (see Tables 9.4 and 9.5):

- Apart from the sizeable increases in textile exports registered by China (PRC) and Chinese Taipei; Japan and Bangladesh (and other South Asian countries) exhibit similar results. India, like virtually all other economies experience looses, with the largest decrease shown by Mexico. In the latter case, the loss of preferential treatment because of the elimination of quotas severely affects Mexico and to a lesser degree Turkey.
- In the case of clothing exports, the massive shift to Chinese sources (+167.84 per cent) is overshadowed by an even larger increase in India's exports (+217.51 per cent). India's increase—which comes onto to a level of exports roughly one seventh of the size of China's (PRC)—can be explained to some extent by the highly restrictive quotas, which prevailed on top of a large domestic industry which could begin to tap into the global potential. However, while India has almost always been viewed as having an export potential in numerous areas, its internal policies have usually been seen as keeping it from being successful. Among all other economies, only Vietnam shows, that it too can profit from the ATC liberalisation.

TABLE 9.4 Impact of Greater China's WTO accession on textile exports—per cent change

	Elimination of ATC[a] quotas				Greater China accession			Total
Economies	WTO members only	China (PRC)	Chinese Taipei	Total	Tariff cuts and services liberalisation[b]		Total	(4)+(7)
					PRC	Taipei		
	(1)	(2)	(3)	(4)	(5)	(6)	(7)	(8)
Hong Kong	−3.20	4.38	−0.12	1.06	1.87	−0.19	1.68	2.73
China (PRC)	2.23	3.86	0.09	6.18	32.51	0.23	32.74	38.91
Chinese Taipei	0.74	7.95	0.00	8.69	1.52	3.86	5.38	14.07
Japan	0.94	7.16	0.12	8.22	3.16	−0.08	3.08	11.30
Korea	2.10	3.08	0.07	5.25	−1.47	−0.17	−1.64	3.61
ASEAN5[c]	7.95	−1.42	−0.08	6.46	−7.58	0.15	−7.42	−0.97
Vietnam	3.94	0.06	0.07	4.08	−9.83	0.64	−9.19	−5.11
India	1.93	1.28	0.05	3.26	−4.26	−0.04	−4.30	−1.04
Bangladesh	17.19	−0.18	−0.02	16.99	−1.45	−0.02	−1.48	15.51
Other South Asia	12.35	0.87	0.13	13.35	−3.18	−0.02	−3.20	10.15
Australia	1.50	1.25	0.04	2.80	−4.48	−0.18	−4.66	−1.87
New Zealand	3.33	0.84	0.06	4.22	−6.68	−0.37	−7.05	−2.83
Canada	−5.08	−4.95	0.23	−9.80	−6.67	−0.11	−6.78	−16.58
United States	−2.86	−3.00	0.09	−5.77	−7.71	−0.04	−7.75	−13.52
Mexico	−6.26	−6.71	0.40	−12.57	−8.04	−0.09	−8.13	−20.70
Brazil	6.02	−2.38	−0.15	3.49	−5.24	−0.03	−5.27	−1.78
Mercosur, other	−0.67	1.59	−0.01	0.91	−2.15	−0.21	−2.36	−1.46
European Union (15)	−1.85	−1.97	0.04	−3.79	−6.67	−0.07	−6.73	−10.52
Turkey	1.94	−2.76	−0.05	−0.88	−6.43	−0.06	−6.49	−7.36
Africa, Mid-East	−3.30	−3.21	0.10	−6.40	−6.69	−0.07	−6.77	−13.17
Rest of World[e]	−2.66	−2.45	0.07	−5.05	−6.56	−0.08	−6.64	−11.69

Notes: [a] ATC = Agreement on Textiles and Clothing. [b] For services a 50 per cent reduction in estimated protection was assumed. [c] ASEAN5 = Indonesia, Malaysia, Philippines, Singapore and Thailand. [d] Pakistan, Sri Lanka, Nepal. [e] Rest of world does not include some parts of Latin America not else wise list. It reflects primarily results for Central and Eastern European countries.
Source: Author's estimatations based on GTAP5 model and Spinanger and Verma 2003.

To put the above changes into proper perspective: alone the increase in clothing exports estimated for China (PRC) would amount to over 25 per cent of total world trade in clothing products in the base year. Given such massive changes the question must be asked whether China (PRC) will be able to accommodate them. In this connection one must recall that numerous other industries in China (PRC) suffered relatively large decreases in output in the course of applying the WTO accession conditions. These highly inefficient industries will help provide the workforce for the newly operating textile and clothing companies. Nonetheless, it does seem to be worthwhile keeping in mind that a rush to the Middle Kingdom, for sure not a rush to the bottom, is something, which is expected to take place over a period of up to seven years. And in seven year's time the necessary adjustments

TABLE 9.5 Impact of Greater China's WTO accession on clothing exports—percentage change

	Elimination of ATC[a] quotas				Greater China accession			
Economies	WTO members only	China (PRC)	Chinese Taipei	Total	Tariff cuts and services liberalisation[b]		Total	Total (4)+(7)
					PRC	Taipei		
	(1)	(2)	(3)	(4)	(5)	(6)	(7)	(8)
Hong Kong	30.18	−19.54	−5.98	4.66	−7.66	0.68	−6.98	−2.32
China (PRC)	−6.41	100.89	−6.66	87.81	79.35	0.67	80.03	167.84
Chinese Taipei	−20.41	−24.63	12.73	−32.31	−30.51	9.76	−20.75	−53.07
Japan	−4.47	1.51	−0.07	−3.03	−16.28	1.65	−14.63	−17.65
Korea	−8.52	−16.09	1.33	−23.29	−21.45	1.33	−20.12	−43.41
ASEAN5 c	28.79	−20.97	−6.14	1.68	−23.98	0.23	−23.76	−22.08
Vietnam	26.92	−7.55	−2.05	17.32	−8.59	3.39	−5.21	12.11
India	337.90	−21.69	−73.67	242.55	−24.86	−0.18	−25.04	217.51
Bangladesh	20.87	−15.97	−3.40	1.51	−9.47	0.04	−9.42	−7.91
Other South Asia	21.93	−18.67	−4.18	−0.92	−17.22	−0.08	−17.31	−18.22
Australia	−5.78	−5.60	0.30	−11.08	−16.29	−0.00	−16.29	−27.37
New Zealand	−1.13	0.06	−0.00	−1.08	−24.43	−0.39	−24.81	−25.89
Canada	−19.86	−24.38	4.75	−39.49	−28.56	−0.09	−28.64	−68.14
United States	2.15	3.90	0.11	6.16	−7.60	0.13	−7.47	−1.31
Mexico	−26.23	−33.73	8.74	−51.21	−36.26	−0.15	−36.40	−87.62
Brazil	12.45	−13.36	−1.71	−2.62	−19.67	0.37	−19.30	−21.92
MERCOSUR, other	−5.63	−5.92	0.32	−11.23	−15.12	−0.15	−15.27	−26.50
European Union (15)	−4.09	−5.14	0.20	−9.03	−18.19	0.10	−18.08	−27.11
Turkey	−4.57	−9.27	0.40	−13.43	−18.43	−0.06	−18.49	−31.92
Africa, Mid-East	−11.79	−12.55	1.46	−22.88	−18.53	−0.10	−18.62	−41.50
Rest of World[e]	−6.57	−11.34	0.73	−17.18	−18.98	−0.08	−19.06	−36.24

Notes: [a] ATC = Agreement on Textiles and Clothing. [b] For services a 50 per cent reduction in estimated protection was assumed. [c] ASEAN5 = Indonesia, Malaysia, Philippines, Singapore and Thailand. [d] Pakistan, Sri Lanka, Nepal. [e] Rest of world does not include some parts of Latin America not else wise list. It reflects primarily results for Central and Eastern European countries.
Source: Author's estimations based on GTAP5 model and Spinanger and Verma 2003.

would seem to be doable. The key question is what India must do to try to ensure that it maintains a competitive position so as to tap the posited gains.

Figure 9.2 illustrates the impact of quota phase-out and Chinese accession on the important textiles and clothing trading nations of the world. The winners and losers have been clearly identified, and India is certainly poised to gain in a big way owing to quota phase-out, although a part of this gain would be wiped out due to Chinese accession into the WTO.

FIGURE 9.2 Per cent impact of ATC phase-out and China's accession on total exports

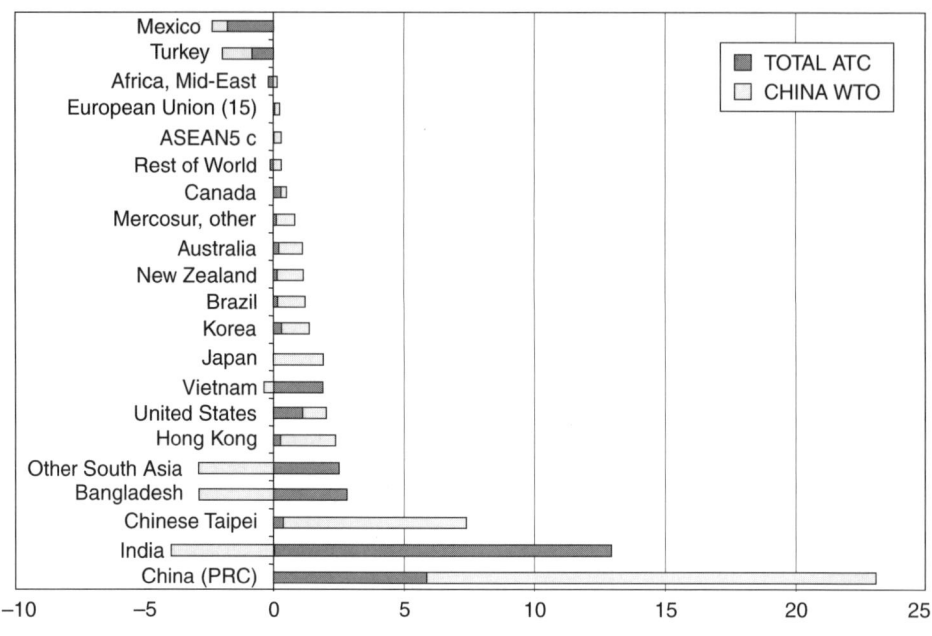

Source: Spinanger and Verma (2003).

DIRECTION OF TRADE

The direction of exports of readymade garments from India to quota countries is provided in Table 9.6.

TABLE 9.6 The direction of exports of readymade garments from India to quota countries

Country 2001–2	Percentage of total exports
US	40.78
EU	41.25
Canada	4.98
OBA (non-Quota)	12.99
Total	100

Source: AEPC (2003).

The Indian industry shifted towards more fashion designs building the ethnicity into a modern style. The government has also taken specific actions for the development of the Indian clothing industry and the creation of domestic brands. However, the sector lacks product diversification, as most of India's exports are concentrated in a few product categories only. This factor along with the sectors' fragmentation, low productivity, high production costs, inappropriate taxation system, and lack of adequate export infrastructure is likely to affect the sector's competitiveness after 2005. A comparison of the estimated annual manufacturing cost in garment marketing is provided in Table 9.7, and it is observed that overhead and capital costs are the two most important components.

TABLE 9.7   Estimated annual manufacturing costs in garment making 1999 (USD '000)

	Direct labour	Supervision	Overheads	Costs of Capital	Total
Hong Kong	2431	829	2809	504	6572
Percentage	37	13	43	8	
China	240	201	1490	508	2439
Percentage	10	8	61	21	
India	91	167	662	566	1486
Percentage	6	11	45	38	
Germany	4337	958	485	510	6290
Percentage	69	15	8	8	

Source: Singh et al. (2004).

It is generally felt that companies focusing on medium-high quality garments will be best placed to benefit from the quota liberalisation, as they will not compete directly with Chinese goods. Recent developments show an increasing interest from large retailers (H&M, GAP, JC Penney, Marks and Spencer, OTTO). In 2002, large Western retailers sourced USD 1500 million of garments from India, up from USD 899 million in 1999. These retailers want to diversify their sources of supply and concentrate more on India.

CONCLUSION

From the above discussion we may draw the following general conclusions on the impact of elimination of quotas. First, the complete elimination of quotas from 2005 is expected to lead to a drastic restructuring of world production and trade in textile and clothing industries. In consequence, intense price competition is inevitable[29] in the global market in textile and clothing goods, which obviously will be consumer welfare improving. This may contribute to a development of 'new protectionism' in developed countries in their effort to shield the domestic industry from the onslaught of price competition.

Second, locational shifts in production may take place, which may also lead to changes in the patterns of trade flows. On one hand, this shift may intensify the long-term drift in production from the Western Europe and the US to Asia and on the other hand, production may be delocalised from the Western developed countries to nearby low cost sources, so as to enable them to compete with the Asian suppliers. This trend will be further boosted by regional integration like NAFTA and the expansion of the European Union to include former Eastern bloc countries.

Third, in an attempt to protect their domestic industry, newer forms of state-led policies are being invoked in developed countries. The attempt to link environment and social issues to trade in goods contains numerous manifestations of this kind.

Fourth, despite ongoing tariff reductions as a result of the Uruguay Round negotiations there exists a sizable section of tariff peaks and spreads, which may play important roles in international trade transactions as well as in negotiations. The integration of the textiles and clothing sectors to the GATT thus appear to imply that trade becomes quota-free but not free in true sense of the term.

Fifth, the sudden end of the 'managed trade' may lead to a deluge in invoking of WTO-sanctioned trade defence mechanisms.[30] One could therefore expect a sudden rise in use of anti-dumping duties and countervailing duties by developed countries on products originating from developing countries. This new protectionism may take the forms of 'ethical' certification of production and processing standards.

As far as India's interests are concerned, the situation however is not so grim, since the textile industry is a key area where India has an opportunity for labour-intensive exports. So India's production and exports are expected to increase as a result of quota elimination. In response, the Indian government, belated though, has taken measures to set appropriate policies at home to exploit its potential advantages in trade. However, ultimately it will be the 'firm' which will have to compete in the global market and therefore the ball squarely lies with the Indian entrepreneurs, to secure for India its rightful place in the international trading regime.

The expected fall in prices is feared to encourage the domestic industry in the developed countries to cry dumping and spark political pressures for greater recourse to alternate forms of protection, especially anti-dumping, exacerbating the problem created by the postponement of any effective liberalisation of the sector to the very end of transitional period.

Although China is expected to become the 'supplier of choice' for most US textile and apparel importers after quotas are eliminated, noting that US imports from China soared by 125 per cent alone in 2002, India, along with Pakistan and Bangladesh may also emerge as 'major suppliers,' primarily in a 'narrower but still significant range of goods.' It is also important to point out here that unlike for all WTO members, quotas on Chinese exports to US and EU may continue until end 2008. And indeed, the recent embargo on exports from China by the two biggest markets of the world—euphemistically called 'Voluntary Export Restraints'—does indicate that the opportunities for non-Chinese textile and clothing exporters to the US and EU is immense, at least for the next couple of years. Besides, if Chinese competitiveness in this sector is partially determined also by domestic and export subsidies, as some evidence suggests, that is additional good news for countries such as India. This is because with WTO accession, China would need to comply with all WTO agreements including those on subsidies, and that would mean a reduction in their state support to this sector, making the industry less competitive, at least in the short run. Indian exporters have thus more than one reason to cheer.

Importance of non price factors cannot be ignored, since the non-price factors of competitiveness are becoming more and more important. Worldwide Responsible Apparel Production (WRAP) and Apparel Industry Initiative (AIP), Clean Clothes Campaign are some of the global movements towards cleansing the global manufacturing and trade in textile and clothing sectors. And this post-consumerism demand has begun to force a large number of exporters from the developing countries to adhere to such norms and get their factories and systems 'ethically certified', before they could be eligible to supply some of the world's biggest retailers. It is in this 'buyer-driven global commodity chain' that India has to position itself.

In the production front, it is observed that employment has marginally increased in the organised private sector and it is expected to further accelerate if some of the rigidities in the labour laws are removed. The Industrial Disputes Act, 1947, Contract Labour

Act, 1970, and Payment of Wages Act, 1936, are some of the legislative instruments that need amendments. Simultaneously, the government is also proposing to bring forth a comprehensive legislation for the welfare of workers in the unorganised sector. Under the Minimum Wages Act, in January 2002, wages were raised for workers of mining and construction sectors, in respect of scheduled employment in the Central sphere.

The large exporters are already seen to invest heavily in modernisation, rationalisation and expansion of capacities. Indian exporters have by and large managed to outcompete through their innovative manufacturing techniques. BPO in Indian apparel, unlike in the software industry, is in its infancy at this stage.

However, in the coming years, there could be a good opening for the Indian exporters to promote India as an outsourcing base to the Far-Eastern countries like Korea, Taiwan and so on, where the labour cost has gone up sky-rocketing, but they still have some very innovative fabrics.

The demand for man-made fibres exceeds supply by about 250,000 tons. India's strong cotton orientation is strength as also a limitation for export. Ability to take advantage of such demands for man-made fibre products requires product diversification in terms of fibre composition. India is currently not well prepared to take advantage of the increasing global demand for blended and synthetic textile and clothing products.

India's domestic market for readymade apparel is estimated at USD 5000 million to USD 7000 million annually. Approximately 20 per cent of the apparel produced in India is branded ready to wear garments. There is a potential to expand the branded ready-made garment segment through better marketing, brand building in the domestic industry and foreign investment in retail.

'It can be said that, *but for quotas*, the exports of Indian fabric to US would have been much lower. In this sense, quotas have indubitably protected the exports of Indian fabric in the US market during the quinquennium. Indian fabric exports have not revealed to be competitive in the US market' (Verma 2002).

In composition of exports to the EU, the main winners are expected to be ready-made garment (upper and middle segments, knitting, made ups, especially bed linen, terry towels and toilet and kitchen linen), although the EU trend of anti dumping allegations could hamper the success of this product. Export of Indian fabric to the EU in future is likely to further slow down substantially. Made-up exports to the EU, like in the US, are a very big opportunity for India. In garments, Indian exports of W&G skirts and suits/ensembles are another big opportunity where India has shown good performance in the EU market over the five years 1995–2000.

With the era of managed trade now being history, and with significant policy reforms in the Indian textile and clothing sector, the ball clearly lies with the Indian entrepreneurs who now must propel the Indian textile and clothing sector to global heights that the sector and its people truly deserve.

Endnotes

[1] Indirectly would include exports to EU and US which are assembled (as apparel) in countries other than where the yarns and the fabrics are produced. It is a common phenomenon in this sector where the manufacturing value chain has been sliced up and each stage is manufactured at cheapest cost location.

[2] Textile would be used to mean fibres, yarn, fabric and made-ups, whereas clothing would stand for ready-made garments. The terms clothing, apparel and garments would be used interchangeably in this paper.

[3] Underhill's discussion on political economy of liberalisation in the Uruguay Round is quite interesting.

[4] The protectionism of the 1970s is referred to 'New Protectionism' largely because it came after the major push for liberalisation in the Kennedy Round, but there was nothing particularly 'new' about the protectionism.

[5] The share of developed country trade in the total trade in textiles and clothing is about 37 per cent.

[6] In the US, these became known as 'Section 807 imports', referring to the relevant clause in one of the trade bills. In the EU, two regimes applied. First—Fiscal Outward Processing Traffic (OPT) regulations—which was similar to US 'Section 807' provisions, where import duty would be charged only on the value added *produced* overseas. Second involves only countries that have signed preferential (zero duty) trade agreements with the EU, such as Turkey, North Africa, and the Central Eastern European countries (PECOs in EU-speak). In this case, re-import was at zero duty if fabric produced in EU member country.

[7] It was scarcely, therefore, surprising that in the US, at the end of the Uruguay Round, while the clothing manufacturers' association was hardly opposed to dismantling MFA, their textile industry counterpart was virulently opposed.

[8] Countries like Bangladesh, Jamaica and Sri Lanka were able to use their quota entitlements to develop their textile and clothing domestic industry, which would not have survived but for quotas.

[9] This section heavily borrows from International Textile and Clothing Bureau (ITCB) documents available on their website

[10] Such as GATT Article XXIV on RTAs and agreements on technical barriers to trade (TBT) and Sanitary and Phytosanitary Agreement (SPS).

[11] ITCB document No CR/33/BRA/4, dated 07 May 2001.

[12] At the beginning of the second stage of integration programme, developing countries mentioned that for integration to be meaningful, the list of integrated products should contain an equitable mix of restrained and unrestrained products and a balanced proportion of sensitive and non-sensitive products, with more emphasis on clothing products. See Bangkok Communique issued following the 23rd session of the Council of Representatives of ITCB held at Bangkok, 20–24 May 1996.

[13] Besides the countries applying restrictions under Art. 2 of ATC, 55 WTO member countries have retained the right to apply Art 6 safeguards, and most of them provided list of products for integration. Nine members, that is, Australia, Brunei Darussalam, Chile, Cuba, Hong Kong, Iceland, Macau, New Zealand and Singapore opted not to retain the right to use the ATC safeguard mechanism. These nine countries are deemed to have integrated 100 per cent of their products at the outset.

[14] Unlike in MFA, Art 6 safeguards cannot be used to avoid real risks of market disruption under ATC. Second, in determining serious damage to domestic industry, ATC takes into account the totality of imports as opposed to imports from a particular source as in MFA. Finally, unlike MFA, ATC has discarded the notion of serious damage caused by low prices. ATC has imposed greater discipline on its use, and reduced the potential for misuse.

[15] Canada, EU, Japan and the US.

[16] This section has been dealt with separately from the section on the ATC implementation because trade defense mechanisms are not—strictly speaking—part of ATC. They follow from other WTO agreements.

[17] Indeed, recourse to GATT Art. XIX was considered to be quite burdensome, and hence the expediency of special arrangement for textiles (transitional safeguard mechanism) was devised to sidetrack such perceived difficulties.

[18] Art. VIII stipulates that these shall not represent an indirect protection to domestic products and recognises the need for minimising the incidence and complexity of trade formalities. Art. XIX also recognises that marking requirements should be reduced to minimum, while protecting the consumers against fraud. Most importantly, any requirement must be made on MFN basis.

[19] According to ITCB, there has not been much authoritative assessment of their actual impact on consumer behaviour, though it appears that not much significant impact has been felt so far.

[20] Core labour standards essential are standards applied to the way workers are treated. The term covers a wide range of things: from use of child labour and forced labour, to the right to organize trade unions and to strike.

[21] For instance, HR 3812 (International Child Labour Elimination Act), HR 3294 (Working Children's Human Rights Act), HR 2065 (Child Labour Deterrence Act) and HR 910 (Socially Responsible Business Practices Act).

[22] This figure corresponds to notifications of new RTAs, as well as of accessions to existing RTAs.

[23] *Differential and More Favourable Treatment, Reciprocity and Fuller Participation of Developing Countries*, Decision of 28 November 1979.

[24] In the year 1999–2000. The data includes the cloth production by Exclusive Weaving Units. The share of composite mills in total cloth manufacture was 36 per cent in 1980–81. Source: Office of Textile Commissioner (2000).

[25] Average investment per machine in a typical garment factory was just USD 250 in India while 1,500 in China and 1260 in Thailand, productivity also being estimated 50 per cent than in China or Hong Kong (see, Business World 2004).

[26] Recently, the government also allowed 100 per cent foreign investment without any export obligations, to spur new investment in the sector.

[27] This section is mostly drawn from Spinanger & Verma (2003).

[28] India's textile exports grew by 10 per cent during period 1990–99, but only by 6 per cent in 1997, and minus 13 per cent in 1999. Office of Textile Commissioner (2000).

[29] Prices are likely to decline by as much as 30 per cent according to some estimates.

[30] One expert argued the collapse of the WTO Dispute Settlement mechanism under heavy burden of disputes that would suddenly be launched by WTO members against China following integration of the sector to the WTO.

References

Baughman, Laura M. and Kara M. Olson. 1997. *Prospects for Exporting Textiles and Clothing to the United States over the Next Decade*, Geneva: International Textiles and Clothing Bureau.

Bhagwati, Jagdish and Arvind Panagariya. 2003. 'Bilateral Trade Treaties are a Sham,. *Financial Times*, 13 July.

Bhardwaj, A., S. Kathuria and W. Martin. 2001. 'Implications for South Asian Countries of Abolishing the Multifibre Arrangement', World Bank Working Paper no. 2721.

Businessworld. 2004. 'Nine Months to go' Cover story, April.

Centre of Social Research. 2003. *Gender Impact of WTO on Women's Livelihood in India: Women Workers in the Textiles and Food Processing Industries*, New Delhi: Centre of Social Research.

Debroy, Bibek. 1996. *Beyond the Uruguay Round*, New Delhi: Sage Publications.

Economist. 2004. 'Rags and Riches: A Survey of Fashion', March.

Elbehri, Aziz. 2004. 'MFA Quota Removal and Global Textile and Cotton Trade: Estimating Quota Restrictiveness and Quantifying post-MFA Trade Patterns', Economic Research Service, USDA, Preliminary Draft Version, 11 May.

ESCAP Secretariat. 1996. 'Agreement on Textiles and Clothing: Progress, Problems and Prospects for Developing Countries of the ESCAP Region', in *Asian and Pacific Developing Economies and the First WTO Ministerial Conference, Issues of Concern*, New York: United Nations.

Financial Times. 2004. 'EU Set to Take New US Trade Spat to WTO', 27 January.

Ministry of Finance. 2004. *Economic Survey 2002–03*, New Delhi: Government of India.

Grether, J. and Marcelo Olarreaga. 1998. 'Preferential and Non-preferential Trade Flows in World Trade', WTO Staff Working Paper ERAD-98-10.

Hoekman, B., N. G. Francis and Marcelo Olarreaga. 2001. *Tariff Peaks in the Quad and Least Developed Country Exports*, Washington DC: The World Bank.

Institut Francais de la Mode. 2004. *Study on the Implications of the 2005: Trade Liberalisation in the Textile and Clothing Sector*, Paris.

ITCB. 2004. Council of Representatives, Presentation and Papers, New Delhi, April.

Kathuria, S., W. J. Martin and A. Bhardwaj. 2002. 'Implications of MFA Abolition for India and South Asia,' in *The WTO for Development: A Strategy for India*, edited by A. Mattoo and Robert M. Stern, New York: Oxford University Press.

Kathuria, S., A Bhardwaj and W. Martin. 2001. 'Implications for South Asian Countries of Abolishing the Multifibre Arrangement', World Bank Working Paper no. 2721, November.

Kathuria, Sanjay and Anjali Bhardwaj. 1998. 'Export Quotas and Policy Constraints in the Indian Textile and Garment Industry', in *Development, Trade and the WTO: A Handbook*, edited by Barnard Hoekman, Aaditya Mattoo and Philip English, Washington DC: The World Bank.

Keesing, D. R. and M. Wolf. 1981. 'Question on International Trade in textiles and Clothing', *World Economy*, March, pp. 79–101.

McKinsey. 2001. *The Growth Imperative*, Mumbai: Mckinsey Global Institute.

Neetha, N. 2001 'Gender and Technology: Impact of Flexible Organisation and Production of Female Labour in Tiruppur Knitwear Industry', V. V. Giri National Labour Institute, Noida.

Olson, Kara M. 2003. 'Sourcing Patterns and the Elimination of Textile and Apparel Quotas' Department of Economics, American University, http://nw08.american.edu/~hertz/fall2003/MFA.pdf.

Oxfam. 2004. 'Stitched Up: How Rich-country Protectionism in Textiles and Clothing Trade Prevents Poverty Alleviation, Briefing Paper no. 60.

Panagariya, A. 1999. 'Labour Standards in the WTO and Developing Countries: Trading Rights at Risk', note served as the basis of author's remarks at the Congressional Staff Forum on International Development, 'Critical Issues for the Seattle WTO Ministerial: Trade and labour Standards', November.

Sathyam Committee. 2001. *Wake-up Call for India's Textile Industry, Report*.

Singh, N., R. Kaur and M. K. Sapra. 2004. *Continents Wide and Layers Deep-The Ready-made Garment Industry in the Times of Restructuring*, New Delhi: NCAER.

Spinanger, D. and Samar Verma. 2003. 'The Coming Death of the ATC and China's WTO Accession: Will Push Come to Shove for Indian T & C Exports?' in *Bridging the Differences: Analyses of Five Issues of the WTO Agenda*, edited by A. L. Winters and P. Mehta, New Delhi: CUTS Publications.

Spinanger, D. 1999. 'Faking Liberalisation and Finagling Protectionism: The ATC at its Best', background paper prepared for WTO 2000 Negotiations, ERF/IAI/World Bank Workshop, Cairo, July.

Stern, Nicholas. 2002. 'Making Trade Work for Poor People', Speech delivered at NCAER, World Bank, November.

SEWA Academy. 2004. 'Globalisation of the Garment Industry and its Impact on Home Based Workers and Small Factor Workers of Ahmedabad City: Recommendations and their Implementation', Workshop in New Delhi on 27 April.

US International Trade Commission. 2004. 'Textile and Apparel: Assessment of the Competitiveness of Certain Foreign Suppliers to the U.S. Market', January.

Underhill, G. R. D. 1998. *Industrial Crisis and the Open Economy: Politics, Global Trade and the Textile Industry in the Advanced Economies*, London: Macmillan.

UNDP. 2003. *Making Global Trade Work for People*, Chapter 8, London: UNDP.

USITC. 2001. 'India's Textile And Apparel Industry: Growth Potential and Trade And Investment Opportunities', Staff Research Study 27, Publication 3401, March.

Verma, Samar. 2002. 'Impact of WTO Agreement on Indian Textile and Clothing Industry', ICRIER Working paper no. 94.

———. 2002a. 'Export Competitiveness of Indian Textile and Clothing Sector', unpublished manuscript, New Delhi: ICRIER.

Section IV

Trade Facilitation and Government Procurement: Singapore Issues of Future Concern

10

Regional Integration through Trade Facilitation: Integrating East India with Bangladesh and North India with Central Asia

Pritam Banerjee, Dipankar Sengupta and Phunchok Stobdan

INTRODUCTION

The basic premise of an efficient global economy is the smooth flow of goods, services, technology and people across borders. This calls for a removal of barriers and reduction in transaction costs for such flows. However, even in a rapidly globalising world economy there are contiguous regions sharing the same geography that have some of the highest barriers and transaction costs to such flows. Prime examples of such a region, and the subject of this analysis, is Eastern India-Bangladesh (EIB) sub-region as well as Ladakh-Central Asia.

While the literature on trade and transaction costs has dealt extensively with the idea of political borders as barriers (Bougheas and Morgenroth 1999), the term trade facilitation (TF) covers all the steps that can be taken to smoothen and facilitate the flow of trade. The term has been used widely to cover all sorts of NBTs, including product testing and impediments to labour mobility, but in the WTO, discussions are limited to 'the simplification and harmonisation of international trade procedures' covering the 'activities, practices and formalities involved in collecting, presenting, communicating and processing data required for the movement of goods in international trade' (WTO 2004). It relates to a wide range of activities at the border such as import and export procedures (for example, procedures relating to customs, licensing and quarantine); transport formalities; payments, insurance, and other financial requirements.

How poorly reality deifies this description and its implications is given by the fact, that where India and Bangladesh are concerned, border crossings are subject to long delays not only due to the fact that they are crossed by relatively small number of roads and rail links leading to bottlenecks, but also inspection and documentation activities that take place at borders are time consuming and often lead to substantial transaction costs (Lakshmanan et al. 2001). Indeed, the borders between India and Bangladesh that dissect the EIB region are one of the worst managed ones and are subject to severe transaction costs. What makes this state of affairs even more ironic, is that prior to the 1947 partition of the subcontinent, Bangladesh and India were in fact a single entity politically, economically and monetarily. The border, with its long history of movements between goods, services, people, cultures, beliefs and ideas was completely unreal from the beginning (Banerjee et al. 1999).

The border disrupted long established economic linkages between the Indian states of Assam and West Bengal and Bangladesh (East Pakistan prior to 1971). The fact that both India and Bangladesh had restrictive trade policies through much of their history up to the 1990's, with high tariffs, quantitative restrictions (quotas) and restrictions on the movement of capital, further exacerbated the problem of diminishing cross border linkages (Lakshmanan et al. 2001).

This chapter aims to the following; it juxtaposes the EIB sub region in the context of sub-regional cooperation, argues that there is an urgent need of such a regional framework in the EIB and discusses how TF may be used to accomplish the same.

In the same vein, it also looks at ways and means to open up through Ladakh, Central Asia (an area from which we are hitherto cut off) using the provision of TF as a device to do so. Just as Bangladesh's economy was integrated with the economy of the present states of West Bengal and Assam, Ladakh too served as a gateway to Central Asia with caravans travelling to and from cities like Lhasa in Tibet and Kashgar in Xinjiang before going off to other cities. While Partition and subsequent political problems with Pakistan and later with Bangladesh, affected trade and transit arrangements, Ladakh's ties with Central Asia were similarly affected given India's problems with China. However with an upsurge in both economic and diplomatic relations with China and the fact that both nations have long shed autarkic policies and actively integrating their economies with the global economy, it is not too soon to consider steps to revive this route as well.

The feasibility of such frameworks have already been established by the success of the Greater Mekong Sub-region (GMS) in South-East Asia under the aegis of the Asian Development Bank (ADB). So far, the literature on sub-regional cooperation suggests that there are five essential pre-conditions for such cooperation to take place (Sohel 2000);

- Economic Complimentarity
- Regional Proximity
- Integrated Infrastructure
- Institutional Cooperation
- Political Will

To these factors, this chapter identifies a sixth: the regime that governs international trade especially aspects of TF that can also help in fostering regional cooperation. This analysis will provide evidence that there is a high degree of economic complimentarity between The Indian states of West Bengal and Assam with Bangladesh. Since the three entities share land borders, and West Bengal and Bangladesh were in fact at one point in history (up to 1947) a single political unit, it makes the case for regional proximity self-evident. The shared linguistic and cultural factors across the borders make this case even more compelling.

The case for linking Ladakh with Xinjiang and Tibet is not immediately obvious. This is because Ladakh being sparsely populated (as indeed are Tibet, Xinjiang and the other Central Asian republics with which Ladakh maybe linked), complementarities in industrial production structure are not meaningful. However, visualised as India's gateway to the land-locked Central Asian states, the importance of acquiring transit routes become obvious and overwhelming. Central Asian as a market and more importantly as a source of energy becomes easily accessible to India with profound implications for India's economic future and energy security. So far India's economic relations with the Central Asian republics have been extremely modest. While the near total collapse of these economies in the aftermath of the dissolution of the erstwhile USSR, is at least in part responsible for this state of affairs, arguably the more important reason is the fact, that trade and transit facilities to these economies to and from India are at present circuitous and lead to high transportation costs. The re-opening and upgrading of these routes from Ladakh to Central Asia are thus absolutely vital for the entire region as not only India's economy and energy security receives a boost, but Central Asian economies too stand to gain enormously from such a move.

It may be again argued that of the six essential pre-conditions for regional cooperation and integration to take place, the first two factors are fulfilled, the next two factors, that is, integrated infrastructure and institutional cooperation will be analysed.

It needs to be stressed that infrastructural integration, broadly referred to as Trade and Transport Facilitation (TTF) serves as the crux of this analysis for a good reason. When sub-regional cooperation in the GMS was initiated, there were doubts expressed as to whether the countries in the GMS would put aside their differences and historical rivalries and make it work. To gain general acceptance and make momentum, ADB first commenced preparatory work on infrastructure projects including transport projects, which would quickly give tangible benefits. The strategy proved to be successful and today, there is overall acceptance that the GMS is a very beneficial initiative, and that it has changed the way the GMS countries do business with each other (ADB 1994).

This brings us to the last, and from the policy point of view, the most important pre-condition to successful sub-regional cooperation; political will as well as the international regime that facilitates it. The paper will offer some ideas on why such political will has been lacking in South Asia, especially in terms of lack of decentralisation of power (India) and political pressure against perceived Indian hegemony (Bangladesh), inability to fathom the nature of changes in Central Asia, as well as the framework under WTO rules that make such cooperation mandatory as long as at least one side wants it.

This paper is will be an attempt to bring all the different ideas represented by the six pre-conditions for sub-regional cooperation to provide an overview of the problem. The policy recommendations that follow will be based on this comprehensive overview. The paper is divided into two sections, the first dealing with West Bengal/Assam and Bangladesh and the second dealing with integration of Ladakh with Central Asia.

SECTION I

Complimentarity between West Bengal/Assam and Bangladesh

While there are no formal studies that map relative comparative advantage (RCA) of West Bengal and Assam with that of Bangladesh,[1] a brief survey of India-Bangladesh imports and exports, the structure of intra-Indian trade and consumption patterns and the production structure of some Bangladeshi export industries provide substantial clues in this area. It also must be kept in mind that complimentarity is just not a function of formally traded goods; it should take into account information on illegal trade, trade in services and trade in infrastructural resources such as transport (transit facilities), electricity and natural gas.

Table 10.1 provides a glimpse of products that can be successfully exported to West Bengal and Assam from Bangladesh. The products in this table were identified in three steps as follows:[2]

- First, identify a subset of products that Bangladesh exports successfully to rest of the world, but not so much to India.
- Second, select a second subset of products from the above list that West Bengal and Assam source from other parts of India that are farther away than to next door Bangladesh.
- Third, select a third subset from within the second, based on consumption patterns in India, that is, the products selected are in sectors that have seen significant average growth in private final consumption expenditure in India between 1995 and 2002.

TABLE 10.1 Potential growth sectors for Bangladeshi exports to West Bengal and Assam

Product	Average annual growth in Private Final Consumption (India), 1995–2002 (in percentage)
Tobacco	13.8
Fish and Fishery products	26.8
Ready made garments	11.7
Natural Gas	54.3
Inorganic Chemicals	6.2

Sources: Centre for Monitoring the Indian Economy (CMIE) State Analysis Service and United Nation Conference on Trade and Development (UNCTAD).

Besides the above listed products Bangladesh can gain enormously from sub-regional cooperation trough transit fees. The port of Chittagong in Bangladesh is the outlet for Assam and other North-East Indian states. Further, the distance between North-East India and rest of the Indian subcontinent will be drastically reduced if transit is allowed through Bangladeshi territory (Map 10.1). This issue is related to TTF and will be discussed in detail in the following section.

The state of West Bengal has a large concentration of heavy industry and happens to be a centre for the production of iron and steel, aluminum and related metallurgy products, machine tools, chemicals, coal and industrial fibers, and yarns.[3] Assam is a centre for silk industry in India and has important facilities in cement and is the primary petroleum producing state in India. It has untapped resources in petrochemicals and processed (and raw) agricultural produce (State Government of Assam 2005).

Based on the production patterns of West Bengal and Assam and primary imports of Bangladesh (top 25 products from India[4] and top 25 products from rest of the world[5]), Table 10.2 identifies sectors that have export potential for West Bengal and Assam to Bangladesh.

While the above tables capture the elements of legal trade across the India-Bangladesh border, analysis of the illegal trade between India and Bangladesh underline similar complementarities. In their path breaking study on illegal trade, Pohit and Taneja (2000) identify cotton yarn and cotton cloth, pharmaceuticals, kerosene, soaps and cosmetics, bicycles, automobile parts and components, machine tools, electronics, cement, pesticides, and iron and steel products as the main Indian illegal exports to Bangladesh, a basket similar to the ones established in Tables 10.1 and 10.2.

MAP 10.1 Trade route between North-East India and the rest of the India through Bangladesh

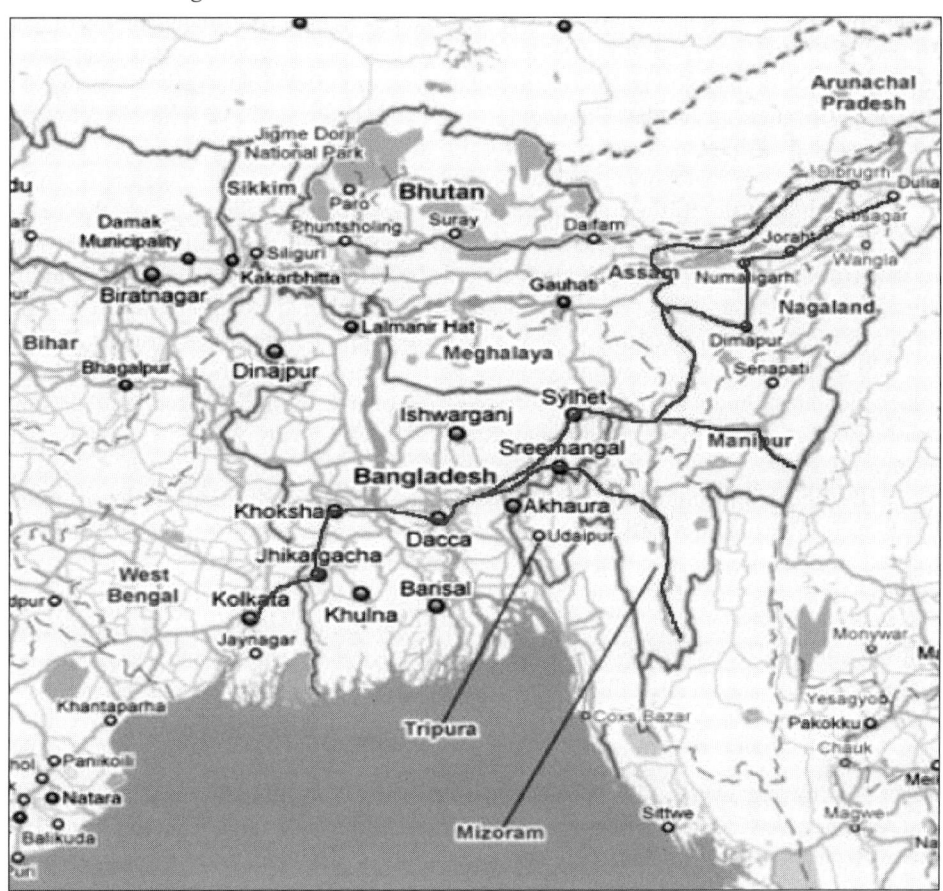

TABLE 10.2 Potential growth sectors for West Bengal and Assam exports to Bangladesh

Products	Indian exports to Bangladesh 2004–5 (million USD)
Rice	196
Agricultural products (raw and processed)	183
Cotton yarn and textiles	133
Machinery and Machine parts	68
Iron and Steel	57
Coal (and coal based products)	54
Aluminum and related products	37
Cement	35
Pharmaceuticals	16

Sources: Director Genral of Foreign Trade (DGFT), UNCTAD, West Bengal Industrial Development Corporation (WBIDC) and State Government of Assam.

Bangladeshi imports from India, a substantial proportion of which comes from West Bengal (CII 2004), have a substantial re-export content in the sense that such imports serve as supply materials and capital goods for finished goods exports from Bangladesh. Almost 30 per cent of the Bangladeshi imports from India go to the export-oriented garments sector of Bangladesh (Rahman 2000). This reliance on imported inputs makes it likely that the competitiveness of Bangladeshi manufacturers, both in terms of lead time and delivered price, is related to the transaction costs (World Bank 2005). In light of this, need for a sub-regional mechanism that works to reduce transaction costs becomes more urgent.

The high intensity in the trade of intermediate products and capital goods also point towards an element of intra-industry trade and supply chain complimentarity between exports from West Bengal to Bangladesh. A study by Research and Information System for Developing Countries (RIS), Ministry of External Affairs, India,[6] point out that the import basket of India and Bangladesh (vis-à-vis each others exports) comprises various products that are amenable to joint venture projects within the region such as paper products, mineral manufactures, wood articles, processed food, pharmaceuticals, and so on. Yet again, sub-regional cooperation on institutional and TTF aspects are crucial to the development of such linkages.

EIB trade is not limited to just goods, several services are also traded. However, the bulk of services exports in EIB region comprises West Bengal's exports to Bangladesh and focused around two main sectors, that is, health and education.

Most of health and education exports from West Bengal are availed by Bangladeshi's coming from rural and semi-urban areas (Rahman 2000). Thus, developments in TTF that will reduce costs for Bangladeshi's to avail these services across the border, will have a salutary effect on the quality of health and education that Bangladeshi people can access.

Trade and Transport Facilitation Problems in EIB Region

There is a growing awareness in international trade literature and policy circles that TTF and related transaction cost issues play a crucial role in fostering trade and development. The major elements of an inefficient TTF system includes institutional bottlenecks (transport, regulatory, and other logistics infrastructure), information asymmetry and administrative power that give rise to rent seeking activities by the officials at various steps of transaction. It is within the realm of the policy makers to reduce this cost through enabling measures in TTF policy (Pohit et al. 2000).

The continuity and future growth of trade in many developing country regions depend on the efficiency and speed of cross border transportation of goods and services and on the harmonisation and simplification of the information processing, related to such flows of goods and services. Therefore, the lack of an efficient TTF system will lead to foregone trade and economic growth (Lakshmanan et al. 2001), something countries and regions of South Asia can ill afford.

The long term benefits of a superior TTF system lies beyond the transaction cost reduction and trade expansion benefits. It opens up greater opportunities for cross border integration of manufacturing and services and the exploitation of economies of scale, skills, and resources. Although such developments take time, they can set in motion a sequence of cumulative processes that lead to falling costs, output increases and incentives for spatial agglomeration. In time these developments lead to self sustaining regional growth.

The India-Bangladesh border procedures remain one of the most cumbersome in the world and in effect reflect the conservative trade policies that characterised the region for decades and the political mistrust among South Asian neighbours. In a study quantifying the costs of overland India-Bangladesh trade Das and Pohit (2003) found that the average time taken for a consignment to cover the 95 km overland distance from Kolkata (West Bengal) through the border crossing at Benapole in Bangladesh is 98 hours, while the ideal best international practices time for a overland border crossing of similar dimensions is 21 hours. One aspect behind this enormous inefficiency is the condition of the border crossing itself. Table three again draws from the work of Das and Pohit and lists the costs arising from problems faced at the border crossing as percentage of the average total cost of shipment.

TABLE 10.3   Transaction costs vis-à-vis shipment value in India-Bangladesh trade

Cost elements	Percentage of shipment value (average)
Delay in customs clearance including parking and queue at the border	5.73
Rent seeking activities of transporters, officials and middlemen	2.50
Delay in obtaining export remittances	2.15
Total	10.38

Source: Das and Pohit 2003.

The main infrastructural and institutional problems related to TTF can at important border crossings can be summarised as presented in Table 10.4 below.

TABLE 10.4   Bottlenecks at the India-Bangladesh border

Facility	Hilli border crossing	Mahadipur border crossing	Petrapole border crossing
Approach road to border customs house	Single lane congested road.	Poor physical condition.	Passes through extremely congested market towns.
Parking lot in Customs border crossing	No Sanitation facilities available. Not secured, problem of thefts.	Discriminatory parking fees, Not secured, problem of thefts.	Inadequate drinking water supply. No Sanitation facilities available. Not secured, problem of thefts.
Warehouse	No government bonded warehousing.	No government bonded warehousing.	No government bonded warehousing.
Other problems	Poor quality of Power supply. Absence of bank collection centre.	Poor quality of power affects efficiency of Customs officials. Absence of bank collection centre. No office space for clearing and forwarding agents.	Irregular power supply with low voltage. Single gate for export, import and passengers. Electronic Data Interchange (EDI) ineffective due to lack of efficient operator.

Source: Das and Pohit 2003.

TTF cooperation between West Bengal, Assam and Bangladesh will not only enhance cross border linkages in the EIB region, but it will also enable the North-Eastern (NE) part of India (of which Assam is the largest state), to effectively access markets in rest of India and the rest of the world. The NE region of India is connected to the rest of the country by a narrow and congested land corridor referred to as the 'chicken's neck' (see map in appendix). The landlocked NE region of India is a natural hinterland to the Bangladeshi port of Chittagong; indeed before partition of the subcontinent in 1947 NE India is to trade mostly through this port.

Since partition, NE India has been forced to use the port of Kolkata for its global exports, adding substantial costs to such a trade. The transportation cost of shipping goods from Assam in NE India to Kolkata includes a trucking distance of more than 1400 kilometers through the land corridor around Bangladesh, using the Chittagong port would cut this distance by 900 kilometers (Lakshmanan 2000).

The costs of transporting goods to and fro between NE India and the rest of the country would also fall substantially, if Indian goods are allowed transit through Bangladeshi territory rather than having to go around it. It has been estimated that Assam was spending almost as much in transporting essential commodities from rest of India as the cost of commodities themselves (Verghese 1996). Table 10.5 below compares the time and cost of moving goods to and fro from NE India through the current route and a possible transit route through Bangladesh.

TABLE 10.5 Comparative time and cost of North-East India routes to rest of the subcontinent

Route	Time taken	Average cost for a 8 ton consignment
Through India (the 'chicken neck' route)	198 hours	1600 USD
Through a transit route cutting across Bangladesh	73 hours	1200 USD

Source: Lakshmanan 2000

Having outlined the issues in TTF in the EIB region in this section, the next section will deal with the institutional aspects of sub-regional cooperation, with a focus on TTF aspects of such a cooperation. The next section also briefly introduces the political backdrop that acts as a barrier for cooperation

Institutional Linkages in Sub-regional Trade and Transport Cooperation

The break up of Indian subcontinent into two sovereign nations, the erstwhile Dominions of India and Pakistan, led to the disruption of commercial and cultural ties that are several millennia old. This was especially true of two provinces in the subcontinent, Bengal and Punjab. Unlike other provinces or regions that went wholly to either India or Pakistan, Bengal and Punjab were divided and portioned off to both. Thus the level of disruption was maximum in these two regions. The old region of Bengal was divided into the Indian state of West Bengal and the Pakistani province of East Pakistan. Intra-regional rail, road and inland waterway linkages were allowed to wither as commercial ties became victims of India-Pakistan hostility. Bengal's traditional routes to Assam went through Bangladesh (that is, East Pakistan) and these were disrupted by Pakistan's refusal to allow India transit through its territory.

East Pakistan, separated from West Pakistan by 3600 kilometers of Indian territory and linguistically and culturally different from their counterparts in the West, opted for independence and became the sovereign nation of Bangladesh in 1971 after a bloody independence struggle. On March 28, 1972, India and Bangladesh signed a trade agreement for a period of one year. Article V of the Agreement provided for 'mutually beneficial arrangements for the use of each other's waterways, railways and roadways for commerce between the two countries and for passage of goods between two places in one country through the territory of the other'.

However, the close relationship and understanding developed between the two countries did not continue. The government of Mujib-ur Rahman (main leader and head of Government of independent Bangladesh) was alleged by the extreme left and right parties to be falling under the policy control of the Government of India. Hence, any talk on bilateral cooperation was viewed as unequal and against interests of Bangladesh (Thapliyal 1999). Keeping this political background that informs much of the institutional linkages in the region in mind, this section offers a brief analysis of such linkages.

Railways and Roadways
Rail links existed between the two countries prior to 6 September 1965, when armed conflict between India and Pakistan broke out. Three different train routes ran between the two countries carrying goods and passengers. These trains routes were cancelled in 1965 and were not restored even after the change in the regional political scenario with the liberation to Bangladesh in 1971 (Indian Council of World Affairs 1983).

There are two major National Highways connecting Eastern India with Bangladesh through West Bengal and Assam. Besides National Highways, a number of state Highways passing through West Bengal and Assam connect East India with Bangladesh. (see map in annex). However, despite the availability of a large number of roads connecting East India with Bangladesh, the institutional arrangements for cross border movement of vehicles act as a barrier to free movement of goods and people. No foreign vehicle is allowed on Bangladeshi roads. As a result all commodities transported by road to Bangladesh have to be transshipped at the border (Lakshmanan et al. 2001). This greatly adds to the congestion, delays and costs as discussed in the last section.

Inland Water Transport (IWT)
Inland waterways provide a potential lower cost alternative for transporting low value cargo in the sub region. On 1 November 1972, a Protocol on Inland Water Transit and Trade was signed in accordance with Article V of the Trade agreement of 1972 for a term of five years, this agreement has been since regularly updated.

The protocol provided for a uniform documentation for vessels, arrangements for settlement, clearance and remittance, uniform toll charges of vessels, and so on. Despite low costs and the absence of cross-border transshipment requirements, inland waterway transport is at a competitive disadvantage because of its low speeds and physical constraints (Thapliyal 1999).[7]

Institutional Arrangement of Authority in India: Federal vs. State
A major impediment for sub-regional cooperation in India is that in almost all areas that need to be addressed for such cooperation, is under the Federal administration. This does

not leave much scope for the State Governments who will be the biggest beneficiaries of sub-regional cooperation to take the initiative. According to the Schedule VII, Article 246 of the Indian constitution, powers in the seven key areas (list below) for sub-regional cooperation are with the Union (federal) administration;

- Foreign affairs; all matters which bring the Union into relation with any foreign country.
- Participation in international conferences, associations and other bodies and implementing of decisions made thereat.
- Railways
- Shipping and navigation on inland waterways, declared by Parliament by law to be national waterways, as regards to mechanically propelled vessels; the rule of the road on such waterways.
- Trade and commerce with foreign countries; import and export across customs frontiers; definition of customs frontiers.
- Inter-State trade and commerce.
- Incorporation, regulation and winding up of trading corporations, including banking, insurance and financial corporations but not including cooperative societies.

The problems with such an arrangement for power sharing are discussed in the next section with greater detail.

A Summing Up: Policy Recommendations

While the political situation in India and Bangladesh has been an impediment to EIB sub-regional cooperation, there is reason to believe that things are changing for the better given certain external as well as internal factors.

First, there has been a radical change in the political alignment in India in the last ten years. Current Indian federal (union) governments are no longer dominated by a single party but are a coalition of several regional parties. This makes the union government more responsive to regional needs.

Second, with liberalisation of the economy, Indian governments have realised global and regional integration is not an option; it's a fact of life. Thereby they are less likely to give into protectionist arguments.

And lastly, the phase out of the MFA that gave Bangladesh easy access to textile and clothing markets in the EU and US has made it imperative that Bangladesh looks for fresh options in the global economy and thereby it can ill afford to ignore possibilities in a rapidly growing market of 200 million people next door.

EIB sub-regional cooperation is now a part of the policy deliberations in Asian Development Bank.[8] and other regional forums like the BIMSTEC.[9] Given the movement in recent years towards an agenda for sub-regional cooperation in South Asia, this section will lay out some of the policy priorities required to move towards an integrated EIB region. The policy priorities will address the problems laid out in the previous sections.

The policy priorities can be put under three categories; that is, infrastructure, institutional reforms and procedural and regulatory reforms.

Infrastructure

Given the poor quality of the transport and TF in infrastructure, huge investments will need to be made to develop state of the art transport corridors. It is obvious that while union and state governments in India and the government of Bangladesh will have to play an important role in finding the resources for such investments, a bigger role for the private sector is definitely possible. Currently regulatory barriers prevent the private sector from effectively taking part in infrastructural development in both Bangladesh and India. Some key areas for deregulation are;

Management functions at land ports and logistics. Private sector activity should extend to the management of land port facilities and services, cargo-handling facilities and services, container operations and dedicated skilled labour services for such functions.

Third party logistics. There is a need for the private sector to provide services, including freight forwarding, customs clearance, financial services, storage and warehousing, and general transit, and shipping services at seaports and land border crossings.

There is a role for organisations like the CII and the Bangladesh Chamber of Commerce to bring together business interests in both countries to explore joint venture possibilities and create a joint lobbying forum with their respective Governments.

The State governments in Assam and West Bengal have an all important role developing their infrastructure. West Bengal is already undertaking a massive overhaul of its State highway system with the help of Asian Development Bank; it needs to synergise such development efforts with future needs and markets in mind, that is, ensure all industrial and urban centers in the State are connected to an EIB regional grid.

Furthermore, state governments can play an enabling role with the help of nodal financial agencies. The state government of West Bengal has established a financial institution, I-WIN, that is a joint venture of the national industrial credit institution (ICICI) and the WBIDC. I-WIN serves as a nodal venture capital institution for private sector infrastructural development projects. The scope of I-WIN needs to be broadened and the Union government needs to infuse some additional low interest funds into I-WIN. Similar organisations need to be incubated in Assam. Joint Ventures between I-WIN and Bangladeshi financial market stakeholders and industrial credit institutions need to be explored with urgency.

Institutional Reform and Decentralisation

As mentioned in the earlier sections, political centralisation of certain administrative functions restricts incentives for seeking proactive regional strategies in India. Of the administrative subjects referred to in section III, the following can be effectively decentralised without taking away the basic control over foreign affairs from the union:

- Participation in international conferences, associations and other bodies and implementing of decisions made thereat.
- Inter-State trade and commerce
- Incorporation, regulation and winding up of trading corporations, including banking, insurance and financial corporations but not including cooperative societies

It is clear that without proper authority to take part in deliberations and making decisions in cross border conferences and associations, the state governments will never be able to take proactive part in sub-regional cooperation. The state governments should also be able to play a major role in the implementation of such agreements to be a truly responsible stakeholder.

The union government can still reserve the right to review and reject by decree any agreement that is detrimental to the collective interests of the Union of India. Moreover, the administrative burden for shipping and navigation on inland waterways should be transferred to the state, with the union playing more of a regulatory role.

Since a bulk of the implementation on all of the issues raised so far, that is, state investment, deregulation, private venture capital in infrastructure, as well as decentralisation needs a responsive bureaucracy; certain institutional bottlenecks need to be addressed. These institutional problems are endemic to the bureaucracy in South Asia and though are not limited to just sub-regional cooperation but is especially relevant to it. These are:

- Lack of a strong institutional framework that can lead to poor coordination and disagreement among government agencies whose approvals and clearances are required. A particular problem is the absence of a single authority to control the process.
- Poor institutional capacity due to a shortfall in expertise in private infrastructure projects. Although civil servants involved in publicly financed turnkey projects tend to be highly skilled in the engineering aspects of the projects, they lack the legal and financial skills to manage a complicated project structure, such as a build-operate-transfer (BOT).
- Lack of transparency in the selection process due to insufficient experience and political cronyism, that often leads to over-reliance on unsolicited proposals. Although, unsolicited proposals that are correctly executed have merit, particularly in terms of speed and directness in developing projects, they lack the transparency, market orientation, and potential efficiency gains of competitive bidding.
- Policy reversal that occurs when the commitments made by a previous government are not honored by the current government. The project developer at best is forced back to the negotiating table or, at worst, faces cancellation of the contract.

Procedural and Regulatory

Certain procedural and regulatory reforms need to be carried out in TF front that will enable safe, quick, and efficient exchange of goods and services across borders. As mentioned before, TF remains the key to sub-regional co operation. The following are an essential list of TF enabling measures (Lakshmanan et al. 2001).

- The use of secure seals for wagons or containers carrying transit cargo, so that few (or no) checks of the cargo are required at different borders.
- Common vehicle inspection and licensing procedures for trucks used to transport cargo across the border.
- Automatic weighing of vehicles at border points.
- The Transport Internationaux Routiers (TIR) system for the carriage of goods approved by customs authorities.
- Round the clock clearance of cargo in high density border crossings like Benapole-Petrapole border.

- Development of a uniform inter-modal transport system that allows integrated use of rail, road, and IWT for the best cost and time advantages.
- Effective Protocol between Indian and Bangladeshi customs.
- Joint checking of cargoes at the origin and destination and/or pre-shipment inspection protocols handled by public (Indian and Bangladeshi customs) and private joint venture operators.
- Electronic Data Interchange (EDI) between customs facilities within the country and across borders.
- Identification numbers, bar codes or other forms of electronic identification for trucks and cargo containers.
- The establishment of a freight operation information system for real time monitoring of trains, wagons and cargo.
- Implementation of smart card system for expediting all transactions associated with cross border movement.

SECTION II[10]

Looking North: Establishing Ladakh as a Gateway to Central Asia

The emergence of Central Asia after the end of the Cold War has been a catalyst for profound changes in Inner Asia, which constitutes multiple geographical, political and economic frontiers. The sceptics describe the unfolding events as the beginning of the New Great Game. In reality however, is that there is a fervent quest for redefining the contours of new relationship across frontiers. But very importantly, a regional cooperative imperative has gained momentum in the China-Central Asia frontiers.

- China has made successful inroads into the region,
- Russia finds new meaning to return to the region,
- The US has legitimised its interests in the aftermath of 9/11,
- The North Atlantic Treaty Organisation (NATO) has included the region into its sphere of interests,
- Japan, Turkey, EU, Iran, Pakistan, and others staked interests in the region,

It is vital that India take steps so not to get left out in this matrix of cooperation.

The major problems that India faces are also problems faced by most countries when dealing with Central Asia.

(a) Transportation is the biggest impediment for any meaningful change. Western analysts have been writing about this since the Iranian Revolution. The states, which remained insular, faced instability and conflict. Afghanistan became glaring example of that. The Western governments and institutions have been focusing on various transformational schemes to integrate many parts of Asia. (It may be noted that the NATO too has widened its charter to include non-traditional security aspects.)

(b) Security is pre-condition for investment and growth. Many countries have rushed to seek security assurance under one umbrella or the other. The NATO's eastward move is to be seen in this context.

The above-mentioned two phenomena together are changing the landscape of Inner Asian world situated in the northern horizon of India. However, India, notwithstanding its strength, has been conspicuously slow in reacting to the new phenomenon across frontiers. Indubitably, India's gain has already been tremendous in building strong bilateral relations but has failed to discern the developments in a regional cooperative framework. For one, India does not belong to any of the regional schemes that involve its interactions with Central Asian states and China. The dynamics evolving in Kazakhstan and Kyrgyzstan are becoming China-centric. The Shanghai Cooperation Organisation (SCO), by facilitating transportation highways, railway lines and pipelines across the Tian Shan and Pamirs has created an area of regional cooperation. Beijing has already prioritised development of western China in its third phase of economic reforms. A web of energy pipelines, including the one from Tarim to coastal China, is going to change the regional economic landscape lying north of India. In the next couple of years China's 'go-west' mentality is going to transform some of the remotest regions of China including Tibet, Xinjiang, Yunnan, and Mongolia.

Given this state of affairs, India has to think how best to use any International Legal tool at its disposa,l whether existing or potential, to turn this situation into her favour to not only gain meaningful access to Central Asia, but also to take advantage of China's `Look West' policy aimed at building up Xinjiang.

Need to Evolve a Look-North Policy

India has been a legitimate player in Central Asia until not so long ago. The British India actively carried out trans-border trade through Ladakh to Xinjiang and beyond. Since the closure of India's Consulate in mid-fifties, India had a thriving trade with Central Asia. India needs to rediscover its lost instruments and re-launch its frontier diplomacy in order to restore its position and economic interests in Inner Asia. It needs to be noted that both China and Pakistan have opened roads through those parts of Jammu and Kashmir (J&K) that lie in their possession to access the region. In fact, in the absence of India's engagement, Xinjiang has opened up trade in Pakistan across Karakoram Highways (Pakistan occupied Kashmir [PoK]). China's PTA, with Pakistan since January 2004, the proposed Free Trade Zones and movements of trucks across frontiers have openned up new opportunities. The completion of Gwadar Port will further boost Pakistan-Central Asia links. It is an irony that Pakistani traders sell Indian goods in Xinjiang market. Similarly, the Tibet-Xinjiang Highway provides China much needed strategic and transportation access.

There is no doubt that only Xinjiang offers a long-distance transportation route. It is therefore vital, that India get access to this hub to access all of Central Asia in the most economical way. But before we discuss how this may be done, it would not be out of order to get a clearer picture. Let us view Xinjiang in geo-economic perspective.

Xinjiang Uighur Autonomous Region (XUAR) is centrally located in the Eurasian continent. It has border with Kazakhstan, Russia, Mongolia, Kyrgyzstan, Tajikistan, Pakistan, Afghanistan, and India. XUAR directly borders with the state of J&K, is strategically located to promote economic interactions with the newly independent countries of Central Asia. Historically, India's interactions with Xinjiang, in the areas of commerce and trade had been enormous. Most of the trade was carried out from Punjab via Kashmir and Ladakh to Xinjiang. The route known as 'Silk Route Extension' (SRE) was most popular during the British era. In fact, British authorities used trading as the most important tool for securing its interests in the region, vis-à-vis Tsarist Russia and China. Leh, the capital town of Ladakh, where the British Commissioner was stationed, was the major crossroad of caravan, where traders from Central Asia, especially from Xinjiang from the north and traders from Kashmir and Punjab from south met for trade transactions. India had a strong political and economic presence in Xinjiang until 1954, when India had to withdraw its Consulate from Kashgar. The SRE from Ladakh to Xinjiang is potentially the most viable and shortest route between India and Central Asia.

XUAR now has sixteen Class A ports, where foreign transport vehicles may deliver goods directly, and eleven Class B ports. XUAR has become the Eurasian Continental Bridge. Several highways and railway lines pass through the region from East to European cities.

XUAR has broadened economic cooperation and trade with Central Asian countries. The border trade has become a pillar and major growth area of XUAR's external trade and its economy as a whole. Xinjiang's own economy is growing and has USD 3000 million foreign trade in 2003.

For Indian policy planners seeking a viable and cost-effective route to Central Asia, the focus of attention should be the ancient Silk Road—a network of roads from China to lands in the west covering hundreds of cities, tombs and Buddhist grottoes. The Jiaohe and Gaochang ancient cities, Loulan Ruins, Qizil Thousand-Buddha Caves, and Tomb of Xiangfei are among the best known worldwide.

Ladakh: India's Economic Springboard to Central Asia

The above-mentioned facts would indicate that XUAR is the natural gateway for many Asian countries to access the outside world through land route. While appropriate regional groupings may be a way forward for India to access Central Asia, *India should also look at WTO regulations that would force China to give India access to Central Asia.* In this context, the potential for Ladakh to become a springboard for India's entry into Central Asia via XUAR is undeniable.

Although, most of the borders between Ladakh and XUAR—in the west along the Karakoram range—mostly forming the PoK, the Shkys-kuum Valley (areas ceded by Pakistan to China), and in the east, along the south of Kun-Lun mountains, the whole of Aksai-Chin is on territory that India considers to be its own under illegal occupation, the traditional route SRE, passing through Nubra Valley into Xinjiang at Daulat Beg Ulde, also known as Karakoram pass, is not under dispute, and forms the direct route between Ladakh and XUAR. Moreover, the Tarim Basin, where most of oil and gas fields are being discovered, is at a very short distance from Ladakh border. It is also important to note that a small land-portion of South-West XUAR separates links between Ladakh and the Central Asian republics of Tajikistan, Kyrgystan and Kazakhstan. In fact, in the recent years, there have been massive developmental projects being envisaged to remove transportation bottlenecks across Chinese-Central Asian sector, which include construction of highways, railway lines, and oil pipelines. Since 1992, Chinese Central Government has been giving a lot of attention on the development of Xinjiang province as a new prosperity zone, bringing in massive overseas investment under the Western China Development campaign. China wants to make XUAR as a major hub of trans-Asian and trans-Eurasian economic activity. Thus India can take advantage of the enormous investments made by the Chinese in this region to access Central Asia.

TABLE 10.6 Xinjiang's transportation links

Countries	Port	Category	Location	Remarks
International	Urumqi Airport	Class A	Urumqi	Istanbul, Sharjiah, Almaty, Tashkent (Moscow, Islamabad)
Mongolia (4)	Takshkent	Class A	Qinghe, Altay Prefecture	Seasonal port, open from the 20 to 30 of each month from April to December
	Hongshanzui	Class A	Fuhai, Altay Prefecture	Seasonal port, open from the 1 to 10 of each month from July to September
	Ulastay	Class A	Qitay, Changji Hui Auto Prefec	Seasonal port, open from 1 to 15 March, June, August, Nov.
	Laoyemiao	Class A	Balikon, Hami Prefecture	Seasonal port, open from 15 to 30 March, June, August, Nov.
Kazakhstan (7)	Korgas	Class A	Huocheng, Ili Prefecture	International seasonal port
	Alataw Pass	Class A	Bortala Mongol Auto. Pref.	International railway/highway
	Baktu	Class A	Tacheng Prefecture	International port
	Jimnay	Class A	Jimnay, Altay Pref.	International port
	Aheytubiek	Class A	Habahe, Altay Pref.	Seasonal port
	Dulart	Class A	Qapqal, Ili Prefe.	Seasonal port
	Muzart	Class A	Zhaosu, Ili Pref.	Seasonal port
Khyrgyzstan (3)	Turgart	Class A	Uqia,Kizilso Kirgiz Pref.	Trade port
	Yearkeshtan	Class A	Kizilso Kirgiz Pref.	Trade port
	Biedieli	Class A	Wushi, Aksu Pref.	Seasonal port
Tajikistan	Kalasu	Class A	Taxkorgan, Kashi Pref.	Seasonal port (open between May 1 and November 30)
Pakistan	Kunjirap	Class A	Tashkurga,Kashi Pref.	Seasonal port (open between May 1 and November 30)
International	Karshi Airport	Class A	Kashi City, Kashi Pref.	Trade with Andjan and Osh
Russia	Kanas	Class A	Burqin, Altay Pref.	
Afghanistan	Tokmans	Class A	TashkurganKashi Pref.	

Source: China.org accessed on 15 December 2004.

Energy Highway

India has been facing tremendous problem in finding direct access to Central Asia for two ways traffic, including transportation of oil and gas supply. For a long time, the option through Afghanistan and Pakistan has been talked without any success. The two energy hungry countries, China and India, are desperately seeking energy supply sources to sustain their economic and industrial growth rates. While China has significantly managed to gain access to Central Asian and Caspian energy reserves for potential supplies, India has been denied supply from the region on accounts of regional instability. Notwithstanding the geographical proximity the constant instability in Afghanistan and Pakistan's hostile approach has so far stymied this process, much to Central Asia's disadvantage.

Like China, India's self sufficiency in oil has become a far cry, as it continues to import over 70 per cent of energy requirements, resulting in large oil import bill and the huge drain on foreign exchange reserves. India's growing dependency on oil imports can lead to increasing vulnerability to supply interruptions. Currently 80 per cent of India's oil supplies, both imports from the Middle East, as well as domestic production in offshore well, have to come across the seas.

It is getting increasingly inevitable, that India has to slowly join China for managing its energy security. Having recognised the supply shortage of oil and gas, ever since China has become an oil importer in 1993, China's National Petroleum Corporation (CNPC) has drawn up several key schemes to boost the energy supply to support its economic growth. Since 1997, China has taken a major step by jumping as a key strategic player in the global oil economics, through production sharing agreements, which are running into millions of dollars. China's embarking on new overseas ventures will have major implications, not only for the management of its industrial and technological revolution, but also for the setting of Asian oil price. As mentioned earlier, China already has invested millions of dollars in developing the Central Asian fields. Similarly, plans are already being drawn up to construct long-distance oil pipelines to link up Chinese growth centres with the major oil and gas producing fields. China is looking for diverse, not only to secure stable oil and gas supply source, but also moving ahead with an objective to achieve a long-term energy supply balance.

India too, since 1997, has been taking several key initiatives to have access to Caspian and Central Asian reserves, but without any success. The route via Afghanistan is unlikely to become a reality for a long time. The US oil giants are no longer showing interest in the Afghan pipeline route. The recently initiated ADB plan for a Turkmenistan-Afghanistan-Pakistan route would also become a non-starter both for technical and political reasons. India's other options such as pipeline via Iran equally face multiple problems. Despite talking for over 12 years now, the gas pipeline projects from Iran or Oman to India has remained feasible only on papers. Venturing for swap transactions with Iran is also not easily available.

The only option now remains to be tried by India are the Central Asia-China routes on which China also already has taken several important initiatives. China since early 1990s has embarked on a several long-distance trans-border oil pipeline projects. These include, gas pipeline from Siberia to China and projects to build a pipeline linking Kazakhstan with China's Xinjiang province. China is also talking about an export pipeline from Turkmenistan to China.

China's new pipeline strategies across the international frontier are ultimately aimed at linking up with its own 'Tarim Basin Energy Development Projects'. The Tarim Basin, located in the heart of XUAR, is the largest onshore basin in the world, covering 560,000 sq. km (a little larger than the size of France). After the discovery of Lunnan field and Tazhong 1 field in 1988/89 in Taklamakan desert, China had set up the Tarim Petroleum Exploration and Development Bureau (TPEDB) in 1989. Since 1993, China opened up the Tarim basin for international companies. It is believed that China has achieved a major break through in developing of over 250 wells in the region. Besides, China is concentrating on a comprehensive transportation infrastructure development across the border with Central Asia and Russia, internally within Xinjiang oil field and finally developing infrastructure to link with eastern Chinese industrial towns. Thus, in a significant way, the pipelines across

Central Asia would be connected to China's own Tarim Basin oil and gas production centers.

Although, China's objective in developing such large scale long-term projects is not profit, but rather to provide energy to the country, it may be argued that it does not have enough resources to develop the infrastructure alone. Central Asia-Xinjiang pipeline route and Tarim Basin oil development fits very well as a viable energy supply route from Kazakhstan to India. However, nothing would be lost if International Law was to be on India's side particularly to make such investments possible and secure.

If one considers the new changes that are fast occurring across our frontiers, India and Kazakhstan must recognise the need to approach China, while making XUAR as an 'Energy-Highway' for a direct link between India and Central Asia, covering a distance less than nine hundred miles and would cost $2000 million only. In this case, oil and gas from Turkmenistan and Kazakhstan could directly come to Ladakh along the SRE or they could be first connected with Chinese pipelines in Tarim Basin, from where a new pipeline can be build up to Ladakh. There is also a plan in the pipeline to have a similar arrangement between Central Asia and Pakistan via Karakoram Highway. But it is confronted with the Chinese anxiety of Pakistani export of Islamic ideology to the Muslim Uighurs in XUAR. However, China would not have any apprehension about threat, ethnic or Islamic, from secular India into XUAR. There are a number of positive points for the consideration of this option.

- The route could be shortest, as it will pass through only one country (China) between Central Asia and India. None of the proposed pipelines from the Caspian and Central Asia to the West or East has such an advantage.
- In comparison to other pipeline routes, which are being confronted with complex regional, ethnic, sectarian, and political instability, Xinjiang route is safer, as China has firmly brought under its control the Uighur Independence Movement in the region. Nor there exists any significant support for the Uighur Movement from the Central Asian states.
- This could also mean the revival of the traditional 'Old Silk Route' that existed between India and China for centuries. Not only will it revive the traditional cultural and economic contacts between the Ladakhis and the Uighurs (also known as Hor by Ladakhis), but will also helps enhancing confidence building between India and China. India's participation in Xinjiang development, however small, should foster greater understanding between the two countries.
- Sooner or later, the border between Ladakh and XUAR will have to be opened up by China and India for trans-border trading, as it becomes highly expensive for China to sustain supplies of basic economic commodities carrying some 7,000 kms from Eastern and Central China to the Western province of Xinjiang. Similarly, India spends formidable amount of resources in lifting essential goods, particularly fuel, to the Trans-Himalayan region of Ladakh.
- The oil pipeline from XUAR to India will not only provide a new source of energy route, but will also cut down on the cost of transportation, incurred in lifting fuel from the refineries to the northern states of India, such as Himachal Pradesh, Punjab, Haryana, and Jammu and Kashmir.
- Conversely, India can supply cheaper goods to XUAR, cutting down transportation costs of bringing goods from the eastern parts of China. Interestingly enough, Indian

goods are extremely popular in XUAR, as demonstrated during the trade-fair held in Urumqi since 1992. Besides, the route would be easiest to get Indian consumer items to Central Asian market. Already, roads up to Ladakh are well maintained by Border Road Organisation (BRO). A small section along the Karakoram needs to be developed to link up with roads in Xinjiang. Leh is located closer to Kashgar and Khotan than Srinagar, Jammu, and Shimla.

- The same pipeline can be further extended to join the Junggar and Turfan-Hami Basins of XUAR, Russian grid in Siberia, and via Mongolia to the Far East, where most of the future resources lie. These could be considered as long-term projects. China and Russia have already signed an agreement for the development of Siberian oil. India should also pull resources and participate in the long-term oil projects signed between China and Russia. A long-term tie-up between Russia, China, and India for exploration of oil, as well as in the field of long-distance pipeline construction across Asia will go a long way in establishing integrated energy security community for Asia. This will not only help to achieve a long-term energy supply balance, but will result in the emergence of a genuine multi-polarity in the international system, crucial for ensuring global security.
- Energy in the form of hydel-power could be available from Kyrgyzstan as well as Tajikistan given their hydel resources and the fact that these two countries cannot consume the entire potential generating capacity.

Unfortunately, this aspect of regional cooperation has so far not received adequate attention in the bilateral Sino-Indian dialogues, although the Governor of XUAR during his visit to New Delhi in 2004, proposed to Indian Civil Aviation Authority to start flights from Urumqi to Delhi. India must stake benefit from China's development plans in Xinjiang and Tibet. The feasibility of constructing oil/gas pipeline from Central Asia along western China connecting to northern India is now well established. Should this happen, it would bring about an unprecedented strategic change, let alone endowing energy supplies to entire northern India. New Delhi must also start pressing Beijing for the re-opening of Indian Consulate in Kashgar, which was closed in the mid-fifties.

WTO and Access to Central Asia

Given the fact that China has now been admitted to the WTO, India can use WTO's legal framework to ensure that China cannot deny India access (at least legally) to Central Asia. Indeed, clause 2 of Article V of GATT (1994) clearly provides for 'freedom of transit through the territory of each contracting party, via the routes most convenient for international transit, for traffic in transit to or from the territory of other contracting parties'. Equally the same clause forbids distinction 'based on the flag of vessels, the place of origin, departure, entry, exit or destination, or on any circumstances relating to the ownership of goods, of vessels or of other means of transport.'

Interestingly enough clause 5 of Article V of GATT 1994 also states that 'With respect to all charges, regulations and formalities in connection with transit, each contracting party shall accord to traffic in transit to or from the territory of any other contracting party treatment no less favourable than the treatment accorded to traffic in transit to or from any third country.' Thus the spirit and letter of the WTO law is clear: China has to allow India the same access to transit facilities that it does to Pakistan!

The problem is that interpretation and application of Article V is not under the jurisprudence or decision of a WTO body. This indeed is a serious lacuna that needs to be rectified. Indeed, even Article I that deals with traffic in transit should be re-written to provide for the right to procure oil/gas through pipelines. Currently Article I provides that

> goods (including baggage), and also vessels and other means of transport, shall be deemed to be in transit across the territory of a contracting party when the passage across such territory, with or without trans-shipment, warehousing, breaking bulk, or change in the mode of transport, is only a portion of a complete journey beginning and terminating beyond the frontier of the contracting party across whose territory the traffic passes. Traffic of this nature is termed in this article "traffic in transit". (GATT 1994)

The spirit of this article clearly also provides for passage of items like hydrocarbons via pipelines or even for that matter electricity through High-tension electricity lines. Clearly a rewording of this clause can make that true for the letter of the law as well. Fortunately, alone among the Singapore Issues, this is an area where progress on a TF Agreement can be expected and Regional Cooperation stemming from a changed International Economic Regime would be an unintended but welcome outcome.

CONCLUSION

The task of integrating East India with Bangladesh and that of linking Ladakh to Central Asia have similarities and differences. The differences lie in the fact that for the former, apart from bilateral trade in complementary goods, integrating production structures is also important. Also, for this region more is known about what needs to be done. The similarity lies in the fact, that a great many steps that are needed for regional integration fall under the rubric of TF.

Another similarity is the unfortunate fact that these various aspects of regional cooperation has so far not received adequate attention be it the case of integration of India's East with Bangladesh or procuring access through Ladakh to Central Asia in the bilateral Sino-Indian dialogues. For example, the Governor of XUAR, Ismail Tiwaldi during his visit to New Delhi in 2004, proposed to Indian Civil Aviation Authority to start flights from Urumqi to Delhi. India must stake benefit from China's development plans in Xinjiang and Tibet. Not much has occurred on this front since. The Kyrgyz offer to sell India hydel power also did not evince much interest in India. The feasibility of constructing oil/gas pipeline from Central Asia along western China connecting to northern India is now well established. Should this happen, it would bring about an unprecedented strategic change, let alone endowing energy supplies to entire northern India. New Delhi must also start pressing Beijing for the re-opening of Indian Consulate in Kashgar, which was closed in the mid-fifties.

If the long shopping list, provided in this chapter, is an indication of the depth of reforms and initiative required to integrate the EIB region and link Ladakh to Central Asia and use the synergies to turn it into a growth zone for all of Asia, then obviously there is a long way to go. But the enormity of the task should not be a source of despair; rather it should be a reason to expedite the process. East India was once the premier hub of economic activity in Asia, bringing together traders and produce from Tibet, South China, South East Asia and the subcontinent. The East India Company was not called so without reason, European traders flocked to the ports of Bay of Bengal from the 17th to the 19th centuries. In the same vein, the Silk Route Extension too had witnessed glorious days. This chapter suggests that by taking steps domestically, as well as by pushing for changes in the international trading regime as exemplified by the WTO, both of which come under the broad rubric of TF, the North and the East of the Region can be integrated with India's neighbours to India's benefit.

Endnotes

[1] Based on the author's findings.

[2] UNCTAD Trade Statistics, http://www.intracen.org/tradstat/main.htm and CMIE indicators.

[3] For maps see, West Bengal Industrial Development Corporation district industrial maps available at http://www.wbidc.com/about_wb/click_map.html.

[4] Directorate General of Foreign Trade (DGFT), Government of India' http://dgft.delhi.nic.in.

[5] UNCTAD, http://www.intracen.org/tradstat/main.htm.

[6] Economic Impact of Trade and Investment Facilitation and Liberalization in South Asia Growth Quadrangle, Research and Information System for the Non-Aligned and Other Developing Countries, New Delhi, December 2001.

[7] Poorly designed warehouses and narrow access roads to river ports.

[8] See South Asia sub-regional cooperation web page of the ADB, available at http://www.asiandevbank.org/sasec/events.asp.

[9] Available at http://www.bimstec.org/.

[10] This section is draws heavily from P. Stobdan's (2003) work, *Evolving a Look North Policy: Conceptualizing Sub-regional Cooperation*.

References

Asian Development Bank. 1996. *Economic Co-operation in the Greater Mekong Sub Region: Facing the Challenges*, Philippines: Asian Development Bank.

Bougheas, Demetrades, and Morgenroth, 1999. 'Infrastructure, costs and trade'. *Journal of Development Economics*, vol. 47, pp. 169–89.

Banerjee, Paula et al. 1999. 'Indo-Bangladesh Cross-Border Migration and Trade', *Economic and Political Weekly*, vol. 34, no. 36, pp. 2549–69.

Confederation of Indian Industry (CII). 2004. *Study of Exports Leaving West Bengal Ports*, www.ciionline.org.

Das and Pohit. 2003. *Quantifying Transport, Regulatory and Other Costs of Indian Overland Exports to Bangladesh*, New Delhi: National Council of Applied Economic Research (NCAER).

Directorate General of Foreign Trade (DGFT), Government of India, http://dgft.delhi.nic.in/.

Economic and Political Weekly. 1999. Commentary, 'India-Bangladesh Cross Border Migration and Trade', 4 September, pp. 1255–62.

Indian Council of World Affairs. 1983. *Studies on Cooperation for Development in South Asia: Transport Linkages: A Regional Synthesis*, p. 28.

Lakshmanan, Anderson and Subramanian. 2001. *Integration of Transport and Trade Facilitation: Directions in Development*, Washington DC: The World Bank.

Manzur, Sohel. 2000. *Growth Zones in South Asia: What can We Learn from South East Asia*, Report no. 20, Centre for Policy Dialogue.
Pohit, Sanjib and Nisha Taneja. 2000. *India's Informal Trade with Bangladesh and Nepal: A Qualitative Assessment*, New Delhi: Indian Council for Research on International Economic Relations (ICRIER).
Rahman, Mustafizur. 2000. *Bangladesh-India Bilateral Trade: An Investigation in Trade in Services*. Bangladesh: Centre for Policy Dialogue, http://www.saneinetwork.net/pdf/SANEI_I/Trade.PDF.
RIS. 2001. *Economic Impact of Trade and Investment Facilitation and Liberalization in South Asia Growth Quadrangle*, New Delhi: Research and Information System for the Non-Aligned and Other Developing Countries.
State Government of Assam. 2005. *Economic Survey of Assam 2003–2004*, http://www.assamgov.org/ecosurvey.
Stobdan, P. 2003. 'Evolving a look north policy: Conceptualizing sub-regional Cooperation'. *Security and Society*, vol. 2, no. 1, pp. 49–57.
Studies on Cooperation for Development in South Asia. 1983. *Transport Linkages: A Regional Synthesis*, Indian Council of World Affairs, p. 28.
Thapliyal, S. 1999. 'India-Bangladesh Transportation Links: A Move for Closer Cooperation', *Strategic Analysis*, IDSA, vol. XXII, March.
Verghese, B. K. 1996. *India Northeast Resurgent: Ethnicity, Insurgency, Governance, Development*. New Delhi: Centre for Policy Research.
UNCTAD. http://www.intracen.org/tradstat/main.htm, accessed August 2006.
World Bank. 2005. *Bangladesh: Growth and Export Competitiveness*. Report no. 31394-BD.
WTO. 2004. 'The Launching of Negotiations on Trade Facilitation', http://www.wto.org/english/tratop_e/tradfa_e/tradfa_negoti_e.htm.

11

Transparency in Government Procurement: A Case Study of India

Sandwip Kumar Das

INTRODUCTION

Article III of the GATT on National Treatment does not apply to government procurement. A code of conduct for central government procurement was introduced in the Tokyo round of multilateral negotiations in 1979. The code applied only to its signatories and most GATT contracting parties, including almost all developing countries did not join the first Plurilateral Agreement on Government Procurement GPA that came into force in 1981 and was amended in 1987. The Uruguay Round extended the coverage of the agreement to include services and additional government entities. The current Agreement on Government Procurement (GPA) was signed in Marrakesh on 15 April 1994—at the same time as the Agreement Establishing the WTO. A Working Group on Transparency in Government Procurement was established after the ministerial meeting in Singapore in 1996, but India and most developing countries have not yet signed the GPA.

The central point of investigation in this paper is whether a greater transparency in government procurement in India would reduce corruption or not. Given that both the officials and firms, may be rent seekers in a system that restricts free entry, there seems to be *a priori* ground for greater transparency. A firm may decide to reduce the competition for contracts by 'rigging' the prices it submits to the government, with the understanding that other firms will take turns in winning government contracts so that they can divide the spoils. Firms could attempt to bribe or otherwise induce government officials to view their tenders favourably. Such corruption has been extensively researched, for instance, by Bardhan (1997) and Rose-ackerman (1999). The general view is that procurement rules should be designed to take account of the danger of corruption, though it may be difficult to make the rules entirely corruption resistant. But a great deal can be done to force public entities to make their decisions in an open fashion, including banning firms who have indulged in bribery, protecting the whistle-blowers and conducting random public and ex-post audits of procurement decisions that explicitly take into account comparisons with similar transactions in the private sector. Box 11.1 provides some instances of the benefits which a developing country may derive from greater transparency in procurement that either reduces corruption or inefficiency or both. In these five case studies cited in the box, either the consumers have gained by paying a lower price or the government has been able to reduce the budget deficit.

> **BOX 11.1** Transparent procurement rules
>
> Transparent Procurement Rules can reduce corruption and save cost:
> (i) 43 per cent saving in the purchase of medicine by Guatemala's Ministry of Health (USAID, 1999)
> (ii) 47 per cent cost saving in the procurement of military goods by the Colombian Ministry of Defence (USAID, 1999)
> (iii) Reduction in pharmaceutical budget of Nicaraguan government from $21 million to $13 million from 1992–93 (Cohen, 2000)
> (iv) A saving of more than $3.1 million for the Karachi Water and Sewerage Board in Pakistan (Transparency International, 2002)
> (v) Reduction of electricity prices at less than US$0.03 per kilowatt-hour in Bangladesh, roughly half the price of directly negotiated deals in Indonesia (Lovei and McKechnie, 2000).

THEORETICAL LITERATURE ON TRANSPARENCY

The theoretical literature (Cartier-Bresson 2000; Kaufman 1997; Klitgaard 1990; Mauro 1997; Rege 2001; Rose-ackerman 1999; Tanzi 1998; Tanzi and Davoodi 1997; Wei 1997, 1999) on government procurement gives one the impression that transparency will definitely promote competition, efficiency, and reduce corruption. However, transparency is costly in terms of monitoring, establishment of new institutions and procurement regimes, training of personnel. What are the possible costs of introducing transparency in government procurement?[1] First, there are the costs of switching over from the existing procurement regime. This depends on the divergence of the existing procurement policies from those required by the GPA and the number of entities involved. For India, these costs could potentially be high in view of its federal structure, the number of sub-central entities and the large number of central and state public sector enterprises. Debroy and Pursell (1997) state that although there would be no problem for India to have joined the Tokyo Round GPA, this is not true for the current GPA (signed in Marrakesh on 15 April 1994) because of its extension to sub-central and other public entities and to the purchase of services. An attempt needs to be made to estimate the changes involved and to examine what exclusions, if any, might be justified on these grounds.

There are some theoretically justifiable arguments for preferential treatment. Developments in international trade theory during the 1980s have showed (Helpman and Krugman 1986), that in the presence of imperfect competition and increasing returns to scale, interventions in trade could be used to shift profits to domestic firms or to generate positive externalities. Some of these arguments can be extended to the case of government procurement. In addition to these, there are some other possible justifications for preferential government procurement. These include the possibility of increasing competition through price preferences (McAfee and McMillan 1989), reducing price-cost margins by expanding domestic output (Chen 1995), problems of contract enforcement (Laffont and Tirole 1991), and economies in the presence of asymmetric information. Although such strategic interventions are difficult to accurately target, and the potential benefits are likely to be small, they are popular with governments and businessmen. Another argument against the GPA suggests that discrimination does not significantly restrict trade and the gains from non-discrimination are consequently small. Mattoo (1996) has pointed out that the benefits may not be insignificant if government demand is large, domestic and foreign goods and services are not perfect substitutes and if there is imperfect competition. The crucial question is whether markets have become more competitive and trade freer, because in that case, it would become easier to conform to the discipline of the GPA. With the public sector being subject to harder budget constraints, procurement by these entities would automatically become more efficient. On the other hand, with trade restricted through tariffs and non-tariff barriers the GPA may not achieve much. Thus, it seems that the effectiveness of GPA depends a great deal on the international trading environment.

From a macroeconomic point of view greater transparency in government procurement has two sides. On one side government saves money and therefore its net spending (budget deficit) goes down. But it is also true that transparency is costly and government ends up spending on system change, training of personnel and so on. It is not very clear what finally happens to net government spending. On the other side, transparency improves the quality of social capital (better roads, bridges and dams) which improves the productivity of the private sector. If transparency reduces corruption, the private sector saves cost. We assume that this raises the marginal productivity of labour in an economy that is not fully employed and cost saving shifts the aggregate supply curve to the right. In the graph, AD and AS are the aggregate demand and supply curves with the price level and real income represented by P and y in the macro economy. Even if a greater element of transparency in government procurement causes a net reduction in government spending (aggregate demand shifting to AD*), real income may rise with a lower price level (y* and P*) if there is a sufficient improvement in labour productivity as well as cost saving shifting the aggregate supply to AS*. Whether this happens or not is an empirical question.

FIGURE 11.1 Transparency in government procurement

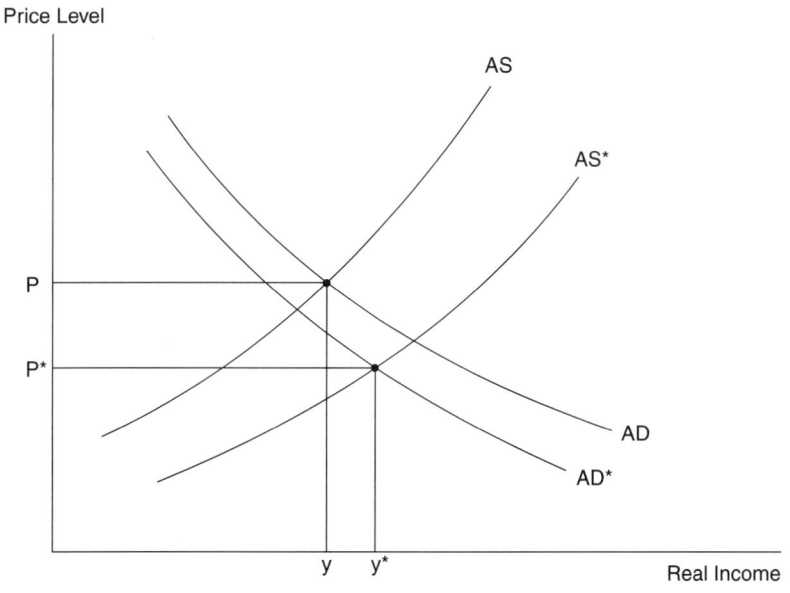

PLAN OF THE STUDY

The paper does an elaborate study on government procurement policy in India and its implementation and explores the role of transparency in reducing corruption in government procurement. Corruption can be proved indirectly if it is shown that transparency leads to an increase in efficiency and cost saving and this is what is done in many OECD studies. Since Indian economy is a federal one, with multiple tiers of government procurement, we will find out whether there is a need for harmonisation of procurement rules and procedures. We will also review the functioning of the regulatory bodies and grievance redressal mechanism. Our objective is to find out the extent to which the government procurement rules and practices are transparent and to suggest measures to improve transparency. Finally, we have interviewed officials (from BSNL (Bharat Sanchar Nigam Limited), DOT (Department of Telecommunications) and Indian Oil) who are either currently or previously connected with government procurement and recorded their views on several aspects of government procurement and graded their answers on a seven-point scale. To get a state-level perspective, we have interviewed some top officials engaged in government procurement in West Bengal. The paper provides a summary of their responses.

GOVERNMENT PROCUREMENT IN INDIA

At the time of independence, procurement was confined to purchase of office equipment and construction of office buildings and roads. Government activity has grown tremendously in the post-independence period, with the setting up of a vast number of public sector undertakings in almost every sector of the economy, in pursuance of the social democracy, planned development and command economy. Public procurement grew exponentially and now covers every type of goods and services and is carried out by a large number of agencies all over the country. Since the nineties the government has embarked upon an economic liberalisation path including gradual dis-investment in the public undertakings. However, the implementation is slow and government procurement continues to remain large in volume and all pervasive. Ministries, departments, municipal and other local bodies, statutory corporations, and public undertakings both in the Center and in the States, carry out procurement of goods and services. The public procurement policies, procedures, and practices of the Center, States and the Public Enterprises have a tremendous impact on the economy and the business community, particularly in the construction sector, which depends largely on public works contracts. The public perception of integrity and efficiency of the government is to a large extent swayed by the transparency and integrity of public procurement. Srivastava (1999) has estimated the size of government procurement in India during 1998–99 and 1999–2000 and the relative size of government procurement works out to be nearly six per cent of GDP. The study also shows the importance of public sector enterprises (PSEs) in government procurement. We have identified the industries that are dominated by PSEs and these can be listed in order of market shares (that is, share of PSEs in total sales of all public sector and private sector firms in the industry in 2000–1). These are Crude oil and natural gas (99.17 per cent), Coal and lignite (98.2 per cent), Financial services (80.3 per cent), Transport service (76.7 per cent), Electricity generation and distribution (73.31 per cent), Communication (62.6 per cent) and Chemicals (64.79 per cent).[2]

The study by Srivastava (1999) also shows significant increases in the share of government expenditure estimates in GDP during 1989–2000. The question that should be asked is whether the government is acquiring more goods and services per rupee spent or not. We have done some rough estimates by looking at total expenditure of the central government, which includes consumption expenditure, gross capital formation, transfer payment to the rest of the economy (current plus capital expenditure), and financial investments and loans to the rest of the economy. Then we have taken the data on gross capital formation from budgetary resources of the central government which includes fixed assets, works stores, increases in the stocks of food grains and fertilizers, and gross financial assistance for capital formation to state governments, public undertakings operated by autonomous corporations and companies, and loans and grants to local authorities for capital formation. The ratio between the two will roughly tell us the value of every rupee spent by the central government and Table 11.1 shows a steady downward trend in this ratio. It should be noted that the decline could not be due to the inflation factor. We could deflate both expenditure and capital formations by separate price indexes if these were available. Deflating both by wholesale price index, which is available, would not alter the ratio. A large part of this decrease in the value of money spent by the central government is caused by the increase in the wages and salaries. But a decrease from 42 per cent in 1981–82 to 19 per cent in 2002–3 does not give much credit to the procurement policy.

TABLE 11.1 Value of government expenditure

Year	Government Expenditure (Rs Crore)	Capital Formation (Rs Crore)	Value for Money (percentage) (Capital formation per rupee spent)
1981–82	25401.2	10799.1	42.51
1982–83	30493.7	12404	40.68
1983–84	35987.7	14701	40.85
1984–85	43878.9	17551.2	40.00
1985–86	53112.4	21477.2	40.44
1986–87	64023.1	24319.7	37.99
1987–88	70304.6	25770.1	36.65
1988–89	81402.3	28977.4	35.60
1989–90	95049.4	33012.7	34.73
1990–91	104972.9	35057.4	33.40
1991–92	112730.7	35164.6	31.19
1992–93	125926.9	37648.6	29.90
1993–94	145788	45050.5	30.90
1994–95	166998.4	54199.9	32.46
1995–96	185232.8	55275.6	29.84
1996–97	211259.6	60950.3	28.85
1997–98	224866	54185	24.10
1998–99	263755	57806.5	21.92
1999–2000	307509.1	67601.5	21.98
2000–1	328264.7	66959.4	20.40
2001–2	361334.7	69238.8	19.16
2002–3	409584.7	77930.5	19.03

Data Source: Economic Survey, 2002–3.

PROCUREMENT POLICIES

India has not passed any law to regulate government procurement but Article 298 of the Constitution authorises the Central and the State governments to contract for goods and services and also requires the executive to protect the fundamental rights of all citizens to be treated equally (while soliciting tenders), but beyond that the constitution does not provide any guidance on public procurement principles, policies, or procedures. There is no Central or State legislation on public procurement, except for two States, Tamil Nadu[3] and Karnataka,[4] which have recently enacted legislation on 'Transparency in Public Procurement'. The Finance Ministry as well as other ministries, such as the Ministry of Industries, issues documents describing policies, procedures, guidelines, and delegation of authority relating to procurement. Therefore, one can say that there is no legal validity of the public procurement procedures that are essentially a set of executive directives. The same laws that govern private contracts govern government contracts. There is no central agency either in the Center or in the states exclusively responsible for public procurement. The Comptroller and Auditor General of India (CAG) carries out ex-post audit of government expenditures and checks whether the expenditure is within the budgetary allocation and whether the laid down procedures are followed or not. The CAG's annual and special reports are published and are discussed in the Parliament and State legislatures. All this shows that India does not have a procurement policy in the form of an act of the parliament. Public procurement is a matter for executive branch of the government. Only two states have recently started to implement transparency acts passed by the respective legislatures.

PROCUREMENT RULES IN INDIA

Ministries such as Finance, Industry, Public Works, Environment, and Agriculture, State Enterprises, issue directives on government procurement with the objectives of encouraging small scale industries, enforcing environmental standards, and setting preferences for state owned enterprises and so on. Initially the Ministry of Supply in the Center and Central Stores Purchase Organisation in the States and the Public Works Department (PWD) in the Center and the States had served as the lead agencies to formulate detailed procedures for the purchase of goods and works respectively. Other departments, agencies and state undertakings followed these procedures. However as the government expanded its activities and a large number of state enterprises were created, each ministry, agency and particularly state enterprise introduced innovations and improvements in procurement rules and procedures. As a result of this, there is no single uniform law that governs procurements by all of these entities.

The scope of government procurement covers purchases of goods and services made by government entities using funds allocated to them from either budgetary resources or international donor agencies as aid (Rege 2001). The central government, the state governments and the three tiers of local government—village, intermediate and district make up the various levels of government in India. In addition, there are centrally and state owned enterprises. The procurement practices of different entities have evolved owing to General Financial Rules (GFRs) of the Ministry of Finance. The Directorate General of Supplies and Disposal (DGS&D) under the Department of Supply is the central purchasing organisation in India. Even though the importance of DGS&D has declined in recent years, it is still used to finalise the rate contracts for common use products. According to a scheme of decentralisation (Ministry of Finance 2003), procurement against ad-hoc indents has been transferred from DGS&D to the indenting Ministries/Departments. The declining importance of DGS&D is however evident from the fact that the purchases made by the directorate have fallen from Rs.24. billion in 1995/96 to Rs. 16.6 billion in 1998/99 (Ministry of Finance 2003). The procedures followed by the state governments are based on the states' financial rules. Multiple rules applied at different levels of the federal government can be regarded as a source of inconvenience for suppliers but it is not necessarily a source of corruption. The current GPA provides for uniform rules of procurement which would require a costly change of procurement regime in India—a point which has been made by Srivastava (1999). We think that the federal economy of India is like a common market and uniform procurement rules will lead to trade creation. There is a strong case for harmonisation of procurement methods and procedures in the federal economy of India.

PROCUREMENT METHODS

The rules provide for purchases based on three types of tendering: advertisements (open tender), direct invitation to a limited number of firms (limited tender), invitation to one firm only (single tender), and negotiation with one or more firms.[5] Indian Trade Journal, a monthly bulletin issued by the DGS&D, publishes tender notices, which are also available on the Internet. For global tenders, notices are also published or disseminated through Indian embassies. In the case of the railways, all tenders above a value of Rs.0.3 million are invited by open advertisements in the national newspapers.

The specifications for procurement are drafted on the basis of national or international standard specifications.[6] The DGS&D registers firms interested in government purchases as approved contractors for supply of stores of various descriptions. Similarly, the National Small Industries Corporation registers such firms in the small-scale sector and Indian Railways also has an analogous registration procedure.

PREFERENCES

In India, all bidders are treated at par and no preference is given to domestic suppliers.[7] According to the Indian government, 'domestic bidders are treated on par with foreign bidders and the ultimate price available to the user department is the determining criterion'.[8] However, with a view to encouraging the small-scale sector, village industries, certain kinds of women's organisations and public enterprises, some preferential treatment is allowed. Generally such preferential treatment discriminates against domestic as well as foreign firms not belonging to these categories and in this sense, foreign firms get 'national treatment'. (Debroy and Pursell 1997) have provided a comprehensive review of this policy. In what follows we briefly discuss the preference system prevailing in India.

Preference for Public Sector

The policies initiated in 1956[9] have led to growth of a large public sector in India. Prior to the reforms initiated in 1991, PSEs were not only protected from competition through reservation, but they also enjoyed both price and purchase preferences from both central government departments and public sector enterprises. The preference for the public sector also applied to construction and service enterprises and was extended to state-level PSEs.

The list of industries reserved for the public sector has now been reduced significantly in the post-1991 years. There were 17 industries reserved in the public sector prior to July 1991. The New Industrial Policy reduced it to eight industries. More industries, namely mining of iron ore, manganese ore, chrome ore, gypsum, sulphur, gold, and diamond and mining of copper, lead, zinc, tin, molybdenum, and wolfram were dereserved since 26 March 1993 and Coal and Lignite and Mineral oils were dereserved from June 1998. Now the reserved list contains only three sectors: Atomic Energy, Minerals specified in Schedule to Atomic energy, and Railway Transport.[10] The system of price preferences has been discontinued. Purchase preference was extended, with some modifications, to orders placed until 31 March 2000. Under this provision, a government enterprise whose bid is within 10 per cent of that of a large private unit is allowed to revise its price downward and is eligible for a parallel-rate contract. Given the emphasis on privatisation and reform of the public sector, such purchase preferences are now an anachronism. Again, this is an issue that is related to preferences and not to corruption.

Preference for the Small-scale Sector

The small-scale sector in India is protected through compulsory purchase and price preference on procurement imposed on central government ministries, departments, and PSEs. The purchase-preference system requires that specified products be procured exclusively from small-scale firms. In addition, a system of price preference exists: if the price offered by the small-scale unit is not more than 15 per cent above the price offered by a large unit, the product has to be purchased from small-scale sector. This condition applies not only to central ministries and departments, but also to central public undertakings. If the competition is with the duty-inclusive price of imports, the implied preferential margin is higher with respect to the duty-free price of imports. As in the case of the public sector, the small-scale sector is exempted from the payment of earnest money and tender fees. So far, the protection of artisans and small-scale firms, and the subsidies and preferences directed to them, have not been touched by the reforms. Between 1994–95 and 1998–99, purchases by DGS&D from the small sector were about 8–10 per cent of the directorate's total purchases.[11]

Preferences for Indigenous Production

Before 1991 there were complicated clearance procedures and controls over the terms of technical agreements between local and foreign firms. Foreign equity participation was restricted to 40 per cent. Government procurement was used directly to favour indigenous production over imports. Both a price and purchase preference in favour of domestic production used to exist. The system of Price Preference was abolished in 1992. Purchase Preference was also scrapped. In some cases, however, the preference for Indian providers of services, if not of goods, continues to apply.

DISPUTE SETTLEMENT MECHANISM

Government of India has constituted Central Vigilance Commission (CVC) in 1999 through an ordinance and it has been strengthened through an act of parliament entitled the Central Vigilance Commission Act 2003. The function of CVC is to investigate offences alleged to have been committed under the Prevention of Corruption Act, 1988 or to act on a reference made by the central government. CVC is a new institution and its role in curbing corrupt practices remains to be seen. The role of CAG is limited to carrying out *ex-post* audit of government expenditures including government and public sector procurements essentially for checking the budget authority for expenditures and adherence to laid down procedures. The Santhanam Committee set up by the central government in 1966 had recommended setting up of an ombudsman in the centre and in every state to investigate charges of corruption against officials and politicians. Some states have set up the mechanism. Others, including the centre, have not done so.

In India, the challenge procedure is rather weak. Assessing Indian financial accountability, analysts from the World Bank (Sahgal and Chakrapani 2002) have stated that incidence of fraud, waste, and abuse of public funds is reportedly widespread. In a World Bank/CII survey of 210 private sector firms carried out in 1999 responded that a bribe of 2 to 25 per cent of the price is necessary to secure government contracts (World Bank 2003).

DISCRIMINATION

India is known for a two-envelope system under which bidders submit all administrative, qualification, and technical response in one envelope and the price in the second envelope. The first envelope is publicly opened first and reviewed, and all bids, which are not in full compliance with tender requirement, are rejected. In the second sitting, the price envelope of the rest are opened publicly, evaluated and decided. There is logic behind this practice as it saves time spent on non-conforming bids. However the procedure suffers from serious disadvantages. In the first place, the delay in opening price envelopes, which can be a week to months in many cases, gives the purchaser the opportunity to switch envelopes. Secondly, the tender conditions and technical specifications may be deliberatively or otherwise skewed in favour of some bidders. In the first round, bids, which do not strictly comply, are rejected and their price envelopes are returned and never opened. The approving authority and auditors are prevented from knowing the additional price paid for a trivial and avoidable technical requirement. The procedure obviously has great scope for discrimination against efficient but not-so-influential suppliers.

PUBLIC WORKS CONTRACTING

The PWD manual is the Bible for works contracting procedures for all government departments, agencies, corporations, and enterprises. The manual outlines procedures that were relevant when contractors were mostly illiterate and essentially labour contractors. Some of the problems in works contracting are elaborated by the World Bank study and are briefly discussed below (The World Bank 2003).

Each PWD maintains a data book, some times district-wise, which provides the rate for each standard item of work. The rates are based on material, labour, and overheads. Departmental estimates for works and the Schedule of Rates for tendering are based on these rates in the data book. However, the data books are generally out of date. The situation varies. The central PWD is reasonably up to date. In most States, the data books have not been updated for years. Also, whenever taken up, often the rates are merely updated for inflation, but not reworked using the new materials, methods of construction, plant depreciation, overheads, and reasonable profit. The result is that the departmental estimates are generally unreliable and out of date. Works are taken up without adequate funding, often under political pressure, which languish for years. Contracts are awarded when land acquisition is far from initiation. Some PWDs even put the responsibility for land acquisition and clearance of the site on the contractor. Advertised tenders are opened only to approved registered contractors, whose qualifications and capacity have been verified. But the registration process has become a vehicle for political patronage and once a contractor is registered, he is automatically deemed qualified. Even for good qualified contractors, the works on hand and consequent available capacity to take on new works is not examined. Bad performers are not systematically eliminated from the list. Powers of approval of awards are linked to the departmental estimates, based on data books, which as mentioned earlier, are outdated. This provides one excuse for negotiation to 'bring prices closer to the departmental estimate'. Even when prices are below the departmental estimate, negotiation is often resorted 'to get further savings to public funds'. Major contractors sub-contract the entire works or a major portion to unqualified sub-contractors with the silent support of the department. The payments are based on entries in 'measurement books' in the handwriting of the supervising departmental engineer, and test checked by his superiors at the site (mostly in theory). Monthly bills are actually prepared by the departmental engineers but signed by the contractors. Every month, each item in the bill of quantities is reentered in the measurement book with full description, and then, the measured quantity. Even if an outside consultant is employed for works supervision, the measurement book is still entered by the department, as stipulated in the 'public works manual'. The whole system is antiquated, repetitive, and based on technology and office systems available fifty years ago, with practically no modernisation.

Contracts do not provide for adequate price adjustment mechanism and fair claim and dispute resolution mechanisms. Contract supervision is spotty and subject to pervasive corruption. In fact, there are frequent press reports of wide spread corruption in many PWDs. It appears from this World Bank study that a part of corruption in public works contracting is due to the fact that the existing rates are outdated and too low for work to be done in today's world.

TENDER DOCUMENTS

There are more than 150 different contract formats used by the government and its agencies (World Bank 2003). Obviously, this causes confusion in the minds of bidders. Also, some are of poor quality. Each ministry/department has a tendency to change the existing document in various ways, destroying the purpose of standardisation and introduce ambiguities and contradictions in the document. The situation in the States is much worse. For the same work, say, for construction of a road, the tender document is different if it is issued by the PWD or the Municipal Corporation or the Metropolitan Urban Development Authority or the State Road Development Corporation. The qualification requirements, selection criteria, the payment terms, the dispute settlement mechanism are all different for no conceivable reason. It is essential to develop and publish a set of Standard Tender Documents and Contract Conditions for mandatory use by all ministries, agencies and enterprises for similar procurements.

NEGOTIATION PROCEDURE

Post-bid negotiation with the lowest bidder and even with other bidders is a standard procedure in India in order to reduce the quoted price further, without any change in the condition of the bid, technical or commercial. Many ministries and agencies issue instructions for post-bid negotiations (DFID 2002). The officials and the auditors believe that negotiation results in savings to the public exchequer. What is not realised, is that all bidders include a cushion in their bid price, which they partly give up when called for negotiation. Negotiation provides the best opportunity for corruption at the cost of the public exchequer. Moreover, the bidders get a chance to make supernormal profit even in a system of competitive bidding. On the other hand, the bidders will quote competitive price if they are sure that no negotiation will take place after the bids are in. World Bank procurement rule prohibits negotiation to merely push down the competitively quoted price. In India, some agencies conduct negotiations with all the bidders requiring them to 'match' the price of the lowest or quote a revised lower price, and then, the quantity in the schedule is divided up, making a mockery of the tender process in which the firm which offered the lowest responsive bid should be entitled to the fill order. According to the World Bank study, once the practice of negotiation (to merely push down the price) is stopped, it will close a major avenue for corruption and result in better prices and real savings to the public exchequer. Negotiation should be permissible only in exceptional cases and only by a committee, and based on mutual concessions.

DELAY IN TENDER PROCESSING AND AWARD

The delay occurs mostly at the time of evaluation and selection. The average time taken in implementation of projects in India is much longer compared to countries like China, Mexico, Indonesia and Brazil mainly due to delays in procurement (World Bank 2003). In procurement, the length of the delay is positively related to the value of purchase. The delay in tender decision invites political pressures and corrupt practices and often results in re-tender which is extremely unfair for the lowest bidder, but an opportunity for the other bidders to manipulate the procurement process. Good bidders are discouraged from participation in re-tender and those who bid increase the prices to reflect added risks and costs in waiting for a decision. Government officials and auditors do not have an adequate appreciation of the cost of delays.

INDIA'S PROCUREMENT POLICY AND THE GPA

There are two models of government procurement. One is UNCITRAL model law published in 1980, which acted as a model for East European and ex-Soviet Union countries. The other is the government procurement agreement of the World Trade Organisation. In defining transparency Evenett and Hoekman (2003) point out—

> A procurement process is said to be transparent if (i) the terms upon which the procurement process will be conducted and the criteria upon which any decisions are to be made are codified to the greatest extent possible and made widely available, (ii) the eventual procurement award decision (and, where possible, any intermediate decisions...) is made publicly available as are the reasons given for these decisions, and

(iii) it is possible to verify expeditiously that the codified procedures and criteria in (i) were indeed applied and that the claims made in (ii) are in fact true.

Effectively, transparency ensures that information be made available to suppliers and in essence, the right to access information in matters of procurement is guaranteed on policies, rules and methods, practices and opportunities.

Procurement system in India significantly differs from provisions of the GPA in respect of the national treatment, transparency, and challenge. Price and purchase preferences allowed in India for government procurement are not in agreement with the requirements of Article III. Article V provides some flexibility to developing countries and exclusions are possible, but the long-term objective of the GPA is to do away with any kind of preferential treatment in purchases. In any case, exclusions are a matter of negotiation. Article XVIII requires that information on winning contracts be made public. It also requires that on information concerning the reasons for rejection and the characteristics and relative advantages of the selected tender be made available on request. India does not have any such provision. India does not have a good reputation so far as transparency in concerned. The GPA's detailed challenge procedure (ArticleXX) has no parallel in the existing rules and procedure in India. An aggrieved party obviously always has access to regular court of law. It is common knowledge that Indian courts are overloaded with litigation and justice is slow. In our view, the absence of a proper challenge procedure is a potential source of corruption. It should however be mentioned, that the state of things in the OECD countries in this regards is only better in some degree. Court proceedings subsequent to procurement appeals have taken as long as one and a half to five years in OECD countries and interim suspension measures are not always granted. The only exception is Canada where appeals are dealt by a quasi-judicial independent review body, the Canadian International Trade Tribunal that is in charge of federal procurement matters (OECD 2003).

INDIAN POSITION ON GOVERNMENT PROCUREMENT IN WTO MINISTERIAL MEETINGS

India did not sign the Tokyo Round GPA and is not a signatory to the current GPA. India, however, has dropped its opposition to a multilateral agreement on transparency in government procurement. Government procurement is one of the four new issues that have arisen from the initiatives of the Singapore Ministerial Conference of December 1996 and is likely to be part of the Millennium Round negotiations. The working Group on Transparency in Government Procurement had been set up by the Singapore Ministerial Conference to study the existing practices and develop elements for inclusion in a suitable agreement. It must, however, be mentioned that in the latest round of talks in Geneva government procurement has been placed on a backburner till 2005.

India refuses to accept the national treatment requirement in any government procurement agreement, on the ground that this requirement will come in the way of promoting the interest of desirable sectors, less privileged social groups and underdeveloped regions of the country. Therefore, the Indian government is only willing to go along with a transparency agreement that does not include market-access issues.

As regards the definition and scope of government procurement and the issue of procurement methods, India is against a broad definition that includes government entities at the sub central level and other public entities and argues that an agreement should be restricted to the central government procurement only, leaving service sector and lease agreements outside the scope of the agreement. Further, there should be no restriction on the choice of procurement method, other than those placed by domestic legislation. India has also argued that review and appeal procedures should not be a part of any transparency agreement and the WTO's dispute settlement mechanism should not deal with disputes related to government procurement. Finally, India wants recognition of the special needs of developing countries in a transparency agreement and insists on a special clause in this regard.[12]

A SUMMARY OF SURVEY RESULTS

In a survey conducted by us we selected some top officials in Indian Oil Corporation (IOC), DOT and BSNL who are either currently or previously associated with government procurement. The officials were interviewed and the discussion with them was centered on the following questions:

(1) What is the extent to which the government achieves its purpose, that is, to provide goods and services not provided by the market?
(2) Government procurement of technically advanced products is based solely based on price criterion. Does this mean that the government does not encourage innovation?
(3) Do government officials favour well-connected firms?
(4) Corporate giants and foreign multinationals influence the decision-making related to the government purchases as they have a big role in government formation. How true is that?
(5) Does the new government honour the prior contractual commitments and obligations of the old government?
(6) How commonly are irregular extra payments or 'bribes' involved in a government purchase deal?

The views of the officials were by and large uniform, even though they were interviewed separately. The summary of their response is as follows:

1. Government procurement may not cater to the real need of the public and may be driven by politics.
2. Price becomes the sole determinant of choice, as there is too much vigilance and lack of trust and the officials are unwilling to take risk.
3. Respondents unanimously reject prevalence of favouritism.
4. The respondents perceive the role of corporate giants and multinationals in influencing government purchase.
5. The respondents seem to think that a change of regime causes chaos and past commitments are not always honoured by the new regime.
6. On the basic question of corruption in government procurement, none is willing to grant its existence in any significant degree.

The state of affairs in government procurement in a state is somewhat different for various reasons. In order to get a state-level perspective, we have interviewed some top officials of PWD in West Bengal. Here the officials openly admit corruption, inefficiency, and lack of transparency. The interview was based on the following questions: (1) Do you think the procurement rules followed by the PWD are outdated and unrevised? (2) Do you think PWD does not take into account the efficiency of the contractors, hence overlooks their past performance? (3) It is alleged that PWD does not take inflation into account while fixing their contract rates. Comment

The basic concern of our interaction with the PWD employees of West Bengal was to find first-hand details about the complexities and problems of their procurement procedures. The fact that policies are completely outmoded and prehistoric is not the only problem; lack of efficiency on the part of the state government is complemented by the lack of funds that are sanctioned by the centre. It is thus surprising not to find a single computer in the office of the high profile Executive Engineer of PW (Road) Department. The amount spent on National Highways, by the center is approximately Rs. two-three crores per kilometer of road constructed, whereas for the same work the state can afford only Rs. 30–40 lacs. In order to get a state government project passed from the center, a huge amount of under-the-table payment is required. Since the state cannot do it, it fixes a contractor in advance and merely plays a role of a middleman! What suffers in the end is quality.

The officials did agree that the procurement rules were outmoded. However, a PWD Schedule is published every year by Presidency Circle I, which includes all the procurement methods, rules and quoted prices. The state makes the best endeavor to keep in line with the existing procurement scenario. But that is not enough as the contractors react depending on how the market behaves. So it is imperative, that the schedule itself is regularly updated, and this is what is not done. The second problem of efficiency has to be looked at in a slightly different manner. PWD does take into account the past performances of the contractors and solely awards the tenders to the lowest bidder. To discern the efficiency level of each contractor, they are registered first. Then the contractors are divided into groups of (say) A, B, C, and D according to their credentials. The contractor who has the maximum credential will be pooled in group A and so on. Now the problem arises from a different angle. PWD designated qualified engineers never verify if the contractors appoint technically sound and capable engineers. Most of the time if a contract is won by a group A contractor, it is not even supervised by a PWD engineer. The third problem of not updating its rates with the level of inflation exists. But this is 'corrected' by a commonly used practice by the contractors in the form of pact contracting. Under this system, the contractors form a group amongst themselves and pre-decide who is going to win the tender. So accordingly, all the bidders bid a certain percentage above the rate fixed by the PWD. Now, since PWD has to award the contract to the lowest bidder, it has but no choice but to award it to that contractor who is bidding the lowest amongst all, although his bid is way above the rate fixed by the government. The contractors definitely want to keep up with the market rates and also make a supernormal profit. So the problem of PWD not updating its rates according to the market, results in this kind of pact contracting. The scope for corruption is obvious in this system. According to the PWD officials, transparency is something that is completely utopist and unachievable.

CONCLUSIONS AND RECOMMENDATIONS

Preference being offered to certain sectors of the economy in government procurement is an issue that can be debated. But there does not seem to be a scope for debate on transparency in government procurement. There is an immediate need for legislation on government procurement providing for uniform rules and procedures for government procurement to be followed by every organ of the government. Such a public procurement law should, as a minimum, cover the objectives, substantive procedural requirements to achieve them, debriefing of unsuccessful bidders, publication of contract awards, and an appeal/challenge mechanism. The law may also cover post award issues in contract implementation, such as securities, timely payment, penalties and damages, dispute resolution, and termination of contract for default or convenience.

Absence of a nodal agency regulating government procurement has resulted in the absence of leadership in the government to deal with public procurement issues with the international financial institutions, bilateral donors, and other international bodies. A Government Procurement Commission along the lines of the recently established Competition Commission may serve as a nodal agency.

Government of India has not shown concern regarding the transparency aspect in any future agreement on government procurement. This shows that the government wants procurement to be corruption-free and the reason for its opposition to GPA lies somewhere else. The government is definitely opposed to market access in order to safeguard the interest of selected economic groups and it is also opposed to uniform rules of procurement for the federal economy. Most developing countries want to offer price and purchase preferences to selected groups that are economically and socially backward. This problem may have a solution in raising the threshold of purchases above which the agreed procurement discipline is applicable. The countries can negotiate higher threshold levels of government purchase in WTO.

The study has clearly established the need of rationalisation and harmonisation of procurement rules. But we could not correlate transparency with lessened corruption. There are studies on government procurement in India claiming prevalence of corruption. But in our opinion poll of officials dealing with government procurement, we get the picture of sporadic rather than pervasive corruption mainly due to the rigidity of the system and fear of vigilance. It should however be mentioned, that a similar survey at the state, local or municipal level may bring out a completely different picture. The broad conclusions of this study are:

1. There is no significant difference between the Indian case and current GPA. Apparently, an agreement on transparency will not make much difference, which is the Indian official position. However, given India's record, greater transparency in government procurement may reduce corruption. A world economic forum survey ranks India 45th out of 49 countries on honesty of its officials and 44th in the effectiveness of laws protecting the shareholders. (*Investor's Business Daily* 1998)
2. An agreement on government procurement is likely to be cost-saving for India and a part of this cost-saving can be taken as saving due to transfer of rent from the corrupt officials to the parties in a transaction who, as a result, do not exaggerate the rates. The macroeconomic impact of improved transparency in government spending is likely to be positive, strengthening the fundamentals in the economy.
3. Divergent procurement rules in the federal economy of India are likely to be a source of inefficiency but not perhaps a source of corruption. Indian's federal economy comprising multiple layers of state-level decision-making is like a

common market. A uniform set of procurement rules followed at all levels would result in efficient purchase as well as trade creation. This requires a drastic change of procurement regime, which is costly but justifiable in the long run.
4. The argument against GPA is a protectionist argument, which loses much of its force in an era of globalisation. India is going through a process of dereservation in public sector and small-scale sector. Disinvestment in public enterprises is the rule of the day and is likely to continue even under the new regime. Since India does not have objection against transparency per se, it can be guessed that India's opposition to GPA is *strategic* in the multilateral negotiations under WTO.
5. Publication of contract awards in news media and the web is a very useful step to improve transparency. The public and the bidders have a right to know the outcome of a public tender. The publication will also reveal the time taken by the purchaser in finalising the award, which will encourage quick decisions. The Tamil Nadu and Karnataka Acts provide for this. The publication can be in the official gazette, bulletin and web site, and for large contracts, in the press as well.
6. Transparency alone may not be able curb corruption or political favouritism. The procuring unit may design the procurement process in favour of a particular firm, interpret the prerequisites with corrupt intensions during the process and manipulate the evaluation process for achieving the desired outcome. A properly designed challenge procedure that delivers justice without delay can go a long way in controlling corruption. The study has identified the inadequate challenge procedure in India as a possible source of corruption in government procurement. But it is doubtful whether a GPA can solve this problem, as the experience of OECD countries in this regard is not very encouraging.
7. Standardisation of tender document is urgently needed. In 1998, the Government of India, Ministry of Finance, in consultation with the World Bank, developed a set of standard documents for National Competitive Bidding (NCB) in Bank projects, and circulated them to the central ministries and the States, advocating their use in non-Bank funded procurement as well. These documents can be the starting point, and can be updated in the light of experience gained in their use.
8. The multi-layered review and approval process, particularly for large value contracts, should be simplified to expedite the process and minimise opportunities for malpractice and corruption. The tender committee alone shall evaluate and compare the bids, and its recommendation should go directly to the approving authority with no intermediate reviewers. The approving authority may seek clarifications from the tender committee or reject the recommendation, giving its reasons for the tender committee to re-examine, but shall not itself re-evaluate the bids. If a decision is not reached within one extension of bid validity, the tender should be cancelled.
9. In line with a study by Transparency International (2002) we recommend frequent public opinion polls on corruption issues to control corrupt practices. The media and the non-governmental organisations can play a constructive role and perform this task.
10. Registration of contractors shall apply only to contracts up to Rs. 10 million. Larger contracts shall be open to all contractors, irrespective of their registration

status, who meet specific qualification criteria in order to be considered. Also registration of contractors should be centralised in one agency.

Endnotes

[1] For a cost benefit study in the Indian context see Srivastava (1999). In this study there are two potential sources of benefit for the signatories to the GPA. One source of gain is through better market access and gains from trade and the second is through the cost saving and quality gains, likely to result from the disciplines imposed by the GPA. The benefit estimates are based on the assumption that gains from market access are likely to be small and that the only significant source of gain is from the potential saving of government resources. The benefits are estimated to be in the range of Rs. 67.5 billion—Rs. 90 billion. The economic costs of switching are predicted to be small. The paper concludes that India should have no hesitation in negotiating a transparency agreement.

[2] Shares are estimated by the author from CMIE's Prowess database.

[3] Tamil Nadu Transparency in Tenders Act, 1998, implemented from 2000.

[4] The Karnataka Transparency in Public Procurement Act, 1999.

[5] The general rules apply to all departments regarding stores required for use in 'the public service'. Special rules apply to Defense, Railways, Post and Telegraphs, Public Works, Central Purchase

[6] The Bureau of Indian standards formulates Indian Standard specifications.

[7] This is not true for all state governments.

[8] See the Government of India's response to Question 9 of the WTO Questionnaire on Government Procurement Services (document S/WPGR/W/11/add.Jan17, 1997).

[9] In March 1998 there were 240 Central PSEs (see Department of Public Enterprises 1998) and almost 1000 State PSEs, including electricity boards, although most the SEBs have been unbundled by now.

[10] Source: Websites of Ministry of Company Affairs and Ministry of Disinvestments (http://www.divest.nic.in).

[11] The year 1997/98 with a 13.3 per cent share is an exception.

[12] Similar to Article V of the current GPA.

References

Bardhan, P. K. 1997. 'Corruption and Development', *Journal of Economic Literature*, vol. 35, no. 3, pp. 1320–46.

Cartier-Bresson, J. 2000. 'Economics of Corruption', *OECD Observer*, vol. a, no. 220, p. 25.

Chen, Xianquin. 1995. 'Directing Government Procurement as an Incentive of Production', *Journal of Economic Integration*, vol. 10, pp. 130–40.

Cohen, J. C. 2000. *The LAC Pharmaceutical Region*, Washington DC: The World Bank.

Debroy, Bibek and Gary Pursell. 1997. 'Government Procurement Policies in India', in *Law and Policy in Public Purchasing: The WTO Agreement on Government Procurement*, edited by Bernard Hoekman and Petros Mavroidis, Michigan: University of Michigan Press.

Department for International Development (DFID). 2002. *Government of Andhra Pradesh— Public Procurement Review*, London: DFID.

Evenett, S. J. and B. M. Hoekman. 2003. 'Transparency in Procurement Regimes: What Can We Expect from International Trade Agreements', in *Public Procurement: The Continuing Revolution*, edited by Sue Arrowsmith and Martin Trybus, London: Kluwer Law International.

Ministry of Finance. 2003. *Report of the Task Force on Revision of Norms for Procurement of Goods and Services by Government'*. New Delhi: Government of India.
Helpman, Elhanan and Paul Krugman. 1986. *Market Structure and Foreign Trade*, Cambridge and Mass.: MIT Press.
Investor's Business Daily. 1998. 'India's Road Ahead', 7 April.
Kaufman, D. 1997. 'Corruption: Some Myths and Facts', *Foreign Policy*, Summer, pp. 114–31.
Klitgaard, R. 1990. *Tropical Gangsters: One Man's Experience With Development and Decadence in Deepest Africa*, New York: Basic Books.
Laffont, J. J. and Jean Tirole. 1991. 'Auction Design and Favouritism', *International Journal of Industrial Organization*, vol. 9, pp. 9–42.
Lovei, L. and A. McKechnie. 2000. *The Cost of Corruption for the Poor: The Energy Sector*, Washington DC: The World Bank.
Mattoo, Aaditya. 1996. 'The Government Procurement Agreement: Implications of Economic Theory', *The World Economy*, vol. 19, no. 6, pp. 695–720.
Mauro, P. 1997. 'Why Worry About Corruption', Economic Issues no. 6, IMF.
McAfee, Preston R. and John Mcmillan. 1989. 'Government Procurement and International Trade', *Journal of International Economics*, vol. 26, pp. 291–308.
Organisation for Economic Cooperation and Development (OECD). 2002. *The Size of Government Procurement Markets*, http://www.oecd.org/dataoecd/34/14/1845927.pdf.
_____. 2003. *Transparency in Government Procurement: The Benefits of Efficient Governance and Orientation for Achieving It*. Paris: Working Party of the Trade Committee.
Rege, V. 2001. 'Transparency in Government Procurement: Issues of Concern and Interest to Developing Countries', *Journal of World Trade*, vol. 35, no. 4, pp. 489–515.
Rose-ackerman, Susan. 1999. *Corruption and Government: Causes, Consequences and Reform*, Cambridge: Cambridge University Press.
Sahgal V. and D. Chakrapani. 2002. 'India: Evaluating Bank Assistance for Public Financial Accountability in the1990s', OED Working Paper, Washington DC: The World Bank.
Srivastava, Vivek. 1999. *India's Accession to the GPA: Identifying Costs and Benefits*, New Delhi: National Council of Applied Economic Research.
Tanzi, V. and H. Davoodi. 1997. 'Corruption Public Investment and Growth', IMF Working Paper WP/97/139, pp. 1–23.
Tanzi, V. 1998. 'Corruption Around the World: Causes, Consequences, Scope and Cures', IMF Staff Paper WP/98/63, pp. 1–39.
Transparency International. 2002. 'Karachi Integrity Pact Saves 75% in Consulting Fees', Press Release.
_____. 2002a. *Corruption in South Asia*, Insights & Benchmarks from Citizen Feedback Survey in Five Countries, pp. 1–42.
USAID. 1999. 'Ensuring Transparency and Accountability in Hurricane Reconstruction and Transformation', USAID Discussion Paper for the Consultative Group for the Reconstruction and Transformation of Central America.
Wei, S. J. 1997. 'How Taxing is Corruption on International Investors?', NBER Working Paper no. 6030.
_____. 1999. 'Corruption in Economic Development: Beneficial Grease, Minor Annoyance, or Major Obstacle', World Bank Policy Research Working Paper no. 2048.
World Bank. 2003. *India: Country Procurement Assessment Report*, Report no. 27859-IN, pp. 1–27.

Section V

TRIPS and GATS

12

The Trips Agreement: Public Health Concerns for India

AMIT SHOVON RAY

INTRODUCTION

The TRIPS agreement under the WTO has been one of the most contentious and highly debated issues, right from its introduction into the Uruguay trade round in the 1980s. Under this agreement, all WTO member nations must provide a uniform standard of protection for a wide range of IPRs including patents, copyrights, trademarks, industrial designs, geographical indications, information and communication designs, and undisclosed information. In this paper, we confine our attention only to the patents provision of the TRIPS agreement.

We begin with a general discussion of the concept of intellectual property, the need to protect such property rights and its implications for economic development from a purely economic theoretic point of view. This would be followed by a more focused discussion of the public health concerns arising out of a TRIPS compatible patent regime in India. This discussion would be carried out against the backdrop of the evolution of Indian pharmaceutical industry post 1970, as well as the WTO driven challenges and adjustments that have been taking place in this industry since 1990.

This will bring us to a discussion of India's healthcare concerns that have been brought to the forefront, following the adjustments and structural changes in the Indian pharmaceutical industry in light of the emerging global order.

THE DEBATE ON INTELLECTUAL PROPERTY RIGHTS

Intellectual property is a form of knowledge that may assign property rights to the owner, along similar lines as rights over physical property. It has been well recognised by economists, right from the nineteenth century, that knowledge has been a key driving force behind economic growth and development. With the modern day scientific and technical advances, especially in the fields of information and communication technology (ICT), biotechnology and so on, knowledge has become even more crucial as source of competitive advantage of industries and nations.

Knowledge has the characteristics of non-rivalry and non-excludability of public goods. One person's use of knowledge does not diminish another's. Also, knowledge is prone to imitation, for example, many products incorporating new knowledge can be easily copied at a fraction of the cost it took to invent it. This leads to market failure. If indeed, one cannot fully appropriate the gains derived from generating new knowledge, there is very little private incentive to push the frontiers of knowledge, which is important for nations to grow and prosper.

IPRs create a legal means to protect knowledge property and to enable the 'creator/owner' of this knowledge, appropriate the gains from it. Intellectual property may be categorised into two broad groups: industrial property (functional commercial innovations) and artistic & literary property (cultural creations). TRIPS covers almost all dimensions of IP. Patents constitute a key industrial property, which we focus on in this paper.

Patents attempt to solve the problem of market failure in knowledge creation by conferring 'temporary' monopoly rights to the inventor, who in turn is expected to recoup his enormous costs of new invention through monopoly pricing. It is believed, that high prices paid by the consumers in the short run (during the patent period) will be more than offset by their long run gains, due to continued research and development and consequent flow of new inventions. In other words, patents are expected to contribute to dynamic efficiency by stimulating technological progress, at the cost of static inefficiency associated with monopoly.

But the rationale for patent protection is not as straight forward and as unambiguous as described above. First of all, it is difficult to arrive at the optimum degree of patent protection. While too weak, a patent protection might limit innovations and technological progress. Too strong, a patent may reduce consumer welfare by allowing patentees to gain profits far in excess of their research and development costs. Moreover, it may also stifle further innovations based on protected knowledge. Indeed, the optimum degree of patent protection is likely to vary widely by product and sector. Another underlying presumption is 'that there is a latent supply of innovative capacity in the private sector waiting to be unleashed by the grant of protection' (IPR Commission 2002). However, in most developing countries, such capacity is often weak. If at all, such capacity is usually in the public rather than private sectors. For these countries, the dynamic gains from patents therefore remain rather uncertain.

Evidently, patent system tends to promote invention and innovation by slowing down the diffusion of new technology. In terms of the Schumpetrian trilogy of invention-innovation-diffusion, as the three constituents of technological progress, patents lay excessive importance on the first two. While this is perhaps appropriate in the context of technologically advanced nations, the technological capability of the developing world rests primarily on the process of learning through reverse engineering, where diffusion plays the most important role. Indeed, it has been argued that strict patents may hinder their process of technological learning by choking off technology diffusion. Accordingly, a weak and flexible IPR is required to acquire technological capability at the initial stages of development, while later with technological maturity and the acquisition of inventive capabilities, a strong IPR may be imposed to facilitate inventions and innovations.

Historical experience shows that countries have used and adapted IP regimes according to their level of development and technological capability to facilitate technological learning and promote their own industrial policy objectives. US, for instance, did not allow patents to foreigners till 1836, and even then it fixed the patenting fees for foreigners at ten times the rate applicable to US citizens. Since patent policies in one country affects the interests of others, there has always been an international dimension to the debate on IPRs.

The Paris and Berne conventions (1883 and 1886) recognised this but allowed sufficient flexibility to countries in designing and adopting their IP regimes, according to their own priorities and context. With the advent of TRIPS, this flexibility is completely removed. All member countries of the WTO are compelled to adopt a uniformly strong IPR regime irrespective of their technological capability levels, notwithstanding the clear evidence and arguments suggesting that the optimum strength (degree) of patent protection depends on the product, sector and nation concerned.

Apart from the general controversy on the role of IPRs in economic development, there has been a serious concern regarding public health implications of imposition of TRIPS in developing nations. Interestingly, the pharmaceutical industry in advanced nations has been a major lobbyist for the TRIPS agreement. It is argued that the pharmaceutical industry in developed countries is more crucially dependent on strong patent protection compared to most other industries, in order to sustain Research and Development for new drug discovery which is characterised by massive investments and high uncertainty. But this is likely to have serious adverse effects on the effort of developing nations to improve public health due to rising drug prices and restricting access to drugs.

This concern was explicitly voiced during the Doha rounds of discussions in November 2001. Indeed, the Doha Declaration on TRIPS and Public Health was a major step forward in recognising 'the gravity of the public health problems afflicting many developing and least-developed countries, especially those resulting from HIV/AIDS, tuberculosis, malaria and other epidemics' and the urgency for 'the TRIPS agreement to be part of the wider national and international action to address these problems.'

We recognise that there are serious imbalances among developing countries with respect to their capability to produce or access affordable medicines for their poor masses. The TRIPS Agreement, therefore, does not pose a single and uniform challenge for the entire developing world. The impact will vary according to the level of manufacturing and research capability in pharmaceuticals acquired by the developing country in question.

We focus our attention on India, a poor developing country with a sizeable pharmaceutical industry, which has reached impressive levels of technological capability. A relatively weak patent regime, introduced in the Indian patent Act of 1970, allowed only process (and no product) patents in pharmaceuticals. In the two or three decades following this Patent Act, there has been a revolution in process of engineering capability in the Indian drug industry. India can now produce cheap generic versions of any new drug introduced globally and has thus been successful in keeping drug prices at one of the lowest in the world. This is going to change with the enactment of the new Patent Act of 2005, complying with TRIPS agreement. A new drug can not be replicated with non-infringing process for a period of 20 years from the date of its patent. The role of 'cheap' generics gets confined to the off-patented segment of the drug industry.

In the remaining part of this paper, we present a discussion of the changing face of the Indian pharmaceutical industry with the imposition of a TRIPS compatible patent act and discuss its public health implications.

THE PATENT ACT OF 1970 AND PROCESS REVOLUTION IN INDIAN PHARMACEUTICALS

1970 marked the beginning of a new era for the pharmaceutical industry in India. With the introduction of the Patent Act 1970, there was a concerted effort at generating indigenous technological capability (in production as well as in research) in the pharmaceutical sector, with the goal of increasing access to drugs at affordable costs. In fact the decade of 1970s witnessed the passage of several government directives directly shaping the growth path of this sector, including the Drug Price Control Orders (DPCO) 1970 and 1979, FERA of 1973, New Drug Policy 1978 and of course, the Patent Act 1970.

The Patent Act of 1970 was a radical departure from the earlier patent law which accorded product as well as process patent protection up to a period of 10 years (extendable by another six years) and acted as a major deterrent to the creation of indigenous technological capability especially through reverse engineering. Patent Act of 1970, by contrast granted only process patent for chemical substances including pharmaceuticals, reduced the duration of patents to seven years from the date of filing or five years from the date of sealing whichever is lower, excluded all imported substances from the domain of patent protection (that is,. only new substances manufactured in India were entitled to patent protection), and placed the burden of proof on the plaintiff in case of infringement.

The spirit of this policy regime of the 1970s was reinforced by Drug Policy 1978 with its three-fold objective of self-reliance in pharmaceutical technology, self-sufficiency in drug production and easy and cheap availability of drugs. This in a sense summarises the policy framework adopted in the 1970s with a clear emphasis on import substitution and self-reliance in the production of bulk as well as formulations and on creating indigenous technological capability of process development (bulk).

Against the backdrop of this policy environment, the pharmaceutical industry in India embarked on a new trajectory of 'technological learning based on reverse engineering', which essentially implies decoding an original process for producing a bulk drug. This involves a detailed understanding of the chemical properties of the active molecule, the excipients used and the chemical process of conversion from the active molecular compound to the final bulk drug. A chemical process incorporates a complex set of parameters, for example, solvent conditions, temperature, time, stirring methods, use of various chemical, and physical substances with different levels of purity and so on, all of which have to be simultaneously optimised in order to arrive at the optimum process specification. It is possible to decode all of these parametric specifications of a process through reverse engineering.

One can make a distinction between *two types* of reverse engineering activities: infringing and non-infringing processes. In case of the former, a reverse engineered process, exactly matches the specifications and design of the original process and therefore, needless to mention, the use of such processes infringes upon the intellectual property rights of the innovator of the original process. Hence the scope of such activities is limited to off-patent drugs only. The second category of reverse engineering activities is somewhat more complex, as it results in the development of non-infringing processes, whereby the same bulk drug may be produced through a different route. Non-infringing processes are relevant only in case of patented drugs, which may be free from product patents but continue to enjoy process patent protection.

With the introduction of the Patent Act of 1970, there has been widespread reverse engineering for non-infringing processes. This is not to suggest that infringing process development (simple imitation) did not taken place. In fact many of the firms began with such simple technological activities (perhaps on off-patent drugs) to acquire more complex capabilities at a later stage. Indeed, the industry acquired substantial technological capability of process development through reverse engineering, both infringing processes for off-patented molecules and non-infringing processes for patented molecules. This phenomenon has been often been referred to as the process revolution in the Indian pharmaceutical sector. As a result, the bulk drug industry grew at a phenomenally high rate of 21 per cent and 11 per cent per annum during the decades of 1970s and 1980s respectively.

Along with process revolution, simple product development in conventional dosage forms which had already started in the post-independence era, continued in the post 1970s. As a result, the formulation industry also registered impressive growth rates of 13per cent and 10per cent per annum respectively, during the same periods. The impetus largely came from the massive expansion of bulk drugs due to the process revolution and the policies to deter captive consumption of bulk.

Indeed there was a marked increase in Research and Development expenditure of the industry during this period: it stood at Rs 50 Crores in 1986 accounting for nearly 2 per cent of the industry's sales turnover compared to less than one per cent prior to 1970.

The policy environment facilitated free entry of a large number of producers of both bulk and formulation, most of them in the small scale and unorganised sector. The resultant market structure was characterised by a limited number of large organised sector units enjoying the lion's share of the market on one hand, and a very large number (thousands) of small producers each producing a microscopic fraction of the total industry sales on the other. This implied a wide variation in the quality and price of a drug in the market and multiplicity of formulations. Problems of spurious drugs and irrational combinations have been a natural outcome of this phenomenon. While the policy environment favoured small producers, lack of adequate quality regulations and control mechanisms often resulted in the supply of sub-optimal and ineffective drugs. Apart from deviations from the quality norms, the norm itself was often kept at a low level by the regulatory authority, to encourage small producers who may not be able to afford sophisticated equipments for various tests/assays. Indeed there has been a noticeable difference in the parameters of acceptable drug quality in India compared to that of the developed world. But most drugs were now available in India at affordable prices, the quality variations notwithstanding.

As an outcome of the policy framework, multi-national corporations (MNCs) became reluctant to launch their new drugs in India. But that did not deprive the Indian patients from the latest drug discoveries without much delay in launching (Bhaduri and Ray 2003). Indian firms introduced these new drugs in the market using non-infringing processes, perhaps with a time lag marginally exceeding the demand lag. Examples are numerous: Ranitidine (Glaxo) and Amlodipine (Pfizer) are two of the glaring examples of this phenomenon.

TRIPS AND THE NEW WORLD ORDER POST-1990: ADJUSTMENS IN INDIA'S PHARMACEUTICAL SECTOR

In tune with a newly emerging international economic order, India's economic reforms process began in the late 1980s/1990. WTO has been the prime architect of the broad framework of this new global order, primarily geared towards free trade and removal of 'policy distortions' in all dimensions of a country's economic activity. The idea is to pave the way for liberalised and market driven international flows of goods, services, capital, and technology in a multilateral framework. Ironically, however, one also finds provisions for bilateral negotiations and unilateral actions built into the WTO framework, especially when it serves the interest of developed countries. Product regulations and standards, anti-dumping and other safeguard measures are examples of WTO provisions which can be misused (mainly by the developed nations) to counter the spirit of multilateral trade liberalisation propagated by the WTO and the proponents of this new world order.

The Patent Act of 2005 has been a direct fallout of the WTO's TRIPS agreements. The salient features of the forthcoming patent regime are summarised below.

- Product patents will be allowed in all fields of technology with a uniform duration of 20 years in pharmaceuticals, food products and agrochemical from the date of application.
- Compulsory licenses will be given by the government only on the merit of each case, and would be granted in case of national emergency. However, the patent holder will be given a hearing and an opportunity to present his case for intellectual protection.
- There will be no discrimination between imported and domestic goods in so far as intellectual property protection is concerned as par the national treatment clause in WTO.
- For process patents, the burden of proof will rest with the party that infringes. This is in contrast with the requirement of the earlier patent regime. In Patent Act of 1970 burden of proof was on the original innovator.

With the enactment of this law, the policy framework encouraging process development, through reverse engineering activities will disappear. But the strong product regime is 'supposed' to encourage basic and frontier research in the industry.

The overall philosophy of the new policy regime is well echoed in the Drug Policy Statements of 1986, 1994 and 2003. Licensing requirements for all bulk drugs and formulations are abolished with a few noted exceptions. Restrictions on import of bulk are largely removed. The earlier policy to deter captive consumption of bulk is reversed. Major thrust is placed on drug quality, acknowledging the need to monitor and regulate quality and promote rational use of drugs. It stresses the need to implement Good Manufacturing Practices (GMP) for all manufacturing units.

Although the Indian pharmaceutical industry has continued to expand both in terms of production and trade during the decade of the 1990s,[1] the new policy environment has posed major challenges to the sector which is evident from rising drug prices, downsizing of employment and closure of production facilities of many units including that of multinationals. As a result, the Indian pharmaceutical industry is going through a turbulent phase of adjustments. In the following section, we will attempt to trace this adjustment process for the organised segment of the industry.

The Challenges

The major challenges posed by the new policy regime of globalisation and reforms to the Indian pharmaceutical industry, especially those in the organised sector, can be synthesised as follows.

Limits to Growth Through Process Development

With the introduction of the new patent regime, the conventional corporate growth strategy, based on non-infringing process development for patented molecules to introduce the latest drugs in the Indian market, adopted by the Indian pharmaceutical industry till now, will no longer be a viable option. Reverse engineering on patented drugs will come to complete halt, raising a big question mark as to how far the Indian pharmaceutical can exploit its process development capabilities acquired through conscious Research and Development efforts during the last quarter of the century. Reverse engineering on off-patent drugs can, of course, continue to give them an edge in the generic market. In fact a market of about US$50b of pharmaceutical products will come off-patent in the next few years.

Limits to the Generic Market

Given that new drugs will now become the exclusive monopoly of the innovating firm, we believe that the generic market will become extremely crowded both in India and the world since all non-innovating firms will have to rely on the generic market.

A further limit on the scope of business development based on the generic market may be posed by the high rate of new drug discovery in the 1990s. Since most these new drugs are not 'new' in the sense of having a pioneering therapeutic use, but are merely replacing existing drugs with better therapeutic efficacy and lower side effects, new drug discovery might reduce the life span of existing drugs. This in turn implies a high rate of obsolescence in the generic pharmaceutical market.

The global pharmaceutical market is becoming increasingly competitive both with respect to price as well as quality. Even with trade liberalisation, the WTO allows for imposition of product regulations and standards to create barriers to free flow of trade. This is being fully exploited by the developed countries to protect their large pharmaceutical markets from low cost imports from the developing world. Therefore new norms of drug quality are being introduced worldwide, which will further limit the scope of access to the world generic market. With a move towards quality harmonisation, drug quality will act as a principal parameter of success, even for Indian firms in years to come.

The Adjustments

To cope with these serious challenges, the Indian industry (organised sector) is going through a major phase of restructuring and adjustments. We intend to analyse and capture some of these. We restrict our analysis to two of the major dimensions of the adjustment process. The first relates to the response of the Indian industry to a new paradigm of drug quality. The second looks at the changing role of Research and Development and technology in this new era of globalisation and reforms.

A New Paradigm of Drug Quality

Drug quality is a complex multi-dimensional concept. First and foremost, quality implies therapeutic efficacy and safety. A high quality drug must be effective and should not produce any toxicity or side effects. In this regard, bio-availability acts as an important parameter of drug quality. A second and most commonly stated parameter of quality pertains to the impurity profile and stability of chemical ingredients. A related quality parameter affecting product purity is contamination during the production process. Not only keeping minimum impurity is important, but also consistency in the specified impurity profile over all batches of production must be adhered to. Detailed documentation of all the production stages along with the quality control operations constitutes an added dimension of quality specification as it creates institutional memory and makes the entire production process transparent to all concerned parties.² The third set of quality parameters stipulates that the production process should be environment friendly and should not create any health hazards within and outside the production unit. The intermediates and excipients of the production process must also be non-hazardous and environment-friendly.³

The relative importance of each of these diverse parameters in the final quality specification would vary from country to country, depending on the composition of their pharmacopoeial committee and socio-economic priorities of the government. This has resulted in divergence of the technical requirements for quality specification and control in different countries, compelling the globalised industry to replicate many test procedures including clinical trials in order to market new products in different countries. To overcome this problem, the governments of the three largest pharmaceutical markets (US, EU and Japan) have jointly initiated a move towards harmonisation of drug quality through the International Conference on Harmonisation (ICH) from the late 1980s. The US Pharmacopoeia (USP) has dominated this harmonisation movement, with an in-built bias towards increasingly stringent norms for impurity profile, through sophisticated instrumentation and analytical methods.

Prior to the 1990s, drug quality in India was loosely defined and remained far below international standards. This is not to suggest that there were no high quality producers even during this period. But quality parameters did not receive much attention by the industry and the regulatory authorities in general. But in the new era of globalisation, characterised by a strict IPR regime, a fast moving technology frontier and a move towards international harmonisation of quality standards, firms will have to explore the growing international market for generic drugs, the US market in particular. Entry into this highly competitive market calls for stringent quality requirements. Indeed with the threat of ICH, not only US but the entire global market may be subjected to stricter quality norms.

In this new era, the Indian manufacturers have to pay intensive attention to the concept of drug quality, which was hitherto largely ignored and adopt the following operational and organisational changes:

- Quality control must be much more rigorous with stricter parameters and sophisticated instrumentation.
- For formulations, the quality of active pharmaceutical ingredients (API or bulk) becomes all important.
- High quality standards as par the multidimensional definition, given above, demand up-gradation of production and quality control technology.
- The environmental dimensions of quality necessitate increased attention towards effluent treatment and proper waste management using modern methods and equipment.
- Detailed documentation is becoming an important facet of production and quality control.
- Finally, quality has added a new dimension to their Research and Development thrust. Firms are now trying to develop new improved analytical methods for quality specification and control. Some Indian firms have already succeeded in developing superior methods, which have been incorporated in the global quality standards like USP and European Pharmacopoeia (EP). In a sense, Indian players have thus contributed to outward shifts in the global frontiers of drug quality.

Most of these elements of higher drug quality entail increased automation of the production process. In many cases, it requires complete overhauling of the plant set-up to install sophisticated (often imported) machinery and equipment for production and quality control.

From 'Business driven Reasearch and Development' to 'Research and Development driven Business'

Technological capability of the Indian pharmaceutical industry can be classified into three broad groups:

- Process development capabilities (bulk drug)—infringing and non-infringing
- Product development capabilities (formulations)—conventional dosage forms (CDF), novel drug delivery systems (NDDS) of first and second generations (NDDS1, NDDS2 respectively) and analytical methods for quality
- New drug discovery research (NDDR)

The industry began with simple product development capabilities in CDF and started producing formulation from imported bulk drug. Eventually, as business expanded, the industry started making explicit efforts towards acquisition of technological capability of process development in post-1970s with the overriding objective of developing non-infringing cost-minimising processes. By the end of the 1980s, the Indian pharmaceutical industry reached new heights of process technology, which acted as the key driving force behind the Indian pharmaceutical revolution. So far the evolution of technological capability followed the conventional trajectory of technological development outlined in the standard economic literature (Katz 198, 87; Lall 1987).

However, in the 1990s we find a renewed emphasis on product development, but this time not on CDF but on NDDS1 (controlled/sustained release dosage forms) and on NDDS2 (targeted release dosage forms) undertaken by a handful of firms only. This movement is dictated by the new policy environment whereby business expansion through non-infringing process development will be severely limited. NDDS1 and NDDS2, catering to the specialised needs of the fastidious patient, are clear signs of a movement towards Research and Development driven business—these new technological developments attempt to open up new dimensions of pharmaceutical business in India.

Advanced product development capabilities (NDDS and analytical methods) paved the way for new drug discovery research (NDDR) in India. The existing skills in chemistry along with strengthening of biology expertise (molecular and structural biology, in particular) required for NDDS research and experience in handling sophisticated equipment facilitated NDDR in India. However, the nature, process and the steps of NDDR in India typically reflect the evolution of technological capability of a typical LDC with limited risk-taking, financial and research capabilities. The me-too type NDDR in India, predominantly focusing on inventing-around an existing inhibitor for a given target, are far less risky and less expensive than finding a new target itself. It has primarily been driven by existing skills and capabilities rather than venturing into new areas of capability building and Research and Development investments.

It is evident from the discussion above, that in the post reforms scenario, Research and Development will play the central role in maintaining successful trajectory of growth and development of the Indian pharmaceutical industry. The industry will now be characterised by Research and Development driven business rather than business driven Reasearch and Development.

HEALTH CARE CONCERNS

The twin pillars of adjustments in the Indian pharmaceutical industry, namely, quality and Reasearch and Development, in the post reforms era, will have serious implications for health care. The health care implications will not only depend on the supply side adjustments in the industry, but also on how the medical profession (constituting the surrogate demand side of the market) absorbs and responds to these changes driven by the new global order. In our analysis of the health care implications, we shall try to incorporate the latter by drawing largely upon the findings of a study on the subject commissioned by the Independent Commission on Health in India (Ray 2004). In this study, a survey was carried out in which around 50 medical practitioners (specialists, general physicians, and quacks) were interviewed in Lucknow and Greater Noida area in order to understand the political economy of medical practice in India in the post reforms era, especially in the context of the adjustments in the Indian pharmaceutical industry.

Our analysis of the health care implications and concerns arising out of the reforms, and WTO-driven adjustments in the pharmaceutical sector, will be discussed under three broad issues: (a) new drugs, (b) existing drugs and (c) drug quality.

New Drugs

A major argument put forward by the proponents of the WTO-driven world order and reforms process, pertains to welfare gains through major technological advances which the new regime is supposed to foster. In the context of the pharmaceutical industry, technological advancement through basic research refers to the discovery of new drugs. Indeed, 'pharmaceuticals is one of the world's most research intensive industries, generating a continuing steam of new products that saves life and raise the quality of life.' (Scherer 2000). In so far as the new world order facilitates, the discovery and introduction of new drugs worldwide and in India, one is perhaps be tempted to make a prima facie case for a favourable health impact of the WTO-driven changes in the pharmaceutical industry. Indeed, it is widely believed that the rate of introduction of new drugs have increased in the last decade. But does it necessarily improve health care in India? This supposition is at best naïve and at worst devoid of any consideration of several conditioning factors, like the therapeutic focus of new drug discovery research and the nature of the new of drugs juxtaposed against the political economy of medical practice in India.

Therapeutic Focus

Given that drug discovery research demands massive research investments and involves a high degree of risks and uncertainty, it is of little surprise that private drug manufactures would prefer to focus on therapeutic areas which commands a large affluent market. Accordingly, non-communicable lifestyle diseases of the affluent western world dominates the large majority of new drug discovery research worldwide, while the poor man's (communicable tropical) diseases of the third world continues to remain largely neglected in the research portfolio of the major pharmaceutical players. Clearly, health concerns of the developing world remain unattended to, notwithstanding the encouragement to drug research provided by the regime.

One may counter argue, that since the new regime is pushing the Indian players into drug discovery research, one may expect them to focus on tropical diseases and other areas of India's needs and priorities. But this has not been the case. Indian firms do not have adequate financial strength and risk taking capability to carry out most of the activities in the developmental phase of NDDR even after getting the lead molecule. As a result they have to tie up with or (sell the lead to) a foreign firm for further development. Accordingly, they have to focus on therapeutic areas with a global market, rather than focussing on tropical communicable diseases. More seriously, even the public sector research laboratories in India (like Central Drug Research Institute [CDRI]) in the post reforms era have been compelled to dilute their social mandate of working on neglected diseases. With the increasing pressure of self-financing and raising resources from 'market' sources, there has been a clear shift in their therapeutic focus away from tropical to 'western' diseases (Ray 2003).

The conclusion is loud and clear. The faster rate of new drug discovery has little to add to the health care needs of the poor third world nations. One exception is perhaps the enormous amount of public money being pumped into research on HIV-AIDS worldwide. This would perhaps cater to the urgent need of some of the African nations suffering from the HIV epidemic.

The Nature of New Drugs: Marginal Improvement Versus Therapeutic Revolution

The last century witnessed a period (1940–55) of major therapeutic revolution with a high rate of drug discovery and the introduction of several new path breaking drugs like penicillin, streptomycin and cortisteroids. By contrast, the new drugs discovered in the 1990s are only believed to be marginally improved versions of existing drugs to combat a disease. In fact, the new drug in many cases may be new molecular entity (NME) with a new mechanism of action (MOA), but with very similar therapeutic effect and perhaps with better toxicity and safety conditions.

Ray (2004) reports that the majority of responding medical practitioners from the qualified categories (non-quacks) feels that, by and large, new drugs that they have been exposed to in the last five years have not replaced existing drugs. Most of them are just an improved version of an existing drug with lower side effects, toxicity and occasionally with greater therapeutic efficacy. As a result, the average lifespan of existing drugs is not reduced due to the faster rate of introduction of new drugs, according to them.

Further, Ray (2004) also notes, that the industry targets to promote the new drugs primarily to specialists in government practice followed by those in private practice. The study also finds that the primary considerations for prescribing a new drug by the medical profession in India are improved therapeutic efficacy, essentiality, and academic reference. Side effects, toxicity, and safety considerations play (not surprisingly) a less important role in the political economy of medical practice in India. Accordingly, the new drugs of the 1990s, primarily aiming at better safety and toxicity, are unlikely to have any major impact in improving India's health care.

The Vicious Cycle of Antibiotics

While it is true that drug discovery research has focussed primarily on non-communicable diseases, at the same new generations of antibiotics are also being introduced in the market. The industry aims to target the antibiotic drugs to non-qualified practitioners in the rural areas (quacks). Given the complex dynamics of rural health care scenario (Ray 2001), these quacks prescribe antibiotics indiscriminately and the unenlightened patient fails to comply with the dosage schedule. This creates resistance problem to existing generations of antibiotics, creating demand for discovering new generations of antibiotics, which when launched are 'pushed' to the market through unethical prescription resulting in the same consequences and completing the vicious cycle. The new world order, pushing the industry to survive through NDDR, tends to perpetuate this vicious cycle, with devastating health care effects.

Existing Drugs

Novel Drug Delivery Systems

We have seen that the new regime is encouraging research by Indian firms on novel drug delivery systems for existing drugs. Clearly the objective is to create (though Reasearch and Development) new dimensions of pharmaceutical business to cater to the needs of affluent and fastidious patients rather than the needs of the masses. In fact, Ray (2004) notes that new dosage forms are yet to take off in Indian medical practice in a major way. The two major considerations in prescribing these are essentiality and affordability. Clearly, the Research and Development effort towards NDDS is, therefore, unlikely to have any major favourable impact on India's health care, at least in the short run.

Prices

We have also discussed how the new regime may foster competition in the generic market. One would normally expect, with rising competition, prices of drugs in the off-patent segment to fall. This would have indeed had a favourable health care impact. But again if we look at the dynamics of medical practice in India, we have reasons to doubt this oversimplified conclusion. Note that this is a sector, with high promotional activities and large price-cost margin. This gives an edge to large firms with greater financial power to capture a larger market share through aggressive promotions at the cost of small low-cost suppliers. This is likely to raise prices of generics.

Ray (2004) finds that for specialists, the choice of brands for a given drug is mainly determined by the reputation of the firm and the persuasive power of the medical representative (MR). Clearly, entry of large firms in the off-patent segment will drive up prices, if indeed they have to convince specialists to prescribe their brands through MR persuasion. Quacks and general physicians seem to suggest that cost effectiveness of a brand is also an equally important consideration in prescribing a brand apart from company reputation and MR persuasion. However, these doctors are more prone to switching brands frequently, often under the influence of MRs (Ray 2004). This implies that large expenditure on promotional activities will also help capture the practice segment of non-specialists and quacks. Overall, the competitive pressure will lead to greater expenditure on brand promotion, leading to rising prices.

Drug Quality

The new paradigm of drug quality, acting as a key parameter of adjustments in the Indian pharmaceutical industry, might have little to do with the health care of its people. The new quality paradigm is driven by the interest lobby of the multinational pharmaceutical giants, in an attempt to create entry barriers to the global generics market. Excessive importance is being placed on safety conditions (impurity profile) through stringent tests and screening using sophisticated instrumentation and analytical methods, and environmental concerns demanding massive investments in up-grading (or overhauling of entire production plant), as per global norms. The question remains, whether or not such strict safety and environmental norms indeed make much difference to patient welfare in terms of the therapeutic impact of the drug.

The medical profession in India, according to Ray (2004), considers therapeutic efficacy and company reputation to be the overwhelmingly important criteria for assessing drug quality. Much less important are the criteria of safety, toxicity (impurity profile) and so on. Indeed, if at all, the specialists are the ones to take these into account, but only as second tier criteria. Therefore, the new paradigm of drug quality dominated by the latter is likely to have little impact on health care, per se.

However, enormous costs are being incurred by the pharmaceutical producers to conform to the new global norms of quality and this is bound to be reflected in the prices. More seriously, so far the Indian regulatory system allowed a spectrum of drug quality in the market, catering to the needs of all segment of society. But with a move towards quality harmonisation, this spread might disappear. Manufacturers with world class production facility conforming to the stipulated global norms will survive. A poor patient who may not be able to afford drugs that are produced as per US Food and Drug Administration (USFDA) norms, for instance, will not have the 'low' quality products to fall back on.[4]

CONCLUSION

The WTO-led new international economic order is going to have a profound impact on the structure and functioning of the Indian pharmaceutical industry with serious implications for India's healthcare.

The new world order of the 1990s, and India's economic reforms driven by the new world order, has placed the Indian pharmaceutical industry at a watershed. Faced with the challenges of globalisation, the industry, especially the organised segment, is undergoing major adjustment and restructuring. We have argued how quality and Research and Development have become the twin pillars of success and survival for the Indian pharmaceutical industry in the post reforms period.

We have shown that while the emerging international economic order is likely to promote the discovery and introduction of new drugs worldwide and in India, it is unlikely to have any perceptible favourable impact on India's health, given the market driven therapeutic focus of new drug discovery research. More alarming is the tendency of the market forces in the new era to perpetuate a vicious circle of antibiotics, through the discovery of newer generations of antibiotics. In addition, we have also indicated that under the new world order, price and quality of drugs will move in a direction that favours the rich and discerning patient, while the poor may be deprived of affordable medicines of acceptable quality.

TRIPS is now a fait-accompli for India and for the entire world. We would like to believe that the new regime will promote new drug discovery research for curing and preventing deadly diseases like AIDS or cancer. But it is also important to recognise the flip side of TRIPS. Active policy interventions are needed to ameliorate these adverse effects. Foremost among these, is a comprehensive health policy, emphasising on a greater government role in ensuring free health and medical care for its poor masses, devising and implementing an effective regulatory framework for quality medical practice based on 'rational use of drugs' and promoting sale and prescription of drugs based on generic rather than brand names to eliminate the unholy nexus between the drug industry and the medical profession. Moreover, there are flexibilities within the TRIPS format (for example, non-significant therapeutic improvement may be kept out of the scope of patents, extract the maximum advantage out of articles 30 and 31 on compulsory licensing, allow pre-grant opposition), which can be leveraged for serving the larger national interest. In fact, it is interesting to note that the amendment to the TRIPS Agreements on 6 December 2005, by the General Council to address public health concerns (by expanding the scope of compulsory licenses) was welcomed by the Hong Kong Ministerial Conference.

Endnotes

[1] See Key Statistics, OPPI, www.indiaoppi.com/keystat.htm, for detail.

[2] Consequently, there has been a rising tendency towards automation of the production technology to eliminate input variations, human touch, and produce consistent batches with detailed computerised documentation.

[3] Increased automation might take care of the problems of 'unsafe' contact of labour with hazardous chemical ingredients and processes. Another way to solve the problem is to replace chemical processes by bio-technological processes as being done in developed nations.

[4] This is not to suggest that we shall turn a blind eye to spurious drugs or drugs manufactured below 'acceptable' quality norms. But one clearly does not need to impose USFDA norms for manufacturing facilities to eliminate spurious and other drugs of 'unacceptable' quality.

References

Bhaduri, S. and A. S. Ray. 2006. 'A Game Theoretic Model of Drug Launch in India', *Health Economics Policy and Law*, vol. 1, no.1, pp. 23–39.
IPR Commission. 2002. *Report of the Royal Commission on IPR*, London: IPR.
Katz, J. 1984. 'Domestic Technological Innovations and Dynamic Comparative Advantage', *Journal of Development Economics*, vol.16, pp. 13–37.
———. 1987. 'Domestic Technology Generation in LDCs: A Review of Research Findings', in *Technology Generation in Latin American Manufacturing Industries*, edited by J. M. Katz, London: Macmillan.
Lall, S. 1987. *Learning to Industrialise: The Acquisition of Technological capability by India*, London: Macmillan.
Ray, A. S. 2001. *The Political Economy of Rural Health Care in India*, New Delhi: VHAI Press.
———. 2003. *A Study of R&D Incentives in India: Structural Changes and Impact*, report prepared for the Department of Science & Technology, Ministry of Science & Technology, New Delhi: Government of India.
———. 2004. *Medicines, Medical Practice and Health Care in India in the Era of Globalisation: Political Economy Perspectives*, ICDHI monograph, New Delhi: VHAI Press.

13

GATS and India: Negotiations in Mode 3

Rashmi Banga

INTRODUCTION

Services sector has acted as an 'Engine of Growth' for India. It grew by almost 8 per cent per annum in the last decade (1994–2004), which is way ahead of agriculture sector (which grew at 3 per cent) and manufacturing sector (which grew at 5.2 per cent), pulling up the growth rate of the economy to 8.1 per cent in 2005–6. It now contributes more than 50 per cent of GDP. Trade in services has played an important role in fuelling this growth. India's exports of services witnessed one of the fastest rates of growth in the world.[1] In 2007–8, services sector grew by 10.8 per cent and contributed 63 per cent of GDP. India accounted for 65 per cent of the global market in offshore Information Technology services and 46 per cent of the global BPO market in 2004–5. Indian services exports grew at a compounded annual growth rate of 17 per cent during 1993–2000 but have grown at a much faster pace recording CAGR of about 24 per cent during 2001–8. There has been rapid growth in the services exports from the year 2002. The exports have grown from US$ 20.8 billion in 2002 to US$ 90.1 billion in 2008. India has also become a reservoir of not only low and semi-skilled service providers, but also high skill workers like doctors, engineers, and so on. Consequently, it is one of the largest recipients of inward remittances in the developing world.

With its services sector growing rapidly, India is playing a pro-active role in the multilateral trade negotiations in services. The framework of these negotiations is modeled in the WTO GATS, which came into force in 1995, as a result of the Uruguay Round negotiations. Unlike many developing countries, India has, in fact, taken an offensive position in these negotiations and has become a demandeur of liberalisation of cross-border supply of services, that is, in information technology (IT) and information technology enabled services (ITeS) (Mode 1). It also seeks greater access to EU and US in terms of the movement of natural persons, that is, temporary migration of people for work (Mode 4). In the process of liberalising its services sector, India has undertaken a number of reforms in the past decade, which include giving market access to foreign firms (Mode 3) in sectors like telecom, finance, computer related services, engineering services, and tourism services. The major sectors in which restrictions on foreign investment still remain are legal, auditing, and accounting and postal services. However, there is now a mounting pressure on India to open its various services sectors to FDI under Mode 3.

An important distinction between commitments undertaken in different modes of services supply, is that commitments with respect to Mode 1 and Mode 4 are horizontal commitments, that cut across different sectors, while commitments undertaken in Mode 3 are sector-specific. Services sector being the most heterogeneous sector (in terms of the required technology, skills, investments, employment and extent of value additions) and also most inter-linked sector (with maximum linkages within and with other sectors), commitments under Mode 3 may have the most widespread implications. Some of the important factors that determine the likely impact of trade liberalisation under Mode 3 are importance of the sector for the economy in terms of its contribution to output and employment, quality of existing domestic regulations in the sector, and the degree of competitiveness of domestic service providers in the sectors. Undertaking higher FDI commitments in a sector, which has large unskilled employment, uncompetitive domestic providers, because of long existing state monopolies and lack of domestic regulations, may lead to larger social costs than economic gains.

While trade under Mode 3 is largely determined by the extent of multilateral commitments undertaken, trade in the other modes is less driven by the policy factors and is more driven by the technology, cost, and demographic factors. Growth in cross-border trade in IT and other business services can largely be attributed to the improvements in ICT infrastructure and reduced communication costs. The off shoring companies are focusing on core competencies and cost savings, through avenues facilitated by technology, which enables them to offer newer, cheaper and more flexible services to their clients. Given India's cost competitiveness in this sector, trade in Mode 1 has happened and will continue to happen with limited scope for improvements through negotiations.

Temporary migration for work, that is, trade under Mode 4, has progressed on the basis of excess demand in the world for these services in the rich countries and excess supply of these services in the developing countries, which in turn has been determined by the demographics of the nations. The requirements of services often determine the immigration policies of the developed countries, which play a significant role in constructing non-tariff barriers, like economic needs tests, lack of recognition of degrees, and so on, to trade in this mode but lie outside the domain of GATS negotiations.

Given the fact that trade under Mode 1 and Mode 4 is largely governed by economic factors, policy with respect to trade under Mode 3, that is, undertaking FDI commitments gains significance. Undertaking higher commitments with respect to commercial presence in some sectors, especially in producer services like banking and insurance, can have far-reaching economic benefits. FDI brings better technology and best practices which improves the efficiency of the sector. These services are heavily used in manufacturing sector and can therefore lead to improvements in its productivity and output growth creating more demand for these services leading to an overall growth in the economy. On the other hand, undertaking FDI commitments in sectors, which have been under state monopolies for a long time, have limited uncompetitive private players and provide large-scale employment to low-skilled workers may lead to more social costs than economic gains. Liberalisation in these sectors must be undertaken in a phased manner, that is, as and when the sector has achieved a level of development, whereby it can benefit from the foreign presence.

In this context, the main objective of this chapter is to develop a negotiating strategy with respect to trade in Mode 3. Competitiveness of different services sectors in India is analysed and an attempt is made to provide a policy framework for identifying the services sectors, which have a potential for further trade liberalisation. Also, those service sectors are identified, where significant domestic constraints exist and therefore any further trade liberalisation must be preceded by considerable domestic reforms.

The chapter is organised as follows: section 2 of the chapter outlines emergence of GATS in multilateral negotiations and highlights its salient features; section 3 discusses the role played by India in GATS negotiations and its current commitments and revised offer; section 4 analyses the significance of different services sectors in terms of their contribution to GDP and employment and assesses their competitiveness vis-à-vis exports and FDI. Section 5 examines the extent of trade liberalisation in different sectors and uses a framework to identify the service sectors that are competitive and where India can benefit from liberalising further; section 6 concludes and provides policy insights with respect to liberalisation of services.

EMERGENCE OF GATS AND ITS SALIENT FEATURES

Emergence of GATS

Historically, services have been considered as non-tradable due to their basic characteristics of non-transferability and non-storability, which made it essential for the user and the provider of the service to interact. Subsequently, services were divided into two categories; first, those that necessarily require the physical proximity of the user and the provider; and second, those that do not essentially require this that is, the long distance services, which were made possible due to technical progress (Bhagwati 1984). Services like banking and insurance fall under this category. However, unlike in the case of goods where factor mobility and trade are distinct phenomena, in the case of services the distinction vanishes, as factor mobility and trade in services are two integral aspects of service transaction. All these characteristics of services have implications for how trade can occur and make international transaction in services conceptually more complex than international transactions in goods.

The first attempt to introduce international rules in trade in services came from the United States at the GATT ministerial meeting of November 1982. The incentive came mainly from the US private-sector service providers, whose motives were to permit rationalisation of service activities, along the lines of comparative advantage. It was thought that trade in services as in the case of goods would expand the sales and profits of those service providers, who were operating from the base of such a comparative advantage.

However, the attempt failed since the European Community was not interested and the developing countries opposed the move, as they feared that since comparative advantages in services lie mainly with the developed countries, especially in modern services, they will not gain much. They also feared that the issue of foreign direct investment would be indirectly included and this was a politically sensitive issue.

Although US was not able to get more than a few references to services trade[2] in the Tokyo Round agreements, it subsequently persuaded the other industrial countries of the OECD to undertake a study on services, with a view to identify areas for future negotiations. Following US efforts, the period 1984 to 1986 saw a surge in national studies on how trade in services should be undertaken.

However, none of the studies was from a developing country. Preceding the Punta del Este, Uruguay Round in 1986, there were four main clusters that became apparent, as discussed by Richardson (1986). These were (1) the United States and some OECD countries, which favoured the original proposal; (2) the European Community, some OECD members, and some developing countries, which were working towards an overall compromise; (3) a group of ten developing countries (the G-10), led by Brazil and India, which strongly opposed the US initiative; and (4) a group of twenty developing countries (the G-20) that were prepared to accept the US proposal depending on the terms.

The inclusion of trade in services in the ministerial declaration was a result of the compromise between these four clusters. Services were finally included in the negotiations in a two-track procedure. Part I covered the negotiations in goods, while negotiations on trade in services were launched in part II of the Punta del Este declaration of September 1986. Part II was drafted as a separate decision by ministers in their capacity as representatives of their governments.

Following the adoption of the Punta del Este declaration, in 1987, the Group of Negotiations on Services (GNS) was established, with a program for the initial phase of the negotiations that aimed at addressing underlying issues, not resolved in the ministerial declaration, while shedding some light on how to fulfill the guidelines and objectives agreed on in Punta del Este. After almost eight years of extensive discussions, the Uruguay Round of multilateral trade negotiations concluded in April 1994.

Participating countries agreed to establish a new WTO, which, among other things, will administer three multilateral trade agreement: the already existing GATT, as amended during the negotiations (the so-called GATT 1994), as well as the new GATS and the agreement on TRIPS.

For the purpose of classifying international transaction WTO under the GATS uses the classification provided by Sapir and Winter (1994 page 27) that is, the Agreement applies to four 'modes of supply'

Mode 1: cross-border supply of service (that is, not requiring the physical movement of supplier or customer)
Mode 2: Provision implying movement of the consumer to the location of the supplier;
Mode 3: services sold in the territory of a Member by (legal) entities that have established a presence there but originate in the territory of another Member; and
Mode 4: provision of services requiring the temporary movement of natural persons.

Salient Features of GATS

GATS established for the first time, legally enforceable rules governing the conduct of world trade in services under four modes. The articles of the GATS, and a set of Annexes, establish some general rules for government measures that affect trade in services. In addition, national schedules of commitments set out specific commitments by each member country. These commitments bind Members not to introduce more restrictive rules, which could have an adverse effect on trade. The schedules are an integral part of the Agreement, as tariff schedules are an integral part of the GATT. While the text of the Agreement applies uniformly to all Members of the WTO, the scheduling of commitments is negotiated by each Contracting Party (member countries or customs territories) with every other Contracting Party.

The text of the GATS consists of 6 parts:

1. Scope and Definition (Article I)
2. General Obligations (Articles II to XV)
3. Specific Commitments (Articles XVI to XVIII)
4. Progressive Liberalisation (Articles XIX to XXI)
5. Institutional Provisions (Articles XXII to XXVI)
6. Final Provisions (Articles XXVII to XXIX)

One of the unique features of GATS, is that it gives the flexibility to each member country, to decide the service sectors in which it will undertake and schedule commitments. It allows the member countries to indicate measures that will be kept in place for that sector, which will act as limitation to market access and national treatment. It also allows countries to undertake commitments that are specified by modes of supply of services. There are essentially five parts to GATS. Article I of GATS sets out a comprehensive definition of trade in services in terms of four different modes of supply: cross-border, consumption abroad, commercial presence in the consuming country, and presence of natural persons.

Part II of GATS sets out general obligations and disciplines. A basic MFN. obligation states that each party 'shall accord immediately and unconditionally to services and service providers of any other Party, treatment no less favorable than that it accords to like services and service providers of any other country'. However, it is recognised that MFN treatment may not be possible for every service activity and, therefore, it is envisaged that parties may indicate specific MFN exemptions. Conditions for such exemptions are included as an annex and provide for reviews after five years and a normal limitation of 10 years on their duration. A second basic principle carried over from the GATT is that of transparency. Other rules in Part II are intended to ensure that benefits under the GATS are not blocked by domestic regulations. Generally-applied measures that affect trade in service sectors, for which a country has made commitments must be applied reasonably, objectively and impartially

Part III of GATS contains provisions on market access and national treatment, which would not be general obligations, but would be commitments made in national schedules.

Thus, in the case of market access, each party 'shall accord services and service providers of other Parties treatment no less favourable than that provided for under the terms, limitations and conditions agreed and specified in its schedule.' The national-treatment provision contains the obligation to accord treatment to foreign service suppliers, which is no less favourable than the treatment granted to domestic service suppliers.

Part IV of GATS establishes the basis for progressive liberalisation in the services area, through successive rounds of negotiations and the development of national schedules. It also permits, after a period of three years, parties to withdraw or modify commitments made in their schedules. Where commitments are modified or withdrawn, negotiations should be undertaken with interested parties to agree on compensatory adjustments. Where agreement cannot be reached, compensation would be decided by arbitration.

Part V of GATS contains institutional provisions, including consultation and dispute settlement and the establishment of a Council on Services. The responsibilities of the Council are set out in a Ministerial Decision. Annexes to the agreement, concern various services like the movement of labour, financial services, telecommunications, air-transport services, and so on.

In Part VI, Article XXVII allows a member to deny benefits under the agreement to services originating in the territory of a non-member, and Article XXVIII defines some key terms used in the GATS.[3]

Although the scope of the GATS is very wide, dealing with 'all measures affecting trade in services', policy measures in some areas are not covered by the GATS disciplines, provided the measures are not used to circumvent their GATS obligations:

- immigration rules; provided they do not contravene commitments on temporary entry under mode 4;
- services supplied under Government Authority;
- fiscal policy and taxation measures (provided the taxes do not discriminate against foreign services or service suppliers.)
- import restrictions on equipment necessary for the supply of a service;
- Restrictions on short term capital movements, or measures that affect property rights (provided they are nondiscriminatory)
- exchange rate management
- privatisation of state owned property, though there are disciplines for state-owned trading entities and monopolies.

Other types of government measures have been put into the GATS work program, though detailed rules are yet to be negotiated:

- safeguard measures
- rules for government procurement
- disciplines on subsidies
- disciplines for domestic regulations

Services negotiations proceed on the basis of requests and offers; that is, countries request each other to consider liberalisation in particular sectors, and respond with offers. Agreement to liberalise is not reached until all participating Members are satisfied with the total package being offered. The offers point towards the direction, in which a Member is willing to liberalise. However, the offers have no legal status and can be withdrawn or amended at any time. In formulating the offers, Members are not obliged to respond positively to any particular request. Nor is there any requirement for reciprocity. Further, the Doha Ministerial declaration reaffirms the rights of members to regulate and to introduce new regulations on the supply of services.

One of the important changes in the negotiating approach that was agreed in the Hong Kong Ministerial meeting on December 18, 2005 is the inclusion of plurilateral approach in addition to bilateral approach requests-offer approach. Under this approach, any groups of Members (with no minimum threshold on number of Members), may present collective requests in any specific sector/mode, identifying: (i) their objectives for negotiations in that sector/mode; and (ii) the Members to whom the requests are made, as the basis for plurilateral negotiations. For each sector/mode, there can be different collective requests from different groups of Members. Like bilateral requests, such collective requests can follow a variety of formats, for example, model schedules, checklists, scheduling guides, and so on. Such collective requests are required to be submitted by an agreed date, with appropriate flexibility provided for developing country Members.

INDIA'S PRO-ACTIVE ROLE IN GATS AND CURRENT STATUS OF NEGOTIATIONS

Given an unprecedented growth in its services sector, India has pursued an offensive rather than a defensive strategy in trade liberalisation of services, especially under Mode 1 and Mode 4. It has been a forerunner in the Doha Round of multilateral trade negotiations under GATS. In the Hong Kong Ministerial Meeting it played a pivotal role in inclusion of Annex C into the main draft, which emphasises three main points:

(a) commitments under Mode one should include removal of existing requirements of commercial presence, which had hitherto militated against developing country suppliers, who find it difficult and expensive to establish companies in the country, where the service is being supplied; (b) there should be new or improved commitments in Mode four on the categories of contractual services suppliers, independent professionals, and others, again delinked from commercial presence, to reflect inter alia removal or substantial reduction of economic needs tests. These had been the demands of several developing countries, including India; (c) commitments on enhanced levels of foreign equity participation as well as 'allowing greater flexibility on the types of legal entity permitted.'

Inclusion of Annex C has implicitly changed the structure of negotiations in GATS, which had hitherto been based on voluntary unilateral commitments or bilateral requests and offers in the various modes. The request-offer negotiations can now also be pursued on a plurilateral basis.

India submitted its initial offer in ongoing services negotiations under GATS in January 2004. The offer indicated India's commitment to liberalise its economy in certain modes of supply, in sectors such as, professional businesses, engineering, tourism, and transport. India's services offer focused primarily on mode one (cross-border supply), two (consumption abroad) and four (movements of natural persons). The offer contained various horizontal limitations on mode three (commercial presence). More specifically, the offer improved market access and national treatment commitments in following sectors and sub-sectors:

(a) accounting and book-keeping services;
(b) construction and engineering services;
(c) computer services;
(d) medical and dental services;
(e) financial services;
(f) tourism services;
(g) maritime transport services.

Market access limitations under mode three were retained in these sectors, including limits on ownership of Indian firms. Moreover, in many cases national treatment commitment in mode three was kept unbound (not committed). With regard to mode four, there were almost no limitations for certain professions including business visitors, intra-corporate transferees, managers, executives, specialists, and employees of foreign companies for short periods of stay (less than one year).

However, in its Revised Offer, submitted in August 2005, there has been a substantial change over the Initial Offer, which reflects India's aggressive approach towards trade liberalisation in services. Eleven sectors and 94 sub-sectors are covered in the Revised

Offer as opposed to seven sectors and 47 sub-sectors in the Initial Offer. In Mode-three (commercial presence), India's Revised Offer covers commitments in many new services. Commitments on FDI levels have also been enhanced in existing sectors such as computer related services, engineering, Research and Development, technical testing, telecom, financial services, construction and related engineering services, and tourism services. The major sectors in which restriction on foreign investment remains are: legal, auditing and accounting, and postal services. However, with respect to retailing the government has now allowed 51 per cent FDI in single brand retailing though no formal commitment has been undertaken in GATS.

Under Mode-four, at the Initial Offer stage itself, India had made substantial improvements in its commitments, by including all the categories of natural persons like intra-corporate transferees, business visitors, contractual service suppliers, and independent professionals, specifically mentioning sectors where access is available. In the Revised Offer, further improvements have been made in the sectoral\coverage of both contractual service suppliers and independent professionals.

So far, 30 countries including India have submitted their Revised Offers. A number of Initial and Revised Offers are still pending. However, in terms of quality of offers the Revised Offers have provided few commercial opportunities and even two rounds of offers, there has been no substantial improvement, especially in areas of interest to India and other developing countries that is, movement of natural persons (mode-four) and cross border supply (mode-one).

India's efforts have been to get binding commitments in cross border supply of services (mode one) and movement of natural persons (mode four). A number of negotiating proposals were tabled at the WTO in furthering India's objectives. As for Mode four, India has been pushing for issues such as removal of the Economic Needs Test (ENT), clear prescription of the duration of stay, provisions of extension, and so on. It has often been noticed, that domestic regulations create barriers for India's service providers, even when the trading partners have taken firm commitments. Disciplining such domestic regulations is necessary to impart effective market access for Indian service providers, especially in mode-four.

With respect to Mode three, India has received many plurilateral requests for opening of a number of services. The US and the EU have made requests under mode three, asking for greater commercial presence rights in more than 10 sectors, including telecommunication, financial services, construction, and energy. However, while the demandeurs have high ambitions in terms of the market access they want, they are not willing to open up their own economies to the same degree. Moreover, whilst the EC is fully committed to the plurilateral process, the US continues to indicate the high importance they give to the bilateral request-offer, possibly because the US is unable to move at all in the Mode four plurilateral request that India et al are now preparing.

COMPETITIVENESS OF INDIA'S SERVICES SECTORS

Given the current status of GATS negotiations and building pressure to open services sectors to foreign commercial presence, it becomes important to analyse at the disaggregated sectoral level the competitiveness of the services sectors. We first examine the importance of different disaggregated services sector in the economy, with respect to their contribution to output and employment. This analysis indicates the extent to which the economy is exposed to trade through a particular sector, that is, the extent to which trade related gains and losses will transmit into the economy. A sector with low contribution to GDP and low employment potential may witness high growth in trade, but may not have a widespread effect.

The aggregate services sector witnessed a phenomenal growth in the decade of 1990s. During 1980s, services sector output grew at the rate of 6.6 per cent per annum, while during 1990s the growth rate increased to 7.5 per cent per annum. In the last ten years (1994–2004), we find, that services sector in India has grown on an average by 7.9 per cent per annum (as seen in Figure 13.1). In contrast to this, we find that in other countries like Thailand, Indonesia and China agriculture sector has grown at an average annual growth of 1.5 per cent, 1.9 per cent and 3.8 per cent, while manufacturing sector has grown at the rate of 7.2 per cent, 6.6 per cent and 12.2 per cent respectively. Corresponding growth in services sector has been 3.9per cent, 4.5 per cent and 8.9 per cent.

FIGURE 13.1 Average sectoral growth rates (1994–2004)

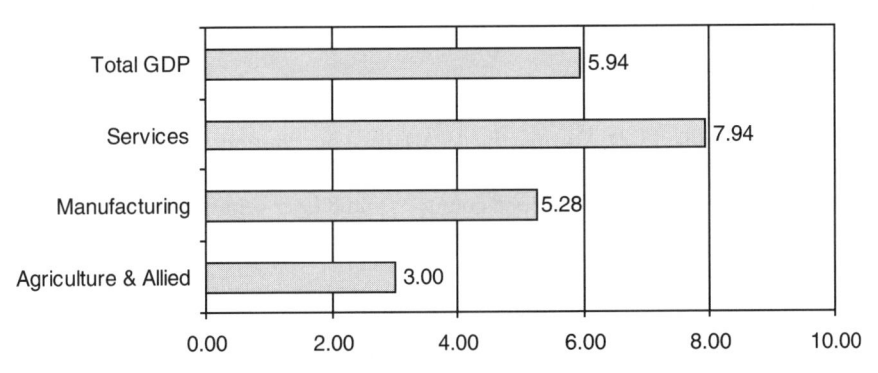

Sector	Growth Rate
Total GDP	5.94
Services	7.94
Manufacturing	5.28
Agriculture & Allied	3.00

Source: Author's estimates using CSO

However, growth in the services sector in India has not been uniform across all services. A closer scrutiny of India's service sector reveals, that amongst services, business services has been one of the fastest growing services in the 1980s closely followed by banking and insurance (as seen in Table 13.1). In the 1990s, we find that a similar trend continues for business services, which grows by almost 20 per cent, but while the growth in banking has increased, growth in insurance sector has slowed down in the 1990s. The prime drivers of growth in services, apart from business services in the 1990s, are found to be communication services (with average growth of around 13.6 per cent) and hotels and restaurants (with average growth of around 9 per cent). But, there is a fall in the growth rates of railways, dwellings and real estate, legal services and public administration, and defense in the 1990s.

Share in GDP

A striking feature of India's growth performance is that in the four decade period, 1950 to 1990, agriculture's share in GDP has declined by about 25 percentage points, while industry and services have gained equally. The share of industry has stabilsed, since 1990

TABLE 13.1 Average annual growth rates in services

	1980s	1990s
Trade (Wholesale trade and retail trade)	5.9	7.3
Hotels and Restaurants	6.5	9.3
Railways	4.5	3.6
Transport	6.3	6.9
Storage	2.7	2
Communications	6.1	13.6
Banking	11.9	12.7
Insurance	10.9	6.7
Dwellings, real estate	7.7	5
Business services	13.5	19.8
Legal services	8.6	5.8
Public administration, defense	7	6
Personal services	2.4	5
Community services	6.5	8.4
Other services	5.3	7.1

Source: CSO.

and consequently the entire subsequent decline in agriculture has been picked up by the services sector (Figure 13.2). During the 1990s, the contribution of service sector to the growth rate of GDP was almost 60 per cent in contrast to 54 per cent in middle income countries, 43 per cent in least developed countries and 34 per cent in China. High share of services in GDP is a unique feature of the Indian economy, as in other developing countries decline in agricultural sector's share has been followed by growth in manufacturing sector's share and the shift towards services sector has occurred only in the final stages of growth.

FIGURE 13.2 Average sectoral contribution to GDP

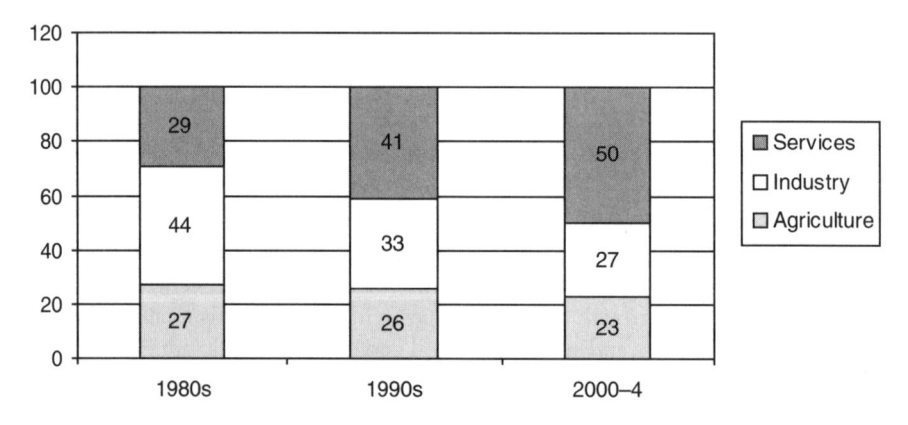

	1980s	1990s	2000–4
Services	29	41	50
Industry	44	33	27
Agriculture	27	26	23

Source: National Accounts Statistics.

Further, we find that increase in the share of services in GDP has not been the same across the board for different services in India [as seen in Figure 13.3]. Figure 13.3 compares share of different sectors in GDP in the last ten years, that is, 1993–94 and 2002–3. The most important services in terms of their share in GDP in early 1990s were trade (12 per cent), insurance (11 per cent), community services (6.5 per cent), but in 2002–3 we find, that the sectoral contributions have changed. Share of trade has increased to 14 per cent and community services to 8.4 per cent. But share of insurance has declined to 7 per cent. Other services that have witnessed a fall in their shares in 2002–3 are railways, real estate and dwellings.

FIGURE 13.3 Share of services in GDP

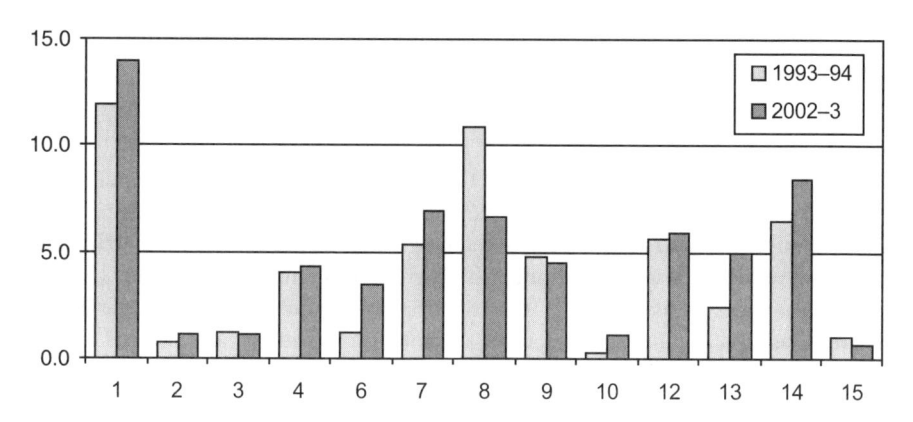

Note: Services with share less than one per cent has not been shown.
Source: Author's estimates based on *Economic Survey* and CSO.

1. Trade (Wholesale trade and retail trade in commodities both produced at home (including exports) and imported, purchase and selling agents, brokers and auctioneers)
2. Hotels and Restaurants (services rendered by hotels and other lodging places, restaurants, cafes, and other eating and drinking places)
3. Railways
4. Transport by other means (roads, water, air transport, services incidental to transport)
5. Storage
6. Communications
7. Banking (banks, banking departments of Reserve Bank of India (RBI), post office4 saving bank, non-bank financial institution, cooperative credit societies, employees provident fund)
8. Insurance (life, postal life, non life)
9. Dwellings, real estate
10. Business services
11. Legal services
12. Public administration, defense
13. Personal services (domestic, laundry, barber, beauty shops, tailoring, others)

14. Community services (education, research, scientific, medical, health, religious and other community)
15. Other services (recreation, entertainment, radio, TV broadcast, sanitary services.

What emerges from the above trends is that, services sector has grown in importance as compared to other sectors in terms of its contribution to GDP and also its growth rates since 1990s. But this growth in share of GDP differs for different services. The most important service, in terms of its share in GDP in the last decade has been wholesale and retail trade. But in terms of growth, we find that business services and communications have experienced the maximum growth in the 1990s, but their share in GDP is still quite low. Community services (which include education and health) on the other hand, have improved their share in GDP and also their growth rates in the 1990s.

Share in Employment

Growth in the share of service sector in GDP, is often followed by a corresponding growth in the share of service sector in total employment in the economy. However, in India we find that though there has been a phenomenal growth in the service sector, this growth has not been followed by a corresponding high growth in employment in the 1990s. And this rise in the share of services in employment has been much slower than the decline in the share of agriculture and manufacturing in total employment (as seen in Table 13.2). This shows that while output generation has shifted to services, employment generation in services has lagged far behind. In the year 2001 services contributed around 25.1 per cent of total employment in contrast to 30 per cent in middle income countries, 70 per cent in Singapore and around 39 per cent in Indonesia.

TABLE 13.2 Percentage distribution of workers in India: 1991–2001

	1991	2001
Agriculture & Allied Activities	66.9	56.7
Mining and Quarrying	0.6	0.6
Manufacturing	9.4	13.4
Electricity, Gas and Water Supply	0.4	0.5
Construction	1.9	3.7
Services	20.8	25.1
Wholesale retail trade; & repair work, Hotels and Restaurants	7.1	9.4
Transport, Storage & Communications	2.8	4.0
Financial Intermediation, real estate, business activities	1.1	2.2
Other Services	9.8	9.5
Total	100	100

Source: *Census of India*, 2001.

While the share of service sector in total employment was around 25.1 per cent in the year 2001, the share of employment differed for different services. In 2001, the share of services in total employment show diverse pattern: share of trade, hotels and restaurant increased from 7.1 per cent to 9.4 per cent; but in other services which include community, social and personal services it declined. Employment in Electricity, gas and water supply, and transport services has increased substantially.

Though lack of corresponding rise in employment is a unique feature of the service-led growth in India, we find that none of the empirical studies exist that explain this. Some of the plausible explanations for the slow growth of employment in the service sector can be:

(a) Are the sectors that have large potential for generating employment growing slowly?
(b) The fast growing services sectors also witness high labour productivity growth. As a result, is the employment potential lower in these sectors?
(c) Is trade positively affecting the growth in those services that do not have large potential for generating employment?

To test the above propositions, we will examine the trends in employment in disaggregated services. A close scrutiny of contribution of different services to employment reveals that the percentage growth of employment differs significantly across services in the period 1994–2000 as compared to the period 1983–94 (as seen in Figure 13.4). There is a fall in the growth of employment in community, social and personal services from 3.85 per cent annual growth rate in the period 1983–94 to –2.08 per cent in the latter period. Fall in employment in this sector has important implications for employment potential of the entire services sector, as this sector witnessed a rise in its growth in this period (that is, it grew by around 7.9 per cent on an average in the period 1994–2004). Another sector that has experienced a fall in its annual employment growth rate is electricity, gas and water supply. To analyse this further we look at the employment elasticities in these sectors.

FIGURE 13.4 Sectoral growth of employment in organised sector

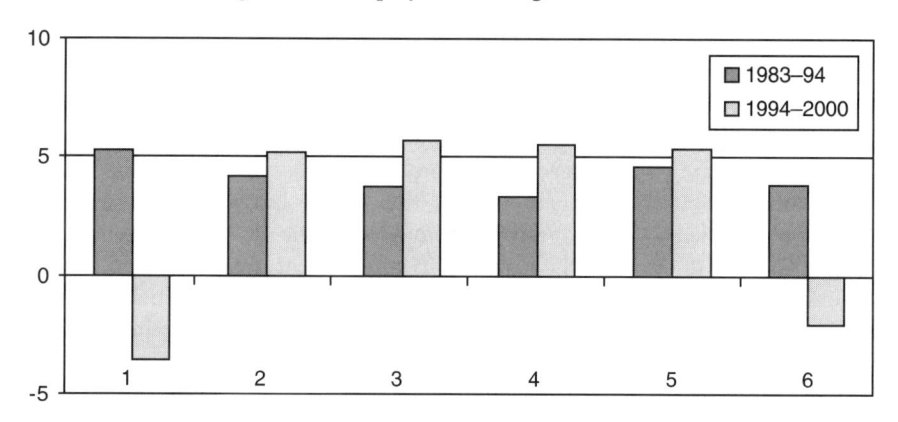

Note: 1. Electricity, gas & water supply
2. Construction
3. Trade, hotels and restaurants
4. Transport, storage & communication
5. Financial services
6. Community, social and personal

Source: Planning Commission.

Trends in employment elasticity of different services are reported in Table 13.3. The trends show, that the overall employment elasticity in the economy declined sharply from 0.41 in the 1980s to 0.15 in the 1990s. But it increased substantially in transport, storage, and communication sector. However, there has been a fall in employment elasticity in sectors that are faster growing sectors, amongst the services and have relatively higher contribution to GDP, for example, community, social and personal services, and financial services. Trade, which provided maximum employment in the service sector also, witnessed a fall in its employment elasticity.

TABLE 13.3 Trends in employment elasticity

Sector	1983–84 to 1993–94	1993–94 to 1999–2000
Agriculture	0.50	0.00
Mining and Quarrying	0.69	0.00
Manufacturing	0.33	0.26
Electricity, Gas and Water supply	0.33	0.26
Construction	1.00	1.0
Trade	0.63	0.55
Transport, storage and communication	0.49	0.69
Financial services	0.92	0.73
Community, social and personal services	0.50	0.07
Total	0.41	0.15

Source: Planning Commission.

A probable reason for fall in employment in faster growing services can be improvements in their labour productivity. But very few studies have estimated productivity growth in services, because of the reasons highlighted above. Of the few studies, a report by Mckinsey et al. (2001) estimates labour productivity in six segments of India's services sector- telecommunication, software, retail banking, housing construction, energy distribution (electricity), and retail distribution. It finds that India's software services have the highest productivity levels amongst all segments, followed by telecommunication, banking, and construction. These are also the services that are growing faster and have high shares in GDP and employment. There is a possibility that higher labour productivity in these segments may have led to slower growth in employment in the services sector. Gordon and Gupta (2004) also attribute the slow rise in employment in services to the fact, that growth in services has concentrated in those services where labour productivity has risen or are skilled labour intensive. Technological improvements and efficiency gains have further reinforced this trend.

To test the proposition, whether trade has led to growth in those services, which have lower potential for employment we examine the share of services in international transactions.

Share in Trade

In the trade mode, services trade has grown at the same rate as goods trade over the 1990s, that is, about 6.5 per cent and its share in total trade is about 24 per cent. Services exports grew by 71 per cent in 2004–5 to USD 46 billion. In 2004, while India's share in world merchandise exports was 0.8 per cent, the corresponding share in world commercial services was 1.9 per cent. India's share in world markets for IT software and services (including BPO) increased from 1.7 per cent in 2003–4 to 2.3 per cent in 2004–5 and an estimated 2.8 per cent in 2005–6 (Ministry of Finance 2007).

Due to the phenomenal rise in India's export of services in the 1990s, India' share in total world exports of services has increased overtime (see Table 13.4). We find that services exports have always been higher than services imports in India.

TABLE 13.4 India's share in world services exports

Year	Exports of India's Services in (USD bn)	Imports of India's Services in (USD bn)	India's Share in World Exports of Services
1998–99	13.20	11.02	0.99
1999–2000	17.60	11.64	1.20
2000–1	20.40	16.39	1.40
2001–2	20.70	16.08	1.30

Source: WTO, Reserve Bank of India (2003).

However, the composition of India's exports of services has changed over the years [as seen in Figure 13.5]. In the period 1990–95 to 1996–2002, we find that the relative shares in total exports of travel has fallen from 39 per cent to 23 per cent, while that of transportation services has fallen from 24 per cent to 15 per cent. On the other hand, there has been a substantial rise in the share of software services from 34 per cent to 60 per cent. In fact, India has become a net foreign exchange earner in total services after 1997–98. Services that are net foreign exchange earners are mainly travel, communication and software services while India is a net importer in services like transport, management and financial services (as seen in Figure 13.6).

FIGURE 13.5 Average share in total services exports

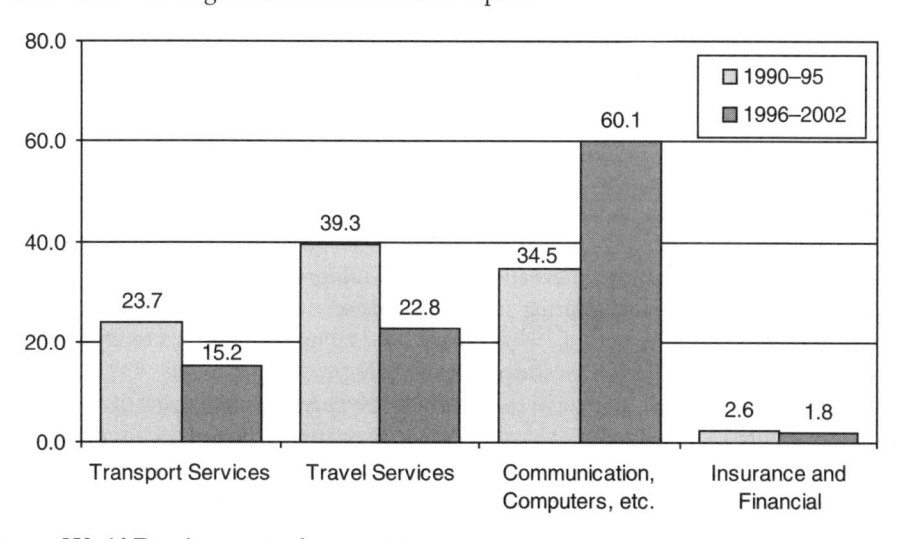

Service	1990–95	1996–2002
Transport Services	23.7	15.2
Travel Services	39.3	22.8
Communication, Computers, etc.	34.5	60.1
Insurance and Financial	2.6	1.8

Source: World Development indicators, 2004.

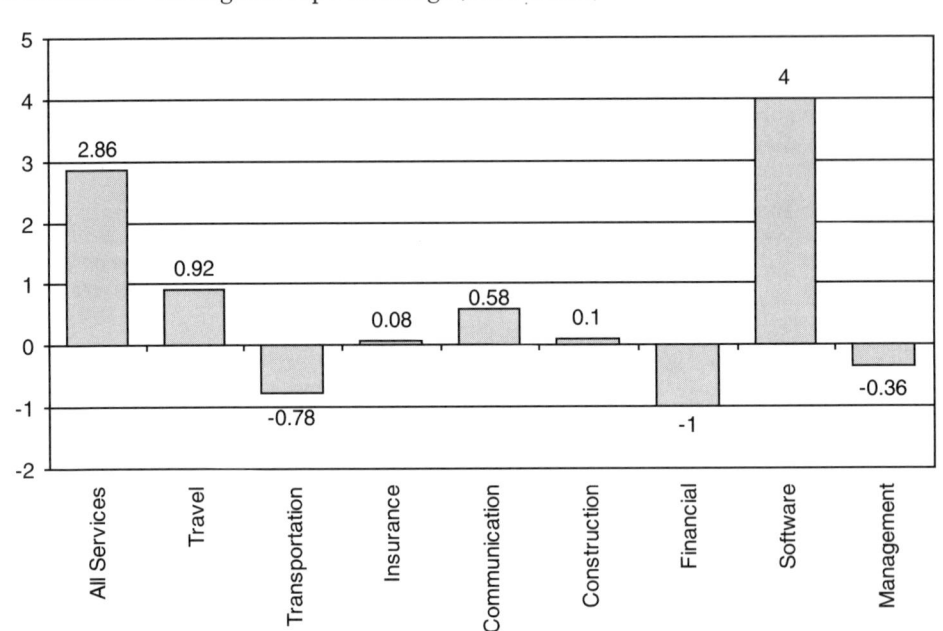

FIGURE 13.6 Average net export earnings (USD billion)

[Bar chart showing values: All Services 2.86, Travel 0.92, Transportation -0.78, Insurance 0.08, Communication 0.58, Construction 0.1, Financial -1, Software 4, Management -0.36]

Note: Average for the period (1998–99 to 2002–3).
Source: Reserve Bank of India.

According to World Bank (2004), India exhibits a strong revealed comparative advantage (RCA) in services as compared to goods. Between 1996 and 2000, the RCA index for services increased by 74 per cent while that for goods declined by 15 per cent. This increase in RCA of services was mainly on account of 'other business services' which include software exports (IT and BPO), finance, communication, management, consultancy, and telecommunication sectors.

Share in FDI

Along with trade, there has been a large inflow of FDI into India since 1990s onwards. India has been ranked in top ten FDI destinations in the World Investment Report (2004). However, this Increase in FDI inflows has been accompanied by a change in the structure of FDI. Following the international trend, FDI inflows into India are also shifting increasingly away from manufacturing sector, towards services sector. The average share of services in total FDI in the period 1990–94 increased from 10.5 per cent to 28.3 per cent in the period 1995–99 (World Investment Report 2004).

But, the inflow of FDI into services sector has been biased towards few of the services sectors (see Figure 13.7). Sectors that have received largest approvals, are telecommunications and financial services. Within telecommunication, the largest recipient is cellular mobiles. One of the striking features of India's FDI flows is the growing proportion of outward FDI from the services sector. The share of services in total FDI outflow increased to around 45 per cent in the period 1999–2003, in which non-financial services constitute around 36 per cent, trade is around 5 per cent and the rest was from financial and other services.

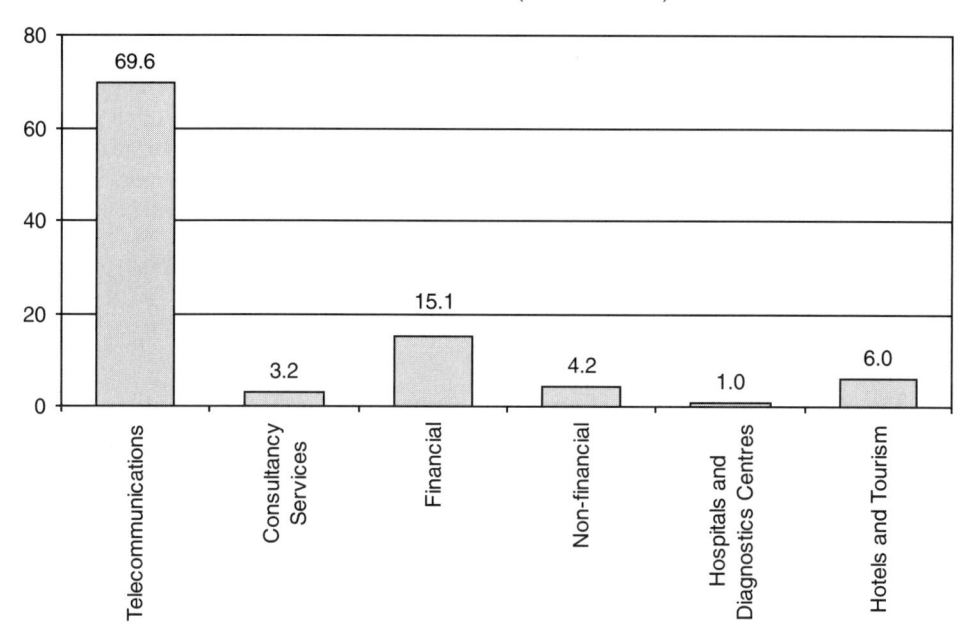

FIGURE 13.7 Share of services in inward FDI (1991 to 2002)

Sector	Share
Telecommunications	69.6
Consultancy Services	3.2
Financial	15.1
Non-financial	4.2
Hospitals and Diagnostics Centres	1.0
Hotels and Tourism	6.0

On the whole, the above trends bring out an interesting picture. Services sector in India has been the fastest growing sector in the last decade. It has contributed maximum to the growth of GDP. But in spite of contributing more than 50 per cent to GDP, it provides less than 25 per cent of total employment and has only around 40 per cent share of total gross capital formation. Within services sector, we find that the fastest growing services sector in the 1990s have been trade, communications, financial services, business services, and community services like health and education. However, out of these sectors, employment elasticity has declined in the later half of the 1990s in trade, financial services and community services. And out of the faster growing services, we find that it is only the communication services that have witnessed growth in their share in exports and FDI during this period. Trade therefore, has not improved the growth of services that have high employment elasticities.

NEGOTIATIONS IN MODE 3: POLICY FRAMEWORK

India's strategy in trade negotiations mainly in Mode three, which is sector-specific, should now be viewed with the competitiveness of the services sectors. The above analysis shows that multilateral trade negotiations undertaken by India in Mode three mainly focus on sectors like telecom, finance, computer related services, engineering services, and tourism services. These are also the services that have grown faster in the previous decade. However, though these services have indirect linkages with the other sectors, they do not directly contribute much to the GDP and nor do they have large employment potential. Trade-led growth in these sectors does not transmit widely and therefore social gains in terms of employment are not achieved to the extent required.

Trade in services can be restricted by external constraints, as well as domestic constraints. Growth in services along with high level of liberalisation point to low external and domestic constraints to the sector. External trade barriers are mainly in the form of limits on foreign equity participation, recognition and licensing of provisions, immigration and labour market regulations, and discriminatory treatment with respect to taxes, subsidies, and other policies. While domestic constraints may result from infrastructure inadequacies, poor quality and standards, lack of clear-cut responsibilities between center and state governments and other policy-related disincentives. The lower the domestic constraints the higher will be the level of competitiveness of the domestic services provider.

To identify the competitive sectors where trade liberalisation under Mode three can be committed and may have a widespread impact in terms of growth in output and employment, we categorise the services sectors in terms of their extent of liberalisation, growth and share in exports (Table 13.5).

The extent of liberalisation of services is captured by the FDI cap and restrictions on trade in Mode four. The period considered for extent of liberalisation is post 1997, as many services were liberalised since and average share in exports is estimated for the period 1997–2003.

TABLE 13.5   Categorisation of services: extent of trade liberalisation and growth

	Substantially Liberalised	Moderately Liberalised	Less than Moderately/Restricted
High growth (10 per cent and above)	Software services ↑ Telecommunication →	Banking →, Insurance →, Travel ↑, Health ↓, Education ↓	
Moderate Growth (5–9 per cent)			Legal ↓
Low growth (0–5 per cent)	Transport (road) ↓	Construction ↓, Air Transport →	Professional services ↓ like Postal, Accountancy, etc. and Rail Transport ↓

Note: ↑ High share in exports of services (10 per cent and above)
→ Moderate share in exports of services (5–9 per cent)
↓ Low share in exports of services (less than 5 per cent)

Table 13.5 shows, that the services that have witnessed substantial to moderate liberalisation, do not necessarily experience high growth rates. Software services, telecommunication services, and road transport have low external trade barriers but though software and telecommunications have experienced high growth rates, road transport has low growth rate. Moderate liberalisation has been experienced by services like banking, insurance, travel, health, education, construction, and air transport services. Though many of these services experienced high growth rates, construction, and air transport services experienced low growth rates. However, services that face high trade barriers have mostly experienced low growth rates, especially professional services and rail transport that are still restricted services.

We also classify services according to their share in total exports of services. The arrows in Table 13.5 indicate the share of services in total exports of services. An interesting picture emerges from this classification. We find that not all services that have low external trade barriers and high growth rates have high share in exports. In particular, we find that health and education services have low external trade barriers and experience high growth rates, but have low share in exports. This reflects high domestic constraints in these services. There exist high potential to trade in these services but domestic policies or infrastructure restricts trade.

Further, we find that there are services that are less than moderately liberalised or are restricted with high external trade barriers and low growth for example, professional services like legal, accountancy and rail transport. These services also have low share in exports, which reflect both domestic as well as external constraints to their trade. Construction services are also found to have low growth and low share in exports though external trade barriers have been somewhat lowered for them.

We now examine the different categories of services identified by the framework and examine in brief the kind of domestic and external constraints which exist in terms of non-trade barriers in these categories.

Substantially Liberalised with High Growth and High Share in Exports: Telecommunications, Financial Services, Software Services and Travel

These services constitute mainly the financial infrastructure of India. A large number of reforms have taken place in these services and these sectors have grown rapidly in terms of their share in GDP, exports and FDI. India's comparative advantage in these services, stems from its endowment of skilled and low cost labour resources. Given the nature of opportunities in these sectors, it is evident that cross-border supply, commercial presence, and movement of natural persons play an important role in exports of these services. Some of the specialised studies on trade in these services are Kathuria (2004) (for telecommunication services), and Ahuja and Juetting (2002) (for insurance services). These studies examine both external, as well as domestic constraints, on trade in these services. We tabulate the major external and domestic constraints to trade in these services as follows:

TABLE 13.6 Major external and domestic constraints to trade

Sector	External Constraints	Domestic Constraints
Telecommunications	Fully owned foreign firms allowed in some segments, though voice telephone services continue to have 49 per cent FDI limit. No restrictions on number of providers.	Some policy uncertainty on tariff, inter-connected regimes, USOs remain. Regulator has established credibility.
Financial services (Insurance)	Somewhat restrictive, with foreign equity limit of 26 per cent in most segments.	Minimum capitalisation norms; Funds of policy holders to be retained within the country; Compulsory exposure to rural and social sectors and backward classes; Penetration remains low.
Financial services (banking)	Private domestic equity limited to 49 per cent and foreign equity limited to 74 per cent with 10 per cent voting rights. FDI and portfolio investment in nationalised banks subject to overall statutory limits of 20 per cent.	Mandatory priority sector lending and rural branch requirements for domestic banks; High operational costs and low profitability in public sector banks; slow privatisation process; insufficient convergence of financial products and services; problems with the legal and regulatory framework, especially with regard to debt recovery and market misconduct.

Moderately Liberalised with High Growth but Low Share in Exports: Health and Education

These services have experienced moderate liberalisation, have high growth but low share in exports. This suggests, that there are substantial domestic constraints to trade in these services, but there is also a high potential to trade in these services. Chanda (2001) has examined the trade in health services, while Deodhar (2001) has examined the trade potential in educational services in India.

At present India's trade in health services occurs mainly from mode four, that is movement of health personnel and mode two, that is, inflows of foreign patients for treatment in India from developed and developing countries. The exports of health services based on mode four is due to the recognition of Indian medical personnel around the world, for their skills and training. India's exports of health services also take the form of consultancy presence and establishments overseas. But trade via cross-border is at present very limited, due to mainly technological and infrastructure constraints. On the import side there is as yet no large-scale foreign commercial presence in India's health service sector. The constraints identified by the studies are as follows:

TABLE 13.7 Major external and domestic constraints in health and educational services

Sector	External Constraints	Domestic Constraints
Health and Education Services	No explicit barriers on commercial presence of foreign firms, but restrictions on foreign service providers under Mode four.	Responsibilities divided between the Centre and States; Absence of a Standardised accreditation system; regulations concerning accreditation and licensing requirements for foreign health service providers; economic and local market needs tests and manpower planning tests

India has potential to expand trade, in both health and education services, under all four modes of supply, provided some of the major constraints are removed. Telecommunication reforms, including reduced connectivity costs and lower tariffs will expand the scope for cross-border supply for these services. However, one should keep in mind that for a developing country, particularly India, increase in outflow of medical personnel could exacerbate the 'brain drain' problem in this sector with adverse implications on the availability and quality of services available. There is a need to ensure that export earnings from this mode are realised and those who go abroad also return. There is also a concern that opening health center may increase the cost of treatment which would in turn have an adverse impact on the poor. Thus, liberalisation should be preceded by the establishment of adequate standards, a quality assurance system, and strengthening of public health care system.

Liberalised with Low Growth and Low Share in Exports: Construction Services and Road Transport

Construction services and road transport constitute a significant share of GDP in many countries. In India, these are important sectors in terms of their employment generation and share in GDP. However, growth in these sectors has been very low and they have low share in trade. Global trade in these services is largely dominated by developed countries, for example, Europe and Japan given their technological capabilities and financial strength. Developing countries have a negligible presence, except for South Korea. Mukherjee

(2001) has examined the trade in construction and consultancy services and identified the following constraints:

TABLE 13.8 Constraints in construction, engineering services and transport

Sector	External Constraints	Domestic Constraints
Construction and related Engineering Services	100 per cent FDI allowed in all segments except real estate where no FDI is permitted.	Price preference to PSUs, as well as a large number of barriers that are external to the sectors: land ceiling; unclear land titles; minimum area restrictions; minimum capitalisation norm; restriction on repatriation; lack of capital; low investments in R&D.
Transport	Restrictions vary significantly across segments. 100 per cent FDI in maritime and road transport but significant restrictions in air and rail transport.	Restrictions on inter state movement of goods; Overlapping responsibilities and coordination issues between government departments (e.g., multi-modal transport).

The main source of comparative advantage for India in construction services are the availability of low cost unskilled and semi-skilled labour and supply of cheap and competent professionals with good command of English. But to exploit these advantages, India needs to upgrade the skills and technology in these areas, strengthen financial base of Indian companies and remove barriers to migration flows. One of the major constraints faced by Indian construction is lack of finance. Most of the international companies invest heavily in research and development and this in turn increases their competitive edge. On the other hand, Indian companies have to depend heavily on import of technology. On the import side, there is considerable scope for expanding India's imports of construction and ancillary services. Commercial presence via joint ventures can have a beneficial impact on the technology and skills in the domestic construction services sector.

Restricted Liberalisation with Low Growth and Low Share in Exports: Legal, Accountancy and Postal Services and Rail Transport

These services are characterised by restricted liberalisation with low growth and low share in exports. Trade in these services is limited by high domestic, as well as, external constraints. One of the common features in these services is that they are under public domain and have limited exposure to both domestic and external competition. Very few studies have examined the constraints to trade in these services. We will provide the constraints identified by Mitra and Zutshi (1999) for trade in legal services; Anant and Zutshi (1999) for trade in accountancy services; and Mukherjee and Sachdeva (2004) for trade in land transport services (Railways)

TABLE 13.9 Constraints in legal services

Sector	External Constraints	Domestic Constraints
Legal Services	Highly restricted. Restrictions on foreign service providers under Mode 4. Prohibitions on partnerships with enrolled professionals of foreign countries.	No effective regulation on non-litigating lawyers; limitations on size and liabilities of legal firms.

(Contd)

(Table 13.9 Contd)

Sector	External Constraints	Domestic Constraints
Accountancy	Foreign service providers not allowed to undertake statutory audits.	Only partnership firms allowed with number of partners limited to 20.
Postal Services	FDI regime open for courier services and closed for postal services.	Price preferences to state postal operators; No functional demarcation between regulator and service provider; Imprecise definition of USO.
Transport (Railways)	significant restrictions in air and rail transport; limited cross country movement of passengers and freight; restrictions on Mode 4.	Public monopoly; Inadequate resources; overstaffing; technological backwardness in freight traffic; high freight charges; high custom duties on rolling stocks.

India's trade in legal and accountancy services is negligible at present, but the prospects of trade are promising. Trade in legal services can expand in many ways. National firms may increasingly employ foreign lawyers. But more importantly, India's legal services exports via mode four can expand considerably given its advantage as a country with British legal culture, lawyers with good command over English, adversarial legal procedures followed by the Indian Bar and the Bench. There is scope for exports of legal services via mode one, that is, via internet. Legal transcriptions, transmission of legal documents via telecommunication devices, and growth in electronic commerce will make possible electronic delivery of many legal services.

On the whole it can be said that infrastructure services in India (for example, transport services and construction) are slow growing services and have low share in trade, in spite of the efforts to lower external trade barriers in these services. This indicates that these services have high domestic constraints that impede their growth and trade. The domestic producers may not be very competitive in these sectors therefore liberalisation must proceed in a phased manner in these sectors.

However, financial infrastructure of India appears to be stronger and services like software, banking, insurance, and telecommunications show low external trade barriers and high growth rates with high to moderate share in total exports. But health and education services though have high potential for trade suffer from considerable domestic constraints that do not allow higher trade in these services. Professional services are restricted and have low growth and low share in trade.

CONCLUSION

India is now in the process of undertaking further trade liberalisation in its services sector. In the on-going plurilateral negotiations, it has submitted requests for opening up of markets in computer services, health services, energy, and architecture and engineering services. Requests have been submitted by the country in two of the four modes, that is, Mode one and Mode four. The EU and US on the other hand have made plurilateral requests to India for greater commercial presence rights, that is, Mode three in more than 10 sectors including telecommunications, financial services, construction, and energy.

Given the options and pressures on India to undertake further commitments under Mode three of trade in services, the chapter has examined the competitiveness and preparedness of different services sectors for undertaking further liberalisation. Domestic as well as external constraints in terms of non-tariff barriers have been highlighted in each sector.

One of the weaknesses in the policy formulation, with respect to services that has probably led to lopsided growth in services sector, is the fact that there is no overall coherent policy with respect to services in India. Due to lack of an integrated services policy, in line with the industrial policy and agricultural policy, reforms in India at the sectoral level have evolved in an ad-hoc manner rather than as part of an overall strategy. Consequently, the depth and pace of reforms lack uniformity across sectors.

There is now a dire need to undertake reforms in a structured manner and accordingly undertake multilateral commitments. Sectors that have high potential for trade, but suffer from domestic constraints should be targeted for further liberalisation but in a phased manner and only after removing the domestic constraints. Some of these sectors are health and education. However, domestic regulations need to be in place before multilateral commitments are undertaken in these sectors. Further, sectors, which have large employment potential; suffer from low growth and have low potential to trade because of long existing state monopolies and corresponding weak domestic producers should be strengthened and exposed to domestic competition, before any multilateral commitments are undertaken with respect to them. Emergence of strong domestic players is needed for the sector to gain from the presence of foreign firms.

Endnotes

[1] 23.2 per cent in 1995–2000, compared to the world rate of 3.7 per cent

[2] Trade Act of 1974 stated that the term 'international trade' includes trade in both goods and services.

[3] The definitions, which could have an important bearing on whether GATS rules were applicable in a particular case, include 'supply of a service' ('production, distribution, marketing, sale and delivery of a service') and 'juridical person' (the definition would not count a legal entity as being owned by nationals of a particular member unless they held 50 per cent of its equity or controlled by nationals of a Member unless they had the power to name a majority of its directors or otherwise to legally direct its actions).

References

Ahuja, R. and Johannes Juetting. 2002. *Design of Incentives in Micro Health Insurance Schemes*, Discussion Paper, Bonn: Center for Development Research (ZEF).

Anant and Zutshi. 1999. *Report on Trade in Accountancy Services*, Project Study sponsored by Ministry of Commerce, Government of India and executed by ICRIER.

Bhagwati, Jagdish N. 1984. 'Splintering and Disembodiment of Services and Developing Nations', *World Economy*, vol. 7, no. 2, pp. 133–43.

Chanda, R. 2001. 'Trade in Health Services', Working Paper no. 70, ICRIER, pp. 1–118.

Deodhar, Satish Y. 2001. 'GATS and Educational Services: Issues for India's Response in WTO Negotiations', IIM-A Working Paper, 3 October 2001.

Gordon, J. and P. Gupta. 2004. 'Understanding India's Services Revolution', IMF Working Paper no. WP/04/171.

Kathuria, 2004. 'Trade in Telecommunications Services Opportunities and Constraints', ICRIER Working Paper no. 14.

McKinsey & Co. 2001. *India—The Growth Imperative: Understanding the Barriers to Rapid Growth and Employment Creation*.

Ministry of Finance. 2007. *Economic Survey 2005–06*, New Delhi: Government of India.

Mitra and Zutshi. 1999. 'Trade in Legal Services', Project Study sponsored by Ministry of Commerce, Government of India and executed by ICRIER, WP 338.9 IND-T.

Mukherjee, Arpita. 2001. 'Trade in Construction and Consultancy Services: India and the GATS', ICRIER Working Paper no. 75.

Mukherjee, Arpita and R. Sachdeva. 2004. 'Trade in Land Transport Services: Railways'. ICRIER Working Paper no. 119.

Sapir, A. and C. Winter. 1994. 'Services Trade', in *Surveys in International Trade, Blackwell Economic Theory and the Role of Government in East Asian Industrialization*, edited by D. Greenaway and L. Winters, Princeton: Princeton University Press.

United Nations. 2004. *World Investment Report: The Shift Towards Services*, New York and Geneva: United Nations.

14

GATS Negotiations in Environmental Services: A Developing Countries Perspective with Special Reference to India

Aparna Sawhney

INTRODUCTION

Environmental services constitute one of the twelve sectors in the GATS targeted for liberalisation since the Uruguay Round. The main *demandeur* of the WTO environmental negotiations in general and environmental services in particular has been the European Commission, supported by Japan, Switzerland and Norway. Few countries, however, made commitments in the environmental services under the GATS in 1994, since the sector was considered to be rather new and wrought with sensitive issues regarding basic services like water and sanitation.

The current WTO negotiating mandate on environmental services, is contained in paragraph 31(i) of the 2001 Doha Ministerial declaration, which seeks 'the reduction or, as appropriate, elimination of tariff and non-tariff barriers to environmental goods and services'. The liberalisation of environmental goods and services is part of the larger environmental agenda in the trade negotiations, whose main *demandeur* the European Commission has had a clear agenda on trade and environment: First to legitimise environmental standards and regulations in goods trade; second to fold in multilateral environmental negotiations into the multilateral trade regime; and third to increase market access in environmental goods and services. At Doha, the scope of the last two issues were narrowed and Members agreed to negotiate: the relationship between existing WTO rules and specific trade obligations set out in the multilateral environmental agreements; and the reduction or, as appropriate, elimination of tariff and non-tariff barriers to environmental goods and services (under paragraph 31, i and iii respectively) with a view to enhancing the mutual supportiveness of trade and environment.

The reduction/elimination of tariff and non-tariff barriers to environmental goods and services is one of the most critical issues in the current Doha negotiations, since this sector is one of the largest and most diffused economic sectors. The negotiation issues and outcome will determine the future rules of the WTO trading regime, and impact a whole host of sectors (like chemicals, engineering, construction, consulting, research and development); and issues (like subsidies, government procurement), which are been negotiated within the WTO separately.

The environmental services industry is a fairly new economic sector in terms of its nomenclature and classification. Indeed the term environmental industry was coined in the 1990s by the OECD in trying to define the sector in its own right, given its rapid growth in the 1980s. The environmental goods and services sector includes a wide range of economic activities, so the OECD and Eurostat defined the environmental industry, to consist of equipment and services which measure, prevent, limit, and correct environmental damage to air, water, and soil, including problems relating to waste, noise, and ecosystems. As the broad definition suggests, the environment sector is diffused across several traditional economic sectors, which makes market estimation rather difficult. Moreover, the provision of environmental services is dispersed across both the public and private sector realms.

During the Uruguay Round, four basic sub-sectors were specified: sewage services, refuse disposal services, sanitation services and other environmental services. The OECD countries, most prominently the European Commission, had pushed for a broader coverage of environmental services in the Uruguay Round classification, beyond the four basic classification under the GATS. Consequently the WTO Secretariat Note in 1998 clarified the initial GATS category of 'other environmental services' to include some of the services listed separately in the OECD/Eurostat classification, like remediation services and noise abatement services. Thus the four basic GATS environmental services segments were clarified as:

A. Sewage services (CPC 9401), *excludes* collection, purification and distribution services of water and construction, repair and alteration of sewers.
B. Refuse disposal services (CPC 9402), *excludes*: dealing and wholesale in waste and scrap; Research And Development services on environmental issues.
C. Sanitation and similar services (CPC 9403), *excludes*: disinfecting/exterminating services for buildings, pest control for agriculture.
D. Other environmental services, including four sub-sectors namely cleaning of exhaust gases (CPC 9404); noise abatement services (CPC 9405); nature and landscape protection services (CPC 9406) but excludes forest and damage assessment and abatement services; and others not classified elsewhere (CPC 9409).

The OECD segments, namely 'water for human use' (collection, purification and distribution services of water); 'recycling services' (under solid and hazardous waste management services) and 'protection of biodiversity', were not included under the GATS classification since they cover services that are sensitive in nature. For instance, in the provision of water for human use, sewerage system for households, social equity needs to be ensured since water and sanitation are essential and basic consumption needs of a population. While privatisation and liberalisation may facilitate the provision of drinking water in an efficient manner, public intervention remains a significant factor in ensuring that, provision of essential services like drinking water is socially equitable. Indeed complete privatisation and liberalisation of the water sector (treatment and purification) is a rare phenomenon.

The GATS negotiations in the environmental services sector began in earnest, following its inclusion in the Doha Ministerial declaration in paragraph 31(iii) in 2001. Since the commencement of the Doha negotiations, several developing countries, including India have offered to open this sector. In the Doha Round, GATS negotiations in environmental services, however, some OECD countries have followed the Eurostat seven-fold classification and included the segments of 'water utilities' and 'recycling' in their initial offers and requests. In a more recent request made to developing countries in 2006, liberalisation in water utilities or 'water for human use' has not been explicitly included. Developing countries nonetheless, continue to encourage privatisation and participation of mature environmental multinational corporations in infrastructure environmental services like water and wastewater management services.

THE GLOBAL ENVIRONMENTAL MARKET AND NEGOTIATING INTERESTS OF WTO MEMBERS

In 2005, the global environmental goods and services sector was valued at US$652 billion, with the environmental services sector accounting for more than half the total value (EBJ, 2006, 1). The global environmental services industry is dominated by the US, Western Europe and Japan, where large multinational service providers have the bulk of the market share. However, emerging economies, including those of Central and Eastern Europe, Latin America, and Asia-Pacific region (especially China and India) have experienced the most vibrant growth in their environmental markets in recent years. In 2005, these emerging economies accounted for 14 per cent of the global environmental market compared to only 8 per cent in 1994 (ibid).

The interests of the negotiating Members on the liberalisation of environmental goods and services are based on the level of maturity of their respective domestic environmental industries. The global Environmental Goods and Services (EGS) industry is dominated by developed countries, with the US, Western Europe and Japan accounting for 85 per cent of the total world market. The most significant environmental services, by value of the total global market, are water, wastewater treatment and solid waste management services. The mature environmental firms from the industrialised countries have a comparative advantage in the export of resource-saving and clean technologies, and in technical expertise in the design and engineering of treatment and purification facilities. As the domestic environment markets in OECD countries reach saturation, exports from the environmental firms in these countries were seen as a significant growth factor.

Moreover, considering the cross-cutting nature of the sector, the environmental sector promises to be one of the fastest growing sectors of the future. Not surprisingly, the EU in its 2005 service liberalisation requests to 103 WTO Members noted that environmental services are a 'key sector' for the European Commission especially since European companies are 'world leaders' in this sector.

In the developing countries, the environmental goods and services sector is still at the stage of initial development. There is little scope for a level playing field for these relatively new and small firms, considering the OECD environmental firms are large multinationals with deep pockets. However, the environmental sector in the developing countries stands to gain from imports of cleaner technology that can be adapted to the local conditions. While developing countries will remain net importers of environmental goods and services, there is scope for some niche exports in both environmental goods and services.

The technological and competitive edge of the environmental service firms in the world market is linked to the stringency of environmental regulations enforced in the parent countries. The environmental industry in Western Europe, Japan and the US took off in the 1970s and emerged as the leading markets in the 1980s, following the enforcement of stringent environmental standards and regulations. The environmental equipment and services industry identified the opportunity to grow as an independent industry driven by a new competitive advantage of less-pollution and green-consumerism in the market.

By the 1990s, however, the industrialised country markets showed signs of maturity and growth rates declined. Not surprisingly, the environmental corporations of these countries began diversifying into other regions with promising market prospects. Growth opportunities in countries of Asia (excluding Japan), Latin America, Africa and more recently Eastern Europe, became of particular interest since the environment sector in developing countries offered double digit growth rates.

In terms of size of the national and regional environmental industry, the US is the largest in the world, followed by the EU, and Japan (see Table 14.1). In 2004, the US accounted for 38 per cent of the global environmental industry by value, while the share of Western Europe and Japan were about 28 per cent and 16 per cent respectively—the three regional markets together accounting for 82 per cent of the global industry (EBJ 2006: 3). The environmental sector in the developing countries of Asia, Latin America and Africa are rudimentary, although growing rapidly. In 2004, the Asian developing countries constituted 6 per cent of the global environmental market. Among the developing countries today, China has one of the fastest growing environmental markets in the world, but much like the other emerging nations it remains dependent on imports for the state-of-the-art technology, largely from France, Germany, Japan and the US.

TABLE 14.1 The global environmental market by region, 2004

Region	US$ billion	Share (percentage)
United States	240.8	38.34
Canada	16.5	2.63
Germany	46.5	7.40
United Kingdom	30.3	4.82
France	27.2	4.33
Italy	18.7	2.98
Spain	12.1	1.93
Rest of Western Europe	45.2	7.20
Japan	98.8	15.73
China	13.4	2.13
South Korea	7.7	1.23
India	4.7	0.75
Taiwan	4.5	0.72
Rest of Asia	7.7	1.23
Brazil	6.6	1.05
Mexico	4.4	0.70
Rest of Latin America	5.6	0.89
Australia, New Zealand	10.1	1.61
Russia	4.5	0.72
Poland	3.7	0.59
Rest of Central & Eastern Europe	4.8	0.76
Middle East	9.4	1.50
Africa	5.5	0.88
Total	**628**	**100**

Source: EBJ 2006, 3.

Environmental services that require large-scale investment due to economies of scale (and that support the emergence of natural monopolies) are provided by a small number of large firms in the global market. In sewerage services for instance, collection and distribution network investment is economical only for a single large operator. Considering the scale benefits due to large capital investments and technological development, there has been a tendency towards increasing concentration in the environmental industry. Small firms are abound in environmental service segments, like analytical services and consulting.

The size distribution from large to small firms in the environmental services industry is found in all countries, developed as well as developing. However, the largest environmental firms in the world are from the industrialised nations, and being mature, these firms are also some of the most competitive globally. While environmental firms from developing nations are also growing rapidly, they remain largely dependent on technology imports from the developed nations.

The largest environmental corporations in the world are from Germany, France, Japan, UK, and the US, and have been exporting equipment, technology and services worldwide (for example, Suez, Veolia, Rheinisch-Westfälisches Elektrizitätswerk). These large environmental multinational firms typically provide integrated products and services, and account for about 50 per cent of the global environment market by value, while the other half is accounted by the smaller firms (UNCTAD, 1998). The large integrated corporations dominate a few environmental service segments, like water and wastewater treatment. On the other hand, specialised environmental services, including analytical services and consulting, are widely provided by both medium-sized and small firms, who are often sub-contractors for large projects.

DEVELOPED AND DEVELOPING COUNTRIES IN THE ENVIRONMENTAL SERVICES NEGOTIATIONS

International trade in environmental services through foreign direct investment (GATS Mode 3 for commercial presence) in developing countries has been the main market access issue in the current WTO negotiations. With mature corporations from developed countries exploring growing markets in developing countries, the developed countries have been requesting for greater market access in Mode 3, and where feasible in Mode 1 (cross-border supply).

Following the Uruguay Round, few countries had made commitments in the environmental service sector under the GATS. By the year 2000, before the Doha Round commenced just about 44 per cent of the WTO Members had made at least one commitment in the sector. Commitments in the sector came mostly from the developed country members. The low number of commitments is comparable to other sensitive social sectors in the GATS, like health and education services.

Up until now, most WTO Members still have not made any commitment in the environmental services sector, especially the developing country members. However, these countries have undertaken liberalisation measures within the sector and also made offers recently to open the sector in the current negotiations, like Argentina, Brazil, India, Indonesia, Malaysia, and Philippines.

Developed countries have a liberal market access regime, in terms of foreign investment for the environmental services sector, and their GATS commitments reflect this. The restrictions, however, feature in terms of movement of natural persons/professionals (Mode 4), as well as cross-border supply (Mode1). Among the developed country Members, the European Commission has made full commitments in environmental services (sewage, refuse disposal, sanitation, and other services) in Mode 3 but kept Mode 4 unbound. In the EC's offer, dated October 2007, Mode 1 and Mode 4 are unbound for most states, while Modes 2 and 3 are open for most states (unbound for the emerging East European Members) (WTO 2007). So while foreign investment has no limitations, environmental professionals face restrictions.

It is important to note that trade in environmental services is closely tied to trade in environmental equipment and technology, since services are often offered in an integrated manner with equipment. The extent of liberalisation in environmental services is determined by both general and sector-specific foreign investment requirements (for example, engineering and construction sector relevant for building waste treatment facilities); and its duty structure for environmental equipment. Within the general investment policy, regulations on the level of foreign ownership and licensing requirements for foreign company operations in sensitive areas of public services (water and sanitation) are especially important.

The typical trade barriers in environmental services include those, that impinge on foreign commercial presence and employment of foreign nationals. Market access limitations in commercial presence or, foreign investment include foreign equity ceilings, exclusivity provisions, type of legal entity permitted and also political sensitivities related to private commercial partnership in the area of infrastructure environmental services like water and sanitation. The Mode 3 restrictions are more significantly imposed by developing countries. Developed countries have imposed Mode 4 restrictions, while otherwise maintaining a more liberal regime in commercial presence.

Considering the different types of market access barriers imposed on the environmental services sector by WTO member countries, the highest incidence is that of restrictions on the nature of legal entity, joint venture requirements, and restrictions on foreign capital participation; followed by limitations on geographical coverage, licensing requirements, and quantitative restrictions like limiting the number of suppliers, operators, value of transactions and number of natural persons (Adlung and Roy 2005, Table 2).

For instance, in countries like Germany, France, UK, and the US, the environmental services sector is open in terms of foreign investment, except for market access restrictions in public environmental services segment (like drinking water) and the movement of environmental professionals. The leading environmental corporations in the world are from Western Europe and the US, and with the home country markets reaching saturation, these corporations have been investing in emerging economies with growing environmental markets. Not surprisingly, the GATS commitments and the current negotiation offers of these developed countries reflect an open regime, and their requests to the developing world ask for greater market access in Mode 3.

Developing countries, by comparison, have not formally liberalised this sector to the same extent as developed countries. However, they have been encouraging foreign investment in environmental infrastructure services like water and sanitation, and importing environmental technology and expertise in this sector. Through the 1990s private participation in infrastructure services was encouraged by Asian and Latin American developing countries, often through multilateral lending agencies.

Foreign direct investment in water and sewerage services in developing countries has closely followed the trend to increase private participation in infrastructure services. Rapid growth was witnessed in the mid-1990s in Latin American and Southeast Asian countries (like Malaysia, Philippines, and Indonesia). However, FDI in these infrastructure environmental services fell off sharply in the late 1990s, following mounting discontent in these developing countries, due to water price hikes and issues of inequity.

Large developing countries like India and China have been unilaterally following a fairly liberal regime in environmental services. Foreign direct investment in environmental infrastructure services like sewage and sanitation have been encouraged in both countries, more so in China in recent years to develop world-class city centers, in the run-up to the Olympic Games in 2008 among other reasons. China also made commitments in several segments of environmental services under the GATS in 2002, after becoming a WTO Member.

The less than full liberalisation in the environmental services sector, followed by developing countries has largely resulted from their apprehensions regarding the privatisation of sensitive services like water and sanitation. Since water and sanitation services are essential services for human livelihood, they have traditionally been in the realm of the public sector. While the developing countries require private capital investment in these infrastructure services, given the paucity of public funds, there is a risk that private businesses may not ensure complete service coverage or an equitable price for these services.

Indeed private-public partnership projects in water and sewerage services witnessed the highest incidence of cancellations or distress among all infrastructure projects with private participation in developing countries during the last fifteen year. By December 2004, since 1990 about 37 per cent of total investment flows into developing countries for water and sanitation, were cancelled or under distress due to difficulties in setting and maintaining the price of water at cost-recovery levels (World Bank 2005b, 3). These difficulties reflect the political economy of infrastructure pricing, since services like water and sanitation are essential services that have to be provided at affordable prices to the public at large, but eventually need to be financed by the consumers through either charges or taxes. Thus initial exercises in liberalising environmental infrastructure services in developing countries especially in East Asia and Latin America witnessed a setback in the late 1990s. Most notably, only China has maintained its liberalisation trend and continues to attract one of the largest foreign investments in environmental services today, besides East European countries.

Thus in the developing countries, the most significant negotiated market access barrier continues to be in foreign investment or commercial presence (Mode 3). Some developing countries have made more liberal offers in Mode 3, notably China, which made a fairly liberal multilateral commitment in the environmental services sector under the GATS in 2002. However, foreign commercial presence (Mode 3) is permitted only in the form of joint ventures, though foreign majority ownership is allowed. There are no restrictions in cross-border supply (Mode 1) of environmental consultation services. Notably China excluded the segment of environmental quality monitoring and pollution source inspection services in its commitments.

Not surprisingly, in current GATS negotiations in environmental services, the developed countries have been requesting for greater market access in Mode 3 (commercial presence), and where feasible in Mode 1 (cross-border supply). In developed countries, like the European Commission, Mode 3 is open but limitations are imposed in Mode 4 (movement of natural persons). In 2006, plurilateral requests from the developed countries (including Australia, Canada, European Commission, Japan, Korea, Norway, Switzerland, Chinese Taipei, and the US) to developing countries specifically asked for the opening up of sewage, refuse disposal, sanitation, cleaning of exhaust gases, noise abatement, nature and landscape protection, and other environmental protection services.

As indicated earlier, in developed countries, like the European Commission, Mode 3 is open but limitations are imposed in Mode 4. Considering the fact that developing countries are typically constrained in capital and net importers of capital, complete liberalisation in Mode 3 abroad does not hold much promise.

Developing country environmental service providers are keen on gaining market access in developed countries, independent of commercial presence. For instance, contractual service suppliers and independent professionals face restrictions in visa and work permit applications. Developing countries have in turn requested European Commission to liberalise Mode 4 for environmental services, including sewage, refuse disposal, and sanitation services. In a recent joint submission at the WTO, several developing countries have sought increased commitments from the developed countries and de-link movement of personnel with commercial presence (Mode 3). The de-linking is particularly relevant for developing countries, which lack capital resources to establish commercial presence and hence find it difficult to exploit Mode 4 opportunities arising out of commercial presence in the host country. (WTO 2005b, 2005c) Such de-linked categories would include contractual service suppliers, and independent professionals.

CASE OF THE INDIAN ENVIRONMENTAL SERVICES AND GATS NEGOTIATING STANCE

Today the water sector, including water purification and wastewater treatment, is one of the key environmental services sector in India. In 2008, the Indian water market was estimated to be more than $4 billion (US Commercial Service 2008, 36). The water transmission and distribution networks are in a state of disrepair, and viewed with significant market potential by foreign multinationals.

During the 1980s, when the environment industry was experiencing rapid growth in the developed countries and gaining maturity, the Indian environment sector was barely taking form. With the establishment of the national environmental regulatory institution in the 1980s in India, and increasing environmental awareness, a market demand for environmental cleanup and pollution prevention began to emerge, and so the domestic environmental goods and services industry began to take shape.

In the 1990s, the government's deregulation policies in private participation in environmental infrastructure services, like water and waste management,[1] and expansion of the domestic environmental legislation have helped increase the demand for environmental services (as well as equipment). In particular, the industry demand for pollution control equipment, along with the associated demand for environmental services in India, has been a result of stricter regulations and laws; while the increase in demand for infrastructure environmental services resulted from the policies of decentralisation and private-public partnerships adopted by the government in the 1990s. As in other developing countries in East Asia and Latin America, large infrasatructure projects in urban water and sanitation have been financed by multilateral and bilateral agencies, though to a lesser degree.

The Indian environmental services industry consists of two sets of firms: large engineering firms offering environmental services as part of their equipment or technology package for pollution treatment; and smaller firms specialising in environmental consulting services. The larger firms offer environmental services as an integrated package through large turn-key consulting projects. Such comprehensive project design and management includes the provision of engineering, construction, equipment, and operation and maintenance of general utility facilities, such as water, pollution, and waste management systems for industrial clients. These Indian firms are typically well developed and large in terms of staff and scale of operations.

Small scale firms, however, dominate the Indian environmental industry making it a rather disorganised sector overall. These small firms lack the resources to invest in research and development, as well as marketing and servicing infrastructure. The small environmental service firms offer consulting services related to environmental management systems facilitation, environmental audits, environmental impact assessment, and development of environmental standards.

The Indian environmental sector also has joint venture companies, as well as wholly owned foreign subsidiaries. Some large Indian firms have entered into joint ventures with Western companies, to facilitate technology and expertise transfer, while some Western companies have also started setting up wholly owned subsidiaries following the government's policy of 100 per cent FDI in environmental equipment manufacturing and consulting/management services. Leading multilateral environmental corporations have been attracted by the growing domestic maket in India. The main exporters of environmental equipment, services and technology are from the US, Germany, Japan, UK, Canada, and Australia. American and West European firms have also established their presence through partnerships with Indian firms. Wholly owned subsidiaries include Pentair Water India Ltd, Hindustan Dorr-Oliver Ltd, IRG Systems South Asia Ltd, and Tetratech India Ltd.

The Indian environmental sector however has limited technological capability, with only the large firms having technology licensing agreements or joint ventures with leading global environmetnal corporations. The Indian environmental services sector is dependent on technology imports from industrialised countries, as domestic research and development remain rather low. For instance, in the water sector the U.S is the principal source of imported water treatment equipment (US Commercial Service 2008, 36)

The existing Indian trade regime allows foreign direct investment in environmental management, and consulting services is allowed with upto 100 per cent foreign equity holding through the automatic route. In July 2005, the government further opened up the environmental infrastructure services in new township construction with 100 per cent equity in 'built-up infrastructure and construction development projects…including city and regional level infrastructure' under the automatic route.[2] The foreign investment in infrastructure environmental services like sewage and sanitation, however, has often been routed through the government's Foreign Investment Promotion Board. Investment under the automatic route in India signifies that central government approval is not required, and reflects the underlying decentralisation and promotion of private participation in infrastructure services at the state and municipal levels.

Despite the encouragement of private partnership in environmental infrastructure projects in India, the cumulative foreign investment in private-public partnership projects in water and sewerage projects during 1992 through 2004 is reported to be only

US$223 million, less than 10 per cent of that in China or Malaysia in the same period.[3] However, unlike the experience of most East Asian and Latin American countries, which witnessed large scale cancellations in infrastructure environmental service projects (notably Philippines), there have been no reported cancellations in India.

In terms of environmental technology imports, India ranks among the top twenty importers for the US, which is one of the leading exporters of environmental technology in the world. In 2004, India's imports of environmental technology from the US were valued at US$257 million having increased by 66 per cent over two years from US$155 million in 2002.[4]

On the whole, the Indian environmental services industry is a rather young sector although growing rapidly. The sector is not quite organised like other mainstream service sectors like banking or transport services. Most of the firms are small, but some large firms have also emerged in the sector. However, in comparison to the leading multinational environmental corporations, the large Indian environmental services firms, are a small fraction in terms of size. The small-size of the environmental firms in India limit their capacity to exploit foreign markets due to the lack of marketing and infrastructure of after-sales services. Moreover, Indian environmental technological capabilities are not recognised nor accepted in the world markets.

The Indian environmental sector, much like other developing countries, largely imports technology from industrialised countries. With Research and Development being low among the domestic firms, indigenous technology development is not yet remarkable and the state-of-the-art technology continues to be imported. The most preferred route of technology-transfer for the Indian industry has been through the joint-venture route. Indeed, joint-venture has been the preferred policy route for China, which allows foreign investment in environmental services only through this arrangement, to ensure the development of the national firms and prevent fully owned foreign subsidiaries from cornering the market.

Finally, due to the lack of market reputation Indian environmental firms face the challenge competing with old established incumbent firms in the global market. The global environmental market is dominated by a few large multinational corporations. The mature firms have the advanatage of an established clientele and can indulge in market practices to keep out new firms. For a new generation of environmental service firms, as in the case of India, the lack of past record, experience and third party guarantees make it difficult for these firms to penetrate the more developed markets in Europe and North America.

Not surprisingly, most of the outward-looking Indian firms have been focusing on exploring foreign markets nearer to home, in the Middle East and Asia, rather than Western Europe or the US. However, the prospective Indian environmental investors face stringent restrictions in Mode 3 in other developing countries. For example, Malaysia, Philippines, Thailand, have equity limitations on foreign investment. Much like India, other developing countries are also dependent on import of environmental technology from the US and Western Europe. Thus, the export potential is somewhat limited, though some Indian firms have been exporting to integrated environmental services to South East Asian countries, as well as the Middle East.

Indian Negotiating Position

India began the environmental services negotiations on a cautious stance, and did not make commitments in the sector under the GATS in 1994. The sector was also excluded in India's initial offer in 2003 under the Doha Round. Yet, unilaterally India has continued to maintain a fairly liberal trade regime and allowed foreign direct investment in infrastructure and non-infrastructure environmental services.

In 2005, however, in the revised offer under the Doha negotiations, India opened the two segments of refuse disposal and sanitation services. The scheduling of these two environmental segments can be seen as a response to repeated requests from the developed country Members, especially the European Commission and US. Considering these segments had been open even before they were scheduled, this does not bring in any major change for the domestic market. However, it does have significant implications in terms of India's negotiating position.

The revised offer in environmental services has signaled to the other WTO Members that India is committed to a more liberalised regime, and that the developed countries need to make a better offer on their part to match her substantially improved offer.

India, along with other developing country Members had made a Mode-4 specific request to a target group of countries (including the US, EU, Australia, Canada, Japan, New Zealand, Switzerland, Norway, and Iceland), which included the three environmental service segments of sewage (CPC 9401), refuse disposal (CPC 9402) and sanitation (CPC 9403) among other indicative service sectors. The collective request sought new and improved market access for contractual service suppliers (CSS) and independent professionals (IP) categories de-linked from commercial presence. Yet, the revised offers by the developed countries have failed to accommodate this request. So to the extent India has made substantial improvement in her revised offer, her negotiating position to ask for greater access in Mode 4 is stronger.

It is also important to note that the two segments excluded in the revised Indian offer are sewage services and other services. The first excluded segment, namely sewage services, is contentious and sensitive by nature since it is related to water for human use, and a segment where there has been widespread discontent (cancellations) in foreign contracts in South East Asia and Latin America. Indeed, in the 2006 plurilateral requests to developing countries, the developed countries (including Australia, Canada, European Commission, Japan, Korea, Norway, Switzerland, Chinese Taipei, and the US) specifically asked for the opening up of sewage, refuse disposal, sanitation, cleaning of exhaust gases, noise abatement, nature and landscape protection, and other environmental protection services—but excluded any request for water for human use (that is, collection, purification, and distribution of natural water). The second excluded segment, namely other services, covers environmental consulting services, which is a rapidly growing domestic segment. So the exclusions can be seen as a part of continued cautious stance.

The impasse in Doha negotiations since July 2006, suggests that the developed countries are unwilling to further liberalise their own markets, as indicated by their stance in the agricultural negotiations. Such a stance is not a welcome sign in terms of its implications for the environmental services sector. In particular, the environmental services is a sector fraught with social equity issues and universal provision (in water and sanitation), and developing countries like India will continue to be net importers while their domestic industries try to reach a more competitive stage.

To make the talks move forward, India needs to explore the coalition route with other developing countries (like the G-20 in agriculture), especially since the developing countries share the similar challenges and concerns in the liberalisation of environmental services. In terms of needs, developing countries have incomplete coverage of essential environmental services of water and sanitation (some more than other), and require capital and state of the art technology. In terms of export interest, developing countries have a comparative advantage in labour-intensive environmental services, which they would like to exploit in the industrialised markets through Mode 4 concessions.

LIBERALISATION OF ENVIRONMENTAL SERVICES AND SUSTAINABLE DEVELOPMENT

The liberalisation of environmental services is inherently connected to the concept of development and sustainability issues since it covers pollution control activities. In particular, environmental services like water and municipal waste management are essential services that need to be provided to every citizen of the country. Similarly, to ensure a basic quality of life of the people, the ambient air quality needs to meet the health standard. Not surprisingly, the provision of these essential environmental services forms an integral part of the Millennium Development Goals.

For instance, in India the current provision level of environmental infrastructure services is rather poor, and there exists inequity in the level of provision of these services between the urban and the rural populations. In 2002, only 30 per cent of the total population had access to improved sanitation (definition of an improved facility range from simple but protected pit latrines to flush toilets with a sewerage connection), with the provision in rural areas particularly lacking where only 18 per cent of the population had such access, while 58 per cent of the urban population improved sanitation (World Bank 2005a). Access to improved water (definition of improved source range from a household connection, public standpipe, borehole, protected well or spring, or rainwater collection)[5] is better by comparison, with 86 per cent of the total population having improved access. The growth of environmental infrastructure services is critical in developing countries in order to improve the basic quality of life of the population.

The growth of the domestic environmental services sector also has direct environmental and ecological benefits. For instance, in India untreated wastewater is perhaps the most widespread pollution problem. Indiscriminate disposal of wastes and effluents in the waterways by both the industry and municipalities has led to severe degradation of surface and groundwater. Improving the treatment facility of local government bodies, both rural and urban, and cleaning up services of contaminated waterways, would go a long way in improving the state of the current environment, and enhance the quality of life of Indians, and reducing the number of productive days lost due to ill-health.

Extending the provision of essential environmental services is only possible through expansion of the supply capacity of the environmental service sector. Such an expansion has direct benefits through employment and income generation, since the sector is quite labour intensive. While the establishment of a water and sanitation network is capital intensive, the maintenance services are labour-intensive. Thus there are both direct health benefits as well as economic benefits through an expansion of the environmental services sector. However, the experience of Latin American and Southeast Asian developingc countries like Bolivia, Malaysia, and Phillippines suggests that the policies of privatisation and liberalisation in environmental services by themselves will not be successful in the ultimate goal of building capacity in essential environmental infrastructure (Sawhney 2007). Other fiscal and developmental measures are required to ensure water and sanitation is accessible for the large sections of poor population within the country.

CONCLUDING REMARKS

At the face of it, liberalisation of environmental services seems to offer a win-win solution to boosting world output and enhancing environmental protection activities directly. Considering the gross under-provision of environmental goods and services in developing countries, liberalisation of this sector seems to be the perfect answer to improving the provision of essential environmental services like clean water and sanitation to the population in these countries.

The negotiations in the liberalisation of environmental services at the WTO, however has proceeded along the lines of typical horse-trading, often reflecting no link with sustainable development. This is primarily driven by the way in which multilateral trade negotiations take place in the WTO, and secondly due to the broad nature of the sector in question. The environmental services sector is one of the largest and most diffused economic sectors, having deep linkages to other sectors like industrial equipment, embedded technology, chemicals, engineering, construction, consulting, research and development. The environmental goods and services negotiation agenda in the Doha Round has shifted gears in recent years to incorporate environmental challenge of climate change. The focus has been turned onto climate change mitigation-related trade liberalisation, with renewable energy technology and equipment being one of the key categories of environmental goods and services now, besides wastewater, solid-waste management services, etc.

Considering the broad scope of economic activities and sectors, the negotiation outcome of liberalisation in EGS will determine the future rules of the WTO trading regime, and impact a whole host of other sectoral negotiations. Not surprisingly, developing countries have treaded rather cautiously, and have refrained from committing or even offering to open up the environmental services sector completely.

The liberalisation of the environmental service sector has to be pursued in the context of the domestic development parameters, including economic, social, and ecological dimensions. While greater liberalisation is often seen as enabling factor for the growth of an efficient sector, it holds true only when there is pure competition. In the case of environmental services, the global market is anything but a perfectly competitive market. The international sector is dominated by a few large and mature corporations. Thus it is unlikely that new and emerging environmental firms of developing countries will face a level-playing field in case the sector is completely opened.

The current impasse in environmental services negotiations in the WTO reflects the unwillingness of the developed countries to further liberalise their own markets in Mode 4 for environmental services. While they have requested developing countries to liberalise trade in equipment (mostly generic industrial products) classified as environmental goods and asked more a more open investment regime for environmental services projects under

Mode 3, they have resisted offering a commensurate freer movement of professionals under Mode 4. Such a stance is not conducive to a successful conclusion of the Doha Round since export interests of developing countries are not adequately reflected nor integrated in that approach. A more attractive negotiation offer from the developed to the developing countries would include better market access in Mode 4 for environmental professionals, since the latter have export potential in labour-intensive services. To reflect the development dimension of the Doha Round and the founding principle of sustainable development of the WTO, the environmental negotiations need to proceed on a more integrated manner, and give due attention to the export interests of developing countries.

Endnotes

[1] The decentralisation policy in India, following the 74th Amendment of the Constitution in 1992, has provided greater autonomy to municipal and local governments to encourage private participation in utilities, including water and saanitation. Financially constrained urban local bodies (ULBs) in particular have welcomed private investment, both domestic and foreign, to expand the service provisions of sewage, sanitation, cleaning of roads and water supply.

[2] The investment is conditional on a minimum size of US$ 10 million for wholly owned subsidiaries and $5 million for joint ventures with Indian partners. Foreign Exchange Management Regulations 2005: Notification No. FEMA 136/2005-RB dated 19 July 2005.

[3] Country Snapshot Reports for 1990–2004, Private Participation in Infrastructure Database, World Bank, http://ppi.worldbank.org.

[4] US Trade Statistics, website http://web.ita.doc.gov/ete/eternfo.nsf/VWQFbySector.

[5] Unimproved sources include vendors, tanker trucks, and unprotected wells and springs. Reasonable access is defined as the availability of at least 20 liters per person per day from a source within one kilometer of the dwelling.

References

Asian Development Bank. 2005. *Asian Environmental Outlook 2005: Making Profits, Protecting Our Planet*, Manila: Asian Development Bank.

Adlung, Rudolf and Martin Roy. 2005. 'Turning Hills into Mountains: Current Commitments under the GATS and prospects for Change', WTO Economic Research and Statistics Division, ERDS-2005-1.

Environmental Business Journal. 2006. 'Global Environmental Markets', vol. XIX, no. 5–6.

Sawhney, Aparna. 2003. 'Liberalization of Environmental Services', Country submission at the UNCTAD Expert Meeting on Definitions and Dimensions of Environmental Goods and Services in Trade and Development, Palais des Nations, Geneva.

———. 2007. 'Building Supply Capacity for Environmental Services in Asia: The Role of Domestic and Trade Policies', Issue Paper no. 5, Geneva: International Centre for Trade and Sustainable Development.

UNCTAD. 1998. 'Strengthening Capacities in Developing Countries to Develop Their Environmental Services Sector', United National Conference on Trade and Development Document no. TD/B/COM.1/EM.7/2, 12 May 1998.

US Commercial Service. 2008. 'India Country Commercial Guide 2008', US Commercial Service, US Department of Commerce, June 2008, http://www.buyusa.gov/india/ccg2008.html.

World Bank. 2005a. *World Development Indicators 2005*, Washington DC: World Bank.
_____. 2005b. 'Public Policy for the Private Sector', Note no. 299, Washington DC: The World Bank.
WTO. 2006. 'Summary Report on the Fourteenth Meeting of the Committee on Trade and Environment in Special Session', Note by the Secretariat, TN/TE/R/14, February.
_____. 2005a. 'Summary Report on the Thirteenth Meeting of the Committee on Trade and Environment in Special Session', Note by the Secretariat, TN/TE/R/13, October.
_____. 2005b. 'Assessment of Mode 4 Offers of Members: Communication from Bolivia, Chile, Colombia, Dominican Republic, Guatemala, India, Indonesia, Mexico, Pakistan, Peru, Philippines, and Thailand', Council for Services Special Session, Job (05)/131, 30 June.
_____. 2005c. 'Environmental Benefits of Removing Trade Restrictions and Distortions', Note by Secretariat (Addendum), WT/CTE/W/67/Add.1, March.
_____. 1998. 'Categories of Natural Persons for Commitments under Mode 4 of GATS: Communication from Argentina, Bolivia, Brazil, Chile, Colombia, India, Mexico, Pakistan, Peru, Philippines, Thailand, and Uruguay', Council for Services Special Session, TN/S/W/31, February.

Section VI

Growth, Poverty and Inequality

15

Trade and Poverty in the Poor Countries

JAGDISH BHAGWATI AND T. N. SRINIVASAN

While freer trade, or 'openness in trade, is now widely regarded as economically benign, in the sense that it increases the size of the pie,[1] the recent anti-globalisation critics have suggested that it is *socially malign* on several dimensions, among them the question of poverty. (see Bhagwati 2002)[2]

Their contention is that trade accentuates, not ameliorates, and that it deepens, not diminishes, poverty in both the rich and the poor countries. The theoretical and empirical analysis of the impact of freer trade on poverty in the rich and in the poor countries is not symmetric, of course. We focus here only on the latter. In doing so, we distinguish between two different strands of argumentation: static and dynamic.

STATIC ARGUMENTS

The central effect on poverty is assumed to come from the effects on real wages of the unskilled workers, endowed with labour, but no human or financial capital. The natural presumption following the Stolper-Samuelson argumentation, would be that, if anything, freer trade should help in the reduction of poverty in the poor countries which use their comparative advantage to export labour-intensive goods. This, in fact, is the central message of Anne Krueger's (1983) findings from a multi-country project on the subject of the effects of trade on wages and employment in developing countries.

Another approach also suggests, that trade is beneficial for poverty reduction in the developing countries. Much empirical evidence suggests that inflation hurts the poor in these countries. It is equally clear that, if a country wishes to maintain an export-promoting, as distinct from an import-substituting, strategy (so that it is generally speaking opting for freer trade), then it will have to maintain macroeconomic stability. Thus, such macroeconomic stability must be regarded as endogenous to the policy choice in favor of freer trade.[3] Therefore, commitment to an outward-oriented trade policy indirectly assists the poor since they are vulnerable to inflation.

DYNAMIC ARGUMENTS

The more direct and salient analysis of the problem, however, has been in the growth context. Here, the central argument has proceeded in two steps: trade promotes growth; and growth reduces poverty.

This article is reprinted from *American Economic Review*, vol. 92, no. 2, May 2002, pp. 180–83.

In regard to the former, there are ample precedents for this hypothesis. Thus, Dennis Robertson (1940) long ago characterised trade as an 'engine of growth.' In regard to the latter, one could go back to Adam Smith (1776 1937, 81), who argued that when society is 'advancing to the further acquisition ... the condition of the labouring poor, of the great body of the people, seems to be the happiest.' In modern times, the favorable link between growth and poverty has been the underpinning of the Indian planning efforts that began as far back as the mid-1950's.[4]

As one can readily imagine, it is easy to write down models which refute each of the foregoing two hypotheses; and in fact there is no dearth of such models. The real question then, as always but even more tellingly here, is which models get at the reality. Here, we would argue that the empirical evidence is more persuasively in support of the two propositions we have just stated. We therefore consider first the theoretical arguments and then the empirical evidence.

THEORETICAL POSSIBILITIES

Theoretical models of the effects of trade and growth, whether in steady state (that is,., long-term) or out (that is, short-term), lead to different possibilities. Thus, in the Harrod–Domar model, if labour remains slack permanently and trade affects only efficiency in the use of resources, the growth rate will be permanently enhanced because of the lasting decline in the marginal capital-output ratio. On the other hand, in the Robert Solow (1956) economy, trade has no permanent effect, and the steady-state growth is independent of it. For an analysis of how trade policy works in different models of exogenous and endogenous growth, see Srinivasan and Bhagwati (2001).

Generally speaking, the effects of trade policy on growth must proceed through links between trade and the two 'fundamentals': accumulation and innovation (in the use and productivity of resources). There are several reasons to think that trade will affect both favourably. Thus, the increased variety of inputs available from trade will enable an economy to get around constraints placed on access to such variety under protection, when absence of scale economies can reduce the available variety from domestic production alone. Then again, high protection is likely to constrain the marginal efficiency of capital by confining sales to domestic markets compared to open economies, where the world defines the market, thereby reducing the rate of investment.[5]

As for the effect of growth on poverty, again different models are possible. If labour is in elastic supply to the growing areas, as in the Arthur Lewis model, then growth will pull more of the reserve army of labour into gainful employment. If growth is modeled in a way such that it does not affect a segmented pool of the poor, as in tribal areas that are not linked to the mainstream or in inner cities which are structurally delinked from the main city where growth is occurring, then growth will pass the poor by. Growth may even immiserise the poor further, when the poor are working on tiny plots of land to produce farm products, whose prices fall because of the larger farms implementing the Green Revolution.

TRADE, GROWTH AND POVERTY: EMPIRICAL EVIDENCE

Regarding trade and growth, the best evidence is to be found in the detailed country studies pioneered by the OECD project directed by Ian Little et al. (1970) and the National

Bureau of Economic Research (NBER) project directed by Bhagwati and Krueger. The recent reliance on cross-country regressions, by contrast, produces mixed evidence in both directions: for example, Jeffrey D. Sachs and Andrew Warner (1995) and Jeffrey Frankel and David Romer (1999) are on the positive side, and Anne Harrison (1996)[6] and Francisco Rodriguez and Rodrik (1999) are skeptical, the latter even leaning to being opposed. However, as we have argued in Srinivasan and Bhagwati (2001), in riposte to the criticisms from Rodrik, the cross-country regressions are a poor way to approach this question. The choice of period, of the sample, and of proxies, will often imply many effective degrees of freedom where one might almost get what one wants if one tries hard enough!

Nonetheless, it is interesting that practically no country that has been close to autarkic, has managed to sustain a high growth performance over a sustained period. Furthermore, the work of David Dollar and Aart Kraay (2002) notes that, if one classifies countries into globalisers and nonglobalisers, by reference to their relative performance in raising the trade share in GNP during 1977–97, the former group has shown higher growth rates. Failure, like success, has many fathers, and no one cause will ever explain big outcomes like growth. Nonetheless, the many reasons why autarky would put a country behind, make these empirical observations quite salient.[7]

The evidence on growth and poverty is best approached through focus on the two countries: China and India. The vast majority of the world's poor live in the rural areas of these two countries. Both countries achieved significant reductions in poverty during 1980–2000 when they grew rapidly. According to World Bank (2000, Table 4–2) estimates, real GDP grew at an annual average rate of 10 per cent in China and six per cent in India during these two decades. No country in the world had as rapid growth as China, and fewer than ten countries exceeded the Indian growth rate. The effect on reduction in poverty in both countries was dramatic, entirely in keeping with the 'Bhagwati hypothesis' of the early 1960's that growth is a principal driver of poverty reduction. Thus, according to the ADB (2000 table 3–1) estimates, the incidence of poverty in China, by standard measures, declined from 28 per cent in 1978 to 9 per cent in 1998. By the Government of India's (Ministry of Finance 2000, Table 5) estimates, poverty incidence fell from 51 per cent in 1977–78 to 27 per cent in 1999–2000.[8]

It is also relevant that these were also the decades in which both China and India increased their integration into the world economy. In fact in the previous three decades (1950–80) India's autarkic policies alongside other damaging policies (such as extreme interventionism and controls and proliferation of an inefficient public sector in economic activity well beyond utilities),[9] were associated with an annual growth rate of only 3.5 per cent, with the natural consequence that the incidence of poverty fluctuated around 55 per cent with no declining trend.

Obviously, the experience of the two giant economies of China and India in achieving faster growth and reduction in poverty, through greater integration into the world economy, treating such integration as an opportunity rather than as a threat, is salutary. According to Dollar (2001), other economies such as Vietnam and Uganda have had similar experiences. Indeed, Dollar (2001, 17) argues that the only developing countries that have registered significant declines in poverty are those that also have integrated faster into the world economy on the dimensions of trade and direct investment. The opponents of trade who allege that it accentuates or bypasses poverty are therefore not credible.[10]

Endnotes

[1] The most prominent skeptic on this question is Dani Rodrik. We have controverted his arguments, at least to our satisfaction, in Srinivasan and Bhagwati (2001).

[2] The social issues and agenda include the impact on gender questions, on democracy, on labour rights or standards, and on culture.

[3] We believe that this is the correct causal way to regard the link between macroeconomic stability and trade performance: there are several cases of macroeconomic stability and absence of a policy of outward orientation, such as the Communist countries and India, but none of successful outward orientation and absence of macroeconomic stability. For an early statement of this view (and an argument that one of the reasons why outward orientation is usually better in overall economic performance than lack of it is due to the macroeconomic stability that it requires), see Bhagwati (1978). We thus reject the argument recently advanced by Rodrik that it is macroeconomic stability, not outward orientation, that matters in better performance: not merely does he ignore the fact that the link has already been discussed in the literature on trade strategy, but we believe he also gets causality wrong.

[4] The link between growth and poverty reduction can be found in the writings of many of India's leaders such as Jawaharlal Nehru. But the precise argument that rapid growth was the principal (though not an exclusive) way of targeting poverty among the bottom three deciles, and assuring them a 'minimum' standard of living, was a result of the work by one of us (Bhagwati) in 1961–62 in the Indian Planning Commission (see Bhagwati, 1988, 2000a).

[5] This argument, explaining the contrasting rates of accumulation and hence growth rates in East Asia and in India, is developed at length in Bhagwati (2000b).

[6] Hanison has a detailed tabulation of, and useful commentary on, the empirical studies up to 1996.

[7] Rodrik has suggested that such associations prove little, since growth may have led to trade, rather than the other way around. The sophisticated in-depth country studies at the OECD and the NBER, however, suggest that trade did matter causally. There are also good reasons to believe that the outward-orientation of the Far Eastern strategy, which led to the Asian miracle, was critical in the story, as developed in Bhagwati (2000h).

[8] A commonly used indicator of poverty is the headcount ratio (i.e., the proportion of the population with monthly consumption expenditure or income per head below a poverty-line expenditure. Angus Deaton (2001) finds that this ratio registered a significant decline in 1999–2000 compared to 1977–78.

[9] The full range of inefficient policies, going well beyond the lack of outward orientation in trade and direct foreign investment, was discussed in the early work of Bhagwati and Padma Desai (1970) and Bhagwati and Srinivasan (1975). An overview is provided also in Bhagwati (1993) and Srinivasan (2000), among several contributions to the analysis of Indian economic policy failings.

[10] We have not considered here the management of trade liberalisation to get to freer trade. A valuable analysis of this problem, to ensure that the poor are not harmed, is provided by Neil McCulloch et al. (2001).

References

Asian Development Bank. 2000. *Asian Development Outlook*, Manila: Asian Development Bank.

Bhagwati, Jagdish. 1978. *Foreign Trade Regimes and Economic Development: Anatomy and Consequences of Exchange Contrast Regimes*, Cambridge, MA: Ballinger.

_____. 1988. 'Poverty and Public Policy' (Vikram Sarabhai Lecture, 1987), *World Development*, vol. 16, no. 5, pp. 539–55.
_____. 2000a. 'Convocation Address', unpublished lecture, Panjab University, Chandigarh, http://www.columbia.edu/-jb38.
_____. 2000b. 'The East Asian Miracle that Did Happen: Understanding East Asia in Comparative Perspective', in *The Wind of the Hundred Days: How Washington Mismanaged Globalization*, edited by Jagdish Bhagwati, Cambridge, MA: MIT Press, pp. 27–49.
_____. 2002. 'Globalization and Appropriate Governance', unpublished Jubilee 2000 Lecture, WIDER, United Nations University, Helsinki, Finland.
Bhagwati, Jagdish and Padma Desai. 1970. *India: Planning for Industrialization*, Oxford: Oxford University Press.
Bhagwati, Jagdish and T. N. Srinivasan. 1975. *Foreign Trade Regimes and Economic Development: India*, New York: Columbia University Press.
Deaton, Angus. 2001. 'Adjusted Indian Poverty Estimates for 1999–2000', mimeograph, Princeton University.
Dollar, David. 2001. 'Globalization, Inequality and Poverty since 1980', background paper, Washington DC: The World Bank, http://www.worldbank.org/research/global.
Dollar, David and Aart Kraay. 2002. 'Spreading the Wealth', *Foreign Affairs*, vol. 81, no. 1, pp. 1–13.
Frankel, Jeffrey and David Romer. 1999. 'Does Trade Cause Growth?' *American Economic Review*, vol. 89, no. 3, pp. 379–99.
Ministry of Finance. 2000. *Economic Survey, 1999–2000*, New Delhi: Government of India.
Harrison, Anne. 1996. 'Openness and Growth: A Time-Series, Cross-Country Analysis for Developing Countries', *Journal of Development Economics*, vol. 48, no. 2, pp. 419–47.
Krueger, Anne. 1983. *Trade and Employment in Developing Countries*, vol. 3, *Synthesis and Conclusions*, Chicago: University of Chicago Press.
Little, I. M. D., Tibor Scitovsky and Maurice Scott. 1970. *Industry and Trade in Some Developing Countries*, Oxford.: Oxford University Press.
McCulloch, Neil, Alan L. Winters and Cirera Xavier. 2001. *Trade Liberalization and Poverty: A Handbook*, London: Center for Economic Policy Research.
Robertson, Dennis. 1940. *Essays in Monetary Ttheory*, London: King.
Rodriguez, Francisco and Dani Rodrik. 1999. 'Trade Policy and Economic Growth: A Skeptic's Guide to Cross-National Evidence', Working Paper no. W708 1, National Bureau of Economic Research, Cambridge.
Sachs, Jeffrey D. and Andrew Warner. 1995. 'Economic Reform and the Process of Global Integration', *Brookings Papers on Economic Activity*, vol. 1, pp. 1–95.
Smith, Adam. 1937. *An Inquiry into the Nature and Causes of the Wealth of Nations* [1776], London: W. Strahan and T. Cadell, reprinted with an Introduction, Notes, Marginal Summary and an enlarged Index by Edwin Cannan, New York: Modern Library.
Solow, Robert. 1956. 'A Contribution to the Theory of Economic Growth', *Quarterly Journal of Economics*, vol. 70, no. 1, pp. 65–94.
Srinivasan, T. N. 2000. *Eight Lectures on India's Economic Reforms*, New Delhi: Oxford University Press.
Srinivasan, T. N. and Jagdish Bhagwati. 2001. 'Outward Orientation and Development: Are Revisionists Right?', in *Trade, Development and Political Economy: Essays in Honour of Anne Krueger*, edited by Deepak La1 and Richard Shape, London: Palgrave, expanded version http://www.columbia.edu/-jb38.
World Bank. 2000. *World Development Indicators*, Washington, DC: The World Bank.

16

Globalisation, Growth and the Poor

T. N. Srinivasan and Jessica Seddon Wallack

INTRODUCTION

Jeffrey Williamson (2002) points out that 'the world has seen two globalization booms over the past two centuries and one bust. The first global century ended with World War I and the second started at the end of World War II, while the years in between were ones of anti-global backlash'.

The per cent of the world population living in extreme poverty (USD1 a day, inflation adjusted), meanwhile, declined from 84 per cent in 1820 (the beginning of the Williamson's first global century) to 66 per cent in 1910 (just three years before its end). The ongoing second global century, which began in 1950, saw this portion decline, from 55 per cent in 1950 to 24 per cent in 1992, and no doubt it is even lower in 2003. In the inter-war period of anti-globalisation backlash, the proportion was probably stagnant on the average. (Bourguignon et al. 2002) Although poverty estimates based on a global poverty line for a time span of more than a century are obviously subject to wide margins of error, other non-income-based indicators, such as those of health, nutrition, and literacy corroborate the broad picture.

The historical association between globalisation and poverty reduction, however, hides substantial variations among countries and also within countries in their experiences with international economic integration. Several decades of rising trade and capital flows, growing numbers of multinational conglomerates, and increasingly globalised cultural interchange have not silenced the public debate over the merits of globalisation. The violent street demonstrations surrounding the ministerial meeting of the WTO and similar protests at World Bank and IMF meetings suggest that this debate is still going strong.

Much of the debate appears to be about whether globalisation has been good for the poor. There is less debate regarding the positive effects of trade liberalisation on growth and the potential growth-accelerating effects of capital market integration, once domestic financial sectors are strengthened. Recent debates have instead focused on whether the benefits of accelerated growth reach the poor and over what time frame they do. Critics claim, that income inequality has risen with globalisation-led growth in many countries (this claim is difficult to assess without more reliable data than are available for many countries) has fuelled some of the skepticism, even though a rise in inequality need not mean that the poor are worse off than before.[1] The recognition, that growth plays an instrumental role in

---

This article is reprinted from *De Economist*, vol. 152, no. 2, June 2004, pp. 251–72.

improving the quality of life and reducing poverty, does not mean that all mechanisms and policies promoting growth also reduce poverty, or that the lags between growth acceleration and poverty reduction are short. However, it seems improbable that growth could harm the poor over the longer run.

Jan Tinbergen thought deeply on the distributional issues in general and in particular on the instrumental role of growth for poverty reduction. He argued: '... the most important single figure representing the set of [goals for improvement of the quality of life] is the rate of growth of real product in the developing world. This is because production is the source of financing social measures, because production implies elements such as food, housing, education, and other social services, because employment is directly dependent on the volume of production envisaged, and because more equal income distribution can be more easily obtained from a high than from a low average income.'

Earlier writers (for example, Lewis (1955): Appendix entitled, 'Is Economic Growth Desirable?') had also examined the pros and cons of growth from the perspective of the poor and concluded that pros outweighed the cons.

Several plausible links in the globalisation-growth-poverty reduction chain can be postulated in theory, yet the reality is far more complicated and many links could be absent in some countries, at some points in time. Agenor (2003), for example, finds that globalisation may have a U-shaped effect on poverty: while extensive integration reduces poverty, small amounts of globalisation may hurt the poor.[2] Even in theory, not all links need be unidirectional; thus, it is possible that in some links, globalisation influences growth positively, but the character of growth increases poverty. This being the case, protesters find it easy enough to blame the process of globalisation for any observed or imagined deterioration in the condition of the poor rather than look for the missing links or for other factors that could have muted or outweighed the beneficial effects of globalisation. Enthusiasts find it equally easy to argue that observed outcomes deviate from globalisations' predicted contributions to poverty reduction, only because globalisation has not gone far enough. It would seem that both sides focus selectively on some aspects of globalisation while ignoring that other processes, besides globalisation, also influence the observed outcomes. (Deardorff 2003)[3] In theory, greater international integration should play an important part in reducing poverty around the world. In practice, it has had mixed effects due to domestic policy shortcomings, continued industrial country protectionism, and limited labour market integration across countries. In practice, many of the ways in which globalisation is perceived as harmful to the poor are not intrinsic aspects of global integration. They reflect, rather, domestic policy failures such as segmented and distorted internal markets, as well as, industrial country protectionism and limited labour market integration across countries.

We have divided the paper into four sections: i) globalisation and growth, ii) growth and poverty reduction, iii) globalisation and poverty reduction, and iv) globalisation for the poor. The first section summarises the underlying theory and empirical evidence for the globalisation-growth linkage, while the second discusses empirical evidence for the connection between growth and poverty reduction sequence. While there are many mechanisms in theory for expecting greater integration to increase growth and reduce poverty, the theory is not without caveats, and the empirical evidence is not conclusive. The effect of globalisation on inequality, in particular, is ambiguous. The third section provides a conceptual analysis of how globalisation could be expected to reduce poverty by reducing market distortions that disproportionately affect the poor. We argue in the last section that remaining industrial country protectionism, particularly in agriculture, as well as continued restrictions on international labour mobility are key areas for reform.

This division simplifies the discussion of the effects predicted by economic theory and the policy changes we need to achieve these effects. There are clearly additional links among the three phenomena and all three are endogenous outcomes of varying economic and social processes of the countries.

The Poor

For most of this paper, we defined the 'poor' as those, whose income or standard of living is below what the society, in which they live, deems a minimum that all its members ought to have.[4] These standards vary widely across nations and the poorest in a rich country may be well-off from the perspective of an average person in lower-income countries. We focused on those whose resources are below country-specific poverty lines, rather than those below a global poverty line (such as USD1 a day), because the latter suffer from serious conceptual and measurement problems.

We also distinguished here between absolute poverty and relative deprivation, or inequality. Inequality can rise, even as the numbers in absolute poverty decline. Understanding effects of globalisation on relative deprivation is important, for understanding some of the obstacles to further integration, but our focus here is on how globalisation affects national poverty.[5]

GLOBALISATION AND GROWTH

The terms 'globalisation' and 'growth' lump together as several different phenomena. Globalisation might mean capital market integration, goods and service market integration, migration agreements, cultural interchange, or some combination of all of these. We referred to these separately. We similarly distinguished between forms of growth in the discussion of theory, though the empirical section does not distinguish between steady state (long-run) growth, and growth during transitions to a steady state.

Theory

There are essentially three sources of economic growth: growth in inputs of production; improvements in the efficiency of allocation of inputs across economic activities; and innovation that creates new products, new uses for existing products, or brings about more efficient use of inputs. The combination of changes in these three dimensions that brings about higher long-run growth (as opposed to short-run transition effects) depends on the characteristics of the economy. Whether or not a change in rate of accumulation of a factor of production or the efficiency of factor allocation, for example, has long-run or only transitional effects on growth, depends in part on the technology of production. An exogenous change in the rate of investment or opening the economy to foreign trade has only a transitional effect on growth in a Solow type two-factor (capital and labour) constant returns-to-scale growth model, if the marginal product of capital declines to zero as capital increases indefinitely relative to labour. On the other hand, if the technology is such, that the marginal product of capital is bounded away from zero, transitional as well as, steady state growth effects could arise from an exogenous change in investment or foreign trade policy. (Srinivasan 1995)

Being open to trade and investment contributes to each of the three sources of growth. Domestic resources are allocated more efficiently when the economy can specialise in those activities in which it has comparative advantage. By being open to capital, labour and other resource flows, an economy is able to augment relatively scarce domestic resources and use part of its abundant resources, elsewhere where they earn a higher return. Clearly, efficiency of resource use in each nation and across the world is enhanced by the freedom of movement of resources. Finally, the fruits of innovation anywhere in the world become available everywhere in such an open world. Empirical studies (for example, Coe et al. 1998) suggest total factor productivity (TFP) in poor countries, which do not have domestic research and development capacities, is higher when their trade with industrialised countries who account for the bulk of research and development in the world is greater.

Theory also suggests that globalisation and growth have a self-reinforcing relationship, in that higher growth spurs a larger volume of trade flows. While the decision to alter policies to further integration is a policy change that harnesses trade as an 'engine of growth,' trade also serves as the 'handmaiden' of growth once policies support freer interchange of goods and services.[6]

Domestic institutions, however, can offset the contributions of liberalisation to growth by limiting labour flexibility, segmenting internal markets, and failing to provide the social infrastructure for education. The traditional argument about static factor price effects and gains from trade, for example, assumes that resources move smoothly and costlessly from import competing to exporting activities. Obviously, if resources cannot or do not move, exporting industries would not expand, while import competing industries surely contract, because of increased competition from imports after trade liberalisation, thus creating unemployment. This somewhat extreme, but elementary argument has been raised by Stiglitz (2002, 59) against trade liberalisation when he says that: 'It is easy to destroy jobs, and this is often the immediate impact of trade liberalisation, as the inefficient industries [those created under the protectionist walls] close down under pressure from international competition.' Since he assumes that no new, more efficient jobs would be created, he concludes that 'moving resources from low-productivity uses [in inefficient industries] to zero productivity [to unemployment] does not enrich any country...' True, but neither does keeping factors in less productive uses forever. There may be a rationale for credibly committing to phase in trade liberalisation over a period, while at the same time, removing impediments to labour mobility, but certainly not postponing liberalisation indefinitely, as is sometimes argued.[7]

Globalisation's effect on short-term growth also depends upon the exact forms of globalisation and pre-existing market distortions. Removing barriers and controls on financial capital flows, for example, may improve resource allocation and give more people access to better-functioning credit markets in the long run. In the short term, on the other hand, it can lead to crisis and lower growth in countries with fragile domestic financial sectors. Capital controls have been advocated by many in the wake of the Asian financial crisis, and some find that controls were useful in helping some countries recover faster than those that had freer capital movements (Mussa 2000; Kaplan and Rodrik 2001)

To sum up, there is no reason to presume that the effects of globalisation on growth have to be the same everywhere and at all times or even if they are similar, that they operate with the same intensity. This variation in country experiences is as important as the expected positive effect of globalisation on growth.

Empirical Evidence

Theoretical formulations of a trade-growth linkage are foundations of the globalisation-growth links. Empirical demonstrations of the linkage go back to the careful and nuanced cross-country studies in the late sixties and seventies sponsored by OECD (Little et al. 197)), and NBER (Bhagwati 1978; Krueger 1978). More recent studies, based on simple cross-country regressions (for example, Sachs and Warner 1995), asserting the same linkage have been controversial, though the questions are more about the magnitude than the sign of the linkage between trade and growth.[8] Wacziarg and Welch (2002) find that the Sachs and Warner's cross-sectional results are somewhat weaker, when the sample period is extended through the 1990s. Their estimates, however, show that openness has positive effects on growth and investment rates within countries.

Nevertheless, the positive effect of trade and growth emerging from the earlier studies appears to be robust when carefully evaluated using more recent data. Dollar and Kraay (2000a) attempt to respond to some of Rodriguez and Rodrik's econometric criticisms in evaluating the trade-growth linkage for countries-mostly developing countries—that liberalised after 1980.[9] They relate *decadal changes* in trade volumes (which they see as a better-though not perfect-proxy for changes in trade policy) and *decadal changes* in growth. Their focus on changes mitigates the effect of geography on growth (and trade) through channels other than trade policy, while their inclusion of 'time dummies' controls for shocks common to all countries included in their analysis. By focusing on *within country* changes in trade and growth, they find a strong positive relationship between the two, and no systematic relationship between changes in trade and changes in household income inequality.

Individual country experiences bear out these cross-country trends. World Bank (2002, Table 1) data show that both China and India enjoyed historically unprecedented average annual rates of growth of GDP of around 10 per cent and 6 per cent, respectively, as the two countries engaged in opening their economies to foreign trade and investment over 1980–2000. The effect is not entirely attributable to 'globalisation,' as both countries also engaged in domestic economic reforms allowing a greater role for markets and the private sector in the economy, but integration no doubt played a larger role.

GROWTH AND POVERTY REDUCTION

Aggregate growth is undoubtedly an instrument for poverty reduction, and it is associated with improvements in the minimum standard of living over some time horizon. Besley and Burgess (2003)'s estimates for the elasticity of poverty with respect to income per capita vary widely across country samples, but all are negative, implying that growth reduces poverty.

This association between growth and poverty reduction, however, could take a long time to be seen. Inequality—which is different conceptually and empirically, though as salient as poverty in the eyes of critics—does not necessarily drop with growth. Although the poor may be becoming better off over time, the rich could gain even more. There are many possible mechanisms through which aggregate growth could affect, positively or negatively, poverty at national or sub-national levels on the one hand, and on the other, how levels and trends in poverty could influence growth, again in either direction. The basic mechanisms behind growth and poverty reduction do not fully overlap, and some policies meant to encourage growth will have little or negative effect on the poor in the short run. These lags can affect the political feasibility of reforms.

It is clear, however, that poverty reduction requires growth, particularly in lower-income countries. The available resources may not, in some cases, provide adequately for all no matter how the country's income is distributed. An early blueprint for development in India, for example, clearly recognised the instrumental role of growth for poverty reduction and specifically estimated the extent of growth necessary to meet a minimum standard of living for all. Its objective:

> was to insure an adequate standard of living for the masses; in other words, to get rid of the appalling poverty of the people... the irreducible, in terms of money, had been estimated by economists at figures varying from Rs. 15 to Rs. 25 per capita per month (at prewar prices)... *[To] insure an irreducible minimum standard for everybody, the national income had to be greatly increased*, and in addition to this increased production there had to be a more equitable distribution of wealth. We calculated that a really progressive standard of living would *necessitate the increase of the national wealth by 500 or 600 per cent*. That was, however, too big a jump for us, and we aimed at a 200 to 300 per cent increase within ten years.
>
> (Nehru 1946, 402–3, emphasis added)

Indian policy makers were by no means unique in seeing rapid income growth as the major instrument for poverty reduction-statements, similar to those of the Indians, could be found in development plans of many other countries.

A positive association between growth and reduction in poverty is seen in several large countries with a high incidence of income poverty, such as China, India, Indonesia (until the financial crisis), and the Philippines. Angus Deaton (2001b) estimated the proportion of poor in India's rural (urban) population in 1987–88 to have been 39 per cent (25 per cent). By 1999–2000, the proportion had fallen to 23 per cent (13 per cent) in rural (urban) areas. Annual data for earlier years suggest that rural and urban poverty proportion fluctuated with no downward trend until 1977–78, when it was 51 per cent (41 per cent) in rural (urban) areas (Datt 1998, 1999). It is no coincidence that significant reductions in poverty since 1980 were associated with a near tripling of per capita GDP growth to an average of around 4per cent per year during 1980–2000 as compared to 1.25per cent during 1950–80.

According to Park and Wang (2001), official data for China show that rural poverty has been virtually eliminated in China, falling from 31 per cent of rural population in 1979 to 10 per cent in 1990, and further to 5 per cent in 1998. The two authors also point out that World Bank estimates (based on a different poverty line and estimation methodology) put rural poverty at 43 per cent in 1990 and 24 per cent in 1997. Although, as is to be expected, given the use of different poverty lines, the estimated level of poverty differs between official and World Bank sources, the trend is similar—namely, a halving of poverty between 1990 and 1998. For the longer period of 1979–98, official data show, an association between rapid growth and poverty reduction.

A few sub-Saharan African countries, such as Botswana and Lesotho, and Mauritius, also enjoyed high growth, resulting in a reduction in poverty of these nations. The association with income growth of non-income facets of poverty is also evident (Table 16.1): there has been a general improvement of life expectancy, rates of infant and child mortality, educational attainments, and so on, although some of the gains achieved are being threatened by the AIDS epidemic in some countries of sub-Saharan Africa and Asia. Many developing countries experienced significant growth only during the 1990s, a time period too short to see significant reductions in poverty.

While these specific cases suggest that growth reduces poverty, systematic statistical results are limited.[10] Dollar and Kraay (2000b) have done perhaps the most careful (econometrical) study.[11] They define the poor as 'the bottom one fifth of the population' so that poverty goes down from their perspective, if and only if, the mean real income of the bottom 20 per cent goes up.[12] Their data on income of the poor and mean income relate to 80 countries covering four decades, providing 236 episodes for evaluating the link between aggregate income growth and poverty reduction. They estimate variants of a basic regression of the logarithm of per capita income, of the poor on the logarithm of average per capita income, control variables and a country fixed effect.[13]

TABLE 16.1 Development outcomes in the 1980s and 1990s, by growth class (unweighted means)

			High growth	Moderate or improved growth	Low growth
Poverty	Per cent with less than USD1 a day	1990s	24.1	31.4	36.9
		1980s	31.0	32.1	30.2
Infant mortality	Per thousand	1990s	29.2	54.3	60.7
		1980s	41.0	66.6	71.0
Illiteracy	Per cent	1990s	17.2	31.2	31.4
		1980s	22.9	37.6	38.8
Life expectancy	Years	1990s	70.0	62.9	59.8
		1980s	66.8	60.6	58.4
Carbon dioxide Emission	Tons per capita	1990s	2.4	2.3	1.7
		1980s	1.5	2.3	1.8
Deforestation	Per cent per year	1990–95	0.83	1.05	1.11
		1980–85	1.08	0.65	1.15
Water pollution	Kilograms per day per worker	1990s	0.16	0.21	0.21
		1980s	0.18	0.21	0.21
GDP growth	Per cent per year	1990s	5.3	4.2	0.3
		1980s	6.5	2.3	2.1
Number of countries			13	53	39

Source: World Bank, 2000, Table 1.2.

Their results suggest that, notwithstanding the variation around the estimated relationship, the positive effect of growth on income of the poor is the same in rich and poor countries. Other findings include, that the incomes of the poor do not fall more than proportionately during economic crises, the poverty-growth relationship is stable in recent years, policies that promote overall growth also benefit the poor, good rule of law and fiscal discipline benefit the poor as much as the rest of the population, inflation is more harmful to the poor than for the rest. Finally, they find no evidence that formal democratic institutions, as well as, public spending on health and education, have systemic effects on the poor.

The lags between sustained acceleration in growth and poverty reduction can create political problems, for the reason that horizons of politicians are almost surely shorter than lags. Policymakers in India, for example, a country whose development plan explicitly stated that its efforts to increase growth were essential instruments for its goals of reducing poverty, debated the extent to which the poor benefited from growth. As early as in 1960, at the end of the Second Five Year Plan, the question of whether growth of the previous decade had improved the lives of the poor was raised by a skeptical socialist member in the Parliament. Prime Minister Nehru responded to this question in introducing the Third Five-Year Plan in Parliament and said:

> Again it is said that the national incomes over the First and Second Plans have gone up by 42 per cent and per capita income by 20 per cent. Now a legitimate query is made—where has this gone? To some extent, of course, you can see where it has gone. I sometimes do address a large gathering in the villages, and I can see that they are better fed and better clothed, they build brick houses and they are generally better off. Nevertheless, that does not apply to everybody in India.
> (Government of India 1964, 1)[14]

Rising inequality can also accompany periods of growth. In contrast to trends in indicators of absolute poverty, those relating to measures of inequality are ambiguous. The data from China and India, for example, suggest that, although poverty at national level decreased during the period of their globalisation and growth, all regions and groups neither grew at the same rate nor did they experience poverty reduction to the same extent. This is not surprising since a change that raises everyone's income and reduces the proportion of the poor in a population could nonetheless increase inequality, if the rise in income accrues first to those with the higher skills and resource bases that allow them to take advantage of the change. Tinbergen (1975) argued that rising average incomes imply reduced inequality, only if education expands faster than the demand for higher skilled workers. His argument is likely to be as true today as then.

There is some evidence that regional disparities widened in China and India as these nations liberalised their foreign trade and introduced other reforms. To a certain extent this is natural: those regions (and individuals) which are better placed initially to take advantage of the opportunities opened up by reforms or, for that matter, by any other factor, such as, for example, the information-technology revolution, are likely to grow faster (and richer). For example, India's phenomenal success in software is still confined to a few cities in the south and west. The real issue is not one of increasing regional disparities, but of whether the socio-economic system would enable the initially disadvantaged regions and individuals to catch up. If it does not, the social and political consequences could be serious and could lead to secessionist threats.

Whether widening disparities are temporary and would be reversed or permanent and entrenched is an interesting issue. At the aggregate level, one approach to this issue is to ask: do regions converge over time to the same level and rate of growth per capita income in the long run without conditioning on any characteristics of the regions, other than their initially different levels of income? This is the so-called 'absolute' convergence hypothesis. It is to be contrasted with the 'conditional' convergence hypothesis, which suggests that each region converges to its own steady state or long-run level and growth of per capita income, which, in turn, depends on the region's characteristics such as its savings rate,

rate of labour force growth and the rate of exogenous technical progress and initial levels of human capital. Under either hypothesis, a region further from its steady state, grows faster than when it is closer. There is a growing literature on testing the hypotheses of absolute and conditional convergence in both China and India. Demurger et al. (2002) and Dayal-Gulati and Husain (2002) find support only for conditional convergence in China. In India, Cashin and Sahay (1996, 1997) found evidence of absolute convergence. Rao and Sen (1997) suggest that, in fact, the findings of Cashin and Sahay should be interpreted as supporting conditional convergence. Clearly, a finding of conditional convergence, since it is consistent with regions growing at different rates in the long run, could mean growing disparities across regions. Coupled with the fact, that the incidence of poverty is higher and the share of the country's population is larger in the latter states, there has been legitimate concern that if sustained in the future, these growth disparities will threaten the stability of India's federal democracy.

GLOBALISATION AND POVERTY REDUCTION

Some individuals or groups in a society may be poor and remain poor because they are disadvantaged in the social and political processes of their society. For example, social institutions such as the caste system in India or forms of racism elsewhere have denied equal access to socio-political processes to lower castes and racial minorities. While recognising the importance of addressing this, we have nothing to add. The economic mechanisms for alleviating poverty could be divided into two broad categories: increasing the resources held by the poor through redistribution and affecting the economic environment that perpetuates poverty. We focus primarily on several ways in which globalisation affects the latter category, as these economic changes have far deeper impacts on reducing poverty over the long run.(Besley and Burgess 2003)[15] While critics focus on globalisation's sometimes negative effects on redistribution, they overlook its potential to reduce economic constraints, that continue to limit the prospects of the poor.[16] Market integration and increased migration limit the extent of poverty-alleviating redistribution in several ways, but their effect on removing the market distortions that perpetuate poverty over the long run, far outweighs these consequences. In the words of Tinbergen (1975: p. 137), the advantage of such mechanisms for poverty reduction is that they 'do not disrupt, but rather shift the equilibrium.'

Needless to say, in the developing world, market distortions are ubiquitous, and their impact on the extent and depth of poverty are often serious. Whether an individual (or a household) has adequate resources to purchase the poverty bundle at the relevant prices at a point in time depends, of course, on what she (or her household) can earn from her assets (land, financial, and physical capital) and most importantly from her (allowing for skills and educational attainments) labour. The functioning of asset and labour markets, as well as, product markets for goods and services bought or sold, obviously influence the earnings from assets and their purchasing power.[17] In this analysis we echo Tinbergen's emphasis that the central issue in alleviating poverty is not to simply offset it with transfers, but to tackle the more difficult issues of removing obstacles the poor face in trading, saving, and investing in their assets for a higher standard of living (see Tinbergen 1962, Section 1.4; 1975: Section 10.2).

The critics of globalisation point to some forms of exploitation of workers in developing countries, such as the frequent use of child labour, the damage that a rapid exposure to global agricultural markets can cause for developing country farmers, and other aspects of the increasingly integrated global economy. However, these are not intrinsic or permanent consequences of globalisation. They often reflect, rather, domestic institutional policy failures as well as continued industrial country protectionism, and the reality that the most powerful forces for alleviation of poverty take time to work.

Redistribution

The critics of globalisation generally point to a decline in state spending on price supports and services for the poor as countries becomes more internationally integrated. Clearly, in a globalised economy, subject to the discipline of international capital markets, fiscal deficits are not sustainable, and taxation of mobile factors will induce their flight. Again, if the growth-accelerating effects of globalisation are strong, the revenue expansion (with a buoyant fiscal system) from growth would enable financing of the needed services for the poor and avoidance of taxing mobile factors.

Increased migration flows are also often thought to reduce domestic demand for redistribution, as the original population may not want to finance services for new immigrants to their country. The rise of nationalist parties, as well as anti-immigrant violence in several industrial countries, reinforces this perception. Razin (2002) shows that immigration generally moves the political voting equilibrium toward less redistribution, unless the new migrants join forces with existing low-income voters in their destination country.

The ramifications of less redistribution for poverty, however, are small relative to potential gains in other areas. Government-led redistribution is one of the more direct, but generally less effective means of reducing poverty in the long run. It has limited effectiveness as a means of affecting the resources that poor households command. It will reduce poverty in the short-run if individuals are poor because the assets they own are too meager. Unless redistribution of income is sustained indefinitely, its poverty reduction effect will be temporary, if the conventional belief that the marginal propensity to consume of the poor is close to unity is correct. On the other hand, if credit markets are absent so that investment is constrained by resources owned and marginal returns to investment diminish, the rich would have a lower marginal return to investment than the poor, if assets are unequally distributed. A redistribution of resources to the poor from the rich would raise the average rate of return to investment and hence the rate of growth of the economy.[18]

Subsidy policies may not even achieve the short-term goals of providing more resources to the poor, as subsidies are not often targeted at the poor or there is hijacking of subsidies intended for the poor by the non-poor. The cost of transferring a dollar to the poor through subsidy schemes (particularly poorly targeted ones) also often exceeds a dollar by a substantial margin. The Indian public distribution system (PDS), through which fixed amounts per person of food grains and a few other essential commodities are sold at subsidised prices, for example, has a negligible impact on rural poverty and the central government alone spends four rupees to distribute one.[19]

Lessening market distortions such as those listed in the next subsections, in contrast, has a dynamic effect in that it not only increases the value of present resources, but encourages greater investment and future accumulation.

Raising the Productivity of the Poor

The chief asset of the poor is their labour. Raising productivity to create a sustained increase in real returns to labour in wage and self-employment would contribute significantly to poverty alleviation. Domestic public policy has a large role to play: increasing the human capital endowments of the poor, perhaps by providing incentives for investment in human capital or through public expenditure on, and improving the access of the poor to, public education and health care programs, raises the productivity of their labour.

Globalisation also contributes to this goal in several ways. First, the growth associated with globalisation will generally create an outward shift in the demand for wage labour and for goods and services produced by the self-employed. Second, returns to the abundant factor, which in most poor countries is unskilled labour, would rise with trade liberalisation.[20] While multinational companies naturally take advantage of the abundance of unskilled workers of the less developed countries, to pay less than they would pay similar workers in their home countries, these wages are often higher than the wages paid by domestic companies in the host countries. Third, more integrated labour markets are important to ensure that workers receive the best return for their work.[21] This last aspect of globalisation has not yet been realised-in fact, national integration is still limited by poor infrastructure, explicit restriction on movement (as in China), and linguistic differences across regions. Unlike commodities, the cost of whose movement within and between countries is primarily determined by costs of transportation and insurance, the cost of mobility of labour involves social and legal barriers, as well as economic ones.

Opportunities for and Returns from Accumulation

Globalisation can also benefit the poor by creating strong competitive pressures for improved financial intermediation. More efficient financial intermediation would have large and long-term benefits for the poor by facilitating their investment in both physical and human capital. Although, this is again partly matter for domestic policymakers, international capital market integration may provide an added incentive to move financial sector reforms faster. Banks facing international competition in their traditional markets may be faster to move into micro-lending or services for small depositors. Similarly, the competition for investment under globalisation encourages governments to focus more closely on providing better opportunities for investment in human capital.

The share of savings used to finance direct investment in physical assets depends in large part on the functioning of the financial system and access to it, which together influence the cost of financial intermediation. The costs faced by the poor are high, and a large share of savings and investment by households in developing countries is currently in the form of physical assets, which they finance on their own, without involving financial intermediaries. This share could be as high as 80 per cent, as in Ghana, or around 50 per cent, as in India. These assets include mostly those related to their production activities and also dual use (that is, production and consumption) assets.

Even though the poor do not save enough to invest in financial markets (particularly in equity markets), they do invest their meager financial savings in the form of deposits in commercial banks, purchase of life insurance policies, and also lending in informal credit markets. Clearly, the returns they realise on such investments depend on the functioning of the financial sector, including the banking system.

The more important effect of improved financial intermediation-via domestic policy changes or spurred by international competition would be in providing greater opportunities for financing education. Just as labour is the major asset owned by the poor, it is their investment in accumulation of human capital that is likely to be the major component of their investment. Although, their poverty limits their saving and investment in any form, it is particularly limiting when it comes to human capital accumulation. Indeed, a major reason that the incidence of child labour is very high in many poor countries of South Asia and sub-Saharan Africa is the poverty of the parents of working children. Such parents cannot afford to forego the income from the work of a child (directly from paid work or indirectly in terms of unpaid contribution to the household's farm or non-farm enterprise). The out-of-pocket costs to the parents for sending their children to school are often substantial.[22]

Lack of investment in education has three serious consequences. First, the earning prospects of uneducated (or less educated) children in their adult working life would be less compared to their competitors in labour markets. Second, unless the labour market conditions improve in their adult life as compared to those that prevailed in their childhood, they are likely to end up as poor as their parents were and, as such, unlikely to educate their own children. The prospect of perpetuation of poverty across generations in such circumstances cannot be ruled out. Third, since some minimal education is often needed for an individual to participate effectively in political and social processes that make decisions affecting his social and economic prospects, these individuals may be in effect unable to exercise their right to participate.

Apart from its beneficial effect on investment in human capital through improved financial intermediation, globalisation has a direct effect on the demand for educated labour in poor countries through outsourcing of some service activities by industrialised countries. Already, China and India have benefited from such outsourcing. Unfortunately, there is a protectionist backlash in the United States against outsourcing. Hopefully, policymakers will not cave in to such pressure.

Product Market Efficiency

Product market efficiency, affected by domestic policies as well as international integration, determines the 'terms of trade' the poor face in attempting to exchange their production for consumption and investment. Needless to say, the extent of integration of national markets and also the competitiveness of exports in world markets depends in large part on whether or not transport and communications infrastructure exists, and functions efficiently, to minimise costs of transportation and of acquiring market intelligence. Insufficient integration would mean the existence of price differentials across markets that cannot be arbitraged away. Also given the uncertainties, not only about harvests, but also about the prices that would rule at harvest time or at any time thereafter, when the harvested output would be sold, it matters whether national markets for forward transactions exist and how costly it is to store commodities for later sale.

Globalisation could have a particularly significant impact on poverty by affecting the prices farmers in developing countries receive for their products and pay for inputs. There are currently two obstacles: lack of competition among intermediaries who aggregate primary products for international trading and continued industrial country subsidies and protection for their farmers. (McMillan et al. 2002)[23]

Economic Institutions

Globalisation can be helpful in mitigating or even overcoming the institutional and market failures that affect the poor adversely.

Governance Quality

Tackling corruption is a major challenge of governance in developing countries, as processes of adoption, enforcement, and effectiveness of policy interventions are often distorted by endemic corruption. Inefficient and corrupt bureaucracies raise transactions costs in asset markets important for the poor. Land and tenancy markets, for example, have higher transactions costs than other asset markets because of the difficulty in establishing a claim of ownership in land when records are poorly maintained and officials who have the authority to certify ownership are corrupt. It is also a phenomenon that has been with us for ages. The *Arthasastra*, a Sanskrit treatise on statecraft dated to fourth century B.C. India, lists more than fifty ways in which officials could be corrupt.[24]

Any extra impetus that globalisation provides toward more transparent institutions will contribute to poverty reduction. The prospect of losing in the race to attract international capital flows, for example, can act as an important impetus to curb corruption. Wei (2000a) finds that corruption's effects on international investment are as if governments were imposing a tax-investors are significantly less likely to invest in more corrupt countries. The direction of causation between corruption, and globalisation, however, is likely to go in the opposite direction for trade: corrupt bureaucrats' bribes act as tariffs limiting imports and exports (Wei 2000b).

Insurance and Credit

Limited access to domestic credit and insurance markets exposes the poor to substantial uncertainty and potentially to consumption volatility. Domestic financial markets in many developing countries are simply not efficient enough to find it worthwhile to extend services to the poor, because it is costly relative to returns to provide small loans to many poor, in contrast to providing large loans to few rich. As mentioned previously, globalisation can create an impetus to improve financial market and offer such credit and insurance opportunities to the poor.

In addition to being dependent on agriculture, the rural poor also have to cope with uncertainties, some of which relate to the environment for production and consumption (for example, weather, disease vectors) and others that are idiosyncratic (for example, health and mortality shocks to humans and livestock). Further, the agricultural production process is one in which inputs have to be committed in advance of the realisation of an uncertain harvest, while the process of consumption is more certain and evenly paced over time. In an economy closed to international agricultural commodity markets, shocks to domestic output and demand have to be absorbed through price changes. To the extent such shocks are not highly correlated across economies, world output and consumption would be more stable than their domestic counterparts. Thus, integration with world markets in effect would provide insurance against price effects of domestic shocks, though not necessarily against their income effects.

It is clear that, even if production and consumption processes were to be free of any risk and uncertainty, still the lack of synchronisation between the two would require means for smoothing consumption over time. It is also clear that achieving such smoothing would be less expensive, compared to each individual holding inventories of inputs and consumption goods, if access to smoothly and efficiently functioning credit markets is available. The need for credit is enhanced also if purchased inputs (for example, fertilizers and pesticides, energy and fuels, hired labour etc.) account for a large share of production costs, as in the case of the cultivation of the so-called 'Green Revolution' varieties of crops. With well-functioning insurance markets, insurable risks would be addressed. However, uninsurable (or more precisely, insurable only at a high cost) risks are also significant in rural areas of poor countries.

For well-known and well-understood reasons of moral hazard, absence of collateralisable assets, poorly functioning legal system for enforcement of contracts and the seizing and sale of whatever collateral that has been pledged, formal credit and insurance markets in poor countries are either virtually absent or costly, if not altogether out of reach, of the poor. On the other hand, informal arrangements substitute in part for transactions in formal markets (Townsend 1994; Udry 1993). However, the cost of informal transactions is not necessarily low arid, in any case, informal arrangements are nowhere near adequate to substitute fully for the incomplete and imperfect functioning of credit and insurance markets.

GLOBALISATION FOR THE POOR

The globalisation discussed in the last section looks substantially different than the partially integrated goods, capital, and factor markets we have today. The most notable departures, and those with the largest negative effects on the poor, are the continued industrial country protection of agricultural and other markets and the lack of integration in labour markets. Porto (2003) estimates that tariff reforms leading to a 15 per cent price increase in agricultural manufactures would lead to 2.5 percentage point decrease in the proportion of Argentines in poverty.[25]

Industrial country protectionism has been a constant part of this most recent wave of globalisation. Tinbergen (1971) noted that decisions regarding trade barriers (and other policies) will 'tend to be based on the short-term interests of that nation, whereas it would have been in the long-term interest to take also into account the interests of others' and that restrictions of the developed countries on trade are 'limiting the possibilities for developing countries to expand their industry and employment'. The fiasco at the recently concluded ministerial meeting of the WTO at Cancun, Mexico confirms Tinbergen's analysis.

The practice of industrial countries to protect vulnerable markets may be thought of as politically difficult to change, but that does not justify acceptance. The answer may be to devote more attention to strengthening international trade policy-making bodies. Tinbergen's (1971) repeated call for more explicit institutional coordination of the world economy appears to be increasingly unlikely to be answered for general cooperation, but it is worthwhile to focus on greater cooperation in specific areas.

Labour market integration has been similarly under-emphasised in the current wave of globalisation. Tinbergen (1971) notes that freer migration may be essential for achieving the goal of smaller differences in wage levels across the world, but the issue has not even been on the agenda in most international trade talks. Rodrik (2002) argues that this is the area with the most significant consequences for developing countries. He estimates that a temporary visa scheme, that allowed migration from developing to developed countries of up to 3 per cent of the labour force of the rich countries would 'easily yield' USD 200 billion annually for developing country citizens.

As if these two changes were not substantial enough, it is also important to emphasise that globalisation alone will not bring about the changes in the economic and institutional environment that are most effective for reducing poverty. It creates additional pressure for such reforms, but these are ultimately domestic decisions.

Endnotes

[1] It is not clear that greater openness is, in fact, associated with increased inequality. Berg and Krueger's (2003) survey of empirical evidence on the linkage between trade, growth, and poverty reduction finds only mixed evidence, with the majority of studies finding that growth does not lead to significant increases in inequality.

[2] The paper presents a variety of theoretical reasons for this finding. The composite index of 'globalisation'—a weighted average of trade and financial openness—is difficult to interpret, however, in the context of his cross-country study.

[3] He goes so far as to suggest that globalisation's critics are motivated by a different understanding of how the world works than the globalisation supporters have.

[4] Operationally, this social minimum is often identified with the value of a specific bundle of goods and services that can be obtained through home production, market purchases and public provisions. Defining a poverty bundle for individuals is difficult enough, but extending the definition to households with many members and differing age-sex compositions is fraught with additional difficulties. Valuation is also difficult: Deaton (2001a), for example, shows that using a price index based on prices actually paid by households rather than an official consumer price index, 'reduces' the number of the poor (as measured by the proportion of population consuming less than the poverty line) in urban India in 1999–2000 from around 254 million to 181 million.

[5] More generally, however, the effects of poverty on human wellbeing include peoples' feelings of deprivation relative to those around them. Sen (1981, Chapter 2) discusses these and other concepts of poverty. Tinbergen (1971) calls for more research on the intensity of peoples' feelings about what others around them are consuming as a way of obtaining more information about individuals' welfare at some consumption level.

[6] The phrases 'engine of growth' and 'handmaiden of growth' are associated with Dennis Robertson (1940) and Irwin Kravis (1970), respectively.

[7] Tinbergen (1962, p.42) suggests, for example, that subsidies be given to retrain workers and facilitate the transfer of capital from declining industries to new, more dynamic sectors.

[8] Rodriguez and Rodrik (2000) are the most recent critics, though Warner (2002) refutes the Rodriguez-Rodrik critique. He essentially argues that their finding that the effect of trade openness on growth is not statistically robust are due to the fact that the forms of protectionism vary across countries so that any single indicator of openness will not describe the effective level of integration for all countries.

[9] Whether or not a country is defined as a globaliser is based on the *decline* in trade-weighted average tariffs and the *increase* in constant price value of trade (exports plus imports) relative to real GDP. Among the top 40 countries according to each of these two criteria, 16 (including Brazil, China, and India) appear on top in both. Unsurprisingly, none of the African countries is among them, though Ghana and Uganda, two African economies that came closest to their threshold were included in the analysis.

[10] Since there are too few observations to do an econometric analysis of the growth-poverty-reduction experience *over time* of *individual* countries, cross country regressions are the only option.

[11] They allow for measurement errors and endogeneity of control variables as well as for the omission of possibly relevant control variables. They also test for over-identifying restrictions.

[12] This *relative* definition of poverty precludes any simple comparison of their results with those of other studies using an *absolute* definition based on national or international (for example, for example, USD1 a day) poverty lines.

[13] Their control variables include proxies for openness, capital account restrictions, rule of law, democratic institutions, inflation rate, government consumption and expenditures on social sectors as a proportion of total government spending, and primary school enrollment.

[14] Nehru followed up his response by appointing a committee to enquire into the distribution of income and levels of living.

[15] Besley and Burgess (2003) discuss the poverty reduction benefits of a similar set of policies, though they do not address the link with globalisation.

[16] Critics often associate globalisation with a reduction in the state's ability to redistribute income. We discuss this point further in the next subsection.

[17] Clearly if there are no distortions in all these markets and all individuals and households face the same prices, the extent of poverty would be determined by the distribution of assets and labour in the economy.

[18] For surveys of relevant analytical and policy issues, see Aghion et al. (1999) and Benabou (1996).

[19] Rao and Radhakrishna (1997) analysed India's PDS from the national and international perspective. They found that in 1986–87, PDS and other consumer subsidy programmes accounted for only about 3 per cent of the per capita expenditure of the poor, and their impact on poverty and nutritional status of the poor was minimal.

[20] There are, empirically, important exceptions to this general theoretical expectation: Harrison and Hanson (1999) present evidence that trade openness in several Latin American and Asian countries has been associated with an increased return to skilled labour relative to unskilled labour.

[21] Wage labour market policies are obviously not a solution for all of poverty. Only a small part of the labour force in many developing countries (less than 20per centper cent in India and South Asia, for example) is in formal wage and salary employment. An overwhelming majority of the labour force is in self-employment (often in subsistence farming, in handicraft activities and household-based production for local markets). For them it is not so much the functioning of labour markets but that of product and credit markets that is more relevant.

[22] National and international attempts to eradicate child labour through restrictions on imports or consumer boycotts of goods produced by children are not likely to succeed unless the basic cause of child labour, namely the poverty of parents, is addressed.

[23] See McMillan et al. (2002) on how domestic market imperfections limited farmers' benefits from liberalisation of the cashew sector in Mozambique.

[24] On the other hand, China, a country in which corruption is thriving, has attracted large flows of investment, particularly from overseas Chinese who apparently are better at operating in a corrupt system! Corrupt practices by transnational enterprises, often with the connivance of the governments in countries of their origin, has received attention in the literature.

[25] The paper points out that although domestic trade reforms in Argentina have larger *marginal* poverty reduction effects, the scope for lowering foreign tariffs is much greater and therefore the *overall* poverty reduction possible from industrial country trade reform is greater than that achievable from domestic reforms.

References

Agenor, Pierre-Richard. 2003. *Does Globalization Hurt the Poor?* Wahington DC: The World Bank.

Aghion, Philippe, Eve Caroli and Cecilia Garcia-Penalosa. 1999. 'Inequality and Economic Growth: The Perspective of the New Growth Theories', *Journal of Economic Literature*, vol. XXXVII, pp. 1615–60.

Benabou, Roland. 1996. 'Inequality and Growth', *NBER Macroeconomics Annual*, vol. 11, MIT Press.

Berg, Andrew and Anne Krueger. 2003. 'Trade, Growth, and Poverty: A Selective Survey', IMF Staff Working Paper WP/03/30, Washington, DC: The World Bank.

Besley, Timothy and Robin Burgess. 2003. 'Halving Global Poverty', *Journal of Economic Perspectives*, vol. 17, no. 3, pp. 3–22.

Bhagwati, Jagdish. 1978. *Foreign Trade Regimes and Economic Development: Anatomy of Exchange Control Regimes*, Cambridge: Ballinger Press.

Bourguignon, Francois, et al. 2002. 'Making Sense of Globalization', CEPR Policy Paper no. 8. London: Centre for Economic Policy Research.

Cashin, Paul and Ratna Sahay. 1996. 'Internal Migration, Centre-State Grants and Economic Growth in the States of India', IMF Staff Paper 43, pp. 123–71.

Cashin, Paul and Ratna Sahay. 1997. 'International Migration, Centre-State Grants and Economic Growth in the States of India: A Reply to Rao and Sen', IMF Staff Paper 44, pp. 289–91.

Coe, David T., Elhanan Helpman and W. A. Hoffmaister. 1998. 'North-South R&D Spill Overs', *Economic Journal*, vol. 107, January, pp. 134–49.

Datt, Gaurav. 1999. *Has Poverty in India Declined Since the Economic Reforms?* Washington DC: The World Bank.

_____. 1998. 'Poverty in India and Indian States: An Update', FCND Working Paper 47.

Dayal-Gulati, Anuradha and Aasim Husain. 2002. 'Centripetal Forces in China's Economic Take off', IMF Staff Papers 49, pp. 364–94.

Deardorff, Alan. 2003. 'What Might Globalization's Critics Believe', Occasional Paper 20, Bureau of Economic Studies, Macalester College, St Paul, MN.

Deaton, Angus. 2001a. 'Counting the World's Poor's Problems and Possible Solutions', *World Bank Research Observer*, vol. 16, no. 2, pp. 125–47.

_____. 2001b. 'Computing Prices and Poverty Rates in India, 1999–2000', mimeograph, Princeton, New Jersey: Princeton University.

Demurger, Sylvie et al. 2002. 'Economic Geography and Regional Growth in China', *Asian Economic Papers*, vol. 1, no. 1, pp. 146–97.

Dollar, David and Aart Kraay. 2000a. 'Trade, Growth, and Poverty', mimeograph, Washington DC: The World Bank, http://www.woridbank.org/research/growth.

_____. 2000b. 'Growth *Is* Good for the Poor', mimeograph, Washington DC: The World Bank, http://www.woridbank.org/research/growth.

Harrison, Anne and Gordon Hanson. 1999. Who Gains From Trade Reform? Some Remaining Puzzles', *Journal of Development Economics*, vol. 59, pp. 129–44.

Government of India, 1964. *Report of the Committee on Distribution of Income and Levels of Living*. New Delhi: Planning Commission, Government of India.

Kaplan, Ethan, and Dani Rodrik. 2001. 'Did Malaysian Capital Controls Work?' mimeograph Kennedy School of Government, Harvard University, Cambridge, MA.

Kravis, Irving. 1970. 'Trade as a Handmaiden of Growth: Similarities between the Nineteenth and Twentieth Centuries', *Economic Journal*, vol. 80, pp. 850–72.

Krueger, Anne. 1978. *Foreign Trade Regimes and Economic Development: Liberalization Attempts and Consequences*, Cambridge: Ballinger Press.

Lewis, W. Arthur. 1955. *The Theory of Economic Growth*, Homewood: Richard D. Irwin, Inc.

Little, I. M. D., T. Scitovsky and M. F. G. Scott. 1970. *Industry and Trade in Some Developing Countries*, Oxford: Oxford University Press.

McMillan, Margaret, Dani Rodrik and Karen Horn Welch. 2002. 'When Economic Reform Goes Wrong: Cashews in Mozambique', mimeography, Kennedy School of Government, Harvard University.

Mussa, Michael. 2000. 'Factors Driving Global Economic Integration', paper presented in at a symposium sponsored by the Federal Reserve Bank of Kansas City on Global Opportunities and Challenges, Jackson Hole, Wyoming, 25 August.

Nehru, Jawaharlal. 1946. *The Discovery of India*, New York: The John Day Company.

Park, A. and S. Wang. 2001. 'China's Poverty Statistics', *China Economic Review*, vol. 23, pp. 384–95.

Porto, Guido. 2003. 'Trade Reforms, Market Access, and Poverty in Argentina', mimeograph, Development Research Group, Washington, DC: The World Bank.

Rao, K. S. and R. Radhakrishna. 1997. *India's Public Distribution System in a National and International Perspective*, Washington, DC: The World Bank.

Rao, M. Govinda and K. Sen. 1997. 'Internal Migration, Centre-State Grants, and Economic Growth in States of India', IMF Staff Paper 44, pp. 283–89.

Razin, Assaf. 2002. 'Tax Burden and International Migration: Political-Economic Theory and Evidence', *Journal of Public Economics*, vol.74, no. 1, pp. 141–50.

Robertson, Dennis H. 1940. 'The Future of International Trade', in *Essays in Monetary Theory*, edited by D. Robertson, London, Staples Press.

Rodriguez, Fransisco and Dani Rodrik. 2000. 'Trade Policy and Economic Growth: A Skeptic's Guide to Cross-National Evidence', *NBER Macroeconomics Annual*.

Rodrik, Dani. 2002. *Feasible Globalizations*, Cambridge, MA: Harvard University.

Sachs, Jeffrey and Andrew Warner. 1995. 'Economic Reform and the Process of Global Integration', *Brookings Papers on Economic Activity*, vol. 1, pp. 1–118.

Sen, Amartya. 1981. *Poverty and Famines*, New York: Oxford University Press.

Srinivasan, T. N. 1995. 'Long-Run Growth Theories and Empirics: Anything New?', in *Growth Theories in Light of the East Asian Experience*, edited by Ito Takatoshi and Anne Krueger, Chicago: University of Chicago Press, pp. 37–70.

Stiglitz, J. 2002. *Globalization and its Discontents*, New York: W. W. Norton and Company.

Tinbergen, Jan. 1962. *Shaping the World Economy*, New York: The Twentieth Century Fund.

Tinbergen, Jan. 1971. *Towards a Better International Order*, United Nations Institute for Training and Research Lecture Series 2, New York: United Nations.

Tinbergen, Jan. 1975. *Income Distribution*, New York: Elsevier.

Townsend, Robert. 1994. 'Risk and Insurance in Village India', *Econometrica*, vol. 62, no. 3, pp. 539–91.

Udry, Chris. 1993. 'Case Studies: Credit Markets in Nolhern Nigeria: Credit as Insurance in a Rural Economy', in *The Economics of Rural Organization: Theory, Practice and Policy*, edited by Karla Hoff, Avishay Braverman and J. E. Stiglitz, Washington DC: Oxford University Press and The World Bank.

Wacziarg, Romain and Karen Welch. 2002. 'Trade Liberalization and Growth: New Evidence', mimeograph, Graduate School of Business, Stanford University.

Warner, Andrew. 2002. 'Once More Into the Breach: Economic Growth and Global Integration', mimeograph, Cambridge, MA: Harvard University.

Wei, Shang-Jin. 2000a. 'How Taxing is Corruption on International Investors?', *Review of Economics and Statistics*, vol. 82, no. 1, February, pp. I–II.

———. 2000b. 'Natural Openness and Good Government', mimeograph, Cambridge, MA: Harvard University.

Williamson, Jeffrey. 2002. 'Winners and Losers over Two Centuries of Globalization', WIDER Annual Lecture 6, UNUIWIDER, Helsinki.

World Bank. 2000. *The Quality of Growth*, New York: Oxford University Press.

———. 2002. *World Development Indicators*, Washington DC: The World Bank.

17

Income Distribution, Structural Change and International Trade: A Developing Countries Perspective, with Special Reference to India[1]

Ananya Ghosh Dastidar

INTRODUCTION

Over the past two decades globalisation has ushered in manifold changes in developing economies world over. All around the developing world, one observes a restructuring of economic policies, with emphasis on reduced state intervention, privatisation, and increased openness, making for greater integration of the domestic, with the world economy. In this context, it is interesting to ask, how the distribution of income in developing countries like India, is likely to be affected by the manifold changes such countries are currently witnessing.

In this paper, we argue that certain structural characteristics of developing countries may have an important influence, on the overall distribution of income and these are likely to affect the way in which income distribution is affected with greater openness to international trade. In particular, our focus is on the overall or personal distribution of income,[2] as we analyse the impact of a particular aspect of globalisation, that is, enhanced exposure of the domestic economy to international trade flows. As such, our empirical analyses explore the relation between income distribution and structural characteristics of developing countries, in an era of trade liberalisation.

In what follows, we begin with a brief survey of the literature that examines the issue of international trade and income distribution, in the context of developing countries (Section 1). Thereafter, we present the analytical framework of our study, which emphasises the importance of studying the process of structural change for understanding the factors that affect the overall distribution of income within a developing nation (Section 2). This is followed by an empirical analysis, where we essentially carry out a cross-country study on a sample of developing countries (which includes India), exploring the relation between income distribution, structural change, and international trade, using two different model specifications and alternative measures of trade openness. Thereafter, we focus on India, where we discuss the nature of structural change that the country is likely to witness in the post-liberalisation era, in light of our findings from the cross-country empirical analysis (Section 3). Finally, we conclude with a summary of the main insights that emerge from our analysis (Section 4).

INCOME DISTRIBUTION AND INTERNATIONAL TRADE: A SURVEY OF THE MAIN ISSUES

Much has been written on the likely impact of globalisation on various aspects of economic performance of developing countries. Of these, perhaps no other issue has received greater attention, than that of poverty and income distribution in these countries.

It's interesting to note, that much of the recent literature on international trade and income distribution in the nineties decade evolved mainly in the context of developed countries, in an attempt to explain the deterioration in the economic position of less skilled workers across the US and Western European nations.

In recent years, particularly in the 1990s, there was a revival of the academic debate on the distributional implications of international trade, mainly in the context of the US and developed countries of Western Europe.[3] Throughout the decade of the 1980s, the economic position of less-skilled workers deteriorated steadily across the developed countries of the 'North'. Over the decades of the 1970s and the 1980s there was a marked increase in unemployment in the manufacturing sectors of all industrialised countries. This was accompanied by a very uneven distribution of the burden of unemployment; unskilled and uneducated workers faced a far greater risk of unemployment than skilled and more educated workers. Where labour laws and minimum wage legislations were largely absent, unskilled workers found employment elsewhere in the economy, although at much lower wages. In such economies, like the US, unemployment figures remained low, but there was a marked rise in income inequality (Freeman 1995).[4] By contrast, in Europe where institutional arrangements prevented wages from falling sharply, countries such as France, Germany, and Italy experienced little or even diminishing income inequality but higher rates of unemployment (OECD Jobs Study 1994).[5]

This period also saw a phenomenal increase in imports of cheap, manufactured goods from labour-abundant, developing countries of the South (such as China, Malaysia, Indonesia, Thailand, India, Bangladesh and Pakistan), to these countries of the developed North. In addition, the decade of the 1980s also saw widespread technological changes (particularly computerisation) sweep across production processes in the North. Both these factors, that is, imports of unskilled-labour intensive products from the South and skill-biased technological change affected adversely, the demand for unskilled labour in the North. Therefore, as economists and policy-makers attempted to explain falling living standards of the unskilled workers, they essentially debated, which of the two factors, among international trade and technological change could be held primarily responsible for these developments in the labour markets of the developed countries.

In this literature, however, there is relatively little discussion on the role of the restrictive macroeconomic policies which were put in place in most countries of Western Europe in the eighties. As these policies sought to restrain inflation, they also tended to affect the labour market, by slowing down the rate of growth of aggregate demand. It can be argued therefore, the restrictive policy regime also contributed to the problem of unemployment, especially in the countries of Western Europe (for discussions on these issues see for example, Nayyar 1996; UNCTAD 1995). With a fall in labour demand in general, less skilled workers would be particularly affected, as arguably, their lack of skills would limit their ability to switch between jobs.

There are two clear-cut positions, taken by economists attempting to explain the falling living standards of unskilled workers, in developed countries of the North (for a survey of these issues see, Burtless 1995; Freeman 1995; Richardson 1995; Wood 1995). One group of economists argued, that the development and spread of new technologies which had a bias towards a more intensive use of knowledge inputs favoured, in particular, the skilled workers in the North (see for instance, Berman, Bound and Griliches 1994; Berman, Machin and Bound, 1996; Bound and Johnson 1992; Krueger 1993). The skill-bias in the new technologies raised the productivity (and wages) and the overall demand for skilled workers, relative to unskilled workers, thereby strengthening the relative economic position of the former.[6]

A second group of economists argued, that the growth of imports of relatively cheap manufactured goods from labour-abundant developing countries (like China, Malaysia, Indonesia, Thailand, Korea and so on), to the developing world, was primarily responsible for the decline in demand for unskilled labour in the developed countries (see for instance Borjas, Freeman and Katz 1992; Murphy and Welch 1991; Sachs and Shatz 1994; Wood, 1994; and so on). The implicit argument was that, the imported goods replaced the domestically produced substitutes, in consumption baskets, in the developed countries. To the extent these import-competing goods used unskilled labour relatively intensively; a cutback in their production affected adversely, in particular, the demand for unskilled labour. However, even in this literature there is considerable dissent regarding the magnitude of the impact of trade. For instance, Krugman (1995) argues, that even though trade with developing countries is likely to depress the demand for unskilled workers, yet such trade is unlikely to be a prime cause underlying the observed increase in wage inequality in the US. For trade with developing nations, constitutes only a very small fraction of total trade (and an even smaller share of GDP) of the developed nations.

Studies Relating International Trade and Factor Income Distributions

The Analytical Framework

The discussion on the relation between trade and income distribution in the context of the United States, essentially focused on factor income distributions. The theoretical framework most commonly used in this literature is the 2 × 2 version of the HOS theory of international trade. In the 2 × 2 version of the HOS model used in this literature, the two countries are the North (that is, all developed countries clubbed together) and the South (that is, all developing countries clubbed together) and the two factors are skilled labour and unskilled labour.[7] In a two-factor world consisting of skilled and unskilled labour, it is assumed that the North is relatively abundant in skilled labour and the South in unskilled labour.[8] In this case the HOS theorem implies, that the North exports skill-intensive products to and imports unskilled labour-intensive goods from the South. Analogously, the South exports unskilled labour-intensive goods and imports skill-intensive products from the North. Trade in manufactures between the developed world (US and Europe) and the developing countries seemed to perfectly fit the pattern of trade, predicted by the factor abundance theorem or the HOS theorem. As such, to many theorists, this appeared to be the most suitable framework for analysing the distributional implications of international trade (see for instance, Wood 1994).

The Stolper-Samuelson theorem is an important corollary of the HOS theorem that embodies the distributional implications of a change in the trade policy regime. According to this theorem, under certain conditions,[9] a reduction in tariffs would hurt the relatively scarce factor and raise the real returns to the relatively abundant factor within the economy. That is, according to the Stolper–Samuelson theorem, in a country that is relatively abundant in skilled labour, a cut in tariff rates would tend to raise the skilled-unskilled wage ratio. This is precisely what was observed in the US over the decade of the 1980s, that is, a rise in the skilled-unskilled wage ratio. In 1963, the weekly wage received by a man in the 90th percentile of the income distribution was about 2.91 times the wage of a man in the 10th percentile of the distribution. This ratio rose to 3.0 by 1969, to 3.47 by 1979 and to 4.42 by 1989 (Kosters 1994). Observing simultaneously, a rise in the skilled-unskilled wage ratio and a rise in unskilled labour-intensive imports, many economists (particularly trade theorists) concluded, that trade related factors had in fact caused the fall in the relative wages of the unskilled workers.

The Empirical Analysis

There are two broad classes of empirical studies that attempt to verify the relation between international trade and factor incomes, on the basis of available data on the US economy.

One class of studies directly attempt to test the empirical validity of the Stolper–Samuelson theorem (see for instance, Lawrence and Slaughter 1993; Sachs and Shatz 1994). Now the Stolper–Samuelson theorem is essentially about the relation between relative commodity prices and relative factor prices. As such, these studies focus on relative price changes. Given that the skilled-unskilled wage rate has risen in the United States, these authors examine whether the relative price of skill-intensive goods has also risen.[10] There is mixed evidence from these studies regarding the nature of change in relative goods prices. While Lawrence and Slaughter (1993) did not find evidence in support of the Stolper–Samuelson theorem, Sachs and Shatz (1994) found that relative prices did actually move in the 'right' direction and they concluded therefore, that trade related factors were primarily responsible for the labour market trends observed in the US.[11]

The second class of studies focuses on the relation between trade volumes and the distribution of income. The basic logic of these studies is quite simple. Imports of low-skill intensive goods are seen as substituting for domestic production. As such imports serve to reduce the demand for low-skilled labour (as compared to say, a zero-imports situation) and thereby contribute to a reduction in the wages of low-skilled workers. Analogously, exports of skill-intensive products raise the demand for, and hence the wages of skilled workers. The basic empirical issue therefore, is to estimate the comparative effects of exports and imports on the relative demands for and relative wages of skilled vis-a-vis unskilled workers. This is the basic principle underlying the 'factor-content-of-trade' methodology, used extensively in these empirical studies (see for example, Borjas Freeman and Katz 1992; Murphy and Welch 1991; Sachs and Shatz 1994; and Wood 1994). These studies broadly conclude, that international trade was an important factor in explaining the fall in employment of low-skilled workers in the US economy. In particular, Wood's study produces by far the largest estimates of the impact of trade on relative factor prices.[12]

We would like to conclude this discussion with a comment on the factor-content methodology used in these studies. This approach draws upon the HOS theory, insofar as the pattern of trade between the developed and less developed countries is concerned (see for example, Wood, 1994). However, while this approach draws a link between trade volumes and relative factor prices, in HOS theory itself trade volumes do not play any role. Rather commodity prices determine factor returns within the 2 × 2 HOS framework. In fact, with the assumption of a small open economy, good prices alone determine the prices of factors of production. In particular, in this model absolute factor endowments do not matter, so far as factor price determination is concerned.

Studies Relating International Trade and the Personal Income Distributions

The Analytical Framework

Personal income distribution refers to the distribution of income across households or individuals in an economy, taking into account incomes from all sources. The basic idea, that the personal distribution of income within an economy is dependent upon the pattern of ownership of factors of production, the economy's endowments of various factors of production and upon the structure of trade protection, can be expressed formally following Bourguignon and Morrisson (1990).

The structure of the Bourguignon-Morrisson model is as follows. It is based on the assumptions of constant returns to scale technology, perfect competition in the product and factor markets, full employment of factors of production, and a small open economy. In this framework the impact of international trade, on the distribution of income depends, not on the 'structure of trade' (that is, which goods are exported and which are imported), but on the 'structure of protection' (that is, the structure of taxes and subsidies on tradeables). For, the latter determines the prices of traded goods in the domestic market, which in turn determines the returns to factors of production and through this the distribution of income. Essentially within this framework, international trade affects the distribution of income via a change in goods' prices. The authors recognise, that domestic demand patterns also play a role in determining prices of goods, whenever non-traded goods exist.

Bourguignon et al.(1990), show that the distribution of personal incomes is dependent upon the endowments of factors of production in the economy, prices of goods, the structure of trade protection, and the structure of factor ownership. In this framework, an individual's income depends upon his endowment of various assets, his income from labour, prices of goods, and on government policy instruments, such as, tariffs that create a wedge between the equilibrium price that would prevail under free market conditions and the actual market price. In their empirical model, the authors assume that all small open economies face the same set of international prices and in this way avoid including a price term as another determinant of cross-country differences in income distribution.

Spilimbergo et al. (1999) extend the Bourguignon-Morrisson framework. Treating the world as an integrated economic unit, they show that international prices are determined by world factor endowments, in the same way as goods prices are determined by factor endowments in a closed economy. Since international prices determine factor prices within an open economy, they show that in an open economy factor prices and hence the distribution of income is determined by (a) internal endowments of factors of production, (b) world endowments of factors of production, (c) the structure of trade protection and (d) the structure of factor ownership. This extension allows Spilimbergo et al. (1999) to do away with a price term and express income distribution solely as a function of factor endowments.

The Empirical Analysis

Empirical studies on the relation between international trade and personal income distributions, mainly use cross country datasets and in each case the dependent variable is a measure of income inequality. For instance, Edwards (1997) and Spilimbergo et al. (1999) all use inequality measures (Gini coefficients and income share of population quintiles) from the Deininger-Squire (1996) data set. The studies differ from each other, in their selection of countries and time periods, and regarding their choice of specific explanatory variables, especially the measures of trade openness used.

In this regard, an important distinction relates to the inclusion of factor endowments as explanatory variables. Studies that include these are linked to Bourguignon et al. (1990). While others do not bring factor endowments specifically into the picture and consider a different set of right hand side variables. We discuss each of these in turn.

Bourguignon et al. (1990) and Spilimbergo et al. (1999) include measures of factor endowments as explanatory variables along with proxy measures for the ownership and distribution of factors of production across the population and measures of trade openness.

Bourguignon et al. (1990) carried out a cross-section analysis for the year 1970, using data on small and medium developing countries. The authors include unskilled labour, skilled labour, capital, export-specific land, non-export-specific land and mineral resources as the main factors of production. Spilimbergo et al. (1999) uses a cross-country panel dataset for their econometric analyses and consider endowments of arable land, capital, skilled and unskilled labour force.

Regarding the relation between trade openness and income distribution, Bourguignon et al. (1990) find that greater trade protection tends to worsen the income shares of the bottom forty and sixty per cent of the population. Spilimbergo et al. (1999) find that the effect openness on inequality is sensitive to factor endowments. They find that inequality increases in countries that are well endowed with skills, when the economy opens (this result is in line with the empirical literature on wage inequality that finds trade openness increases the premium for skilled workers). While inequality decreases in countries that are relatively well endowed with capital, when the economy opens (this result is interpreted as being in line with the rent-seeking literature dating back to Krueger (1974) that argues that rents from the ownership of capital decreases when the economy opens up). Spilimbergo et al. (1999) uses seven alternate measures of trade openness[13] and their basic result regarding income distribution and openness is fairly robust to the choice of indices, that is, the impact of trade openness upon income distribution will differ, depending upon the economy's endowment of skilled labour.

Another class of empirical studies, simply test the effect of trade protection on the distribution of income, without bringing in factor endowments specifically into the picture (Savvides 1998; Edwards 1997). Both studies use alternate measures of trade protection and income distribution data from the Deininger-Squire data set. In Edwards (1997) the dependent variable is change in the Gini coefficient over time and this is regressed on an openness indicator, the initial level of GDP, the rate of growth, the rate of inflation, and change in the proportion of population with at least secondary schooling. Edwards focuses only on developing countries and finds no evidence linking openness or trade liberalisation to increases in inequality. Savvides (1998) carries out a similar empirical exercise, regressing change in the Gini coefficient on a measure of openness, the rate of growth, secondary schooling rate and a developing country dummy. He finds that, trade liberalisation tends to increase income inequality in developing countries, but has no such effect for developed countries. There is mixed evidence from the second set of studies (Savvides 1998; Edwards 1997) regarding the relation between trade openness and inequality. Clearly this indicates there is scope for further research in this area.

The first set of studies discussed above, serve to underscore the importance of factor endowments in influencing the relation between trade openness and income distribution. However, we shall argue that the 'endowment-based' approach is not entirely appropriate in the context of developing countries (see Dastidar 2006). Primarily this is because, the justification for including factor endowments as right hand side variables stems from a model based on assumptions that do not conform to the reality observed in developing countries. In particular, in developing countries the presence of surplus labour in the Lewisian sense, may actually lead to a breakdown of the relation between relative factor endowments and relative factor returns, that is obtained in full employment models.

Our approach in this paper, is to examine the hypothesis that certain structural features of developing countries may have an important influence on the overall distribution of income in such countries. Our analytical framework, presented in the following section, builds on this basic point.

INCOME DISTRIBUTION, STRUCTURAL CHANGE AND INTERNATIONAL TRADE: EXPLORING THE LINKS

As in any research work on personal income distributions, the starting point of our analysis is also Kuznets (1955). We begin by exploring the implications of the process of structural change that accompanies industrial transformation, for the overall distribution of income in a developing country. Thereafter, we analyse how international trade is likely to affect the process of structural change, and via this channel the overall distribution of income, in the current era of globalisation and trade liberalisation in these countries.

In this context a study by Li et al. (1998) provides interesting insights into the factors affecting the overall distribution of income within an economy. Li et al. (1998) have carried out a detailed study of the Deininger Squire (1996) dataset, which is a compilation of available data on measures of overall income distribution, such as Gini coefficient, income shares of population quintiles, and so on. They note, that the distribution of income tends to be relatively stable over time within countries, while it varies widely across countries. They conclude that this is basically due to a set of political economy factors and due to certain institutional factors, like the existence of credit market imperfections. Hence, inequalities in income distribution tend to persist over time within countries and differ widely across countries, with different credit market conditions and political institutions.

While Li et al. (1998) focus on political economy and institutional factors as important determinants of the overall distribution of income, they do not bring out the importance of structural change per se, which also occurs relatively slowly over time, within a country and even within a group of developing countries. The nature and pace of structural change may vary widely depending on a host of institutional, political, and socio-economic factors. We argue, that structural change could also be an important factor that influences the distribution of income and it is important to study the implications of trade liberalisation for structural change, in order to understand the direction and nature of change in the distribution of income in a globalising world.

Structural Change and Income Distribution

The literature on the determinants of overall distribution of income within an economy has evolved around the concept of the 'Kuznets Curve'. Kuznets (1955) advanced the hypothesis, that in the course of development, it is expected that income inequality in a society will increase. This trend will continue until the economy attains a certain (high) level of per capita income after which, the trend in income inequality is reversed. Thereafter, income distribution becomes more and more equitable (the gap between income shares of the higher and lower population percentiles declines) even as higher and higher levels of per capita income are attained. Plotting this relation on a graph with per capita income, on the horizontal axis and the Gini coefficient (or some other measure of income inequality) on the vertical axis yields a curve that takes the shape of an inverted U—this is commonly referred to in the literature as the Kuznets curve.

Kuznets (1955) argued intuitively that as the process of development progresses, one might reasonably expect such a relation to be true, particularly in the context of developing countries. The basic model of development implicit in his argument, is the traditional Lewis-type dual economy model (Lewis, 1954)—countries at a low level of development are characterised by large agricultural sectors (that is, the agricultural sector employs the majority of the population) and a relatively small manufacturing sector. Also in the tradition of the Harris-Todaro (1970) model of rural-urban migration, workers migrate from rural areas to urban areas motivated by expectations of higher earning levels.

Basically within the dual economy framework, development proceeds by an increase in the size of the manufacturing sector and a movement of the labour force from agriculture to industry. This is accompanied by a rise in urbanisation as, typically, industrialisation starts off in and promotes the growth of cities. Agricultural wages are typically stagnant and much below the wages earned by workers in the industrial sector, where labour productivity tends to be significantly higher, compared to agriculture. Therefore, as society progresses, with increasing numbers of workers moving from agriculture to industry, it is expected that initially, the distribution of income will worsen.

At least two explanations for the increase in inequality are immediately apparent. First, the gap between rural and urban incomes grows as due to industrialisation, urban incomes rise while rural incomes remain stagnant. Second, as industrialisation progresses, the dynamics of capitalism come into play and incomes within the industrial sector become more unequal as fortunes are made and profit rates increase, widening the gap between incomes of workers and capitalists. Kuznets himself accounts for the change in the distribution of income in terms of differential marginal propensity, to save of the rich and the poor. Those with higher incomes generally have a higher propensity to save. The concentration of income within the industrial sector is thus accompanied by a concentration of savings and hence accumulated wealth in the hands of relatively few. These phenomena explain the upward sloping arm of the Kuznets curve.

However, as industrialisation proceeds further and the transition made from an agricultural to an industrial society, it is expected that the initial trend in income inequality will be reversed. As industry will now employ a much larger share of the population than before, an increasing number will now enjoy higher incomes and standards of living. Further the continuous movement of labour from agriculture to industry will reduce overcrowding on land. As disguised unemployment in agriculture falls, the marginal product of labour within the sector rises and so do agricultural incomes. Moreover, as Kuznets points out, the dynamics of an industrial economy will itself unleash forces that tend to move society towards a more egalitarian distribution of income. In a dynamic society, with a high rate of technological change, typically wealth is not concentrated within the same business family for more than one or two generations (though, of course, there are exceptions). Therefore, as investors in the old industries lose their wealth, newer ones take their place, as economies continues to grow. All these factors tend to make the distribution of income more egalitarian, as society attains higher and higher levels of income—this explains the downward sloping arm of the inverted U curve.

The Kuznets Curve

In the discussion that follows, we will examine the literature that has developed around the Kuznets curve hypothesis in order to see, apart from the level of income, which other factors have been identified as the primary determinants of income distribution. In our study, it will be important to control for these other factors, which influence income distribution, as we shall attempt to isolate the impact of structural change and international trade.

Over the years, an enormous amount of work has been done on the Kuznets curve relation (See Kanbur 2000). Most of this has focused on testing the existence of an inverse U-shaped relation between income distribution and the level of income, using cross-country data on measures of income inequality (typically Gini coefficients) and levels of GDP. Earlier, empirical studies of this kind were seriously hampered by problems related to data availability. Since time-series data on income distribution was not available for most countries, empirical tests have been based on cross-country comparisons, at a given point of time.

An important early contribution in this field remains that of Chenery and Syrquin (1975) who used data on 55 countries and found evidence of the Kuznets relation. They regressed the income share of the bottom 40 per cent of the population on the level of GDP and on the square of the level of GDP. A negative (and significant) coefficient on the former and a positive (significant), one on the latter confirmed that the share of the poorest 40 per cent of the population first declines and then starts to rise as a country's GDP rises. They carried out a similar regression, with the income share of the top 20 per cent of the population and again the coefficients were significant while the signs were reversed, seeming to support a Kuznets curve type relation.

More importantly for our purpose, Chenery et al. find significant coefficients on three other variables in their income distribution regressions. These are the share of agriculture in GDP, the share of primary exports in total exports and the percentage of school enrollment. All three variables have been regarded as standard indicators of development in the literature. In comparison with developing countries, countries at advanced stages of development are expected to have a relatively lower share of agriculture in GDP, of primary exports in total exports, and a higher share of the population with at least secondary level education. A low share of agriculture and primary exports will generally be achieved in countries that are well on their way to making a transition from an agrarian to an industrial society. Such societies have a high level of income and in terms of the logic underlying the Kuznets relation, income inequality is falling in these economies. Income inequality will also decline in economies in which a larger proportion of the population are educated upto the secondary level, for at least two reasons. First, since expenditure on education does not yield immediate returns, in general, countries with higher levels of income, which face relatively lower opportunity cost of resources, tend to spend more on education. Since, by the Kuznets curve logic, richer countries tend to have a more egalitarian distribution, this gives an inverse relation between education level and the degree of income inequality as well. Second, education serves as a tool which a person may use to improve upon his or her economic prospects. Thus societies in which a higher proportion of the population is educated (till at least the secondary level) will have a less skewed distribution of income.

The subsequent literature in this genre, (Kanbur 2000) does add newer variables to income distribution regressions, but the general idea remains the same. Most of the variables added, for example, extent of urbanization, are proxy measures of the levels of development of the countries. In our regression analysis we propose to control for differences in countries' levels of development, using the indicators of development used in the Chenery et al study, as we will attempt to assess the effect of trade openness on income distribution. In addition, we shall include a measure of the redistributive policy of the government that is, income and profit taxes, as this can affect income-inequality directly by re-distributing income from the rich to the poorer classes. The assumption we make is that, governments tax the rich and use the proceeds primarily (if not solely) to make income transfers to the poorer sections of society, either directly through transfer payments or via employment generating projects.

International Trade, Structural Change and Income Distribution

Greater openness to trade flows can affect the distribution of income, by affecting the process of structural change or industrial transformation in the following manner. As countries become more open, protective barriers (such as tariffs) are reduced; imports increase and presumably so do exports. The dismantling of trade barriers can have a beneficial impact on domestic incomes via two channels: (a) Removal of import barriers may lead to an increase in non-compteting, intermediate imports and thus boost domestic production and the demand for factors. This is likely to have a positive effect on factor incomes;[14] (b) a more open trade regime generally leads to an increase in production for exports. This will also tend to have a positive effect on factor incomes, via an increase in the demand for factors. In so far as the tradables consist mainly of manufactured goods, in this case trade liberalisation would actually tend to reinforce the process of industrial transformation and in the medium term this may actually lead to an increase in income inequality.

However, greater trade openness may also have a negative effect on domestic incomes, if import competing sectors decline under pressure of competition as barriers to entry are dismantled and the domestic market is thrown open to international players. When imports out-compete domestically produced goods in the market, domestic demand is switched from domestically produced goods to cheap (or otherwise attractive) imports, leading to a fall in domestic production, factor demands and thus factor incomes. If this effect is not counterbalanced by an increase in production for exports, then greater openness may even have a negative impact on incomes of specific economic sectors and worker groups, at least in the short to medium term, till such time as the resources are reallocated to some alternate use. The impact of trade openness on the distribution of aggregate incomes may therefore, be either positive or negative depending on the specific circumstances involved.

Thus the basic model, which we test empirically, is based on the notion that, the distribution of income, in general, is a function of the level of aggregate income, the extent of openness of the economy to international trade flows (as measured by the volume of trade), structural parameters that characterise the economy (measured by the relative sizes of the agricultural and manufacturing sectors and the share of primary exports in total exports), the redistributive policies of the government, and the average educational attainment of the population (measured by the share of people with at least secondary level education).

The discussion in the following section focuses more specifically on the econometric methodology and the data sources that we use.

AN EMPIRICAL ANALYSIS

Till recently, research on income distribution issues had been seriously hindered by the lack of reliable data. However, time series data on income distribution (Deininger and Squire, 1996) is now available. The Deininger-Squire data set has time series data on Gini Coefficients and income shares by population quintiles for 108 countries, with about four or more high-quality observations for 58 countries and about six or more observations for 40 countries. This is the most extensive and reliable data set available till date; as a result it is now possible to construct a cross-country panel, in order to study the effect of trade openness on income distribution. This is precisely what we will do, in the first part of our regression analysis. In the second part of our regression analysis, we shall check the robustness of the results, regarding openness and the distribution of income, by using an alternate model and two different measures of trade openness.

The Fixed Effects Model

The statistical methodology used is fixed effects panel regression. Panel regression is often the most appropriate estimation technique used with 'panel' data, where we have time-series observations on a large cross-section of individuals or countries. There are at least two reasons for this. First, it helps to address the problem of 'omitted variables bias' (OVB), which arises, when the error term in the regression equation is correlated with one or more regressor(s). In this case, using OLS regression gives rise to biased estimators. Fixed effects panel regression, corrects this problem, by using dummy variables to control for unobserved, country-specific, time invariant, 'fixed' effects, and yields unbiased estimators. Second, panel regression makes the most optimal use of the time-series and across-country information in panel data sets. In panel data sets, we have observations across a large number of countries (or individuals) with several observations on each country, taken at different points in time. Thus, we have both 'within country' (over time) as well as 'between country' variation in the variables under consideration. It can be shown, that OLS regression gives equal weightage to both 'within' and 'between' country variation, while random effects panel regression, weights this information optimally (minimising the variance of the estimator). Fixed effects regression on the other hand, uses the 'within' information fully, but does not make any use of the 'between' country information. This is a drawback of the fixed effects regressor, but we still prefer to use it over the random effects estimator, as it eliminates the OVB in our estimator. Further, even though the random effects estimator appears more efficient in the way it uses the available information, it is more difficult to justify its use in terms of purely economic logic.

The basic econometric model we are trying to estimate is the following:[15]

$$\text{gini}_{it} = \beta_1 + \beta_2 \text{gdp}_{it} + \beta_3 \text{gdp2}_{it} + \beta_4 \text{open}_{it} + \beta_5 \text{agr}_{it} + \beta_6 \text{mfg}_{it} + \beta_7 \text{primx}_{it} + \beta_8 \text{tax}_{it} + \varepsilon_{it}$$

[16]

where the subscript 'i' stands for country, 't' for time-period and the other variables are the following:

gini = gini coefficient (the most commonly used measure of income inequality)
gdp = Per Capita Gross Domestic Product
gdp2 = Square of **gdp**
open = Percentage share of exports plus imports in GDP (measure of trade openness of the economy)
agr = Percentage share of value added in the agricultural sector in GDP
mfg = Percentage share of value added in the manufacturing sector in GDP
primx = Percentage share of food and non-food primary exports in total merchandise exports
tax = Percentage share of income and profit taxes in total tax revenue
ε = random error term

We would like to note a couple of points at this juncture. First, apart from gini, we use one other measure of income inequality, 'ineq', which is the ratio of the income share of the top 20 per cent of the population to that of the bottom 40 per cent. While the gini coefficient indicates, how the overall distribution of income is affected within the economy, across all income classes, the second measure of inequality serves to highlight specifically the income gap between the richest and the poorest sections of society. Moreover, in order to examine how the income shares of various sections of the population are affected, we also use the income shares of the bottom 40 per cent ('poor'), the middle 40 per cent ('mid') and the top 20 per cent ('rich') of the population as dependent variables in our regression.

Secondly, the square of the GDP, gdp2 is included among the regressors, in order to test for evidence of a Kuznets Curve type relationship between the level of income and income-inequality, on the basis of time-series data across countries.

Our panel consists of 34 countries and the time period of our study is 1970 to 1990.[17] On an average, we have tried to include five observations across time for each country.[18] The observations are five year apart, that is, for each country we have observations at five points in time, 1970, 1975, 1980, 1985, and 1990. This gap of five years helps reduce the problem of serial correlation, which arises inevitably in a panel, with annual observations on each country.

We use fixed effects regression, where the random error-term ε contains a country-specific component v_i that is fixed for each country over time, in addition to a random component μ_{it} that varies over each country and for each period of time. That is, in the above regression the equation is, $\varepsilon_{it} = v_i + \mu_{it}$. The reason we have used fixed effects regression is, because this helps to get rid of omitted variables bias in our estimated coefficients. Income distribution is endogenously determined by the interplay of a host of economic forces. We have tried to control for what we have identified as the principal determinants of income inequality. But there still remains scope for omitted variables bias in our specification. For instance, a country's past history (for example, whether it was once a British/French colony or not) determines quite often, whether or not and to what extent, it is a primary product exporter; a country's resource endowments determine the nature of its comparative advantage and thus its overall structure of production and trade. These factors, which determine the structural characteristics of an economy are obviously correlated with the size of its manufacturing and agricultural sectors, the extent of openness of the economy, and the composition of its imports and exports. In so far, as we fail to control explicitly, for these factors, their effect will be captured by the random error term and give rise to non-zero correlation between the error term and the regressors. In this case, ordinary least squares (OLS) estimation will yield biased coefficients, as the condition for unbiasedness (that is, zero correlation between the error term and the regressors) is clearly violated. Using fixed effects panel regression helps in this situation. The country-specific component in the error term controls for the omitted structural variables in this case and helps obtain unbiased estimates of the regression coefficients.

The Fixed Effects Results

The results of the fixed effects regression are described in Table 17.1. At the very outset we must note, that our exercise yields rather negative results, in the sense, that in most cases, the estimated coefficients are statistically insignificant at accepted levels of significance. In fact other than primx, the coefficients of none of the other regressors (including the level of GDP) can be said to be significantly different from zero.

TABLE 17.1 Results of fixed effect panel regression

Dep. Var. → Indep. Var. ↓	gini	ineq	poor	mid	rich
constant	40.29 (5.76)	2.54 (1.47)	0.16 (2.89)	0.39 (7.9)	0.45 (5.15)
gdp	−0.00 (−0.88)	−0.00 (−0.73)	5.87 (0.75)	−8.63 (−0.12)	−5.01 (−0.39)
gdp2	−1.18 (−0.26)	−3.74 (−0.38)	1.74 (0.00)	4.29 (1.53)	−4.29 (−0.87)
open	0.00 (0.06)	−0.00 (−0.04)	0.00 (0.29)	−0.00 (−0.16)	0.00 (−0.09)
primx	0.16 (2.85)	0.04 (3.05)	−0.00 (−2.30)	−0.00 (−2.02)	0.00 (2.55)
agr	0.32 (1.82)	0.06 (1.59)	−0.00 (−0.92)	−0.00 (−1.44)	0.00 (1.38)
mfg	0.04 (0.26)	0.01 (0.29)	−0.00 (−0.11)	−0.00 (−0.26)	0.00 (0.21)
tax	−0.03 (−0.47)	0.14 (1.042)	−0.00 (−0.08)	−0.00 (−0.32)	0.00 (0.23)
yr70	−11.15 (−3.48)	−1.93 (−2.79)	0.05 (2.24)	0.04 (2.21)	−0.09 (−2.62)
yr75	−8.46 (−3.70)	−1.62 (−3.32)	0.04 (2.53)	0.03 (2.49)	−0.07 (−2.96)
yr80	−4.56 (−2.89)	−1.10 (−3.25)	0.02 (2.26)	0.03 (2.89)	−0.05 (−3.02)
yr85	−2.61 (−2.46)	−0.62 (−2.77)	0.01 (1.96)	0.01 (2.21)	−0.28 (−2.45)
R^2 (within)	0.23	0.23	0.15	0.20	0.19
No. of Countries	34	34	34	34	34
No. of Observations	114	103	103	103	103

Note: t-statistics are in parenthesis; yr70, yr75, yr80 and yr85 are time dummies, which take the values one for the years 1970, 1975, 1980,1985, respectively, and zero otherwise; R^2 (within) measures the correlation coefficient for the 'within' regression, which is the appropriate one to look at in this case, since fixed effects regression uses only the information 'within' each country group.

The coefficient on primx has the expected positive sign, suggesting, an increase in the share of primary exports over time, is associated with increasing income inequality (whether measured by ineq or by gini). In each case, the coefficient is significant and for gini and ineq they are positive and non-negligible (0.16 and 0.04 respectively). For the individual income classes however, the coefficients are very small in magnitude (ranging between -0.0007 on mid to 0.0015 on rich). Our results suggest, that primx does have some effect on the overall distribution of income. As the share of primary exports in total exports increases, the overall distribution of income within an economy tends to become more unequal and the gap between the richest 20 per cent and poorest 40 per cent of the population widens. The signs of the coefficients for rich, poor, and mid suggest, an increase in the primary export share reduces the income shares of the poor and the middle-income classes and raises the share of the richest income group. However, these latter effects are extremely small in magnitude.

Regarding openness, our results indicate that trade openness has absolutely no effect whatsoever, on the distribution of income within the economy. Not only is the coefficient on openness not statistically significant, but it is almost equal to zero in each of the cases considered. The coefficient of open ranges from -0.00004 (in the mid and rich regressions) to 0.002 (in the gini regression). Therefore, there is no evidence in the data for the hypothesis, that trade openness systematically affects the distribution of income within an economy. And this result is robust to alternate measures of income inequality and income-shares of different quintiles of the population.

Regarding the Kuznets Curve relation, we find no evidence of this in the data. This echoes the general finding in the literature that there is little evidence of a inverted-U on the basis of time-series data (Bruno et al 1998; Ray 1998). Instead, we find some evidence that inequality tends to decrease with increasing levels of income, the income share of the poorest class tends to increase with income (the coefficient of gdp and gdp2 are positive in the poor-regression), while that of the richest, to decrease with income (the coefficients of gdp and gdp2 are negative in the rich-regression). Further, for the income share of the middle income group (mid) there is evidence of an inverted U-shaped relation. However, the coefficients are not statistically significant in any of these cases. So, at best we can say that there is some weak support in the data for the hypothesis, as the level of income increases, the distribution of income within economies tend to become more egalitarian.

Finally, we would like to highlight one more result that emerges from the fixed effect regression. The tax variable enters the ineq-regression with a positive coefficient. This is somewhat counter-intuitive, as it indicates that a rise in the share of income and profit-taxes will widen the income gap between the poorest and the richest sections of the population, instead of reducing it. Though the coefficient is very small and not statistically significant, yet given its sign, it seems worthwhile to focus on it. The sign on the coefficient seems to suggest that, while the lower income groups do share the burden of taxation (on incomes and profits) to some extent, the tax proceeds do not benefit these groups directly. Rather the richest income classes seem to enjoy the benefits of tax proceeds. However, these are only very tentative conclusions based on estimates whose magnitudes are very small and which are statistically insignificant.

Thus the results of our fixed effects regression suggests, that once we make use of time-series information, none of the variables suggested in the literature have much impact on the extent of income inequality (whether measured by the gini coefficient or by the relative income shares of the richest and poorest sections of the population) within an economy. In particular, the openness variable that we suggest might have an impact on income distribution, fares very poorly. It seems to have no effect whatsoever either, on the overall distribution of income or on the income shares of particular sections of the population. In fact, the only variables worth focusing on as determinants of income inequality in future studies seems to be the level of income (which has the largest estimated coefficients in our regressions) and the share of primary exports in total exports (which is the only variable with statistically significant coefficients).

A Specification Analysis

We had started off by assuming that the fixed effects model would be the most appropriate one for analysing changes in trade openness on the distribution of income. However our results indicate that there is no such effect worth reporting. In this section we check if our results are being driven by misspecification of the model itself. To do so we run the Hausman Specification Test for each of our fixed effects regression. This test helps us decide whether a fixed effects or a random effects model is more appropriate for our case. The Hausman test involves testing the null that the correlation between the error term and the regressors is zero, against the alternative hypothesis that it is non-zero. Therefore whenever we fail to reject the null, it is more appropriate to use a random effects model for our regression, as in the random effects model, the country specific error term v_{it} is not systematically correlated with the other regressors, rather it varies randomly just like the other component of the error term, μ_{it}. Failure to reject the null indicates the absence of any correlation between the error-term and the regressors and thus of any omitted variables bias in the estimated coefficients.

We find that the null of zero correlation is rejected at the 5 per cent level in the regressions, with rich and mid as the dependent variable, while it is rejected at the 10 per cent level in the regressions, with gini and ineq as the dependent variables. Thus overall our specification of the fixed effects model seems to have been correct. Only in case of the regression with poor as the dependent variable, do we fail to reject the null of zero correlation between the regressors and the error term. Running random effects regression (column 1, Table 17.2) with poor as the dependent variable does not change our results in any way however. The coefficient of primx remains negative (though almost zero) and significant, while that on open is positive (and almost zero) though insignificant. Regarding the income share of the poorest 40 per cent of the population, the results of the Hausman test seem to indicate that there is no omitted variables bias in our regression. That is the income share of this group is not systematically affected by any factor other than the ones we have specified in the regression. Rather, the income of this poorest group in society is subject to random, country-specific shocks. Typically, the poorest classes in all societies, have the least amount of income-protection and this makes their incomes the most likely to be affected by random shocks—interpreted this way, the statistical results do tend to make some intuitive sense.

We also run the full set of regressions using pooled least squares. In most cases, this yields biased coefficients owing to the presence of omitted variables bias (in all cases above, in which the Hausman test suggested that the fixed effects model is more appropriate, we may expect the pooled regression variables to be biased). The results are reported in Table 17.2, column 2 onwards. Regarding openness, the results are no different from the fixed effects model. The coefficient of open in the gini and ineq-regressions are negative, but insignificant and almost zero, indicating that even on the basis of cross-country

TABLE 17.2 Results of random-effects and pooled least squares regression

Dep. Var. → Indep. Var. ↓	Poor	gini	ineq	poor	mid	rich
constant	0.13 (3.33)	57.52 (9.14)	6.51 (5.31)	0.09 (2.61)	0.27 (9.71)	0.64 (10.97)
gdp	4.55 (0.89)	0.00 (−2.42)	−0.00 (−2.42)	7.25 (1.51)	0.00 (3.16)	−0.00 (−2.37)
gdp2	−5.49 (−0.23)	3.59 (0.76)	1.63 (0.19)	−8.15 (−0.32)	−1.24 (0.64)	2.06 (0.49)
open	0.00 (0.39)	−0.01 (−0.62)	−0.01 (−2.47)	0.00 (1.55)	0.00 (1.49)	−0.00 (−1.62)
primx	−0.00 (−2.81)	0.16 (4.29)	0.02 (3.73)	−0.00 (−4.00)	−0.00 (−2.73)	0.00 (3.68)
agr	0.00 (1.38)	−0.62 (−4.56)	−1.12 (−4.53)	0.00 (3.85)	0.00 (4.88)	−0.01 (−4.58)
mfg	0.00 (0.97)	−0.15 (−1.05)	−0.01 (−0.42)	0.00 (0.99)	0.00 (0.64)	−0.00 (−0.89)
tax	−0.00 (−0.55)	−0.03 (−0.65)	−0.00 (−0.33)	−0.00 (−0.70)	0.00 (0.34)	0.00 (0.27)
yr70	0.02 (1.39)					
yr75	0.01 (1.55)					
yr80	0.01 (1.32)					
yr85	0.01 (1.06)					
R^2	0.20	0.37 (0.33)	0.33 (0.28)	0.27 (0.21)	0.54 (0.50)	0.39 (0.35)
No. of Countries	34	34	34	34	34	34
No. of Observations	103	114	103	103	103	103

Note: t-statistics are in parentheses; Column 1 reports random effects regression results with poor as the dependent variable—in this case the figures in parentheses are standard normal statistics; R^2 represents the overall correlation coefficient for the random effects regression since this uses *both* 'between' and 'within' country information and weights them optimally. Columns 2 to 6 report the results of pooled regressions—for these the R^2 in parenthesis is the adjusted correlation coefficient.

comparisons, we cannot say anything about the nature of income distribution within an economy, based on information about its degree of trade openness. The coefficient of primx is significant in each case, but its value is again very small (ranging from 0.0004 in mid to 0.001 in the rich-regression), except for the gini and ineq-regressions for which the values are 0.16 and 0.02 respectively.

Our results also suggest, that as the level of income rises, there is not much impact on either overall inequality or on the income shares of either the middle-income or high-income groups (the coefficient of gdp is almost zero and significant for the gini, ineq, mid and rich-regressions). Only the income share of the poorest 40 per cent of the population seems to increase with income at the initial stages (the coefficient of gdp is comparatively quite large, 7.25, though insignificant). Regarding the Kuznets Curve relation, we find some evidence of just the reverse kind of a relation in the data—the coefficient of gdp is negative (though not significant)—while that on its square term (gdp2) is positive (again not significant) in the poor-regression.[19] Thus using the recent Deininger-Squire data set on inequality, we find little evidence of the Kuznets curve relation, even on the basis of cross-country data.

Alternate Model Specification and Measure of Openness

We will now use cross-country data and two different measures of trade openness, to check the robustness of our results, regarding the relation between income distribution and international trade.[20]

We will use the trade-gdp ratio as before and a second, readily available measure of openness proposed in Sachs and Warner (1995). The Sachs-Warner trade openness index classifies countries as open or closed over the period 1970–89, using five different criteria associated with the degree of restrictiveness of the country's trade regime.

The five criteria that Sachs and Warner propose are the following:

(i) Non-tariff barriers covering 40 per cent or more of trade;
(ii) Average tariff rates of 40 per cent or more;
(iii) A black-market exchange rate that is depreciated by 20 per cent or more;
(iv) A socialist economic system;
(v) A State monopoly on major exports.

If a country meets at least one of these criteria, it is classified as 'closed'; it is classified as 'open' otherwise, over the period 1970–89. As such this classification essentially yields a dummy variable measure of trade openness, 'opensw' which assumes the value 'zero' for all years when a country followed a closed trade regime and 'one' for the years when it adopted an open trade regime.

Before using this measure, we would like to point out that this has a few problems. The choice of 40 per cent and 20 per cent as the thresholds for tariff (and non-tariff) barriers and black market premium respectively, seems totally arbitrary. Indeed, the authors do not try to justify their choice of these figures at any point. Further, the decision to classify countries as closed if they have a socialist regime is also arguable.[21] In spite of these problems however, we use the Sachs-Warner openness criteria because it is based on a large number of criteria that closed economies usually do satisfy. Therefore, it should not do too badly as a measure of openness of a country's trade regime.

We have carried out a cross-country analysis, using data on 48 countries[22] with all the explanatory variables used in the panel regression (the results are reported in Tables 17.3 and 17.4). In addition we have used data on the coverage of secondary education as well. For the cross-country regression, our dependent variable is Δgini, which is the change in income inequality, as measured by the gini coefficient; between 1970 and 1989 (a positive value for this variable indicates an increase in overall income inequality over this period). We also looked at a second measure of income inequality that is, the ratio of the income share of the top 20 per cent of the population to that of the bottom 40 per cent. This variable, Δineq, measures the change in relative income shares between 1970 and 1989. We also look at how the income shares of the bottom 40 per cent (Δpoor), middle 40 per cent (Δmid) and top 20 per cent (Δrich) of the population changed during our period of study, in order to decide to what extent these changes can be attributed to the nature of the trade regime.

Our regression equation is the following:

$$\Delta gini = \beta_1 + \beta_2 \, gdpgr + \beta_3 (\Delta \, primx) + \beta_4 (\Delta agr) + \beta_5 (\Delta tax) + \beta_6 (\Delta \, edu) + \beta_7 (\Delta mfg) + \beta_8 \, opensw + \varepsilon$$

where:

gdpgr = the growth rate of GDP over the period 1970–89.
Δ primx = change in the percentage share of food and non-food primary exports in total merchandise exports over the period 1970–89
Δagr = change in the percentage share of value-added in the agricultural sector in GDP over the period 1970–89

Δmfg = change in the percentage share of value-added in the manufacturing sector in GDP over the preiod 1970–89

Δtax = change in the percentage share of income and profit taxes in total tax revenue over the period 1970–89

Δedu = change in the percentage share of secondary school enrollment in gross school enrollment over the period 1970–89

opensw is the Sachs-Warner measure of openness of the trade regime. It is a dummy variable, which takes the value one if the country is open, zero if closed. In our first set of regressions, we have used this dummy variable measure of openness and use the various measures of income inequality discussed above, as the dependent variables. In the second set of regressions, we have used the change in percentage share of imports and exports in GDP (Δopen), as our measure of openness and we compare the two sets of regression results to see if this makes any difference to our basic result regarding the effect of trade on income distribution.

The reason we have focused on first-differences in the variables, rather than averages, is related to the basic nature of the question we pose. We are interested in asking how *changes* in the openness of an economy affect *changes* in its distribution of income. So our dependent variable, is a measure of the change in income inequality between 1970 and 1989 and we use first differences for our independent variables as well.

In this specification, we have made no attempt to test for the Kuznets Curve hypothesis, the results of the previous section and those reported in Bruno et al. (1998) and Ray (1998) show that this relation gets little support in the data, using the Deininger and Squire (1996) data set. Instead, we have included the rate of growth of GDP as an explanatory variable, to see if this affects income inequality in a systematic way. In particular, we shall examine if there is evidence to support the hypothesis that economic growth affects adversely the income shares of the poorest classes in society.

The results from running OLS regression using the Sachs-Warner criteria for openness, are reported in Table 17.3. The coefficient on opensw turns out to be quite small, in each of

TABLE 17.3 Results of least squares regression using the Sachs-Warner measure of openness

Dep. Var. → Indep. Var. ↓	Δgini	Δineq	Δpoor	Δmid	Δrich
constant	2.19 (0.84)	0.53 (0.98)	−0.02 (−1.22)	−0.01 (−0.53)	0.02 (1.19)
opensw	−0.41 (−0.17)	−0.40 (−0.81)	−0.01 (−0.47)	0.02 (0.93)	−0.01 (−0.52)
Δgdpgr	1.77 (0.93)	0.48 (1.10)	−0.00 (−0.49)	−0.01 (−0.76)	0.02 (0.94)
Δagr	−0.29 (−0.16)	0.03 (0.67)	0.00 (0.19)	−0.00 (−0.13)	−9.4 (−0.01)
Δmfg	−0.83 (−0.43)	−0.06 (−1.54)	0.00 (1.52)	0.00 (0.14)	−0.00 (−1.03)
Δprimx	0.16 (2.23)	0.01 (0.78)	−0.00 (−0.99)	−0.00 (−1.80)	0.00 (2.14)
Δtax	−0.41 (−0.43)	0.01 (0.72)	0.00 (0.40)	−0.00 (−0.69)	0.00 (0.35)
Δedu	−0.01 (−0.12)	−0.01 (−0.39)	0.00 (1.24)	−0.00 (−0.73)	−0.00 (−0.12)
R^2	0.35 (0.13)	0.37 (0.08)	0.43 (0.17)	0.24 (−0.11)	0.42 (0.15)
No. of Observations	29	23	23	23	23

Note: t-statistics are in parenthesis; The R^2 in parenthesis are the adjusted correlation coefficients.

our regressions and in each case it is statistically insignificant. This suggests that in general there is no systematic relation between the openness of the trade regime a country and the nature of income distribution within its economy. That is, on the basis of cross-country data we cannot say that more open economies tend to have a more (or less) egalitarian distribution of income in comparison with relatively closed economies.

Regarding the growth rate of gdp also, we cannot conclude anything on the basis of our data. The coefficient on gdpgr is positive in the Δgini- and Δineq-regressions, suggesting that countries that experienced faster growth rates experienced an increase in income inequality. However, in both cases the coefficients are statistically insignificant. Thus we really cannot come to any conclusion regarding the relation between income growth and income inequality based on our sample.

The coefficient on the education variable, which we have added in the cross-country regression, has the expected negative sign in the Δgini- and Δineq-regressions, but in each case the size of the coefficient is extremely small and it is statistically insignificant. Thus we cannot draw any conclusion regarding the effect of education on income inequality also, on the basis of our results.

Exactly the same pattern of results emerges from our second set of cross-country regressions, using percentage trade-shares (Δopen) as our measure of trade openness (these results are reported in Table 17.4). The only significant variable, once again is the share of primary exports in total exports, just as in case of the results from our panel regressions.

TABLE 17.4 Results of least squares regression using trade shares as a measure of openness

Dep. Var. → Indep. Var. ↓	Δgini	Δineq	Δpoor	Δmid	Δrich
constant	2.26 (0.88)	0.43 (0.81)	–0.02 (–1.46)	–0.00 (–0.28)	0.02 (1.09)
Δopen	–0.03 (–0.45)	–0.01 (–0.69)	0.00 (0.88)	–0.00 (–0.15)	–0.00 (–0.39)
Δgdpgr	1.98 (1.00)	0.48 (1.01)	–0.01 (–1.02)	–0.01 (–0.34)	0.02 (0.89)
Δagr	–0.02 (–0.10)	0.04 (0.84)	0.00 (0.20)	–0.00 (–0.25)	0.00 (0.10)
Δmfg	–0.09 (–0.49)	–0.06 (–1.41)	0.00 (1.806)	–0.00 (–0.13)	–0.00 (–0.94)
Δprimx	0.16 (2.59)	0.01 (0.55)	–0.00 (–1.38)	–0.00 (–1.50)	0.00 (0.00)
Δtax	–0.03 (–0.38)	0.01 (0.69)	0.00 (0.06)	–0.00 (–0.40)	0.00 (0.32)
Δedu	–0.01 (–0.12)	–0.01 (–0.29)	0.00 (0.96)	–0.00 (–0.55)	–0.00 (–0.08)
R^2	0.35 (0.14)	0.37 (0.08)	0.45 (0.19)	0.20 (0.17)	0.42 (0.15)
No. of Observations	29	23	23	23	23

Note: t-statistics are in parenthesis; The R^2 in parenthesis are the adjusted correlation coefficients.

Therefore, on the basis of cross-country analysis and using alternate measures of trade openness also we come to the conclusion that trade openness and income distribution are not related in any systematic manner across countries.

Implications for India

An important feature of income distribution in India, is the remarkable stability of the distribution over time. A number of authors have commented on this (see for instance, Bruno et al. 1998). Till now relatively few observations are available for the post liberalisation period. However available evidence indicates, that in the post-liberalisation phase, the extent of inequality in the overall distribution of income has increased (Jha 2000), even as measured poverty seems to have declined (Sundaram and Tendulkar 2003).[23]

On the basis of our regression results, we cannot draw any direct implications regarding the nature of change in income distribution in India, as the country pursues policies of liberalisation. However, we can make some surmises regarding the direction of change on the basis of the foregoing analysis and available secondary data sources. Several forces can be identified that may actually accentuate income inequality in India in the post-liberalisation phase. In particular we focus on a few factors that affect: (a) rural-urban disparities and (b) inter-regional disparities within the country.

India has a federal structure with 28 major states and there is a large literature that examines the growth of inter-regional disparities in the country, by focusing mainly on the growth of inter-state differences in per capita incomes and other socio-economic indicators (CII, 2002; Das and Barua 1996; Datt and Ravallion 1998; Ravallion and Datt 2002 and so on). Evidence from this large body of literature indicates that inter regional disparities in the country are increasing, with growing inter-state disparities, especially with respect to manufacturing growth rates.

In this context, we would like to discuss a particular aspect of globalisation that may actually enhance inter-regional disparities in India even further. This relates to the increasingly widespread phenomenon of business process off-shoring or outsourcing, that is being practiced by manufacturing firms across the developed world and by multi-national corporations in particular. A closely linked and equally widespread phenomenon is the inflow of FDI into developing countries like India. Even though FDI coming into India is still less than that going into China, yet the amount of FDI that the country currently receives is still significant and growing at a fast pace. It is interesting to note, that there is a regional bias in the pattern of FDI, with the better off states like Maharashtra, Gujarat, Tamilnadu, Karnataka and Andhra Pradesh, receiving a far greater share of foreign investments than the others. Investment flows into these states can be explained in terms of certain advantages they possess in terms of necessary industrial infrastructure, including labour.

The implication of a growing volume of FDI would therefore be to enhance existing regional disparities as foreign investment is targeting those regions which are already relatively better off. Insofar as the inflow of investment leads to an increase in manufacturing activity in the region, this would tend to enhance inter-regional disparities in the country. The ultimate effect of this phenomenon would be to exacerbate inequality in the overall distribution of income, which reflects income disparities among the population settled across various regions of the country.

An inevitable fallout of growing FDI flows, may also be to increase the extent of rural-urban disparities in the distribution of income, especially insofar as these flows tend to be urban-centric. This tendency would actually tend to be reinforced by the outsourcing phenomenon, which also tends to be urban-centric. A lot of the outsourcing, especially business process outsourcing (BPO) carried out especially by American and European firms is being located in India in order to take advantage of the country's vast skilled labour force. Although, only a small fraction of the Indian population are educated, yet in terms of absolute numbers this is a significant resource base, that can be employed at far lower wage rates than those available in the developed countries. As such, increasingly foreign capital is relocating to India in order to hire the services of its educated and mostly urban workforce. Given the open door policies being followed in the country with respect to the inflow of foreign capital, and given that such inflows may actually be associated with growing rural-urban income disparities, overall inequality in the country may actually increase further in the near future.

However, there may also be a tendency for overall inequality to be dampened, insofar as liberalisation policies affect exports, especially agricultural exports in the country. Increasing agricultural production for exports and also growing links between agricultural production and the food processing industry are both likely to enhance rural incomes. While this would most certainly lead to increasing inequities within the rural sector, it may, especially in the long run, reduce overall inequality by narrowing the gap between rural and urban per capita income levels.

Finally, it is fast becoming apparent that education may well become an extremely important instrument for enhancing incomes in the Indian context. This is especially so, in the light of the nature of opportunities that are opening up in the BPO sector. However as of now it appears that this sector is affecting the incomes of relatively only a small section of the population and the future of this sector remains uncertain given the backlash against outsourcing activities in the developed countries and the growing competition among developing nations to attract foreign capital.

CONCLUSION

The empirical analyses in this paper suggests, that a-priori there is no reason to expect that open economies will have a more (or less) unequal distribution of income, as compared to less open or closed economies. While our brief analysis of the Indian situation points to several factors, that may actually enhance overall income inequality in the economy in the context of a developing country that is beginning to open up to international capital flows.

Our empirical results indicate, that the extent of trade openness of an economy, per se, does not exercise any systematic influence on the distribution of income within the economy. Taken in this sense, it seems that the widely expressed pessimism regarding the effects of globalisation on poverty and income inequality is actually unwarranted. However, our conclusions are at best tentative because the data set we have used has a lot of problem areas, particularly related to missing data points, which tend to limit the size of our sample. Further, our study is based on a few data points for a limited number of countries and our results indicate that in general, there is no reason to expect that openness will affect income distribution in a particular way. However, country studies that use time-series data on a particular country might reveal more useful information, as has been the case for the empirical studies carried out in the context of the US. Finally, our measure of trade openness itself can be criticised. We have seen that the Sachs-Warner openness index is somewhat arbitrarily defined, while the trade-shares we use for the rest of our analysis can be criticised because it fails to separate the exogenous, from the endogenously determined component of trade. After all, the volume of trade (which we focus on) is determined endogenously along with other economic aggregates, within a general equilibrium set up, in the real world.

An important result that emerges from our analysis is, for primary product exporters, increasing dependence on primary exports tends to make the existing distribution of income more unequal. At one level this result seems to echo the Singer-Prebisch hypothesis regarding deteriorating terms of trade for primary-product-exporting countries in the long run. Basically, it indicates that the composition of exports might constitute an important determinant of the way in which international trade affects the distribution of income. Further research is needed before we can say anything more, regarding the exact nature of the relation between the extent of a country's dependence on primary exports and changes in its distribution of income.

Finally, another result emerges in the course of our analysis. There is no evidence of a Kuznets-Curve type relation between income levels and the degree of inequality, in the data. In fact we find that most of the variables suggested in the literature (which has evolved around the Kuznets Curve concept) are quite ineffective in explaining changes in the distribution of income in a systematic way. This seems to suggest, the need for more work, especially at a theoretical level, on the determinants of the distribution of income within an economy.

Endnotes

[1] I would like to thank Dale Jorgenson, Deepak Nayyar, Dani Rodik and Romain Wacziarg for their help and valuable comments on this paper. The usual disclaimer applies.

[2] On the topic of income distributions, one could either talk about the *functional* distribution (that is, the distribution of income across various economic categories, such as wages, rents, profits and so on) or about the *personal* distribution which refers to the distribution of income across households (or individuals) from all sources.

[3] In this context, for an insightful discussion of the various questions that can be raised on the issue of international trade and the distribution of income see Deardorff and Hakura (1994).

[4] The real hourly wages of men with 12 years of schooling dropped by about 20 per cent between 1979 and 1993.

[5] The rate of unemployment was 2.9 per cent in Europe in 1973. From 1983 to 1991 however, the average unemployment rate rose to 9.3 per cent.

[6] At one level technological change has actually helped create job opportunities for the less-skilled. This point has received relatively little to almost no attention in the existing literature. Consider one such instance of technological change. In supermarkets across the developed world, bar-code machines at payment counters are so equipped that those working at the counter require little 'skills', other than basic familiarity with the 3 Rs to qualify for this post.

[7] In the standard textbook version of the 2 × 2 HOS trade model, typically labour and capital are identified as the two factors of production.

[8] In this framework, the implicit assumption seems to be that 'capital' is essentially produced using skilled labour relatively intensively. As such, skilled labour abundance implies capital abundance.

[9] The main results of the HOS theorem and its corollaries hold under certain assumptions, such as: (a) perfect competition in the goods and factor markets, (b) constant returns to scale technology, (c) incomplete specialisation in production, (d) at least as many factors of production as there are goods and (e) full-employment of all factors of production.

[10] In the 2 × 2 version of the HOS model, with the assumption of a small open economy, it can be shown that relative factor prices change only when there is a change in relative goods prices. Given this, if the Stolper–Samuelson theorem were true (under the small open economy assumption), then if a change in relative factor prices is observed, it *must* be the case that relative goods prices have also changed.

[11] One reason for the difference in the estimates of relative price changes in the two studies was due to the fact that Sachs and Shatz excluded computer prices from their series of prices of high-skill-intensive goods. These authors argued that the massive decline in computer prices in the 1980s would tend to distort the overall pattern of price change in the US economy.

[12] Wood (1994) actually adopts a variant of the factor-content methodology where he makes several adjustments, especially for differences in production techniques between the developed North and the developing countries of the South. His calculations indicate that the net impact of North-South trade on manufacturing employment in the US is roughly ten times what standard factor content estimates imply.

[13] The authors develop a new 'endowment-corrected' measure of trade openness and use six existing indices of trade openness.

[14] Though the exact response of factor demand on factor incomes will depend on the nature of the factor supply function.

[15] Data on GDP and Trade shares (percentage share of exports and imports in total GDP) is taken from the Penn World Tables (version 5.6). Data on all the other variables, that is, percentage shares of value-added in agriculture and manufacturing sectors in total GDP; percentage share of food and non-food primary exports in total merchandise exports; percentage share of income and profit taxes in total tax revenue of the government; the percentage of secondary school enrollment as a percentage of gross school enrollment; are taken from the World Development Indicators CD-Rom.

[16] We do not include a measure of secondary education as an explanatory variable in our panel regression because of lack of continuous time-series data on this variable, in the World Development Indicator CD-Rom.

[17] We do not focus on the 1960s decade at all because we are constrained by the availability of time-series data on our explanatory variables, for which the starting date for the observations is 1970.

[18] However there is a problem with missing data, arising partly from the fact that continuous time series data is not available, especially on income distribution, for all countries in our sample. For the income distribution variable, when an observation is missing for a country for a particular year, we replace it by an observation from the closest year available in the preceding five years. Since the distribution of income within an economy tends to be relatively stable over short periods of time, this should not affect our results significantly.

[19] Bruno et al. (1998) report finding a similar U-shaped relation using time series data on gini coefficients and growth rates for India.

[20] Using a panel dataset and a fixed effects (and random effects) model we did not find a significant relation between openness and income inequality, so we use a simple cross-section dataset to see if there is any change in the results and in particular check if the results are sensitive to change in the measure of trade openness.

[21] However, this criteria can be justified on the grounds that most erstwhile socialist countries did have highly restrictive trade regimes.

[22] However, due to a large number of missing data points in our final data set the actual cross-country regression is carried out on only 29 countries, with the gini coefficient as the

measure of income inequaltiy and only 23 countries with relative quintile shares as the measure of income inequality. Most of the problem with missing data arises due to the lack of time-series data on income distribution over our period of analysis.

[23] However, there is still some debate on the extent of poverty reduction that has actually taken place (Sen et al. 2003).

References

Berman, E., J. Bound, and Z. Griliches. 1994. 'Changes in Demand for Skilled Labour within US Manufacturing: Evidence from the Annual Survey of Manufactures', *Quarterly Journal of Economics*, vol. 109, pp. 367–97.

Berman, E., S. Machin, and J. Bound. 1996. 'Implications of Skill-Biased Technological Change', mimeograph, Boston: Boston University.

Borjas, G., R. Freeman and L. Katz. 1992. 'On the Labour Market Effects of Immigration and Trade', in *Immigration and the Workforce*, edited by G. Borjas and R. Freeman, Chicago: University of Chicago Press.

Bound, J. and G. Johnson, G. 1992. 'Changes in the Structure of Wages in the 1980s: An Evaluation of Alternative Explanations', *American Economic Review*, vol. 82, pp. 371–92.

Bourguignon, F. and C. Morrisson. 1990. 'Income Distribution, Development and Foreign Trade', *European Economic Review*, vol. 34, pp. 1113–32.

Bruno, M., M. Ravaillon and L. Squire. 1998. 'Equity and Growth in Developing Countries: Old and New Perspectives on the Policy Issues', in *Income Distribution and High-Quality Growth*, edited by V. Tanzi and K. Chu, Cambridge: MIT Press, pp. 117–46.

Burtless, G. 1995. 'International Trade and the Rise in Earnings Inequality', *Journal of Economic Literature*, vol. 33, pp. 800–16.

Chenery, H. and M. Syrquin. 1975. *Patterns of Development, 1950–1970*, London: Oxford University Press.

CII. 2002. *How are the States Doing?* New Delhi: CII.

Das, S. K. and Alokesh Barua. 1996. 'Regional Inequalities, Economic Growth and Liberalisation: A Study of the Indian Economy', *Journal of the Development Studies*, vol. 32, no. 3, pp. 364–90.

Dastidar, A. G. 2006. 'International Trade and Personal Income Distribution in Developing Countries: Some Issues and Concerns', *Arthaniti*, vol. 5, nos 1–2, pp. 64–80.

Datt, G. and M. Ravallion. 1998. 'Why have some Indian States Done Better than others at Reducing Rural Poverty', *Economica*, vol. 65.

Deardorff, A. V. and D. S. Hakura. 1994. 'Trade and Wages: What are the Questions', in *Trade and Wages*, edited by J. Bhagwati and M. H. Kosters, Washington DC: AEI Press, pp. 76–107.

Deininger, K. and L. Squire. 1996. 'A New Data Set Measuring Income Inequality', *World Bank Economic Review*, vol. 10, pp. 565–91.

Edwards, S. 1997. 'Trade Policy, Growth and Income Distribution', *American Economic Review, Papers and Proceedings*, pp. 205–10.

Freeman, R. B. 1995. 'Are Your Wages Set in Beijing?', *Journal of Economic Perspectives*, vol. 9, pp. 15–32.

Harris, J. R. and M. P. Todaro. 1970. 'Migration, Unemployment and Development: A Two-sector Analysis', *American Economic Review*, vol. 60, pp. 126–42.

Jha, R. 2000. 'Reducing Poverty and Inequality in India: Has Liberalization Helped?', Working Paper no.204, Sweden: WIDER.

Kanbur, R. 2000. 'Income Distribution and Development', in *Handbook of Income Distribution*, vol. 1, edited by A. B. Atkinson and F. Bourguignon, North Holland: Amsterdam, pp. 791–841.

Kosters, M. H. 1994. 'An Overview of Changing Wage Patterns in the Labour Market', in *Trade and Wages*, edited by J. Bhagwati and M. H. Kosters, Washington DC: AEI Press, pp. 1–35.

Krueger, A. B. 1993. 'How Computers have Changed the Wage Structure: Evidence from Microdata 1984–89', *Quarterly Journal of Economics*, vol. 108, pp. 33–60.

Krueger, A. O. 1974. 'The Political Economy of the Rent Seeking', *American Economic Review*, vol. 4, pp. 291–303.

Krugman, P. 1995. 'Growing World Trade: Causes and Consequences', *Brookings Papers on Economic Activity*, vol. 1, pp. 327–62.

Kuznets, S. 1995. 'Economic Growth and Income Inequality', *American Economic Review*, vol. 45, pp. 1–28.

Lawrence, R. Z. and M. J. Slaughter. 1993. 'Trade and US Wages: Giant Sucking Sound or Small Hiccup?', *Brookings Paper on Economic Activity*, vol. 2, Washington DC: Brookings Institution, pp. 161–226.

Lewis, W. A. 1954. 'Economic Development with Unlimited Supplies of Labor', *The Manchester School of Economic and Social Studies*, vol. 22, pp. 139–91.

Li, H., L. Squire and H. Zou. 1998. 'Explaining International and Intertemporal Variations in Income Inequality', *The Economic Journal*, vol. 108, pp. 26–43.

Murphy, K. M. and F. Welch. 1991. 'The Role of International Trade in Wage Differentials', in *Workers and their Wages: Changing Patterns in the United States*, edited by M. H. Kosters, Washington DC: AEI Press, pp. 39–69.

Nayyar, D. 1996. 'Free Trade: Why, When and For Whom', *Banca Nazionale del Lavoro Quarterly Review*, vol. XLIX, pp. 333–50.

OECD. 1994. *The OECD Jobs Study: Evidence and Explanation*, Paris: OECD.

Ray, D. 1998. *Development Economics*, Princeton: Princeton University Press.

Ravallion M. and G. Datt. 2002. 'Why has Economic Growth Been More Pro-poor in Some States of India than Others?', *Journal of Development Economics*, vol. 68, pp. 381–400.

Richardson, J. D. 1995. 'Income Inequality and Trade: How to Think, What to Conclude', *Journal of Economic Perspectives*, vol. 9, pp. 33–55.

Sachs, J. and H. Shatz. 1994. 'Trade and Jobs in US Manufacturing', *Brookings Paper on Economic Activity*, vol. 1, Washington DC: Brookings Institution, pp. 1–84.

Sachs, J. and A. Warner. 1995. 'Economic Reform and the Process of Global Integration', *Brookings Paper on Economic Activity*, vol. 1, pp. 1–118.

Savvides, A. 1998. 'Trade Policy and Income Inequality: New Evidence', *Economic Letters*, vol. 61, pp. 365–72.

Sen, A. and Himangshu. 2003. 'Poverty and Inequality in India: Getting Closer to the Truth', mimeograph, Centre for Economic Studies and Planning, New Delhi: Jawaharlal Nehru University.

Spilimbergo, A., J. L. Londono and M. Szekely. 1999. 'Income Distribution, Factor Endowments and Trade Openness', *Journal of Development Economics*, vol. 59, pp. 77–101.

Sundaram, K. and S. Tendulkar. 2003. 'Poverty has Declined in the 1990s: A Resolution of Comparability Problems in the NSS Consumer Expenditure Data', *Economic and Political Weekly*, vol. 38, 25 January.

UNCTAD. 1995. *The UNCTAD Report on Trade and Development*, New York: United Nations.

Wood, A. 1994. *North-South Trade, Employment and Inequality: Changing Fortunes in a Skill-Driven World*, Oxford: Clarendon Press.
____. 1995. 'How Trade Hurt Unskilled Workers', *Journal of Economic Perspectives*, vol. 9, pp. 57–80.

18

Trade Liberalisation and Income Inequality: An Analysis of Inter-Regional Income Inequality in India

ALOKESH BARUA AND PAVEL CHAKRABORTY

INTRODUCTION

India had undergone a series of tariff liberalisation policies since the 1990s but the extent and the coverage of tariff reductions and the pace with which lowering of tariffs were carried out ever since it had joined the WTO in 1995 had never been so phenomenal before. For instance, India's economy-wide average applied tariff rate fell from around 125 per cent in 1990–91[1] to 14.5 per cent in 2007 (WTO 2008). The average applied tariff rate for the non-agricultural goods was 11.5 per cent, which was even lower, though the same for the agricultural goods being 34.5 per cent (WTO 2008) was relatively much higher. Such significant fall in tariff barriers was expected to lead to reallocation of resources towards the sectors in which the country had comparative advantages. In consequence, income distributional changes were expected to favour the abundant factor which, in case of India, was the unskilled labour. However, trade liberalisation also must have led to changes in the distribution of income across regions, an issue which has not received its due attention in the standard literature on international trade theory and income distribution.

It is by now quite well recognised that opening up an economy to international trade may often lead to changes in inter-regional income distribution, and, in fact, there are a number of empirical studies which have highlighted upon this issue. In response to the growing evidence of the effect of trade liberalisation on inter-regional income inequality, new developments in trade theory have taken place with the explicit recognition of how geography can shape trade patterns and economic developments (Krugman, 1995). In this paper we shall attempt to analyse the impact of trade liberalisation on inter-regional income inequality in India. It is an important issue because growing inter-regional inequality is certainly not desirable in a federal economy on grounds of economic and political stability. Further, it may directly hamper the speed of the liberalisation process itself if the stakeholders particularly in the backward regions were to believe that the cause of their increasing miseries lies in trade liberalisation. In democracies, consensus building is an important component determining policy changes. More often than not we hear the dissenting voices against the WTO-induced liberalisation for rising poverty[2] and growing inter-regional income inequality[3] in India. Certainly, such voices may eventually pose to be a big challenge for the future of trade liberalisation in India.

The present paper will examine the impact of trade liberalisation on regional income inequality in India. The paper is divided into seven broad parts which will: summarise the literature on growth, convergence and regional inequality in the context of the Indian economy; analyse the patterns and trends of regional income inequality in India covering data till 2006; try to establish the causality between inter-regional income inequality and the inequalities of its various components, such as agriculture, manufacturing and services, etc; try to extend the causality analyses further by using a model of structural change based on the Chenery-Syrquin hypothesis (Chenery and Syrquin 1977); summarise results on trade liberalisation and inter-regional inequality; and conclude with a broad analysis of the findings.

GROWTH, CONVERGENCE AND REGIONAL INEQUALITY

In recent years the debate on the income distributional implications of trade, particularly in the context of the developing countries, has shifted its focus from relative to absolute income inequality. That is, whether globalisation leads to a decline or rise in poverty. The shift in focus of the impact of globalisation on absolute rather than relative income distribution makes the issue of income inequality politically more sensitive. There is no a priori reason however to believe that trade may lead to increase in poverty and in fact economists tend to believe that it may even reduce poverty by its effects on growth and technical change. The trade-growth nexus and its impact on poverty have been considered both at theoretical and empirical levels by Bhagwati and Srinivasan, and by Srinivasan and Wallack in this volume (chapters 15 and 16 respectively). Trade liberalisation, by providing incentives for a more efficient allocation of resources in the economy, may contribute to sustained growth (Bannister and Thugge 2001). The static efficient allocation of resources may boost growth via increased efficiency of investment, as well as may enable a country to expand at constant (rather than diminishing) returns for a longer period through access to markets (Ventura 1997). It may also help achieving higher rate of domestic saving and/or foreign capital inflow and higher real return to capital in unskilled labour abundant countries. Further, exposures to ideas and innovations being generated in other countries may also increase productivity. The theory of long run economic growth also claims that openness raises the steady state level of income along with the growth rate of a country via efficient resource allocation (Berg and Krueger 2003).

Trade-Growth Nexus: Convergence or Divergence?

As far as empirical evidence of the relationship between trade and growth is concerned, a large number of studies, including Dollar and Kraay (2001a, 2001b), Barro and Lee (1994), Frankel and Romer (1999) and others, have concluded that openness to trade is a significant explanatory variable for the level or the growth of rate of real output per capita. The issue of interest for us is whether trade-led growth is regionally converging or diverging.

There are several studies looking at the inter-regional divergences in growth rates in India. For instance, Mathur (1987) try to explain why growth rates diverge between regions while Dholakia (1994) observed marked tendencies of convergence of long term economic growth rates for the period of 1960–61 to 1989–90 for twenty Indian states. The same conclusion was also drawn by Cashin and Sahay (1996). But, at the same time, Cashin and Sahay also reported that the dispersion of real per capita income had increased during the period. The study by Rao, Shand and Kaliranjan (1999) suggested that per capita Net State Domestic Product (NSDP) in the states have tended to diverge rather than converge. Nagraj et al. (1997) considered the growth performance of the Indian states during 1960–94 and found evidence of conditional convergence i.e. convergence relative to state-specific steady states. In contrast, some studies that have discerned tendencies of divergence are Majumder and Kapoor (1980), Bajpai and Sachs (1996), Marjit and Mitra (1996), Raman (1996), Rao et al. (1999), Dasgupta et al. (2000), and Sachs et al. (2002). What was being observed was the existence of a clear dichotomy between the 'forward' and 'backward' states, the former having higher levels of per capita income, better infrastructure, higher resource flows and private investment as well as better social and demographic indicators compared to the latter group. Some of the studies also have attempted to address the impact of trade on the issue of regional divergences in India (Sachs et al 2002, Ahluwalia, 2002). For instance, Ahluwalia (2002) analysing the differential economic performances of Indian states in the 1990s under the influence of the forces of globalisation found no evidence of unconditional convergence, although he had found some evidence of conditional convergence. Looking at the period 1990–91 to 1998–99, Singh and Srinivasan (2002), on the contrary, concluded that the evidence does not permit one to reach very definite conclusions on convergence or divergence across Indian states.

Trade and Regional Inequality

The analysis of per capita income convergence or divergence as discussed above and the analysis of inter-temporal regional inequality measures essentially pertain to explain the same phenomenon. There is however a difference between the two approaches. The former is based upon certain theory of dynamic growth processes whereas the latter is an absolutely statistical artefact devoid of any theoretical underpinning. The advantage of the latter approach is that while the former merely is a test of falsification (or validation) of a particular theory of growth, the latter leaves it opens for testing to any contestable proposition in regional growth theory. Further, the former has other disadvantage; as per capita income is a poor measure of growth (Agarwal and Basu 2005).

In an interesting paper, it has been shown that restrictive and inward looking policies in a country may cause concentration of production in a region enjoying any small advantage (Elizondo and Krugman 1992), which might be either due to better infrastructural facilities for large-scale production or existence of manpower training institutions or facilities for smooth financial transactions and marketing. It has been argued that opening up of such an economy may weaken the traditional backward and forward linkages and lead to a more even distribution of economic activities across regions along with expansion of foreign trade. Thus, regional inequality may decline as a result of trade liberalisation. However, Paluzie (2001), on the contrary, suggests that trade may actually serve to increase, not decrease, urban concentration within developing countries and claims that regions with some initial advantage may be the ones to benefit disproportionately from trade liberalisation with the result of reinforced regional inequalities. Analysing the trends in regional inequalities across different countries, Shankar and Shah (2001) had concluded that the experiences of both unitary and federal countries do not show up unidirectional patterns. While certain countries have shown increasing regional inequalities, there are others for which a decline in regional inequalities can be seen.

There are a few studies where attempts have been made to relate regional inequality to trade liberalisation. According to Hanson (1997), the formation of NAFTA resulted in a less concentrated spatial distribution in Mexico. This is because firms found it more profitable to locate along the border to US rather than in the old industry belt cantered on Mexico City. However, Sjöberg and Sjöholm (2004) have shown that even during the period (1980–96) when Indonesia was liberalised substantially, concentration of manufacturing activities did not decrease. In a recent paper Barua and Chakraborty (forthcoming) have argued that regional concentration in both trade and manufacturing in India had been increasing even after significant extent of trade and industrial liberalisation.

REGIONAL INEQUALITY IN INDIA

There has been a proliferation of studies as reported above showing rising inter-regional inequality rather unabatedly in India. Some more recent studies are by Barua and Bandyopadhyay (2005) and Barua and Chakraborty (forthcoming). Of late, economists find it convenient to claim that the WTO-led trade liberalisation policies undertaken in India since the mid-1990s are chiefly responsible for sharp increase in inter-regional inequality in income. Thus, instead of breaking the monopoly of the more advanced states (Elizondo and Krugman 1992), trade in India has, in effect, accentuated concentration in manufacturing in the more advanced state leading to rising inter-regional or inter-state income inequality in the country.[4] The states that had a first-mover advantage and were already industrially prosperous could use trade as an engine of growth and grow faster while those that were laggards earlier saw their situation worsen and went further behind the former group. In what follows we first try to provide an up to date estimate of inter-regional income inequality in India and then attempt to explain whether there is any inherent tendency within the economy which may cause it to rise and diminish over time.

Theil Measure

We use the Theil measure to estimate inter-state income inequality in India and for this we use the inter-state data provided by the CSO.[5] The Theil index of inequality is defined as:

$$E_x = \Sigma\, x_i \log (x_i / p_i) \tag{1}$$

where x is an indicator such as per capita NSDP, agriculture, manufacturing, services, infrastructure etc; i = regions i.e. state's of India; p_i = region i's share in total population and x_i = region i's share in various economic activities of India like NSDP, agriculture, manufacturing, etc. The inequality measures E_x, take non-negative values. An equal distribution is denoted by $E_x=0$, which happens when every region's population share and its share in the economic indicator are equal. A rise in the value of E_x over time means that inequality is rising. Since the estimates of the E_x lie between 0 and 1, for visual convenience therefore we multiply all values of E_x by 100.[6]

TABLE 18.1 Inequality index at constant prices for 20 regions (1993–94=100)

Year	Income	Agriculture	Primary activities	Agriculture and Primary Activities	Manufacturing	Registered Manufacturing	Unregistered Manufacturing	Infrastructure	Services
1980–81	5.26	4.58	44.50	6.18	20.02	30.06	14.04	12.30	11.88
1981–82	4.89	4.27	27.45	3.78	17.93	24.89	13.48	13.85	11.15
1982–83	5.72	5.95	24.08	5.42	18.67	26.82	12.52	13.33	11.20
1983–84	4.71	4.22	24.38	3.81	16.10	21.31	14.21	14.52	10.75
1984–85	5.23	3.40	25.84	2.95	19.00	25.36	14.39	16.82	11.55
1985–86	5.52	4.48	26.64	4.14	19.32	26.38	13.69	14.79	11.75
1986–87	5.56	4.08	24.14	3.47	18.10	23.58	13.82	13.58	11.83
1987–88	6.67	4.07	24.80	3.84	18.45	23.59	15.05	13.84	11.73
1988–89	6.29	4.72	21.56	4.06	16.86	20.77	14.27	14.20	11.51
1989–90	6.83	4.77	22.78	4.33	17.88	22.72	14.24	14.55	11.42
1990–91	6.97	4.91	19.66	4.01	18.01	22.63	14.91	14.75	13.49
1991–92	7.95	4.94	17.95	4.06	19.76	23.92	16.70	14.65	13.76
1992–93	8.82	5.91	17.39	4.68	23.71	27.42	20.93	12.81	14.91
1993–94	7.25	5.12	14.36	4.06	22.43	22.58	20.00	12.23	11.34
1994–95	7.57	4.71	14.46	3.68	22.63	21.58	22.17	13.30	12.40
1995–96	8.29	5.88	14.40	4.76	22.16	21.57	20.62	13.01	12.56
1996–97	8.01	5.51	13.63	4.34	23.44	22.16	22.02	14.29	13.10
1997–98	8.33	5.60	13.85	4.40	18.92	18.91	17.07	14.61	13.82
1998–99	8.74	4.88	10.93	3.70	21.58	20.61	22.42	14.16	14.49
1999–2000	8.37	5.67	11.31	4.18	20.12	17.78	24.49	13.05	14.26
2000–1	8.80	6.50	11.65	4.59	22.16	19.77	23.71	13.90	14.07
2001–2	8.95	5.73	12.39	4.41	23.35	21.53	23.46	13.44	14.31
2002–3	9.08	5.98	12.79	4.20	22.35	20.06	26.21	13.65	15.03
2003–4	9.54	6.74	12.90	5.25	22.50	21.00	24.94	15.08	15.38
2004–5	9.95	6.21	13.62	4.80	23.13	21.76	25.56	15.82	15.87
2005–6	10.34	6.78	13.31	3.44	23.15	21.19	25.02	15.74	16.17

b. Trends in Regional Inequality

The Theil index has been calculated for income (NSDP) as well as for all other components of income such as agriculture, manufacturing, services, primary goods and infrastructure. Table 18.1 gives the Theil entropy measure for all the 20 states over the period from 1980–81 to 2005–6. The values as shown in Table 18.1 indicate that inequality has increased in almost all counts except for the primary sector, registered manufacturing and agriculture and primary combined.

The estimates of the Theil inequality trends have been analysed in Table 18.2 where the trends are given for the entire period, that is, 1980–81 to 2005–6 as well as for the two sub-periods, 1980–81 to 1991–92 (as the pre-1991 period) and 1993–94 to 2005–6 (as the post-1991 period) respectively.

TABLE 18.2 Inequality trends (1993–94=100)

Variable/Inequality Index	Time Period	Average Annual Growth Rate	t-value	R-square
Income	1981–2006	2.90724	17.71***	0.9025
	1981–92	3.90138	5.73***	0.7776
	1993–2006	1.96579	3.75***	0.7069
Manufacturing	1981–2006	1.11526	6.56***	0.5422
	1981–92	−0.11507	−0.20	0.0044
	1993–2006	0.09234	0.30	0.0039
Registered Manufacturing	1981–2006	−1.09901	−4.62***	0.4910
	1981–92	−1.74437	−2.29**	0.3704
	1993–2006	−1.02621	−1.50	0.1894
Unregistered Manufacturing	1981–2006	3.10164	16.36***	0.8732
	1981–92	1.35736	2.62**	0.4979
	1993–2006	2.01059	6.03***	0.5214
Agriculture and Primary Activities	1981–2006	0.12258	0.22	0.0037
	1981–92	−1.65362	−0.97	0.0971
	1993–2006	0.10781	0.11	0.0015
Agriculture	1981–2006	1.76260	5.17***	0.5920
	1981–92	0.54122	0.55	0.0204
	1993–2006	1.76806	3.05***	0.4476
Primary Activities	1981–2006	−4.28731	−8.41***	0.8347
	1981–92	−4.97056	−3.21***	0.6473
	1993–2006	−1.51142	−2.17**	0.2830
Infrastructure	1981–2006	0.16395	0.76	0.0276
	1981–92	0.81157	1.62	0.1527
	1993–2006	1.41491	5.05***	0.5896
Services	1981–2006	1.42279	12.75***	0.7651
	1981–92	1.35017	2.24**	0.4464
	1993–2006	1.85192	2.87***	0.5928

Notes: *** Significant at 1 per cent level; ** Significant at 5 per cent level; * Significant at 10 per cent level.

The annual average rate of growth of inequality of income for the entire period has been found to be 2.91 per cent and this was highly significant. Considering the two periods separately, we find that the income inequality had been increasing in both the sub-periods separately considered but rate of growth of inequality during the post-1991 period being 1.96 per cent turns out to be much lower than the growth rate of inequality during the pre-1991 period, which was 3.9 per cent.

As for the components of the NSDP, we can see from Table 18.2 that the growth rates of inequality except for the primary sector had been increasing for all other sub-sectors of NSDP. The primary sector has shown that the inequality trend had been declining significantly at –4.3 per cent. The manufacturing inequality has been rising at a significant 1.1 per cent per annum although the regression coefficients for the two sub-periods were not significant. However, the signs of the coefficients tell us that while it has declined during the pre-1991 period, the post-1991 period had shown increasing trends. Interestingly, however, we get a different picture by breaking the manufacturing sector into registered and unregistered sectors. While in the former case we observe that the inequality trend was significantly declining, in the latter case however the inequality trend showed a significant increasing trend. In fact, the un-registered manufacturing had witnessed the highest rate of growth of inequality (3.1 per cent) in comparison to all the other subgroups although the inequality growth for the post-1991 period was much higher (2 per cent) in comparison to the pre-1991 period (1.36 per cent). The stories of agriculture and service sectors are almost the same as that of the unregistered manufacturing. In this case, the inequality trend has been significantly rising for the entire period as well as for the two sub-periods with of course a caveat that the post-1991 period had witnessed much higher rate of growth of inequality. In contrast, the infrastructure sector shows that inequality trend for the entire period as well as for the pre-1991 period did not show any significant rising trend but the post-1991 period had witnessed a very significant rising trend of inequality.

We now turn to examine if there exist non-linearity in the behaviour of inequality over time. Table 18.3 gives the results of estimation of non-linear trends in the relationships between inequality and time.

TABLE 18.3 Non-linearity of inequality index, 1980–81 to 2005–6 (1993–94=100)

Dependent variable	Time-period	Constant	T	T2	T3	R-SQ	F-Statistic	N
E (Income)	1981–2006	4.51 (14.63)***	0.24 (4.49)***	–0.01 (–0.55)		0.92	135.50	26
		4.48 (9.93)***	0.25 (1.73)*	–0.01 (–0.16)	0.02 (0.08)	0.92	86.43	26
E (Manufacturing)	1981–2006	17.56 (16.88)***	0.19 (1.08)	0.01 (0.20)		0.55	13.95	26
		19.15 (13.21)***	–0.46 (–1.00)	0.06 (1.54)	–0.01 (–1.53)	0.59	10.62	26
E (Registered Manufacturing)	1981–2006	27.71 (21.99)***	–0.59 (–2.75)***	0.01 (1.60)		0.54	13.55	26
		27.50 (14.89)***	–0.50 (–0.87)	0.01 (0.09)	0.01 (0.16)	0.54	8.66	26

(Contd)

(Table 18.3 Contd)

Dependent variable	Time-period	Constant	T	T2	T3	R-SQ	F-Statistic	N
E (Unregistered Manufacturing)	1981–2006	11.96 (10.94)***	0.38 (2.05)**	0.01 (1.08)		0.88	83.23	26
		14.38 (10.04)***	−0.60 (−1.34)	0.10 (2.52)**	−0.02 (−2.35)**	0.81	68.39	26
E (Agriculture and Primary Activities)	1981–2006	4.71 (10.97)***	−0.10 (−1.37)	0.03 (1.42)		0.08	1.01	26
		5.70 (10.23)***	−0.50 (−2.86)***	0.04 (2.69)***	−0.01 (−2.47)**	0.28	2.86	26
E (Agriculture)	1981–2006	4.45 (12.72)***	−0.01 (−0.13)	0.01 (1.70)*		0.65	21.41	26
		4.75 (9.40)***	−0.13 (−0.82)	0.02 (1.09)	−0.02 (−0.83)	0.66	14.30	26
E (Primary Activities)	1981–2006	36.64 (18.78)***	−2.19 (−6.57)***	0.05 (4.13)***		0.85	65.34	26
		36.71 (12.83)***	−2.22 (−2.46)**	0.10 (0.68)	−0.01 (−0.03)	0.85	41.67	26
E (Services)	1981–2006	11.23 (22.65)***	0.04 (0.46)	0.01 (1.81)		0.79	44.11	26
		11.07 (15.27)***	0.10 (0.45)	−0.01 (−0.01)	0.01 (0.30)	0.79	28.27	26
E (Infrastructure)	1981–2006	14.41 (21.09)***	−0.11 (−0.97)	0.01 (1.20)		0.08	1.04	26
		12.42 (15.39)***	0.70 (2.75)***	−0.07 (−3.18)***	0.02 (3.45)***	0.41	5.00	26

Notes: Figures in the parenthesis are t-values; *** Significant at 1 per cent level; ** Significant at 5 per cent level; *Significant at 10 per cent level.

It can be seen from Table 18.3 that in most of the cases the higher terms of time are not significant thus implying that no significant non-linearity exist in the time path of inequality for income as well as most sub-sectors except for unregistered manufacturing, agriculture and primary combined and infrastructure sectors for which the higher order of the time coefficients were found to be significant. The above results of non-linearity make it clear that the linear time paths of inequality correctly describe the inequality trends for all sectors except for infrastructure, unregistered manufacturing and primary-agriculture combined. Let us have a look at the graphs for the two important sectors—unregistered manufacturing and the infrastructure sectors.

We can see from the above graphs that the unregistered manufacturing had been growing all along though the rate of growth had slowed down during the post-1991 period. On the other hand, the infrastructure inequalities while decreasing initially, there is a clear tendency of increasing the rate of growth of inequality in infrastructure after the liberalisation of the economy.

Trade Liberalisation and Income Inequality

FIGURE 18.1 Unregistered manufacturing

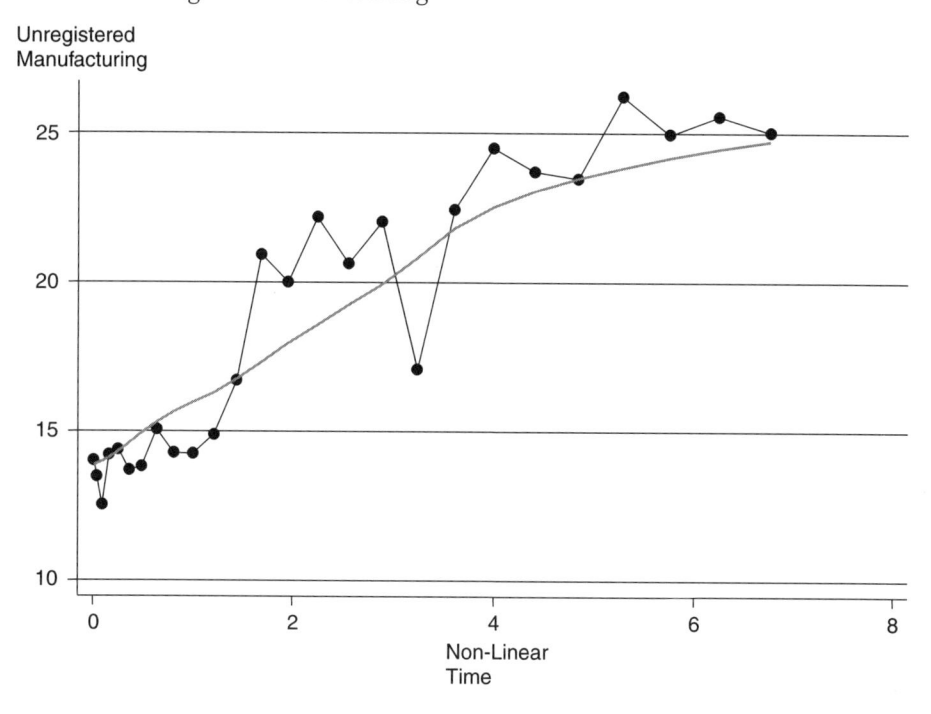

FIGURE 18.2 Infrastructure

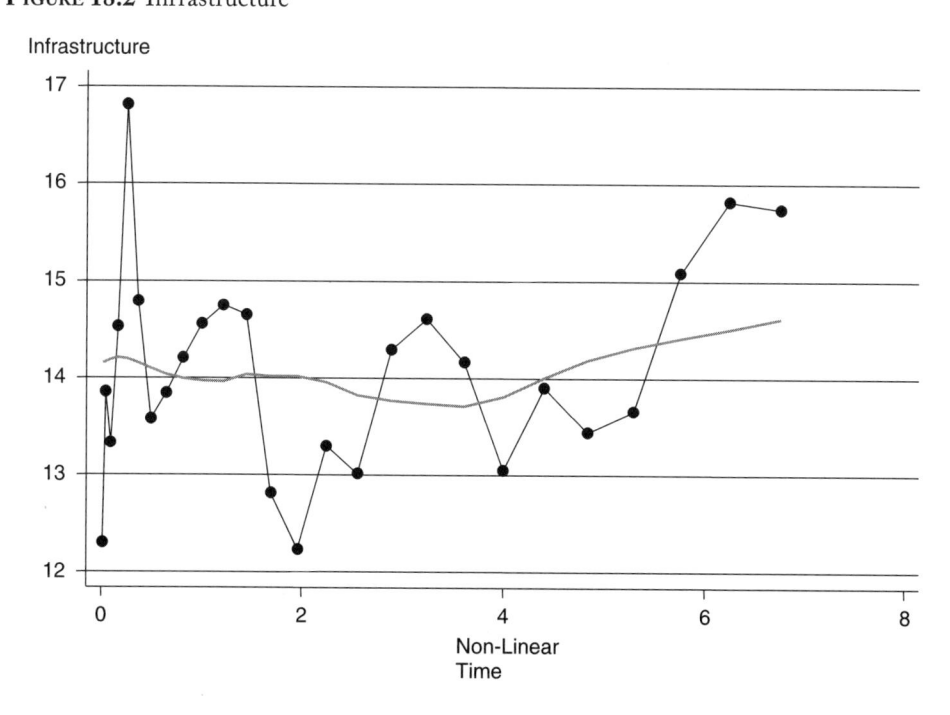

CAUSALITY ANALYSIS

As noted above, the measure of inter-regional income inequality was a mere statistical construct and therefore it does not by itself provide any explanation of the causes of increasing trend of inter-regional income disparity in India. Therefore, in an attempt to make a preliminary investigation into the relationship between income inequality and the inequalities in various components of income we have estimated the regression equation of income inequality on inequalities in manufacturing, services, agriculture and primary, etc. We have found that manufacturing and infrastructure inequalities are highly correlated (the correlation coefficient is 0.713) and therefore, we run two separate causality regressions using manufacturing and infrastructure separately to avoid the problem of multi-colinearity. In Table 18.4, the Model 1 takes into account only manufacturing inequality ignoring infrastructure inequality and Model 2 takes infrastructure inequality by ignoring manufacturing inequality.

TABLE 18.4 Causality of inequality for 20 regions, 1980–81 to 2005–6 (1993–94=100)

Variables	Model (1): Dependent Variable- Income Inequality	Model (2): Dependent Variable- Income Inequality
Manufacturing	0.118 (2.77)***	
Infrastructure		−0.086 (−1.06)
Agriculture	0.321 (1.85)*	0.359 (1.73)*
Primary Activities	−0.063 (−5.81)***	−0.070 (−4.86)***
Services	0.527 (7.04)***	0.626 (5.80)***
Trade Dummy 2000	0.19 (−0.98)	−0.214 (−0.87)
Constant	−2.28 (−1.72)*	−0.0211 (−0.01)
R-Square	0.9511	0.9412
F-Statistic	94.36	69.4
N	26	26

Notes: Figures in the parenthesis are t-values; *** Significant at 1 per cent level; ** Significant at 5 per cent level; * Significant at 10 per cent level.

The regression results in Table 18.4 clearly show that the inequalities in agriculture, manufacturing and services are positively and significantly causing the rising inter-regional income inequality in India over time, while the primary sector was negatively and significantly affecting income inequality. However, in terms of their relative importance as causes of rising income-inequality, the most important factor seems to be the service sector inequality followed by manufacturing and then agriculture. On the other hand, both primary and infrastructure inequalities are showing decreasing impact on inter-regional income inequality in India, although the latter effect has shown to be statistically insignificant. Using the year 2000 as a dummy we have tried to find if openness has any significant impact on the inequality trend. The regression coefficient though negative is not significant and hence we may conclude that openness apparently has no impact on inequality. But there is a caveat. The impact of openness may not be directly observed as much from the inequality measure as it may be seen indirectly through its impact on the share of manufacturing, agriculture and services, the three dominant forces of causing rising inter-regional income inequality in India. Therefore, in what follows, we shall make an attempt to examine the behaviour of the two most important explanatory variables of income inequality—manufacturing and service sectors inequalities—within a model of structural transformation of an economy based on the Chenery-Syrquin analysis.

AN EXPLANATORY MODEL OF INEQUALITY

The results of the above regression provide us with some explanation of the rising inter-regional income inequality in India. One, inter-regional income inequalities are caused by the inequalities in agriculture, manufacturing and the service sectors. Two, inequalities in the primary and infrastructural sectors have led to a decline in inter-regional income inequalities. What conclusions can we draw from this information? We can perhaps argue that if in the process of economic growth, the share in manufacturing, agriculture and the service sectors grew disproportionately across the states (regions) then it may lead to rising inter-regional income inequalities. In order to examine the behaviour of the shares of these three sectors in NSDP we consider below an analysis of structural transformation of an economy based on the well-known Chenery-Syrquin hypothesis (Chenery and Syrquin 1977). We restrict our analyses to the two dominant sources of rising inter-regional income inequality—manufacturing and the service sectors—on the ground that the share of agriculture and primary goods in NSDP in any case had been declining over time. This may have happened due to two reasons: First, the operation of Engel's law which states that as income rises people tend to consume less of agricultural and primary goods and more of luxury goods such as manufacturing and services. Second, if an economy like India is opening up to the forces of international trade, the patterns of resource allocation will change. That is, resources will be moved away from agriculture and the primary sectors to manufacturing and the service sectors. This is because India is a resource poor and labour abundant (in both unskilled and skilled) country. Therefore, India's comparative advantages should lie in the manufactures and the service sectors and the export of these goods and services should increase over time. Further, in many ways both manufactures and services are complements to each other. Hence, with the process of trade liberalisation, India is expected to experience a rise in the production of manufactures and services and a decline in the production of primary and agricultural goods. As a result, India's exports of manufactures and the tradable services should increase over time in India's total exports.

However, there are vast differences in factor proportions across the regions and therefore we expect that with the growth of an economy and trade liberalisation the shares of manufactures and services will experience different growth trajectories.

The Model

We hypothesise that the shares of manufactures and services in NSDP are determined by three factors, namely, aggregate demand, population size and shares of trade to NSDP. We consider the regression equation as given below to analyse the pattern of structural changes across the Indian states:

$$x_{it} = a_{it} + \beta_1 * \log y_{it} + \beta_2 * (\log y_{it})^2 + \gamma_1 * \log N_{it} + \gamma_2 * (\log N_{it})^2 + \delta * T_{it} + u_{it} \quad (2)$$

In the above equation (2) the variables x, y, N and T are defined for each of the 20 states as follows: x is the share of manufacturing (services) in NSDP, y is per capita NSDP (income per capita), N is population size and T is the share of trade in NSDP. In a cross-section-time series analysis represented by equation (2), the trade share (T) variable captures the impact of openness on the growth of manufacturing (service) sector of the country. The argument goes as follows: as a country is opening up to the stimuli of external trade under tariff liberalisation, different states (regions) are likely to experience differential impact of such exposures on their economies depending on the strength of the variables. For instance, a state with a relatively high per capita income is likely to experience a relatively higher share of manufactures and services. Similarly, a large population size provides the advantages of economies of scale and thereby allows the particular state to enjoy a higher share in manufactures and services in NSDP. While the per capita income and population growth are the two major internal stimuli for growth in manufactures and services, major external stimuli is coming from international trade. Let us examine how trade affects the growth of manufacturing and service sectors in an economy. The key role here would be played by the comparative advantages of the states in manufacturing as well as the service sector. India is a labour abundant and per capita resource poor country and therefore it is not expected that India could ever be able to specialise in resource intensive goods like agriculture and primary production. What is expected is that as liberalisation proceeds, the resources will be shifted away from agriculture and primary to the manufacturing and service enterprises. Trade liberalisation will therefore lead to a rise in the share of manufactures and services in NSDP across all states and hence each state should experience a rise in its per capita income as argued above. However, trade may increase or decrease income inequality depending on whether the impact of trade on manufacturing specialisation is unevenly or evenly spread out across the states. For instance, if manufacturing requires better infrastructure, marketing networks, and speedy and swift transportation and communication facilities then trade may lead to increasing concentration of manufacturing production in the well developed states. As against this, we may state an alternate hypothesis emphasising the fact that since the backward states enjoy the advantages of lower wages and since India presumably has comparative advantage in labour intensive exports, trade liberalisation may lead to dispersal of manufacturing activities to the interior states resulting in decreasing inter-regional income inequality.

Thus, the well developed states (regions) within India are relatively at a disadvantageous position in comparison with the relatively backward states in terms of labour cost. The rural-urban differences in wage structure are further accentuated by imperfect factor mobility particularly with respect to labour across the states. While the skilled labour has a strong preference for the metropolis, the unskilled labour mobility is constrained by low income, information asymmetries and strong family ties. Unlike the labour market, however, the capital market is highly integrated. An obvious reason for this is the intervention of the central government. For instance, there exists uniform rate of interests across all the regions due to the existence of nationalised banks and other financial institutions. So, we should expect a dispersal of industrial spectrum across the states so that the backward regions experience a higher growth in their shares of manufactures. On the other hand, the metropolis will specialise in providing services in which cheap capital and skilled labour are important and which are relatively abundant in the metropolis. The relative strength of these two factors will determine the trends in inter-regional income inequality. We may conclude the following two possible outcomes: one, both the developed and the backward regions should experience a rise in income per capita with the rise in the share of manufacturing in NSDP. Two, if the service sector grows at a faster rate in the metropolis and if this sector has a relatively stronger influence on income, then the income in the developed and the backward regions will increase disproportionately resulting in rising in inter-regional inequalities over time. Third, if the manufacturing sector, on the other hand, rises at a relatively faster rate in the backward regions due to the impact of trade liberalisation, we may experience a convergence of per capita income across the states and hence a decline in inter-regional income inequality. The net outcome will therefore be a question of empirical verifiability.

As against the above neo-classical type of analysis of the impact of trade liberalisation on regional income inequality, we may yet consider an alternative hypothesis following the location theoretic analysis of trade put forwarded by Elizondo-Krugman (1992). This model argues that in a closed economy manufacturing production is concentrated more in the metropolis resulting in inequalities across regions. However, with the opening up of trade, the hegemony of the metropolis breaks down and manufacturing production as a result gets evenly distributed across regions, which then would lead to a fall in the inter-regional income inequalities.

The neo-classical position may not be in conflict with the Elizondo-Krugman type analysis if the relative advantages of wage differences in the neo-classical framework may outweigh the locational advantages due to the proximity to the market. However, if the market proximity impact is more pronounced in the neo-classical analysis then conclusions based on the neo-classical analysis and the Elizondo-Krugman location theoretic analysis may be in conflict with each other. The resolution of the issue therefore would lie in its empirical verification.

The Estimation of the Model

We thus estimate equation (2) separately for manufacturing as well as the service sectors to find how the different factors, namely, demand, population size and trade intensities are affecting the share of these sectors in NSDP over time. For estimating the above-specified equation, with the cross-section and time series data for various states, our major problem was to find data on exports and imports for each state of India, which unfortunately is not available. What in fact we have are the aggregate trade data for exports and imports for the country as a whole. Therefore, we have used in our study a proxy rule to estimate the export-import data for each state.[7] The openness variable will then be defined as total trade (that is, export plus import) as a percentage of the NSDP for each of the state. Since we are able to find trade data only from the year 1991, we have conducted our analysis of structural changes only for the period 1991–2006.

On the basis of the availability of data, we have estimated the equation by using the standard Feasible Generalized Least Square Method (FGLSM). With the pooled sample we estimated both the Fixed and the Random Effect models, and, by taking the Hausman test on the desirability of the application of Fixed Effect or Random Effect, we have accepted the statistically desirable model. The Hausman test confirms that the desirable testing procedure should favour the Fixed Effect model. However, we prefer to adhere to the Random Effect Model results because of the better significance of the coefficients of the independent variables and the fact that the overall results are very different. Accordingly, we report our results in Table 18.5 below for both the manufacturing share and the services share equations:

TABLE 18.5 Structural change equation: Random effect model, (1990–91 to 2005–6)

Variables	Model (1): Dependent Variable-Manufacturing Share	Model (2): Dependent Variable-Services Share
Log (Income)	−0.601	1.333
	(−2.79)***	(6.19)***
(Log (Income))^2	0.0379	−0.0693
	(3.24)***	(−5.88)***
Log (Population)	−0.4546	−0.4171
	(−6.56)***	(−2.35)***
(Log (Population))^2	0.0140	0.0127
	(6.54)***	(2.32)***
Total Trade/NSDP	0.0813	−.0129
	(4.12)***	(−0.63)
Trade dummy 2000	−0.0611	0.0269
	(−8.08)***	(4.35)***
Constant	6.132	−2.598
	(5.35)***	(−1.28)*
R-Square		
Within	0.2925	0.3914
Between	0.6521	0.0208
Overall	0.5741	0.0782
Wald Chi-Square (5)	301.05	177.60
	0.000	0.000
N	320	320

Notes: Figures in the parenthesis are t-values; *** Significant at 1 per cent level; ** Significant at 5 per cent level; * Significant at 10 per cent level.

Table 18.5 above gives the estimates of the coefficients of the random effect regression model where we have regressed both manufacturing and services share on per capita income, the square of the per capita income, population size and its square and for representing the openness variable, we have used the total trade as a proportion of the NSDP across all 20 states and over the period of time 1990–91 to 2005–6. The results show that model is good with statistically significant (at 1 per cent) Wald Chi-square with 5 degrees of freedom and both the demand and the population variables are significantly determining the share of manufactures and services in the NSDP. Interestingly, the openness variable appear to having significant impact on the manufacturing, its impact on the service sector turns out to be insignificant. Lastly, in order to find if there is any structural shift in the regression due to the lagged effect of openness, we have introduced the year 2000 as a dummy for capturing the openness effect on the shift. We found that time dummy is statistically significant in both the models and it has negative impact on share of manufacturing and positive impact on share of services.

Analysis of the Results

Let us now consider separately the effects of the three main determinants of the rise in the shares of manufactures and services over time, namely, the per capita levels of income, the size of the population and trade openness.

Per Capita Income and the Shares of Manufactures and Services

On the basis of the estimates as reported in Table 18.5, we depict the effects of the demand captured by the per capita income and the population variables on both manufactures and services in terms of Figures 18.3 and 18.4 respectively as given below:

The manufacturing share as can be seen in Figure 18.3 is steadily increasing only after the per capita income level reaches the threshold limit of Rs 5000 and it reaches the peak when income level reaches approximately Rs 17000 and then after the manufacturing share starts declining. On the other hand, there is no threshold lower limit for the share of the service sector to rise as we can observe in Figure 18.4. However, unlike the manufacturing share which shows a gradual increase, the service share increases at a much faster rate as the per capita income rises. Yet, the service share too starts declining after a certain levels of income as in the case of manufacturing. This scenario seems to support our hypothesis that the low income states may perform relatively better in terms of their manufacturing orientation due to their advantages of having lower labour costs. On the other hand, the

FIGURE 18.3 Manufacturing share and per capita income (structural change results, 1991–2006)

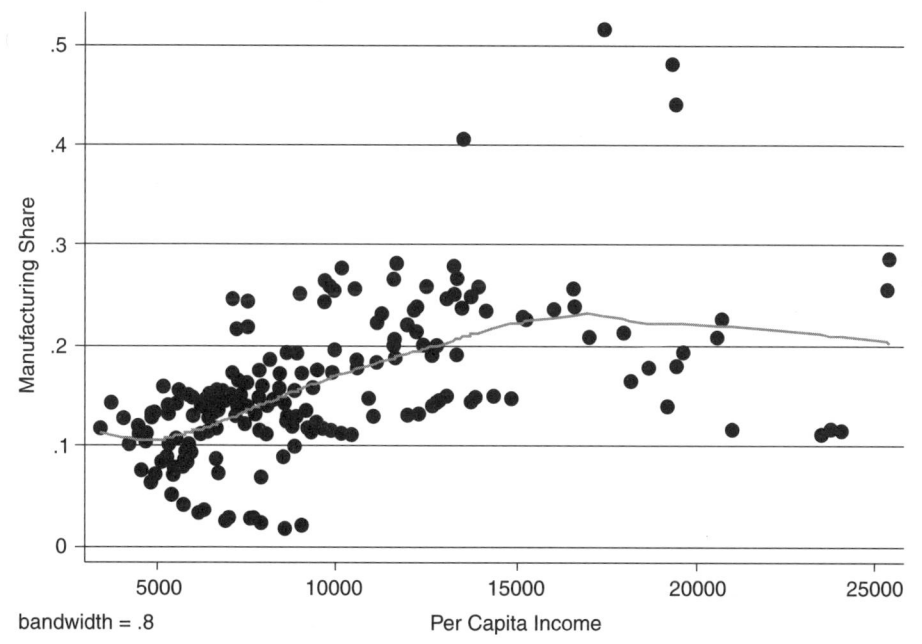

Figure 18.4 Service share and per capita income
(structural change results, 1991–2006)

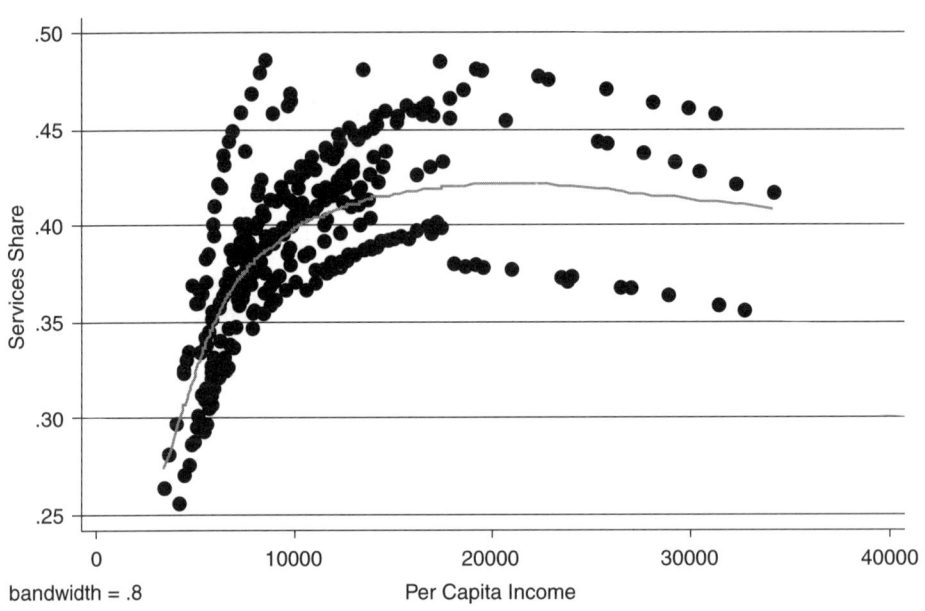

service sector is expanding at a much faster, nearly exponential, rate in the lower income states. Thus, the over all situations seem to indicate that the dynamics of growth are more visibly favouring the low income states than the high income states. That is, if this scenario continues for a relatively longer period of time then at some point in time in future we may see a down turn in the rise of inter-regional income inequality in India. Despite such disproportionality in the behaviour of both the shares of manufactures and services, we observe however that during the post-1991 period the concentration of manufactures and trade had increased as measured by the Herfindahl index of concentration (See Barua and Chakraborty, forthcoming). This could be because of the fact that the high income states are better equipped for manufacturing location and also to serve trade due to its efficient and reliable infrastructural facilities. As shown in Figure 18.2, the increasing infrastructural inequality lends support to this. Thus, during the initial phase of trade liberalisation it is likely that inter-regional inequality may increase despite the favourable impact of liberalisation on the shares of manufactures and services in the lower income states. But certainly this trend is bound to be reversed over time with the increase in the share of manufactures and services in income in the low income states provided the low income states make efforts to improve their infrastructure. Let us now turn to examine the impact of the size of the states determined by the levels of population in the determination of the shares of manufactures and services over time.

Population Size and the Shares of Manufactures and Services

The impact of population size on the shares of manufactures and services are shown separately in Figures 18.5 and 18.6. The graphs show that the shares of both manufactures and services are decreasing for the states with smaller population while they are increasing

Trade Liberalisation and Income Inequality 363

FIGURE 18.5 Manufacturing share and population
(structural change results, 1991–2006)

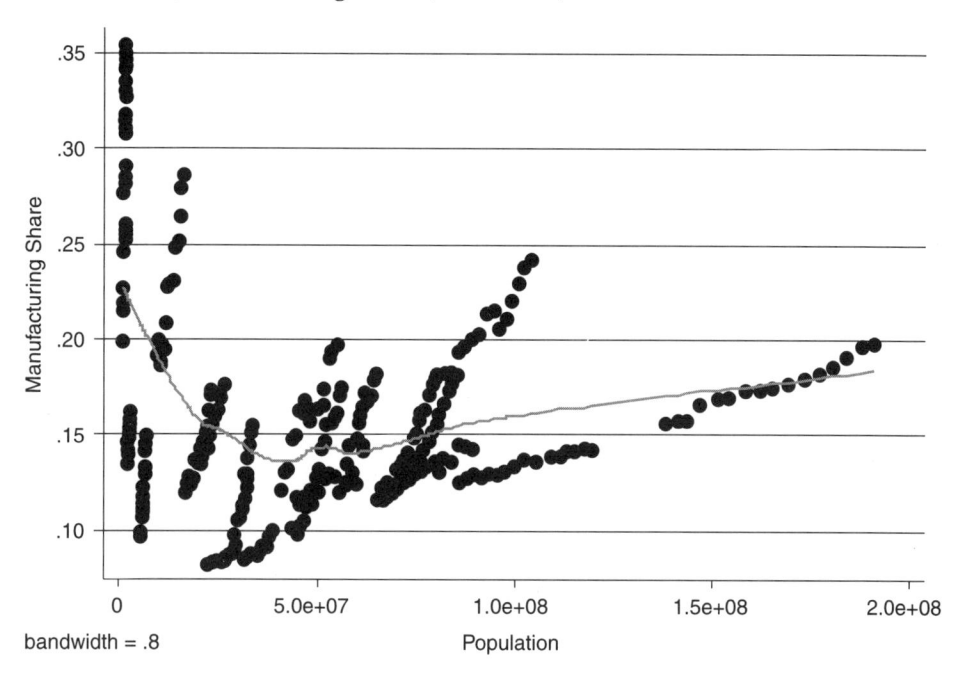

FIGURE 18.6 Services share and population
(structural change results, 1991–2006)

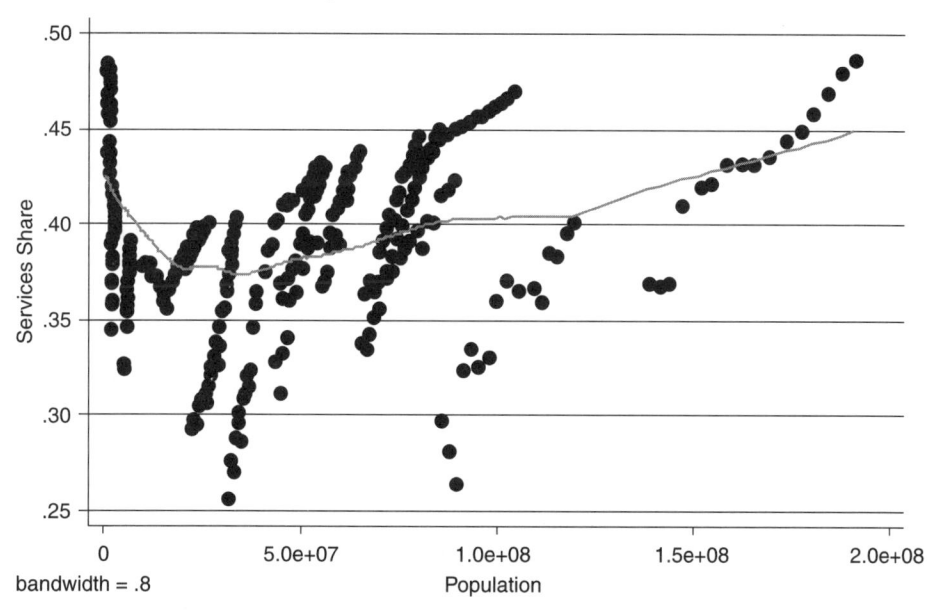

at a faster rate with the rise in the size of population. The obvious implication of this is that the size of the population is a major determinant of the expansion of manufactures and services. That is, the larger states irrespective of their income are experiencing a much faster growth in the shares of both manufactures and services.

The above analysis of structural transformation of the Indian economy over time suggests that there are two opposite forces affecting the trends in inter-regional income inequality in India. These two forces are the income effect and the population size effect. While the former effect tends to reduce income inequality, the latter tend to increase. To the extent that most of the large sized states also happen to be the very high income states, the inter-regional income inequality may even rise further until diminishing returns to scale sets in motion in the highly populated states.

The Impact of Trade Openness on the Shares of Manufactures and Services

The openness variable as captured by the TRADE:NSDP ratio shows that it has differential impact upon the share of manufactures and services. Its impact on the share of manufacturing is significant and positive implying that openness has a favourable impact in increasing the share of manufactures in NSDP. On the other hand, trade openness has negative but insignificant impact on the share of services. Thus, the impact of openness on income growth provides us a mixed scenario. We have also incorporated an openness dummy to show if post-2000 period gives any evidence of structural shift in the behaviour of both the shares of manufactures and services. Interestingly, the dummy coefficient for manufacturing shows negative and significant effect while the same for the service share equation shows positive and significant effect. The dummy thus reveals that the post-2000 period did not show any conclusive implications of openness on growth of income.

STRUCTURAL TRANSFORMATION AND INTER-REGIONAL INEQUALITY

The results of the forces driving the structural transformation of the regions in India do provide some evidence to our causality results of rising inter-regional inequality as reported in Table 18.4. As noted above, the inequalities in manufactures and services are positively and significantly increasing inter-regional income inequality in India. Therefore, unless there is a process of disproportionate changes in the share of manufactures and services across the lower and higher income states, we should not expect any reversal of the trend in regional income inequality. In essence, if the lower income states are undergoing a relatively faster rate of growth in manufactures and services compared to the higher income states, we should expect a reversal in the trend of rising inter-regional income inequality. The question is: does the process of structural transformation indicate any tendency to increase or decrease in the inequalities in manufactures and services? The answer is that it is not conclusive. While it is true that the process of structural transformation contributed to increasing the share of both manufactures and services in NSDP across the states, there is some evidence as shown in the Figures 18.3 and 18.4 that the impact of the structural transformation has been disproportionate across the states of India as far as the impact of per capita income is concerned. That is, the lower income states are experiencing a relatively faster growth in these shares over time. On the other hand, the effect of the population size is just the opposite as shown in Figures 18.5 and 18.6. Thus, to the extent that the high income and the large size go together (for instance, Maharashtra, Gujarat, Tamilnadu and West Bengal), the structural transformation may tend to increase inter-regional inequality. But there are some states which are very low in income levels but are much bigger in terms of the size compared to the above mentioned states. The examples of such states are like Uttar Pradesh, Bihar, Madhya Pradesh and Rajasthan. For these states, the message of structural transformation is very clear that their relative income inequality should be declining over time. However, the lower income smaller sized states are under the influences of both the opposite forces—one trying to pull up their income and the other to pull down. Thus, the overall impact of structural transformation for these states does not provide us any clear picture. Their relative inequality may increase or decrease, although their impact on the national average level of inequality may not be very much perceptible as their sizes are very small.

The above analysis of structural transformation while provides some insights regarding the long run tendency of inter-regional income inequality in India, it does not conclusively resolve the impact of openness on the *average regional income inequality*. For this we consider a regression analysis based on regressing the estimated levels of average levels of inter-regional income inequality as measures by the Theil indices on the TRADE/NSDP ratio, which captures the effects of openness on inequality.

The three regression equations given in Table 18.6 provide the results of the estimates of the regression equations of income, manufacturing, services and agricultural inequalities respectively being regressed on the trade openness variable. We also introduce an openness dummy taking the year 1995, the year, in which India became a signatory of the WTO. The results of Table 18.6 indicate that the elasticity of the income, manufacturing, agriculture and services inequalities with respect to the trade-NSDP ratio are positively and strongly significant, with the exception of the manufacturing inequality, which is only significant at 10 per cent confidence interval level. The role of declining registered manufacturing inequality may be valid reason to withstand this phenomenon. Thus, we may conclude that trade liberalisation has not resulted in any decline in inter-regional income inequality in India. The only saving grace is that the co-efficient of the openness dummy turns out to be negative and significant for income and agricultural inequalities implying that trade liberalisation is perhaps acting as a force to lowering down the rate of growth of inter-regional income inequality in India.

TABLE 18.6 Elasticity openness with openness dummy (1991–2006)

	Constant	Log (Trade/NSDP)	Openness	R-sq	F Statistic	N
Log (Income Inequality)	2.471 (31.89)***	0.237 (10.23)***	−0.108 (−1.68)*	0.7920	88.96	16
Log (Manufacturing Inequality)	3.189 (33.67)***	0.084 (1.81)*	−0.027 (−0.35)	0.2027	2.46	16
Log (Agriculture Inequality)	2.112 (20.49)***	0.256 (5.14)***	−0.148 (−2.00)**	0.6780	24.00	16
Log (Services Inequality)	2.931 (24.20)***	0.190 (4.96)***	−0.124 (−1.29)	0.5160	32.83	16

Notes: *** Significant at 1 per cent level; ** Significant at 5 per cent level; * Significant at 10 per cent level.

In order to be able to say a little more about the impact of openness on inter-regional inequality trends, we have estimated the same regression equations in non-linear forms and the results are shown in Tables 18.7. It is clear from Table 18.7 that we should reject any non-linearity in the relationship between inequality and openness except for the services sector. In the case of the service sector, the relationship is depicted in Figure 18.7 below which shows that the service inequality may decrease with further increase in openness of the economy. In other words, one of the key determinants of rising inter-regional inequality, the service sector inequality, may contribute to dampen the further rise in inequality with the increase in the openness of the economy. We may thus conclude from this empirical observation that notwithstanding the favourable impact of liberalisation on increasing income in the lower income states, the *average levels* of inequality are still increasing. The only way this process could be reversed is by adopting policies to reduce infrastructural inequalities across the states via massive investments on roads, transport, education and communication in the relatively backward states. Such investments will work as catalytic agent to decrease concentration in both manufacturing and trade across the states. The liberalisation effect then would lead to dispersal of economic activities across the states more favourably towards the lower income states of the country. Similarly, rising costs of land and labour in the higher income states may also lead to relocation of industries in the backward regions due to diseconomies of scale.

TABLE 18.7 Non-linear estimates of inequality measure on trade/NSDP ratio (1991–2006)

Inequality Index	Constant	TRNSDP	TRNSDP^2	TRNSDP^3	R^2	F-Statistic	N
Income	7.619 (6.66)***	−1.534 (−0.22)	12.867 (0.93)	−8.679 (−1.05)	0.8081	215.54	16
Manufacturing	17.980 (4.17)***	23.743 (0.79)	−44.974 (−0.74)	28.375 (0.77)	0.1925	2.51	16
Agriculture	28.375 (5.95)***	−1.638 (−0.23)	10.730 (0.64)	−7.791 (−0.71)	0.6269	14.91	16
Services	15.862 (11.57)***	−25.126 (−2.62)**	66.376 (3.17)***	−42.646 (−3.18)***	0.6537	23.03	16

Notes: TRNSDP= Trade/NSDP ratio; TRNSDP^2 and TRNSDP^3 are higher order of Trade/NSDP ratio; *** Significant at 1 per cent level of confidence; ** Significant at 5 per cent level of confidence.

CONCLUSION

We may thus draw our conclusions as follows: One, regional inequality in India has been increasing in all components of income except for the primary sector where we observe a persistent decline in inter-regional inequality in India. Two, regressing income inequality on the inequalities in various components of income, we find that only manufacturing and service sector inequalities do significantly and positively affect income inequality. Third, our structural change analysis shows that the shares of both manufacturing and services were increasing at a relatively faster rate in the middle income level states as compared to the high income states as per capita income rises. In fact, the high income states are

FIGURE 18.7 Services inequality and trade/NSDP

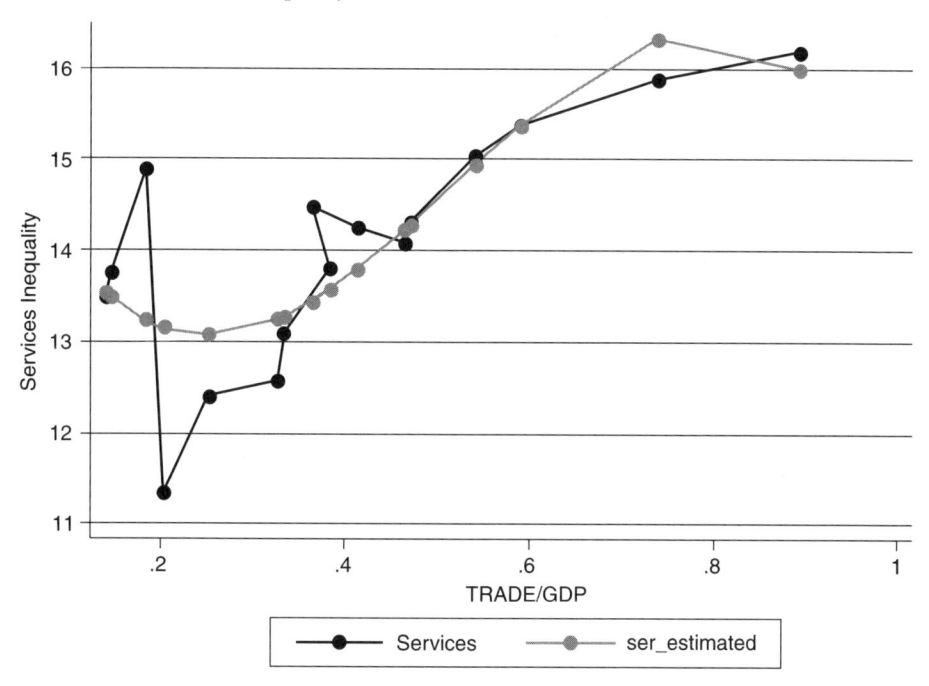

showing somewhat decreasing shares as per capita income rises. On the other hand, the population size variable is favourably affecting the large sized states. Therefore, to the extent the large sized states and the high income states coincides (for instance, Gujarat, Maharashtra, Tamilnadu and West Bengal), structural changes are contributing to increase in their income and consequently leading to increasing inter-regional inequalities. On the other hand, in case of the states such as Bihar, Uttar Pradesh, Madhya Pradesh and Rajasthan which are large in size and also low in per capita income, the structural changes are favouring the rise in their incomes and thereby contributing to dampen their relative income inequality vis-à-vis the high income states. The low income small sized states are experiencing advantages as well as disadvantages due to the opposing effects of income and the size. The net effect on the average income inequality as measured by the Theil index will therefore depend upon the relative impacts of increasing income due to structural changes in these three different sets of countries. In a nutshell, the manufacturing and service shares in income, the two main forces of increasing inter-regional income inequality, are showing a disproportionate tendency to grow over time at different levels of income. If this trend continues the long run inter-regional income equality is bound to taper off as time passes. The size factor though is a major hindrance to such equalisation process, the large sized states are bound to face diseconomies of scale and in fact many big cities in the high income states are already showing the impact of rising rent and labour cost resulting in the dispersal of industries from these cities to the backward areas. We may therefore conclude from the structural transformation analysis that in the long run inter-regional income inequality may decline provided certain proactive policies are adopted by the government. Fourth, the structural transformations results though provide us with some insights about the long run tendency of inter-regional income inequality, it does not show conclusively how openness has impacted upon the *average inter-regional inequality* in India. For this we regress the inequality measures on the openness variable. The regression results indicate that openness increases the average inter-regional income inequalities in all spheres of economic activities like manufacturing, services and agriculture in India. Obviously, we should therefore expect that openness increases the over all income inequality as well. But such conclusions of the impact of globalisation on inter-regional income inequality may not be correct since it fails to depict the dynamics of development. As we have observed from our structural transformation analysis, the smaller states are experiencing somewhat dramatic impact of globalisation on their economies insofar as both manufacturing and service shares were increasing steeply for these states while the high income states were lagging behind. If this trend continues then such disproportional growth in the shares of manufactures and services in income may turn the die in favour of the low income states in the long run so that the inter-regional income inequality may eventually decline. Of course, a faster development of infrastructure in the lower income states may enhance this process of economic transformation resulting in a decline in the concentration of both trade and manufacturing in the high income states, which may help the country to escape from otherwise inescapable trap of rising inter-regional income inequality.

Endnotes

[1] India's peak tariff rate was 355 per cent in 1990–91. The peak tariff rate in 1993–94 was 85 per cent, which was further reduced to 50 per cent in 1995. The peak tariff rate was reduced to less than 30 per cent since 2005. See Haider A. Khan, 2005.

[2] It has been observed that 'trade liberalisation led to an increase in poverty rate and poverty gap in the rural districts of India where industries more exposed to liberalisation were concentrated. The effect is quite substantial.' See Topalova 2007, p. 293.

[3] There are many studies showing that trade liberalisation has led to increasing inter-regional income inequality in India. See Sachs et al, 2002; Zhang, Xiaobo and S. Fan, 2002; Barua and Chakraborty, 2010, forthcoming.

[4] In our analysis a state of the Indian Union represents a region.

[5] The National Accounts Statistics (NAS) brought out by the CSO is the main source of data for various regional economic activities in India. The regional income data are however complied by the statistical departments of various regions (that is, the States). But, the data for economic activities is available at 2 different base year prices: (1) 1980–81 prices and (2) at 1993–94 prices. The CSO gives us both the current as well as constant price data. As mentioned above, there are two constant price series—one for 1980–81 prices and the other for 1993–94 prices. Since we did not obtain the constant price series for the entire period of our analysis at 1980–81 prices, we have therefore converted the data from 93–94 onwards till 99–00 (the end period of our analysis) available at 93–94 prices to 1980–81 prices using the price indices correction analysis and used this data for our calculations. The outputs of economic activities for all the regions' are given in Rs Lakhs.

[6] For details on this measure, see Das and Barua, 1996.

[7] The trade data that we have used for our analysis have been sourced from India Trades Database-CMIE, and DGCIS. We have used the trade data based on HS-Code classification from 01 to 99. On the basis of availability of data, we have restricted our analysis from the period of 1990–91 till 1999–2000. The trade values which are also been given in Rs Lakhs.

Methodology:
We considered the entire trade series for India based on HS-Code classification ranging from 01 to 99 into two broad categories: (a) 01–24 has been classified as agricultural items and (b) 25–99 has been has been considered as manufacturing items. As all the items belonging to the latter category needs to be manufactured in some way or the other before trading, so we have accumulated the entire series into one broad head.

In order to calculate state i's manufacturing (agriculture) exports, firstly, we computed state i's manufacturing (agriculture) share in India's total manufacturing (agriculture) output, which is the summation of manufacturing (agriculture) output of all the states. Next, from the CMIE data we assessed the total manufacturing (agricultural) exports of India i.e. the summation of the trade values of items ranging from HS-Code 25 to 99 (1 to 24). The state i's manufacturing (agriculture) share has been multiplied by India's total manufacturing (agriculture) exports in order to get an estimate of state i's manufacturing (agriculture) exports. We termed it as the 'rule of thumb' in calculating the different state's export figures. But, we have used a different way in order to calculate the imports of manufacturing (agricultural) items for each of the state. We divided total imports of manufacturing (agriculture) by India's population to get per capita manufacturing (agriculture) imports. Subsequently, the above share has been multiplied with the respective state's population in order to estimate each respective state's import figures for manufacturing (agriculture). This is based on the assumption of homothetic preference for imports across all states. Finally, the exports and imports figure for each of the state estimated are added to arrive at the total trade for a state.

Measurement of the degree of openness of any state has been done by calculating the state's total trade balance, exports and manufacturing trade as a percentage of the NSDP of that state. We understand that these are not the actual trade figures from the state but since no data is available for trade from the state, we can perhaps use these estimates as proxies.

References

Ahluwalia, M. S. 2002. 'State Level Performance under Economic Reforms in India', in *Economic Policy Reforms and the Indian Economy*, edited by Anne Krueger, Chicago: University of Chicago Press.

Agarwal, Manmohan and Sudip Ranjan Basu. 2005. 'Development Strategy and Regional Inequality in India', in *India's North-east: Developmental Issues in a Historical Perspective*, edited by A. Barua, New Delhi: Manohar and CSH Publication.

Bajpai, N. and J. Sachs. 1996. 'Trends in Inter-State Inequalities of Income in India', Discussion Paper no. 528, Harvard Institute for International Development, Harvard University.

Banister, G. J. and K. Thugge. 2001. 'International Trade and Poverty Alleviation', IMF Working Paper no. 01/54, Policy Development and Review and African Departments, Washington DC: IMF.

Barro, R. and J. W. Lee. 1994. 'Sources of Economic Growth', Carnegie-Rochester Conference Series on Public Policy.

Barua, A. and Arindam Banyopadhyay. 2005. 'Structural Change, Economic Growth and Regional Disparity in the North-East: Regional and National Perspectives', in *India's North-east: Developmental Issues in a Historical Perspective*, edited by A. Barua, New Delhi: Manohar and CSH Publication.

Barua, A. and Pavel Chakraborty. Forthcoming. 'Does openness affect Regional inequality? A Case Study for India', *Review of Development Economics*, Special Issue.

Berg, A. and A. Krueger. 2003. 'Trade, Growth and Poverty: A Selective Survey', IMF Working Paper no. WP/03/30 February.

Cashin and Sahay. 1996. 'Internal Migration, Centre-State Grants, and Economic Growth in the States of India', IMF Staff papers, vol. 43, no. 1, pp. 123–71.
Chenery, H. and M. Syrquin. 1977. *Patterns of Development, 1950–1970*, Washington DC: The World Bank and Oxford University Press.
Das, S. K. and A. Barua. 1996. 'Regional Inequalities, Economic Growth and Liberalization: A Study of the Indian Economy', *Journal of Development Studies*, vol. 32, no. 3, pp. 364–90.
Dasgupta, D. et al. 2000. 'Growth and Interstate Disparities in India', *Economic and Political Weekly*, vol. 35, July, pp. 1637–48.
Dholakia, R. 1994. 'Spatial Dimensions of Acceleration of Economic Growth in India', *Economic and Political Weekly*, vol. 24, no. 35, pp. 2303.
Dholakia, R. H. 1985. *Regional Disparity in Economic Growth in India*, Delhi: Himalaya Publishing House.
Dollar, D. and A. Kraay. 2001a. 'Growth is Good for the Poor', Policy Research Working Paper no. 2587, The World Bank.
———. 2001b. 'Trade, Growth, and Poverty', Policy Research Working Paper no. 2199, The World Bank.
Elizondo, R. L. and P. Krugman. 1992. 'Trade Policy and the Third World Metropolis', NBER Working Paper no. 4238.
Frenkel, J. and D. Romer. 1999. 'Does Trade Cause Growth', *American Economic Review*, vol. 89, no. 3, pp. 379–99.
Hanson, G. H. 1997. 'Increasing Returns, Trade, and the Regional Structure of Wages', *Economic Journal*, vol. 107, pp. 113–33.
Khan, Haider A. 2005. 'Assessing Poverty Impact of Trade Liberalization Policies: A Generic Macroeconomic Computable General Equilibrium Model for South Asia', ADB Institute Discussion Paper no. 22.
Krugman, P. 1995. 'Growing World Trade: Causes and Consequences', *Brookings Papers on Economic Activity*, vol. 1, Washington, DC: Brookings Institution, pp. 327–62.
Majumder, G. and J. L. Kapoor, 'Behaviour of Inter-state Income Inequalities in India', paper presented at the Twelfth Conference of the Indian Association for Research on National Income and Wealth, 1980.
Marjit, S. and S. Mitra. 1996. 'Convergence in Regional Growth Rates: Indian Research Agenda', *Economic and Political Weekly*, vol. 31, no. 33, pp. 2239–42.
Mathur, A. 1987. 'Why Growth Rates Differ within India: An Alternative Approach', *Journal of Development Studies*, vol. 23, no. 2, pp. 167–99.
Nagraj, R., A. Varoudakis, and M. A. Veganzones. 1997. 'Long-run Growth Trends and Convergence across Indian States', mimeograph, Mumbai: IGIDR.
Paluzie, E. 2001. 'Trade Policy and Regional Inequalities', *Papers in Regional Science*, vol. 80, pp. 67–85.
Raman, J., 1996. 'Convergence or Uneven Development: A Note on Regional Development in India', mimeograph, Valparaison University, US.
Rao, M. G., R. T. Shand and K. P. Kalirajan. 1999. 'Convergence of Income across Indian States: A Divergent View', *Economic and Political Weekly*, vol. 34, no. 13, pp. 769–78.
Sachs, J., N. Bajpai and A. Ramiah. 2002. 'Understanding Regional Economic Growth in India', CID Working Paper no. 88, Harvard University.
Shankar, R. and A. Shah. 2001. *Bridging the Economic Divide within Nations: A Scorecard on the Performance of Regional Policies in Reducing Regional Income Disparities*, Country Evaluation and Regional Relations Division, Washington DC: The World Bank.

Singh, N. and T. N. Srinivasan. 2002. 'India's Federalism, Economic Reform and Globalization', paper prepared for CREDPR project on Globalization and Comparative Federalism.

Sjöberg, Ö and F. Sjöholm. 2004. 'Trade Liberalization and the Geography of Production: Agglomeration, Concentration, and Dispersal in Indonesia's Manufacturing Industry', *Economic Geography*, July.

Topalova, Petia. 2007. 'Trade Liberalization, Poverty and Inequality: Evidence from Indian Districts', in *Globalization and Poverty*, edited by Ann Harrison, Chicago: University of Chicago Press.

Ventura, J. 1997. 'Growth and Interdependence', *Quarterly Journal of Economics*, vol. 112, no. 1, February.

WTO. 2008. *World Tariff Profiles 2008*, Switzerland: WTO.

Bibliography

Abed-el-Rahman, K. 'Firms Competitive and National Comparative Advantages as Joint Determinants of Trade Composition', *Weltwirtschaftliches Archiv*, vol. 127, 1991, pp. 83–97.
Agarwal, Manmohan and Alokesh Barua. 'Trade Policy and Welfare in Segmented Markets', *Keio Economic Studies*, vol. 30, vol. 2, 1993, pp. 95–108.
_____. 'Effects of Entry in a Model of Oligopoly with International Trade', *Journal of International Trade & Economic Development*, vol. 3, no. 1, 1994, pp. 1–13.
_____. 'Firm and Industry Response to Liberalization in India: Theory and Evidence', paper presented in an international seminar organised by the CSH on Globalization of Firms: India, China and Russia, 19–20 December 2002.
_____. 'Entry Liberalization and Export Performance: A Theoretical Analysis in a Multi-market Oligopoly Model', *Journal of International Trade and Economic Development*, vol. 13, no. 3, 2004, pp. 287–303.
Agarwal, Manmohan and Sudip Ranjan Basu. 'Development Strategy and Regional Inequality in India', in *India's North-east: Developmental Issues in a Historical Perspective*, edited by A. Barua, New Delhi: Manohar-CSH Publication, 2005.
Agarwal, Manmohan. 'South-South Trade: Building Block on Bargaining Chip', in *Rules, Power and Credibility*, edited by J. Whalley, Toronto: MacMillan, 1991.
_____. 'Regional Trading Arrangements in the Era of Globalizations: An Indian Perspective', *International Studies*, vol. 41, no. 4, 2004, pp. 411–23.
Agenor, Pierre-Richard. 'Does Globalization Hurt the Poor?' mimeograph, Washington DC: The World Bank, 2003.
Aggarwal, Aradhna. 'Anti-Dumping Law and Practice: An Indian Perspective', ICRIER Working Paper no. 85, April 2002.
Aghion, Philippe, Eve Caroli and Cecilia Garcia-Penalosa. 'Inequality and Economic Growth: The Perspective of the New Growth Theories', *Journal of Economic Literature*, vol. XXXVII, December, 1999, pp. 1615–60.
Ahluwalia, M. S. 'State Level Performance under Economic Reforms in India', in *Economic Policy Reforms and the Indian Economy*, edited by Anne Krueger, Chicago: University of Chicago Press, 2002.
Ahuja, R. 'Design of Incentives in Micro Health Insurance Schemes', forthcoming as Center for Development Research (ZEF) Discussion Paper, Bonn: ZEF, 2002.
Anant and Zutshi. 'Report on Trade in Accountancy Services', project study sponsored by the Ministry of Commerce, Government of India and executed by ICRIER, WP 382.92 IND-T, 1999.

Anant, T. C. A. 'India and the WTO: Flawed Rejectionist Approach', *Economic and Political Weekly*, vol. 36, no. 46 & 47, November 2001, pp. 4243–45.

Andresen, Martin A. 'Canada, the United States and NAFTA: The Effects on Trade Patterns', Working Paper, Department of Economics, Simon Fraser University, 2001.

Aquino, Antonio. 'Intra-industry Trade and Inter-industry Specialisation as Concurrent Sources of International Trade in Manufactures', *Weltwirtschaftliches Archiv*, vol. 114, 1978, pp. 275–96.

Asian Development Bank. *Economic Co-operation in the Greater Mekong Sub region: Facing the Challenges*, Manila: Asian Development Bank, 1996.

———. *Asian Development Outlook*, Manila: Asian Development Bank, 2000.

Aturupane, Chonira, Simion Djankov and Bernard Hoekman. 'Determinants of Intra-industry Trade between East and West Europe', draft paper, Washington DC: World Bank, 1997.

Azad, N. A. 'Trade Performance and Trade Distribution: A Study of North Vs South,' PhD. thesis, New Delhi: Jawaharlal Nehru University, 1992.

Bajpai, N. and Sachs, J. 'Trends in Inter-State Inequalities of Income in India', Discussion Paper no. 528, Harvard Institute for International Development, Harvard University, 1996.

Balassa, Bela. 'Tariff Reductions and Trade in Manufactures among the Industrial Countries', *American Economic Review*, vol. 56, 1966, pp. 466–73.

Banerjee, Paula, Sanjoy Hazarika, Monirul Hussain and Ranabir Samaddar, 'Indo-Bangladesh Cross Border Migration and Trade', Commentary, *Economic and Political Weekly*, vol. 34, no. 3, September 1999, pp. 1255–62.

Banister, G. J. and K. Thugge. 'International Trade and Poverty Alleviation', IMF Working Paper no. 01/54, Policy Development and Review and African Departments, Washington DC: International Monetary Fund, May 2001.

Bardhan, P. K. 'Corruption and Development', *Journal of Economic Literature*, vol. 35, no. 3 September 1997, pp. 1320–46.

Barro, R. and J. W. Lee. 'Sources of Economic Growth', Carnegie-Rochester Conference Series on Public Policy, 1994.

Barro, R. and X. Sala-i-Martin, *Economic Growth*, New York: McGraw Hill, 1995.

Baru, Sanjaya. 'India Launches FTA Spree Before Cancun', *The Financial Express*, Friday, 20 June 2003, http://fecolumnists.expressindia.com/print.php?content_id=36543.

Barua, A. and Arindam Banyopadhyay. 'India's North-east: Developmental Issues in a Historical Perspective', New Delhi: Manohar-CSH Publication, 2005.

Barua, Alokesh and Debashis Chakraborty. 'Liberalization, Trade and Industrial Performance in India: An Empirical Study', paper presented in the seminar entitled WTO Negotiations: India's Post-Cancun Concerns, jointly organised by Planning Commission and International Trade and Development Division, JNU, 18–19 October 2004.

Baughman, Laura M. and Kara M. Olson. 'Prospects for Exporting textiles and Clothing to the United States over the Next Decade', Geneva: International Textiles and Clothing Bureau, March 1997.

Benabou, Roland. 'Inequality and Growth', *NBER Macroeconomics Annual*, vol. 11, 1996.

Berg, A. and A. Krueger. 'Trade, Growth and Poverty: A Selective Survey', IMF Working Paper no. WP/03/30, February 2003.
Berman, E., J. Bound and Z. Griliches. 'Changes in Demand for Skilled Labour within US Manufacturing: Evidence from the Annual Survey of Manufactures', *Quarterly Journal of Economics*, vol. 109, 1994, pp. 367–97.
Berman, E., S. Machin and J. Bound. 'Implications of Skill-Biased Technological Change', mimeograph, Boston: Boston University, 1996.
Bernard, A. and J. B. Jensen. 'Exporters, Jobs, and Wages in U.S. Manufacturing: 1976–1987', *Brookings Papers on Economic Activity and Microeconomics*, Washington DC: Brookings Institution, 1995, pp. 67–119.
Besley, Timothy and Robin Burgess. 'Halving Global Poverty', *Journal of Economic Perspectives*, vol. 17, no. 3, 2003, pp. 3–22.
Bezruchka, Stephen A. 'Fertility Table', *OECD Social Indicators 2005*, http://mailman1.u.washington.edu/pipermail/pophealth/2005-March/001071.html and http://www.oecd.org/dataoecd/34/28/34542290.xls.
Bhaduri, S. and A. S. Ray. 'A Game Theoretic Model of Drug Launch in India', *Health Economics Policy and Law*, vol. 1, no.1, 2006, pp. 23–39.
Bhagwati, J. 'Splintering and Disembodiment of Services and Developing Nations', *World Economy*, series no. 2, vol. 7, June 1984, pp. 133–43.
Bhagwati, J. and Ruggie. *Powers, Passions and Purpose, Prospects for North South Negotiations*, Cambridge MA: MIT Press, 1984.
Bhagwati, Jagdish and Arvind Panagariya. 'Bilateral Trade Treaties are a Sham', *Financial Times*, 13 July 2003.
———. 'Defensive Play Simply Won't Work', *Economic Times*, 29 August 2003.
Bhagwati, Jagdish and Padma Desai. *India: Planning for Industrialization*, Oxford: Oxford University Press, 1970.
Bhagwati, Jagdish and T. N. Srinivasan. *Foreign Trade Regimes and Economic Development: India*, New York: Columbia University Press, 1975.
Bhagwati, Jagdish. *Foreign Trade Regimes and Economic Development: Anatomy and Consequences of Exchange Contrast Regimes*, Cambridge MA: Ballinger, 1978.
———. 'Splintering and Disembodiment of Services and Developing Nations', *World-Economy*, vol. 7, no. 2, June 1984, pp. 133–43.
———. 'Poverty and Public Policy', Vikram Sarabhai Lecture, 1987, *World Development*, vol. 16, no. 5, May 1988, pp. 539–55.
———. 'The East Asian Miracle that Did Happen: Understanding East Asia in Comparative Perspective', in *The Wind of the Hundred Days: How Washington Mismanaged Globalization*, edited by Jagdish Bhagwati, Cambridge MA: MIT Press, 2000, pp. 27–49.
———. 'Convocation Address', unpublished lecture, Punjab University, Chandigarh, India, 2000, http://www.columbia.edu/~jb38.
———. 'Globalization and Appropriate Governance', unpublished Jubilee 2000 lecture, WIDER, Helsinki: United Nations University, 2002.
Bharadwaj, R. 'Factor Proportions and the Structure of Indo-US Trade', *Indian Economic Journal*, vol. 10, October 1962.

Bhardwaj, A., S. Kathuria and W. Martin. 'Implications for South Asian Countries of Abolishing the Multi-fibre Arrangement', World Bank Working Paper no. 2721, 2001.
Bhattacharyya, B. 'Non-Tariff Measures on Indian Exports: An Assessment', Occasional Paper no. 16, New Delhi: Indian Institute of Foreign Trade, 1999.
Bhattacharyya, R. 'India's Intra-Industry Trade: An Empirical Analysis (1970–1987)', *Indian Economic Journal*, vol. 42, no. 2, 1994, pp. 54–74.
Bhattarcharjea, Aditya. 'Trade, Investment, and Competition Policy', in *India and the WTO*, edited by A. Mattoo and R. M. Stern, Washington DC: Oxford University Press and The World Bank, 2003.
Blinova, Natalia, Nicolas Dorgeret and Razvan-Florian Maximiuc. 'The EU in the Complex WTO', paper presented at the WTO seminar, Geneva, 11–13 May 2006, http://hei.unige.ch/sections/sp/agenda/wto/wto2006/Paper%20-%20EU%20%20in%20the%20complexWTOr.pdf.
Borjas, G. J., R. J. Freeman and L. F. Katz. 'On the Labor Market Effects of Immigration and Trade', in *Immigration and the Workforce*, edited by G. Borjas, and R. Freeman, Chicago: University of Chicago Press, 1992, pp. 213–44.
Bougheas, Demetrades, and Morgenroth. 'Infrastructure, Costs and Trade', *Journal of Development Economics*, vol. 47, 1999, pp. 169–89
Bound, J. and G. Johnson. 'Changes in the Structure of Wages in the 1980s: An Evaluation of Alternative Explanations', *American Economic Review*, vol. 82, 1992, pp. 371–92.
Bourguignon, F. and C. Morrisson. 'Income Distribution, Development and Foreign Trade', *European Economic Review*, vol. 34, 1990, pp. 1113–32.
Bourguignon, Francois, et al. 'Making Sense of Globalization,' CEPR Policy Paper no. 8, London: Centre for Economic Policy Research, 2002.
Bruno, M., M. Ravaillon and L. Squire. 'Equity and Growth in Developing Countries: Old and New Perspectives on the Policy Issues', in *Income Distribution and High-Quality Growth*, edited by V. Tanzi and K. Chu, Cambridge MA: MIT Press 1998, pp. 117–46.
Bureau of Economic Analysis,. *Savings Data*, US: Department of Commerce, various years, http://www.bea.gov/national/nipaweb/Nipa-Frb.asp.
Burtless, G. 'International Trade and the Rise in Earnings Inequality', *Journal of Economic Literature*, vol. 33, 1995, pp. 800–16.
Businessworld. 'Nine Months to Go', Cover Story April 2004, www.businessworldindia.com.
Cartier-Bresson, J. 'Economics of Corruption', *OECD Observer*, 2000.
Cashin, Paul and Ratna Sahay. 'Internal Migration, Centre-State Grants, and Economic Growth in the States of India', IMF Staff Paper, vol. 43, no. 1, 1996, pp. 123–71.
Cashin, Paul and Ratna Sahay. 'International Migration, Centre-State Grants and Economic Growth in the States of India: A Reply to Rao and Sen', IMF Staff Paper, vol. 44, 1997, pp. 289–91.
Centre of Social Research. 'Gender Impact of WTO on Women's Livelihood in India: Women Workers in the Textiles and Food Processing Industries', New Delhi: Centre of Social Research, 2003.

Chadha, R, B. Hoeckman, W. Martin, A. Oyejide, M. Pangestu, D. Tussie and J. Iarrouk, 'Developing Countries and the Next Round of WTO Negotiations', *The World Economy*, vol. 23, no. 4, 2000, pp. 527–42.

Chadha, R. et al. 'Computational Analysis of the Impact on India and the Uruguay Round: The Doha Development Agenda Negotiations' edited by Mattoo, Aaditya and Stern, '*India and the WTO*', World Bank and Oxford University Press, 2003, pp. 13–46.

Chaisse, Julien and Debashis Chakraborty. 'Disputes Resolution in the WTO: In the Light of Chinese and Indian Involvements', in *Future Negotiation Issues at WTO: An India-China Perspective*, edited by Bibek Debroy and Mohammad Saqib, New Delhi: Globus Books, 2004, pp. 377–432.

Chakraborty, Debashis and Arnab Kumar Hazra. 'Preferential Trade Agreements and India: A Review of Issues', New Delhi: RGICS Working Paper no. 48, 2005.

Chakraborty, Debashis and Dipankar Sengupta. 'Learning Through Trading? India's Decade-Long Negotiation Strategy at WTO', *South Asian Survey*, vol. 12, no. 2, 2005, pp. 223–46.

———. 'IBSAC (India-Brazil-South Africa-China): A Potential Developing Country Coalition in WTO Negotiations', CSH Occasional Paper no. 18, December 2006.

Chakraborty, Debashis and Julien Chaisse. 'Trade Policy Review Mechanism and Dispute Settlement System: A Cross-Country Analysis of Enforcing WTO Rules between Negotiations and Sanctions', in *WTO at Ten: Looking Back to Look Beyond*, edited by Bibek Debroy and Mohammad Saqib, New Delhi: Konark Publishers, 2005, pp. 210–78.

Chakraborty, Debashis and Pavel Chakraborty. 'Indian Exports in the Post-Transitory Phase of WTO: Some Exploratory Results and Future Concerns', *Foreign Trade Review*, vol. XL, no. 1, 2005, pp. 3–26.

Chakraborty, Debashis. 'India's Intra-industry Trade: An Analysis of the Pre-reform and Post-Reform Trends', Unpublished M.Phil Dissertation, International Trade and Development Division, SIS, Jawaharlal Nehru University, 2002.

———. 'The Changing face of Indian Negotiation Strategy in WTO', paper presented in the seminar on NDA Government's Foreign Policy, organised by SPANDAN in association with Ministry of External Affairs, Government of India, Jawaharlal Nehru University, New Delhi, 30 July 2003.

———. 'Recent Negotiation Trends on Agriculture under WTO', New Delhi: RGICS Working Paper no. 47, 2004.

———. 'India's Participation in WTO Negotiations: The Changes in Attitude and Emphasis', *Taiwanese Journal of WTO Studies*, vol. 3, 2005, pp. 119–63.

———. 'India's Negotiations on Trade and Environment Issues at WTO: A Decade Long Experience', *GALT Update*, vol. 1, no. 2, March 2007, pp. 12–17.

———. 'Misuse of Anti-Dumping Provisions: What do the WTO Disputes Reveal?', in *Anti-Dumping: Global Abuse of a Trade Policy Instrument*, edited by B. Debroy, and D. Chakraborty, New Delhi: Academic Foundation, 2007, pp. 155–83.

Chand, Ramesh and Linu, Mathew Philip. 'Subsidies and Support in Agriculture: Is WTO Providing Level Playing Field?', *Economic and Political Weekly*, vol. 36, no. 32, August 2001, pp. 3014–16.

Chand, Ramesh. *WTO, Trade Liberalization and Indian Agriculture*, New Delhi: Mittal Publications, 2002.

———. 'India's Agricultural Trade during Post-WTO Decade: Lessons for WTO Negotiations', paper presented at the conference on Off the Starting Block to Hong Kong: Concerns and Negotiating Options on Agriculture and NAMA for India, organised by CENTAD, New Delhi, 22 July 2005.

Chanda, R. 'Trade in Health Services', Working Paper no. 70, ICRIER, 2001.

Chen, Xianquin. 'Directing Government Procurement as an Incentive of Production', *Journal of Economic Integration*, vol. 10, 1995, pp. 130–40.

Chenery, H. and M. Syrquin. *Patterns of Development, 1950–1970*, London: Oxford University Press : London, 1975.

Chisti, Sumitra. 'Restructuring of International Economic Relations: Uruguay Round and the Developing Countries', New Delhi: Concept Publishing Company, 1991.

CII. *How are the States Doing?*, New Delhi: CII, 2002.

———. 'Study of Exports Leaving West Bengal Ports', 2004, www.ciionline.org.

CII-ICMF. *Indian Textile Industry: The Road Ahead*, New Delhi: CII-ICMF, April 2003.

Cline, W. *Trade and Income Distribution*, Washington DC: Institute for International Economics, 1997.

———. 'Trade, Immigration and Wage Distribution,' in *The Causes and Consequences of Increasing Inequality*, edited by F. Welch, Chicago: University of Chicago Press, 2001, pp. 227–67.

Coe, David T., Helpman Elhanan and W. A. Hoffmaister. 'North-South R&D Spill Overs', *Economic Journal*, vol. 107, January, 1998, pp. 134–49.

Cohen, J. C., *The LAC Pharmaceutical Region*, Washington DC: The World Bank, 2000,

Commonwealth Business Council, *Developing Countries and the WTO Trade Debate: Compelling Case for Full Participation in the New Round*, London: Commonwealth Business Council, 2001.

Council of Representatives. Presentation and Papers, New Delhi: ITCB, April 2004.

Das, Bhagirath, 'Implementations and Implications—The WTO and the Multilateral Trading System: Past, Present and Future' Third World Network Publication, www.twn.org.

Das, D. K. 'Manufacturing Productivities under Varying Trade Regimes: India in the 1980s and 1990s', ICRIER Working Paper no. 107, July 2003.

Das, Deb Kusum. 'Quantifying Trade Barriers: Has Protection Declined Substantially in Indian Manufacturing?', ICRIER Working Paper no. 105, July 2003.

Das, S. and S. Pohit, 'Quantifying Transport, Regulatory and Other Costs of Indian Overland Exports to Bangladesh', National Council of Applied Economic Research (NCAER), New Delhi, 2003.

Das, S. K. and A. Barua. 'Regional Inequalities, Economic Growth and Liberalisation: A Study of the Indian Economy', *Journal of the Development Studies*, vol. 32, no. 3, 1996, pp. 364–90.

Das, S. K., A. Barua and M. N. Ghosh. 'Interstate Economic Inequality in India: Some Implications for Development Strategy', Discussion Paper, International Trade and Development Division, Jawaharlal Nehru University, New Delhi, 1993.

Das, S. P., 'An Indian Perspective on WTO Rules on Foreign Direct Investment', in *India and the WTO*, edited by A. Mattoo, and R. M. Stern, Washington DC: The World Bank and Oxford University Press, 2003, pp. 141–68.

Das, Satya P. 'An Indian Perspective on WTO Rules on Foreign Direct Investment', in *India and the WTO*, edited by A. Mattoo and R. M. Stern, Washington DC: Oxford University Press and The World Bank, 2003.

Dasgupta, D., P. Maiti, R. Mukherjee, S. Sarkar, and S. Chakrabarti. 'Growth and Interstate Disparities in India', *Economic and Political Weekly*, July 2000.

Dasgupta, Subhendu. 'Their Rules, Our Rights: Intellectual Property Rules and Right to Health', in *WTO and TRIPS: Indian Perspective*, edited by Byasdeb Dasgupta, et al., Kalyani: University of Kalyani, 2003, pp. 27–41.

Dastidar, A. G. 'International Trade and Personal Income Distribution in Developing Countries: Some Issues and Concerns', *Arthaniti*, vol. 5, no.1–2, 2006, pp. 64–80.

Datt, G. and M. Ravallion. 'Why Have Some Indian States Done Better than Others at Reducing Rural Poverty', *Economica*, vol. 65, 1998.

Datt, Gaurav. 'Poverty in India and Indian States: An Update', *FCND Working Paper*, vol. 47, 1998.

———. 'Has Poverty in India Declined Since the Economic Reforms?' mimeograph, Washington DC: The World Bank, 1999.

Dayal-Gulati, Anuradha and Aasim Husain. 'Centripetal Forces in China's Economic Take off', IMF Staff Paper, vol. 49, 2002, pp. 364–94.

Deardorff, A. V. and D. S. Hakura. 'Trade and Wages: What are the Questions', in *Trade and Wages*, edited by J. Bhagwati and M. H. Kosters, Washington DC: AEI Press, 1994, pp. 76–107.

Deardorff, Alan V. and Robert M. Stern. 'Enhancing the Benefits for India and Other Developing Countries in the Doha Development Agenda Negotiations', paper presented at the conference, The WTO and India: Issues and Negotiating Strategies, Cotton College, Guwahati, 11–12 August 2004.

———. 'Designing A Pro-Active Stance for India in the Doha Development Agenda Negotiations', paper presented in the seminar entitled WTO Negotiations: India's Post-Cancun Concerns, jointly organised by Planning Commission and International Trade and Development Division, Jawaharlal Nehru University, 18–19 October 2004.

Deardorff, Alan. 'What Might Globalization's Critics Believe,' Occasional Paper no. 20, Bureau of Economic Studies, Macalester College, St Paul, 2003.

Deaton, Angus. 'Computing Prices and Poverty Rates in India, 1999–2000', mimeograph, Princeton: Princeton University, 2001.

———. 'Counting the World's Poor's Problems and Possible Solutions', *World Bank Research Observer*, vol. 16, no. 2, 2001, pp. 125–47.

Debroy, Bibek and A.T. Santhanam. 'Matching the Codes of the ITC (Revision 2) with the ITC (Harmonized System)', *Foreign Trade Bulletin*, January 1992.

———. 'Concordance between National Industrial Classification and India Trade Classification (Revision 2), *Foreign Trade Bulletin*, Indian Institute of Foreign Trade, July 1992.

———. 'Matching Trade Codes with Industrial Codes', *Foreign Trade Bulletin*, July 1993.

Debroy, Bibek and Debashis Chakraborty (eds). *The Trade Game: Negotiation Trends at the Multilateral Level and Concerns for Developing Countries*, New Delhi: Academic Foundation, 2007.

Debroy, Bibek and Gary Pursell. 'Government Procurement Policies in India', in *Law and Policy in Public Purchasing: The WTO Agreement on Government Procurement*, edited by Bernard Hoekman and Petros Mavroidis, Michigan: University of Michigan Press, 1997.

Debroy, Bibek. *Beyond the Uruguay Round*, New Delhi: Sage Publications, 1996.

Deininger, K. and L. Squire. 'A New Data Set Measuring Income Inequality', *World Bank Economic Review*, vol. 10, 1996, pp. 565–91.

Demurger, Sylvie, Jeffrey Sachs, Wing Thye Woo, Shuming Bao, Gene Chang and Andrew Mellinger. 'Economic Geography and Regional Growth in China', *Asian Economic Papers*, vol. 1, no. 1, 2002, pp. 146–97.

Deodhar, Satish Y. 'GATS and Educational Services: Issues for India's Response in WTO Negotiations', 2001, http://www.iimahd.ernet.in/publications/data/2001-10-03SatishDeodhar.pdf.

Department for International Development (DFID). 'Government of Andhra Pradesh: Public Procurement Review', United Kingdom: Department for International Development, 2002.

Dhar, Biswajit and C. Niranjan Rao. 'Third Amendment to 1970 Patent Act: An Analysis', Commentary, *Economic and Political Weekly*, December 2004.

Dholakia, R. *Regional Disparity in Economic Growth in India*, Delhi: Himalaya Publishing House, 1985.

———. 'Spatial Dimensions of Acceleration of Economic Growth in India', *Economic and Political Weekly*, vol. 29, no. 35, 21 August 1994, p. 2303.

Dixit, Avinash and Joseph Stiglitz. 'Monopolistic Competition and Optimum Product Diversity', *American Economic Review*, 1977, pp. 297–308.

Dollar, David and Aart Kraay. 'Growth *Is* Good for the Poor,' mimeograph, Washington DC: The World Bank, 2000.

———. 'Trade, Growth, and Poverty', mimeograph, Washington DC: The World Bank, 2000.

———. 'Growth is Good for the Poor', Policy Research Working Paper no. 2587, Washington DC: The World Bank, 2001.

———. 'Spreading the Wealth', *Foreign Affairs*, vol. 81, no. 1, January–February 2002, pp. 1–13.

Draper, Peter and Razeen Sally. 'Developing-Country Coalitions in Multilateral Trade Negotiations', paper presented in the seminar entitled WTO Negotiations: India's Post-Cancun Concerns, jointly organised by the Planning Commission and International Trade and Development Division, Jawaharlal Nehru University, 18–19 October 2004.

Dubey, M. 'India and WTO Negotiations in the Doha Round', paper presented at the seminar on The Indian Experience of Liberalisation, Institute for Advanced Studies, Shimla, 2005.

Economic and Social Commission for Asia and the Pacific. 'Non-tariff Measures with Potentially Restrictive Market Access Implications Emerging in a Post-Uruguay

Round Context', *Studies in Trade and Investment* no. 40, New York: ESCAP, United Nations, 2000.
Economist, 'Rags and Riches: A Survey of Fashion', March 2004.
Edwards, S. 'Trade Policy, Growth and Income Distribution', *American Economic Review, Papers and Proceedings*, 1997, pp. 205–10.
Elbehri, Aziz. 'MFA quota Removal and Global Textile and Cotton Trade: Estimating Quota Restrictiveness and Quantifying Post-MFA Trade Patterns', Preliminary Draft, Economic Research Service, USDA, 11 May 2004.
Elizondo, R. L. and P. Krugman. 'Trade Policy and the Third World Metropolis', NBER Working Paper no. 4238, 1992.
ESCAP Secretariat. 'Agreement on Textiles and Clothing: Progress, Problems and Prospects for Developing Countries of the ESCAP Region', in *Asian and Pacific Developing Economies and the First WTO Ministerial Conference, Issues of Concern*, New York: United Nations, 1996.
Ethier. S. *Modern International Economic*, New York: W.W. Norton and Co., 1983.
Evans, John W. *The Kennedy Round in American Trade Policy: The Twilight of the GATT*, Cambridge, Mass.: Harvard University Press, 1971.
Evenett, S. J. and B. M. Hoekman. 'Transparency in Procurement Regimes: What Can We Expect from International Trade Agreements', in *Public Procurement: The Continuing Revolution*, edited by Sue Arrowsmith and Martin Trybus, US: Kluwer Law International, 2003.
Faustino, H. C., J. R. Silva and R. V. Carvalho, 'Testing Intra-Industry Trade between Portugal and Spain: 1990–1996', Instituto Politenico De Portalegre Working Paper, 1999.
Financial Times. 'EU Set to Take New US Trade Spat to WTO', 27 January 2004.
Finger, J. M. 'Implementing the Uruguay Round Agreement: Problems for Developing Countries', *The World Economy*, vol. 24, no. 9, September 2001 pp. 1097–108.
Finger, J. M. and J. J. Nogues. 'The Unbalanced Round Outcome: The New Areas in Future WTO Negotiations', *The World Economy*, vol. 25, no. 3, March 2002, pp. 321–40.
Francois, J. R., B. MacDonald and H. Nordstorm. 'The Uruguay Round: A Numerical Based Qualitative Assessment,' in *The Uruguay Round and Developing Economies*, edited by W. Martin and L. A. Winters, Cambridge: Cambridge University Press, 1996.
Frankel, Jeffrey and David Romer. 'Does Trade Cause Growth?', *American Economic Review*, vol. 89, no. 3, June 1999, pp. 379–99.
Freeman, R. 'Are Your Wages Set in Beijing ?', *Journal of Economic Perspectives*, vol. 9, 1995, pp. 15–32.
———. 'Will Globalization Dominate U. S. Labour Market Outcome', paper prepared for the Brookings Conference on Import, Export and the American Workers, January 1996.
Ganuza, E., S. Morley, S. Robinson and R. Vos. 'Are Export Promotion and Trade Liberalisation Good for Latin America's Poor?', *Development Policy Review*, vol. 23, no. 3, 2005, pp. 385–403.
Gary, Sampson and Richard Snape. 'Identifying the Issues in Trade in Services', *The World Economy*, series no. 2, vol. 8, June 1985, pp. 171–82.

Globerman, Steven and J. W. Dean. 'Recent Trends in Intra-industry Trade and their Implications for Future Trade Liberalization', *Weltwirtschaftliches Archiv*, 1990, pp. 25–49.

Goldar, Biswanath. 'Productivity Trends in Indian Manufacturing in the Pre- and Post-Reform Periods', ICRIER Working Paper no. 137, July 2004.

Gordon, J. And P. Gupta. 'Understanding India's Services Revolution', IMF Working Paper no. WP/04/171, September 2004.

Goswami, et al. *Competitiveness of Indian Manufacturing, Results from a Firm-Level Survey*, New Delhi: CII-The World Bank, 2002.

Government of Assam, *Economic Survey of Assam 2003–2004*, Guwahati: Government Press, 2004, http://www.assamgov.org/ecosurvey.

Government of India, *Report of the Task Force on Revision of Norms for Procurement of Goods and Services by Government*, Ministry of Finance, New Delhi: 2003.

———. 'Kamal Nath Constitutes FTA Cell to Deal with Industry Grievances', Press Release, 7 January 2005, http://www.commerce.nic.in/Jan05_release.htm#h7.

Greenaway, David, Robert Hine and Chris Milner. 'Vertical and Horizontal Intra-industry Trade: A Cross Industry Analysis for the United Kingdom', *Economic Journal*, vol. 105, 1995, pp. 1505–18.

Grether, J. and Marcelo Olarreaga. 'Preferential and Non-preferential Trade Flows in World Trade', Staff Working Paper ERAD-98-10, WTO, 1998.

Grimwade, Nigel. 'The GATT, the Doha Round and Developing Countries', in *The WTO and Developing Countries*, edited by H. Katrak and Roger Strange, New York: Palgrave Macmillan, 2004.

Grossman, G. M. and E. Helpman. 'The Politics of Free Trade Agreement,' *American Economic Review*, vol. 85, no. 4, September 1995, pp. 667–90.

Grubel, Herbert G. and P. J. Lloyd. *Intra-industry Trade: The Theory and Measurement of International Trade in Differentiated Products*, Hampshire: Macmillan Press Limited, 1975.

Gulati, Ashok. *Agriculture and the New Trade Agenda in the WTO 2000 Negotiations: Interests and Options for India*, New Delhi, Institute for Economic Growth, 1999.

———. 'India,' in *Agriculture, Trade and WTO in South Asia*, edited by D. I. Merlinda, Washington DC: The World Bank, 2003.

Haberler. *Trends in International Trade*, report by a panel of experts, Geneva: GATT, 1958.

Hanson, G. H. 'Increasing Returns, Trade, and the Regional Structure of Wages', *Economic Journal*, vol. 107, no. 440, 1997, pp. 113–33.

Harris, J. R. and M. P. Todaro. 'Migration, Unemployment and Development: A Two-sector Analysis', *American Economic Review*, vol. 60, 1970, pp. 126–42.

Harrison, Anne and Gordon Hanson. 'Who Gains From Trade Reform? Some Remaining Puzzles', *Journal of Development Economics*, vol. 59, 1999, pp. 129–44.

Harrison, Anne. 'Openness and Growth: A Time-Series, Cross-Country Analysis for Developing Countries', *Journal of Development Economics*, vol. 48, no. 2, March 1996, pp. 419–47.

Harrison, G. W., T. E. Rutherford and D. G. Tarr. 'Quantifying the Uruguay Round', in *The Uruguay Round and Developing Economies*, edited by W. Martin and L. A. Winters, Cambridge: Cambridge University Press, 1996.

Hazra, Arnab Kumar. 'Industrial Disputes Act: A Critical Appraisal', RGICS Working Paper Series no. 29, 2001.
Helpman, Elhanan and Paul Krugman. *Market Structure and Foreign Trade*, Cambridge and Mass.: MIT Press, 1986.
Helpman. 'Innovation, Imitation and Intellectual Property Rights', *Econometrica*, vol. 6, no. 6, November 1993), pp. 1247–80.
Hindustan Times. 'US May Walk Out of WTO', 16 February 2006.
_____. 'US Refusal to Bring Down Subsidies May Extend Deadlock on Trade Talks', 31 May 2006.
_____. 'Trade Talks Gain Momentum with Ministers' Conclave', 22 July 2006.
_____. 'India Plans Alternative Strategy with EU, Japan', 26 July 2006.
_____. 'US May Make India Pay for WTO Intransigence', 9 August 2006.
Hoekman, B. and K. Saggi. 'Assessing the Case for Extending WTO Disciplines on Investment-Related Policies', *Journal of Economic Integration*, vol. 15, no. 4, 2000, pp. 629–53.
Hoekman, B., A. Mattoo and P. English (eds). *Developing Countries: Turning Participation into Influence, Development Trade and the WTO: A Handbook*, Washington DC: The World Bank, 2002, pp. 485–92.
Hoekman, B., N. G. Francis and Marcelo Olarreaga. *Tariff Peaks in the Quad and Least Developed Country Exports*, Washington DC: The World Bank, 2001.
Hoekman, Bernard M. and Petros C. Mavroidis. 'WTO Dispute Settlement, Transparency and Surveillance', in *Developing Countries and the WTO: A Pro-Active Agenda*, edited by B. Hoekman and W. Martin, Oxford: Blackwell Publishers, 2001.
IMF and World Bank. 'Market Access for Developing Country Exports: Selected Issues', Approved by Timothy Geithner and Gobind Nankani, Geneva: The World Bank, September, 2002.
Institut Francais De La Mode. *Study on the Implications of the 2005 Trade Liberalisation in the Textile and Clothing Sector*, Paris: Institut Francais De La Mode, 2004.
International Food & Agricultural Trade Policy Council. 'Twenty-Five Ways to Improve the Derbez Draft on Agriculture', 10 February 2004, http://www.agritrade.org/Doha/Derbez/Assessment%20Paper.pdf.
International Labour Organization. 'Textiles, Clothing, Leather and Footwear, Sectoral Activities Programme', 1999, www.ilo.org.
IPR Commission. *Report of the Royal Commission on IPR*, London: IPR Commission, 2002.
Jaitley, Arun. 'Will we step out and drive at Cancun?', *Economic Times*, 29 August 2003.
Jha, R. 'Reducing Poverty and Inequality in India: Has Liberalization Helped?', WIDER Working Paper no. 204, Sweden, 2000.
Joshi, Vijay and I. M. D. Little. *India Economic Reforms 1991–2001*, New Delhi: Oxford University Press, 1998.
Josling, T. 'Developing Countries and the New Round of Multilateral Trade Negotiations: Background Notes on Agriculture', paper presented at conference on Developing Countries in the next WTO Trade Round, Harvard University, November 1999.
Juma, C. 'Intellectual Property Rights and Globalization: Implications for Developing Countries', paper presented at conference on Developing Countries in the Next WTO Trade Round, Harvard University, November 1999.

Kanbur, R. 'Income Distribution and Development', in *Handbook of Income Distribution*, vol. 1, edited by A. B. Atkinson and F. Bourguignon, Amsterdam: North Holland: 2000, pp. 791–841.

Kantawala, Bhavana S. 'Inter and Intra-industry international trade among SAARC countries: 1981–1992', *Foreign Trade Review*, vol. XXXII, no. 1&2, 1997, pp. 29–72.

Kaplan, Ethan, and Dani Rodrik. 'Did Malaysian Capital Controls Work?', mimeograph, Kennedy School of Government, Harvard University, 2001.

Kathuria, S., A. Bhardwaj and W. J. Martin. 'Implications for South Asian Countries of Abolishing the Multi-fibre Arrangement', World Bank Working Paper no. 2721, November, 2001.

Kathuria, S., W. J. Martin and A. Bhardwaj. 'Implications of MFA Abolition for India and South Asia,' in *The WTO for Development: A Strategy for India*, edited by A. Mattoo and R. M. Stern, New York: Oxford University Press, 2002.

Kathuria, Sanjay and Anjali Bhardwaj. 'Export Quotas and Policy Constraints in the Indian Textile and Garment Industry', in *Development, Trade and the WTO: A Handbook*, edited by Bernard Hoekman and A. Mattoo and Philip English, Philip, Washington DC: The World Bank, 2002.

Kathuria. 'Trade in Telecommunications Services Opportunities and Constraints', ICRIER Working Paper no. 14, 2004.

Katz, J. 'Domestic Technological Innovations and Dynamic Comparative Advantage', *Journal of Development Economics*, vol.16, 1984, pp. 13–37.

———. 'Domestic Technology Generation in LDCs: A Review of Research Findings', in *Technology Generation in Latin American Manufacturing Industries*, edited by J. M. Katz, London: Macmillan, 1987.

Kaufman, D. 'Corruption: Some Myths and Facts', *Foreign Policy*, summer 1997, pp. 114–31.

Keesing, D. R. and M. Wolf. 'Question on International Trade in Textiles and Clothing', *World Economy*, March 1981, pp. 79–101.

Khan, Amir Ullah and Bibek Debroy. *Intellectual Property Rights Beyond 2005: An Indian Perspective on the Debate on IPR Protection and the WTO*, Kottayam: D C School of Management and Technology, 2004.

Klitgaard, R., *Tropical Gangsters: One Man's Experience with Development and Decadence in Deepest Africa*, US: Basic Books, 1990.

Kosters, M. H. 'An Overview of Changing Wage Patterns in the Labour Market', in *Trade and Wages*, edited by J. Bhagwati and M. H. Kosters, Washington DC: AEI Press, 1994, pp. 1–35.

Kravis, Irving, 'Trade as a Handmaiden of Growth: Similarities between the Nineteenth and Twentieth Centuries', *Economic Journal*, vol. 80, 1970, pp. 850–72.

Krishna, Pravin and Devashish Mitra. 'Trade Liberalisation, Market Discipline and Productivity Growth: New Evidence from India', *Journal of Development Economics*, vol. 56, 1998, pp. 447–62.

Krueger, A. B. 'How Computers have Changed the Wage Structure: Evidence from Microdata 1984–89', *Quarterly Journal of Economics*, vol. 108, 1993, pp. 33–60.

Krueger, A. O. 'The Political Economy of the Rent Seeking', *American Economic Review*, vol. 4, 1974, 291–303.

Krueger, Anne, *Foreign Trade Regimes and Economic Development: Liberalization Attempts and Consequences*, Cambridge, Ballinger Press, 1978.

———. *Trade and Employment in Developing Countries*, vol. 3, *Synthesis and Conclusions*, Chicago: University of Chicago Press, 1983.

Krugman, Paul R. 'Increasing Returns, Monopolistic Competition and International Trade', *Journal of International Economics*, vol. 9, no. 4, 1979, pp. 469–79.

———. 'Scale Economies, Product Differentiation, and the Pattern of Trade', *American Economic Review*, no. 5, 1980, pp. 950–59.

———. 'Growing World Trade: Causes and Consequences', Brookings Papers on Economic Activity no. 1, Washington DC: Brookings Institution, 1995, pp. 327–62.

KSA Technopak. *Implications of the Phase out of the MFA on Indian Exports of Textiles and Apparel*, New Delhi: FICCI, 2001.

Kurian, N. J. 'Widening Regional Disparities in India: Some Indicators', *Economic and Political Weekly*, vol. 35, no. 7, February 2000, pp. 12–18.

Kuznets, S., 'Economic Growth and Income Inequality', *American Economic Review*, vol. 45, 1995, pp. 1–28.

Laffont, J. J. and Jean Tirole. 'Auction Design and Favouritism', *International Journal of Industrial Organization*, vol. 9, 1991, pp. 9–42.

Lakshmanan, Anderson and Subramanian, 'Integration of Transport and Trade Facilitation', in *Directions in Development*, The World Bank, 2001.

Lall, S. *Learning to Industrialise: The Acquisition of Technological capability by India*, London: Macmillan, 1987.

Lancaster, K., 'A New Approach to Consumer Theory', *Journal of Political Economy*, vol. 74, 1966, pp. 132–57.

———. 'Intra-industry Trade under Perfect Monopolistic Condition', *Journal of International Economics*, vol. 10, 1980, pp. 151–75.

Lawrence, R. Z. and Slaughter, M. J. 'Trade and US Wages: Giant Sucking Sound or Small Hiccup?', *Brookings Paper on Economic Activity*, vol. 2, Washington DC: Brookings Institution, 1993, pp. 161–226.

Lewis, W. Arthur. 'Economic Development with Unlimited Supplies of Labor', *The Manchester School of Economic and Social Studies*, vol. 22, 1954, pp. 139–91.

———. *The Theory of Economic Growth*, Homewood: Richard D. Irwin Inc., 1955.

Li, H., L. Squire and H. Zou. 'Explaining International and Intertemporal Variations in Income Inequality', *The Economic Journal*, vol. 108, 1998, pp. 26–43.

Little, I. M. D., T. Scitovsky and M. F. G. Scott. *Industry and Trade in Some Developing Countries*, Oxford: Oxford University Press, 1970.

Little, I. M. D., Tibor Scitovsky and Maurice Scott. *Industry and Trade in Some Developing Countries*, Oxford: Oxford University Press, 1970.

Lovei, L. and A. McKechnie. *The Cost of Corruption for the Poor: The Energy Sector*, Washington DC: The World Bank, 2000.

Majumder, G. and J. L. Kapoor. 'Behaviour of Inter-state Income Inequalities in India', paper presented at the Twelfth Conference of the Indian Association for Research on National Income and Wealth, 1980.

Manzur, Sohel, *Growth Zones in South Asia: What can we learn from South East Asia*, Centre for Policy Dialogue, Report no. 20, 2000.

Marjit, S. and S. Mitra. 'Convergence in Regional Growth Rates: Indian Research Agenda', *Economic and Political Weekly*, vol. 31, no. 33, 17 August 1996, pp. 2239–42.

Maskus, K. E. and D. E. Konan. 'Trade Related Intellectual Property Rights: Issues and Exploratory Results', in *Analytical and Negotiating Issues in the Global Trading System*, edited by A. Deardorff and R. M. Stern, Michigan: Ann Arbor, 1994.

Mathur, A. 'Why Growth Rates Differ within India: An Alternative Approach', *Journal of Development Studies*, vol. 23, no. 2, 1987, pp. 167–99.

Mattoo, Aaditya and Arvind Subramanian. 'India and the Multilateral Trading System Post-Doha: Defensive or Pro-active?', in *India and the WTO*, edited by A. Mattoo and R. M. Stern, Washington DC: The World Bank and Oxford University Press, 2003.

Mattoo, Aaditya. 'The Government Procurement Agreement: Implications of Economic Theory', *The World Economy*, vol. 19, no. 6, 1996, pp. 695–720.

Mauro, P. 'Why Worry About Corruption', IMF, 1997, imf.org.

McAfee, R. Preston and John McMillan. 'Government Procurement and International Trade', *Journal of International Economics*, vol. 26 1989, pp. 291–308.

McCulloch, Neil, L. Alan Winters and Xavier Cirera. *Trade Liberalization And Poverty: A Handbook*, London: Center for Economic Policy Research, 2001.

McMillan, Margaret, Dani Rodrik and Karen Horn Welch. 'When Economic Reform Goes Wrong: Cashews in Mozambique', mimeograph, Kennedy School of Government, Harvard University, 2002.

Mehta, Dewang. 'Non-Tariff Trade Barriers in IT Trade', paper presented in WTO Information Technology Symposium, Geneva, 16 July 1999, www.wto.org/english/tratop_e/inftec_e/mehta.ppt.

Mehta, Rajesh and J. George (eds). *Food Safety Regulation, Concerns and Trade: The Developing Country Experience*, New Delhi: Macmillan India, 2005.

Mehta, Rajesh. 'Non-Tariff Barriers Affecting India's Exports', RIS Working Paper no. 97, June 2005.

Mehta, Rajesh. 'Tariff and Non-Tariff Barriers of Indian Economy: A Profile', RIS Working Paper, July 1999.

Ministry of Commerce. 'G-20 Ministerial Declaration', Government of India, http://www.commerce.nic.in/wto_sub/g20/min_decln.htm.

_____. *India and the WTO*, Newsletter, New Delhi: Government of India, various issues.

_____. various submissions made to WTO, Government of India, http://www.commerce.nic.in/indian_wtopaper.htm.

_____. *Non-Tariff Barriers Faced by India*, Preliminary Report, New Delhi: Government of India, 1999.

Ministry of Finance. *Economic Survey*, New Delhi: Government of India, various years.

_____. *Economic Survey, 2002–03*, New Delhi: Government of India, 2004.

Ministry of Labour. *Second Labour Commission Report*, New Delhi: Government of India, 2002, http://labour.nic.in/lcomm2/nlc_report.html.

Mitra and Zutshi, 'Trade in Legal Services', Project Study Sponsored by Ministry of Commerce, Government of India, ICRIER WP 338.9 IND-T, 1999.

Mukherjee, Arpita and R. Sachdeva. 'Trade in Land Transport Services: Railways', ICRIER Working Paper no. 119, January 2004.

Mukherjee, Arpita. 'Trade in Construction and Consultancy Services: India and the GATS', ICRIER Working Paper no. 75, November, 2001.
Murphy, K. M. and F. Welch. 'The Role of International Trade in Wage Differentials', in *Workers and their Wages: Changing Patterns in the United States*, edited by M. H. Kosters, Washington DC: AEI Press, 1991, pp. 39–69.
Murray, T. *Trade Preferences for Developing Countries*, New York: John Wiley and Sons, 1977.
Mussa, Michael. 'Factors Driving Global Economic Integration', paper presented at a symposium on Global Opportunities and Challenges, sponsored by the Federal Reserve Bank of Kansas City, 25 August 2000.
Nag, Biswajit and Debashis Chakraborty. 'India's Approach to Asian Economic Integration', paper presented in the conference on Globalization, Blocization and East Asian Economic Integration, Center for WTO Studies, National Chengchi University, Taipei, 31 March 2006.
Nagraj, R., A. Varoudakis and M. A. Veganzones. 'Long-run Growth Trends and Convergence across Indian States', mimeograph, IGIDR, Mumbai, 1997.
Naik, Gopal and Yashika Singh. 'Doha Round Negotiations: Agriculture', Working Paper no. 217, Indian Institute of Management, Bangalore, November 2003.
Narlikar, Amrita. 'International Trade and Developing Countries: Bargaining Coalitions in the GATT and WTO', London: Routledge, 2003.
Nayyar, D. 'Free Trade: Why, When and For Whom', *Banca Nazionale del Lavoro Quarterly Review*, vol. XLIX, 1996, pp. 333–50.
Neetha, N. 'Gender and Technology: Impact of Flexible organisation and Production of Female Labour in Tiruppur Knitwear Industry', NOIDA: V. V. Giri National Labour Institute, 2001.
Nehru, Jawaharlal, *The Discovery of India*, New York: The John Day Company, 1946.
Nordas, Hildegunn Kyvik. *The Global Textile and Clothing Industry Post the Agreement on Textile and Clothing*, Geneva: WTO, 2004.
OECD. *The OECD Jobs Study: Evidence and Explanation*, Paris: OECD, 1994.
———. *The Size of Government Procurement Markets*, Paris: OECD, 2002.
———. *Transparency in Government Procurement: The Benefits of Efficient Governance and Orientation for Achieving It*, Paris: Working Party of the Trade Committee, 2003.
Office of the United States Trade Representative. 'Trade Facts. Charting a Course to Prosperity: WTO Agrees on Detailed Plan to Open Markets, Expand Trade', 31 July 2004, www.ustr.gov.
Olson. Kara M. 'Sourcing Patterns and the Elimination of Textile and Apparel Quotas', American University, Department of Economics, 2003, http://nw08.american.edu/~hertz/fall2003/MFA.pdf.
Oxfam. 'Stitched Up: How Rich-Country Protectionism in Textiles and Clothing Trade Prevents Poverty Alleviation', Oxfam Briefing Paper no. 60, 2004.
Paluzie, E. 'Trade Policy and Regional Inequalities', *Papers in Regional Science*, vol. 80, 2001, pp. 67–85.
Panagariya, A. 'Labour Standards in the WTO and Developing Countries: Trading Rights at Risk', note served at the conference Critical Issues for the Seattle WTO Ministerial: Trade and labour Standards, on the basis of author's remarks at the Congressional Staff Forum on International Development, November 1999.

_____. 'The Millennium Rouild and Developing Countries: Negotiating Strategies and Areas of Benefit', paper presented at Conference on Developing Countries in the next WTO Trade Round, Harvard University, November 1999.

_____. 'India at Doha: Retrospect and Prospect', *Economic and Political Weekly*, 26 January 2002.

Pant, Manoj and Alokesh Barua. 'India's Intra-Industry Trade: 1960–80', Discussion Paper no. 8, International Trade and Development Division, SIS, Jawaharlal Nehru University, 1986.

Pant, Manoj and P. Nunnenkamp. 'Why the Case for a Multilateral Agreement is Weak', Working Paper no. 400, Kiel Institute for World Economics, March 2003.

Pant, Manoj. *FDI in India: The Issues Involved*, New Delhi: Lancer Books, 1995.

_____. 'TRIPS and TRIMS: India's Threat Perceptions', in *Egypt and India in the Post Cold War World*, edited by M. E. Selim, Centre for Asian Studies, Cairo: Cairo University, 1996.

_____. 'First the Stick and Now the Carrot: Labour Standards in WTO', *Economic Times*, vol. 3, August 2002.

_____. 'Millenium Round of Trade Negotiations: A Developing Country Perspective', *International Studies*, vol. 39, no.3. 2002, pp. 1–32.

Park, A. and S. Wang. 'China's Poverty Statistics', *China Economic Review*, vol. 23, 2001, pp. 384–95.

Planning Commission,. *Report of the Committee on Distribution of Income and Levels of Living*, New Delhi: Government of India, 1964.

Pohit, Sanjib and Nisha Taneja, 'India's Informal Trade with Bangladesh and Nepal: A Qualitative Assessment', Indian Council for Research on International Economic Relations (ICRIER) Report, 2000.

Porto, Guido. 'Trade Reforms, Market Access, and Poverty in Argentina', mimeograph, Development Research Group, Washington DC: The World Bank, 2003.

Rahman, Mustafizur. 'Bangladesh-India Bilateral Trade: An investigation in Trade in Services', Centre for Policy Dialogue, Bangladesh, 2000.

Raizada, B. K. and Javed Sayed. 'IPR and Drugs and the Pharmaceutical Industry: Concerns for Developing Countries', in *Salvaging the WTO's Future: Doha and Beyond*, edited by Amit Dasgupta and Bibek Debroy, New Delhi: Konark Publishers Pvt. Ltd., 2002, pp. 274–89.

Raman, J. 'Convergence or Uneven Development: A Note on Regional Development in India', mimeograph, Valparaison University, US, 1996.

Ranjan, Prabhash. 'How long can the G-20 Hold Itself Together? A Power Analysis', Working Paper no. 1, Centre for Trade and Development, An Oxfam GB Initiative, New Delhi, February 2005.

Rao, K. S. and R. Radhakrishna. *India's Public Distribution System in a National and International Perspective*, Washington DC: The World Bank, 1997.

Rao, M G., R. T. Shand and K. P. Kaliranjan. 'Convergence of Income across Indian States: A Divergent View', *Economic and Political Weekly*, vol. 34, no. 13, 27 March 1999, pp. 769–78.

Rao, M. Govinda and K. Sen. 'Internal Migration, Centre-State Grants, and Economic Growth in States of India', IMF Staff Papers no. 44, 1997, pp. 283–89.

Rao, Padma Arti. 'A Study of the Determinants of Firm profitability in Selected Industries in Post-Reform India', unpublished M.Phil. dissertation, Delhi School of Economics, University of Delhi, 2001.
Ravallion M. and G. Datt. 'Why has Economic Growth Been More Pro-poor in Some States of India Than Others?', *Journal of Development Economics*, vol. 68, 2001.
Ray, A. S. *A Study of R&D Incentives in India: Structural Changes and Impact*, report prepared for the Department of Science & Technology, Ministry of Science & Technology, New Delhi: Government of India, May 2003.
Ray, A. S. *Medicines, Medical Practice and Health Care in India in the era of Globalisation: Political Economy Perspectives*, ICDHI monograph, New Delhi: VHAI Press, 2004.
Ray, A. S. *The Political Economy of Rural Health Care in India*, New Delhi: VHAI Press, 2001.
Ray, D. *Development Economics*, Princeton: Princeton University Press, 1998.
Razin, Assaf. 'Tax Burden and International Migration: Political-Economic Theory and Evidence', *Journal of Public Economics*, vol. 74, no. 1, 2002, pp. 141–50.
Rege, V. 'Transparency in Government Procurement: Issues of Concern and Interest to Developing Countries', *Journal of World Trade*, vol. 35, no. 4, 2001, pp. 489–515.
Research and Information System for the Non-Aligned and Other Developing Countries. *World Trade and Development Report 2003: Cancun and Beyond*, New Delhi: Academic Foundation, 2003.
Richardson, J. D. 'Income Inequality and Trade : How to Think, What to Conclude', *Journal of Economic Perspectives*, vol. 9, 1995, pp. 33–55.
RIS. 'Economic Impact of Trade and Investment Facilitation and Liberalization in South Asia Growth Quadrangle,' Research and Information System for the Non-Aligned and Other Developing Countries, New Delhi, December 2001.
Robertson, Dennis. *Essays in Monetary Theory*, London: King, 1940.
———. 'The Future of International Trade,' in *Essays in Monetary Theory*, edited by D. Robertson, London: Staples Press, 1940.
Roderick, D. 'Globalization and Labour', in *Market Integration, Regionalism and the Global Economy*, edited by R. E. Baldwin, D. Cohen, A. Sapir and A. Venables, Cambridge: Cambridge University Press, 1999.
Rodriguez, Francisco and Dani Rodrik. 'Trade Policy and Economic Growth: A Skeptic's Guide to Cross-National Evidence', Working Paper no. W708 1, National Bureau of Economic Research, Cambridge, MA, April 1999.
Rodrik, D. 'Imperfect Competition, Scale Economies, and Trade Policy in Developing Countries', in *Trade Policy Issues and Empirical Analysis*, edited by R. E. Baldwin, Chicago and London: University of Chicago Press, 1988.
———. 'Trade and Industrial Policy Reform', in *Handbook of Development Economics*, vol. III, edited by J. Behrman and T. N. Srinivasan, 1995, pp. 2925–82.
———. *Making Openness Work: The New Global Economy and the Developing Countries*, Washington DC: Overseas Development Council, 1999.
———. 'Globalization and Labour, or: If Globalization is a Bowl of Cherries, Why are There So Many Glum Face around ahe Table?' in *Market Integration, Regionalism and the Global Economy*, edited by R. E. Baldwin et al., Cambridge: Cambridge University Press, 1999.

Rodrik, Dani. *Feasible Globalizations*, Cambridge MA: Harvard University, 2002.
Rose-ackerman, Susan. *Corruption and Government: Causes, Consequences and Reform*, Cambridge: Cambridge University Press, 1999.
Rowntree, S. *Poverty: A Study of Town Life*, London: Macmillan, 1901.
Sachs, J. and A. Warner. 'Economic Reform and the Process of Global Integration', *Brookings Paper on Economic Activity 1*, Washington DC: Brookings Institution, 1995, pp. 1–118.
Sachs, J. and H. Shatz. 'Trade and Jobs in US Manufacturing', *Brookings Paper on Economic Activity 1*, Washington DC: Brookings Institution, 1994, pp. 1–84.
Sachs, J., N. Bajpai and A. Ramiah. 'Understanding Regional Economic Growth in India', CID Working Paper no. 88, Harvard University, 2002.
Sahgal V. and D. Chakrapani. 'India: Evaluating Bank Assistance for Public Financial Accountability in the1990s', OED Working Paper, The World Bank (2002).
Saint-Mezard, Isabelle. 'The Look East Policy: An Economic Perspective', in *Beyond the Rhetoric: The Economics of India's Look East Policy*, vol. II, edited by Frederic Grare and Amitabh Mattoo, New Delhi: Centre de Sciences Humaines and Manohar, 2003, pp. 21–43.
Sally, Razeen. 'Developing Country Trade Policy Reform and the WTO', *Cato Journal*, vol. 19, no. 3, Winter 2000, pp. 403–23.
Sapir, A. and C. Winter. 'Services Trade', in *Surveys in International Trade, Blackwell Economic Theory and the Role of Government in East Asian Industrialization*, edited by D. Greenaway and L. Winters, Princeton: Princeton University Press, 1994.
Savvides, A. 'Trade Policy and Income Inequality: New Evidence', *Economic Letters*, vol. 61, 1998, pp. 365–72.
Scherer, F. M. 'The Pharmaceutical Industry', in *Handbook of Health Economics*, vol.1, edited by A. J. Culyer and J. P. Newhouse, US: Elsevier 2000, pp. 1297–336.
Sen, A. and Himangshu. 'Poverty and Inequality in India: Getting Closer to the Truth', mimeograph, Centre for Economic Studies and Planning, New Delhi: Jawaharlal Nehru University, 2003.
Sen, Amartya. *Poverty and Famines*, New York: Oxford University Press, 1981.
SEWA Academy. 'Globalisation of the Garment Industry and Its Impact on Home Based Workers and Small Factor Workers of Ahmedabad City: Recommendations and their Implementation', Workshop, New Delhi: SEWA Academy, 27 April 2004.
Shankar, R and A. Shah. 'Bridging the Economic Divide within Nations: A Scorecard on the Performance of Regional Policies in Reducing Regional Income Disparities', Country Evaluation and Regional Relations Division, Washington DC: The World Bank, November 2001.
Sharma, Devinder. *GATT-WTO: Seeds of Despair*, New Delhi: Konark Publishers Pvt. Ltd., 1995.
Silva, J. A. and R. A. Leichenko. 'Regional Income Inequality and International Trade', *Economic Geography*, July 2004.
Singh, N. and T. N. Srinivasan. 'India's Federalism, Economic Reform and Globalization', paper prepared for CREDPR project on Globalization and Comparative Federalism, 2002.
Singh, N., R. Kaur and M. K. Sapra. 'Continents Wide and Layers Deep-The Ready-made Garment Industry in the Times of Restructuring', NCAER Working papers 2004.

Singh, Swaran. 'Factoring Taiwan in India's Look East Policy', in *India and ASEAN: Foreign Policy Dimensions for the 21st Century*, edited by K. Raja Reddy, New Delhi: New Century Publications, 2004.

Singh, Yashika. 'EU Trade: Tariff and Non-tariff Hurdles', RGICS Working Paper no. 13, New Delhi, 2000.

Singh, Yashika. 'India at the Fourth Ministerial Meeting in Doha: Déjà vu again?' RGICS Working Paper no. 32, New Delhi, 2001.

Sjöberg, Ö and F. Sjöholm. 'Trade Liberalization and the Geography of Production: Agglomeration, Concentration, and Dispersal in Indonesia's Manufacturing Industry', *Economic Geography*, July 2004.

Smith, Adam. *An Inquiry into the Nature and Causes of the Wealth of Nations*, London: W. Strahan and T. Cadell, 1776; reprinted (with an Introduction, Notes, Marginal Summary, and an Enlarged Index by Edwin Cannan) New York: Modern Library, 1937.

Solow, Robert. 'A Contribution to the Theory of Economic Growth', *Quarterly Journal of Economics*, February 1956, vol. 70, no. 1, pp. 65–94.

Spilimbergo, A. J. L. Londono and M. Szekely. 'Income Distribution, Factor Endowments and Trade Openness', *Journal of Development Economics*, vol. 59, 1999, pp. 77–101.

Spinanger, D. 'Faking Liberalisation and Finagling Protectionism, the ATC at its Best', background paper prepared for WTO 2000 Negotiations, ERF/IAI/World Bank Workshop, Cairo, July 1999.

Spinanger, D. and S. Verma. 'The Coming Death of the ATC and China's WTO Accession: Will Push Come to Shove for Indian T & C Exports?' in *Bridging the Differences: Analyses of Five Issues of the WTO Agenda*, edited by A. L. Winters and P. Mehta, Jaipur: CUTS Publications, 2003.

Srinivasan, T. N. 'Long-Run Growth Theories and Empirics: Anything New?,' in *Growth Theories in Light of the East Asian Experience*, edited by Ito Takatoshi and Anne Krueger, Chicago: University of Chicago Press, 1995, pp. 37–70.

———. *Eight Lectures on India's Economic Reforms*, New Delhi: Oxford University Press, 2000.

———. 'India in the Doha Round', *Financial Express*, 4 September 2003.

———. 'Indian Economy, Economic Reforms and Change in Government', presented at CREDPR Annual Conference on the Indian Economy, Stanford, 1 June 2004.

Srinivasan, T. N. and Jagdish Bhagwati. 'Outward Orientation and Development: Are Revisionists Right?' in *Trade, development and Political Economy: Essays in Honour of Anne Krueger*, edited by Deepak Lal and Richard Shape, London: Palgrave, 2001, expanded version 4 available online at http://www.columbia.edu/-jb38.

Srivastava, Vivek, 'India's Accession to the Government Procurement Agreement: Identifying Costs and Benefits', in *India and the WTO*, edited by A. Mattoo and R. M. Stern, Washington DC: Oxford University Press and The World Bank, 2003.

Srivastava, Vivek. Pooja Gupta and Arindam Datta. *The Impact of India's Economic Reforms on Industrial Productivity, Efficiency and Competitiveness: A Panel Study of Indian Companies, 1980–97*, New Delhi: National Council of Applied Economic Research, 2001.

Stern, Nicholas. 'Making Trade Work for Poor People', speech delivered at NCAER, November 2002.

Stiglitz, Joseph. 'The Causes and Consequences of the Dependence of Quality on Price', *Journal of Economic Literature*, vol. 25, 1987, pp. 1–48.

_____. 'Two Principles for the Next Round or, How to Bring Developing Countries in from the Cold', in *Developing Countries and the WTO: A Pro-Active Agenda*, edited by B. Hoekman and W. Martin, Oxford: Blackwell Publishers, 2001.

_____. *Globalization and its Discontents*, New York: W. W. Norton and Company, 2002.

Stobdan, P. 'Evolving a Look North Policy: Conceptualizing Sub-Regional Cooperation', *Security and Society*, vol. 2, no. 1, pp. 49–57.

Subramaniam, A. 'Putting Some Numbers on the TRIPS Pharmaceutical Debate', *International Journal of Technology Management*, vol. 10, no. 10, 1994, pp. 252–68.

Sundaram, K. and S. Tendulkar. 'Poverty has Declined in the 1990s: A Resolution of Comparability Problems in the NSS Consumer Expenditure Data', *Economic and Political Weekly*, vol. 38, 25 January 2003.

Tangermann, Stefan. *An Assessment of the Uruguay Round on Agriculture*, report prepared for the OECD's Agricultural Directorate, Paris: OECD, 1994.

_____. 'Agriculture: New Wine in New Bottles?' in *The World Trade Organization Millennium Round: Freer Trade in the Twenty-First Century*, edited by K. G. Deutsch, and Bernhard Speyer, London: Routledge, 2001, pp. 199–212.

Tanzi, V. 'Corruption around the World: Causes, Consequences, Scope and Cures', IMF Staff Paper, 1998.

Tanzi, V. and H. Davoodi. 'Corruption Public Investment and Growth', IMF Working Paper, 1997.

Tata Services Limited, *Reforms and Productivity Trends in Indian Manufacturing Sector*, Mumbai: Department of Economics and Statistics, 2003.

Thapliyal, S. 'India–Bangladesh Transportation Links: A Move for Closer Cooperation', *Strategic Analysis*, vol. XXII, March 1999.

The Hindu, 'G-20 adopts New Delhi Declaration', Sunday, 20 March 2005, http://www.thehindubusinessline.com/2005/03/20/stories/2005032001810300.htm.

Tinbergen, Jan. *Shaping the World Economy*, New York: The Twentieth Century Fund, 1962.

_____. *Towards a Better International Order*, United Nations Institute for Training and Research Lecture Series 2, New York: UN, 1971.

_____. *Income Distribution*, New York: Elsevier, 1975.

Topalova, Petia. 'Trade Liberalization and Firm Productivity: the Case of India', Yale: Yale University, Press 2003, www.econ.yale.edu/seminars/NEUDC03/topalova1.pdf.

Townsend, Robert. 'Risk and Insurance in Village India', *Econometrica*, vol. 62, no. 3, 1994, pp. 539–91.

Transparency International. 'Karachi Integrity Pact Saves 75% in Consulting Fees', press release, 2002.

Trotman, LeRoy. 'The WTO: The Institutional Contradictions', in *Doha and Beyond: The Future of the Multilateral Trading System*, edited by M. Moore, Cambridge: Cambridge University Press, 2004.

Tussie, D, and D. Glover (eds). *The Developing Countries in World Trade: Policies and Bargaining Strategies*, Boulder: Lynne Riennes Publishers, 1993.

Tussie, D. and M. Lengyel. *Developing Countries and the WTO Participation versus Influence*, Buenos Aires: Latin American Trade Network/Facult and Latin America Canada Cencios Social, 2001.

Udry, Chris. 'Case Studies: Credit Markets in Nolhern Nigeria: Credit as Insurance in a Rural Economy,' in *The Economics of Rural Organization: Theory, Practice and Policy*, edited by Karla Hoff, Avishay Braverman and J. E. Stiglitz, Washington DC: Oxford University Press and The World Bank, 1993.

UNCTAD. *Trade and Development Report*, Geneva: UN, 1993.

_____. *The UNCTAD Report on Trade and Development*, Geneva: United Nations, 1995.

_____ and WTO. *Market Access Development since the Uruguay Round: Implications. Opportunities and Challenge*, Geneva: UN, 1997.

Underhill, G. R. D. *Industrial Crisis and the Open Economy: Politics, Global Trade and the Textile Industry in the Advanced Economies*, London: Macmillan, 1998.

UNDP. *Making Global Trade Work for People*, Chapter 8, 'Textiles and Clothing', New York: UNDP, 2003.

Unel, Bulent. 'Productivity Trends in India's Manufacturing Sectors in the last Two Decades', IMF Working Paper no. WP/03/22, 2003.

United States Trade Reprehensive. 'National Trade Estimate: Foreign Trade Barriers', report on 'India', various issues, www.ustr.gov.

US International Trade Commission, 'Textile and Apparel: Assessment of the Competitiveness of Certain Foreign Suppliers to the US Market', January 2004.

USAID. 'Ensuring Transparency and Accountability in Hurricane Reconstruction and Transformation', USAID Discussion Paper for the Consultative Group for the Reconstruction and Transformation of Central America, 1999.

USITC. 'India's Textile and Apparel Industry: Growth Potential and Trade and Investment Opportunities', Staff Research Study 27, Publication 3401, March 2001.

Veeramani, C. 'Intra-Industry Trade under Economic Liberalisation: The Case of Indian Capital Goods Industries', *Journal of Indian School of Political Economy*, vol. 11, no. 3, 1999, pp. 455–73.

_____. 'India's Intra-Industry Trade under Economic Liberalisation: Trends and Country Specific Factors', Working Paper no. 313, Centre for Development Studies, 2001.

Ventura, J. 'Growth and Interdependence', *Quarterly Journal of Economics*, vol. 112, no. 1, February 1997.

Verghese, B. K. 'India Northeast Resurgent: Ethnicity, Insurgency, Governance, Development', New Delhi: Centre for Policy Research, 1996.

Verma, Samar. 'Export Competitiveness of Indian Textile and Clothing Sector', unpublished manuscript, New Delhi: ICRIER, 2002.

_____. 'Impact of WTO Agreement on Indian Textile and Clothing Industry', ICRIER Working paper no.94. 2002

_____. 'How Big is the Bang for India: Market Access in Textiles Post 2004', paper presented in the seminar entitled The WTO and India: Issues and Negotiating Strategies, jointly organised by JNU, ICSSR and Cotton College, Gwahati, 11–12 August 2004.

Virmani, A., B. Goldar, C. Veeramani and V. Bhatt. 'Impact of Tariff Reforms on Indian Industry: Assessment Based on a Multi-sector Econometric Model', ICRIER Working Paper no. 135, July 2004.

Wacziarg, Romain and Karen Welch. 'Trade Liberalization and Growth: New Evidence', Graduate School of Business, Stanford University, Palo Alto, CA. Mimeo, 2002.
Warner, Andrew. 'Once More Into the Breach: Economic Growth and Global Integration', mimeograph, Cambridge MA: Harvard University, 2002.
Wei, S. J. 'Corruption in Economic Development: Beneficial Grease, Minor Annoyance, or Major Obstacle', World Bank Policy Research Working Paper no. 2048 1999.
Wei, Shang-Jin. 'How Taxing is Corruption on International Investors?', *Review of Economics and Statistics*, vol. 82, no. 1, February 2000, pp. I–II.
_____. 'Natural Openness and Good Government', mimeograph, Cambridge MA: Harvard University, 2000.
Whalley, J. 'Developing Countries and Systems Strengthening in the Uruguay Round,' in *Uruguay Round and the Developing Economies*, edited by W. Martin and A. Winters, Washington DC: The World Bank, 1999.
_____. 'Note on Textiles and Apparel in the Next Trade Round', paper presented at conference on Developing Countries in the Next WTO Trade Round, Cambridge MA: Harvard University, November 1999.
Williams, M. *International Economic Organisations and the Third World*, New York: Harvester Wheatsheaf, 1994.
Williamson, Jeffre. 'Winners and Losers over Two Centuries of Globalization', WIDER Annual Lecture 6, Helsinki: WIDER, 2002.
Willmore, L. N., 'Free Trade in Manufactures among Developing Countries: The Central American Experience', *Journal of Economic Development and Cultural Change*, vol. 20, 1972.
Winham Gilbert, R, *International Trade and the Tokyo Round Negotiation*, Princeton: Princeton University Press, 1986.
Winters, Alan and P. Mehta (eds). *Bridging the Differences*', Jaipur: CUTS Centre for International Trade, Economics and Environment, 2003.
Wood, A. *North-South Trade, Employment, and Inequality: Changing Fortunes in a Skill-driven World*, Oxford: Clarendon Press, 1994.
_____. 'How Trade Hurt Unskilled Workers', *Journal of Economic perspectives*, vol. 9, 1995, pp. 57–80.
_____. 'Globalisation and the Rise in Labour Market Inequalities', *Economic Journal*, vol. 108, 1998, pp. 1463–14.
Wood, Adrian and Ridao-Cano Cristobal. 'Skill, trade and international inequality', *Oxford Economic Papers*, vol. 51, 1999, pp. 89–119.
World Bank. *World Development Indicators*, Washington DC: The World Bank, various issues.
_____. 'Trade Blocs Policy Research Report', New York: Oxford University Press, 2000, http://www.worldbank.org/research/trade/pdf/trade_blocs2.pdf.
_____. *The Quality of Growth*, New York: Oxford University Press, 2000.
_____. *Global Economic Prospects and the Developing countries 2002: Making Trade Work for the World's Poor*, Washington DC: The World Bank, 2002.
_____. *India: Country Procurement Assessment Report*, Washington DC: The World Bank, 2003.
_____. *Bangladesh: Growth and Export Competitiveness*, Report no. 31394-BD, Washington DC: The World Bank, 2005.

World Trade Organization. *WTO Annual Report*, New York and Geneva: WTO, various issues.
———. *WTO: Trading into the Future*, Geneva: WTO, 1999.
———. *Trade Policy Review*, Geneva: WTO, 2000.
———. 'Market Access: Unfinished Business—Post-Uruguay Round Inventory and Issues', Special Studies no.6, Geneva: WTO, 2001.
———. 'India', in *Trade Policy Review*, Geneva: WTO, 1998 and 2002.
———. *World Investment Report*, New York and Geneva: WTO, 2004.
———. The World Trade Organization in Brief, Geneva: WTO, 2004, www.wto.org.
———. 'Members OK Amendment to Make Health Flexibility Permanent', press release, http://www.wto.org/English/news_e/pres05_e/pr426_e.htm.

Contributors

ALAN V. DEARDORFF is currently Professor of Economics and Public Policy, University of Michigan, Ann Arbor.

ALOKESH BARUA, is currently Professor and Chairperson, Centre for International Trade and Development, School of International Studies, Jawaharlal Nehru University, New Delhi.

AMIT SHOVAN RAY is currently Professor, Centre for International Trade and Development, Jawaharlal Nehru University, New Delhi.

ANANYA GHOSH DASTIDAR is currently Assistant Professor, Department of Business Economics, University of Delhi.

APARNA SAWHNEY is currently Associate Professor, Centre for International Trade and Development, School of International Studies, Jawaharlal Nehru University, New Delhi.

ARVIND PANAGARIYA is currently Jagdish Bhagwati Professor of Indian Political Economy, School of International & Public Affairs, Columbia University.

ASHOK GUHA is currently Professor of Economics, Indian Institute of Technology, New Delhi.

CHAKRABORTY PAVEL is currently PhD Student, Department of International Economics, Graduate Institute of International and Development Studies.

DEBASHIS CHAKRABORTY is currently Assistant Professor, IIFT, New Delhi.

DIPANKAR SENGUPTA is currently Professor, Department of Economics, Jammu University.

JAGDISH BHAGWATI, is currently University Professor, Economics and Law, Columbia University and a Senior Fellow in International Economics at the Council on Foreign Relations, US.

JESSICA SEDDON WALLACK is currently Director, Centre for Development Finance, Institute for Financial Management & Research, Chennai.

MANMOHAN AGARWAL is currently Senior Visiting Fellow, Centre for International Governance Innovation, Waterloo, Canada.

MANOJ PANT is currently Professor, Centre for International Trade and Development, Jawaharlal Nehru University, New Delhi.

PHUNCHOK STOBDAN is currently Senior Fellow, Institute for Defence Studies & Analyses, New Delhi.

PRITAM BANERJEE is the Head of International Trade and Policy, Confederation of Indian Industry, New Delhi.

RAMESH CHAND is currently Director, National Centre for Agricultural Economics and Policy Research, New Delhi.

RASHMI BANGA is currently Senior Economist, UNCTAD-India Program, New Delhi.

ROBERT. M. STERN is currently Professor of Economics and Public Policy, Gerald R. Ford School of Public Policy, University of Michigan, Ann Arbor.

SAMAR VERMA is currently Policy Advisor, South Asia, OXFAM, New Delhi.

SANDWIP KUMAR DAS is currently Visiting Faculty, Department of Economics, Skidmore College and State University of New York.

T. N. SRINIVASAN is currently Samual C. Park Professor of Economics, Yale University.

Index

accountancy services, share in exports, 274–45
Agarwal, Manmohan, 18, 53, 151
Agenor, Pierre-Richard, 303
Agreement on Agriculture (AOA), of WTO, 20–21, 35–36, 37, 40, 123, 124, 130, 131
   implementation of, 125, 138–40
   market access, 137
Agreement on Procurement (GPA), 221, 223, 227
   India's procurement policy and, 231–32
Agreement on Textiles and Clothing (ATC), 20, 22, 40, 112, 145, 170–71
   implementation of 172–75, 179
   quantitative restrictions under, 174
agriculture(al), agreement on, in WTO, 20–21
   export subsidies 89, 131, 134
   import of, 128–30
   India and WTO negotiations on, 123ff
   liberalisation of trade in, 16, 59, 89, 97, 125, 126
   markets, 131–33
   products, global prices of, 126–27
   reduction in domestic support, 131–32
   share in GDP, 329
   subsidies, 48, 57
   tariff reduction, 40
   taxation on, 131
   trade before and after WTO, 125–30
   US and EU liberalization of, 68
Ahluwalia, M. S., 349
Ahuja, R. 273
American Textile Manufacturing Industry (ATMI), 37
AMS, 136
Anant, T. C. A., 66, 275
'Anglo-French Textiles', revenue of, 179

Anglo-French Treaty of 1860, 1
anti-dumping 48, 71, 99
   India as victim of investigation, 70
   measures, 79–80, 145, 179–80
Apparel Industry Initiative (AII), 190
Asia/Asian, economic development in, 47
   financial crisis, 305
   miracle, 46, 47
Asian Development Bank (ADB), 200, 209, 215, 299
Association of Southeast Asian Nations (ASEAN), 35, 38, 79

Bajpai, N., 349
Balance of payments, problem 55, 56
Bandopadhya, Arindam, 350
Banerjee, Pritam, 23, 199
Banga, Rashmi, 24, 255
Bangladesh, infrastructure in, 209
   link with East India, 207, 218
   trade policy between India and, 199, 200
   West Bengal/Assam and, 201–4
Bangladesh Chamber of Commerce, 209
Bangladesh-India-Myanmar-Sri Lanka-Thailand Economic Cooperation (BIMSTEC), 208
banking sector, reforms in, 146
Bardhan, P. K., 221
Barro, R., 348
Barua, Alokesh, 1, 21, 26, 142, 151, 156, 347
Basmati rice, patenting of, 67
Bay of Bengal Initiative for Multi-sectoral Technical and Economic Cooperation (BIMSTEC), 79, 83n
Berne Convention (1886), 243
Besley, Timothy, 306

Bhagwati, Jagdish, 25, 92, 93, 101, 297, 299, 348
Bhattacharya, Aditya, 102, 156
'Big Bang', in trade and clothing trade, 22, 170
biological diversity, protection of, 72
The Blair Home agreement, 59
Border Road Organisation (BRO), 217
Bourguignon, F., 325, 326
Brazil, open economy in, 60–61
Britain, end of mercantilism in, 2
   free trade in, 2
   trade liberalization policy of 1
Bruno, M., 338
Burgess, Robin, 306
Bush administration, 113
BOP 74, 162
business process outsourcing (BPO), 255
   in India 71, 340, 341
   in US 58

Café au Lait group, 53, 58, 59
Cairns group, 35, 36, 53, 58, 59
Cancun Ministerial meeting/Round (2003), 13, 16, 17, 39, 41, 61, 101, 102, 124, 145, 146
   India's negotiating strategy at 68
Cashin, Paul, 310, 349
Central Asia, Ladakh and 199–201, 211–12, 218
   WTO and, 217–18
Central Asian and Caspian energy reserves, 214, 215
Central Vigilance Commission (CVC), India, 228, 229
Central Vigilance Commission Act, 2003, 228
Chadha, 100, 150
Chakraborty, Debashis, 19, 21, 65, 142
Chakraborty, Pavel, 21, 26, 142, 156, 347
Chand, Ramesh, 21
Chanda, R., 274
Chenery, H., 329, 330
China, admission to WTO, 117, 217
   environmental liberalisation/market in, 282, 285
   exports to US and EU, 190
   growth rate in, 299, 306
   incidence of poverty in, 299
   liberalisation in, 61

National Petroleum Corporation (CNPC) in, 215
Preferential Trade Agreement with Pakistan, 212
regional disparities in, 309
Western China Development campaign in, 213
and WTO accession on clothing and textiles exports, 185–87
Clean Clothes Campaign, 190
Clinton, Bill, 12, 13, 58
coalition formation, negotiating stage and, 57–59
Cold War, end of, 211
Committee on Regional Trade Agreements, 108
Committee on Rules of Origin, 112
Committee on Trade and Environment, 108
Comptroller and Auditor General of India (CAG), 220
   on government expenditure, 226
Confederation of Indian Industry (CII), 209
Congress Party, Common Minimum Programme (CMP) of, 102, 103
construction services, growth and share in exports 274–75
   share in GDP, 274
Contract Labour Act, 1970, 191
Convention on Biodiversity (CBD), 38
Corn Laws, repeal of, in Britain, 2
cotton, at the AOA, 138
   fabric processing in India, 182–83
   -subsidisation schemes, 68
   see also textiles
credit and insurance markets, globalisation and access to, 314–15

Darjeeling tea, patenting of, 67
Das, Sandwip Kumar, 23, 205, 221
Das, Satya P, 102
Dasgupta, DE. 349
Dastidar, Ananya, 26, 321
Daton, Angus, 307
Dawood, Abdul Razak, 113
Dayal-Gulati, Anuradha, 310
Deardorff, Alan V. 19, 88, 92
Debroy, Bibek, 155, 222

decentralisation, institutional reform and 209–10
Deininger, K., 326, 327, 338
Demurger, Sylvie, 310
Deodhar, Satish, 274
Depression of 1930s, 2
'Derbez Draft', 68, 69
developed countries, agricultural safeguards in, 125
  environmental services negotiations by, 283–86
  liberalisation in, 58
  subsidies to farmers in, 132–33
developing countries, and ATC, 174–75
  balance of payments and foreign exchange crises in, 16
  and Doha Round, 37–38
  economic growth of 15
  in economic negotiations, 55–57
  environmental goods and service sector in, 281, 282
  environmental services negotiations by, 283–86
  globalisation in, 321
  governance in, 314
  as members of GATT, 15
  and most-favoured-nations (MFN) status, 14
  and reciprocity policy, 4
  role in WTO negotiations, 10, 18
  special and differential treatment for, 137
  tariff reduction in industrial products, 143
Directorate General of Singapore and Disposal (DGS & D), India, 226–27, 228
Dispute Settlement Body (DSB), 70, 179
dispute settlement mechanism, under GATS, 259
  in India, 228–9
Dispute Settlement Understanding and Agreement, on TRIPS, 113
Doha Agreement, 118
Doha Declaration, 38, 107–9, 114, 115, 117, 260, 279
  on TRIPS and Public Health, 243
Doha Development Agenda (DDA), 13, 17, 18, 19–20, 68, 74, 124
  India's stance at, 88ff

Doha Ministerial meeting/Round (2001), 5, 13, 14, 17, 21, 34, 39, 61, 66–68, 74, 123, 145, 280
  Decision on Implementation-Related Issues and Concerns, 106–7, 110, 112
  division among developing countries in 37–38
  India at 66–68, 106ff, 114
  multilateral trade negotiations, 261
  negotiation on environment, 289
Dholakia, R., 349
Dollar, David, 299, 306, 308, 348
drinking water, services in, 280
drug(s), conventional dosage forms (CDF), 249
  generic market in, 247
  new drug discovery research (NDDR), 249
  novel drug delivery system (NDDS), 249
  quality control in, 247–49, 253
  research and development in, 249–50
Drug Policy Statements, India, 246
Drug Price Control Orders, India, 244
Dunkel Draft, 35, 66

East Asia/Asian, development in 46
  'miracle', 16
  tigers, 34
East India Company, 219
Eco-labeling schemes, 180–1
economic growth, 17, 304
  in developed countries, 16
  in developing countries, 16
  see also growth
education, investments in, 313
  services, share in exports, 274
Edwards, S., 326
Elizondo, R. L., 359
employment, in India, 266–68
energy supplies, India and China seeking, 214–17
environmental goods and services, in India, 286–90
  investments in, 287
  technology imports in, 288
Environmental Goods and Services (EGS) industry, global, 281

environmental services, commitments in, 283–84
   in developing countries, 290
   elimination of tariff and non-tariff barriers to, 279
   GATS negotiations on, 279ff
   global market for, 281–83
   liberalisation of, 281, 285, 290–91
   negotiations, 25, 72
   sewage service, 283, 289
   trade barriers in, 284
Europe, environmental industry in, 281, 282
   industrialisation in, 2
European Common Agricultural Policy, 62n
European Community (EC), environmental services in, 284
European Union (EU), 12, 35–37, 102, 107, 175
   agricultural subsidies and tariffs in, 17, 118
   anti-dumping duty by, 179
   domestic subsidies in, 17
   environmental industry in, 282
   export subsidies in, 134
   India's export of fabrics to, 191
   market access to clothing and textiles in, 22
   tariff rates on ATC products, 176
   textile import by, 170
Eurostat, on environmental industry, 280, 281
Evenett, S. J., 231
export(s), competition and subsidies, 134, 137
   from India, 152, 153
   industry in India, 98, 151
   -led strategy, of growth, 16
   markets, liberalisation of, 67
   subsidies, elimination of, 139

factor income distribution, 323–5
fertility rate, 45
financial services, reforms in, 273
Five-Year Plan, Third, 309
fixed effects model, for income distribution, 331–35
Food Corporation of India (FCI), role in price administration, 134
food security, India's, 134, 135, 139
foodgrains, quantitative restrictions (QR) on imports, 128, 133

Fordney-McCumber Tariff Act, US 3
foreign direct investment (FDI), commitments to 255, 256, 262
   in environmental equipment services, 287
   inflow into India, 5, 73–74, 146, 152, 270–71, 340
   policy, in India, 163n
   in water and sewage services in developing countries, 284–85
Foreign Exchange Regulation Act (FERA), 1973, 244
Foreign Investment Promotion Board, India, 287
France, tariff rates in, 2
Frankel, Jeffrey, 299, 348
free trade agreements (FTA)agreements, 3, 83n, 100, 118

G-6, 70
G-8, 89
G-10, 57
G-20 group, 18, 39, 40, 41, 81, 117, 124
   on agricultural subsidies, 146
   draft, 68
   formation of, 80
G-33, 69
G-110, 69
Gahrton, Per, 115, 116
General Agreement on Tariffs and Trade (GATT), 3–4, 6, 7, 10, 13, 17, 23–25, 33, 112, 123, 147, 170, 171, 172, 189, 257
   Article III on National Treatment, 221
   India at, 65–66
   protection to agriculture under, 20
   rules, 56
General Agreement on Trade in Services (GATS), 7, 37
   emergence and features of, 257–60
   India's role in, 255ff, 261–62
   negotiations on environmental services, 279ff
General Financial Rules (GFRs), in India, 226
Generalised System of Preferences (GSP), 4, 56, 70
Geneva Ministerial meet, of WTO, 66
   India's role at, 145

Global E-commerce Agreement, 18
  India as part of, 145
Global Trade Analysis Project (GTAP) 5
  model, 185
globalisation, growth, and the poor, 302ff
  and inequality, 303
  for the poor, 303, 315–16
  effects on poverty, 25, 302, 303, 310–15
Gmbel, 156
Good Manufacturing Practices (GMP), 246
Gordon, J., 268
Gore, Al, 13
government procurement, UNCITRAL model
  of, 231
government procurement, in India, 224–25
  corruption in, 224, 235, 236
  transparency in, 221ff
GPA, 237n
  India on, 235, 236
Great Depression, 34
Greater Mekong sub region (GMS), in South
  East Asia, 200, 201
'green revolution', 298, 315
gross domestic product (GDP) 16, 34, 225
  services sector's share in, 263–66
  share of manufacture in, 26
Group of Negotiations in Services (GNS), 258
growth, globalisation and the poor, 302ff
  and poverty reduction, 298, 299, 303, 306–
    10
  rates, 44, 46–47
Guha, Ashok, 17, 44
Gupta, P., 268

handloom industry, in India, 182
Hanson, G. H., 350
Harris, J. R., 328
health/healthcare, 250–53
  antibiotics, 252
  growth and share in exports, 274
HIV/AIDS, research on, 251
Hockman, B. M., 231
Hong Kong Declaration, 135–38
Hong Kong ministerial meeting (2005), of
  WTO, 13, 40, 61, 65, 68–70, 80, 125, 145,
  146
Hull, Cordell, 3

human rights, WTO and, 9
Husain, Asssim, 310

immigration policies, in developed countries,
  256
imperfect competition, 156–59
Imperial preferences, 34
'implementation issues', India's demands under,
  112–13
import substitution industrialisation strategy
  (ISI), 54, 55, 60, 65
income, distribution in India, 339–41
  distribution and international trade, 322–
    27
  distribution, trade and structural change,
    327–31
  inequality, 329, 337, 338, 339
Independent Commission on Health in India,
  250
India, agricultural sector in, 96–97
  anti-dumping action by, 99
  and ASEAN countries, 79, 83n
  and Bangladesh, border procedures, 205
    road and inland water link with, 207
    trade policy, 199, 200
  and coalition in multilateral trade
    negotiation, 53ff
  at Doha, 106ff
  and DDA negotiations, 88f, 92–97
  eastern, link with Bangladesh, 218
  economic liberalisation/reforms in, 224,
    253
  environmental services and GATS
    negotiations, 286–90
  exports from, 62, 67, 94
  exports and earnings from agriculture 125–
    27
  FDI flow into, *see* foreign direct investments
  at GATT negotiations, 19, 65–66
  GATS and, 255ff, 261–62
  government expenditure in, 225, 226
  government procurement in, 221ff, 226–27
  and GPA, 231–32
  growth performances of 46
  growth rates in, 306
  imports to, 152, 154
  income distribution in, 321ff, 339–41

liberalisation in, 126, 341
as member of P-5, 61
negotiating position of 60–2, 65ff, 109–10
north-east, transporting goods to and from, 206
oil supplies in, 215
and Pakistan hostility, 206, 207
Patent Act in, 243–5
policy reforms in, 92–94
procurement policy in, 23
reforms of 1991 in, 21, 104n
regional inequality in, 309, 347ff, 350–35
role in WTO meetings, 17–18, 19
tax on agriculture, 94
trade scenario of, 76–78
and US FTA, 100
workforce in, 266
at WTO, 145–49
WTO agricultural negotiations and, 123ff
WTO induced reforms, 146–48
Indian economy, 26, 104, 147, 162, 208
industrial countries, low tariffs in, 20
Industrial Dispute Act (1947), 165, 190
industrial tariffs, 111–12
reduction in, 3
industry, efficiency scale in, 161
intra-industry trade (IIT), 151, 156–9
level analysis, 159–62
and trade performance, 142ff
inequalities, 308, 309, 328
income, 329, 337
regional, 26–27, 309
information and communication technology (ICT), 241
Information Revolution, 46–47
Information and Technology (IT), software, and services, 255, 268–70
infrastructure, inequality and income inequality, 353–37, 362, 366, 368
investments in, 366
intellectual property rights (IPRs), 4, 5, 11, 24, 48, 70, 101, 241–43
International Conference on Harmonisation (ICH), 248
International Development Assistance (IDA), 56

International Labour Organization (ILO), 9, 114
international trade, and income distribution, 322–27
structural change, income distribution and, 327–31
intra-industry trade (IIT), in India, 21

Jaitley, Arun, 96
Japan, environmental industry in, 281, 282
Juetting, Johannes, 273
'July Package' of 2004, 124, 138, 140

Kaliranjan, K. P., 349
Kamal, Yussef Hussain, 108
Kapoor, J. L., 349
Kennedy Round negotiations, 3, 54
knitwear sector, in India, 183
Kraay, Aart, 299, 306, 308, 348
Krueger, Anne, 297, 299
Krueger, A. O., 326
Krugman, Paul, 46, 156, 323, 359
Kuznets, S., 327, 328
Kuznets Curve relations, 329–30, 335, 336, 338

labour productivity, 183–84
labour standards, WTO and, 9
Ladakh, and Central Asia, 199–201, 211–12, 218
and XUAR, 213
Lamy, Pascal, 13, 69, 115
Lancaster, 156
Lau, Lawrence, 47
Lawrence, R. Z., 100, 324
Lee, J. W., 348
legal services, share in exports, 274–75
less developed countries (LDCs), 12
manufactured exports from, 34
Li, H., 327
liberalisation, 14, 61, 66, 272
in developed countries, 58
see also China, India
Like Minded Group (LMG), India as part of, 66

Little, Ian, 298
'Look East' policy, of India, 152, 212–13

macroeconomic stability, and trade performance, 297, 300n
Majumdar, G., 349
manufactured products, export of, 159
    and income inequality, 353–56, 366
    India's trade in, 155–56
    liberalisation of, 98
    per capita income and, 361–62
    population size and, 362–64
    trade openness and, 364
manufactured sector, India's 142
    and market access, 142–45, 150–56
Maran, Murasoli, 81n, 82n, 109, 110, 114, 115, 117
Marjit, S., 349
market access, for agriculture, manufacture and textiles, 20–22, 67
    to developed countries, 56, 139
    for environmental services, 283, 284
    for exports, 77
    impact on manufacturing, 150–56
    issues for agricultural and non-agricultural products, 66, 69
    and national treatment under GATS, 259
    for textiles, 170ff
Marrakesh meet, of WTO, 66–68, 221
Mathur, A., 348
Mattoo, Aaditya, 67, 92, 94, 98, 99, 101, 223
Mckinsey, 268
The Medicines and Related Substances Control Amendments Act, 70
Mercosur, agreement, 12
Millennium Development Goals 290
Minimum Wages Act, 2002, 191
Mitra, S. 162, 275, 349
Mode 1, negotiations on trade, 256
Mode 3, negotiations on trade in services, 255, 256, 261, 262, 271–73, 276, 284
Mode 4, for environmental services, 284, 286
    negotiations on services, 81
Modigliani, Franco, 45
Monopolies and Restrictive Trade Practices (MRTP) Commission, 146

Moore, Mike, 12, 115, 116
Morrison, C., 325
most favoured nations (MFN), treatment under GATS, 2, 3, 23, 34, 92, 142, 184, 259
Mukherjee, Arpita, 274, 275
Multi-Fibre Arrangement (MFA), 4, 7, 22, 34, 35–37, 40, 63, 116, 170, 208
    dismantling of, 22, 62, 70, 112, 101, 171–72
    quotas, and India's exports, 184
Multilateral Agreement on Investment (MAI), 38, 39
multilateral environmental agreements (MEA), 108
multilateral investment agreement, 48
multilateral negotiations, 17, 48, 80
    theory of, 31–34
multilateral tariff reduction, 33, 34, 35
multilateral trade negotiations (MTNs), India and, 53

Nagraj, R., 349
Nath, Kamal, 118
Nato, 211
National Competition Bidding (NCB), India, 236
national environmental regulatory institution, India, 286
National Highways, India's expenditure on, 234
NSDP, 352, 353
    share of agriculture in, 357
    share of manufacturing in 357–60, 364
Nehru, Jawaharlal, 300n, 309
New Drug Policy, 1978, India, 244
new industrial policy, India's 146, 228
New International Economic Order, 53, 253
Non-Agricultural Market Access (NAMA), 40, 69, 71
non-tariff barriers (NTBs), 7, 34, 77, 81, 145
    on India's exports, 149
North American Free Trade Agreement (NAFTA), 12, 35, 37, 98
    impact on India's exports, 100
    and less regional inequality, 350
North-South trade, 35

Novel drug delivery system (NDDR), 251, 252

'Old Silk Route', 216
Organization for Economic Co-operation and Development (OECD) countries, 45, 46, 74, 125, 224
  agricultural exports from, 127
  Code for the Liberalization of Capital Movements, 75
  on environmental industry, 280, 281
  government procurement in, 232
  India's agricultural export to, 140
  MFA and, 171
  subsidies to farmers in, 132–33
Organisation of the Petroleum Exporting Countries (OPEC), 61

Pakistan, and China trade, 212
  and India hostility, 206, 207
Paluzie, E., 349
Panagariya, Arvind, 19, 20, 92, 93, 101, 104, 106
Pant, Manoj, 16, 31, 156
Paris Convention (1883), 243
Park, A., 307
Patent Act, 2005, 243, 246
patents, 38, 242
Payment of Wages Act, 1936, 191
per capita income, share of manufactures and services in, 361–62
personal income distribution, and international trade, 325–27
pharmaceuticals, Patent Act of 1970 and, India, 243–45
  quality and R & D in 250
plant life, patenting of, 38
Pohir, 205
'poor', definition of, 304
  globalisation and, 302, 313, 315–16
  growth and the, 302
population, growth, 17
  living in extreme poverty, 302
  size, and share of manufactures and services, 362–64
Portman, Rob, 69

Porto, Guido, 315
postal services, share in services, 274–75
poverty, estimates, 302
  growth and 25
  and inequality, 26
  liberalisation and, 347, 348
  trade and, in poor countries, 287ff
preferential government procurement, 222
preferential trading areas/arrangements (PTA), 2, 75, 100–1, 181
Prevention of Corruption Act, 1988, 228–29
Price Preference, abolition of, in India, 228
procedural and regulatory reforms, India, 210–11
product, market efficiency, 313
  patent regime, 72
public distribution system (PDS), 311
public health, 72, 146
  TRIPS and, in India, 241
public sector enterprises (PSEs), 224, 227–28
public works, contracting in India, 229–31
Public Works Department (PWD), India, 229–30, 234
Punta del declaration, 258
Pursell, Gary, 222

quota, abolition, impact of, 181–89
  access 173–74
  restrictions, dismantling of, 172–73

Rahman, Mujibur, 207
rail transport service, share in exports, 275–76
Raman, J., 349
Rao, M. Govinda, 310, 349
Ray, Amit Shovon, 24, 241, 251, 252, 253
Ray, D., 338
Razin, Assaf, 311
readymade apparel, India's domestic market for, 191
  export trade in, 188–89
Reciprocal Trade Agreements Act, US, 3
reciprocity policy, 1, 4–6, 92
regional income inequality, in India, 347ff
  trade and, 349–50
  trends in, 353–55
regional trade blocs, 75–79

Index

Regional Trading Arrangements (RTA), 35, 37, 38, 75–76, 145, 181
Rhodesia, economic sanctions against 9
Ricardo, David, 2
Richardson, 257
Ridao-Cano, 150
road transport, share in exports, 274–75
  share in GDP, 274
Robertson, Dennis, 298
Rodrik, Dani, 150, 159, 160, 299, 315
Romer, David, 299, 348
Rose-Ackerman, Susan, 221
Roosevelt administration, US, 3
Roy, Sanchari, 26

Sachdeva, R., 275
Sachs, J., 299, 324, 337, 338, 349
Sahay, 349
Sanitary and phyto-sanitary (SPS) measures, 134
Santhanam, 155
Santhanam Committee, India, 229
saving rates, 44–6
Savvids, A., 326
Sawhney, Aparna, 25, 279
Seattle ministerial meeting (1999), of WTO, 11, 12, 17, 66, 145
Sen, K., 310
Sengupta, Dipankar, 23, 199
services sector, 255–56, 262–71
  contribution to GDP, 263–6, 271
  export from, 268, 269, 272
  inflow of FDI into, 270–71
  liberalisation under GATS, 259
  share in total employment, 266–8
  share in trade, 268–70
service trade, liberalisation of, 55, 89, 98–9
  India's stand on liberalisation, 71, 72
Shah, A., 350
Shand, R. T., 349
Shanghai Cooperation Organisation (SCO), 212
Shankar, R., 350
Shatz, H., 324
'shrimp-turtle' case, 6, 8
'Silk Route Extension', 212–13, 219

'Singapore issue' 39, 40, 59, 69, 102, 107–10, 114, 117
Singapore ministerial meeting (1996), of WTO, 17, 22–23, 66, 232
  India's role at, 145
Singh, N., 349
Sinha, Yashwant, 111
Sjoberg, O., 350
Sjoholm, F., 350
Slaughter, M. J., 324
small scale sector, 228
Smith, Adam, 2, 298
software services, 268
  reforms in, 273
Solow, Robert, 298
South Africa, economic sanctions against, 9
South Asia Free Trade Agreement (SAFTA), 79
South Asian Association for Regional Cooperation (SAARC), 38
South East Asia, crisis in, 147
Special and Differential Treatment (S & DT) provision, in GATT, 4, 41, 66, 69, 81, 139
'special safeguard measures' (SSM), 69
Spilimbergo, A., 325, 326
Spinanger, D. 173, 185
Squire, L., 326, 327, 338
Srinivasan, T. N., 25, 26, 92, 97, 99, 100, 101, 103, 297, 299, 302, 348, 349
Srivastava, Vivek, 102, 225, 227
state trading enterprises (STEs), 134–35, 137, 139
Stern, Robert M, 1, 19, 88, 92
Stiglitz, J., 156, 305
Stobdan, Phunchok, 23, 199
structural transformation, and inter-regional income inequality, 327–31, 364–66
Subramanian, Arvind, 67, 92, 94, 98, 99, 101
sustainable development, environme4ntal services and, 290–91
Syrquin, M., 329

tariff, on industrial products, 111–12
  in India, 68, 175–79
  levels, 33, 54
  reduction, 137, 150, 175–79

reforms, 143–44, 146, 147, 347
tariff reduction policies, under WTO, 5, 21, 37
Tarim Petroleum Exploration and Development Bureau (TPEDB), 215
technology, in Asia and the West, 47
  transfer, in developing countries, 73
telecom reforms, 273, 274
textiles (sector), impact of quota abolition, on India, 181–3
  market access in 170ff
  trade, and labour standard, 181
  as unorganised sector, 182, 183
textiles and clothing products, exports from developing countries, 22–23
  international trade in, 177–79
  restraints on exports, 185
therapeutic focus, drug manufacturers on, 250–51
Tinbergen, Jan, 303, 309, 310, 315
Tiwaldi, Ismail, 218
Todaro, M. P., 328
Tokyo Round negotiations, of WTO, 4, 34, 221, 232
trade, barriers, 20, 272, 273, 330
  defence mechanism, 179–80
  disputes in, 148–9
  and environment, 107, 108
  facilitation, 22, 23, 72, 89, 102, 199ff, 218
  and growth nexus, 348–49
  and industrial performance, 142ff
  and investments, 73–75
  and NSDP, 358, 360, 365
  policy in India, 148, 149
  and poverty in poor countries, 297ff
trade liberalisation, 1, 24, 26, 58, 59, 62, 90–92, 107–8, 150–52, 159, 256, 272
  impact on income distribution, 326, 330, 334, 335, 347ff
  and inter-regional inequality, 366
Trade Promotion Authority (TPA), of USTR, 118
Trade Related Intellectual Property Rights (TRIPS) Agreement, 7, 12, 23, 24, 35, 36, 37, 38, 54, 60, 66, 72, 79, 101–2, 146, 148, 172, 258

General Council of, 254
  obligations, 111
  and public health, 69, 106, 107, 110, 111, 241ff
Trade Related Investment Measures (TRIM), 35, 36, 37
Trade and Transport Facilitation (TTF) policy, 201, 204, 205–6
traditional knowledge (TK), patent right over, 72
Transnational National Corporations (TNCs), 35
Transparency International, 236
travel, reforms in, 273
turtle-exclusion devices (TEDs), 8

Uighur Independence Movement, China, 216
United Nations Conference on Trade and Development (UNCTAD), 34, 56, 65
United Progressive Alliance (UPA), government in India, 102, 103
United States, Africa Growth and Opportunity Act, 181
  agricultural import tariffs in, 17
  agricultural subsidies in, 118
  -Cambodia Textile Agreement, 181
  environmental industry in, 281, 282
  export subsidies in, 134
  preferential trading arrangements in 8
  rules on trade in services, 257
  -Singapore Free Trade Agreement, 175
  subsidies in, 17
  tariff policy in, 3, 34, 176
  textile import by, 170
  trade and income distribution in, 323
  on 'war on terror', 39
United States Trade Promotion Authority 13
USTR, 89
Uruguay Round negotiations (1986–94), 3, 4, 5, 6, 11, 15, 16, 17, 20, 22, 23, 24, 34–37, 41, 53, 54, 57, 60, 66, 92, 107, 109, 110, 221, 255, 258, 279
  on environmental sector, 280
  India's services commitments in, 98

Multilateral trade negotiations, 142, 170
see also Agreement on Agriculture,
Agreement on Textiles and Clothing
(ATC)

Verma, Samar, 22, 170, 185

Wacziarg, Romain, 306
wage structur, in urban-rural areas, 358
Wallack, Jessica S, 26, 302
Wang, S., 307
Warner, Andrew, 299, 337, 338
water and sewage service, investments in, 285
Wei, Shang-Jin, 314
Welch, Karen, 306
West Bengal, and Bangladesh, 201–4
  heavy industry in, 202
  I-Win, 209
West Bengal Industrial Development Corporation (WBIDC), 209
Williamson, Jeffrey, 302
Wood, A., 150, 324
World Bank, 56, 299
  study, 229, 230, 231
World Trade Organization (WTO), 12, 14, 279
  access to Central Asia, 217–18
  critics of, 10–11
  design and mission of, 90–92
  dispute settlement mechanism (DSM)/panel, 6, 7, 9, 10, 106, 145, 148, 149
  establishment of, 6–7, 258
  General Council, 124, 135
  General Council Decision 2004, 22
  and globalisation, 7, 8
  India and, 145–49, 232–33
  India's 'negotiation strategy' at 65
  Ministerial meetings, 11–14
  objections to, 9–11
  and right on environment, 9
  rules, 99–102, 107, 108, 116
  Secretariat, 115
  'Single understanding' clause in, 16
  and trade negotiations, 31ff
  Working Group on Transparency in Government Procurement of, 232
  and world economy, 44ff
Worldwide Responsible Apparel Production (WRAP), 190

Xianjiang, India's political and economic presence in, 212, 213
  transport links in, 214
XUAR, as 'energy-highway', 216

Young, Alwyn, 47

Zoellick, Robert, 113
Zutshiv, 275